KITCHENER

ARCHITECT OF VICTORY,
ARTISAN OF PEACE

KITCHENER

ARCHITECT OF VICTORY,
ARTISAN OF PEACE

———

JOHN POLLOCK

CARROLL & GRAF PUBLISHERS, INC.
New York

Carroll & Graf Publishers, Inc.
19 West 21st Street
New York
NY 10010-6805

The Road to Omdurman first published in the UK by
Constable and Company Ltd 1998
Copyright John Pollock © 1998

This combined edition first published in
the UK by Constable 2001
First Carroll & Graf edition 2001
Copyright John Pollock © 2001

A copy of the Cataloging in Publication Data
for this title is available from the Library of Congress.

ISBN 0-7867-0829-8

Printed and bound in the EU

CONTENTS

CONTENTS

VOLUME II: SAVIOUR OF THE NATION

CONTENTS

CONTENTS

ILLUSTRATIONS

VOLUME I: THE ROAD TO OMDURMAN

Captain Henry Horatio Kitchener, aged 37 (*Mrs Julian Fellowes*)

Fanny Kitchener (*née* Chevallier) with her three elder children, 1851 (*Earl Kitchener*)

Herbert aged 18; aged 28; and with 'Chevally', 'Millie' and Walter before Millie's wedding (*Earl Kitchener*)

General Gordon, Kitchener's hero (*Mrs Elizabeth Blunt*)

William Stavely ('Monkey') Gordon (*Mrs David Gordon*)

Colonel Herbert Kitchener Pasha, 1890, aged 40 by Sir Hubert von Herkomer (*National Portrait Gallery*)

Kitchener's masters: Lord Salisbury and Lord Cromer (*Miss M. H. Raitt*)

Archie Hunter, 'Kitchener's Sword Arm' (*Mr A. A. de C. Hunter*)

Rex Wingate, Kitchener's Chief of Intelligence (*Mr David Gordon*)

Walter Kitchener's immediate sketch of Mahmud in the Berber 'triumph' (*Mrs Peter Hall*)

Photographs snapped on the Omdurman Campaign by Captain the Hon. Edward Loch, Grenadier Guards, afterwards Major-General 2nd Lord Loch (Sir Hugh Stucley, Bt)
Wingate interrogates Mahmud; 'Friendlies' ready for action; Sudan Military Railway: Gunboat sections; Early morning toilet; The Memorial Service for Gordon; A Lancer and a Grenadier hold Gordon's telescope; Father Brindle, DSO, the best loved man in the Expedition.

'Monkey' Gordon's sketch before demolishing the Mahdi's tomb (*Mr David Gordon*)

VOLUME II: SAVIOUR OF THE NATION

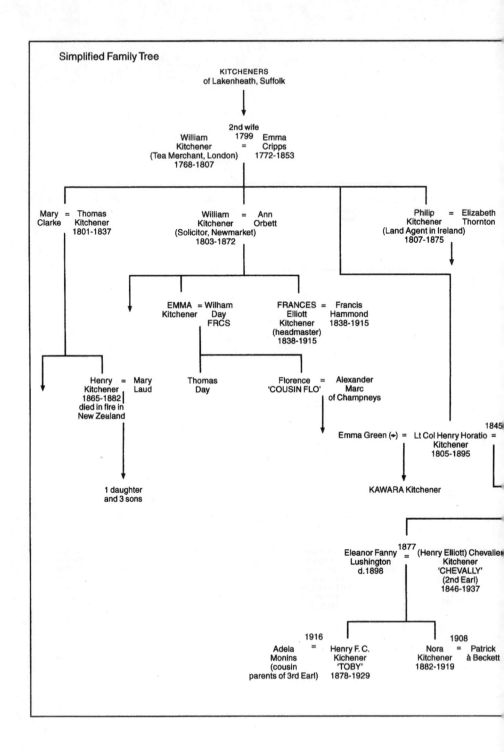

Simplified Family Tree

KITCHENERS
of Lakenheath, Suffolk

William
Kitchener
(Tea Merchant, London)
1768-1807
=
2nd wife
1799
Emma
Cripps
1772-1853

Mary = Thomas
Clarke   Kitchener
1801-1837

William = Ann
Kitchener   Orbett
(Solicitor, Newmarket)
1803-1872

Philip = Elizabeth
Kitchener   Thornton
(Land Agent in Ireland)
1807-1875

EMMA = Wilham
Kitchener   Day
FRCS

FRANCES = Francis
Elliott   Hammond
Kitchener   1838-1915
(headmaster)
1838-1915

Henry = Mary
Kitchener   Laud
1865-1882
died in fire in
New Zealand

Thomas
Day

Florence = Alexander
'COUSIN FLO'   Marc
of Champneys

1 daughter
and 3 sons

Emma Green (♦) = Lt Col Henry Horatio =
Kitchener
1805-1895

1845

KAWARA Kitchener

Eleanor Fanny
Lushington
d.1898
= 1877
(Henry Elliott) Chevalier
Kitchener
'CHEVALLY'
(2nd Earl)
1846-1937

Adela
Monins
(cousin
parents of 3rd Earl)
= 1916
Henry F. C.
Kitchener
'TOBY'
1878-1929

Nora
Kitchener
1882-1919
= 1908
Patrick
à Beckett

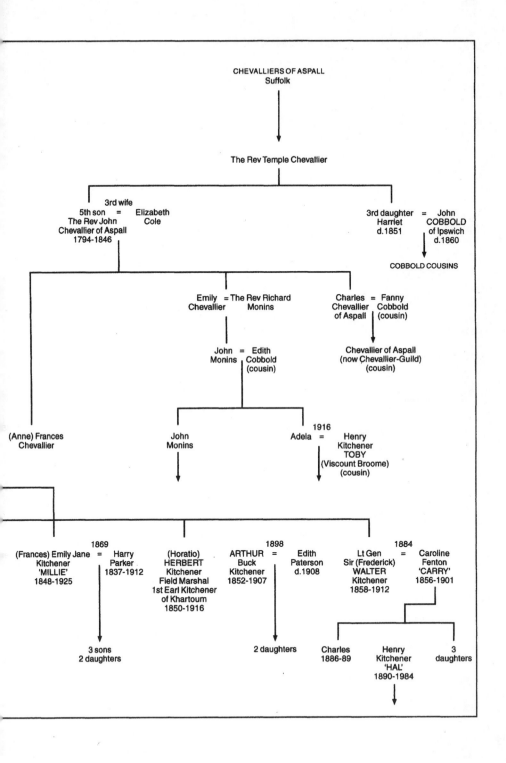

CHEVALLIERS OF ASPALL
Suffolk

The Rev Temple Chevallier

3rd wife
5th son = Elizabeth
The Rev John Cole
Chevallier of Aspall
1794-1846

3rd daughter = John
Harriet COBBOLD
d.1851 of Ipswich
d.1860

COBBOLD COUSINS

Emily = The Rev Richard
Chevallier Monins

Charles = Fanny
Chevallier Cobbold
of Aspall (cousin)

John = Edith
Monins Cobbold
(cousin)

Chevallier of Aspall
(now Chevallier-Guild)
(cousin)

(Anne) Frances
Chevallier

John
Monins

1916
Adela = Henry
Kitchener
TOBY
(Viscount Broome)
(cousin)

1869
(Frances) Emily Jane = Harry
Kitchener Parker
'MILLIE' 1837-1912
1848-1925

(Horatio)
HERBERT
Kitchener
Field Marshal
1st Earl Kitchener
of Khartoum
1850-1916

1898
ARTHUR = Edith
Buck Paterson
Kitchener d.1908
1852-1907

1884
Lt Gen = Caroline
Sir (Frederick) Fenton
WALTER 'CARRY'
Kitchener 1856-1901
1858-1912

3 sons
2 daughters

2 daughters

Charles
1886-89

Henry
Kitchener
'HAL'
1890-1984

3
daughters

ACKNOWLEDGMENTS

Both volumes in this combined edition are based mainly on the very extensive Kitchener Papers now in the Public Record Office. They were deposited in 1959 by the Field Marshal's great-nephew, the 3rd Earl Kitchener of Khartoum and of Broome. I am most grateful to Lord Kitchener for allowing me unrestricted use of this material, which is his copyright, and for his great encouragement and the provision of material not in the PRO.

The Kitchener family made the research and writing a delightful experience. In addition to Lord Kitchener, I particularly wish to thank Lady Kenya Tatton-Brown; the Hon. Mrs Charles Kitchener and her daughter and son-in-law, Emma and Julian Kitchener-Fellowes. Julian most kindly read the book in typescript and made excellent suggestions. Mrs Peter Hall, granddaughter of General Sir Walter Kitchener, the Field Marshal's youngest brother, let me copy her valuable collection of letters, loaned me books and pictures and helped in other ways. Mrs Harriet King, great-granddaughter of their sister, Millie Parker, let me copy Kitchener's letters to her. Mrs Ralph Toynbee (*née* Monins) shared childhood memories of her cousin, the Field Marshal. Mr John Chevallier-Guild and his mother, Mrs Cyril Chevallier-Guild, showed us round their moated manor where Fanny Kitchener (*née* Chevallier) was born and brought up.

The Royal Archives continued to be a mine of fresh material, and I gratefully acknowledge the gracious permission of Her Majesty The Queen

[xv]

to quote from the journals of Queen Victoria, King George V and Queen Mary and from letters written by them and King Edward VII, and to make use of other material in the Royal Archives and of material not in the Royal Archives but of which the copyright belongs to Her Majesty. I thank Mr Oliver Everett CVO, Librarian at Windsor Castle, and the Registrar, Lady de Bellaigue, LVO, and her assistants, whose welcome and efficiency made my research for both volumes a great pleasure.

The Royal Engineers, Kitchener's Corps, have been very helpful and generous, and I thank warmly the Secretary of the Institute, Colonel M. R. Cooper, his predecessor, Colonel J. Nowers and Dr John Rhodes and their staff.

For permission to quote or use copyright material (manuscript or printed) I thank the Marquess of Salisbury (and his archivist, Mr Robin Harcourt-Williams, FSA), Lord Birdwood, Lord Gainford, Lord Hardinge of Penshurst, Sir Hugh Stucley, Bt., General Sir Anthony Farrar-Hockley, GBE, KCB, DSO, MC, Mr Duncan H. Doolittle, Mr Archie Hunter, Mrs R. Lambert, Mr Henry Keown-Boyd, Mr Philip Mallet, Mr Richard Marker, Mr Kenneth Rose, CBE, Colonel A. H. W. Sandes, Mr Charles Sebag-Montefiore (Magnus Papers), Magdalene College, Cambridge (Inge Papers), Pembroke College, Cambridge (Storrs Papers), the Lord Kitchener National Memorial Fund and Scholars' Association, and the National Army Museum (and Dr Peter B. Boyden, Head of Archives). I have not been able to trace all copyright owners and apologize to any not contacted.

I have been very grateful for advice and encouragement from Dr George H. Cassar, author of *Kitchener: Architect of Victory*, and other fine studies of the First World War. Readers who wish to delve deeper into incidents and strategies will find Dr Cassar's books most valuable.

Miss Mary H. Raitt of Washington DC kindly researched for me in the National Archives and the Library of Congress, and I thank her warmly.

Whilst writing both volumes, I have had the help of many people and would like to thank especially: Lady Anne Bentinck, Miss Constance Biddulph, Mr Peter Basset-Smith, Mr Richard Butler-Stoney, OBE, Mr Julian Byng, Sir Howard Colvin, Mr John D'Arcy, Colonel G. S. H. Dicker, CBE, TD, the Reverend Alan Duke (Rector of Barham, Kent), Mr Hugo von Dumreicher, Lady Dunboyne, the late Mr Peregrine Fellowes, Mr Otto Fisher, Brigadier Denis FitzGerald, DSO, OBE,

Desmond FitzGerald, Knight of Glin, Mr David Gordon, Mr Jeff Gibbons (Private Secretary to the Lord Advocate), Miss H. H. Harper, Professor Cameron Hazlehurst, Mr John Hussey, Colonel Victor Humphreys, OBE, Sir Peter Laurence, KCMG, MC, Mr Iain MacKenzie (Admiralty Library), Mr F. R. Maloney, Mrs Peter MacKinnon, Sir John and Lady Mogg, and Brigadier Nigel Mogg, Mr Nigel Nicolson, MBE, The Diocesan Archivist of Nottingham (the Rev. Father A. P. Nolan), Mrs Lindsay Phillips, Mr Timothy Price, Sir Godfrey Ralli, Bt., Sir Maurice Renshaw, Bt., Lord Richardson, LVO, FRCP, Mr John N. Ross, Mr Trevor Royle, the Reverend Canon Michael Saward, Lady Soames, DBE, Mr R. C. Stanley Baker, Mr Richard Taylor and his daughter, Mrs Deborah Hinsch, Colonel John Walker, Mr David C. C. Watson, Mrs Janet Winchester, Mr Allan Woodliffe and Mr Philip Zeigler, CBE.

I am grateful to the following institutions: the Regimental Headquarters of the Coldstream Guards and of the Irish Guards; the Museums of the 9th/12th Royal Lancers, of the Royal Norfolk Regiment, of the Queen's Royal Surrey Regiment, of the Worcestershire Regiment, of the Royal Army Chaplain's Department and of the Army Medical Services; the Admiralty Library of the Ministry of Defence and the Army Historical Branch; Birmingham University Library Special Collections, the City Library of Dinan, France, the Local Studies Library of Dover, the Sudan Archive of the University of Durham Library, Exeter City Library, Lambeth Palace Library, Liddell Hart Centre for Military Archives (King's College, London), the London Library, Nuffield College, Oxford, Magdalene College, Cambridge, Pembroke College, Cambridge and the Wellcome Institute for the History of Medicine.

A special word of thanks to the staff of the Public Record Office, especially Dr Alexandra Nicol and Mr Andrew McDonald.

For photographs and maps I am indebted to the kindness and generosity of the Marquess of Salisbury, Earl Kitchener, The Hon. Mrs Charles Kitchener, Mrs Peter Hall, Miss Elizabeth Blunt, Dr George H. Cassar, the Reverend Anthony Creery-Hill, Mr and Mrs Julian Kitchener-Fellowes, Mr David Guzdon, Mr A. A. de C. Hunter, Mrs Harriet King, Sir Hugh Stucley, Bt., Mrs Bridget Toynbee, Mr Allan Woodliffe, the Tasmanian Museum and Art Gallery, Hobart, the Lord Kitchener National Memorial Trust and the Institute and the Officers of the Royal Engineers.

To all these, and to any inadvertently omitted, my warm thanks, and to Mrs J. E. Williams of Bideford who, as always, impeccably typed my manuscript; and finally a very warm thank you again to Mr Benjamin Glazebrook, my publisher, and his team at Constable, especially for their patience, as this book took much longer than I forecast.

JOHN POLLOCK
Rose Ash
Devonshire

PROLOGUE

THE GREAT WAR, as contemporaries called it, had been raging for a year and ten months when King George V, on a morning of early June 1916, left London by special train for one of his numerous inspections of troops.

Two brigades, totalling 1,300 soldiers and sailors, were drawn up on the landing ground of the Royal Naval Air Station at Felixstowe in Suffolk. While the King was receiving senior officers before mounting his horse, his equerry was called urgently to the telephone. He returned with a grave, shocked face to report to the King, privately, that Lord Kitchener, Secretary of State for War and his staff had been drowned.

They had embarked from Scapa Flow for a short official visit to Russia. HMS *Hampshire* had been sunk off Orkney in a violent storm 'either by a mine or a torpedo' at about 8 p.m. the previous evening.

The King rode round the troops, took the salute and returned to London in shock and grief. By the time he was being driven from the railway terminus, the news had been released and he saw men and women standing stunned on the pavements. At Buckingham Palace he found a note from Queen Mary, who had left to inspect a hospital at Woolwich and could not be home before him. '12.45 June 6. My darling, I am miserable at this dreadful news about dear Ld K, so what must you feel. Such a loss to you & the nation, it is indeed terrible.' A letter had also come over from Queen Alexandra at Marlborough House. 'My beloved Georgie boy,' his mother wrote, 'What *fearful* news are these! – I feel quite stunned & collapsed at these *dreadful* and *awful* news of our beloved

Kitchener's untimely loss – at *sea* too! On his way to Russia! which I feel I told you only last Sunday was unnecessary at this very important moment too . . . He had the whole Empire's confidence and did so splendidly. My poor Georgie boy I am sorry for you indeed.'[1]

That night Queen Mary wrote in her diary: 'Went to G who was dread-fully upset. Stayed some time with him & we saw Sir George Arthur who had been working for Ld K for the last 22 months. Spent a very sad evening.' And the King's comment in his diary highlights their utter sense of loss: 'It is indeed a heavy blow to me & a great loss to the Nation & the Allies. I had every confidence in him & he was a great personal friend. Saw Bigge on my return. The Prime Minister came to see me, he is much upset, but we shall redouble our efforts to win the war. George Arthur came to see me. That charming FitzGerald was of course with K & is lost.'[2]

The news shook the nation to the core. In camps where 'Kitchener's Armies' were training, in the trenches of France and Flanders, especially among those who had answered their country's need in response to his pointing finger in the famous poster, in factories and fields, villages and city offices, men and women felt a personal sense of loss. Not since the death of Queen Victoria had Britain known such national grief. The diary of Kitty Inge, wife of the Dean of St Paul's, echoes the general desolation. The news had been whispered to the Dean by the Prime Minister's wife when she arrived late for the baptism of her step-grandchild, Raymond Asquith's baby son. When Inge returned to the Deanery he told his wife: 'I have heard the most terrible news . . .' Kitty later went for a walk in Temple Gardens, pushing her baby son, and saw shocked faces on rich and poor. Stores had closed, blinds were drawn, flags were at half-mast. She commented: 'The idol of the people – our greatest Englishman – so straight & honourable & unambitious . . . O! the sorrows wh. have come upon us. The heavens indeed are black.'[3]

Some of his Cabinet colleagues were not so sure. They had wanted Kitchener out of the way, though not tragically, either because they had concluded that his faults now outweighed his merits, or because his single-minded dedication to winning the war hindered their political ambitions: these wept 'crocodile tears', as one friend put it.

But none felt the loss more deeply than those who had served on his personal staff. Sir William Birdwood ('Birdie'), commanding the Anzac troops on the Western Front, as previously in Gallipoli, wrote at once to Clive Wigram: 'I am simply overwhelmed & feel for the moment that I am left alone in the world. The news Creedy has just wired to me is just too awful, though I fear at present I cannot grasp all it means to the country, I am selfishly taken up in my own grief.' He recalled how he had worked under Kitchener for nine years, hardly ever away from him, 'so I suppose I knew him better than almost any other human being – but even then I hardly realized what a complete blank his death would mean.' Birdie recalled Kitchener's visit to Gallipoli 'when he showed his pleasure at seeing me again, so very much more than was his usual custom . . . I was writing to him only last week telling what we thought of the yapping curs in the House of Commons round the old lion.'[4]

Far away in the Sudan, Sir Reginald Wingate, Kitchener's successor as governor-general, who had been with him throughout the reconquest and when setting up a regime of peace and justice which lasted sixty years, wrote from Khartoum: 'We are all dreadfully distressed about Lord Kitchener's loss. Personally I feel it greatly for he was one of my oldest & best friends and we had served more or less together for close on 30 years . . . The people of the Sudan, who were devoted to him, have sent hundreds of telegram of sympathy & condolence.'[5]

And in Egypt, where Kitchener had been *de facto* ruler until the outbreak of war, Lord Edward Cecil described to his wife in England the great memorial service in Cairo where the Christian and Muslim clergy sat together on the dais. He had been so busy with arrangements that he did not feel emotional 'until the Last Post which took my entrails out of me. I ran about for him as I used to do and for the last time & I was awfully glad to do it.

'The effect in the country is extraordinary – everyone really depressed for everyone has lost a true friend.'[6]

Kitchener left an indelible mark on his generation and on British history. Although his posthumous reputation has varied from contempt to high praise, he was by any standard one of the towering personalities of his age.

His height and strong build, with his famous moustache, thick brown hair and impassive face, gave Kitchener a somewhat alarming appearance. His eyes were blue, with a slight cast in the left eye which, with a scar from a war wound, enhanced the effect of sternness until he smiled. He was

painfully shy and loathed personal publicity and was therefore often misunderstood. His great friend Edward Stanley, Earl of Derby, said that 'to
many he was an enigma, and some have likened him to a sphinx . . . Only
those who knew him well really understood him.'[7]

References and Notes

1 RA GVD 6 June 16; Queen Mary to George v, RA GV CC 8/198; Queen
   Alexandra to George v, 6 June 1916, RA GV AA 34/54. The King arrived
   at Felixstowe at 11.30 a.m. The Admiralty had received confirmation of K's
   death at 10.30 a.m. It was publicly released at 1.40 p.m.
2 RA QMD 6 June 1916; GVD 6 June 1916.
3 Mrs Inge, Diary, 6 June 1916. Inge Papers, Magdalene College, Cambridge.
   Dean Inge had stopped his own diary in August 1914 and did not resume
   until 1 January 1917. Duff Cooper in *Old Men Forget*, 1953, describes the
   scene at the baptism.
4 Lieutenant-General Sir W. Birdwood (later Field Marshal Lord Birdwood)
   to Lieutenant-Colonel Clive Wigram (later Lord Wigram), 6 June 1916. RA
   GV Q 2521/56.
5 General Sir Reginald Wingate to Lieutenant-Colonel Clive Wigram, 14 June
   1916. RA GV Q 2522/257.
6 Lord Edward Cecil to his wife, 14 June 1916. Bodleian Library. Cecil
   Papers, U 1599. c 73/70.
7 Lord Derby, tribute read for him at unveiling of memorial in Lakerheath
   parish church, 23 July 1917.

Volume I

The Road to Omdurman

for

Henry Herbert
3rd Earl Kitchener

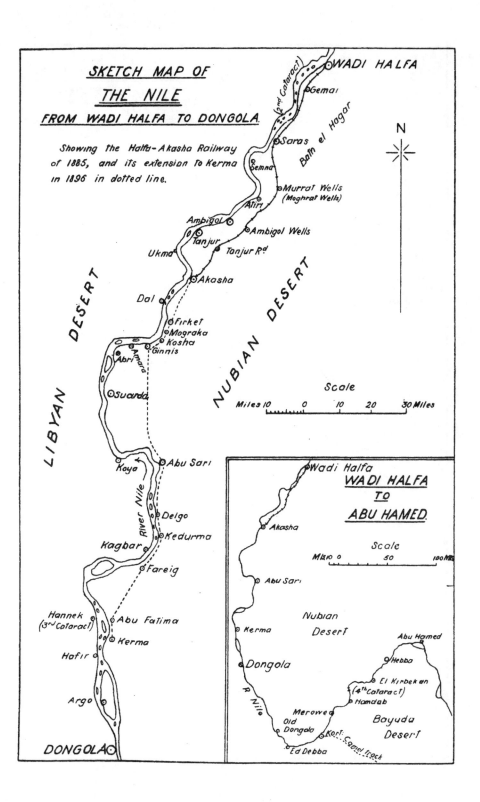

SKETCH MAP OF
THE NILE
FROM WADI HALFA TO DONGOLA.

Showing the Halfa-Akasha Railway
of 1885, and its extension to Kerma
in 1896 in dotted line.

N

WADI HALFA
(2nd Cataract)
Gemai
Bain el Hagar
Saras
Semna
Murrat Wells
(Moghrat Wells)
Atiri
Ambigol
Ambigol Wells
Tanjur
Ukma
Tanjur Rd
Akasha
Dal
Firket
Mograka
Kosha
Ginnis
Amara
Abri
Suarda

LIBYAN DESERT
NUBIAN DESERT

Scale
Miles 10   0   10   20   30 Miles

Koya
Abu Sari
River Nile
Delgo
Kedurma
Kagbar
Fareig
Hannek
(3rd Cataract)
Abu Fatima
Kerma
Hafir
Argo

DONGOLA

Wadi Halfa
WADI HALFA
TO
ABU HAMED.

Scale
Miles 10 0   50   100 Miles

Akasha

Abu Sari

Nubian
Desert

Kerma

Dongola

Abu Hamed
Hebba
El Kirbekan
(4th Cataract)
Hamdab
Merowe
Old
Dongola
Kort: Camel Track
Ed Debba
Bayuda
Desert

R. Nile

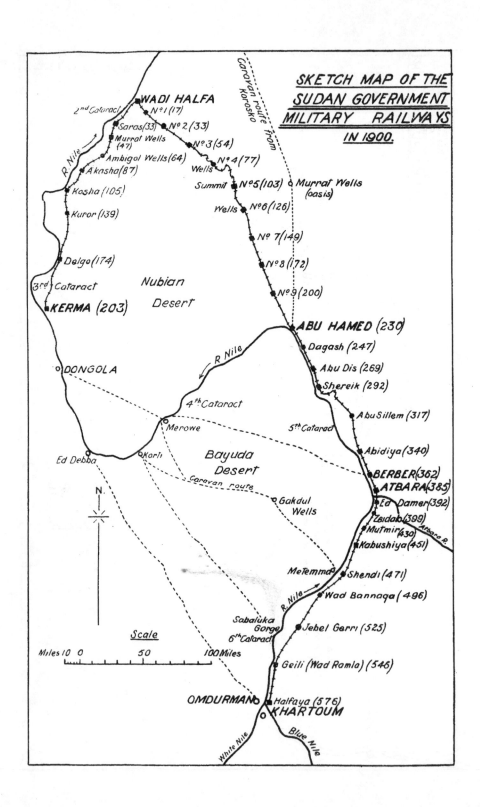

SKETCH MAP OF THE
SUDAN GOVERNMENT
MILITARY RAILWAYS
IN 1900.

WADI HALFA
Nº 1 (17)
2nd Cataract
Saras (33)
Nº 2 (33)
Murrat Wells (47)
Nº 3 (54)
Ambigol Wells (64)
R. Nile
Nº 4 (77)
Aknsha (87)
Wells
Summit
Nº 5 (103)
Murrat Wells (oasis)
Kosha (105)
Wells
Nº 6 (126)
Kuror (139)
Nº 7 (149)
Delgo (174)
Nº 8 (172)
3rd Cataract
Nubian Desert
Nº 9 (200)
KERMA (203)
ABU HAMED (230)
Dagash (247)
R. Nile
DONGOLA
Abu Dis (269)
Shereik (292)
4th Cataract
Abu Sillem (317)
5th Cataract
Merowe
Abidiya (340)
Ed Debba
Korti
Bayuda Desert
BERBER (362)
Caravan route
ATBARA (385)
Ed Damer (392)
Gakdul Wells
Zaidab (399)
Mutmir (430)
Atbara R.
Kabushiya (451)
N.
Metemma
Shendi (471)
Wad Bannaga (496)
R. Nile
Sabaluka Gorge
Jebel Garri (525)
6th Cataract
Scale
Geili (Wad Ramla) (546)
Miles 10 0   50   100 Miles
OMDURMAN
Halfaya (576)
KHARTOUM
White Nile
Blue Nile

Caravan route from Korosko

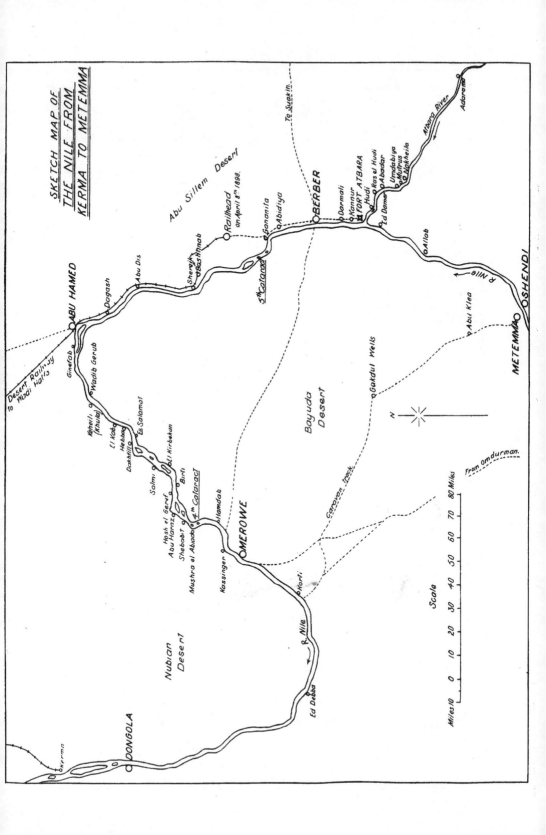

SKETCH MAP OF
THE NILE FROM
KERMA TO METEMMA

To Suakin.

Abu Sillem Desert

Railhead
on April 8th 1898.

Gonanita

Abidiya

BERBER

Darmali
Kannur
FORT ATBARA
Hudi

Atbara River

Adaroma

Ras el Hudi
Abadar
Umdabiya
Mutrus
Nakhheila

Ed Damer

Sherijik
Bashhnab

5th Cataract

Ginefab
Wadib Gerub

ABU HAMED

Dagash
Abu Dis

Aliab

Desert Railway
to Wadi Halfa

Netteili
(Khulai)

El Kabo
Hebba

Es Salamat

Dakhili

Ali Kirbekan

Salmi

Hosh el Geruf
Abu Hamza

Shebabit

Birti

4th Cataract
Hamdab

Mushra el Abaoab

Kassinger

MEROWE

Kerma

DONGOLA

Nuban
Desert

R. Nile

Ed Dabba

Korti

Bayuda
Desert

Gakdul Wells

Abu Klea

METEMMA
SHENDI

R. Nile

Caravan Track.

From Omdurman.

N

Scale

Miles 10   0   10   20   30   40   50   60   70   80 Miles

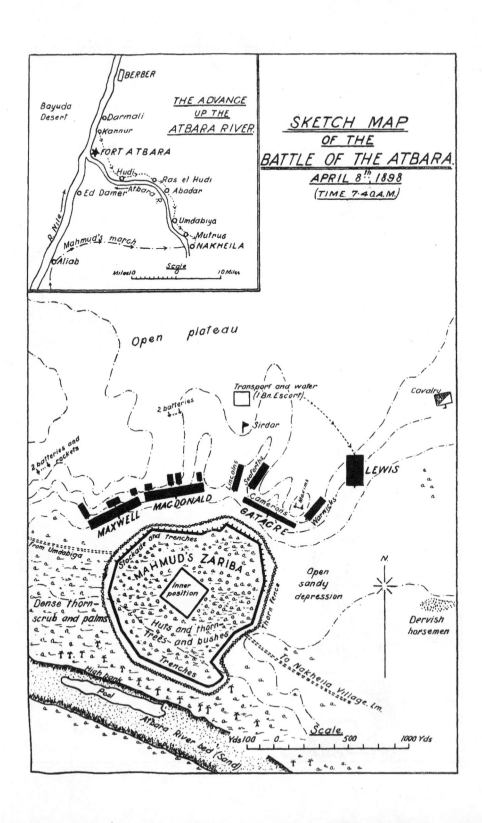

BERBER

THE ADVANCE
UP THE
ATBARA RIVER.

Bayuda
Desert

Darmali

Kannur

FORT ATBARA

Hudi
Ras el Hudi
Ed Damer Atbara Abadar

Umdabiya
Mutrus
NAKHEILA

Mahmud's march

Aliab

R. Nile

Scale
Miles 10   10 Miles

SKETCH MAP
OF THE
BATTLE OF THE ATBARA.
APRIL 8th, 1898
(TIME 7·40 A.M.)

Open plateau

Transport and water
(1 Bn. Escort)

Cavalry

2 batteries

Sirdar

2 batteries and
rockets

LEWIS

Lincolns
Seaforths
Maxims
Camerons
Warwicks

MAXWELL MACDONALD GATACRE

From Umdabiya

Stockade and trenches

MAHMUD'S ZARIBA

Inner position

Open
sandy
depression

N.

Dense thorn-
scrub and palms

Huts and thorn-
Trees and bushes

Trenches

Thorn fence

To Nakheila Village. 1m.

Dervish
horsemen

High bank

Pool

Atbara River bed (Sandj)

Scale
Yds 100   0   500   1000 Yds

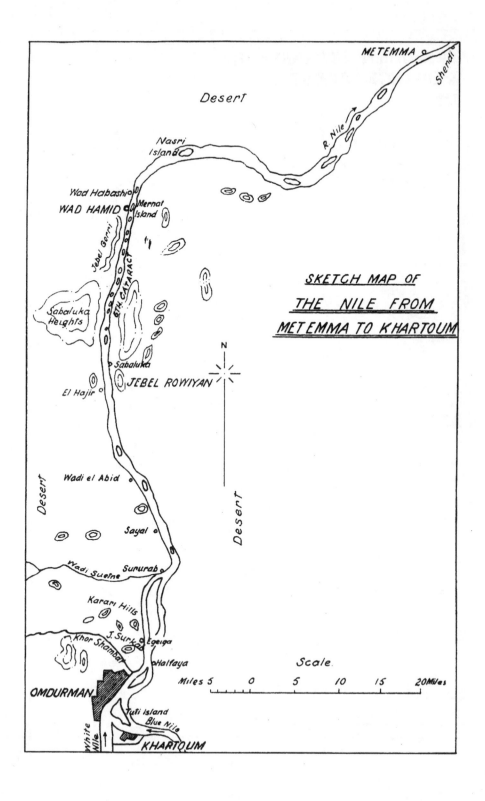

METEMMA

Shendi

Desert

R. Nile

Nasri
Island

Wad Habashi

WAD HAMID

Mernat
Island

Jebel Gerri

6TH CATARACT

Sabaluka
Heights

Sabaluka

El Hajir

JEBEL ROWIYAN

N

SKETCH MAP OF

THE NILE FROM

METEMMA TO KHARTOUM

Desert

Wadi el Abid

Sayal

Desert

Wadi Sueine

Sururab

Karari Hills

J. Surkab

Egeiga

Khor Shambat

Halfaya

Scale

Miles 5   0   5   10   15   20 Miles

OMDURMAN

Tuti Island

Blue Nile

White Nile

KHARTOUM

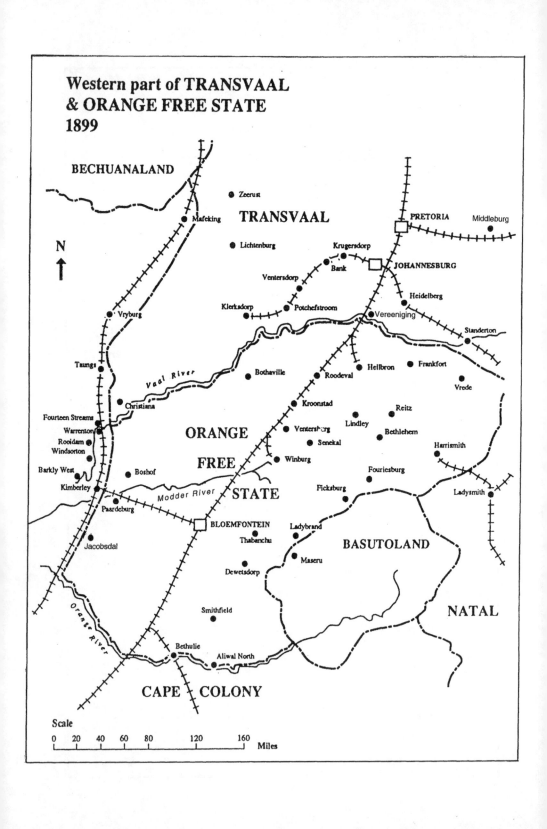

PART ONE

'What a fellow Herbert is'

1850–1883

I

A LOVING,
AFFECTIONATE CHILD

In the autumn of 1849 Lieutenant-Colonel Henry Horatio Kitchener, newly retired, crossed over to Ireland and bought a bankrupt estate on the banks of the Shannon.

In the aftermath of the Great Potato Famine the British Parliament had passed the Encumbered Estates Act to attract fresh owners, whether Irish or English, who had capital to invest in the decayed and depopulated countryside. Colonel Kitchener was wholly English.

His first recorded ancestor was a Hampshire yeoman, Thomas Kitchener, born at Binsted near Alton in 1666. At the age of twenty-seven he was offered a chance to better himself when the local magnate, Sir Nicholas Stuart of Hartley Maunditt, who was already seventy-seven and lived to be ninety-three, needed a resident agent for his distant manor of Lakenheath in north-west Suffolk, on the edge of the fens. In 1693, therefore, Thomas Kitchener moved more than a hundred miles from Alton to manage the manorial lands for the rest of his life. He married, bought a farm of his own (or was given it by Sir Nicholas) and founded a new Kitchener dynasty in East Anglia.

His grandson Thomas kept the Lakenheath land but became also a dealer in tea at Bury St Edmunds, the nearby market town. He outlived his own eldest son, William, born at Lakenheath in 1768. William Kitchener migrated from Suffolk to London and became a prosperous tea merchant in the China trade. He rose in the social scale by marrying the daughter of a clergyman from an old Suffolk county family, but she died five years later leaving two sons. In 1799 he married Emma Cripps, again a clergyman's daughter, well connected in Lincolnshire and Yorkshire. Through her mother, née Catherine Buck, Emma Kitchener was a first cousin of Sir Francis Wood, father of the first Viscount Halifax, and of the wife of Thomas Clarkson, the Abolitionist.

Emma brought up her stepsons and gave William sons of their own in quick succession. Two had died in infancy and two were in the nursery of their house in Bunhill Row in the City, the street where Milton had written *Paradise Lost,* when she gave birth to another son on 19 October 1805, two days before the Battle of Trafalgar. Inevitably, with their East Anglian connections, they gave him Nelson's name.

Henry Horatio Kitchener was only two years and eight months old when his father died suddenly, aged thirty-nine. The widow was left in comfort, and her elder stepson, who rose to be Master of the Clothworkers' Company, was generous, so that when Henry was twenty-four and decided to enter the army they helped him purchase a commission as a cornet in a cavalry regiment, the 13th Light Dragoons. His peacetime soldiering brought him no active service or distinction. He purchased his promotion to lieutenant, glorious in whisker and the regiment's distinctive blue, yellow and gold. To achieve his captaincy he exchanged into a less costly regiment, the 29th Foot (Worcestershires) in January 1841. He sailed with them to India in May 1842, landing near Calcutta in August.

He was already in love. He had often stayed with his next elder brother, William, in Newmarket. William's little girl Emma was his favourite niece. At the age of twelve, Emma went to share a governess with her great friend Fanny Chevallier (rhyming with *cavalier*) at Aspall Hall, a moated manor near Debenham in Suffolk. Henry Kitchener visited Aspall to see Emma and fell in love with Fanny, who was not yet old enough to marry.[1]

The Chevalliers were descended from the sixteenth-century Huguenot scholar Anthony Chevallier (who had also taught French to the future Queen Elizabeth I) and were settled in Jersey until 1702, when Clement Chevallier bought the Aspall estate with its small Jacobean mansion. In 1728 he had sent to Normandy for a special stone wheel for crushing apples to make the Aspall cyder that became famous in East Anglia and later was widely exported. His descendant, Fanny's elderly father, the Reverend Dr John Chevallier, was both squire and parson ('squarson') of Aspall, a practical landowner who first cultivated the celebrated Chevallier barley. He had qualified as a physician before ordination and earned a doctorate of medicine for work on mental

affliction, then little understood: he was one of the earliest to treat it by kindness. He added a storey to the house, putting his family upstairs and the
patients in the best rooms on the first floor, each with an inspection window.
In 1842 he had eleven boarders, three being certified lunatics. Fanny
Chevallier grew up accustomed to deranged or depressive patients wandering
in the garden. She was the youngest of a large family, as the reverend doctor
had been twice widowed before marrying Fanny's mother.[2]

Fanny (Anne Frances) was not quite nineteen when Captain Henry
Kitchener, aged thirty-nine, came back on home leave and married her at
Aspall in July 1845. They sailed at once, taking eighty-seven recruits for the
regiment, which Kitchener rejoined outside Lahore in February 1846, having
just missed the two battles of the brief but bloody First Sikh War. He was soon
promoted major, without purchase, on the death from wounds of Major Barr.
Six months afterwards he exchanged into the 9th Foot (later the Royal
Norfolks). The Kitcheners were stationed at Kussowrie in the foothills below
Simla when their eldest son was born in October 1846 and christened Henry
Elliott Chevallier. He was always known by his third name, pronounced
Chevally as the family had pronounced their name until the Napoleonic Wars.

The climate of India did not suit Fanny. Major Kitchener loved the army,
but he loved Fanny more and brought her back to England. Their second
child Frances Emily Jane ('Millie') was born in London in 1848. Battling
with ill health, his wife's and his own, he purchased a lieutenant-colonelcy and
went on half-pay, a form of reserve, and looked around for a livelihood.[3] To
recover his health he went to south-west Ireland on a visit to his younger
brother Phillip, who had recently become land agent to the Earl of Dunraven
at Adare in County Limerick, close to the Shannon estuary. Phillip suggested
setting up as a landowner in the neighbourhood since Irish land was so cheap
after the famine. In April 1850 Henry sold his commission and bought a bankrupt estate on the southern shore of the estuary between the little fishing ports
of Tarbert to the west and Glin in the east, about 160 miles from Dublin.
Called Ballygoghlan, it lay partly in the parish of Ballylongford, County
Kerry, and partly in County Limerick, 'a property', the colonel described it,
'beautifully situated but in a wretched state of farming,' so much so that the
agreement allowed him to pay by instalments over ten years.[4] The rambling
residence, formed by several detached buildings, stood in decay on a wooded
hill above the meadows sloping down to the estuary, with the shores of Clare
beyond.

The colonel began to restore it. Fanny was pregnant again. The ham-mering and sawing must not stop, so when her time neared in June 1850 he took her with four-year-old Chevally and two-year-old Millie a short distance to stay with a retired clergyman, Robert Sandes, and his wife at Gunsborough Villa, four miles north-west of Listowel. Here, on 24 June 1850, Fanny gave birth to her second son, whom they named Horatio Herbert but called him Herbert. He was not christened until December, when they were fully settled at Ballygoghlan and could ask the Sandes to come over to their Church of Ireland church outside Ballylongford, at Aghavallen. Two years later Fanny had a third son, Arthur Buck Kitchener, born at home.

Meanwhile the colonel was making a success of Ballygoghlan. Determined to farm much of it himself, he evicted a number of the small tenants on gener-ous terms. He was not the cruel landlord of later legend. He waived the half-year's rent due, paid their rates and charges and bought their crops at valuation. Those who decided to emigrate to America could sell him their stock; those who wished to farm elsewhere could leave their cattle on his land until suited. He got 'all the land I wanted without any trouble, generally receiv-ing the blessing of those who are represented in England as ready to murder under such circumstances'.

He used the smaller tenants as labourers, paying some seventy-five men and women to drain the land, make roads, carry turf and do other work under his Scots steward, who kept a sharp eye since they were inclined to be lazy. The land was fertile, and Kitchener soon found that under proper farming he could get good crops. He pioneered the use of lime on the land; he brought lime by the river and built a lime kiln, still standing, and sent off his crops by water. He also built a brick kiln and a pottery.

'I have received the greatest kindness from all ranks', he wrote in a letter to *The Times*, in which he urged more Englishmen to 'come over with capital to employ the poor and improve the land'. He had good neighbours of the Ascendancy, plenty of game, with 'yachting close by', and, confident of success, he was sinking 'all I am worth in the venture'.[5]

He brought in two young Englishmen to learn farming and assist him, but according to local legend he began to increase rents on tenant land which he had improved by draining, clearance and liming, and like many landlords of the time he would evict those who would not or could not pay. One of them, Seán MacEniry, was a poet who lampooned him in verse, claiming that the colonel stank when he sweated and that to be thus afflicted by 'the Devil's fire' was a sign of utter depravity.

In 1854 the neighbouring Castle Glin estate, with the ancient title of Knight of Glin, passed to the highly eccentric John Fraunceis Eyre FitzGerald, who made the colonel his pet aversion. The peculiarities of 'The Cracked Knight' were famous. He would ride into neighbours' front halls, he would drink porter out of a chamber-pot, he used his horsewhip freely. He set his dogs on the bailiffs summoned by the colonel to evict tenants whose families had once been his own tenants, and later challenged him at Tralee races to a whipping match when he disgraced the colonel to the amusement of the crowd. The Knight of Glin called him 'Colonel Stinkener'; but this not uncommon affliction of stinking sweat (*bromidrosis*) is not mentioned by any of the colonel's family in later life, though they wrote frankly about him between themselves.[6]

By 1857 the colonel had prospered enough to buy a second, more profitable estate, twenty miles south-west. Crotta House, built in the reign of Charles I by a branch of the Anglo-Irish Ponsonbys, stood a mile and a half from the village of Kilflynn, half-way between Listowel and Tralee. The small mansion, in Elizabethan style, had beautiful well-timbered grounds and, being close to the hills, was better for Fanny's health. Crotta became the main Kitchener residence, the family migrating in summer to Ballygoghlan, which the children loved best, their first home, where each had a little garden to cultivate as they liked: Herbert showed early his love of flowers.

At Crotta, in September 1858, Fanny gave birth after a six-year gap to her youngest son Walter (Frederick Walter Kitchener, a future major-general and colonial governor). She was never really well again. 'Consumption' (tuberculosis) was gradually taking hold. Fanny was also rather deaf, presumably a congenital deafness because four of her five children were hard of hearing as they grew older. But the deafness skipped Herbert. His hearing was normal or he might never have been a field marshal.

In the autumn of 1858 a young woman joined the household as nanny, on her way to a career in schoolteaching. Sixty years later, as Mrs Sharpe, she wrote at Millie's request her memories of Herbert between the ages of eight and ten. She provides the earliest clear picture, although perhaps coloured a little by hero-worship, of the late field marshal, 'my ideal of all that was noble and good in manhood'.[7]

Writing at the age of eighty or more, she recalled with delight her arrival at Crotta, 'their beautiful home in sight and sound of the Kerry mountains covered with broom or heather with the waves dashing at the foot'. Chevally was now twelve and Millie ten. Her special charges were the two younger brothers and the baby, and of these three 'Herbert soon had an absorbing inter- est for me . . . the little boy with his serious face asking questions'. He had a fair complexion, light brown hair (which became darker as he grew up, but was always distinctively brown) and small pearly teeth; 'a sweet smile, grey penetrating eyes, which looked you through and through and a very soft deliberate *Yes*', which remained a characteristic. His eyes were generally con- sidered blue rather than grey, and a very slight cast in one of them would become more noticeable after a war wound.

'He was a very loving, affectionate child,' remembered Mrs Sharpe, 'very reverent and earnest in everything he did and always ready to do a kind action, truthful and honourable to a degree in a little child of 8 or 9'.[8] Nanny did not find him solemn or lacking in fun, but he was specially tender-hearted to towards his invalid mother, who knew she was unlikely to see her children grown up and was particularly concerned for Herbert.

One day Nanny missed him, then found him hiding under a bed crying quietly because a heavy stone had fallen on his hand. She bathed and bound it and he then slept. At six o'clock, when she collected the children for them to see their mother lying on her couch in her bed-sitting-room, Herbert tore off the bandage, saying, 'Oh, please don't tell Mother'. He hid his hand all the time they were with her. His young Nanny said nothing at the time but, duty- bound, mentioned it the next day. His mother commented: 'Herbert is so very reserved about his feelings, I am afraid he will suffer a great deal from repres- sion'. She had spotted a lifelong facet of his character.

The colonel certainly expected a stiff upper lip. He ran the household with military order and discipline, backed by forceful language.[9] He was a stickler for punctuality. He scolded a servant who brought breakfast to the dining-room one minute after eight, and Nanny saw the lady's maid, Sarah, standing outside Mrs Kitchener's room with the breakfast tray on one hand and a watch in the other, awaiting the precise hour to enter. Mrs Sharpe was not surprised, years later, to hear that her former charge was a rigid disciplinarian: 'it was bred in him'.

No firm evidence suggests that the colonel was a tyrant, frustrated by missing the Crimean War or the Indian Mutiny; he was training his boys for the army. The children respected and a little feared him. Once Nanny went to fetch Herbert and found him with dirt on his hands and pinafore, hair ruffled, not at all a young gentleman. He often dirtied himself helping the farm labourers to sort potatoes or pack peat ready for the winter fires. The steward, Stephens, said he would rather have Master Herbert pack the turf than any man on the estate: 'he is particular about making them fit in so that they never fall'. This evening he had been in a barn trying to do a kindness to bats. Nanny told him that the colonel was in the hall talking to the Kilflynn shoemaker. She hoped Herbert could slip by, 'but nothing escaped the colonel's quick eye. "Come here, sir." The poor boy hung his head. "A nice pickle you are!"'

The colonel turned to Nanny and said they had better get a sack, make holes for his arms and tie it around Herbert's neck. 'Then he smiled so the poor boy knew he was not angry'. Nanny recounted the incident to Mrs Kitchener. 'Let him wear it,' she said. 'He is different from other boys. He does not need to do it now, the knowledge may be useful in years to come. At any rate, there is the kindly action'.

Their mother encouraged Herbert and Arthur to recount the events of the day and each to recite a hymn or read a New Testament passage which she would then explain. Herbert was not a good reader, but Nanny, as devout a Christian as her mistress, noticed that he was quick to grasp a truth or an idea and would never forget what he was told if it were important – an early indication of an exceptional memory. One evening, after several doctors had been at Crotta for a consultation and servants' gossip had exaggerated his mother's danger, Herbert was 'very thoughtful and very tenderly said, "Are you better, Mother?"' She replied that she was a little easier and asked if he had anything to tell her. Herbert had chosen a verse from a hymnbook on Nanny's table about 'a calm, a sure retreat . . . found beneath the mercyseat'.[10] His mother explained the mercyseat (an Old Testament symbol). 'It means,' she said, 'being alone with God in prayer. Try and remember all through life in any trouble, any difficulty, any perplexity or sorrow, go alone in prayer to the mercyseat. Do you understand me?'

That night he asked Nanny if he might say his prayers alone instead of in her hearing, the custom in most nurseries. 'Then I knew he wanted to be alone with God'. Next morning he found his mother looking no worse and was happy, unaware that 'consumption' had then no permanent cure.

The children were affectionate among themselves. 'I never remember hearing them quarrel', Nanny Sharpe recounted. 'They led a very simple country life, no playfellows, no expensive toys'. They all rode and hunted with the local packs, and as children of a soldier they probably played out mock campaigns in the woods and seem to have imposed pretence field punishments on each other if the story is true that Herbert was once found pegged out under a hot sun, tied uncomplainingly to croquet hoops in lieu of the wagon wheel of Field Punishment No. 1.[11]

As for education, the colonel would not send his elder sons away to public school in England or Dublin. Many gentry families of the period still preferred to use tutors, yet the colonel's choice of Church of Ireland clergymen was not a success. A clever young nephew, Francis Elliott Kitchener, came to stay. He was on the threshold of an academic career as Fellow of Trinity College, Cambridge, assistant master at Rugby under Temple and then headmaster of a Staffordshire high school.[12] The colonel asked Frank to examine the boys. He reported of Herbert that he had never known a boy more totally devoid of any groundwork of education but that he was quick to appreciate a work of art.[13]

If devoid of classical knowledge, Herbert was learning about estate man-agement and rural improvement, about cattle and horses, crops and timber. He took a particular interest in his father's operations to drain the marshes and add to his fields. Even fifty years later, when Herbert, now a field marshal and peer, revisited Crotta, he could remember the Irish names of all the fields.[14] As he grew taller, though not yet strong, he liked working with the farm hands. Taking for granted his parents' assumption that Protestant landlords were superior to Catholic peasantry he was the reserved young master, who could not display the warmth he would always feel for the poor.

When he became famous any local memory of 'Colonel Kitchener's boy' would tend to be linked to Herbert. Thus a Kerryman recalled that on market-days the landlord of the Listowel Arms hotel had instructions to refuse the boy breakfast until he had sold the cattle.[15] 'The boy' was more likely to have been Chevally, nearly seventeen, than Herbert, who was aged about twelve. And the boy who rode up to the estate workers as they felled timber and was dis-pleased and struck young Jamesey Sullivan with his riding crop sounds like Chevally. Jamesey, temper flaring, knocked the young master off his horse; he fell against a tree and landed insensible, to the horror and fear of the men, who might all be dismissed, if not prosecuted. The sequel, however, sounds like Herbert, for when he came round he made light of it and won the respect of the men by refusing to tell his father or have Jamesey punished.[16]

By 1863, with Herbert turning thirteen, his father was more accepted as an agricultural expert and the land was improving, but Fanny Kitchener was declining.* The doctors insisted that she could never recover, in the moistness of south-west Ireland. They urged Switzerland where the mountain air was a standard cure for tubercular and bronchial diseases before the discovery of penicillin. The colonel did not hesitate. He sold Crotta and beloved Ballygoghlan.

Thus Herbert Kitchener left Ireland before his thirteenth birthday. He never thought of himself as Irish or Anglo-Irish, his parents having come to Ireland only a few months before his birth. His Irish years had given him an unusual if deficient early education, with an emphasis on mathematics and history rather than on the classics. His home had moulded him to be at ease with his close-knit family but shy with others. He had absorbed a simple Christian faith from his mother and Nanny and the eager if small congrega-tion of Kilflynn church. His future attitudes suggest that he did not feel estranged from those who worshipped differently.

He had absorbed the social structure of home and neighbourhood. He accepted his father's right to command him and the peasantry's duty to obey him, yet he must oversee every detail. And his mother had taught him to care for the poor.

---

* The legend that the colonel contributed to her decline by insisting that they sleep in sheets of newsprint and not in linen is nonsense. He adopted this foible only several years after her death. Madge Kitchener to Sir Philip Magnus, 3 November 1958. Magnus papers. Another view in the family is that the habit should be attributed to his eldest son, not to the colonel.

2

NO CRICKET
AT 'THE SHOP'

DAVOS WAS NOT identified as the best place for consumptives until 1865. In 1863 the Kitcheners went to the little spa of Bex above the right bank of the Rhône as it left the Valais to flow to Lake Geneva. The three elder boys were sent to a French school at the other end of the lake near Geneva. Their Chevallier blood helped them to pass from the stilted schoolroom exercises of Crotta to an easy fluency in French, with passable German.

Bex failed to halt Fanny's disease. The Kitcheners moved the few miles to Montreux on the northern lake shore, where the pure air, soft climate and mountain views had attracted a British colony of invalids and retired officers or their widows. Fanny continued to decline. The boys were summoned. During the summer of 1864, when Herbert was turning fourteen, the mother he adored and trusted, who understood his shyness and his hopes, died at the age of thirty-nine and was buried in the graveyard of Christ Church, Clarens, the English church of Montreux. (In the 1930s the land was required for railway lines and she now lies in Aspall.)

Her death was the great sorrow of his life. Ever after, he sought to live as she would have wished. He placed women on a pedestal, to be honoured as he had honoured her. Her death increased his shyness and his tendency to repress which his mother had noticed, and his inner loneliness; perhaps retarded his sexual development. The full effect cannot be measured because he revealed so little of his feelings.

Chevally went to England to a crammer and then to the Royal Military College at Sandhurst. The colonel decided to stay on in Montreux with Millie and placed Herbert, Arthur and seven-year-old Walter at the English board-ing-school run by Bennett, the chaplain of Christ Church, at the Château de Grand Clos, five miles to the south in the village of Rennaz, outside Villeneuve. Bennett specialized in educating boys who were expecting to work away from England; other pupils were the sons of British subjects living in Switzerland. With such a disparate lot, the shock for the half-educated Kitcheners was probably less than if they had been thrown into an English public school.

The next two and a half years are a biographical shadowland with no con-temporary evidence except a brief undated letter from the Rennaz school in which Herbert tells his father that Walter has stomach ache.[1] A curious item in the George Arthur papers may indicate that Herbert hated the school and washed it from his memory.[2] To make matters worse, he and Walter soon had no home, for the colonel went off to New Zealand. He had used capital from the sale of his Irish properties to invest in land in the South Island. Gold had been found in the province of Otago and he was persuaded that raising sheep would be profitable. After purchasing a commission for Chevally in the 46th (Duke of Cornwall's Light Infantry), the colonel decided to inspect and develop his New Zealand estate.

Before leaving Switzerland he married Millie's music mistress, (Mary) Emma Green, at Berne on 10 January 1867. He took her and Millie, now eighteen, and Arthur, but not Herbert or little Walter. Herbert had set his heart on the Royal Engineers (his father would have preferred the cavalry but agreed), and a voyage to New Zealand would disrupt his preparation. Arthur, on the other hand, had no wish for the army; he wanted to be a mining engineer or an agriculturalist and ended by being both. New Zealand, and the excellent high school at Dunedin, would be useful to Arthur. Walter, aged eight and destined for the army, was left at de Grand Clos in the care of Herbert.

The colonel settled at Waihemo Grange, north-west of Palmerston and below the Horse Range hills. The next run was owned by Sir Francis Bell, one of the pioneers of New Zealand, an expert on Maori affairs and a member of the first representative ministry after the grant of self-government. Late in 1867 the colonel's only child by his second marriage was born in New Zealand and christened Henrietta Emma Kawaru. She was always known as Kawaru, after the Kawaru gorge and river in the centre of Otago province, where perhaps they had spent a holiday.

With their father on the other side of the globe, Herbert and Walter would have spent the holidays at Aspall with their grandmother and Uncle Charles, now the 'squarson'. Herbert always had a great love for Aspall. Uncle Charles had married a Cobbold, of the rich Suffolk brewing family who were already related to the Chevalliers, so that Herbert had many Cobbold cousins. He would also have stayed with his Aunt Emily, his mother's sister, who had married a Suffolk clergyman, John Monins.* Their son, John, became Herbert's great friend.

In 1867 Herbert left the Swiss school to cram for Woolwich, staying partly with his cousin Frank Kitchener at Rugby or in his rooms at Trinity College, Cambridge, before Frank had to vacate his fellowship on marriage, and partly in Kensington with a well-known crammer, George Frost.

Between them, with his own hard work, they educated him enough to pass the examination and win a place at the Royal Military Academy, coming twenty-eighth in a list of sixty successful candidates.[3] In February 1868 he joined the army as a gentleman-cadet at Woolwich, aged seventeen years and seven months.

The Royal Military Academy (nicknamed 'the Shop') stood on Woolwich Common a short distance south of the arsenal and the old dockyard on the Kentish bank of the Thames. The Shop prepared youths for commissions in the Royal Regiment of Artillery and the Corps of the Royal Engineers. Future gunners and future sappers trained and drilled together. Discipline was strict, hours long, but over the preceding twenty years, after various riots and reforms, the food and living conditions had improved. The age of entry had risen. The Shop was less of a cross between a public school and a recruit barracks and growing more like a university college under arms. Inevitably there was plenty of horseplay, but less bullying, and because their commissions could only be earned, not purchased as in the cavalry and infantry, cadets at Woolwich had a strong incentive to work.

The records of Kitchener's career at the Shop were lost with almost all records in the fire of 1873. They would not have been remarkable. The other boys in Kitchener's batch did not spot that he had a great future. When his official biographer trawled for memories he found a tinge of annoyance that Kitchener 'should have become famous without giving them early warning of

* Pronounced *Munins*.

it'. They thought him quite an ordinary youth, with plenty of common sense, a plodder at his books but a slow learner. His great height was not yet matched by strong physique. He did not play cricket or football but was 'a very good rider'. His shyness, increased by the rough-and-tumble and strangeness for someone who had not been at an English public school, made him difficult to know well, yet he was not unsociable 'and never unpopular'.[4]

Other cadets did not realize that he was handicapped. His squint was scarcely noticeable and his blue eyes were clear. But he could not see straight. During the rebuilding of Khartoum thirty years after he had left Woolwich, Major-General Lord Kitchener happened to be discussing recreations with a young sapper officer, Lovick Friend. In a rare admission of any weakness, Kitchener told him:

> Throughout my life I have been much handicapped, owing to my defective eyesight. I have never been able to compete with any boys or men in *any* games. It is not that I cannot see, but that my eyes do not work together, and one eye has to follow the other, and in any games played with a ball my eyes work too loosely to enable me to take part.[5]

He was also a bad shot, perhaps explaining why he later named three gundogs 'Bang', 'Miss' and 'Damn'.

At the Shop he disguised this defect but as he grew older he would find that he might address one person and be answered by another or by both. A hostile journalist in the Boer War thought him devious, not answering questionners by looking them straight in the eye. His Cabinet colleagues in the Great War were often uncertain whom he addressed.[6] The defect added a touch of mystery since he would never admit to it in public.

Among those senior to him at Woolwich was Prince Arthur, Queen Victoria's third son, afterwards Duke of Connaught. Although only seven weeks older than Kitchener, he had entered a year earlier and was treated more as a prince than a cadet. He was a Knight of the Garter already. In old age he recalled Gentlemen-Cadet H. H. Kitchener as 'a tall lanky young man, very quiet and unassuming'. 'I have always liked him very much', he told King George V in 1916, 'and we always got on well together'.[7]

During the summer vacation of 1868 Kitchener went down to Cornwall, soon after his eighteenth birthday, to stay with a Mr Henderson whose two sons were about his age.

The young ladies in Truro quite indulged his vanity, he wrote to Millie in New Zealand. They saw 'so very few young gentlemen that they are very different from les belles de Londres', who probably scorned him as gauche and shy, although smartly dressed, at the balls given by the Shop or by the gunners across the common. In Truro were 'some nice people called the Chilcots – very pretty and nice girls. We went to several croquet parties there'. After about a week of very hot weather the Chilcot household prepared for the family holiday at Newquay on the North Cornwall coast. On the last evening Kitchener and the Hendersons were invited to croquet as usual, and at dusk they all went in and the four girls sang. As the carpets were already up, and the folding doors open between the music- and the drawing-room, Kitchener sug- gested dancing. They got a candle and began, but the Henderson boys were no dancers: 'one wouldn't and the other would but couldn't so almost all the dancing devolved upon your humble slave'.

He asked Millie to imagine the hot evening and then to

think of me with four young ladies, each longing for her turn. I really thought I should break a blood vessel or do something dangerous as they each caused great strain upon my legs. However I got over it and enjoyed it very much as the candle which lighted us was put out (quite by accident) and we got on very well without it.

After the Chilcots left, the boys found amusement picking up the arrows for the ladies at the archery butts, and they went down the river with five young ladies through beautiful scenery to Falmouth and visited a man-of-war lying offshore. Next they made a walking tour to the Lizard peninsula and round by Land's End, 'very fine cliffs, beautiful coves and caves but nothing so awfully grand as the Alps'. Back in Truro they had another excitement. Henderson was captain of the fire brigade, and one night it was called to a burning haystack. The boys followed on foot as fast as they could and had 'some very good fun'. They helped pump water from the engine, and after the fire was out they woke up the farmer who plied them all with brandy.[8]

Kitchener returned to Woolwich for the next term on 7 August and con- tinued his hard plod. His handwriting at this time was still a typically Victorian longhand, which might have become more difficult to read as he grew older and wrote faster, but he was becoming interested in survey work and gradually developed the very clear script that he kept all his life, a biographer's delight.

His great friend at this time, though senior, was another intending sapper with skill in surveying. He had first met Claude Reignier Conder at the crammer. Eighteen months older than Kitchener, Conder was the son of a civil engineer and grandson of Josiah Conder, a prominent nonconformist writer and editor in the early years of the century. Like Kitchener, Conder had some French blood, being descended from the French-born sculptor, Louis Roubiliac, celebrated for his statue of Isaac Newton at Trinity College, Cambridge, and fine monuments in Westminster Abbey. Conder was attracted to the languages of the Near East. He invited Kitchener to join him in learning Hebrew, thus laying a linguistic foundation and increasing their understanding of the Old Testament. Conder was to exert a strong influence on Kitchener's early career.

At the turn of the year or early in 1869 the colonel brought the family back from New Zealand after placing the Waihemo Grange estate in the hands of a manager. A few years later he gave the post to his nephew, Captain Henry Kitchener, on his retirement from the army, a choice to prove disastrous for the estate and for Henry.

The colonel did not stay in England. Probably for economy, since his capital was tied up in the South Island, he settled in north-east Brittany, near the almost unspoiled medieval town of Dinan, perched above the Rance some eighteen miles up river from St-Malo, with its ferry to England: Dinan had a large English colony. He bought the château of Le Grandcour in Tressaint outside the ramparts.[9] The boys came over when they could, Chevally from his regiment, Herbert from the Shop. Arthur was about to enter the School of Mines in London, and Walter, still at de Grand Clos, would go to Bradfield, one of the newer public schools, as soon as he was old enough. Millie was with them at Dinan but not for long. Not yet twenty-one, she had become engaged in New Zealand to an English landowner, Harry Parker, who had come out to farm with his brother Ned in another part of Otago: they had met at a ball in Dunedin. Harry Parker was thirty-two and lord of the manor of Rothley in Leicestershire. His parents were dead. His father, Sir James, had been a judge and his mother the daughter of Thomas Babington, MP, of Rothley Temple, a close friend of Wilberforce and uncle of Thomas Babington Macaulay (Lord Macaulay), the historian. Millie had made an excellent match materially, especially as she was an expert horsewoman and would be able to hunt in the shires when they settled at Rothley. But both loved New

Zealand. Harry Parker was coming back to claim his bride, and then they would return to Otago.

A letter written by Kitchener to Millie a few weeks before her wedding at Weybridge on his nineteenth birthday, 24 June 1869 (two days after her twenty-first), gives another glimpse of him at the Shop. He was now a cadet sergeant, 'and you would be amused at my military swagger with a stick about 5 inches long and as upright as a flagstaff. I think you would be also amused at my giving the orders which I do in a very imposing voice', despite having a false tooth 'which feels as if it was always going to fall out and is not very comfortable'.

The RMA had recently had a sports day in beautiful weather. Kitchener did not compete in the high jump or long jump but ran in three races without winning cup or medal. For the steeplechase they had dug out a hole 'about 20 ft square and five feet deep filled with water. Nobody being able to jump it everybody went in – some dived in and swam across, others stumbled through it'. The Prince of Wales was on a stand where he could see the fun and Kitchener thought the water jump 'a most amusing sight except for those who were in the water like me'.

Before the sports the Shop gave a magnificent lunch for 1,500 in the gymnasium, with silver vases and flowers all up the five long tables. The Prince of Wales, Prince Arthur, six generals and about a hundred officers of all the regiments of the Woolwich garrison came in full dress: 'the horse gunners with all their gold lace made a grand show and there were crowds of ladies'.

Kitchener got tickets to the lunch for 'Sir R Jarvis who honoured us with his company and the Gordons and party'.[10] Kitchener had been welcomed into the Woolwich home of (Sir) Henry Gordon, a senior official of Ordnance who was soon to be commissary-general. The Gordons had a large family, some being about Kitchener's age, and he was the eldest brother of Colonel Charles George Gordon, Royal Engineers. And thus, through Sir Henry, Kitchener met the hero of his life.

'Chinese' Gordon, as he was known to all, was only thirty-six but famous for his brilliant campaign in China, six years earlier, which had ended the Taiping Rebellion.

Returning to England a Chinese field marshal, Charley Gordon had refused to be lionized. He was now in the comparatively lowly post of Commanding Royal Engineer at Gravesend, a few miles down the Thames from Woolwich, and spending most of his spare time relieving the poor and

sick, and teaching poor or destitute boys, to whom he was always most generous. Rather small, he had the prominent and penetrating blue eyes which were
a Gordon family trait. He seemed almost to stare when conversing, and the
Sudanese later would say they never could tell a lie in his presence.

Gordon disliked social occasions but was fond of his brother and his
nephews and nieces. He was also a close friend of Prince Arthur's governor,
Major Howard Elphinstone, and would sometime ride on Woolwich
Common with him and the prince. Moreover, the new governor of the
Academy, Major-General Sir Lintorn Simmons, was Gordon's former commanding officer on the Armenian boundary commission. Gordon was thus
well known to the cadets and especially to any who, like Kitchener, were
welcome at the Henry Gordons.

'Chinese' Gordon's exotic fame, his whimsical humour and his obvious
love for those around him (unless they disobeyed an order) were captivating to
a young man, and he had a vibrant Christian faith. 'I had unbounded admiration for your brother', Kitchener would write to Augusta Gordon after his
death.[11] In that summer of 1869 neither man could imagine how closely and
tragically their lives would be intertwined fifteen years later. Moreover, if
young Kitchener could not fail to notice Gordon, Gordon did not notice
Kitchener among the other cadets. His awareness sprang later from
Kitchener's skill and achievement as a sapper, not knowing they had met; for
eight years afterwards he wrote a note to another officer: 'Let me introduce to
you Lieut. Kitchener (whom I have never seen). Introduce him to L'Estrange
and do not go sitting up and talking the "Langwidge".'[12]

3

HEART AND SOUL

KITCHENER LOST ONE term through an unspecified illness but passed out successfully from the RMA in December 1870. He crossed the Channel to Dinan for Christmas and to await his commission.

France was engulfed in the closing stages of the disastrous Franco-Prussian War. The emperor and his best army had been captured at Sedan in September. Paris was under siege. The new Republic had ordered a *levée-en-masse* and the young men of Dinan were conscripted to the Army of the Loire. French tradition insists that Kitchener enlisted as a private in the 6th Battalion of the *Gardes Mobile* of the Côtes-du-Nord, the local Reserve.[1] This is doubtful, for as late as 26 January he and another young Englishman, Harry Dawson, were still at Dinan looking for a means to reach the front, where they would offer their services. Colonel Kitchener found a staff officer about to leave who took them by diligence to Rennes, the capital of Brittany, some forty-five miles south. Next day they went a further forty-five miles eastwards in a train 'crammed with soldiers, and there were several officers in our compartment. They were very civil and polite to us', wrote Dawson.

At Laval they were admitted to the headquarters of General Chanzy, who had been summoned from Algeria after the disaster of Sedan. He was France's best soldier, of indomitable will, but he had been defeated in a three-day battle around Le Mans because his Breton reservists ran away. Despite heavy casualties he had executed a skilful retreat and was now re-forming. The battle of Le Mans had ended seventeen days before Kitchener reached the army, disproving claims that this was his baptism of fire and that he saw the slaughter

[24]

of large numbers of men and horses without showing emotion.[2] His baptism of war would have been only the harrowing sights of field hospitals and walking wounded and the chaos of a defeated army re-forming. Chanzy had received fresh, if raw, troops and was preparing a fresh offensive. 'We expect the sound of cannon at any moment', wrote Dawson on 27 January. They were still trying to obtain horses to ride to the front when, next day, the news came that Paris had fallen, the French government had asked for an armistice and the war was over.[3]

Kitchener accepted an invitation from a French officer to go up in a balloon to see the distant German lines. But he did not take enough warm clothing and caught a chill in the late January air. The chill turned to pleurisy and pneu-monia. Harry Dawson, refusing the offer of a commission in the French artillery to stay with him, sent an urgent wire to Colonel Kitchener, who arrived to find his son lying in great pain in an insanitary village inn.

As soon as Herbert could stand the journey, his father took him back to England for better treatment. He had nearly died and took many months to throw off the effects. He also nearly had his commission revoked for unneutral activity in France. He was ordered to present himself before the Commander-in-Chief at the Horse Guards. The officers of the British Army in 1871 were a close-knit family, very much soldiers of the queen. Queen Victoria signed every commission, and if an officer were court-martialled the Judge Advocate General had to report the verdict to her in person. It was therefore not sur-prising that the Commander-in-Chief, HRH the Duke of Cambridge, should personally rebuke a new and insignificant twenty-year-old lieutenant of the Royal Engineers, especially as the duke had only lately relinquished the titular governorship of the Shop.

The duke tongue-lashed Kitchener with a plentiful flow of the oaths for which he was famous; told him he was a disgrace to the British Army, a deserter, had behaved abominably, did not deserve a commission, etc. Kitchener stood ramrod straight and never said a word, although inwardly impenitent, holding that as he was domiciled in France, had left the RMA yet not received his commission, he was entitled to do what he liked. His logic was a little flawed, for he had known that the queen's commission as a lieuten-ant, RE, would arrive at Dinan any day. When received, it was dated 4 January, so that he was a serving officer of neutral Britain when he joined Chanzy.

The flow of oaths continued. Then the duke paused and 'with a funny sort of twinkle' murmured: 'I am bound to say, boy, that in your place I should have done the same thing'.[4]

In April 1871 Lieutenant Kitchener reported to the great barracks at Brompton, above the Medway close to Chatham, which was the depot of the Corps of Royal Engineers and its School of Military Engineering. For the first time, he walked in the spacious grounds where his own equestrian statue would stand, and dined in the magnificent mess with its portrait of Gordon in the robes of a Chinese mandarin. His own portrait, in the khaki of his campaign that avenged Gordon, would be placed near it a quarter of a century later.

At Chatham he went through the normal training of a young officer, including the making of a survey of twenty square miles, with two men under him. 'It is jolly in this weather', he told Millie, now back in New Zealand with her husband, when congratulating her on 'my promotion to the ranks of uncle. It must be awfully jolly for you. I suppose my nephew is like his father with his mother's eyes. All babies are'.[5]

The family meant much to Herbert. Arthur had returned to New Zealand with the Parkers but was now nearly home. When Herbert saw their father, over in England to meet Arthur, he invited both to Chatham. A few days later the colonel announced Arthur's arrival but absent-mindedly addressed his letter to Woolwich. 'On my not answering this unreceived epistle he takes umbrage and will not let Arthur come down and see me'. Fortunately, Herbert wrote again when Arthur did not turn up and was able to catch him in London before father and son went to France. Arthur later returned to London to study chemistry, and Herbert was able to give him an occasional day's hunting. Young Walter, now at Bradfield, also came to stay, a jolly boy who has 'greatly grown and perhaps will overtop me'.[6]

Except with the family, Kitchener still kept rather to himself, preferring long rides on his mare to jaunts with brother officers, partly because he had nothing except his pay and a small legacy from his mother. His father could not provide an allowance when his capital was tied up in New Zealand and yielded little. 'The Gov. is very hard up'.[7] Frugality became natural to Herbert Kitchener.

He made one very good friend soon after arrival at Brompton barracks. Not yet fully recovered from the illness contracted during the Franco-Prussian War, he had been glad to find himself given a room of his own and made it comfortable. He had hardly settled in when he and the subaltern next door received orders to quit. A new instructor, Captain R. H. Williams, required both rooms. Kitchener was upset and rushed to William's office.

A very tall and very slight youth burst into the room and blurted out:

> 'My name is Kitchener, and I am ordered to move out of my little room because you want it. I know you would not wish for such a thing, sir.' He was looking terribly ill, and his evident distress caused me to offer him one of my two rooms. In a week we understood one another, took our daily exercise in company, sat next each other at mess, went to evensong together, became inseparable.[8]

Williams was a High Churchman. As they talked, rode and worshipped together, Kitchener came to love more ritual and to give a higher place to the Eucharist. Ferment in the Church of England over vestments, incense and lights had led recently to a Royal Commission which had ruled against many of the pre-Reformation practices which were being reintroduced by the Oxford Movement, to which Kitchener became an enthusiastic adherent. He and Williams kept festival and fast, Kitchener finding an ingenious way to keep a 'fast' in an officers' mess: 'We must find something unpleasant', he would whisper as they sat down.[9]

As his batch neared the end of their course (he did not do too well in exams) Kitchener dreaded being posted to India, perhaps because India had broken his mother's health. The only consolation would be a hope of meeting Millie and Harry Parker on their way home if he went out by North America and Japan. Millie had asked him to be godfather to her second son, the future Parker Pasha.

In the spring of 1873 the general at the War Office who was to attend the Austro-Hungarian manoeuvres selected Kitchener as his aide-de-camp, perhaps because of his height and military bearing. General Greaves promptly fell ill in Vienna, so that Kitchener, twenty-three, found himself representing the queen, mingling with foreign generals and sitting next to Emperor Franz Josef at meals. The emperor allowed him to study Austrian military bridging, very useful for a report he was writing at Chatham.

His posting came through – not to India but to Aldershot, to join the mounted Telegraph Troop which was training to lay and operate electric telegraph lines on campaign, a fairly new skill for the Royal Engineers.

'Aldershot Camp', as it was generally known, had been laid out less than twenty years before in the Crimean War around a small village in the little-populated Hampshire heathlands where parades, exercises and manoeuvres could take place unhindered. By 1873 it was still a dreary landscape of barrack squares and lines of mostly wooden buildings which became the centre of a vast tent town when companies, battalions and volunteer formations from all over southern Britain arrived for summer camp.

Except for the hunting and tent-pegging Kitchener disliked the place, although he enjoyed a rain-drenched exercise down on distant Dartmoor. That October the Commanding Officer of RE troops at Aldershot in his confidential report described Kitchener as 'A most zealous and promising officer – thoroughly acquainted with his special work, and performs his duties to my entire satisfaction'.[10] The Commanding Officer was Lieutenant-Colonel Sir Howard Elphinstone, who combined regimental duty with his work as comptroller to Prince Arthur, now Duke of Connaught: Kitchener dined with them occasionally. Elphinstone's great friend Gordon was twice briefly in England at that time, before taking up his dangerous post as governor-general of the equatorial southern Sudan, the first step by which 'Chinese' Gordon became 'Gordon of Khartoum'. Young Kitchener could have again come under his spell.

When Captain Williams was also posted from Chatham to Aldershot, 'We were very happy', Williams recalled, 'in a never-to-be-forgotten brother-hood of keen Churchmanship brought to high pressure under a remarkable man, Dr Edghill'. John Cox Edghill was senior chaplain at Aldershot and later chaplain-general for sixteen years. He had taken over a gaunt 'tin taber-nacle' as garrison church. Williams, Kitchener and others helped him make it 'better fitted for Church worship, with an enlarged Altar and seemly sur-roundings, an organ and a choir'.

During the summer camps they must have gone round to different units to persuade them to drop Sunday church parades in their own lines and march instead to Edghill's church, for Williams says that 'the original congregation of 30 quickly grew to one of 800 assembled inside, with another hundred or two waiting outside. Officers and men were equally enthusiastic and a sung Eucharist was well attended'. Since Edghill was more of a ritualist than most army padres of the day, and the newspapers were full of the vestments dispute, 'there was just enough persecution to keep us all at white heat'.[11] Kitchener could never express his deepest feelings and hated any 'undressing' of soul, but he could show his faith by externals. And when in 1874 Disraeli's new government responded to widespread public fears and episcopal dislike of 'Roman' practices by passing the ill-advised Public Worship Regulation Act, Kitchener became a member of the English Church Union which defended them.[12]

Professionally, Kitchener was very ambitious, determined to reach the highest rank. 'You are too tall', said his father. 'Only little men get to the top!'[13] He was probably thinking of Napoleon and possibly Havelock or Wolseley, just becoming famous. Little 'Bobs', the future Lord Roberts, was still unknown to the general public, but Wolseley, was 'the very model of a modern major-general', and was forming his expedition to put down the murderous King of Ashanti. Kitchener volunteered. 'At least', he told Millie in New Zealand, 'I have said if they order me I shall be glad to go. So the next thing you may hear will be my slaying niggers by the dozen'.[14] His services were not required.

The Royal Engineers at that time carried out many works that in a later age would be done by civil engineers and surveyors. Although in peacetime the cavalry, brigade of guards and gunners despised sappers as mere professionals, the letters RE after an officer's name carried great prestige. Kitchener's commandant at the Shop, Lintorn Simmons, a future field marshal, had masterminded the expanding railway system of Britain before the Crimean War, and Gordon had demarcated the new frontiers between the Ottoman and Russian Empires after it. Sappers had first begun to survey the Holy Land in 1864. The Palestine Exploration Fund (founded in 1865) paid and reaped the glory, while the War Office welcomed detailed knowledge which could be used in war. Kitchener's old friend, Lieutenant Claude Conder, was now in command of the survey.

While waiting for an opportunity, Kitchener accepted two months' leave (by no means unusual for home forces) in January and February 1874, which he spent in Dinan for reasons of economy. The colonel had sold the château and bought a house in Rue Saint-Charles known as L'Ancien Presbytère. Here Kitchener improved his stamp collection and taught himself the still-complicated art of photography. He was also training what became a remarkable memory, in the spirit of his words to Millie about her small son: 'Above all things work at his memory when he is young, make him learn things by heart. Euclid is a good thing for that'.[15]

But his father and stepmother were falling out: 'there is always an element of discord which drives one wild'.[16] A year or two later they separated, though never divorced. The colonel lived in England. His wife made L'Ancien Presbytère her home with Kawara, who was much loved by her father and half-brothers and Millie. Mrs Kitchener survived three of her stepsons, dying in 1918, honoured in Dinan for the hospital work of mother and daughter in the Great War.[17]

Herbert did not return to Dinan for his next, shorter leave in the summer of 1874. He went to Hanover to improve his German and to study fortifications. In Hanover he heard from Conder in Palestine. Conder had been assisted by a civilian, Charles Tyrwhitt-Drake, who although only twenty-eight was already a distinguished explorer and naturalist. Tyrwhitt-Drake had died on 23 June. Conder urged Kitchener to apply and had strongly recommended him. This was the very post Kitchener had wanted. 'I am one fully determined to do so many things which never come off that it is quite surprising to be able to say, what I intended is accomplished'.[18]

4

'THE FOOTSTEPS
OF OUR LORD'

KITCHENER ENTERED HANOVER railway station and was standing on the platform beside his japanned uniform case marked with his name and rank when a well-dressed English youth shyly approached. The boy confessed that he had recklessly broken his journey from the University of Lüneburg to dine and sleep and hear a famous singer at the opera, which had all cost more than he had expected: he was stranded.

Kitchener asked his name, cross-examined him severely, then bought his ticket to London, kept him under his eye, fed him throughout the journey and, so the young man's brother related many years later, 'finally saw him and his luggage into a cab for home'.[1]

In London, the Palestine Exploration Fund's sponsors, including Sir George Grove, more celebrated for creating the Royal College of Music and *Grove's Dictionary*, and the secretary, (Sir) Walter Besant, better known to contemporaries as a novelist, were impressed by Kitchener, who then took a course in Arabic. He saw his eldest brother Chevallier ('Chevally'), now passed staff college, and Walter, still at Bradfield. Arthur was 'a little put out' because his father had chosen a thirty-six-year-old nephew to manage the New Zealand estate instead of a twenty-two-year-old son. His motive probably was to safeguard Arthur's career as a mining engineer; Arthur went off to Mexico, while Captain Henry Kitchener began his ruinous career in New Zealand. The colonel himself and his second wife were still living in France.

Early in November, 'having left everyone perfectly well and happy, I started with a clear conscience and a ticket for Venice'. The Fund paid all expenses.

Kitchener spent a day's sightseeing at Venice, then embarked at Trieste in an Austrian-Lloyd steamer for Alexandria, with a rather grand Egyptian pasha, a German family, an Englishman and an American couple – a dull husband and a wife who 'was fun, such quaint expressions and mannerisms I never met'. After they had all recovered from a bout of rough weather, she scandalized the pasha and charmed the rest by 'singing on deck by the light of the moon Yankee Doodle and such like'.[2]

After sightseeing in Alexandria with the eagerness of a first-time tourist and watching a dance of coal-black Nubians, he took the Jaffa steamer.

Next day Sunday 15th November I got up early to see the sun rise over the Holy Land. It was glorious more from association than anything else, seeing for the first time that land which must be the most interesting for any Christian. The sun rose in a golden halo behind the hills and we rushed on towards it through the deep blue sea.[3]

The ship anchored outside the harbour. Kitchener was rowed to the beach and carried ashore by half-naked Arabs.

His luggage from England arrived two days later, and he left the bazaars and orange groves of Jaffa that evening, having bargained for two mules, a horse and a guide, and rode the forty miles up through the hills. (He does not say why he chose to travel at night: possibly to avoid robbers.) 'Such a ride over terribly rough country'. The guide, with a better horse, kept cantering away into the darkness 'while I blundered on, trusting entirely to my horse. We went all the short cuts' and sometimes had to jump from ledge to ledge of rock as the road climbed steeply. Kitchener was very thankful when they reached Jerusalem and the hotel at 4 a.m. Conder came later that morning, and next day they rode out of Jerusalem through the stony hills of southern Judaea to the survey camp.

Palestine at that time was a corner of the Ottoman Empire, thinly populated by Muslim Arab shepherds and farmers and rather neglected by the Turkish rulers. In the north were many Maronite Christian villages, but the massacre of 1860 had reduced the number of Christians. Orthodox monasteries had long existed here and there. Pilgrims could visit the holy sites, and small colonies of Germans and Americans awaited the Second Coming of Christ. Jewish refugees from Eastern European pograms were coming in, supported mostly by charity raised in the West.

Biblical archaeology was in its infancy. The Royal Engineers' map would be an essential tool. Conder and Kitchener, Sergeants Armstrong and Black and one corporal worked closely together, supported by thirteen servants, six tents, seven mules and seven horses: Kitchener's horse was a little arab named Salem, 'all mane and tail'.

The work was highly demanding. They were not making sketch maps but an ordnance survey of the most precise accuracy. They would rise at seven for tea and bread, ride out and survey, with a break at noon for a substantial break, fast, brought with them on a mule, then back at four. 'Dinner at 6, a cup of tea at 8 and very early to bed'. Heavy rain, high winds, and fever among the servants drove them back to Jerusalem, but Kitchener managed to photograph the rugged valley where King Saul's son Jonathan had climbed alone except for his armour-bearer and routed the Philistines.

On New Year's Day 1875, with the weather better, the expedition took the dreary road from Jerusalem down to Jericho, then a mere 'collection of hovels inhabited by extremely dirty Arabs' surrounded by trees and the fertile green, ery of the Jordan plain. After the cold of Jerusalem in winter, the semitrop, ical warmth made surveying delightful, and when they saw the Dead Sea 'the water looked so blue and nice we were soon stripped and in it. The sensation is extraordinary . . .' They could only float and the salt got into their eyes.

Kitchener 'paid dearly' (in Conder's words) for their visit to the Jordan plain. On their return to Jerusalem he went down with 'Jericho fever', the worst of the local varieties, almost certainly malaria, since swamps still lay on the edge of the town. The term is unknown to medical textbooks.[4] Conder feared that Kitchener might be invalided home, but he was saved by the English doctor, Chaplin, and Conder as 'a capital nurse' and by downing a glass of light beer at a critical moment. Chaplin kept him convalescent in the expedition's curious house in the Jewish quarter, with thick stone walls between the rooms, while Conder resumed the survey on 25 February.

Kitchener worked up their notes and resumed his sightseeing. He revelled in the colours and excitement of the East. He visited the Wailing Wall and a service at a synagogue, he walked about the Arab quarter, wholly oriental in noise and movement, and secured a permit to the Muslim Dome of the Rock on the site of the Temple and marvelled at its beauty. But 'the Holy Sepulchre was naturally the first place I visited'. He was not impressed by the different sects who jealously guarded their corners of the church, and he doubted the authenticity of the traditional sites: 'I think divine wisdom has been shown in hiding them. Such fearful scenes of fighting and bloodshed could never be allowed round the sacred spot of our Lord's sacrifice and His tomb'; and the place where the church was built, he held, could not have been outside the city wall, whatever clever men might write. It would be left to Gordon, eight years later, to make famous an alternative site on the skull-like hill beyond the present saracen walls, afterwards known as Gordon's Calvary.

On 7 March, waiting alone for lunch, Herbert opened his heart to Millie:

> . . . I find that writing letters to one's friends is almost as delightful as receiving them. It brings before one old times, happy days. Their faces seem to gleam through the inner self and smile, their voices again talk with the same tones sweet and low and so one is apt to dream away a morning while writing a letter. What a glorious land this is when one can see it through the spectacles of imagination – those grand old knights, so fierce in war, so gentle in religion.

He saw the old Crusaders, each a Lion and a Lamb, leaving pleasant homes to undergo most terrible privations to fight in their quaint armour for their God against a far superior force and probably to die amid a heap of corpses.

'*After lunch*. I have read over the preceding remarks and laughed to find how spiritual fasting makes you'. He was inclined to tear it up but it would provide variation in a long letter.[5]

Six days later, on the evening of 13 March, Conder recorded that Kitchener rejoined him, 'with Habib, the groom, the little dog Looloo, her new puppy, and the baggage. The camp was once more increased to six tents, and the meeting was cheerful'.[6]

Fit again, Kitchener threw himself into the work, scrambling over stony country on little Salem, taking angles, setting up the camera here, sketching a little there, or exploring a ruin to record inscriptions, 'but principally feeling an interest in the donkey with the grub . . . Then coming back in the evening satisfied with a good day's work to our tents'.

On 5 April they were at Askelon on the coast and went for their daily bathe in the sea. Conder was caught in an undertow and would have been drowned had not Kitchener, a strong swimmer, reached him in time and dragged him back to shore. They next worked in Galilee. When Kitchener passed his twenty-fifth birthday on 24 June he was thoroughly enjoying the life. Conder and he were on excellent terms. A French archaeologist who saw them from time to time noted Kitchener, as tall, slim and vigorous, 'a frank and most outspoken character, with recesses of winsome freshness'. His 'high spirits and cheeriness', contrasting with Conder's sadder disposition, might sometimes lead to headstrong acts, but his 'ardour for work astonished us' and he showed 'marked proficiency' as an archaeologist.[7] His identifications were not always confirmed. He made an impassioned appeal to save the ruins of the synagogue of Capernaum, 'hallowed by the footsteps of our Lord', but excavations many years later proved that the site was not where he contended.[8]

The survey had been aware of latent suspicion among the Arab country folk, based on fears that Christians had designs on their lands, but no serious incident occurred until 10 July 1875 in the hills of upper Galilee, at Safad, a fanatical Muslim town. On arrival, Conder had sent the Imperial Ottoman prescript, an imposing document, to the local Turkish governor, who would then at his leisurely convenience pay a courtesy call. The surveyors had just laid out their camp in an olive grove when an elderly sheikh or headman arrived with a small crowd, brandishing shotguns and shouting anti-Christian blasphemies. When he tried to steal a revolver hanging on a tree, Conder arrested him and tied him up to await the Turkish authorities. This enraged the crowd, who advanced yelling. Conder prudently untied the sheikh and tried to calm matters, but within seconds a battle began with a shower of stones and a charge. The unarmed Europeans had nothing to hand but their hunting crops and canes: Conder laughed as he saw Sergeant Armstrong all ready to repel a charge, holding the camera obscura legs as if a rifle and bayonet. Soon matters were desperately serious. A huge black slave whirled a nail-studded club and would have smashed Conder's skull if he had not dodged and butted so that the club fell on his neck in a damaging wound. The slave was about to strike again. 'I must inevitably have been murdered, but for the cool and prompt assistance of Lieutenant Kitchener', whose thigh was severely bruised by a stone yet managed to reach Conder under a hail of blows and stones and fight off the slave with his cane.

Other villagers were coming through the olive grove and vineyards, converging on the Europeans. 'Unless the soldiers arrived at once we must all die'. Conder gave orders to bolt back to a hill a hundred yards off, Kitchener covering the retreat with his now-broken steel-handled hunting crop, while a bullet whistled by his ear.

The Turkish soldiers ran up. The crowd dropped their stones and pre-tended to be innocent sightseers.[9]

Conder brought forward the planned three-week holiday on Mount Carmel above Haifa, then suspended the survey, since the expedition could not work anywhere safely until the Safad rioters were punished: moreover, a cholera epidemic had broken out in northern Palestine. Conder's wound had not healed, and he handed over command to Kitchener. The rioters, after a long trial, received derisory sentences and fines (given to the Fund) which were increased after diplomatic pressure.

With the cholera unabated, Conder still wounded and Kitchener and the sergeants suffering from fever, they decided in October to go home temporarily. Kitchener insisted on their riding the forty miles down to Jaffa in one day. He fell off his horse unconscious as they reached the garden of the German hotel. Conder hurried for help, returned to find no sign of him, and was relieved to discover him in bed, having come round and then crawled through the garden.

For Christmas leave he crossed to Dinan, where despite the worsening domestic discord he completed *Lieutenant Kitchener's Guinea Book of Photographs of Biblical Sites*, the only book he ever produced. When Besant cut it from fifty photographs to twelve, he wrote back 'utterly disheartened and disgusted', then apologized in his next letter: 'You know I daresay what it is to be seedy and cross, and I was very much of both when I last wrote'.[10]

They had expected to return to Palestine early in 1876, but as Conder was not fit they spent the entire year based on London. Using rooms in the hideous muddle of buildings off the Cromwell Road which then comprised the South Kensington Museum (renamed the Victoria and Albert when rebuilt) they worked up the map and compiled 'Memoirs', copious notes on Palestine's flora, fauna, topography, archaeology and other matters, seven composite volumes in all, some by Kitchener, most by Conder.

The year was lightened for Kitchener by the Parkers' return from New Zealand. Kitchener was able to meet his godson, his two other nephews and a niece before Millie and Harry took a castle in Ireland while waiting for tenants to vacate Rothley Temple and they could settle down in Leicestershire. Some years later, Harry's bad management of his estate caused him to sell up and take them all back to New Zealand.

Early in that year of 1876 Kitchener joined a new brotherhood, the Guild of the Holy Standard. Major Wyndham Malet of the Horse Guards, a clergyman's son, had found that many young men who had been communicants of the Church of England abandoned their religious practices after enlistment, through fear of ridicule or from the pressures and temptations of the barrack-room and the public houses outside. He therefore founded the guild in 1873, with John Edghill (Kitchener's padre at Aldershot) and others, to protect and encourage men by binding them to a voluntary rule. Guild Brothers of the Holy Standard pledged themselves to support one another and set a Christian example, 'to be sober, upright and chaste; to be regular in their private prayers; to receive the Holy Communion at least three times a year, to be reverent during services, to avoid immoral books, to pray for other people, help the chaplains and promote the religious and social welfare of soldiers and their families'. Kitchener became a Brother on 1 January 1876 and, as the obituary in the guild magazine tactfully stated, 'he remained a silent member till the day of his lamented death'.[11]

Conder was still not passed fit by the end of 1876. Kitchener replaced him in command and was given a larger expedition.

Before he left England he met Gordon again, back briefly from the Sudan. Gordon had long planned to spend a year in Palestine, meditating and studying the holy sites, and Kitchener may have expected to show his hero many of them. But Gordon's hopes of the Holy Land were postponed for another five years. The persuasions of the Khedive of Egypt, backed by the orders of the Duke of Cambridge (and a little sortilege) sent him out again to the Sudan as governor-general of the entire country with powers greater than those of a viceroy of India. Gordon admired Kitchener's fine presence and his character. He heard much about him later as one of the best of officers – with a cool head and a hard constitution; but the turn of the year 1876–7 was the last time they could have met face to face in England.[12]

Kitchener went out by Constantinople, where he made useful contacts, and reached Beirut on 6 February 1877, went up to Damascus and then to Jerusalem. In the next months he surveyed in northern Palestine, where they had been abused, and had a triumphal return to Safad, where he graciously remitted the remainder of the fine.

He now had a strong party of eighteen men ('quite a little army to feed'). 'I have six horses and a number of dogs as companions', he wrote to a friend of the family early in May. 'My time is fully taken up with work from morning to night. I enjoy the life amazingly'.[13] A few days earlier he had learned that Turkey and Russia were at war. He felt no cause for alarm. He realized that

Disraeli's England might be drawn into the conflict but almost certainly on the Turkish side. Nevertheless the outbreak of war brought urgency: he must finish the survey as fast as possible lest it be stopped by the Turks or he was recalled for special service.

He urged on his men. Where Conder had been short-tempered, quick to beat a slow servant, Kitchener had the gift of evoking enthusiasm. He was always in anxiety because he had Christian servants and Muslim soldiers (placed under his command for the expedition's protection). One day in June, when the temperature was 105°F in the shade, he had to break up a knife-fight between two servants by pulling them apart. 'A sound thrashing and summary dismissal settled their business. In this hot weather it is unpleasant to have to scrimmage with one's servants'.[14]

That summer was the hottest in Palestine for fifteen years, and he was often in the saddle for over eight hours. In late August, on the way down from the Lebanon mountains, where he had rested the party and worked up his notes and measurements,

> the sun was dreadfully hot and I got a slight sunstroke. I had to lie under a tree for 2 hours with water being poured over my head. I then tried to get on but was so weak I had to stop wherever there was the least shade. I got to Sidon at 12.30 a.m. and had dinner at 1 in the morning. My dogs nearly died on the road and everyone suffered considerably.[15]

During these months Kitchener came into his own. He was physically hard with great powers of endurance. The work of the ordnance survey had increased his mastery of detail and his thoroughness. Negotiating with Arabs and Turks, with civil authorities and suspicious Muslim imams, and with Christian priests and patriarchs had developed his natural tact and diplomacy (the Orthodox patriarch was particularly difficult about preserving Jacob's Well). He was proud that by careful preparation and use of resources he kept within his budget, no mean feat in a Middle Eastern land.[16] He and Conder added many hundreds of placenames and identified sites, so that Besant could fairly claim for the survey that 'nothing has ever been done for the illustration and right understanding of the historical portions of the Old and New Testament, since the translation into the vulgar tongue, as this great work'.[17]

On 2 October 1877 Kitchener reported in a biblical phrase that the mapping was finished 'from Dan to Beersheba'. Many discoveries remained to be examined in more detail, while the distant war and the rumbles of revolt made the country more dangerous and officials less helpful, probably because any Western European was believed to be an ally of Russia. At Nablus on 3 November the expedition was stoned. The acting governor rejected Kitchener's complaint, so he had several offending boys tied up and beaten publicly, as if to emphasize that a British officer's innate authority counted for more than a minor official.

On 26 November Kitchener paid off the servants, saw his sappers into a steamer for home – and hurried to Constantinople and onwards to Bulgaria to see the fighting. He had many adventures which he afterwards described in *Blackwood's Magazine*. He saw scores of Bulgarian corpses hanging by their necks – the 'Bulgarian horrors' that Gladstone would soon make famous in his 'bag and baggage' pamphlet – and reached the frontline head-quarters of Valentine Baker Pasha. Baker had commanded the 10th Hussars for thirteen years with great success, then made a notable journey in Central Asia. When assistant quartermaster general at Aldershot he was sent to prison for assaulting a young woman in a railway carriage. He was therefore cashiered. He was now a Turkish pasha winning glory but had ruined a promising career in the British Army and was a marked man. Ambitious young British officers were told that they should not become closely involved with him, a fact which was to be awkward for Kitchener six years later.

Kitchener next helped to rescue two British newspaper correspondents about to be shot as spies, one of whom described him as 'lean as a gutted herring, as active as a panther and tanned ... to the blackness of an Arab complexion'.[18] Kitchener ended his war as a stowaway in a troop train returning to Constantinople, to the amusement of the Turkish officers who discovered him under the seat. And so to England, just too late for Christmas.

'Herbert is home again', wrote nineteen-year-old Walter Kitchener, on leave from Sandhurst, to Amy Fenton, an older sister of the girl he would not be allowed to marry for nearly another seven years, continuing:

We had not heard from him for a long time and only knew he had gone to see some fighting; of course we were in a tremendous fright and were just merging from the passive to the active state when he suddenly appears among us ...

You've no idea what a fellow Herbert is, I don't think there *is* anyone a bit like him. Talking to him does one good, it has something like the same effect as staying at Clanna* — it changes one altogether and leaves one full of determination.[19]

* The house at Lydney, Gloucestershire, where the Fentons were then living.

5

THE CYPRUS SURVEY

When disraeli and Lord Salisbury brought back 'peace with honour' from the Berlin Congress of June 1878 they also brought Cyprus. Predominantly Greek with a Turkish minority, it would remain nominally in the Ottoman Empire, but under British administration, and needed an accurate survey. Thomas Cobbold MP, a former diplomat, recommended to Lord Salisbury that Lieutenant Herbert Kitchener, his cousin through the Chevalliers, was the right man to make it.

Recommendations through Parliamentary 'interest' were then normal. Kitchener wrote to Cobbold 'to thank you for a most delightful appointment . . . It is exactly what I like and will be a great advancement for me professionally when I have done it. I expect I shall take 2½ to 3 years to finish it'.[1] His instructions were to make a detailed ordnance survey map at one inch to the mile, with larger scale where necessary, and he was allotted a twenty-three-year-old sapper subaltern, Richard Hippisley, and four NCOs and men. Kitchener was particularly pleased that he was to report direct to Salisbury, the Foreign Secretary.[2]

Still working on the Palestine map and notes, Kitchener was living with his father in Albert Mansions, Victoria Street, one of the first tall buildings in London to be designed as 'flats'. Young Walter, on leave from the Curragh and soon to sail with his regiment for India and the Afghan War, told Hetty Fenton: 'He has a room fitted up entirely in Eastern fashion where he sits cross-leged [sic] and receives his friends at afternoon tea'.[3] He wore an early version of a neat imperial beard (for a short time) and the famous moustache.

[41]

Herbert handed over the completed Palestine map, receiving highest praise, and hurried out to Cyprus with Hippisley to reconnoitre. After landing at Larnaka they dined with the Bombay Sappers and Miners 'and slept or rather laid awake scratching' in the house of a Greek then travelled by mail cart through the lower eastern mountains and down to Nicosia, where Kitchener found Britain's first High Commissioner (and Commander-in-Chief) of Cyprus encamped in a monastery garden. Lieutenant-General Sir Garnet Wolseley, famous already for the Ashanti campaign and his reforming zeal at the War Office, was 'very agreeable and pleasant though I don't like his manner much or that of his staff. I hope eventually to have very little to do with them'. Kitchener put his finger at once on the trouble with empire-builders: 'It is just what I expected – the English have come with English ideas in every-thing and a scorn for native habits or knowledge of the country. The result is fatal – they work hard and do nothing absolutely except mistakes, absurd laws etc that have to be counter-ordered. All is in fact chaos'.[4]

As soon as HMS *Humber* arrived (late) on 17 October with the sappers and equipment, Kitchener began the survey, starting a baseline, climbing moun-tains to fix points and finding the existing maps of the interior 'excessively wrong'.[5]

He liked the island, the life and the inhabitants and did not expect to be bothered much by staff officials; but very soon the Treasury in London was grumbling at the expense, and Wolseley became tiresome. Herbert wrote to Millie on 2 February 1879: 'The survey goes pretty well – lots of worries, I am quite losing my sweet temper. Lady W. they say drives the coach. I don't much like her. Sir G. is very civil but they are all a dangerous lot saying one thing and meaning another, like women eh!' Wolseley summoned Kitchener and over his almost insubordinate protests ordered him to limit the survey to a chart of the land instead of the map he had been ordered to create with exact con-tours, buildings and archaeological sites. Kitchener soon hoped Wolseley would be posted to South Africa, where the Zulu War went badly, and indeed he was, but not before he had suspended the survey altogether for financial reasons. The surveyors were two days' journey from Nicosia by bullock wagon in early May when they were recalled.

Kitchener deplored the decision on both public and personal grounds. The acting governor's assurance that their work was highly approved did not lessen Kitchener's distress. He wrote at once to Lord Salisbury that 'the whole of my prospects as a surveyor are injured by the sudden recall'. He implored his lordship to let him bring his work home for inspection and not allow it to be lost. Years later Wolseley admitted 'handsomely and openly' that he had been wrong. He had already noted Kitchener as a highly professional if tiresomely independent soldier.[7]

Kitchener returned to England and stepped straight into another appoint, ment. Articles 61 and 62 of the Treaty of Berlin had enjoined the Ottoman Empire to reform its administration in Anatolia (Asia Minor) and to relieve oppressions, ensure religious freedom for Armenian and other Christian com, munities and prevent atrocities by Circassians and Kurds. Four British mili, tary vice,consuls and a consul,general would oversee the reforms and report back.

The Foreign Office had appointed as consul,general the sapper who had founded the Palestine Survey, Lieutenant,Colonel Charles Wilson, who six years later would achieve unfortunate fame as commander of the force that arrived two days too late to save Gordon. Wilson knew Kitchener well enough to secure his services as one of the four vice,consuls.

In August 1879 Kitchener left London nonstop by ferry and train for Vienna, his diplomatic courier's pass most useful for passing Customs and obtaining comfortable carriages. He went down the Danube and by the Black Sea to Constantinople and the ambassador's summer residence, the wooden palace at Therapia, 'a charming place on the Bosphorus. I dined and spent the night in no end of luxury'.[8] Some years earlier, Therapia palace had been the setting of the fateful meeting with Nubar Pasha which had sent Gordon to the Sudan.

The British Ambassador was now Sir Henry Layard, better known to pos, terity as the archaeologist who excavated Nineveh the ancient Assyrian capital. He immediately asked Kitchener to investigate Circassian atrocities at Ada Bazar in the nearer part of Anatolia, 'rather annoying' as his baggage had gone by sea direct to Sinop and his intended base at Kastamonu. Instead, he went by train with a cook and an interpreter to Izmit (Nicea), where he was put up by the Armenian bishop, who rode with him next day through beautiful scenery towards Ada Bazar. The first deputation of welcome awaited him four hours from the town. By the time he reached the gates he had about a hundred horsemen and several cartloads behind him. 'The streets were crowded with thousands of people and I had to go bowing right and left. A lot of little boys with banners went singing in front, then came 4 soldiers, then myself, then the

Bishop and a crowd of notables. All the church bells were ringing'. He held a reception at the bishop's house, shaking hands and making speeches.

On the Sunday he had to attend the Armenian cathedral in state where the bishop officiated in an enormous mitre and 'preached an eloquent sermon about the Queen and the reforms that were to be introduced'. Kitchener was seated 'in a great chair and was specially prayed for'.[9] He spent much of the week receiving petitions from people who had been robbed by soldiers or dis-possessed, or whose relatives were among the seventeen people whose throats had been cut by Circassians 'and the authorities did nothing'. Next Sunday he attended the service of the Presbyterian community of some three hundred converts, who sang 'God Save the Queen' and prayed for him in English.

When he reached his own consular area round Kastamonu he received almost royal honours wherever he went, with crowds to see him arrive, officials backing out of his presence, and peasants pathetically expecting immediate relief and reforms. The reports he wrote were damning: bribery in the law-courts; speculation and misappropriation; blackmail and extortion. Petitioners against corrupt officials must first pay high fees, while complaints about robbers would bring them back with a vengeance after they had squared the police. No reforms had been made in the police, prisons or in education. Kitchener's heart was specially touched by a group of refugees who had nothing to give their children except vegetables, soon to be all eaten. 'They have no houses and sleep under trees'. He urged the Foreign Office that the Turkish government should act for the safety of the district and to 'prevent these people dying of want'.[10]

He hated the cold of his first winter for many years. 'My house is all windows and consequently all draughts, it is impossible to warm it', he wrote with 'frozen' hands.[11] Yet he delighted in Anatolia, 'with its lovely scenery and the glorious feeling of being the biggest swell in the country',[12] for alongside the ardour of his spiritual mission to bring justice to the poor, sat a slightly contradictory love of social prominence. When an invitation came early in 1880 to return to Cyprus, after only five months as vice-consul, he was tempted to refuse it and stay on under Wilson – and soon would have been unemployed, for after the British General Election that spring the victorious Gladstone reversed Disraeli's forward policy and withdrew the military consuls.

Major-General Sir Robert Biddulph, who had been Wolseley's deputy, suc-ceeded him as High Commissioner of Cyprus and recognized that the survey must be made. He appointed Major Lloyd of the Indian Survey Department to resume it temporarily and asked for Kitchener,[13] who returned to Nicosia on 2 March 1880. On 18 April he wrote to Millie: 'What do you think they sent me from Kastamunia! a little bear! Such a funny little brute. I mean to teach him all sorts of tricks'.

Kitchener was sharing a house in Nicosia with a daredevil young Scotsman, Lord John Kennedy of the Royal Scots Fusiliers, the Marquess of Ailsa's son, who soon had the bear making happy mischief; but when the bear took a bathe in a bath prepared for Kitchener and proceeded to dry himself by climbing into his owner's bed he was banished.[15]

By Kitchener's thirtieth birthday on 25 June the survey was going well. In the first six months Kitchener and his men surveyed 1,058 square miles, including the lands of 197 villages, 19 monasteries and 16 farms.[16] As Land Registrar in addition to his work as Director of Survey, he computed them for revenue. His wide travels in the island convinced him that Cyprus, when handed over, had been in 'a thoroughly exhausted and ruined condition', for the Turkish system took all it could and gave nothing in return. The British were creating a new and happier land.[17]

In August he was at the camp, about 6,000 feet above the sea among pine trees on a 'rather narrow ridge' below Mount Troovos, which the government and military pitched as a summer capital. The views all around were magnificent and the climate 'simply heavenly'. 'There are a good many ladies up here now', he told Millie. 'Lady Biddulph came up last week, had a fearful journey'. He dined with the Lancashire Fusiliers on their annual celebration of the battle of Minden (1 August 1759) and was amused that 'we drank the *health!* of the heroes who fell in solemn silence. The band then marched round the table playing the Minden March'.[18]

Late in September he arranged to work near Limassol on the southern coast because his brother Arthur had promised to break his journey to New Zealand. Arthur had left Mexico, refusing a better mining position, to take charge of the New Zealand estate, Colonel Kitchener being unhappy with his nephew' reports. 'Herbert came off in a boat to meet me', Arthur wrote to their father. 'He looks wonderfully well – broad, strong, very sunburnt, and in capital spirits'. He had pitched camp under trees close to the sea. 'The tent is about the best thing of the East I have ever seen, plenty of room, nicely carpeted and furnished, and of very brilliant oriental colours'. The brothers bathed in the sea, ate figs before breakfast, then rode into the countryside wherever

Herbert's duties as Surveyor or as Land Registrar might call, then dined with the local garrison. 'Everyone here seems awfully jolly and like the place', wrote Arthur, while Herbert was 'awfully glad' that Arthur had come.[19]

Arthur resumed his voyage to New Zealand, where he found Waihemo Grange in decline and his cousin Henry secretly drinking and behaving badly to his wife Mabel and his six children. His contract not renewed, Henry settled in Dunedin and went to the bad. Mabel tried to run their home as a boarding-house, but it burned down on 1 July 1882. Three of their small children lost their lives in the fire, and Henry and the baby died of their burns soon after. Arthur rushed to Dunedin and did all he could. 'It is a sad sad story. To be reduced to poverty, and disgrace, by Henry's misconduct and then finally to have four children swept away, it seems almost too dreadful'.[20]

Arthur had seen his brother at his most relaxed, his chest much broader than he remembered from their last meeting some years back. To a colleague in Cyprus Herbert Kitchener seemed

> very slight in figure and spare for his height. The thick brown hair was parted in the middle; clear blue eyes looked straight and full at you; a shapely moustache concealed the upper lip, while the upright figure and square shoulders gave an impression of vigour and alertness which was not belied by a manner decidedly shy and reserved.[21]

He joined in the social life of Nicosia when not upcountry surveying. He was a whip to the garrison hounds, hunting hare, and rode in the races. The mare Salem, which he had brought from Palestine, was not too successful, but the following year he won two races with Kathleen, 'a well bred Arab'. In the Welter Steeplechase, recorded the *Cyprus Herald*, 'Kathleen kept the lead, the neat way in which she took her fences standing her in good stead'. She won by four lengths from Derviche, ridden by Charles King-Harman, Biddulph's Private Secretary and future son-in-law.[22]

When the garrison put on theatricals, Kitchener had a long part. He attended balls and went out to dinner.[23] When one military couple, the Bovills, were to be stationed in Leicestershire near the Parkers, who had returned from New Zealand to The Temple, Rothley, Herbert wrote to Millie: 'I am sure you will like her and both she and her husband have been *most kind* to me out here'.[24]

[46]

But he signs off the letter as 'Your affectionate brother, unmarried and unlikely to be'. Victorian officers were discouraged from marriage before their later twenties: they must put the service first. Kitchener was now over thirty but too dedicated to his profession to want a wife. When his second-in-command, Grant, came back married, Kitchener grumbled that they would probably have lots of children and put them before the work.

He was thoroughly happy in his surveying and land registering and as a sideline seized opportunities to excavate ruins, with such skill that the British Museum invited him to superintend the excavations at Nineveh. He was tempted if he could match his present generous salary. He suggested ingenu-ously that he double as British consul in Mosul. The Foreign Office was not amused.

Cyprus also brought him an abiding passion for collecting, especially ceramics. The British administration had activated an Ottoman law, hitherto a dead letter, by which archaeological finds were divided between the owner of the land, the finder (who usually bought out the owner) and the state. Kitchener helped to found the Cyprus Museum and was its first secretary. He also sent pieces to the South Kensington Museum and kept less valuable items to form the nucleus of his own collection. He had already brought early pottery back from Palestine. When his father had moved house he wrote to Herbert: 'Your "crockery" had a narrow escape – other things were smashed but your treasures are safe. Hurrah!'[25]

In July 1881 Herbert took his three-month home leave and found the family in uproar over the secret engagement of young Walter, still in India, to Caroline ('Carry' or 'Cary') Fenton, youngest of the three daughters of Captain Charles Fenton, their father's best friend. All three were in love with Walter and he was in love with Carry. She was older than Walter and not in the least economical. Fenton had consented, subject to the colonel's approval, but neither he nor Walter told the colonel, who considered that an early mar-riage at twenty-three would be ruinous to Walter's military career. Worse, the colonel discovered the engagement shortly after he had left Albert Mansions to share the Fentons' pleasant new home near Lymington in Hampshire. 'We ought to be grateful that such charming people can take him and make his life more cheerful', Herbert had written to Arthur, but on discovering that Fenton had consented behind his back the colonel removed himself at once to Millie and Harry at Rothley, where Herbert found him 'very much upset'.[26] He asked Chevally and Herbert to advise. They wrote stiff letters to Fenton before he would agree that Walter remained free, and to Walter that 'the Governor' disapproved but that if Walter worked hard and became a captain and adjutant they could marry, but not correspond meanwhile.

Once Fenton had agreed to consider the engagement suspended, Herbert took the colonel back to Lymington, where he found Carry quietly determined and wearing Walter's presents. Herbert was sure they would marry but doubted she would make a good wife; but when they married in Bombay in 1884 the marriage was supremely happy until her tragic death in South Africa during the Boer War. Of sweetest character, devoted to Walter and their children she became a recognized artist of Indian scenes in oils and watercolour.

'I am very thankful', Arthur had written during the uproar, to his father 'that you have Herbert with you, his clear way of looking at matters will I feel sure bring things right'.[27] The 'Governor' became cheerful again, despite worsening eyesight, but living with the Fentons did not prove happy, as Herbert had foreseen. Instead, Millie and Harry offered 'the Governor' a house on their estate, Cossington Manor, where he lived the rest of his life. Herbert had returned to Cyprus. His father wrote to him that Cossington was rather larger than he needed but it was nice. 'I wish you were here; you seem to have the knack of making any place I am in comfortable'.[28] And indeed his dedicated soldier son had a fastidious eye for porcelain, furniture, carpets and flowers which critics long after would seize upon as evidence of a sexual bent which would have horrified Herbert.

In Cyprus, his third tour of duty was uneventful except that one December day he was shot at by a brigand who missed. But stirring events were occurring in Egypt. Kitchener, restless that he had seen no active service – the only way to the top – took a step that might have brought his military career to an abrupt end.

6

ARABI AND AFTER

Egypt was a province of the Ottoman Empire which was self-governed under a hereditary khedive or viceroy. Khedive Ismail II's imperial ambitions and extravagance had forced him to sell to Britain his shares in the newly opened Suez Canal, yet he went deeply into debt to Britain and France. They formed a Commission of the Debt – to give the creditors a first claim on the revenues of Egypt and the Sudan, where Gordon, seconded to the khedive's service from the British Army, was attempting to rule for the benefit of the Sudanese rather than for Egypt and to bring peace and good government and to suppress the slave trade.

The khedive had summoned him to Cairo to help reorganize his finances, but Major Evelyn Baring, as the British Commissioner of the Debt, had out-manoeuvred Gordon and forced Ismail to abdicate in favour of his son, Tewfik. Before long, Gordon, in despair at being thwarted at every turn, resigned the governor-generalship of the Sudan, which soon lapsed back into the venal corruption he had fought.

In 1882 the increased control of Egypt by the European creditors had incensed a large group of nationalists, who staged a revolt under the Minister for War, Arabi Pasha. Khedive Tewfik fled from Cairo. The Egyptian Army supported Arabi, who seized Alexandria. The large European and Levantine communities were engulfed by riot, looting and arson. The free passage of the Suez Canal was in danger.

Kitchener was too junior and too far away to have the slightest influence on these events, but news of the riots and destruction in Alexandria, and the assembling in Cyprus of a small British force to secure the Suez Canal, made him itch to see action. Detained at Nicosia by a bout of malaria, he sent a request to the High Commissioner in the tented capital in the hills for a week's leave of absence, which Sir Robert Biddulph granted, assuming that Kitchener would convalesce by the sea or in the hills.

Kitchener went to Limassol in plain clothes, not uniform, and took the weekly steamer to Alexandria. He made no secret of his destination (the *Cyprus Herald* reported it on 5 July) and maintained for the rest of his life that as he worked under the Foreign Office and could go wherever he liked in Cyprus, 'leave of absence' implied absence from the island. But he did not tell Biddulph that he was going to Alexandria. This omission prompted Charles King-Harman (echoing Biddulph's view) to remark in later years that though he sensed that Kitchener would one day achieve a great position, if conscience came into conflict with self-interest, self-interest would win.[1]

At Alexandria Kitchener boarded the flagship, HMS *Invincible*, and sought out the Military Liaison Officer, Lieutenant-Colonel Tulloch, who was pleased to see 'a tall, thin subaltern of engineers' who said he spoke fluent Arabic and Turkish and offered his services. 'Certainly', replied Tulloch. 'I hope you will be able to stay with me'. Few British officers spoke Arabic in 1882 as the army had not yet served in Arabic-language lands.

Together they went on a dangerous reconnaissance by train in Arab-held territory. Tulloch disguised himself as a Levantine official since he might be recognized, and indeed a few days later a fair-bearded Syrian was dragged out of the train and his throat cut in the belief that he was Tulloch. Kitchener went in his own plain clothes.[2] They returned safely in time to witness from HMS *Invincible* the great bombardment of Arabi's new forts and batteries on 11 July after the expiry of Admiral Seymour's ultimatum. Kitchener watched as the forts of Alexandria fired back, salvo after salvo, doing little damage to the twenty-eight British ironclads which pounded them remorselessly until the last fort was silenced after ten and a half hours. The admiral signalled the cease-fire; but *Invincible*'s armament included an experimental ordnance that could be only be unloaded at risk to its gun-crew. The admiral gave permission for this one final shell to be fired, and it hit the upper works of a fort exactly on target. A cloud of dust and debris darkened the air. 'But', Kitchener would recall with amusement, 'when this cleared away, an old woman rushed franti-cally from an outhouse and chased in some fowls!'[3]

Kitchener was not allowed to accompany shore parties to spike the guns because he was not in uniform, but he persuaded Admiral Seymour (nick-named 'the Ocean Swell' for his genial ways and dressy attire) to wire for an extension of leave. Biddulph refused: Kitchener was absent without leave and must return by the next steamer, which he missed because Tulloch did not hand him the telegram until the steamer had sailed. He returned at the very first opportunity, arriving six days after his leave had expired to find that a furious Biddulph had talked of a court-martial. 'No one was so ludicrously astonished as I was', Kitchener later told a brother officer, 'when I arrived in Cyprus to find I was in disgrace. I had never dreamt of having done anything insubordinate'. He reported to Biddulph and tried to explain that as a 'civil-ian' he had acted correctly. 'The General was so angry about the matter that I dropped the subject, but I little knew then what damages he would do me in the W.O. I hear I am put down as a most insubordinate character and that Lord Wolseley has a special black mark against my name'.[4]

'Herbert is all right', wrote Colonel Kitchener to Arthur on 7 August. 'He is back in Cyprus having got a wigging from Sir R. B. What was wrong was he was attached to nobody'.[5]

Herbert wrote to Biddulph: 'I have been very much pained ever since my return at the view you took of my absence in Alexandria'. He was 'extremely anxious' to see service in Egypt and mentioned a post on the intelligence staff which was kept open for him (by General Sir Archibald Alison). He assured Biddulph of his ambition to finish the survey but feared his career would suffer if he remained in civil work, because a soldier's first duty was to serve in the field and not to remain at ease while others were fighting. Kitchener added, somewhat ingenuously, that he had not sought the post but if he were asked for and Biddulph opposed, 'it would absolutely capsize all my hopes in the service for the future'.[6]

When the Liberal government decided to suppress Arabi's rebellion, Alison did indeed ask the High Commissioner to release Kitchener for the expedition that led to Wolseley's victory of Tel-el-Kebir on 13 September 1882.[7] Biddulph refused without telling Kitchener, who wrote in all inno-cence to Arthur on 30 September:

I did my utmost to get over again to Egypt to be in the row but all unsuccess-ful, there was no place for outsiders with everyone in England trying to go. I had just a chance of being sent with the Turkish troops but now they are not going and all is over. It has been an exciting time here so close to the scene of action and Cyprus has been made use of a good deal which will do the Island good. When I have finished here I should not mind a berth in Egypt, but I must stay here to finish the map and that will take at least another year unless the publisher puts on much more steam than at present.[8]

Biddulph gave Kitchener full credit for his 'great professional skill' in car-rying out the survey and noted in his Confidential Report (always seen and signed by the officer concerned) that he had considerable self-reliance, very good general ability and good professional acquirements; but he added that Kitchener was 'a well-informed officer of active habits, rather impulsive and does not always foresee results'.[9]

Biddulph and his secretary King-Harman (a year younger than Kitchener) regarded him at this time as rather superficial. As strong Evangelicals they probably assumed that his love of ritual masked a shallow faith, but they thought his whole character lacked depth. He was still a young man, and King-Harman in old age recognized warmly that the Herbert Kitchener he had known in Cyprus had not yet undergone the desert experiences, physical and spiritual, which would lead to greatness.[10]

Kitchener continued his Cyprus survey. He won golden opinions from the Greek Orthodox Church for his fairness and patience in the land registration, and he had grown to love the Greek liturgy, although he could not attend often because of Orthodox suspicion of Protestants and because he must support the English chaplaincy. He was popular also with the Turkish and French communities.[11]

Meanwhile Gladstone's government in London had decided to re-create the Egyptian Army, disbanded after its defeat by Wolseley, under British lead-ership. Major-General Sir Evelyn Wood, VC, a fifty-year-old veteran of the Crimea, the Mutiny and the Ashanti and Zulu Wars, one of Wolseley's 'Ring', was appointed to command with the title of Sirdar, the Anglo-Indian word for 'leader'. Wood was to select twenty-five British officers as Commanding Officers and seconds-in-command of the twelve regiments and corps to be formed. Fifteen of his twenty-five rose to general's rank or above in the British Army.

Sir Evelyn Wood owed his appointment to Gordon's recommendation. Gordon also recommended Kitchener as one of the twenty-five, telling Reginald Brett, Parliamentary Private Secretary at the War Office, of his fine physical presence and character, his cool head and hard constitution.[12] Wood reached Cairo shortly before Christmas 1882. On 28 December he wired to 'Captain Kitchener, Cyprus' (although the promotion was not gazetted until 4 January): 'Will you join me for soldier's duty being spoiled five hundred and fifty no allowances except forage two years engagement. Wood.' Kitchener wired back: 'Very sorry present work will not permit me leave Cyprus for one year'. On 30 December Kitchener received a second wire from Wood: 'Write your plans as we wanted you for second in command cavalry regiment'.[13]

A story did the rounds (leaving no documentary evidence) that when Wood had stopped briefly in Cyprus Kitchener had arranged with the aide-de-camp for an immediate follow-up telegram, knowing that Biddulph would refuse to release him on the first.

With Biddulph's blessing he crossed to Cairo. A British journalist saw him early one morning standing in the centre of a circle of riders – Egyptian former officers and non-commissioned officers – trying to keep their seats, although some had not ridden much or at all. With his long boots, dark cutaway coat and tarboosh (fez) he only needed a long whip to look like a circus master as he and his Commanding Officer, Taylor of the 19th Hussars, slowly selected fifteen for training as cavalry officers. Kitchener hardly said a word. 'He's quiet', murmured Taylor to the journalist, 'that's his way . . . he's clever'.[14]

Back in Cyprus to clear up and hand over the survey, although he would retain overall responsibility for publication, Kitchener wrote to Millie: 'I feel pretty well satisfied I did right in accepting although it is not a paying billet, still I want to do some soldiering now having been a civilian for so long and I could not get a better chance than the present'.[15]

On 21 February 1883 he began service as a *bimbashi* (equivalent to major) in the new Egyptian Army. 'I am getting on all right', he wrote to Millie a month later, 'and rather like my new life. It is a tremendous change of course from being a civilian to becoming all at once a sort of sergeant major'.[16] He worked with an intensity that did not make him too popular. Arthur Kitchener had written from New Zealand: 'I have the character of being a very hard task-master – and I am glad of it, as I am sure it is just what these people want, if they only knew it'.[17] This too was Herbert's attitude. He was already drawn to his Egyptians, many of whom were *fellahin* (peasants), but he kept his warm feelings locked behind a stern exterior. And easygoing British officers disliked his devotion to work, although one wrote later with tongue in cheek that at first they had hated the sight of him because he was a sapper (only one other sapper had been chosen) and because the light blue uniform he designed for his cavalry was finer than theirs. But later 'We got fond of him'.[18]

He joined in the cosmopolitan social life of Cairo, telling Millie of balls and dinners, and how at a great parade he had charge of the harem enclosure, 'which was very pleasant as some of the Egyptian princesses are very pretty and amiable. How would you like a dusky sister-in-law?'[19]

When his regiment moved out to Abbasia barracks on the edge of the desert a few miles north-east of the centre of Cairo he joked that the only two British ladies on the station were 'followed about by a long train of generals and colonels so that there is no chance of speaking to them hardly. As they are both ugly this is not much to be regretted'.[20]

In that year of 1883 he became a Freemason, being initiated at Cairo in La Concordia Lodge, Number 1226, English constitution. Two years later in London he was founder-member of the Drury Lane Lodge, Number 2127, and kept a lifelong involvement in the Craft at home and abroad, rising to high masonic rank.[21]

The hard work of Kitchener and his Commanding Officer was rewarded when the Sirdar inspected. Sir Evelyn Wood was delighted by their regiment, saying they had showed him a wonderful performance, whereas one infantry regiment was so poor that he stopped its colonel's leave.

In November Kitchener left Egypt to spend his own leave surveying the Sinai Desert at the invitation of the Palestine Exploration Fund, with an Oxford geologist who found him an agreeable companion and most useful for his knowledge of Arabic and local customs. He often worked away from the main party and once returned to find Professor Hull confronted by a sheikh who had refused to let him climb Mount Nebo and was demanding a large entrance fee to Petra. Kitchener trumped the sheikh by producing the Ottoman sultan's *firman*, provided in Cyprus, requiring all his subjects to give free access and assistance to Kitchener and his party wherever he wished to go.[22]

On 31 December the surveyors and geologists were near the Dead Sea when four Arabs, who had ridden post-haste from Egypt by camel, handed Kitchener an urgent letter from Sir Evelyn Baring, the former British Commissioner of the Debt who had returned from India to be British Agent and Consul-General. A simmering rebellion in the Sudan under the leadership of the thirty-five-year-old Muhammad Ahmad, a mystic who had proclaimed himself el-Mahdi (the Expected One), had become dangerous. The

Mahdi had trapped and slaughtered an expedition of the new Egyptian Army under Hicks Pasha, was raising the country and advancing on Khartoum. Kitchener must return at once with all speed.[23]

Disguising himself in Arab dress as an Egyptian official with the name of Abdullah Bey, he set off on his small horse to ride two hundred miles across country, alone except for the four Arabs on their camels. The tribes were not too loyal, so he could not wear his tinted spectacles which would have betrayed him as a Westerner, and his eyes 'burned'. They lost the clear blue of his youth, and the slight squint became a little more pronounced and fearsome. The last two days were the worst, with a strong west wind blowing the sand in their faces and almost stopping the camels. He marvelled at the skill of the Arabs, using no compass yet missing the way only once. Kitchener's endurance, riding ten hours daily without stopping, gave rise to further legend, in which he crosses the Sinai Desert alone, gets lost, and only by great self-control recovers his route.[24]

And thus, by an epic desert ride, he came to his destiny.

PART TWO

Gordon's Land

1884–1899

7

BLOOD BROTHERS
OF THE DESERT

UNAWARE OF ADVENTURES to come, Kitchener began 1884 tamely at Abbasia barracks. Colonel Taylor had been ordered to join a British contin-gent for the defence of Suakin on the Red Sea coast of the Sudan. Kitchener had been recalled to take temporary command of their Egyptian cavalry regi-ment. With war in the offing, he put men and horses through rigorous train-ing, including early-morning steeplechases.

He shared a house on the edge of the desert with his second-in-command, Captain La Terrière, who found his chief's devotion to duty rather trying, with irregular hours, meals and sleep. Thanks to the dry heat Kitchener was now extremely fit, so slender that he seemed even taller than he was, so sun-burned that his brown moustache looked almost white. He could be brusque, and the 'curious cast in his left eye gave you the feeling that he saw right through you', but La Terrière recalled him as 'in many ways just a boy – with a boy's hearty laugh and cheery manner'.

Off duty he was working up his 2,000 square miles of Sinai survey. He could seldom spare time for polo or the station's paperchases or their jaunts to Cairo, but in these congenial surroundings he was less shy, 'nor did he run away from the ladies', noted La Terrière. 'He had a few friends of his own, his taste in womankind tending rather to the motherly and "unsmart".' La Terrière thought him most unworldly because not interested in the fleshpots of Egypt.[1] Besides, he had fallen in love, or at least was attracted to a beautiful girl.

Hermione Baker was rising seventeen, the elder of the two daughters of the celebrated Valentine Baker, hero of the Russo-Turkish War whom Kitchener had met in the Balkans, and niece of Sir Samuel the explorer and administrator whom he also knew. Valentine Baker Pasha might have been selected rather than Wood as first Sirdar of the new Egyptian Army had he not been cashiered from the British. He was away in the eastern Sudan commanding an Egyptian column sent against the Mahdi's ally, Osman Digna. At the first battle the Egyptian conscripts ran away. Baker thus lost the fight through no fault of his own but saved his life by a supreme act of courage. His wife, with Hermione and her sister Sybil, were living at Cairo's Shepheard's Hotel, where Kitchener visited them. The Bakers certainly believed that he was in love with Hermione and that they would marry when her age and his service allowed.[2]

In after years his cousin Edith would deny that Herbert loved Hermione; but Valentine Baker's disgrace in the British Army would be a serious handicap to any officer married to his daughter. The ambitious, self-controlled Kitchener would surely have kept himself from close involvement with the Bakers unless he were in love.

Late on 24 January Kitchener was attending a Royal Engineers dinner in Cairo when the senior officer present, Major-General Sir Gerald Graham, was handed a message that General Gordon, his dearest friend, and Lieutenant-Colonel Donald Hammill-Stewart as Chief of Staff would soon be arriving at Cairo railway station. Gordon had been sent out by the British Cabinet at very short notice in response to the national clamour of 'Gordon for the Sudan' but with confused instructions. He had been ordered to Suakin to report on the situation, but Baring had dispatched Wood to Port Said to divert him to Cairo, where he would be made governor-general with executive powers to effect the evacuation of the Egyptian garrisons and of civilian families, of whatever race, who wished to leave, and to select a Sudanese successor.

Gordon was Kitchener's hero. Stewart was a close friend since they had been vice-consuls together in Anatolia. The quiet Scot was five years older than Kitchener and, despite long service in a smart cavalry regiment, shared his taste for a rough life under canvas and boiled rice in the desert rather than the delicacies of an officers' mess. They were together again in Egypt in 1883 when Stewart was writing up his report after being sent hastily round the garrisons in the Sudan to advise on response to the Hicks disaster.

General Graham immediately left the dinner for the railway station, and Kitchener surely would have been among the small party of officers which went with him to greet Gordon and Stewart. During their twenty-four hours in Cairo Kitchener had no part in the round of conferences and calls which confused, even more, the exact purpose of Gordon's mission, but he can reasonably be assumed to have spent at least an hour or two with Stewart and to have met Gordon again, with his penetrating blue eyes and a sense of mystical power, faith and dedication. Neither Kitchener's intense loyalty in the tragic months ahead, and his lifelong veneration, nor Gordon's admiration for Kitchener can be explained if their only contact was through telegrams and native runners.

Kitchener was too junior to be at Wood's farewell dinner but probably stood among the well-wishers at the railway station to see them off on the night of 25 January, with Gordon looking upset because he had been refused the Sudanese ex-slave-trader, Zubair Pasha, his surprising but inspired choice as right-hand man and potential successor, a refusal that contributed to disaster.

Two weeks later, while Gordon was still on his way to Khartoum, Kitchener was ordered to hand over his regiment temporarily. He went by railway to Assuit, then by Thomas Cook's regular steamer to Keneh (Qena) in Upper Egypt, where the Nile is closest to the Red Sea. Taking a local escort, he rode across the desert by camel to Kosseir on the coast, assessing whether the wells, the terrain and the tribes of the caravan route would allow the passage of an Anglo-Egyptian army. Cairo assumed that if Gordon were unable to achieve evacuation by his personal influence and diplomacy, Gladstone would authorize a sufficient force to support him, as Gordon himself believed.

Kitchener exceeded his brief and made a thorough study of the friendly Ababdeh tribe, more nearly related to the Berbers of north-west Africa than to the Semitic Arabs of the Sudan: blue eyes like Kitchener's were not unknown; he could pass as one of them. He recommended the formation of an Ababdeh Field Force to assist in future operations. His report was approved warmly in Cairo and London.

By then he was back with his regiment and restless, his thoughts with Gordon and Stewart in Khartoum. They had been sending civilians down-river to safety, but the Mahdi's forces were closing in while the British Cabinet dithered. Herbert wrote to his father on 20 March:

We are going on pretty much as usual, drifting through very exciting times for Egypt . . . You know much more in England what is going on than we do here. I do not think England will stand Gordon being deserted. It is the most disgraceful thing I ever knew, had they taken anyone's advice that knew anything about the country Gordon would be safe now.[3]

Baker's defeat was reversed by General Sir Gerald Graham, who trounced Osman Digna in two battles near Suakin, though with grievous British casu‑ alties at Tamai on 13 March. Graham wired to Cairo for permission to lead his victorious force across the desert to Berber and up the Nile to reinforce Gordon and complete the withdrawal. Twelve days later Kitchener was ordered to undertake a special mission to Berber to open the Suakin caravan route and make contact with Gordon, now isolated by the cutting of the tele‑ graph line. 'It is a very important job', he told his father, 'and I am very glad to go' despite the heat and hard work. Leslie Rundle, a quiet gunner some years his junior ('a charming fellow'), was to go with him. [4]

They set off by train and steamer. Kitchener was confident: 'I expect we shall have English troops at Berber before long and begin a Sudan campaign next autumn'. But at Aswan they were ordered to wait, 'through the utter incompetence of the Cairo and home authorities to make up their minds for 5 minutes consecutively . . . I feel quite sure if we go on much longer in this way Gordon's blood will be on the G.O.M.'s head. How the English people can stand it I cannot understand'.[5] Gladstone refused to let Graham march. Berber surrendered, and less than a year later the English people would reverse Gladstone's nickname of GOM ('Grand Old Man') to MOG. ('Murderer of Gordon'). Graham would regret bitterly that he had not advanced into the desert, far from the telegraph, without waiting for orders.

At Aswan Kitchener and Rundle raised the Ababdeh Field Force. They worked well together. Kitchener discovered by chance that Rundle was in love with a Leicestershire girl, daughter of a neighbour of Millie's, but they could not get engaged through lack of means. Kitchener remembered the girl and urged Millie to organize a grand family party when they got home 'and let these poor lovers meet'.[6] As for his own love‑affair, he was able to visit Hermione when recalled to Cairo briefly in May to report. He found her father recover‑ ing from facial wounds received at Tamai, and Hermione ill. On Kitchener's last hurried visit the wife and ten‑year‑old daughter, Bonte, of Professor Shelton Amos, a judge who lived next door to Shepheard's Hotel, were about to enter Hermione's room with her beef tea.

Many years later Bonte recalled how a tall young officer came up and spoke hurriedly to her mother, who drew back and they waited on a couch. 'But why?' asked young Bonte. 'Doesn't she want her beef tea?' 'Yes, but Major Kitchener is going to marry her, and wants to see her quietly'.[7] No unmarried male would have been admitted to a young lady's sickroom unless either a close relative or a fiancé.

He never saw her again. Eight months later, on 13 January 1885, she died during an epidemic of typhoid fever. He was deep in the Sudan. Whether they had written to each other cannot be known because Kitchener destroyed most of his personal correspondence. Her sister Sybil (Lady Carden) was never in doubt that Hermione's death was a great tragedy in Kitchener's life, and her first cousin Annie (Lady Wood), 'who had an extremely accurate mind, was quite certain that it is true that K and Hermione were in love'.[8]

Hermione's mother died of typhoid less than a month later. Valentine Baker gave Kitchener a gold locket containing a miniature of Hermione which may have been worn by her mother. He wore it under his shirt (not, probably, on active service). Before his last voyage in 1916 he sent it to the Baker family for safekeeping; it is believed to lie in the sarcophagus supporting his effigy in St Paul's Cathedral.[9]

In mid-May the Sirdar ordered Kitchener, Rundle and their Abadeh Field Force further upriver to Korosko in Upper Egypt, known as the gates of hell for its summer heat.

Together they organized a line of desert strongpoints between the Nile and the Red Sea, about 200 miles long. Kitchener had been made Special Commissioner for the Arabs. He had over 1,500 men under his command 'and am charmingly independent'.[10] He gathered intelligence and secured the loyalty of tribes by the careful distribution of subsidies. Heavily bearded, wearing a turban and Arab robes, he rode about with an escort of twenty men 'all dressed in white on good camels with lances bearing green banners – all picked men who will go anywhere with me'.[11] They had made him their 'blood brother' and had taken an oath, administered by a holy man with their hands crossed on the Koran, that 'his enemies should be their enemies and his friends their friends',[12] an oath they never betrayed. The Sirdar (Wood) and the Commander-in-Chief of the British Army of Occupation (Sir Frederick Stephenson) were most impressed by Kitchener's influence on the Ababdeh, whose loyalty was essential to the safety of the lines of communication up the Nile. They admired his 'very great tact, energy and great devotion'. The frontier duty, Stephenson told the War Office when recommending Kitchener for promotion, 'required the exercise of those qualities in a high degree, and I know of no other officer in the Egyptian Army – there is certainly none in the English – capable of performing it so well'.[13]

His field force chased and nearly caught a marauding emir sent by the Mahdi to harry Egypt, and Kitchener warned headquarters that unless the home government acted quickly the day would come when Egypt would be invaded and 20,000 men would be needed to reconquer the Sudan, a figure near the total which he himself would command fourteen years later. His warnings were passed to London and not believed.

In late July Cairo urgently wanted to encourage the wavering mudir (governor) of Dongola, about three hundred miles up the Nile from Korosko. Only an Egyptian, they believed, could reach him, since the river route included two long cataracts and would be too slow: he must ride six days across the desert, through possibly hostile tribes.

An Egyptian officer volunteered to go if given an escort of 1,200 men and a reward of £10,000, so high was the risk. Kitchener offered to go for nothing, alone except for his faithful twenty. He was sure that to send more than one Englishman would be fatal, though Rundle, to be left in command at Korosko, dearly longed to go too.

During this long desert ride, and others later, Kitchener's sense of eternity deepened: the silence, the vast vistas; the escorts' faithfulness in stopping for Muslim prayers; the knowledge that he was doing it all to help Gordon, a man of profound faith. From now on, Kitchener seemed to see life through desert eyes. When, a few months later, he was a member of the headquarters mess of the Relief Expedition, with excellent food at low cost, he commented: 'I have grown such a solitary bird that I often think I were happier alone.'[14]

On 2 August he reached Dongola. The mudir would not have received him had he not come in Arab dress. Mustafa Yawar was a white Circassian, like many in the Egyptian service. Kitchener's diplomatic skills and authority to promise subsidies swung him away from a half-formed desire to change sides; a few weeks later he repulsed a dervish raid. But Kitchener reckoned him an intriguer, untrustworthy and probably corrupt. He was a fanatical Muslim. 'We Christians are dogs', Kitchener discovered, 'but are to be tolerated until we have bitten the adversary!'[15]

After two days with the mudir Kitchener went upriver to the town of Debbeh in the lush strip of vegetation beside the Nile. Debbeh had a ramshackle Turkish garrison of rapacious, cruel bashibazouks (irregulars) serving the khedive and robbing the locals. With Debbeh as his base, he went out again among the tribes, sometimes with the mudir and his cumbrous entourage, more often alone except for his escort. He encouraged the sheikhs and detected where loyalty wavered. He knew that when he entered an uncertain camp he might be seized as a spy. His probable fate was brought home to him when he returned once to the mudir's camp to find a dervish spy being flogged with a rhinoceros-hide whip until he died. The sight and sound prompted Kitchener to carry a phial of poison.

8

LIFELINE TO GORDON

MAJOR KITCHENER, just thirty-four, was the link between Gordon and the outer world. The telegraph line being cut, Gordon could no longer cause corrupt officials to jump to attention and salute when a telegraph clerk deci-phered a Morse-coded message: 'It is I, Gordon Pasha. I see along the wire. I am watching you. Do not demand that bribe. Let that man go'. Another story that Kitchener heard concerned a bey whom Gordon wanted promoted to pasha. Cairo refused; Gordon persisted. The exchange ended when Gordon requested cancellation of previous wires 'as I have had occasion to hang the man'.[1]

No wires came now from Gordon. Kitchener organized undercover mes-sengers who went and came back (or did not) by the desert or river routes, with letters and telegrams and small personal necessities. If he were glad to push his career, telling his father to feed the press morsels from his letters, the dominant motive was to save his hero, to be the first to reach him and help him complete the evacuation of the garrisons and to leave a settled government.

The more Kitchener cross-examined his men when they returned from Khartoum, the more grew his admiration for Gordon: his skill in organizing the defence and maintaining the morale of the mixed-race population, his improvisations, his love for the Sudanese, whom he had ruled with such success in the previous decade, his unwavering Christian faith.* Kitchener

---

* For Gordon in Khartoum, see the present writer's *Gordon: The Man Behind the Legend*, Constable, 1993, pp. 288–317.

commented to Millie soon after Gordon's death: 'His character will hardly ever be really understood for it had no smallness in it'.[2] At that time, and in after years, whenever he reminisced at a dinner table, his hearers were left in no doubt of his 'veneration little short of hero worship'.[3]

Gladstone spread the long-enduring myth that Gordon had disobeyed orders, had turned a mission of peace into an occasion of war (Kitchener knew better). Public opinion, pressure from Lord Wolseley, as he had become after Tel-el-Kebir, and finally a threat of resignation by the Secretary of State for War forced the Prime Minister's hand. On 5 August he asked Parliament for funds to send out what became known (to Gordon's indignation) as the Gordon Relief Expedition. It left England on 26 August 1884, and on 9 September Wolseley arrived in Cairo. Kitchener had been fortifying Debbeh, laying in stores for the arrival of British troops while maintaining the tenuous link with Khartoum. His name was mentioned to Queen Victoria when Downing Street explained plans to her Private Secretary and concluded: ' . . . by this means we may have reasonable hope under Kitchener's intelligent supervision, of communicating with Gordon, and finding out what he wants and what he proposes to do' (about evacuation when reinforced).[4]

The Sirdar ordered Kitchener to report on the expedition's alternative routes from Debbeh to Khartoum, 'it being of course understood that as you will not be able to traverse the routes yourself, you must be dependent on what you hear'.[5] But compiling information was not enough for his adventurous spirit. Having decided that the route across the Bayuda desert was probably best, he determined to test it. He persuaded three sheikhs to escort him to within three days' march of Khartoum and back.

Soon afterwards he heard that Gordon intended to take the offensive. A force under Stewart, in the steamer *Abbas* and ten boats, would burn occu-pied Berber. Stewart in the *Abbas*, carrying Gordon's journal and code-books and a mass of letters, would continue downriver to give accurate information to the expedition, which Gordon optimistically supposed was already coming up the Nile. Kitchener wired the news to Cairo and was told to stop Gordon burning Berber and to help Stewart all he could. Kitchener wired back that he could do so if allowed to take Turkish troops from Debbeh and if a steamer lying idle at Dongola could be ordered far upriver to Merowe to awe the unreliable Monasir tribe before Stewart's steamer entered their territory.[6]

Red tape was still keeping Kitchener from carrying out his plan when he learned that Stewart had started. In alarm, Kitchener immediately sent out letters to the Hannaniyeh tribe in the Bayuda desert and the Monasir sheikhs along the Nile, ordering them to protect and assist. Sure that a trap was planned, he sent a spy to intercept Stewart at Berber with an urgent warning to take the desert route and not to continue downstream. Stewart never received it.[7]

On 2 October a runner reached Debbeh, sent on by the mudir's deputy higher up the Nile, with news that Stewart's steamer had grounded on a rock near the start of the Fourth Cataract in the Monasir country, seventy miles from safety. The runner did not know what had happened to Stewart and his party, but the steamer was stuck fast near the village of the young sheikh Suleiman Numan wad Qamar, whom Kitchener rated unreliable.

He sent the runner back with a message to Suleiman: 'If any harm befall Stewart, for every hair of his head I will have a life'.[8] Rumours of disaster swept the Debbeh bazaars. Kitchener was alone, with no Englishman to consult, with no authority to move Turkish troops. Worrying how to save his friend, he spent almost sleepless nights, each morning sending almost insub-ordinate wires to his faraway superiors urging plan after plan. 'I did all I knew to help him'.[9]

After two days another spy reached Debbeh with news that Stewart and his companions were dead, murdered two weeks earlier before Kitchener had even heard they were in trouble. Trusting Suleiman's offer to supply camels to complete their journey, they had accepted an invitation to enter the nearby house of a blind man for coffee and dates. When asked to leave their escort outside and enter unarmed (except for Stewart's revolver), they had relied on the law of Arab hospitality. But the blind man was a fanatical Mahdist and had persuaded young Suleiman to betray the law. Hidden dervishes rushed in, seized the revolver and cut at them with swords. Stewart and others fought with their fists until overcome. Then their soldiers and the crew were surrounded and slaughtered, though some were believed to be alive.

Kitchener begged Cairo to allow him to rescue the survivors by diplomacy. 'I would promise to do nothing rash. Please ask General Wood if I can be trusted in this respect'. The request was refused.[10]

Kitchener was deeply upset by Stewart's death, 'a dear friend of mine and the finest soldier I have ever met. It is terribly sad that he suffered such a fate but he died trying to save others. His name will live as a hero for ever'.[11] His death had a lasting effect on Kitchener. He realized that the powerful emotions he had experienced, of worry, devotion and grief, could have affected his military judgement. More than ever, he must rigidly control the warmth and tenderness of his heart.

Not until almost two months later, on 1 December 1884, could Kitchener write to his father from Debbeh: 'The steamer is now in sight bringing 200 men of Sussex under Colonel Tolson so I give over my command here. It has been rather amusing being OC Troops here'.[12]

Lord Wolseley, for valid reasons, had rejected the shorter route across the desert and was sending the Relief Expedition up the Nile, a slower and more laborious task than he had expected, even had he not lingered in Cairo waiting for Canadian *voyageurs* to help him with the boats. On 24 November Kitchener had been 'still waiting here for the Expedition. What a time they take getting up'.[13] As commandant of Debbeh he was receiving and transshipping 'stores, hospitals etc' arriving in advance.

Even more important, he was still the only link with Gordon. Telegrams would arrive from Sir Charles Wilson, now chief of intelligence and Kitchener's immediate superior: 'November 16. A message for Gordon will be sent to you tomorrow. Please find messenger who will start at once and [in cypher] *promise good pay*'.[14] Not every messenger reached Khartoum; Gordon complained in his journal of lack of news. Moreover, he could not read cypher telegrams as he had sent the cypher-book with Stewart. And when Kitchener sent newspapers wrapped around some goods, Gordon nearly missed them.

But he was grateful. He wrote in his journal, sarcastically, 'It is delicious to find not one civil word from any official personage except Kitchener', and pasted in a letter he had received from Sir Samuel Baker, former governor-general of equatorial Sudan, Hermione's uncle: 'I like Baker's description of Kitchener. "The man whom I have always placed my hopes upon, Major Kitchener, R.E., who is one of the few *superior* British officers, with a cool and good head and a hard constitution, combined with untiring energy . . ."' That same evening (26 November) Gordon added: 'Whoever comes up here had better appoint Major Kitchener governor-general for it is certain after what has passed, *I am impossible* (what a comfort!).' Twice more he recorded his belief that Kitchener would be 'the best man'.[15]

Gordon would go up on the roof of the palace with his telescope in vain. As Kitchener wrote in Debbeh: 'The expedition is rather dragging'.[16]

Wolseley had formed two camel corps from volunteers of the British heavy cavalry and the Household Division (foot guards and Household cavalry). His plan was to concentrate at Korti and Amuskol, further up the Nile, then send the camel-mounted column under Sir Herbert Stewart (no relation of the murdered Colonel Stewart) by the short cut across the Bayuda desert. The main body would continue up the Nile, punish the murderers, recapture Berber and meet the desert column at Metemmeh. The whole expedition would then advance on Khartoum.

Kitchener (now again in British uniform, without beard and with a moustache smaller, he thought, than shown in the illustrated papers) had been appointed to Stewart's staff as head of intelligence. He hoped to be the first to shake hands with Gordon. Then a wire reached him at Stewart's camp near Korti that Wolseley did not wish him to go. A disappointed Kitchener supposed that 'My Lord Wolseley has not forgotten or forgiven'[17] his long-ago insubordination in Cyprus. And certainly Wolseley, before leaving England, had rejected Cairo's recommendation that Kitchener be promoted from captain to brevet-major in the British Army. Cairo had repeated the recommendation even more strongly, and the Duke of Cambridge approved it after Wolseley had left.[18]

But Kitchener had misjudged him. When Wolseley arrived at Korti by river, at dusk on 16 December, so Kitchener told his father,

I was on the bank in a crowd of soldiers and officers – almost the first thing I heard was Ld.W. saying 'Is Major Kitchener there' – then some one said 'Yes' and he then said 'Let him come on board at once, I wish to see him'. I had to go down a broad flight of steps and on board he shook hands and asked the news which I told him. Next day I met him walking about and he called me and said some very nice things about my services – I dined with him the same evening.

Writing on 26 December, Kitchener went on:

However the greatest honour was done to me last night, Xmas, the men had a bonfire and sang songs. Lord W. and everyone was there. After the songs cheers were given for Ld. W., Genl. Stewart, and then someone shouted out 'Major K.' So 2,000 throats were distended in my honour. I am very proud of that moment and shall not forget it in a hurry. After that Genl. Buller was cheered. I expect we shall be at KHARTOUM before you get this letter – Genl. Sir H. Stewart is an awfully nice man and I like him very much – he has been very civil and kind to me – he will command the troops advancing across the desert.[19]

Kitchener would be there after all; Wolseley had decided to let him go.

At sundown on Wednesday 7 January 1885 Kitchener and his escort left Korti as advance scouts of a convoy of a thousand camels under the inefficient command of Colonel Stanley de Astel Calvert Clarke, equerry to the Prince of Wales ('Nothing could be worse managed', was Wolseley's comment).[20] Stewart's main body left the following day in excellent order. They all reached the wells of Gadkul a week later, but Kitchener was unable to contact the local tribe. Then, to his renewed disappointment, an express messenger summoned him back to Wolseley's camp, where he arrived on 16 January after a hard ride by camel. Wolseley needed him to handle communications with Gordon, such as they were, and Kitchener therefore missed the short but bloody battle of Abu Klea when the ansars (dervish cavalry) broke into the British square before being repulsed. Colonel Fred Burnaby, famous as a traveller in Central Asia, was killed. Two days later, in a minor engagement when they reached the Nile, Stewart was mortally wounded. The command of the column fell on Colonel Sir Charles Wilson, a distinguished surveyor and intelligence chief but with no experi⁄ence of directing a campaign.

Wolseley received news of Abu Klea and of Stewart's wound, but no more. The main body working upriver had been held up, but Lord Charles Beresford's gunboats had passed Berber, with some damage, and met Stewart's force. Gordon's own steamers had fought their way down to meet it.

Wolseley therefore sent his Chief of Staff, Redvers Buller, to take over from Stewart. He also sent the Royal Irish Regiment, 'magnificent looking men, wiry and strong',[21] as reinforcements. They marched off on foot in the small hours of 29 January after a dust storm had dropped. Kitchener went with them as chief intelligence officer and expected to see Gordon within days.

Kitchener made a great impression on the Royal Irish. After the regiment had returned home, a young priest in Plymouth was visiting Catholics in the local jail and and entered the cell of a soldier. The soldier chatted about the Sudan and mentioned a remarkable officer: 'Oh, he is not known, sir. But if you wish really to know, he is only a major in a black regiment'. The priest asked him name. 'Kitchener, sir. If you like to follow him, sir, he will *own the whole of the British Army*!' When asked what sort of man, the soldier used the Irish slang for excellent (like the Scottish 'grand'): 'A terrible man, sir!'[22]

During the six-day march Kitchener came to know the best-loved man of the whole expedition, the Roman Catholic padre of the Royal Irish, Father Robert Brindle. A Liverpool man aged forty-seven, he always marched with the men instead of riding with the officers, and with blistered hands and neck had been stroke-oar of the boat on the upward Nile journey which won Wolseley's prize of £100 for the first to arrive without loss. He was a man of great humour. His favourite story was of the sermon he preached on the first Sunday in Lent, telling the men that he could not ask them to fast on a campaign, but 'It would please our Lord and me very much if this Lent you gave up *bad language*'. A few minutes after the service he happened to walk on the sand behind a group of privates and heard one say: 'That was a b⁓⁓y good sermon the f⁓⁓g Father gave us this morning!'[23]

Thirteen years later Father Brindle would be with Kitchener at a highly emotional moment.

And one morning on that march on the well-trodden caravan route a young, very small but smart staff officer, rather sore from his early efforts to master his camel, was riding alone when 'a tall officer, with bronzed face and piercing blue eyes, ranged himself alongside of me and said pleasantly that, as we were both for the time unattached, we might as well ride together'. Sir George Arthur (a baronet) introduced himself. After some trivial chat he drew from Kitchener an exciting account of his doings and learned of his 'desperate efforts to save Stewart from the trap laid for him' and of his veneration for Gordon.[24] Arthur, a great favourite in London society, was a High Churchman like Kitchener. Their friendship, begun that day, would culminate in Arthur's becoming Kitchener's Private Secretary (civil) in August 1914.

The march reached the wells of Gadkul, where on 2 February they were horrified to be told that Khartoum had fallen. After a three-day delay (for which Kitchener never blamed Wilson) the steamers had fought their way to within sight of Khartoum, one day too late. They withdrew under fire and learned later than Gordon had been killed.

'The shock of the news was dreadful, and I can hardly realise it yet', Kitchener told his father more than a month later. 'I feel that now he is dead, the heart and soul of the Expedition is gone'.[25]

9

HIS EXCELLENCY

ON THE LAWNS of Osborne House, Isle of Wight, at noon on a very hot 14 July 1885, the sixty-six-year-old Queen Victoria stepped down from her carriage and paid the Heavy and Guards Camel Corps (their camels left in the Sudan) and the staff officers who had travelled home with them the signal honour of walking down every rank. The *Australia* had anchored that morning in Cowes Roads, and they had at once been commanded to march to Osborne House to receive her thanks. If she was a trifle disappointed that they had hastily darned and brushed their war-soiled uniforms, they were more than a little disappointed, despite being thrilled by the honour, that the Household had forgotten they would be thirsty.[1]

All officers were presented, and thus Lieutenant-Colonel Herbert Kitchener (brevet gazetted 15 June 1885) met his sovereign for the first time. She had heard much of him and again when the Foreign Secretary asked Baring to obtain his views on the policy of retreat from Korti, to Wolseley's indignation: 'Such a request is unheard of', he complained to the Queen; it should have been made through him.[2]

After the death of Gordon, Kitchener had marched with Buller to the Nile. Then they had been ordered to withdraw to the wells of Abu Klea, where they had wondered whether the Relief Expedition would re-form, take Berber and recapture Khartoum, or retire. Kitchener wrote to his father, 'Some say it has been a dismal failure . . . Altogether the organization of the Expedition has been very bad', and to a friend a month later, 'Nothing up here but mismanagement and mistakes'.[3] One mistake, which would have brought disaster on Buller's column, was put right by Kitchener himself. He had learned that a large dervish force was advancing on the wells of Abu Klea. Buller decided to retreat across the desert, but when Kitchener urged that the wells be filled in so that the dervishes could not pursue, the kind-hearted Buller was aghast: to deprive an enemy of water in a desert was against the rules of war. The staff supported Kitchener until at last Buller agreed reluctantly that they could fill in the principal well. Kitchener jumped up: 'Verner, you know the biggest well. Get some men at once and fill it in'. Turning to another officer: 'Fill in the biggest well you can find. I'll go and see about the rest'.[4]

The expedition re-formed at Korti on the Nile.[5] Wolseley failed to secure permission to advance on Khartoum. Early in May Gladstone found an excuse to order total evacuation. Kitchener wrote: 'It is a sad end to the campaign. I wish I had been taken ill with any disease sooner than stay and see it'.[6] The welfare of the Sudanese, the safety of Egypt and the canal, the memory of Gordon cried out against it. Kitchener was sure it must be reversed one day, probably at great cost. The failure of the campaign drove deep into Kitchener the fundamental need for exact and thorough preparation at every level.

All these last weeks Kitchener had been compiling the official report on the fall of Khartoum and the death of Gordon. He had been touched to receive a kind letter from Gordon, written many weeks earlier, which had been sent down the Nile with his journal and other papers in the last steamer to leave before the end. 'It is the best reward that I shall get for many months hard work', he told his father, 'so please keep it most carefully'.[7] Unfortunately he lost it.

Kitchener examined refugees from Khartoum as they trickled in across the desert or down the Nile. He believed, on the evidence then available, that when the Mahdi's men broke through the weakened defences Gordon had been killed by rifle fire when walking with his escort from the palace to the armoury in the former Austrian mission, where he planned a last stand. Later evidence suggests that he was killed by a thrown spear on the palace stairs, as in the famous picture, though the truth can never be known.

As Kitchener compiled his report he was more than ever impressed by Gordon's 'indomitable resolution and resource' in maintaining the defence for 317 days. 'Never was a garrison so nearly rescued, never was a commander so sincerely lamented'.[8] Kitchener was determined to avenge him.

After the parade at Osborne came two months' leave, which included visits to Leicestershire to stay with his father and with Millie and her family. He also made two lifelong friends. Pandeli Ralli, a bachelor five years older than Kitchener and of Greek extraction, was a partner in the great trading firm of Ralli Brothers. A close friend of the murdered Colonel Donald Stewart, he had written as a stranger to Kitchener in the Sudan for details. This mutual friendship brought them together in London. Ralli's fine London house in Belgrave Square would become Kitchener's home on later leaves. And he was invited to Taplow Court near Maidenhead by the celebrated oarsman, athlete and Member of Parliament, 'Willy' Grenfell, who had swum Niagara twice and climbed the Matterhorn by three different routes. They had first met two years earlier when Grenfell had visited his younger brother Charles, serving in Egypt with the 10th Hussars. More than thirty years later Willy Grenfell (Lord Desborough) recalled the Kitchener of that time, before the Sinai Desert ride had affected his eyes, as 'a most striking figure, tall and spare, with the most wonderful piercing bright blue eyes, set very far apart'. At Taplow Court in 1885, Grenfell, who was not yet married and knew nothing about Hermione's recent death, noticed a strange atmosphere of loneliness about him.[9]

Most of the leave was spent in London, studying oriental law. Kitchener was one of the few whose reputation had been enhanced by the Gordon Relief Expedition. In Cairo the khedive, when decorating him, had made 'some very nice remarks which he started in English, tried hard to bring out in French and then relapsed into Arabic in which he was fluent in my praise which will not bear translation being oriental in character'.[10] But the Royal Engineers did not like their officers to be away too long from regimental duty. Kitchener expected to build barracks in Ireland. Gordon, after his triumphs when seconded to the emperor of China, had spent five years at Gravesend renovating Thames forts, happily giving his spare time to the poor and the sick and to poor boys. Kitchener's shyness would not have encouraged him along that path, but he wanted to return to Egypt 'where I have a pet scheme for getting the Fellaheen out of their financial difficulties'.[11] He had been concerned that poor peasants in the hands of moneylenders could be left destitute when a creditor foreclosed. Kitchener wanted to prevent this, but twenty-eight years would pass before he had the authority to bring in a law himself.

Instead of Egypt he received orders for Ireland. A few days later these were revoked. The Foreign Office required his services again.[12] He found himself briefly caught up in the 'scramble for Africa' as British representative on the Zanzibar Boundary Commission. On 29 November 1885 he landed in

Zanzibar, the island of cloves and port of the slave trade (still active, if clandestine, harried by the British Navy), and was welcomed by the legendary Sir John Kirk, once Livingstone's fellow explorer, now the British consul and dominant influence on the sultan.

The sultan of Zanzibar considered himself suzerain of the mainland which would later be Tanganyika and Kenya. Germany had been annexing much of it by treaties not recognized by Britain and France; but until the powers settled exactly how far inland lay the sultan's boundaries, they could not carve up the rest.

Kitchener thought the German representative shifty and difficult, and by the new year, still stuck in Zanzibar in the yellow flatroofed consulate, he was longing for the work to be over: 'One is dreadfully cut off from the world without the satisfaction of a wild life'.[13] Later, in January 1886, the commission sailed some forty miles along the coastline, taking evidence at each harbour but not penetrating the interior, the land of plenty and beauty which Kitchener would later come to love.

The commissioners argued among themselves and sent long dispatches to their governments, only to have the matter settled in the capitals of Europe behind their backs. Kitchener suggested Mombasa as a British naval base. Otherwise, the Zanzibar commission had wasted energy and time, although it brought him the Foreign Secretary's warm approval and a CMG.*

In August 1886 he had at last started home when at Suez he was handed a wire appointing him His Excellency the GovernorGeneral of the Eastern Sudan and the Red Sea Littoral – a resounding title which meant nothing but control of the coastline by ships of the British Navy, plus the port and town of Suakin and some fifteen miles of hinterland; Osman Digna had recovered much territory when Sir Gerald Graham's large force had been withdrawn in 1884. Suakin and the littoral were essential to the safety of the route to India and to prevent arms being landed for the Mahdists. The governorgeneral also commanded 2,500 British and Egyptian troops, with the local rank of colonel. The previous governorgeneral had been removed after only a few months as useless in command.[14]

A small naval vessel took Kitchener back down the Red Sea and through

* Companion of the Most Distinguished Order of St Michael and St George. He had hoped for a CMG for his Cyprus map (published at last in April 1885), and no doubt that and his Sudan service counted.

the narrow difficult channel, some two miles long, to the safe basin between Suakin island and the mainland, where he found the squalid little town in sweltering heat and 'a large rambling ruined house' which was His Excellency's residence – 'it is quite good enough for me and I have made myself to be fairly comfortable'[15] – together with his aide-de-camp, Peel, and the garrison engineer, young William Staveley Gordon, 'a nice little chap' nick-named 'Monkey'.[16] The late general's nephew, he had the family's large, rather staring eyes. 'Oh, you have Gordon's eyes!' exclaimed Kitchener.

The Mahdi had died less than five months after Gordon, of smallpox or pos-sibly poison, and had been succeeded by the caliph who had directed the siege, known to the British as the Khalifa.[17] His rule was already proving brutal and arbitrary, he was bleeding the country to maintain a huge army, and Kitchener soon found that many of the local tribes were less certain of their allegiance to the Khalifa and his local subordinate, the redoubtable Osman Digna.

Kitchener employed a policy of tact and the offer of forgiveness for any rebel who would come in. He had a slogan placed on the gate: 'Peace to those who enter and who leave this place'. 'I always did my best', he wrote, 'to use all kindliness, justice and truth to those under my rule'[18] After he had recaptured Tamai, up the coast, he wrote letters to the neighbouring sheikhs. When they came to see him and complained of the unsettled state of the country, he replied that they could follow Mahdism if they liked but to secure peace they should abandon this false creed (which most Islamic leaders held to be hereti-cal and the Mahdi a false Messiah).[19] 'Kitchener', wrote the new Sirdar, Sir Francis Grenfell, 'first succeeded in detaching the tribes from Osman and making an anti-Dervish league. He got to know every sheik personally and completely gained their confidence and respect. It is most disgusting to see him held up to abuse'.[20]

For when he stopped trade with the interior he was attacked in *The Times* and in letters to Lord Salisbury by Augustus Wylde, a trader who had been ruined by the rebellion and wanted to trade with the Mahdist empire, and William Fox, a Quaker engineer who believed that if he were allowed to build a railway from Suakin to Berber, all would be peace, that every shot fired at a Sudani was wicked, and Kitchener's whole policy was wicked and wanton.[21] Baring himself, misled by the British consul, the quarrelsome Donald Cameron, was doubtful of Kitchener's policy at first, 'but I must confess', he wrote after visiting Suakin, 'that all I have heard and seen lately has impressed me very favourably with him'.[22]

Kitchener was carrying out Lord Salisbury's policy under Baring's instructions. But one initiative backfired. Cut off from world news, Kitchener had persuaded Baron Reuter to extend his wire service to Suakin, promising in return 'the most wonderful and thrilling news from the Sudan'. But when Reuter's reported a speech of Lord Salisbury in which he said that Egypt was only justified in holding Suakin as a means to end the slave trade, Kitchener suppressed the paragraph because the loyalty of the people would not be encouraged if safety from Osman Digna depended merely on humanitarian feelings in England.[23]

When not away on operations or diplomacy Kitchener Pasha kept up a liberal establishment at Government House, spending all his considerable pay to do so. He gave frequent dinners, mainly male affairs since only three white women (one a bride) were resident.

Each day he would rise early and ride, inspecting troops and fortifications to keep both to his high standards; then go to his office at 8 a.m. until 5 p.m. except for lunch, 'settling all sorts of questions for everything has to come to me'. At five o'clock he would ride down to watch tennis or sometimes to play polo. In one match they had 'a most dreadful' accident when his brigade major's pony fell and rolled over him fatally. 'It was a great loss to me as well as everyone', Kitchener told his brother Arthur, 'as he was a most charming little fellow and we hit it off exactly'.[24]

Arthur Kitchener was coming home from New Zealand on leave and to work out details of their father's decision to amalgamate his sheep run with Sir Francis Bell's. Herbert was most disappointed that Arthur's ship did not stop at Aden so that he could not reach Suakin. Herbert tried to persuade Millie to come out on a winter visit, and he wrote regularly to his father, who was going blind. 'Thank you', wrote the old colonel, 'for writing so big and plain . . . your letters are the only ones now I can read . . . your beautiful big hand – it must take you long to do but helps me much'.[25]

In late 1887 Osman Digna, strengthened by appropriating the trading caravans before Kitchener had stopped the trade, had been laying waste the nearby country and sending raids almost to the suburbs of Suakin. 'Monkey' Gordon built a wall of coral, at great speed, and several outlaying forts. The loyal tribes were angry with Osman, and in early January 1888 Kitchener saw an opportunity of catching him at his base in the village of Hardub and liberating a large number of slaves. Kitchener secured the Sirdar's permission to attack, provided he used no regular British or Egyptian troops but relied on friendly tribesmen, Turkish irregulars (bashibazouks) and Egyptian police.

He concentrated his force of four hundred men in the middle of the night. His second-in-command, T. E. Hickman, noticed a suspicious number of Black Sudanese regulars (who hated Mahdism) dressed in shirts and drawers and pretending to be scallywags. 'Shall I turn them out or turn a blind eye?' he asked Kitchener. 'Turn a blind eye!'

The night march took the Mahdists by surprise and nearly caught Osman, but when the enemy counterattacked from the rear the tribal friendlies and the bashibazouks bolted, while the liberated slaves ran in all directions. The Blacks and Egyptians rallied on a hillock. Both sides were pouring a hot fire at each other. Kitchener rode forward, intending to lead the Blacks in a final charge to win the day. As he turned along the line a bullet hit the lobe of his right ear, splintered a piece of his jaw and lodged close to the throat. He had missed death by an inch. He kept his seat, and the medical officer, Galbraith, rode up and tied a handkerchief around the jaw since Kitchener dared not dismount.

The Blacks never charged. The raid failed. Kitchener, barely able to speak, handed over command to Hickman, who conducted a fighting retreat under heavy fire. By the time Kitchener was helped off his horse at Government House he was in great pain. On examination Galbraith found the jaw unbroken but a splinter of bone had lodged near the windpipe, tonsils and glands. The neck had swollen, and he could not find the bullet, which moved later and nearly choked Kitchener until he managed to swallow it, or so he always claimed.

The deputy commandant, A. B. Makepeace Shakespear, wrote to Millie: 'Your poor brother has a very nasty wound in the face. He is anxious to make light of it but that is all nonsense'. Shakespear described the injuries. There was no cause for alarm but 'it is too severe a wound for him to remain here so I am sending him up in the Starling and he will leave today. I have taken over his duties until his return but I dare say you will see him at the Temple before I shall see him back at work here. The Queen has just telegraphed to ask after him. We are able to say there is an improvement this morning though the improvement is slight. The fact is he is a bad patient. He worries himself about his work here and about leaving it. I shall be glad to hear of him arriving in Cairo where he will have all the comforts of the grand hospital they have in the Citadel',[26] where the Sirdar visited him and laughingly said he supposed he ought to court-martial him as the names of several Sudanese regulars were on the comparatively short casualty list.

No one seemed to mind that Hardub was a defeat. Wolseley wrote from the War Office. 'Everyone here was extremely grieved to hear of your wound and all wish you a speedy recovery. We shall be badly off at Suakin until you are well enough to return there which I hope and trust for your own sake as well as the country's may be very good [sic, a slip for 'soon'].'[27] In his reply Kitchener praised the hospital and asked Wolseley to write and thank the three army doctors and the sister concerned.

At Suakin Kitchener's ADC wrote to Millie three weeks after the battle: 'You can guess how terribly cut up we all were about your brother, and it is very pleasing that the whole town felt it very much and they never cease to enquire how he is getting on'. Millie came out briefly to Cairo and when Kitchener returned in mid-March to Suakin he told her of 'a most cordial reception from the people who all turned out when I landed and illuminated the town in the evening'.[28]

On 11 April he was not only promoted colonel (brevet) but Queen Victoria was personally[29] pleased to appoint him one of her aides-de-camp. This, he commented to Millie, was a most unexpected surprise. 'It is another jump successfully negotiated on the rather tiring course through this life'.[30] The Sirdar had written a glowing report: 'His garrison has been kept in perfect order, while he has worked hard at his civil duties. He has great influence with native tribes, speaking Arab fluently'. His capacity for command was 'very great'.[31]

Kitchener was on his way to the top. But fame was never so strong a spur as duty and the will of God.

10

SIRDAR

THE WOUND REFUSED to heal. In the spring of 1888 Kitchener took early leave, and in London the doctors cured him. But the handicap of 'one eye following the other' became a little heavier. Moreover, the honourable scars now gave his face a somewhat cruel look, which those who did not know him, or its cause, supposed an indication of character. To others he seemed to scowl, or glare or frown. He was happy to exploit his face to keep unwanted people at a distance, but the harsh look disappeared when he smiled.

While on leave he was summoned by the Prime Minister, Lord Salisbury, who was his own Foreign Secretary. Salisbury was 'much impressed with him', recalled Lord Edward Cecil, his fourth son. 'That I clearly remember, for my father was not often impressed'.[1] Lord Edward, a twenty-one-year-old ensign in the Grenadier Guards, met Kitchener for the first time when Salisbury followed up his official interview by the rare honour of an invitation to stay a weekend at Hatfield, his Jacobean mansion in Hertfordshire. As Kitchener climbed the Grand Staircase he would have seen the Duke of Wellington's trophy from his early Indian wars, Tipu Sahib's sword which the Duke had given to an earlier Lady Salisbury, a spur to any ambitious young commander.

Although Kitchener astonished the household by his early rising, since the day began late at Hatfield, he immediately found himself at home among the Cecils. Their unusual blend of intellectual pursuits, politics, science and fun, with no inhibitions between the generations, and a strong but unself-conscious Christianity, was well able to encourage a gauche and shy soldier on the verge of great achievement. The eldest son, Jem (Viscount Cranborne), and his young wife became particular friends. Jem, twenty-seven, was a Member of Parliament, a keen officer in the Militia and a zealous churchman, so they had much in common.

His wife, born Lady Alice Gore, daughter of an Irish earl, was then twenty-one. She had dark hair and a rather severe beauty which belied her delightfully happy personality. Like Kitchener she had lost her mother in childhood. She had been brought up by her grandmother, Lady Joscelyn, a woman of charm and beauty who had been one of Queen Victoria's Coronation trainbearers. Lady Joscelyn was a fervent Evangelical but full of sorrows: her husband and four children all died in her lifetime. The gloom of the Cross rather than the joy of the Resurrection pervaded Alice's childhood. Her own sincere faith came to its fulness in the relaxed atmosphere of Hatfield and a most happy marriage. She had gifts of understanding which would mean much to Kitchener in the years ahead. She was in tune with his desire to help the poor, for the great philanthropist Lord Shaftesbury had been her great-uncle by marriage and she loved to follow his example.

Kitchener would find a sympathetic correspondent in Lady Cranborne (it was always 'Dear Lady Cranborne,' never 'Dear Alice') and she kept his letters, written to be shown to her husband too, but most unfortunately he destroyed hers with almost all his private archive.

At Hatfield that week-end Salisbury offered Kitchener the post of Adjutant-General of the Egyptian Army, second-in-command to the Sirdar (the appointments were controlled by the Foreign Office, not the War Office). Kitchener wrote to Arthur in New Zealand: 'I do not much like the change as I shall not be so independent but I believe it is best to accept, which I have done.'[2] When he went on to Cossington, where the colonel was well but had aged and was very blind, he found his eldest brother Chevallier, still a major, and wrote to Arthur: 'I cannot understand him, he seems more queer than ever and is I feel very jealous of my promotion, a funny thing for a brother to be.'[3] Harry and Millie were about to revisit New Zealand, promising to stay with Herbert in Cairo on the way back. Herbert finished his leave by shooting in Scotland, where he got his first stag 'and a good many grouse'.

Before he could settle down in Cairo in the spacious house allotted to the Adjutant-General, he went with Grenfell and reinforcements to Suakin, where Osman Digna had been strengthened by Baring's mistake in revoking Kitchener's ban on trade with the interior. Grenfell defeated Osman in a brief campaign. Kitchener handled the cavalry well. By late January 1889 Sirdar and Adjutant-General were in Cairo.

In the hot weather that year Kitchener was on leave in England when he was summoned back to find the Sudanese frontier aflame. The dervishes were assembling for an invasion of Egypt. He wrote from Aswan on 24 July to Millie, now returned from New Zealand: 'What a change it was, in only 12 days from London gaieties to organizing a force here with the thermometer at 110 in the shade.' The dervishes had brought their women and children but no food, 'so they leave them to starve, the poor creatures come in to us in the most ghastly state, mere walking skeletons'.[4]

Nine days later, on 3 August 1889, the dervish invasion was totally stopped by Grenfell at the battle of Toski, Kitchener again commanding the cavalry, who headed off a dervish flanking movement. Western firepower inevitably wrought a great slaughter.

Grenfell's confidential report for 1890 noted Kitchener's strengths and weaknesses:

> . . . a very capable, active clear-headed officer. Can drill with all arms. A good brigadier, very ambitious, his rapid promotion has placed him in a somewhat difficult position. He is not popular, but has of late greatly improved in tact and manner and any defects in his character will in my opinion disappear as he gets on in the service. He is a fine gallant soldier and a good linguist, and very successful in dealing with orientals.[5]

He hoped to succeed Grenfell as Sirdar. Then Baring, early in 1890, asked him to reorganize the Egyptian police. Kitchener demurred, saying that acceptance might injure his career. 'My dear Colonel,' replied Baring, 'if you do not accept posts that are offered you, you may have *no* career!'[6] Kitchener accepted, reorganized the police to Baring's satisfaction and resumed the Adjutant-Generalship.

The Grenfells had shown no sign of moving 'so I go on waiting', he had written to Millie. 'It is a poor game, but perhaps it is worth it. Anyway, unless something v. good turns [*sic*] I think I ought to stick on.'[7]

One year later, in January 1892, Khedive Tewfik died after a short illness through the incompetence of native doctors. He was succeeded by his eighteen-year-son, Abbas Hilmi II, fresh from an Austrian military school in Vienna. The British government decided to recall Grenfell after seven years as

Sirdar. The English officers of the Egyptian Army hoped that the pasha in command at the frontier, Jocelyn Wodehouse, would succeed, being genial and a fighting soldier, but Baring (who became Lord Cromer this same year) recommended Kitchener. Cromer knew from his own early military experience that an administrator rather than a fighter was required for the reconquest of the Sudan, if ever approved. It would depend more on thorough organization, training and strict economy than on strategic brilliance. Kitchener was not yet forty-two, young to be 'a full blown Sirdar and a brigadier-general'.[8]

Lord Cromer thought that twenty more years might pass before the reconquest could be attempted, for no money was available from the Egyptian treasury and none likely from the British, especially when Lord Salisbury was defeated at the General Election of 1892 and Gladstone returned. Kitchener, however, determined to be ready. He set himself to enlarge the Egyptian Army without asking for more money. He appointed 'Monkey' Gordon as Director of Stores, who quietly prepared all manner of equipment to avenge his uncle. Kitchener promoted Reginald Wingate to be Director of Intelligence. Wingate had already mastered all aspects of Mahdism and set up a network of spies, whose evidence of the maladministration and misery of the Sudan was overwhelming. His final estimate was eight million dead by execution, rebellion, disease or hunger. Wingate had made contact with Rudolf Slatin, the Khalifa's prisoner in Omdurman, and engineered his escape, accomplished by Slatin's own courage and resource.

Ten years earlier in Cyprus General Biddulph and Charles King-Harman had concluded that the young Kitchener went for the popular line, for immediate rather than long-term results. These characteristics had been rubbed away by his desert experience. Since the Gordon disaster his eye was on the distant horizon. He saw already how to reconquer the Sudan and all else must be secondary. 'Comfort, affections, personalities, all were quite inferior considerations', noted Lord Edward Cecil, whose close observation came a little later but was true already. The aim came before everything. 'He felt he was defrauding the Almighty if he did not carry out his task'.[9]

He could be 'brutal in his methods', thought Cromer's Third Secretary, Horace Rumbold, 'and would get the last ounce of work out of a man'. To Rumbold, not knowing him well, he seemed 'quite devoid of emotions or sentiment'.[10] Easy-going officers criticized him for not playing tennis or racquets. He would not reveal the reason, his inability to focus both eyes. Inspecting the ranks, he never spoke to a private soldier, but he would not disclose why, that if he addressed one, another might answer. He cared for them but did good by stealth.[11]

He weeded out the inefficient. On his annual leave in England he would interview promising young officers attracted by the higher rank, better pay and prospect of action. He insisted on an undertaking that they would not marry for two years or even get engaged. The service must not be hindered by domestic ties. In Egypt he could not prevent casual sexual liaisons, but he himself was chaste, scorning those who had mistresses or visited brothels. He put women on a pedestal and was hurt when he knew of any treated as chattels.[12] He enjoyed feminine company when duty allowed. He flirted mildly with Ellen Peel, his former ADC's sister but cooled off when she hoped for a proposal. She married one of his officers. Daisy Rogers, sister of a swell dragoon, fell in love with Kitchener but her landowner father suppressed any romance with a mere sapper. Daisy never married.

He also had the social life of Freemasonry. By 1895 he was a member of five Lodges in Cairo, and held the rank of Past Senior Grand Warden of Egypt.[13]

Each year Cairo became a winter capital of European society, including rich and aristocratic Britons, several of whom became Kitchener's friends. He told Lady Cranborne that he had plenty of room; she and Jem could bring whom they wished.[14] With his strong family feeling, he longed for Millie. When the Parkers were going to New Zealand, he wrote: 'I hope you are not going through without staying with me, that would be *too bad* and you promised. The Khedive is continually asking after you'.[15] Another year he suggested she come for the three winter months with her two girls. 'My house wants looking after and I find a lady is quite necessary but it is too difficult to find one to marry'. Later he was half-jokingly threatening her: 'If you do not do something in the way of helping in the entertaining I shall be driven into some rash alliance of a matrimonial nature, so you have your warning and better look out'.[16]

When he liked, Kitchener was a good host, even giving fancy-dress balls, but he kept ambitious mothers and their eligible daughters at a distance. One winter visitor was Margot Tennant, then twenty-eight. Daughter of a Scottish industrial magnate and future second wife of Asquith, she wrote in her sharp-edged journal:

I had heard a good many stories of Colonel Kitchener but never met him till he took me in to dinner at the Residency, after which he came several times to see me. He is not popular, and I can see that neither Mr. Milner nor Sir Evelyn Baring like him; but I found him an interesting study; not really *interesting*, but a study. Though a little underbred, he is not at all vulgar, and though arrogant is not vain; but he is either way very stupid or very clever, and never gives himself away.[17]

The new young khedive was strongly nationalistic and chafed at the British occupation. During 1892 Lord Cromer needed all his experience and tact to prevent Abbas undermining the balance of power in the eastern Mediterranean. In the summer of 1893, while Cromer was in Scotland, Abbas appointed a crony, Maher Pasha, as deputy war minister, who at once showed anti-British prejudice and signs of subverting the loyalty of the Egyptian Army to its British officers. Fearful of another rebellion like Arabi's, eleven years earlier, with massacres of foreigners and disruption of the economy, Cromer was seeking an occasion to bring Abbas to heel.

In January 1894 the khedive announced his wish to inspect the Nile garrisons between Aswan and Wadi Halfa. Kitchener made every preparation to honour him and display a smart, efficient army, but before the khedive and Maher arrived a secret document was betrayed to Wingate. It revealed the khedive's deliberate intention to humiliate the Sirdar and to force British officers out of the Egyptian Army. Forewarned, Kitchener ordered Wingate to keep an official diary of the inspection. The Sirdar would provide details when Wingate was not in ear shot.

Knowing that Abbas was little more than a boy, Kitchener reacted calmly when the khedive criticized a smart Sudanese battalion for holding their rifles wrongly: Abbas later insulted a black Sudanese officer and complained at having to give commissions to negroes. The following morning, on parade, he remarked loudly, that the Sirdar knew nothing of the finer points of arms drill, and when the German attaché praised the drilling he was ignored. Next, the khedive complained that the British surgeon-general was incompetent and ignorant. Kitchener respectfully replied that the khedive had not had opportunity to make any judgement and that Surgeon-General Graham was exceptionally able. Abbas praised every Egyptian, criticized every Briton.

The climax came at Wadi Halfa as the entire garrison marched past. Whenever a British-led formation passed the saluting base, the khedive abused it to the Sirdar. Finally, as they rode from the parade, he exclaimed: 'To tell you the truth, Kitchener Pasha, I consider it is disgraceful for Egypt to be served by such an army'.

Kitchener, fully aware of the tensions between Cromer and the khedive, replied in a most respectful tone: 'I beg to tender Your Highness my resignation'. The khedive was aghast but the Sirdar held his ground: 'Your Highness, I am not in the least angry, but in resigning I consider I am only doing my duty'. He told the khedive that all the English officers would probably resign and no replacements would volunteer. Three times, to make his point, the Sirdar stated his intention to resign.

The khedive by now was alarmed at what he had done, and begged the Sirdar to withdraw his resignation. The Sirdar, making no definite promise, wired Cromer the facts. Cromer supported him immediately. Backed by Lord Rosebery, the Foreign Secretary (and soon to be Prime Minister), he demanded that the khedive apologize to the army and dismiss Maher. Kitchener withdrew his resignation.[18]

To show their confidence, the British government promptly advised the Queen to knight him. He became Sir Herbert Kitchener, KCMG, CB.* 'So glad my dear old father has lived long enough to be pleased', wrote Herbert to a cousin.[19] The old colonel was now wholly blind. That August of 1894, with Kitchener, on leave, at his bedside in Cossington Manor, he died after several days in a coma. The others were all in India (where Herbert had spent one leave with Walter at Poona) or New Zealand. Their half-sister Kawara came over from Dinan and their cousin Frank Kitchener, now a headmaster, and a few surviving friends attended the funeral, which was 'quietly but nicely done . . . I was able to secure a very nice place for his grave just under the East window of the church here'.[20] Herbert then paid off the servants, sold up and settled 'the governor's' small estate in England by the end of the month, writing long, affectionate letters to Arthur about the debt-ridden New Zealand land. Herbert worried that Arthur would spoil his own career as an engineer if he stayed, yet they must sell up first and the times were bad.[21]

Herbert had thought he might go out to New Zealand on his next annual leave but greater events supervened.

On each leave in England he had lobbied for an advance into Dongola province, which would begin the reconquest of the Sudan. He had lobbied

* He had been made a Companion of the Bath in 1889 for his part in the battle of Toski.

so hard in 1894 that Cromer, on leave in Scotland, 'did not like it. Now I have to be quiet for a while', Kitchener told Wingate.[22] In June 1895 Lord Salisbury returned to power. On Kitchener's annual weekend at Hatfield that summer he thought Salisbury sympathetic but in no hurry to commit British troops or money.

Back in Cairo, Kitchener found another block to his plans. A report on the vital question of irrigation in the Nile Delta had proposed a dam at Aswan in Upper Egypt, near the island that Kitchener had sought as a country retreat and experimental farm, still known as Kitchener Island. The official in charge of irrigation, (Sir) William Garstin, was determined to have the Aswan dam. Early in 1896 his proposal had a firm claim for any available funds, despite a worry that the French in Central Africa might annex the equatorial province of the Sudan where the Mahdist hold was weak. A Captain Marchand was preparing an expedition to reach the Upper Nile at Fashoda and claim it for France. This remote threat did not displace the dam's priority.

Suddenly, on 1 March 1896, the situation changed. Far away in the mountains of Abyssinia (as Ethiopia was then known) an Italian army, advancing from their colony of Eritrea, which they had annexed six years earlier, was soundly beaten and almost wiped out by a huge army of Abyssinians in the battle of Adowa. While the surviving Italians were being marched into captivity (some having been castrated), the Italian ambassador in London begged Lord Salisbury to stage a diversion on the Nile lest the Mahdist regime in the Sudan seize the opportunity to attack the Italian garrison in Kassala on the western border of Eritrea. On the evening of 12 March, following two Cabinet meetings and consultation with Lord Wolseley, Salisbury sent a telegram to Cromer with a copy to the Sirdar, while the War Office sent another to General Knowles, commanding the British Army of Occupation. Although differing in detail, their effect was to order an advance into Dongola, the northernmost province of the Sudan.[23]

Salisbury's cypher telegram reached the Egyptian War Office after midnight. It was taken for decoding to Lord Athlumney of the Coldstream Guards and Jimmy Watson, 60th Rifles, Kitchener's ADC, both in the Egyptian Army, who were living at the Turf Club. Excited by the decoded message, they each set out in different directions to find the Sirdar, who might still be attending the social functions to which he was engaged, for late hours were kept in Cairo. Finding that he had gone home, Watson hurried to the palatial Sirdarieh, where Kitchener lived alone with his already impressive collection of ceramics, armour, carving, screens and antiquities (which aston-ished his brother Walter when he saw them).[24] The servants' quarters were in the garden. It was now 3 a.m. on 13 March 1896.

Kitchener awoke to hear pebbles rattling at the window. Annoyed, he lit a lamp and threw open the window to see the night watchman standing respect-fully beside Captain Watson, who was waving a piece of paper. Kitchener came down in his pyjamas and read the decoded telegram. When Athlumney arrived a few moments later he saw the Sirdar, a lamp in one hand and the tele-gram in the other, dancing a gentle jig with Watson.[25]

II

ADVANCE UP THE NILE

AT THE RESIDENCY lights were burning and Cromer was drafting orders, although annoyed that Salisbury had forced his hand two years before he was ready. Together, Cromer and Kitchener sent out the orders in the khedive's name to the khedive's army, then remembered that he had not been told. They hurried to the Abdin Palace; Abbas was still asleep.[1]

No time could be lost if the Expeditionary Force were to be far enough upriver to use the Nile's high-water season, when transports could move freely and gunboats support the final assault on Dongola. Cromer worked on the Commissioners of the Debt to produce the money.[2] He obliged a reluctant khedive to reject the Ottoman sultan's veto on the use of the Egyptian Army. Kitchener put into motion the plans he had already drawn up.[3]

Only three days after Lord Salisbury's telegram, a mixed column moved into the Sudan and in four days, almost unopposed, reached the village of Akasha, eighty-seven miles higher up the Nile, and immediately fortified the village and made it into the advanced base. Meanwhile, unknown to Kitchener until the matter was settled, the War Office was trying to give the command to General Knowles, until Salisbury ordained that the Sirdar should command, reporting to Cromer and thus to the Foreign Office, not to Wolseley at the War Office.[4] No British troops were to be used except for Maxim machine-gunners of the Connaught Rangers and one battalion (North Staffords) in reserve. At Kitchener's urgent request an Indian brigade freed the Egyptian garrison at Suakin for service on the Nile.

Success would depend on men and supplies reaching the front without interruption from cataracts or low water. The ruined railway of 1885 must therefore be relaid. Troops, convicts and locals were put to repairing the old bed through the wild country of the Womb of Rocks (or Belly of Stones – Batan el Hagar). Kitchener remembered that after the withdrawal from the Sudan, which he had so deplored, many railway sleepers had been used to roof barracks at Wadi Halfa. He ordered the roofs to be stripped and the sleepers relaid as the line advanced. Sleepers were found in native huts; the dervishes had built gallows with others. Every relaid sleeper helped the budget that Cromer had set at a minimum. Kitchener had to improvise and command-eer. He was able to boast that he made one stretch of ten miles for nothing. ('What slave-driving and sweating!' was the comment of one of Queen Victoria's ladies.)[5]

Kitchener summoned a young sapper lieutenant from Woolwich, a French-Canadian who had worked on the Canadian Pacific railway. Percy Girouard proved to be a genius at railway repair and construction, and with his trans-atlantic background was not afraid of Kitchener. On one occasion after the line had reopened, the Sirdar, in a hurry, became impatient when a crazy old engine would not pull a heavily laden train as fast as he wanted. He mounted the footplate, left half the train behind and told the driver to 'go like hell'. They rattled and rocked over the corkscrew line until the Sirdar emerged at his destination exclaiming: 'What a dreadful journey we've had, Girouard! Terrible, terrible!' Girouard, twenty-nine years old, adjusted his eye-glass and faced the Sirdar: 'You will break the record and your own neck one day!' Kitchener damned him, then grinned, for he loved a man who would speak his mind. He learned much from Girouard.[6]

Before the railway could be ready, and afterwards for operations, camels were essential. Kitchener was determined not to repeat the wastage of camels from the inexperience of British officers during the Gordon Relief. His brother Walter had worked with camels in the Second Afghan War. Walter came from India to be Director of Transport. He was efficient and hard-working, rather deaf, and not afraid of Herbert although greatly admiring him. And the always spruce Herbert's brotherly affection tolerated Walter's untidiness.[7]

Lord Salisbury, however, was worried when he heard that the Sirdar had bought large numbers of camels. 'I would much rather see him without them', fearing they would tempt him to make a dash for Khartoum, whereas a railway 'can't move'; the Cabinet had not yet decided whether the money would run to an advance beyond Dongola province. Cromer reassured him, repeating his

earlier verdict that Kitchener 'is cool and sensible and knows his job thoroughly, and is not at all inclined to be rash'.[8] Yet on 1 May Salisbury told
Cromer with some amusement that several Cabinet ministers were still scared
'that Kitchener meditates an expedition into the wilderness at the head of a
string of camels. I do not share their apprehensions – tho' I have as much
horror of the camel as they have'. Wolseley had even wanted to send out 'some
great English General'.

Salisbury's misreading of Kitchener, despite an avuncular interest, and his
ignorance of the demands of the terrain would soon be rectified. Long ago
Lord Edward Cecil (Nigs to his family, Ned to his friends) of the Grenadier
Guards had daringly asked Kitchener to take him as an ADC if the opportunity offered. Knowing that Cecil had proved a good ADC to Wolseley, the
Sirdar sent a wire. So keen was he to have a direct line to Salisbury that he
ignored his own veto on married officers, for Cecil had a wife and a son of six
months. The High Church Cecil had married the atheist Violet Maxse after
a whirlwind courtship, against the advice of his parents. The rather caustic,
gloomy Nigs and the bohemian Violet were ill-matched. Cecil may have been
glad to get away.[9]

Jimmy (or Jemmy) Watson continued as senior ADC, and Kitchener's
choice of him is a comment on his own character. For Watson went through
life laughing and telling ridiculous stories and making up limericks to lighten
tensions at the worst moments. He had the kindest of hearts and was universally popular as well as protective of his Sirdar, who trusted him implicitly.
Watson kept a diary, but only of the briefest chronological kind, so that pos-
terity has lost the stories he could tell and is left with the gloom of Cecil's
private, almost illegible diary of the campaign and his perceptive, sympathetic
essay of twenty years later. Watson had won a reputation for bravery and cheerfulness with the 60th Rifles in India. Accepted for the Egyptian Army, it was
he who first identified at Wadi Halfa a scruffy nervous vagabond in Arab dress
as Rudolf Slatin, known to have escaped from Omdurman. Watson fetched
a glass of beer: an Arab would have refused it; a thirsty Austrian gulped it
down.[10]

For Chief of Staff Kitchener had Rundle, his old companion of 1884, but
left him at Wadi Halfa to deal with base affairs and acted virtually as his own
Chief of Staff. As second-in-command he had the remarkable and outstanding Archie Hunter, eight years younger than himself, a brave, rather
quiet Scot who gloried in fighting and had great experience in Arab warfare

and was a clever tactician. More popular than Kitchener, many wished at first that he were in command. The strait-laced Cecil thought him licentious. He may have boasted of the Abyssinian mistress he had kept when governor of Suakin (he shocked brother officers who put their native mistresses into back-street lodgings by having her to stay at Shepheard's Hotel). He was not wanton, and like other staff officers had learned not to talk of such things before the chaste Sirdar. Hunter was inclined to be impulsive where Kitchener was cautious. A journalist dubbed him 'Kitchener's sword-arm' but his part in planning Kitchener's battles may have been exaggerated.

Even more important to the success of the expedition was Reginald Wingate, Chief Intelligence Officer, with Rudolf Slatin as his deputy. Rex Wingate was dubbed 'the White Knight' (from the *Alice* books) for the bits of equipment that tended to hang about him. He had kept up his remarkable network of spies and contacts. The Khalifa believed that the Sirdar never made a move without consulting Wingate, who would come every evening to the Sirdar's tent to report and advise.[11]

Almost the whole Egyptian Army was engaged in the campaign. Each battalion's lieutenant-colonel (El Kaimakam) and company commanders (El Bimbashi) were British, with Egyptian and Sudanese officers under them, and a sprinkling of British among the warrant-officers and sergeants. The brigade commanders (El Miralai) were all British, the most colourful being 'Fighting Mac', Hector MacDonald, a former sergeant-major in the Gordon Highlanders who had been promoted from the ranks by Roberts in Afghanistan for his courage and leadership, with the exceptional honour of a commission in his own regiment.[12] Of middle height, broad-shouldered and trim he had a determined jaw and steely eyes, and a 'smile so winning that when his white and perfect teeth showed beneath the closely trimmed moustache the whole face was lit up as by a sunbeam'.[13] He had already distinguished himself in frontier battles commanding the 11th Sudanese, now in his brigade. Unlike the lighter-skinned Egyptians, who were Arabs and almost all Muslims except for a few Coptic Christians, the Sudanese came from the equatorial south, and with their negroid features and very dark skin were affectionately known as 'the Blacks'. Many had left the Sudan as children when Gordon evacuated the families of his loyal southern soldiers in 1884 before the Mahdi closed the route; older ones had either taken part in the attempted relief of Khartoum or had escaped from the Mahdist regime. Mostly animists (from later fruitful fields for the Christian gospel), they revered

Gordon almost as a god because he had put down the slave trade. Irrepressible, they adored fighting (and looting if they got the chance). Off duty they liked to strip down to the national dress of their Shilluk and Dinka tribes – stark naked. War correspondents who saw them bathing in the Nile marvelled at these well-endowed young Hercules. Their women and children were camp followers in the African and eastern way, and when the Sirdar once ordered that the women should stay behind a deputation called on him. Their language was so explicit that with his mastery of colloquial Arabic he was seen to blush under his brick-red sunburn.[14]

The Blacks hated the Khalifa and his tribe, the Baggara, who formed the core of his army, and so did the Ababdeh tribesmen who provided Kitchener's 'friendlies' of 1884, and the Jaalin of the lands north of Khartoum: the campaigns of 1896–8 were as much a civil war as an invasion. And although the Mahdi had been born in Dongola, Wingate was now receiving many secret messages from sheikhs in Dongola with one refrain: 'We long for you to come'.[15]

Early in April Wingate reported that an advance force of the enemy lay at Firket, some sixteen miles upriver from Akasha.

Anxious to know whether the Egyptian and the Sudanese battalions would fight well enough to ensure victory, Cromer had asked Kitchener to bring the dervishes to battle at the earliest opportunity. Back in March, after examining the logistics, Kitchener had told him that he would fight on 7 June.

On 1 June, with 10,000 troops south of Wadi Halfa, the Sirdar ordered Hunter to ride by night until he could see into the enemy camp at dawn, and plan its capture. Undetected, Hunter found the enemy concentrated before Firket village, which straggled along the east bank of the Nile, with a hill rising about half a mile behind Hunter. He came back to Akasha at about eleven in the morning, wrote out detailed orders and then rode north to meet Kitchener 'and explained the whole thing to him which he accepted in toto'.[16]

During the night of 6 June two columns set out. The River column commanded by Hunter, which Kitchener accompanied, marched on Firket from the north, between the Nile and the hill. The Desert column, which included the cavalry, swung out into the desert beyond the hill and approached from the south-east to cut off the enemy's flight. Despite the distances, the two columns attacked simultaneously at dawn on 7 June 1896.

Surprise was complete. The enemy, in their uniform of white *jibbah* (smock) with black or dark blue patches, fought hard but were overwhelmed. Some fell back to the houses and resisted to death, many surrendered, others threw away their weapons and swam across the river, naked and unarmed. A number of horsemen fled through an undetected gap. Kitchener ordered his cavalry to pursue but not to intercept; he wanted none of his own men killed by dervishes brought to bay.

More than eight hundred dervish dead were counted, including their commanders, to trifling Egyptian loss and no British officer killed. Slatin had the curious experience of finding the bodies of several of his former tor-mentors. He assured Queen Victoria, who had given him the privilege of writing direct to her, that the enemy's wounded were cared for and the prison-ers well treated: 'They were astonished at the clemency and the mercy', since many had murdered innocent people.[17]

The army had proved it could fight, and the Sirdar that he could win without wasting lives and material. 'Kitchener has done the whole thing admirably', Cromer wrote on 20 June. 'I always felt confident he would do so, as he is a first rate man'.[18] Cromer and the British press gave Kitchener the credit for the night march and Hunter's brilliant tactics, 'and quite right too', Hunter assured his brother. 'He was responsible and if it had failed he would have been blamed, and so I am quite satisfied he will do me justice when the proper time comes – I know he trusts me. He knows I am as keen for his success as he is himself, in fact we sink or swim, and so does everyone in the show, together, and we are a united and not an unhappy family'.[19]

Hunter and Wingate wanted the Sirdar to make a dash for Dongola town, more than two hundred miles upriver, believing it could now be seized without a shot. Kitchener may not have known of Salisbury's worry about a string of camels in the wilderness, but he would not risk being counterattacked and besieged at the end of an overlong line of communication and without his gunboats. Instead, he sent Hunter back to bring the gunboats up the difficult and dangerous nine miles of the Second Cataract, a gorge of great granite steps under surging water. Hunter succeeded but resented Kitchener's refusal to come to see him do it. The Sirdar had given his orders, trusted his subordinate and saw no need to pat him on the back for doing his duty. Hunter in old age claimed that the Sirdar had never thanked him.[20] But by the end of Hunter's operation Kitchener was under intense pressure.

Before Hunter had left for the railhead and the Second Cataract Kitchener had selected a site at Firket for the army to await the gunboats and fresh supplies.

Hunter pointed out that it was too near the place where they had buried the dervish dead and persuaded him to move it some miles upstream to Kosheh.

Hunter ascribed Kitchener's mistake to his 'cursed bad eyesight'.[21] Eyestrain gave constant headaches. He wore glasses for office work but not outside. One of Wingate's intelligence officers, Nevill Smyth of the Bays (who was a brother of Ethel Smyth the composer and would win the VC at Omdurman), thought Kitchener's eyes his most notable feature.

> They appeared to look from a kind of ambush, not a stealthy ambush, but a courageous and strategic ambush, and to scan the distance above and beyond the faces or the foreground which he was actually contemplating. His eye was often likened to a lion's, and this illusion was helped a little by the colour scheme of light blue orbs in a dark ruddy face and the straight line of the eyebrows. His expression was generally grave and thoughtful, his smile flattered the fancy, he was very fond of humour, and his eyes sparkled when he was amused and in battle.[22]

Three months would pass before he was in battle again, months of unexpected near-disasters.

12

DONGOLA, 1896

Soon after the battle of Firket the force was afflicted by dysentery and then by a severe epidemic of cholera. Whether it came down from Egypt or up from the Sudan, it spread rapidly in the base and forward camps. Doctors worked hard but were too few and medical supplies too short.[1] At Akasha the cholera patients from the North Staffordshires were crowded into one tent in the high summer heat, to suffer the stench and misery of vomit and bowel, followed too often by death. Of the total of 411 casualties of all ranks, Egyptians and British, of the entire six-month Dongola campaign, 364 died of disease and only 47 from enemy action. In this cholera epidemic Father Brindle and his Anglican counterpart worked selflessly.

The cholera subsided but the seasonal north wind failed that year, preventing wind-driven craft from taking men and supplies up the Nile, already much lower than normal. Then came an unexpected and scorching wind from the south; July and August were hell for man and beast, creating the most demanding period in Kitchener's forty-six years, on body, mind and spirit.

He was a light sleeper, needing only four hours.[2] At forward or base headquarters he was out of bed before dawn. As a brother of the Guild of the Holy Standard he had promised not only to be 'sober, upright and chaste' but regular in private prayer. His favourite prayer was the Collect for Whit Sunday: '. . . Grant us by the same Spirit to have a right judgement in all things, and ever-more to rejoice in his holy comfort . . .' 'Use the Whitsun collect and it will help you through life', he told a young cousin.[3]

He would then walk around in his pyjamas between 5 and 6 a.m. to the tents or huts of his staff officers, who must always live near him, and dictate his orders so that they could be telegraphed and carried out that day; thus no one's sleep would be disturbed on the next night unless in emergency.[4]

He would then dress and 'wander off', recalls Cecil,

at that curious stalking stride of his soon after dawn to the railway yard, the embarkation place, the store yards, or whatever interested him for the minute. He saw everything – nothing escaped him; but he officially saw or did not see as much as he chose. Sometimes he seemed to like one with him, but more often he liked to walk ahead, plunged apparently in sombre meditation.[5]

He would return to his office and put in three hours' work before breakfast at ten. He always looked clean and neat (thanks presumably to his soldier servant) despite sand and sweat and it was a myth that papers did not stick to his arms as they did to other men's. But his office was a mess. Papers were on tables, chairs, windowsills and the floor. Only he knew where to find a list or report, and he would let no one touch the muddle except Jimmy Watson and thirty-eight-year-old Staff Sergeant William Bailey of the East Lancashire Regiment, the Chief Clerk. The Sirdar trusted Bailey absolutely and obtained a commission for him a few months later, to continue as his administrative staff officer.[6] Yet the Sirdar hardly needed to look at a paper: he had an extraordinary memory and grasp of detail, thus allowing him to be virtually his own Chief of Staff but causing difficulties to subordinates when he kept his intentions or movements to himself and then blamed his ADC for letting him slip away unaccompanied.

His meals would be at any hour, a probable cause of the chronic indigestion that made him grumpy. In the extreme heat of that terrible summer he might keep his staff waiting for dinner until ten, then eat it in solemn silence if something were on his mind. Cecil (in the privacy of his diary) called him the Great White Czar. 'Nigs' may have expected the deference due to a lord, for he complained (to the diary) of insults. Fifteen years later he became a close and admiring colleague in the government of Egypt but he did not like his chief in 1896. Kitchener seemed uncouth to an Old Etonian Grenadier and was living on his nerves as he wrestled with the problems of an army to be transported, supplied and victorious on too little money in extreme heat. He could be inconsiderate and rude. 'He was always inclined to bully his own entourage, as some men are rude to their wives. He was inclined to let off his spleen on those round him. He was often morose and silent for hours together'.[7]

But except in a crisis he liked to stop work for an hour at six and chat to his staff over a gin and tonic, his 'most human time', with plenty of humour, mixed however with cynicism. Long experience of Arabs had made him affect to be a cynic. He was inclined, to Cecil's observation,

> to disbelieve that any action sprang from motives other than those of self-interest – or rather, he affected to be. He had in reality the greatest confidence in those who were worthy of it, and he was rarely if ever taken in. His cynicism was in a large measure a part of the curious shyness which declined to show any inside portion of his life or mind. He loathed any form of moral or mental undressing. He was even morbidly afraid of showing any feeling or enthusiasm, and he preferred to be misunderstood rather than be suspected of human feeling.

Cecil forgot, writing years later, that he was present on at least one occasion when Kitchener's deep feelings broke through in public. And shyness was cloaked by an almost childlike simplicity 'both in his outlook on life and his display of what most of us hide with care'.[8]

Kitchener's ambition to reach the top was displayed deliberately. Arab sheikhs who had no interest in patriotism or liberating the oppressed could understand fame as a spur. So the Sirdar freely asked them to help him win a great name. This offended his own people who did not display their ambition. He was too shy to tell them of his dominant desire to do the will of God.

He could be maligned far beyond anything that his defects of character might deserve in this time of supreme testing. In late August, when the high water of the Nile had allowed four gunboats and three steam transports to reach Kosheh, where the railway had also arrived with its antiquated rolling stock, Kitchener ordered Hunter to send MacDonald's brigade forward to the next stage before Dongola and to take the shorter desert route, not the curve of the Nile bank. As they marched, a renewed south wind made the desert a raging furnace of sand and dust; eight Blacks died of sunstroke before they could reach the first water depot prepared by Walter Kitchener's camel men. The brigade reached its objective in considerable distress. Lewis's brigade, sent to reinforce, and accompanied by Hunter, suffered even worse from heavy unseasonable rain with unrelenting heat. The British war correspondents dubbed it 'the Death March'. Cecil thought Hunter irresponsible in not turning back at the first watering place, but Hunter wrote to his brother in Cairo a furious put-down of the Sirdar:

> I have plumbed to the bottom of Kitchener now – he is inhuman, heart-less; with eccentric and freakish bursts of generosity specially when he is defeated: he is a vain egotistical and self-confident mass of pride and ambition, expecting and usurping all and giving nothing: he is a mixture of the fox, Jew and snake and like all bullies is a dove when tackled.[9]

Hunter sent a dispatch that virtually accused the Sirdar and Rundle of murder. (He ignored their financial and political restraints.) He wrote an insubordinate letter telling Kitchener how to be a general and look after his men.

Probably he never sent it.[10]

If he did, Kitchener would not have seen it; for another crisis had blown up. On the evening of 29 August, after prolonged rain, he heard at Kosheh that twelve miles of the railway embankment had been washed away by the worst floods and torrents for fifty years. Rails were dangling, sleepers scattered and the army had only five days' supplies in the forward area. Without the railway the campaign must stop. Cromer and Salisbury might even order an ignominious withdrawal.

Kitchener saddled up and rode all night. As Smyth recalled, 'The Sirdar made a practice of always appearing on the scene of any difficulty or disaster'. He reached Akasha at dawn. He organized battalions, some to mend the embankment, others to find and replace the sleepers. He took off his coat and helped lay out curves with his own hands. As Smyth continued:

> The men worked night and day at this vital work. Just as the efforts of all concerned were flagging and the troops were becoming exhausted by the great heat, the Sirdar rode along the line during the hottest part of the day on the 31st August and inspired all ranks to continue the work with renewed vigour. He spoke to many of the men in Arabic and encouraged some of the 15th Battalion who were working under Sergt. Butler, the champion boxer of Cairo and fencing instructor of the Gloucestershire Regiment, who set a fine example in carrying large rocks to build up the embankment.[11]

The line was relaid within a week, wild flowers bloomed in the desert and Kitchener returned up the line ready for the crowning act of his preparations for the assault on Dongola. Before the campaign, Kitchener and Burn-Murdoch, commanding the Egyptian cavalry, had designed a new iron-clad stern-wheeler gunboat, the *Zafir*, with more firepower, better protection for troops on deck and shallower draught than the four older gunboats. The *Zafir* had been built in London in eight weeks, sent out in sections to Egypt and up the railway to Kosheh, where it had been reassembled day by day, to the great interest of any free to watch.

By 7 September her boilers and cylinders had been inserted and the Sirdar and his staff boarded to join Colville, the naval commander, and his second-in-command, the dashing Lieutenant David Beatty, future hero of Jutland. Kitchener, standing on the bridge, was beaming: not only was *Zafir* his special toy, but he reckoned her worth more than a battalion of infantry 'because its armament insures that I can make a landing anywhere I want to in face of Dervish opposition'.[12]

Zafir steamed majestically into mid-stream. Suddenly they heard a muffled explosion below and *Zafir* stopped: her low-pressure cylinder had burst. She would be out of action until a replacement could arrive, perhaps weeks away.

Kitchener stared straight ahead, his mouth twitching. Then he said: 'By God, Colville, I don't know which of us it's hardest luck on – you, or me!' [13] He ordered the guns and Maxim machine-guns to be transferred to another steamer, left the ship and disappeared into the cabin of another. Cecil found him in tears. He threw up his arms: 'What have I done to deserve this?'[14]

All the strain of the past months came to a head at what Cecil thought trivial, but Kitchener knew it to be grievous because the Nile was falling and he could not afford delay. Cecil tactfully kept away. Kitchener recovered and ordered the advance to begin on the day he had planned, 11 September. The British battalion, the North Staffordshires which he had kept in reserve, had now arrived. Dervish activity had been negligible except for patrols which cut the telegraph wire, unaware that the messages went by a cable below the bank or in the water.

A week later the main body had joined the forward troops and they were approaching the fortified village of Karma, 110 miles upstream from their starting-point. Some battalions had marched, others 'steamered' (as the phrase was) in transports and gunboats which navigated the forty-five miles of the

Henry Horatio Kitchener, aged 37, when Captain, 29th Foot, by George Richmond
(sittings 1842 before HHK left for India; delivered 1843)

Fanny Kitchener (*née* Chevallier) 1851. Herbert on her lap;
Chevallier ('Chevally') and Emily ('Millie')

Herbert aged 18, a keen rider

Herbert (right) with Chevally, Millie and
Walter 1869, before Millie's wedding

Herbert at 28,
on return from Palestine, 1878

General Gordon,
Kitchener's hero

'Monkey' Gordon, his nephew, Kitchener's
Director of Supplies

Colonel Herbert Kitchener Pasha, CB, CMG, 1890, aged 40,
by Sir Hubert von Herkomer

Lord Salisbury (3rd Marquess)

Lord Cromer (Sir Evelyn Baring)

Archie Hunter
'Kitchener's Sword Arm'
(later General Sir Archibald Hunter)
(from a *Vanity Fair* cartoon)

Rex Wingate
Kitchener's indispensable chief of
Intelligence (later General Sir
Reginald Wingate)

Walter Kitchener's immediate sketch of Mahmud in the Berber 'triumph'.
He was *not* lashed

gentler but rocky Third Cataract: one gunboat struck a rock and was temporarily stranded.

Wingate had reported that the dervish Emir Bishara Rayda, the Khalifa's
relative, had concentrated his troops at Karma. Kitchener's men had made
good their losses from cholera and storms and were eager to engage. The
Sirdar, unlike Hunter, was not bloodthirsty but determined to bring Bishara
to battle in the open, to avoid street-fighting in Dongola.

At dawn on 19 September Kitchener rode with the advance guard of the
Egyptian cavalry to reconnoitre the enemy personally, only to find that Bishara,
knowing he was outnumbered, had cunningly shipped his force across the
wide river during the night, to fortified positions at Hafir. The scene was awe-
inspiring, the fortifications were clearly visible, with thirty small boats (*gyassas*)
and one steamer moored to the banks covered by a mile of rifle pits and three
batteries of guns. Behind, some 3,000 dervishes, mounted and on foot, could
be seen in the desert beyond.

At 6.30 a.m. the Egyptian horse artillery fired the first shot in the battle of
Hafir. The gunboats engaged the forts. Infantry could do nothing, except for
those in the gunboats, who much felt the absence of the *Zafir* and its armour.
On *Tamai* a British machine-gunner was killed and Commander Colville hit
in the wrist. *Tamai* withdrew 'to report to the Sirdar' but was smartly returned
to the fight. Anglo-Egyptian firepower was inflicting heavy casualties and
Bishara was wounded, but two of the gunboats had been holed, though not
dangerously, and the Sirdar began to fear he might lose one gunboat if this
inconclusive duel continued. Young Lieutenant David Beatty, future hero of
Jutland, Admiral of the Fleet and First Sea Lord, spotted the answer: make a
dash upstream for Dongola itself. Kitchener gave him leave, and since the Nile
above Hafir narrows to six hundred yards he moved his artillery to give covering fire. Beatty led his flotilla with typical panache to the open water and
beyond.

The wounded Bishara suspected a ruse to cut him off from his base, for even
if the bombardment died down he could not remain at Hafir because his boats
with reserves of food and ammunition were within range of the Egyptian
guns. That night he abandoned Hafir and withdrew to Dongola.

Next day Kitchener used the boats to ferry the force to the western bank.
Dongola lay thirty-five miles upstream. Without haste, and allowing a rest-
day at Argo island, Kitchener advanced.

On 22 September he was ready for the final battle. 'The Sirdar's love of fighting was known to all ranks of the Egyptian Army', recalled Smyth. 'Without being foolhardy, he always took the same risks as those who were most exposed to the enemy's fire, and during all the advances such as that upon Dongola on the 22nd September 1896, he moved in advance, close to the contact squadron of cavalry'.[15] His entire force was advancing on the dervish army, which could be seen, a mass of horse and footmen, with banners waving and drums beating, on the plain before Dongola. The Staffordshire men in the centre had been ordered to wear their red tunics, perhaps because Gordon had said that if British redcoats had arrived at Khartoum the siege would have been lifted.

Beatty's gunboats, with the newly repaired *Zafir*, were bombarding the town and the massed ranks. Suddenly a dervish wing turned and rode off the field. Kitchener, Hunter and Wingate supposed it a tactical withdrawal. None of them ever discovered that Bishara had ordered a frontal assault which his emirs reckoned suicide. They arrested, bound him and carried him away.[16] The dervish army melted into the desert, their flight so hasty that the Sirdar's cavalry found groups of men dead from thirst in the desert, and dead and dying babies dropped by their mothers: 'The cavalry and horse artillery came back laden with black and brown babies'.[17]

Many important emirs surrendered, along with seven hundred Sudanese Blacks who joyfully offered their services to the conquerors. The best were re-enlisted, the others sent to the railway labour battalions. Several guns, much ammunition 'and loot of all sorts' were captured.

The Sirdar entered Dongola unopposed, welcomed by the populace, who hated the Khalifa and his Baggara tribesmen.

Next morning, 23 September 1896, a staff officer recalled that on that very day Queen Victoria became Britain's longest-reigning monarch. Wingate drafted a signal that the Sirdar signed: 'On this auspicious anniversary of her Majesty's reign . . .'[18]

13

THE IMPOSSIBLE RAILWAY

ON 18 November 1896 Queen Victoria commanded Sir Herbert Kitchener, newly promoted to major-general 'for distinguished services in the field',[1] to dine and sleep at Windsor. During the rather solemn dinner, sitting some way from the queen, he was at his most shy and gauche. One of the Queen's ladies wrote to her husband that in spite of their many and strenuous efforts 'he would hardly utter to us ladies', and concluded he was 'either a woman-hater or a boor'. Knowing nothing of the facial disfigurement caused by his wound, Marie Mallet continued: 'My impression of Kitchener (which may be quite wrong) is that of a resolute but cruel man, a fine soldier no doubt, but not of the type that tempers justice with mercy'.[2]

After dinner, when brought up to the Queen he was expansive. She found him 'a striking, energetic-looking man, with rather a firm expression, but very pleasing to talk to'. His staff had sent a consignment of armour, shields, flags and other trophies from Dongola for the Queen, which had been laid out in the corridor. He had never seen them, but when she asked to be told about each he made it up as he went along, so that she wrote down in her journal that the sword was a Crusader sword although the inscription of the blade was in English and thus inevitably of later date (a sword with a hilt like a cross was often loosely termed Crusader).[3]

Later the men of the Household took Kitchener to their smoking room where, Arthur Bigge told Marie Mallet, 'under the influence of whisky and tobacco he thawed and gave an appalling account of the young Khedive. He says he could not possibly be more wicked, cruel and weak. He hates the

French, and the Turks; the Sultan most of all, and openly asked why we do not assassinate the Sultan. He simply longs for murder and executions would be his greatest joy were he to have his own way in Cairo. The Egyptians detest him and if we left the country his reign would not be long'.

Kitchener had come to England on duty to secure money from the Treasury to continue the campaign. He was determined to reach Khartoum and end the miseries of the Khalifa's misgovernment. But while in England he learned that the money produced by the Commission of the Debt must be refunded by the Egyptian government after a ruling by the Mixed Tribunal.[4] This money, now spent, and the finance for a further campaign could come only from Britain. The Chancellor of the Exchequer, 'Black Michael' Hicks-Beach, was not known for liking forward movements which cost money. Kitchener set out to persuade, helped by evidence of French intentions to control the Upper Nile basin, which Britain could not allow.

Salisbury told Cromer: 'His campaign against the Chancellor of the Exchequer was not the least of his triumphs. But all his strategy is of a piece. The position was carried by a forced march and a surprise'. On his last day in England, 21 November, he had been to Windsor again for luncheon, after which Queen Victoria knighted him as a Knight Commander of the Bath. He hurried back to London, produced his detailed estimates and persuaded the Chancellor. Salisbury had 'to give my approval at the end of a moment's notice, when the train by which Kitchener was to go away was already overdue. I need not say I was very glad to do so'.[5] Gordon would be avenged.

Kitchener returned to Egypt and the Sudan to carry out a daring plan: 'it is his idea and his only', Hunter told his brother.[6] He had decided to build 230 miles of railway across the Nubian Desert to cut out the vast curve of the Nile between Wadi Halfa and Abu Hamed, reducing the distance to Khartoum by hundreds of miles and three difficult cataracts. Even Gordon, who in his earlier reign as governor-general had ordered plans for a railway along the Nile (cancelled for want of money), had not dared to propose a desert line. Experts told Kitchener that it could never be built, especially when studies and surveys he had commissioned in 1895 caused him to reject a line following the caravan road from Korosko to Abu Hamed through the Murrall Wells oasis, which Gordon and Stewart had ridden on their way to Khartoum in 1884. He chose instead a more southerly line, starting at Wadi Halfa, which would allow easier construction but had no surface water.

Kitchener chose a twenty-four-year-old sapper, Edward Cator, to find the best route up to the low summit of the desert and down the other side. Knowing that Cator was a water diviner, he marked a sketch map in two places. Cator divined water in both and drew blank at eight others. He came back marvelling at 'Kitchener's luck' but caught typhoid and died. They dug a well and found water at the first place. The second required much trouble and ingenuity, but at last a bottle was brought back to Wadi Halfa. The commandant, Maxwell, decided to 'have some fun with the Sirdar when he arrives'. He offered him a whisky and soda. The Sirdar tasted it and made a face. Maxwell then told him that the 'soda' was water found seventy-two feet below ground. Kitchener was delighted at the joke. Success was now assured.[7]

He had come back from England well pleased at laying orders for engines himself. Girouard cross-examined the Sirdar, then pronounced that his engines would be too light and weak. The Sirdar therefore sent him off to Europe to find better, saying, 'Don't spend too much, Girouard. We are terribly poor.'[8] Girouard borrowed from Cecil Rhodes some heavy locomotives which Rhodes had ordered for South Africa. Kitchener had already selected a wider gauge than Cromer had wanted, so the Sudan Military Railway (SMR) could one day form part of the Cape to Cairo railway of Cecil Rhodes's dream.

The first sod of the yards at Wadi Halfa was lifted on 1 January 1897[9] and laying the track began in February. At the seventeenth mile a siding was added, a ragged tent went up, a field telephone installed, and Station Number One was ready. Eleven miles were laid in April. Then, with a large reinforcement of labour brought over from the other line, which had been laid close to the Nile, progress was faster. Enthusiastic young officers of the Royal Engineers under Girouard surveyed, designed and directed the operation. They became known throughout the army as 'the band of boys'.

The Sirdar never seemed far away. At the harbour, railway yard and workshops of Wadi Halfa he would often appear early in the morning in his dressing gown as rails, engines and rolling stock were unloaded from Nile steamers. Once he saw a large engine standing idle. The civilian works manager explained that the boiler was cracked and could be dangerous. The Sirdar said sadly that dangerous or not it might haul a heavy load to the railhead. 'After all, we aren't particular to a man or two!' The works manager knew him well enough not to take that seriously.

The Sirdar would travel up the line with a train carrying rails, sleepers and always tanks of water for the labour force and for its own steam engine:

Kitchener had investigated electric traction but found it too expensive. At the great, movable tented city at the railhead he would be out among the eight thousand Egyptian troops and convicts who formed the labour force, deal with any questions raised by Girouard or his band of boys, and then continue to the rail-end, the farthest point reached by the track layers, with the labourers ahead preparing the bed, the surveyors farther ahead still, the mirages all around, and patrols of the friendly Ababdeh tribe keeping watch out of sight.

A story that was long told among sappers had the Sirdar at one of the sta-tions in a hurry to reach another: stations were about twenty-three miles apart. An engine stood in the siding but no driver could be found. A sapper clerk manning the telephone said he did not know how to drive a train.

The Sirdar retorted, 'You are an Engineer. Any Engineer should be able to drive an engine.' (Starting and stopping presents no problem but handling a heavy locomotive on the road needs training.) Together they mounted the foot-plate, got up steam, pushed this lever and that until the engine was not only in motion but at speed. They reached the next station without mishap.[10]

As the spring of 1897 turned into summer the great heat did not hinder the band of boys. Their skills, experience, improvisations and refusal to be deflected by difficulties, their sense of humour and their leadership conquered the desert despite a mobile enemy never far away. Several of them rose to be generals, but all gave the chief credit for the desert railway to Kitchener, himself a sapper. He took the risk and the responsibility. He organized the preparations, was the mastermind and the driving force. He would listen to advice, some-times acted on, often rejected. The band of boys saw themselves cheerfully 'as pawns on a chess board, moved from square to square as the game demanded'.[11]

Kitchener was back in Cairo in time for the great military parade on 22 June 1897 to celebrate Queen Victoria's Diamond Jubilee. An hour or two later Hunter wrote to his sister-in-law in America sentiments that Kitchener would never have expressed but deeply shared:

> It was a wonderful event and one cannot help a glow of pride at the thought that today, as the sun broods over the Earth and across the sea, in every land and on every ocean from one end to the other, a salute of 60 guns at noon will remind all hearers that we are the greatest Nation the Universe ever saw ... And, the whole world today will realize the truth and advantage that ours is 'The Power, the Kingdom and the Glory' and that we exercise

our Might in the interests of humanity which no other Power has succeeded in doing yet.[12]

Hunter had just returned from leave in Scotland, during which he had broken off his engagement. Like Kitchener, he had reached a conviction that the Sudan and marriage did not mix. He and the Sirdar made a wager: whoever married first would give the other £100. Fourteen years later General Sir Archibald Hunter handed £100 to his best man, Field Marshal Viscount Kitchener of Khartoum.

During the days after the jubilee, while Jimmy Watson seized the opportunity for plenty of squash, polo and bicycling,[13] the Sirdar, Cromer and Hunter planned in strict secrecy a lightning campaign.

The new railway line was creeping steadily across the desert, but its intended terminus on the Nile at Abu Hamed was still in dervish hands. After the capture of Dongola, the Anglo-Egyptian Army had advanced upriver, unopposed, to Kitchener's old base of 1884 at Debbeh and on to Merowe near the western end of the long Fourth Cataract. Hunter, now military governor of Dongola province, had quickly established civil control over wide areas, but the advance towards Khartoum could not resume until the next rise of the Nile in August. By then, Abu Hamed must be captured and the railway touch the Nile.

On 6 July the Sirdar and his staff left for the frontier and arrived at Karma, the railhead of the river line, six days later. Wingate had warned Kitchener that the Khalifa's young nephew and best general, Mahmud Ahmad, had left Omdurman with a strong force and was threatening Metemmeh, chief town of the Jaalin tribe which loathed the Mahdist rule and had sent urgent requests for guns and ammunition. These were still crossing the Bayuda desert when Kitchener reached Debbeh and received news that Metemmeh had fallen. The town had been sacked. 'Women and children and all men put to the sword', recorded Watson. 'Only the young girls spared'.[14] A Jaalin sheikh, Ibrahim Muhammad Farah, had fled to Dongola some time earlier and had raised an irregular force of Jaalin and other tribesmen, known as the 'Friendlies'. Kitchener now wanted him to advance into the desert towards Berber, but he kept delaying because the days were unlucky. The Sirdar sent for him, and with a 'prophetic air but in a very forcible way', said: 'All days are made by God and must be equally lucky. You are going in a good cause and will leave tomorrow'.[15]

Sheikh Ibrahim, his mind at rest, led the Friendlies south into the Bayuda desert while Hunter and a strong Egyptian force covered the 132 miles to Abu Hamed in eight days, marching at night by a badly mapped rocky track above the Fourth Cataract, resting by day without tents or shade. Kitchener could but wait, riding most mornings with Watson, sometimes relaxing in the evening with him at a game of piquet. At noon on 9 August came a message that Abu Hamed had been captured. That night a dispatch arrived from Hunter describing the brilliant action by which the garrison had been surprised at 6.30 a.m. and the place stormed. But two British officers had been killed in the street-fighting. They were the only British officers of the Egyptian Army to be killed in the entire campaign of 1896–8.[16] One was the thirty-two-year-old Edward FitzClarence, a grandson of King William IV's eldest illegitimate son by the celebrated actress Mrs Jordan: Edward's twin, Charles, would win the VC in South Africa three years later.

The gunboat flotilla was already taking advantage of the rising Nile to navigate the cataract: on 4 August David Beatty had a lucky escape when his gunboat capsized. On 29 August the flotilla steamed into Abu Hamed. Four days later Kitchener at Merowe heard that the Friendlies had taken Berber, the most important town before Omdurman. Hunter had already sent a flying column of 350 Blacks to consolidate the capture and reopen the caravan route to Suakin on the coast.

Kitchener moved his forward base to Abu Hamed. He must bring the rest of his army up the cataract before the Nile fell again. He must complete the railway to Abu Hamed to shorten his lines of communication. He was outnumbered by the dervish armies who could move against him. The pressures were mounting. When Arthur Renshaw, the solicitor and family friend, wrote from England offering to look after his financial affairs, Kitchener accepted gladly as 'I have my hands full and a lot of anxious work in this most damnable country where every obstruction the Creator could conceive has been put in our way and has to be got over'.[17]

He was becoming an even harder taskmaster, driving his officers without thanking them, ruthlessly sending back any who went sick too often or failed. On 11 September a transport capsized in the cataracts with loss of life. Kitchener blamed Lieutenant-Colonel E. F. David, Royal Marines, in sole charge of passing the troop steamers up to Abu Hamed, and sacked him. Colonel David had led a brigade with distinction in the Dongola campaign and asked for an interview. Kitchener refused, saying there was no point. He appointed David to the miserable post of commandant at Debbeh, where he had no British shoulder to weep on. The tragedy of the transport preyed on his mind; he went off his head and died the following year.[18] Lord Roberts would have seen him and helped put matters into perspective: Gordon had the gift of being at once stern and sympathetic. Kitchener gained a reputation for want of sympathy. Wingate recognized that 'K's seeming indifference — arising from shyness and dislike of scenes — was not real, but other officers did not know this'[19] or know about the inner turmoil he was now enduring behind the mask.

On 6 October Kitchener wrote a despairing letter to his friend Clinton Dawkins, a government official in Cairo:

> You have no idea what continual anxiety, worry, and strain I have through it all. I do not think that I can stand much more, and I feel so completely done up that I can hardly go on and wish I were dead. Before next year's work in the field begins I must get some leave, or I shall break down. I have had none for three years now.[20]

Everything seemed to conspire against him. Cromer, who had been in Scotland (remarking that he might as well shoot grouse while Kitchener shot dervishes), wanted to delay any advance on Khartoum. The War Office had sent out Grenfell, the former Sirdar, to command the enlarged British Army of Occupation. Kitchener was 'worried to death' (in Wingate's phrase)[21] that Grenfell, a much senior general, would supersede him as Wolseley superseded Wood in 1884. Kitchener admired and liked Grenfell but longed to lead the men he had trained and fought with to the glory of taking Khartoum. (Salisbury had told Cromer that Kitchener must remain in sole command in the Sudan, but Cromer had failed to tell Kitchener.) Next he learned that the Italians wanted to evacuate Kassala on the border of Sudan and Eritrea. To protect his flank he must garrison the place; yet he had neither the troops nor the money. On 12 October Grenfell in Cairo noted in his diary: 'Received a long and despondent letter from Kitchener which I took to Lord Cromer and I have arranged some of the matters which disturbed him'.[22]

That week the gunboats steamed far into dervish territory and shelled Metemmeh under fire: *Zafir* was struck under the shield on the lower deck.[23] But at Abu Hamed Kitchener received a telegraphed demand from the Finance Ministry that he reduce expenditure. In despair he wired his resignation.

Resigning was not a cynical ploy to get his way. George Gorringe, RE, ADC in Watson's temporary absence, was taking the telegram for encoding when he realized the state the Sirdar was in. 'That evening I induced him to come out duck shooting with me, a thing he rarely did, and it took his mind off his worries'.[24]

Cromer ignored the telegram, merely telling Salisbury that 'my Sirdar is a changed man' and that the letter to Dawkins which arrived the same day as the wire was the product of a sick man who had lost his nerve. 'Those who know Kitchener best tell me that he is liable to fits of extreme depression from which, however, he rapidly recovers. In the meantime his frame of mind causes me some anxiety, for everything depends on his keeping his head, and judging calmly of the situation'.[25] Cromer was still against an advance to Khartoum.

On the afternoon of 1 November Kitchener arrived in Cairo. 'We rode to meet him', recorded Grenfell. 'He looked rather cross but was very pleasant to me'.[26] Cromer told him to hand over his command temporarily to Hunter and spend a month in Egypt to sort matters out and recover his health, with a visit to the Red Sea coast to arrange the takeover of Kassala. The Sirdar hurried back to the Sudan, sent Watson ahead to open up the Cairo Sirdarieh (Watson travelled overnight to Wadi Halfa by the new line and thought it excellent)[27] and arrived in Cairo again on 18 November. Grenfell 'thought him rather depressed and ill. Assured him of my desire to help him in every possible way'.[28] His morale rose when Reuter reported that Hicks-Beach had told the House of Commons, to cheers, that the advance would continue to Omdurman and Khartoum at the next high water in 1898: French progress towards the Upper Nile had swung the Cabinet.

The change of air and scene and the temporary lifting of pressure restored the Sirdar's health, though in telling Renshaw on 9 December that he was off for the frontier in a day or two he added: 'no rest for the weary'.[29] He left Cairo with the firm promise that he could have a British brigade whenever he asked.

On the last day of 1897 Wingate landed at Wadi Halfa, the rear base for the campaign, and went up to the Sirdar's pleasant bungalow. The Sirdar had already made a swift tour of his far-flung front. Wingate found him nursing a heavy cold and 'in a state of considerable perplexity owing to conflicting news'.[30] Hard on Wingate's heels came telegrams from Hunter at Berber and Rundle in Dongola confirming that the Khalifa had amassed almost his whole army outside Omdurman ready to move down the Nile to recapture Berber.

Wingate urged Kitchener to call for the British brigade at once. Kitchener was not sure. If it came too soon, his supply problems at the end of a long line would be vast. If too late, he could be defeated. They had a long discussion. Kitchener agreed at last. Wingate was astonished 'to see the difference in the Sirdar once he had made his decision; he became quite light hearted and cheery. I think he is very happy that he has made up his mind'.[31] His cup ran over when Cromer wired that he hoped to arrange for Kitchener to be in sole command of the whole offensive expedition to Khartoum: 'K immensely pleased', noted Wingate.[32]

Wingate did not, at that stage, hero-worship Kitchener. He was genuinely fond of him but knew his foibles. A week later, when Wingate refused to reject Colonel Frank Rhodes, elder brother of Cecil, as a war correspondent and Kitchener had to do so himself, 'K furious with me . . . K is the quintes-sence of a coward and was afraid to tell Rhodes he did not want him'. A few hours later an opportunity came to induce Rhodes to withdraw. 'K greatly relieved but episode only serves to further lower that time-server character in my eyes'.[33] Wingate had not remembered that Cecil Rhodes might refuse more rolling stock for the SMR if Kitchener personally offended Frank. (He was allowed after all to represent *The Times*.)

Again, when the Sirdar found refugees and prisoners arriving without food or water at Abu Hamed because Hunter had disobeyed orders at Berber, yet would not rebuke him, Wingate grumbled in his diary: 'The long and short of it is that K is afraid of Hunter but I suppose that situation will last out until Omdurman is taken'.[34]

Kitchener's wire to Grenfell to send a British brigade and to prepare a second brought a rush of activity in Lower Egypt, where the brigade commander, William Gatacre, had trained it to a peak of fitness and excellence and earned the nickname of 'Back-acher'. The brigade moved down the SMR. By early February the bulk of the Anglo-Egyptian force was concentrated north of Berber. The railway was still under construction. The British regi-ments – Warwicks, Lincolns and Cameron Highlanders, with the Seaforths arriving later – had marched the last thirty miles across sand and rock, and their boots wore out and must be replaced. Walter Kitchener's camels remained important for transport where low-water or the Fifth Cataract made the Nile useless. He joked to his wife in England about brotherly correspondence:

You'd be amused at the wires between me and Herbert. Of course I have a good deal of work direct with him now. He gets fairly shirty at times and is horribly obstinate – whereas as you know I am only firm and have a knack of expressing myself a bit more than I mean. I heard through Blunt that he had sent my saddle to Assouan [Aswan] for new camels, so I ended my wire of expostulation 'I had hoped at last to get a camel that would not require 2 months patching up', which drew him properly. He deserved it.[35]

The Sirdar had asked Grenfell for an additional staff officer. Grenfell sent him a thirty-four-year-old baronet, Sir Henry Rawlinson of the Coldstream, whose late father had been eminent as an Assyriologist and diplomat. Rawlinson had come on leave to Egypt for his wife's health and cannily had brought his gear. He proved a great help to Kitchener and became a friend. Early in February, soon after their meeting for the first time, Rawlinson described the Sirdar as a curious and very strong character.

I both like and admire him, but on some minor points he is as obstinate as a commissariat mule. He is a long-headed, clear-minded man of business, with a wonderful memory. His apparent hardness of nature is a good deal put on, and is, I think, due to a sort of shyness. It made him unpopular at first, but, since those under him in the Egyptian army have come to realize what a thoroughly capable man he is, there is a great deal less growling than there used to be . . .

The one serious criticism I have is that this is too much of a one-man show. If anything were to happen to the Sirdar there would be chaos, as no one but he knows the state of preparedness in which the various depart-ments are. He keeps all information regarding the details of railways, trans-port, steamers, supply and intelligence, in his own hands, and shows wonderful skill in working the various strings.

Wingate was writing in his diary on almost the same day: 'K irritates me by keeping his movements secret from me'.[36] Rawlinson concluded: 'Everything works smoothly and well as long as he is at the head of affairs but he does too much and may break down if he is not hit'.[37]

Shortly afterwards Kitchener came to the crux of his career.[38]

14

CRUX OF A CAREER

Kɪᴛᴄʜᴇɴᴇʀ sᴇɴᴛ ʀᴀᴡʟɪɴsᴏɴ on short compassionate leave when his wife's health worsened. He returned on 18 March 1898 to the vast tented city that had sprung up south of Berber, and on to Fort Atbara, a strong defensive position that the Sirdar had built at the point where the Atbara river (dried up at that season) entered the Nile. Rawlinson found them 'all in a state of great excitement at the prospect of an early engagement with the enemy, the coolest and most deliberate being the Sirdar himself who had the whole situation at his finger ends', partly because unlike most generals he messed together with his staff, not in splendid isolation.[1]

The young Emir Mahmud had advanced north down the Nile boasting that he would recapture Berber. He had 18,900 fighting men and large numbers of camp followers and women: other wives had been left at Shendi opposite Metemmeh where he had massacred the inhabitants. With Mahmud was Osman Digna, the veteran of the Suakin campaigns, but the Khalifa had not given him overall command and the two disputed. Mahmud wanted to march north beside the Nile and meet the Sirdar head on. Osman advised swinging out into the desert to outflank him. When the gunboats harried the river march, Mahmud accepted Osman's advice, marched away from the Nile until his army, exhausted by lack of water, stopped near a village beside a stagnant pool in the dried up Atbara, forty miles from its confluence. Kitchener had already moved some way up the Atbara to forestall him. Osman urged Mahmud to base his force many miles further up the river bed but he refused.

Egyptian cavalry patrols reported that Mahmud had constructed a circular zariba (defensive encampment) of thorns and stakes, a thousand yards wide, above the river bed. Deserters revealed to Wingate and the Sirdar, who loved to examine them himself, that the zariba was only a first line. The dervish encampment had a stockade, trenches and numerous blockhouses of dried mud. Kitchener waited. Even with desertions, Mahmud had more than 16,000 defenders, many with women, children and slaves, and when food ran short he would come out to do battle. but he remained in his stronghold.

Kitchener continued to wait, his force camped in an excellent site, shaded by dom palms, some thirteen miles away. Walter looked on his brother's waiting 'as a very fine display of strength and knowledge. All of course', Walter told Arthur in New Zealand, 'urged him on, the chance of Mahmud clearing off untouched was a terrible risk to him as it would have made a fool of him before the world at large'.[2] And he would have an unbeaten enemy on his flank as he advanced towards Khartoum. But the Sirdar's knowledge of the Arab mind assured him that Mahmud would never face his women if he slipped away like a coward.[3]

Mahmud's zariba looked impregnable from a distance. A clever foray by his cavalry almost trapped a reconnoitring company of the Sirdar's. They were saved by Maxim machine-guns and the quick thinking of Douglas Haig, who thus came to Kitchener's attention.

Still waiting, Kitchener sent gunboats upriver to land at Shendi, destroy the base and bring back the women left behind, in hopes that their men would desert. Not many did. The women were welcomed by the Sirdar's Blacks and by Berber men whose wives had run off to follow the drum.

With Hunter and Gatacre to advise on tactical details, he planned an order of battle which could either repulse Mahmud if he sallied out or assault him. In the three weeks since the arrival of the British brigade he had trained and welded his force so that every officer and man knew his exact task in battle – and knew his Sirdar, whose great distinctive moustache was a talisman, like Monty's beret before Alamein.

'Herbert is a real King out here, I tell you', wrote Walter in his letter to Arthur, continuing:

'Sirdar's order' is an expression equivalent to 'Czar's decree' in Russia and overrides every regulation and law. He certainly is a wonderful man. He never keeps any record of his telegrams (all is done by wire) and yet remembers everything. He has *no* staff officer except an ADC and an intelligence man and attends to every detail himself . . . Herbert looks 'the Sirdar' all over. He rides lovely arabs and has a perfect seat.[4]

He was deeply respected and trusted, though never seeking the affection that Lord Roberts, with his very different character, had won from his men in India. Yet in the words of a staff officer of the British brigade, 'There has probably never been a force in the field which has been bound together by a better feeling of good comradeship, and in which quarrels and rivalries have been so conspicuously absent'.[5]

By 31 March Kitchener had to decide whether to follow his instinct and assault the zariba. He called a council of war, with Hunter, Wingate and the brigadiers. The fire-eating Gatacre, with little experience of the Sudan, favoured assault. But Hunter now advised against: Gatacre possibly changed his opinion to accord with Hunter's, for sixteen years later Ronald Storrs recorded after dining alone with Kitchener: 'K said the crux of his own career as a general was at the Atbara, when all his advisers were against his giving battle, and he gave it and won it in their teeth. The thought of taking an army out to fight 40 miles in the desert had completely destroyed his night's rest and he had determined, if defeated, never to return himself.'[6]

His memory had exaggerated the distance but not the agony of decision. His numbers, though great, were too low by contemporary military wisdom to assault a well-defended fortress. His British brigades might be exhausted by the night march and the heat. His superiority in small arms would be of no avail. If he failed, or incurred heavy losses, the political and military consequences could be crippling.

In the morning he decided to seek a fresh mandate from his political masters. He wired to Cromer: 'I am rather perplexed by the situation here . . .' and set out the options to fight or not to fight. Cromer showed the wire to Grenfell and sent it to London. Salisbury consulted Wolseley, who answered: 'You have a first rate man in command. Trust him and let him do as he thinks best.'

Grenfell told Cromer it was impossible to advise, but Cromer wired caution. Before his wire arrived, Hunter had withdrawn his objection.

Afterwards, when the result had been 'all that the most critical could desire', Wolseley told Kitchener:

Were I in your place, I would not however ask such a question. You must be a better judge than Lord Cromer or me or anyone else can be. You have your thumb upon the pulse of the Army and can best know what it is capable of. This is my only criticism and I give it for what it is worth.[7]

The Sirdar had a second, brief hesitation when he realized that the fight would take place on a Friday, which he usually avoided as the Muslim holy day, not from superstition. One of the staff pointed out that 8 April 1898 was Good Friday, 'a good day for an act of liberation'. The Sirdar laughed and agreed. 'I have been two years bringing you face to face with these fellows. Now go in and fight it out.'[8] He had already warned the force not to slaughter the wounded, and had ordered that the British battalions be taught the Arabic word and symbol for surrender. Quarter should always be granted, though most dervishes would fight to the death.[9] He added a final word: 'The Sirdar is absolutely confident that every officer and man will do his duty, he only wishes to impress upon them two words: "Remember Gordon." The enemy before them are Gordon's murderers.'[10]

At first light on 8 April Mahmud saw a great line of Egyptian, Sudanese and British troops spread in a semi circle about 600 yards to the north of his zariba, with their guns about 30 yards in front. He rode around the perimeter to check that riflemen and spearmen were in place and that every emir knew what to do. He retired to his underground command post. Within the zariba a great cloud of dust arose as men dug pits for their donkeys, tying their legs to prevent them running amok in the battle. Osman Digna, certain of disaster, slipped away with fifty of his own cavalry.

At 6.16 a.m. the Anglo-Egyptian batteries pounded the zariba, with the Maxim machine-guns in support. The dervishes disappeared from the parapets. Shells smashed parts of the thorn and earthwork defences and started fires. Shrapnel killed Mahmud's gun-crews, so that his guns were silent when most needed. 'Herbert was a bit anxious but did not show it – gave very few orders – stuck in one place and let the gunners do their work without bothering them.'[11]

After three-quarters of an hour the shelling stopped as planned. Kitchener could not keep his infantry, especially the British, waiting longer in the strengthening sun. He ordered the Advance to be sounded on the bugles. To Charles à Court of his staff, writing five days later, 'It was a truly magnificent sight as the twelve battalions swept forward in perfect order and beautiful alignment to within 300 yards of the zariba'.[12] They halted and fired volley after volley at the parapets now crowded again with dervishes, who directed a hot fire from rifles and elephant guns at the ranks in the open without cover. The Camerons particularly suffered. After twelve minutes the Advance sounded again. The massed troops moved forward, with bands playing and pipes swirling. The British marched as if on parade, which caused them casualties but terrified the defenders as they saw cold steel drawing slowly nearer. The Egyptians and Sudanese ran at the zariba, with Hunter riding and waving his sword at the head of Maxwell's brigade. The line crashed through the thorn fences and the pallisades to cries of 'Remember Gordon'. The next half-hour in the labyrinth of trenches, pits and blockhouses was a hell of blood, screams and pain, a savage nightmare of hand-to-hand fighting. Blacks wreaked vengeance on Arabs for the despoiling of tribal homelands far away to the south; kilted, unshaven Highlanders and English boys in their first fight almost lost control of themselves as they thrust and parried and fired. More than twenty thousand men were locked in brutal combat within less than a square mile. Frank Scudamore of the *Daily News*, who covered almost every Sudan fight from 1884 to 1898, thought it the hottest of all.

Blood lust rose on both sides. Arabs slaughtered deserters and escaping slaves. Walter, who had ridden to the reserve brigade with a message, rejoined the Sirdar 'just as he was trying to stop black troops shooting down men who came out to give themselves up. I saw some of these shot at a yard off as they ran forward with bits of palm held up in their hands – but "Tommy" was just as bad as the blacks'.[13]

By 8.20 the line had reached the river bed. Mahmud's army had ceased to exist. Two thousand were dead, thousands more lay wounded, others were being rounded up as prisoners (many of whom were happy to change sides and fight for the Sirdar). Hundreds streamed into the desert.

The victorious brigades re-formed outside. The Sirdar rode up as the British, almost mad with excitement and glee, were coming out. 'They gave Herbert a grand reception', grouping around him and cheering so loudly that his words of thanks and praise were drowned. Charles à Court remembered it as 'a scene of . . . tremendous and tumultuous enthusiasm', and Walter was reminded of the Diamond Jubilee when the Queen came by. 'Herbert is tremendously popular with the British'.[14] He was beaming, his eyes lit up as he exclaimed his delight at victory.[15]

As sporadic firing continued he ordered the Cease-fire to be sounded. Detachments were left inside to search and mop up. The Sudanese found that Mahmud's men had burdened themselves with loot. The Sirdar gave his Blacks leave to loot as permitted by the rules of war after a fortress fell by assault. Ancient chain armour, helmets, spears, prayer mats, robes, numerous flags and banners were soon being distributed around to the victors by purchase or gift. An officer's horse was led past the Sirdar laden with loot. He stopped it, used his collector's knowledge to pick out the best and told an ADC to take it to General Gatacre with his compliments and thanks for fine leadership.[16]

The Sirdar rode on across the field with Hunter. An officer galloped up with news that Mahmud was a prisoner, saved from Sudanese bayonets by a young gunner officer. They wheeled their horses and saw a Sudanese sergeant leading a tall, proud man in an ornate bloodstained jibbah, his hands bound behind his back. He scowled at them, which annoyed Hunter.

'This is the Sirdar', said Hunter angrily in Arabic. Kitchener quietly ordered Mahmud to sit, the recognized prelude to beheading or pardon in the Sudan. But instead of kneeling to learn his fate, Mahmud sat down cross-legged, the attitude of an equal.

Kitchener on his horse, the Egyptian flag carried beside him, looked down on Mahmud.

'Why have you come into my country to burn and to kill?' asked the Sirdar.

'Same as you', replied Mahmud. 'I must obey the Khalifa's orders as you the khedive's'. Kitchener smiled and remarked to his staff, 'Rather a good answer'.

Further questions followed, which Mahmud answered without fear. As he was taken away he shouted at the Sirdar: 'You will pay for all this at Omdurman. Compared with the Khalifa, I am but a leaf'.[17]

By now the Sirdar had a headache. He dismounted and lay on the ground while his orderly splashed water on his face. The stink from the stricken zariba was dreadful in the heat of the day. Many enemy bodies were being buried in the trenches where they fell. One officer counted a heap of sixty in the river bed, evidently deserters cut down by their own cavalry. Numbers of wounded had fled or crawled into the bush or the desert, where many died, for wounds were fearful. Gatacre had ordered his brigade to file the tops of their bullets to make the dreaded scooped-out dumdums that were never used against a white enemy and were later outlawed by international convention. Men who died in the desert were left unburied: six months later the Duke of Connaught was astonished to see bodies of men, donkeys and camels preserved by the dry heat.[18]

A hospital was set up to tend the wounded until they could be carried back to the Nile, but the British brigade's medical side was poor compared with the Egyptian 'and K was furious', wrote Rawlinson to his wife: 'He had a pretty anxious time from the beginning of the night march until the end of the battle, but the only thing I saw him disturbed about was the treatment of the British wounded, who, from lack of proper arrangements, suffered unnecessarily from the heat and from thirst'.[19]

Kitchener had lost only 74 men killed, mostly British (3 officers and 57 other ranks), with 499 wounded: He attended the British funeral that after-noon. He stood impassive but tears rolled down his cheeks. An English officer, who knew him only from afar as the 'Sudan machine', said the Sirdar was human for more than fifteen minutes.

They began their return to the Nile, the wounded being carried on Walter's camels by a Sudanese battalion which volunteered. Hunter stayed on the field until late at night, searching for wounded who had been overlooked. They all rested on the Saturday, and on Easter Sunday held thanksgiving services after which the Sirdar read out telegrams of congratulation from Her Majesty and others including the Kaiser.

By any reckoning the battle of the Atbara had been a remarkable victory, at minimal cost to the Sirdar's army and devastating loss to the enemy. 'There's no doubt he is a wonderful man', Walter enthused to Arthur.

> I think all felt it might not have been quite the same under any of the men that would take his place were he knocked over. Hunter would have just gone straight in and would have got off lucky with a butcher's bill of 1,000 instead of our 500. Old Gatacre would have fussed about until no one knew what was wanted of them. No! there can be no doubt Herbert is a wonderful administrator and, for a fight, the very best.[20]

Four days after the battle Kitchener rode with Hunter beside him at the head of his Sudanese and Egyptians (but not the British – sent tactfully to summer quarters) down the wide main street of Berber through cheering, clapping crowds. Flags and colourful garments decorated trees. G. W. Steevens, the *Daily Mail*'s war correspondent, thought it like a Roman triumph as he watched the Sirdar, 'tall, straight and masterful in his saddle'.[21] Behind him rode the brigadiers and staff officers, then a cavalry escort. The people pressed forward more eagerly , noted Steevens, as 'farther behind, in a clear space, came one man alone, his hands tied behind his back. Mahmud! Mahmud, holding his head up and swinging his thighs in a swaggering stride – but Mahmud a prisoner, beaten, powerless. When the people of Berber saw that, they were convinced'. Women hurled insults at the butcher of Metemmeh whose approach had brought fear a few weeks before. Now they hooted at the satirical slogan in Arabic held over his head by two Sudanese soldiers: 'The Conqueror of Berber'.[22]

Mahmud was displayed with a long line of bound prisoners to convince the populace that he was beaten – in battle. He was not lashed as he marched or whipped to keep up with cavalry, as a late-twentieth-century writer alleged. The bound hands (Mahmud had no shackles on his legs) were the traditional symbol of defeat, but for a defenceless captive emir to be lashed in a public procession would be a humiliation so contrary to Sudanese custom – and to British fair play – that eyewitnesses would have recorded it and folklore never forgotten. Contemporary evidence, including Walter's sketch, done the same day, rejects such brutality. 'The Dervish leader', reported Bennet Burleigh of *The Daily Telegraph*, 'was not in the least downcast, but walked with head elate, as a central personage in the parade. He was gibed and hooted in the oriental way as he passed the crowds of those who had but recently cowered before him.'[23]

Mahmud was sent north, in chains, by a saloon carriage of the SMR, talking volubly to British journalists who knew enough Arabic. He died in captivity at Rosetta aged forty in 1906.

The battle of the Atbara gave the army and the Sirdar a surge of confidence. Kitchener became the hero of the British people as they read exuberant accounts by the war correspondents, which quite embarrassed some of the soldiers, who knew that they owed most to the Maxim machine-guns and the field guns. Senior officers discussed tactics, Gatacre being privately criticized by Hunter, but Charles à Court, who knew far more about military affairs than Walter Kitchener and was unaffected by family feeling, wrote within days of the victory a verdict that endorses Walter's: 'I consider the Sirdar is as good in the field as he is in administration, head and shoulders above all his subordinates here'.[24]

Kitchener's own view, expressed to Wolseley some months later, was unequivocal: 'I had such good men under me that it would have been difficult to go wrong'.[25] Good men – and Maxim machine-guns, the decisive factor.

With Mahmud's army eliminated, Kitchener could estimate how many extra troops he would require to take Khartoum. He told Neville Smyth, soon to win the VC, that he had been repeatedly asked by the War Office 'but I could not make the estimate until now'. Smyth knew that 'Kitchener's power of visualizing the future was so great that many of the wild Arabs with whom he had to deal in the Sudan credited him with prophetic powers'.[26]

15

APPROACH MARCH

A<small>T ABOUT</small> 5 a.m. on an August morning the train of cattle trucks which had carried the 1st battalion Grenadier Guards 385 miles from Wadi Halfa across the desert and beside the Nile drew into Atbara. Colonel Simon Hatton jumped down in his pyjamas. He was astonished and abashed to find the Sirdar, spruce as always, beside the train to greet the battalion.[1]

The Grenadiers, from Gibralter, were the last to arrive of the four infantry battalions which made up the 2nd British brigade, together with Maxims, gunners and the 21st Lancers. They brought Kitchener's force up to approx-imately 20,000 men. They soon found that desert country in the rainy season could test even the discipline of Grenadiers. 'The dust storms were awful', wrote one officer, Captain Humphrey Stucley. 'Great dust devils would rush through camp, overturning tents right and left, and all would be pitchy dark for half an hour or more.'[2] Heavy rainstorms sometimes soaked equipment while the expedition was organizing for the final march on Omdurman and Khartoum.

The Sirdar had used the four months since the battle of the Atbara to rest and refresh his force. Walter Kitchener was one of those who were delighted to be sent on a month's leave in England, where Carry and the children were living at Dover. He returned a few days ahead of time, to the approval of Herbert, who had gone no further than Cairo and then was back, organizing everything. Walter was most impressed that Herbert had accumulated two months' supplies at forward bases, less than a hundred miles from Khartoum. Against a strong current and a south wind the Egyptian and Sudanese troops had dragged barges and cut wood for steamers; they had never seemed to tire and 'every man a guardsman in physique'.[3]

Three new armoured gunboats, twin-screwed, had arrived in sections from England. At Wadi Halfa 'Monkey' Gordon loaded them on to the desert railway. At Abadiya, near Berber, George Gorringe and his men assembled them. The Sirdar loved hurrying to the dockyard in the early mornings to help, not always usefully. When he hammered a rivet a sapper would quietly mark it with chalk so that it could be properly hammered after he had left.[4] And one morning when Gorringe was on some vital job inside a perilous crib-pier of sleepers supported by a girder with a rope attached, he was horrified to hear the familiar voice saying, 'Now then, you men. What are you waiting for? Haul on that rope!' Choosing mutiny to death, Gorringe swore at the unseen Sirdar, then heard: 'Wingate, perhaps we had better go and have breakfast!' Shortly afterwards Gorringe was invited to join them.[5]

The desert railway which brought gunboats also brought new staff and special service officers. The fashionable military world vied for the honour and glory, rather to the resentment of those who had borne the heat and burden. The sprinkle of princes, peers and heirs made Walter laugh at Herbert's 'brilliant' staff. Herbert, however, would have no one not 'a real workman'. He selected Lord Roberts's only son, Freddy, a man of dedication, efficiency and charm who the next year in South Africa would win a posthumous VC saving the guns at Colenso; and he took a thirty-one-year-old grandson of Queen Victoria, Prince Christian Victor, a keen professional soldier in the 60th Rifles (and a first-class cricketer). But when the Prince of Wales, who could not be refused, personally recommended an excellent officer for whom Kitchener had no vacancy, the letter was mysteriously lost.[6] The Egyptian Army already had Prince Francis of Teck, a brother of the Duchess of York, the future Queen Mary. Tall, handsome, with the gaiety, kind heart and extravagance of his mother, Princess Mary Adelaide of Cambridge, Frank Teck was a favourite with all who knew him. When he died comparatively young, twelve years later, Kitchener felt it 'deeply as he was such an old friend of mine both on service and at home'.[7]

The Sirdar would not have Winston Churchill, then aged twenty-three, serving in India with the 4th Hussars. Winston's mother, Lady Randolph, had tried for the Dongola campaign. Kitchener had sent her a polite assurance of bearing him in mind. In 1898 she left no stone unturned and no cutlet uncooked, in Winston's own apt phrase. Sir Evelyn Wood, Adjutant-General, agreed to press his case. In February the Sirdar replied to her that he had noted her son's name and 'I hope I may be able to employ him later in the Sudan'. Winston took this as a promise and when no appointment came he grumbled, 'He may be a general – but never a gentleman'.[8]

Churchill was unpopular with brother officers for unrestrained belief in his manifest destiny and for writing an excellent book about a frontier campaign in which he had fought. But Kitchener objected to Churchill's using the campaign as (to adapt Churchill's later remark about the Mother of Parliaments) a public convenience on his path to politics and journalism. The Sirdar wished to keep coveted places for soldiers of military promise. He was not pleased when Churchill managed an attachment to the 21st Lancers at the last moment through the intervention of Lord Salisbury.

Churchill also had a commission from the *Morning Post* to report the coming battle. Fifteen full-time war correspondents had already arrived. Kitchener shared Hunter's opinion that journalists got in the light, over used the telegraph lines, quarrelled among themselves and drank too much,[9] despite this being officially a 'dry' campaign. However, the story that the Sirdar kept them waiting in the hot sun and then strode out of his tent exclaiming 'Out of my way, you drunken swabs' has no contemporary source and is out of character. He would have preferred to restrict them to base, but when he noticed them he was courteous, especially as he would need their help to fulfil a vision not yet disclosed. He enjoyed the company of little Frank Scudamore of the *Daily News* and appreciated George Steevens of the *Daily Mail*, as 'such a clever and able man. He did his work as correspondent so brilliantly and he never gave the slightest trouble. I wish all correspondents were like him'.[10]

Two other observers were the Italian and German attachés. Captain Baron Adolf von Tiedemann, whose sartorial elegance caused amusement, found the Sirdar 'generally reticent and unapproachable, but occasionally most amiable and positively charming, on these occasions showing a keen and ready wit' and whatever he was doing, 'always perfectly natural'.[11]

By mid-August all was ready. Kitchener packed his men, horses, supplies and ammunition into the gunboats, transports and barges, ignoring the Plimsoll line ('Plimsoll's dead') and accepting the dangers of overcrowding, the stink and the sweat. 'The river is just full and *rushing* by', wrote Walter. 'The new steamers (*Melik*, *Sultan* and *Sheik*) make very poor fight against it.'

The transport steamer *Ambigole* stuck on a sandbank. Eight hundred and sixty men and officers of the Lancashire Fusiliers had to strip and wade ashore for the vessel to be refloated. Later, the ill-fated *Zafir* gunboat that had brought the Sirdar to tears in Dongola sprang a leak as she approached the Shabluka gorge (Sixth Cataract) and sank, without loss of life. Meanwhile, the Camel Corps, Walter's camel transport and the cavalry marched on shore, followed by the inevitable women and children of the Egyptian and Sudanese troops.

At the final point of disembarkation, when all had arrived safely by water or land, the Sirdar reviewed his army. The previous day Walter 'went for a ride with Herbert this morning – he is very cheery and in great fettle'.[12]

For the last two days of the approach to Omdurman and the ruins of Khartoum, Kitchener marched his 20,000 men (including 8,200 British) in fighting formation on a front of nearly three miles on the western bank of the Nile, followed by Walter's 2,300 camels. These looked like a solid wall a mile long. 'With his usual luck', wrote Walter, 'Herbert had the most perfect two cool days of the year', so that the army covered twelve miles a day, from 5 a.m. to 1 p.m., 'without knocking up the British'.[13]

They passed through an area of thick bush. In Gordon's day it had been fertile pasture; now it was covered by mimosa scrub up to twelve feet high. They had expected the Khalifa to defend it or harry their flanks, but even the villages were empty. They approached the low Karari hills. MacDonald's Sudanese were merry and talkative at the thought of action, but the hills were not defended and the summit gave a first limited view of the spread-out city, dominated by the Mahdi's tomb and, in the distance, the ruins of Khartoum and Gordon's palace.

Shortly before midday on 1 September the Sirdar encamped his army round the village of El Egeiga on the western bank of the Nile. The cavalry formed a screen ahead, accompanied by Royal Engineers with a heliograph. Behind, on the Nile, were the gunboats, which had begun bombarding the city. On the farther bank the Friendlies were ranging, rather murderously, under the command of Edward Stuart-Wortley who in 1885 had been on the gunboat that penetrated nearest to Khartoum, saw that Gordon's flag no longer flew from the palace and realized that the city had fallen.

Kitchener's troops were erecting the defensive zariba. His plan was to advance early the following morning and defeat the Khalifa's huge army outside Omdurman. His fear was that the enemy would refuse a major fight, retire within the city and defend it street by street, inflicting heavy casualties.[14]

He was sitting on a wall in the scanty shade eating his lunch when the heliograph began to flash from a small hill (Jebel Surgham, at 328 feet) which rose to the south-west between his position and the city: a very large dervish army was advancing.[15]

16

OMDURMAN

THE SIRDAR FINISHED his lunch, remounted his white arab and galloped with his ADCs towards the hill. An officer riding down from the detachment of the 21st Lancers reported more detail. And thus Herbert Kitchener and Winston Churchill met for the first time.

Kitchener rode to the top. Soon afterwards Hunter met him 'just come down from the hill, looking as if he had seen a ghost and no wonder, for he said the Enemy were only 5 miles beyond the hill, advancing 50,000 strong against us'. Hunter said they must dig in and all would be well.[1]

The Sirdar immediately deployed the infantry in a wide arc beyond the village and zariba, personally laying out the general line of the perimeter, allotting the British to the left and the Egyptians and Sudanese to the centre and the right: they dug trenches but the British made a thorn hedge. The desert gave a clear field of fire. Then the dervish army stopped about three miles short.

Walter made his camels snug in the village and rejoined headquarters at about 5 p.m. With darkness coming, he expected the Sirdar to withdraw into the original close-packed zariba, according to normal practice. When he did not 'It fairly took my breath away'.[2] Walter had been sure

Herbert would reform into the zariba for the night, but his ways are not common men's ways; all lay down where they were, and the information (quite correctly) was that they intended to attack at night. I have seldom put in such a bad night. I could see *nothing* that could prevent their getting through our weak line and once well amongst us there would have been the most hideous mêlée ever seen. I asked Herbert about it next day, and to my astonishment he admitted at once, 'O yes! I think they would have got through us,' but he sent word by spies that we were going to attack them and instead of coming on and scuppering us, they sat up all night waiting for our attack. To be able to accept a risk like that means simply extraordinary nerve. Of course to have formed close zariba would have had a very bad effect on our troops – they had had a hard day and it would have caused infinite confusion and loss of rest. As it was at dawn all were in their places and fresh, and with baggage loaded ready for anything.[2]

Gunboat searchlights had played all night under a full moon, though a drenching storm passed through. Villagers and camp followers, placed out in the open, would have given warning. Except for one false alarm nothing had happened, but many officers shared Hunter's feelings: 'When the sun rose on 2/9/98 I never was so glad in all my days.'[3]

By then, Kitchener had set them in battle line, fresh, fed and eager, with field guns and Maxims in support. He had put on his white uniform, and on his white arab he stood out beside the prevailing khaki.

A squadron of 21st Lancers reported that the dervish army was advancing across the Karari plain. Soon the Sirdar, with his field glasses, could see Broadwood's cavalry retiring as ordered towards the Karari hills to the north, and the glint of the sun on thousands of spears and banners. They were moving north across the front. Whether following Broadwood, or misled by Wingate's spies or bad advice, they appeared to suppose that the Sirdar's main force lay behind the hills, not beside the Nile. They were gaining on Broadwood's cavalry. At 6.23 a.m. the Sirdar sent a staff officer to order the guns to fire, at a range of 2,700 yards. The gunboats joined in. Shrapnel shells burst above the distant horde with no clearly visible effect until suddenly a great segment of the dervish army wheeled and bore down towards the zariba.

To the defenders it looked as if the whole world were come against them. Rawlinson, on his horse behind the Sirdar, thought it 'a magnificent sight, those thousands of wild brave savages advancing to their destruction. We could plainly hear their yells and see them shaking their spears, but they did not think so small a party, as we were, worth shooting at. They kept a wonderfully good line in their advance.'[4] Kitchener trotted to a position behind the Cameron Highlanders, at left-centre of the line, and sat impassively on his arab, field glasses in constant use. His staff brought messages and answered his stream of quiet questions, then galloped off with his orders.

The horde drew nearer, a wide arc of white-smocked warriors led by emirs on horseback and chanting ceaselessly, '*La llaha illa llah wa Muhammad rasul Allah.*'* 'Immediately our guns opened', recalled Stucley of the Grenadiers, 'and I saw the first shell burst right in the middle of the advancing mob. There was a flash, a cloud of dust and then just a space, where a few seconds before had been a densely packed mob of howling, cursing human beings.'[5]

Then the Maxims opened, and at eight hundred yards the infantry fired volleys by company. For Walter it was 'a case of binoculars and a bad time for the Dervishes – cruel slaughter of very brave men'. As the bodies piled up 'one's feelings went over to the enemy – they just struggled on. As far as I could judge the standard bearers were the only men who seemed to be able to live under it. One man with a white and red flag getting to within 200 yards or possibly less – the reason being I suppose, that he was aimed at!'

The Khalifa had played into the Sirdar's hands and caused terrible loss of life by choosing the worst possible course against modern firepower. But when Wilfrid Blunt, the poet, philanderer and friend of all nationalists, wrote a furious letter to *The Times*, contrasting Kitchener's slaughtering with Gordon's renowned clemency, he forgot that otherwise the Sirdar's men would have been massacred. Yet as Walter wrote, 'All the pluck was displayed by the Dervishes, our side had no chance of showing anything but discipline'.

While the approaching horde faltered and died by thousands on the plain of Karari, Kitchener knew that Broadwood's cavalry might be in difficulties from the huge other wing of the dervish army, and he sent Lord Tullibardine to order Broadwood to retire on to the zariba. Tullibardine galloped back with a message from Broadwood: he was too far for a retirement; he would draw them into the desert beyond the hills. The Sirdar sent Tullibardine to the fighting Camel Corps, between Broadwood and the Nile, with an order to retire towards the Nile. Swinging his binoculars he saw them hard pressed and sent Freddy Roberts to signal to 'Monkey' Gordon in the *Melik*, who steamed inshore, brought his guns to bear and saved the Camel Corps.

By 8.30 a.m. the dervish assault on the zariba had petered out in a misery of

* 'There is one God and Muhammad is the Messenger of God.' Both sides were relying on God, an irony that would be even more marked in South Africa the following year and sixteen years later in Europe.

wounds and death and with ghastly piles of bodies, at the price of a comparatively small number of casualties for the Sirdar, including one British officer
killed – the tallest in the expedition, hit in the temple.

The way was open to Omdurman. Walter was 'just beginning to think
Herbert was going to fall into the over-cautious trap and throw away his
chance when the "Advance" sounded and on we went'. As the brigades
moved forward, with MacDonald's Sudanese on the right, the Sirdar sent an
order to the 21st Lancers on his left to reconnoitre over the ridge between the
higher Jebel Surgham and the Nile and make contact with the retreating
enemy. 'Annoy them as far as possible on their flank,' he told Colonel Martin,
'and head them off if possible from Omdurman.'[6] The Lancers (with
Winston Churchill from the 10th Hussars leading a troop) trotted off.

The 21st Lancers were a new regiment, determined to win glory. Martin
made a detour to attack a small group of the enemy and thus led his regiment
into a trap laid by Osman Digna, who had secreted a large number of warriors in a *khor* (shallow depression). Martin did not hesitate. The charge of the
21st Lancers, a brief saga of supreme valour, became the most famous incident of the battle. Yet like the charge of the Light Brigade at Balaclava it
achieved nothing. Robin Grenfell, the former Sirdar's nephew, was killed and
twenty lancers. Twenty-two horses were killed or had to be destroyed. Two
VCs were won. Winston Churchill wrote an immortal account.

The Sirdar was annoyed at unnecessary loss of life, at Martin's failure to
report a large force that he should have seen, and that later the exploit rang
around the world to steal glory from MacDonald, the real hero of the battle.
Walter, however, probably represents the more general feeling when he wrote:

> Of course the charge was unnecessary, but they came up to find an oppor-
> tunity and they seized a real good one and did the work in real cavalry style.
> Old Martin, to my mind, deserves infinite praise all through . . . 'Ce n'est
> pas la guerre' no doubt – but good work and sound for recruiting.

While the Lancers were out of sight the Sirdar advanced. He knew that the
Army of the Black Flag under the Khalifa and his brother Yakub had been
waiting beyond the hill (Jebel Surgham), but he must get between them and
Omdurman and reach the city before the fleeing remnant from the assault on the
zariba. When Walter (who knew nothing of the Black Flag) returned to headquarters after getting his camels on the move, he heard Herbert say to Gatacre:

'Get on – get on, step out for that ridge and you've got them' – and old Gatacre to the Colonel of the Guards – 'Now Colonel Hope [*sic*, i.e. Hutton] address your men – a few words you know.' – What the few words were to be to prelude rapid volleys at 1,000 yards into a crowd of unarmed fugitives, struck me as possibly embarrassing for the Colonel but very much 'Gatacre'. It was *picturesque and safe*, which is my idea of what a battle should be!

For MacDonald and his mainly Sudanese brigade of 3,000 men on the far right, the battle was picturesque but not safe. The 17,000 warriors of the Black Flag were coming at him. Far away to the right the Green Flag armies (15,000 men) were pouring out of the Karari hills: Osman Sheikh el Din and Ali Wad Helu had turned back from their fruitless chase after Broadwood's cavalry. MacDonald sent a message asking Taffy Lewis,[7] moving his Egyptian brigade behind, to reinforce him, but Lewis would not disobey his orders to proceed to Omdurman. MacDonald could see, as he wrote to General Knowles after the battle:

> that the force in front of me was a very large one and I knew that the one on my right was a very large one and I determined to defeat if possible the nearer force before the other could join. At a range of 1,100 yards I brought forward the artillery and opened fire, the infantry which were advancing in fours from the flanks of companies forming line. No sooner had we opened fire than up went innumerable standards, amongst them a prominent black one, the Khalifa's, and they opened a furious fusillade and at once bore down upon us. Their advance was very rapid and determined and though they appeared to be mowed down by the artillery and Maxims they still pressed on in such numbers and so quickly that I brought up the infantry into line with the guns, but in spite of the hail of lead now poured at effective ranges into their dense masses they still pressed forward in the most gallant manner until between 300 and 400 yards when they practically melted away leaving the Khalifa's black flag flying alone within 250 yards of Jackson's Bn. A fine performance truly for any race of man.[8]

Kitchener heard the firing but could not see MacDonald from his position with Maxwell's[9] brigade. Harry Pritchard, one of 'the band of boys', galloped up with a message from MacDonald: should he attack the Green Flags and could Lewis's brigade alter direction to help? The Sirdar refused. 'Cannot he see that we are marching on Omdurman? Tell him to follow on.' Pritchard tried to explain MacDonald's dangerous situation without effect, 'so I had to take this cold comfort back to MacDonald'.[10]

Kitchener immediately galloped to a higher vantage point. For various reasons the landscape was less masked by smoke than most battlefields. He saw the situation, suspended the march on Omdurman, and by a rapid flow of orders wheeled the brigades so that Yakub's army was caught in a pincer between Lewis and MacDonald, who thus saw the enemy melt away. The speed of the Sirdar's change of front had justified his unorthodox habit of giving orders direct, not through the usual channels of command. He also told Maxwell to send a company to seize Surgham hill.

During Yakub's attack MacDonald, now in much pain from the kick of a horse which broke bones in his foot, was anxiously watching the movements of the enemy on his right, the Green Flag armies 'whom I now saw advanc-ing in huge masses, and I was just in time to bring a Battery onto the new front to open fire at 800 yards'.[11] Had these masses arrived simultaneously with Yakub's, MacDonald might have been overwhelmed. Instead, by an extraor-dinary feat of drill and discipline he made a complete change of front at the double, battalion by battalion, in such a way that the fighting remnants of Yakub were held off on one front while the fresh hordes of the Green Flag were faced on the other. During the movement about a hundred of Yakub's cavalry charged to the death, 'a heroic deed'. Yakub died facing the enemy.

Two Green Flag columns, densely packed, were drawing closer: MacDonald rejected an agitated Hunter's order to retire, made his excitable Blacks hold their fire until the enemy columns were almost on them, and then broke the columns by disciplined firepower. They 'slunk away to the west'. By the time the Lincolns, famed for marksmanship, had doubled up to help, the last dervish assault was almost over.

Kitchener was later criticized by students of strategy, including Douglas Haig, for advancing on the city while the Green Flag armies were at his rear; critics claimed that MacDonald had adjusted the Sirdar's blunder and saved the day. But Kitchener knew that the Green Flag thousands were in the field. He must get to Omdurman before them: that was his winning card. Knowing the danger, he had moved MacDonald to the flank instead of Lewis's less steady Egyptians; his trust was not misplaced.

At 11.15, from the height of Surgham hill, Kitchener swept his gaze around the ghastly ruin of the dervish armies then shut away his binoculars. 'Well,' he said, 'we have given them a good dusting!'[12]

The Sirdar sounded the Advance. The cavalry raced ahead around the land-ward side of the city, hoping to catch the Khalifa. The main army swept forward on a wide front across the Karari plain with its shallow depressions. 'We passed over hundreds of dead and wounded Dervishes', recalled Stucley of the Grenadiers, 'approaching all with caution, as they would feign death till one passed and then jump up and spear one'.[13] He saw a gunner speared while sitting on a timber as the guns drove forward. In another part of the field two war correspondents had ridden ahead and dismounted to loot bodies (as some said) when an enormous dervish sprang up and charged them with a spear, ignoring their panic pistol shots as they turned tail. He was about to strike when Neville Smyth of the Bays ran between, received the charge with a wound in his elbow and killed the man. Smyth was awarded the VC, though to spare the blushes of the press the citation disguised the correspondents as 'camp followers' and the warrior as 'an Arab who ran amok'.

This incident did not stop an Oxford don and temporary war correspondent claiming in an article three months later that Kitchener had given an order that the wounded be killed. Inevitably British soldiers and their allies were prone to take no chances – 'It's you or me, mate, and it won't be me' – but Kitchener categorically denied the accusation, and although Churchill believed it the Italian attaché, Major Count Luigi Calderari, an independent witness much better placed to know the truth, denied 'in the most absolute way' that wounded or prisoners were molested except in legitimate defence'.[14]

Kitchener himself nearly lost his own life when some nearby Sudanese took no chances. 'A wounded man had jumped up in front of the line to "kill his man",' Walter told Arthur, 'and a whole company were firing straight in our direction, and worst of all not aiming at us. It was quite extraordinary some of the crowd were not hit. We legged it back to behind the British real smart I can tell you.' Steevens of the *Daily Mail* and little Scudamore of the *Daily News* rode up at that moment after covering MacDonald's fight, 'just in time to hear the great man give vent to some of the most violent expressions of disgust and anger – in English and Arabic – that probably he ever used in his life'.[15]

After watering their horses in the fouled Khor Shambat, the Sirdar and his staff rode at a trot with Maxwell's Sudanese brigade, a British battery and Maxims, to enter the wide main street of Omdurman; troopers carried his

own flag behind him, with the captured Black Flag of the Khalifa, embroi-
dered with verses from the Koran. The street was empty except for an elderly
sheikh and his entourage who stood across their path. He asked whether the
Sirdar intended to massacre the women and children. On being assured to the
contrary, he presented an enormous key, and the roofs of the houses suddenly
filled with women screaming a welcome.

As the Anglo-Egyptian troops entered from different directions (one
Sudanese battalion forded the main sewer) and penetrated deeper, 'the streets
were all a huge latrine', noted Stucley, 'and dead men, women and donkeys at
every few yards, the result of the bombardment. The smell was beyond words.'
The Grenadiers' chaplain, Reginald Moseley, vomited. They passed gallows,
one with a recent corpse. No organized resistance was met but many pockets
of warriors would not surrender.[16]

The Sirdar reached the Sur, the Khalifa's citadel dominated by the cupola
of the Mahdi's tomb, damaged by gunboat shells. He entered through a breach
as Hunter rode up in great excitement, shouting to Kitchener that he could be
Lord Khartoum if he wished, and that the government should give him a big
sum. All earlier criticism forgotten, Hunter felt that 'Kitchener deserves all he
gets. He has run the show himself. His has been the responsibility. Some of us
have helped too.'[17] Walter shared Hunter's opinion, as he wrote to Carry a
fortnight later: 'It has been a well managed show and Herbert has run it
absolutely off his own bat. His staff were not given a chance of remembering
the most ordinary details. As a matter of fact I think he was afraid to trust any
of them, and he was just about right.'

The Sirdar, with Hunter, Walter and the staff rode into the great walled
area of the Khalifa's quarter, which had only just been captured from his tribal
bodyguard, and passed a great storehouse of corn and rotting dates and along
a causeway over pools drawn from the Nile; then through an archway into the
wide square of the Iron Mosque, littered with red leather-bound copies of the
Koran. Ahead stood the Khalifa's house and the Mahdi's tomb. A Sudanese
battalion had failed to capture the Khalifa, who fled with his women as they
entered, and were happily looting his chickens. They stopped at once, tucked
chickens into their belts 'and stood grinning in wide-mouthed devotion
towards their beloved Chief', as Scudamore saw.[18]

Then Kitchener nearly lost his life again. A shell burst overhead and shrapnel rained down. Hunter picked up a fragment and saw it was from one of
their own guns, but another splinter had tragically killed Hubert Howard, the

Earl of Carlisle's daredevil (and teetotal) younger son who was covering the campaign for newspapers. 'Then came two more shells,' wrote Walter, 'and we all skiddadled smart by the way we came.'

Kitchener was determined to find and release Charles Neufeld and the Khalifa's other Western prisoners. With a company of Blacks they had a 'most exciting afternoon' working their way through the city. They never knew whether the next wall would be held. They went through narrow alleys. Sometimes shadowy figures 'potted at Herbert through windows and it was wonderful luck his not being hit ... Herbert just did all he could to get himself shot and wouldn't stop till well after dark.' By then, most of the staff had dropped off. Herbert and Walter pressed on, with a guide and an escort of half a dozen Blacks until they found the jail, high walled with only one door, which was fast shut.

> After considerable parley through the door the Jehadier guard came out (some twenty men) and laid down their arms — and Herbert, *very keen*, pushed into the low inner court-yard which was full of prisoners. The moon was up now and it made quite an impressive picture when Neufeld was, after some delay, brought out of a dark inner mud hut, so heavily chained he could hardly walk and then only swaying from side to side — in jibbeh and Dervish cap, but unsunburned white face — he hobbled forward to shake hands with Herbert.

Despite the chains he had not been badly treated and had refused to leave his native wife when Wingate had contrived an opportunity for escape.

That night, outside the city on what they discovered afterwards to be the execution ground, the Grenadier officers had the curious sight, by a campfire, of the Sirdar lying on his back on a rough bed dictating telegrams for the Queen and Cromer to Wingate, who was lying on his stomach on the ground. Two ADCs were providing light from a succession of thick wax matches which Scudamore happened to have. A few feet away an armourer was filing off Neufeld's steel chains.[19]

Kitchener finished his despatches. As he prepared for a brief sleep he said: 'I thank the Lord of Hosts for giving us victory at so small a cost in our dead and wounded.'[20] And, if the Sirdar's actions next day and his lifelong attitudes are a guide, his thoughts ranged also to the suffering of the other side.

17

'HEROIC SOUL
WHOSE MEMORY WE HONOUR'

KITCHENER NAMED the victory the Battle of Khartoum but was overruled by the War Office, who named it officially as Omdurman; to the Sudanese it is the Battle of Karari. On the morning after, the Sirdar appointed one of the prisoners he had liberated, an Egyptian physician named Hassan Effendi Zeki, to be General Superintendent for the care of the dervish wounded, later estimated at 16,000. Zeki set up a hospital in a central position where more than 400 of the worst cases were tended and out-patients flocked in daily. The military field hospitals had to give priority to the expeditions's wounded but did what they could for dervishes. Uncounted numbers were carried to their homes by relatives, since every Omdurman male who could march had been conscripted for the fight.[1] Some wounded undoubtedly had been slain in the night by looters, whether from the city or camp followers, and others would have died of wounds before being found in the very extensive battlefield. Kitchener categorically rejected 'cruel and disgraceful' accusations, made three months later, of inhumanity. 'Considering the condition of the troops and the means at my disposal, I did all that I could to relieve suffering amongst the enemy.'[2]

Kitchener also ordered a count of dervish bodies, which came to a horrifying 10,883. Eighteen years later nearly double that number of British soldiers would be killed on the first day of the Battle of the Somme, three weeks after Kitchener's death.

While the divisional generals were reorganizing their troops, the Sirdar took Ned Cecil and Walter, with no escort except orderlies, in a gunboat the three miles up the Blue Nile to set foot in the ruins of Khartoum, the city that had been the lodestar of his life for fourteen years. Walter was 'dead beat and the river trip was delicious'. He was even able to have a tub bath on board, 'which quite pulled me together'. On landing, they explored the ruins of Gordon's palace. Kitchener was much moved as he identified the site of the stairs where Gordon had been killed and where his body had lain unburied. Gordon's old gardener came up with a present of oranges, weeping lest he be dismissed after fifty years' service. Cecil saw Kitchener gentle and kind, 'as he always was to the poor'. He reassured the gardener that he would tend the roses in the garden of the palace soon to be rebuilt: Kitchener was already planning the new Khartoum, but his eyes were on the south, to complete Gordon's work by bringing peace and liberty to the tribes.[3]

They re-embarked and went a mile or two upstream before turning back to Omdurman. Kitchener now drafted a memorial service for Gordon, to be conducted next day, Sunday, by chaplains of each Christian denomination in the expedition. But when an ADC took the form of service to the senior Anglican chaplain, A. W. Watson, he objected that as Gordon had been Church of England he alone should officiate; or, in Walter's words, 'unless he *ran* the service he'd not play'.[4] The Sirdar was amused rather than irritated. He had other Anglican chaplains if Watson were out of the way, and after check-ing with 'Monkey' Gordon that his nominally Anglican uncle had wor-shipped with any sincere Christian (and had been ahead of his times in friendship with Roman Catholics) the Sirdar sent for Padre Watson. As Walter put it, the parson 'was given his choice of Khartoum or Cairo – and gave in'.

Next morning detachments from every battalion were ferried by gunboat to Khartoum and drawn up on what had been the lawn, facing the broken wall of the palace, its windows filled with the rubble of years, where Gordon had paced and prayed and looked through his telescope for the relief that never came. Two flagstaffs had been erected; the expedition was operating under two flags as a temporary answer to the problem that the Mahdist rebel-lion had been caused by Egyptian bad government before and after Gordon. Two officers stood by each flagstaff. Anchored immediately behind the troops lay the *Melik*, commanded by 'Monkey' Gordon, with other gunboats nearby. The generals, and the German and Italian attachés, stood at the head of the troops.

The Sirdar raised his hand. An enormous Union Jack flew out. All presented arms or saluted, the *Melik* fired a gun and the band of the Grenadier Guards played 'God Save the Queen'. The Blacks, from the far south, were excited and delighted.

The Sirdar raised his hand again. The Egyptian flag flew out. The gun fired and the khedival anthem was played. The Sirdar called for three cheers for each monarch, but when General Wauchope, commanding the British division, called for three cheers for the Sirdar the noise was deafening.

Then the four chaplains, Anglican, Roman Catholic, Presbyterian and Methodist, stepped forward and faced the parade. The Guards' band played the Dead March from *Saul* to commemorate Gordon, as the gunboats fired solemn minute guns: they had no blanks so fired upriver into the Nile. To Rawlinson

the moan of the shell hurtling through the still air added a weird and unusual note to the ceremony, which marked it, in my mind, as being not an occasion for triumph but for solemn resolve . . . We had pledged ourselves to complete the work for which Gordon died thirteen years ago, and to free this land from brutality and tyranny.

The band of the 11th Sudanese then played Handel's march from *Scipio* ('Toll for the Brave') in memory of the Blacks and Egyptians who had died with Gordon and those massacred after the fall of the city. About a hundred survivors and locals had gathered at the far end of the lawn.

As the last shot was fired, the Anglican chaplain led the congregation in the Lord's Prayer, and the Presbyterian read the fifteenth Psalm: 'Lord, who shall dwell in thy tabernacle? Who shall rest upon thy holy hill? He that walketh uprightly, and worketh righteousness, and speaketh the truth in his heart . . .'

The pipes of the Camerons and the Seaforth Highlanders then played the Coronach lament, with a muffled roll of drums, at which the local survivors cried with a shrill lament of their own.

'Abide with Me', known to almost every Briton present and believed to be Gordon's favourite hymn, was played by the band of the 11th Sudanese, to Monk's famous tune 'Eventide', which they afterwards renamed 'Khartoum' and played wherever they performed, immediately before the National Anthem.

The emotion, for the British, was already almost unbearable. Then Father Brindle, with his floating white hair and white beard, the best-loved man in the army, stepped forward, put his helmet at his feet and read from a sheet of paper the benediction prayer he had specially written:

O Almighty God, by whose providence are all things which come into the lives of men, whether of suffering which Thou permittest, or of joy and gladness which Thou givest, look down, we beseech Thee, with eyes of pity and compassion on this land, so loved by that heroic soul, whose memory we honour before Thee this day. Give back to it days of peace — send it rulers animated by his spirit of justice and righteousness — strengthen them in the might of Thy power that they may labour in making perfect the work to which he devoted, and for which he gave, his life.

And grant to us, Thy servants, that we may copy his virtues of self-sacrifice and fortitude, so that when Thou callest we may each be able to answer, 'I have fought the good fight.'

A blessing which we humbly ask — in the name of the Father, the Son and the Holy Ghost. Amen.[5]

'By then there was not a dry eye', recorded Rawlinson in his diary. The Sirdar 'who is, as a rule, absolutely unmoved, had great round tears on his cheeks'. Men's shoulders were shaken by sobs, wrote Prince Frank of Teck to his sister Princess May (Queen Mary) that evening. 'One leant over Brindle and cried like a child — in fact it was terribly affecting.'[6]

Teck's detail may be doubted but Kitchener was too overcome to dismiss the parade. He signalled to Hunter.

Afterwards the senior officers shook the Sirdar's hand, silently, one by one according to rank, and then they wandered about the garden and Gordon seemed almost as if among them. Charles à Court came up to Kitchener to congratulate him.

He was very much changed; the sternness and the harshness had dropped from him for the moment, and he was as gentle as a woman. He spoke in affecting words of Gordon, and of the long years which had been spent in recovering the lost Sudan, and of all he owed to those who had assisted him. The lines of thought had gone out of his face. His manner had become easy and unconstrained. He was very happy.[7]

[141]

Then he summoned the war correspondents and unfolded his great vision for a Gordon Memorial College, to be built facing the Blue Nile a little upstream from the restored palace, to educate Sudanese tribesmen's sons, from the Muslim north and the animist (and later largely Christian) south, 'to give them the intellectual force to act as governors of their own destinies'. Gordon had done so much for poor boys in England and the Sudan that a college would be after his heart, a twin, as it were, to the Gordon Memorial School in England.

'Now, gentlemen', the Sirdar said after explaining his plan, 'you can help me. I require £65,000 to put this scheme through, and I believe that if you give me your help in your papers, I can get it at once from the British public.'

He looked around at each of them, 'with his usual half-commanding, half-whimsical smile', and rested his glance on little Frank Scudamore, his friend since Debbeh in 1884. Scudamore said: 'Why £65,000, sir? At this height of your success you can just as well ask a hundred thousand and put your scheme beyond risk of failure.'

'Well, Scudamore, if you think that is so, put forward an appeal for a hundred thousand, and God bless you if you get it.'[8] He would find that he needed even more for this, his own special cause.

Back in Omdurman the Sirdar said farewell to the British wounded as they left in barges towed by steamers for Abadan, where a hospital had been prepared. Then he wrote to Queen Victoria's Private Secretary. As the Royal Engineers had run out of telegraph wire (the Sirdar must have missed a detail) the message had to be carried by steamer downriver to be telegraphed from Nasri island and only reached Balmoral on the following evening, 5 September. The Sirdar's plain prose so excited the Queen that she described it in her journal as 'a most touching account, and most dramatic, of his entry into Khartoum and of a memorial service held to the memory of poor Gordon on the spot where he was killed! Surely he is avenged!'[9]

The Queen, who had already sent a telegram of congratulation which had been read to the troops,[10] wired at once to Lord Salisbury suggesting a peerage for Kitchener. 'I should much like to announce it to him myself if you propose it'[11] – an exceptional honour. Salisbury concurred warmly in a telegram the next morning. Victoria wired her announcement at once, in the first, not the usual third person, another exceptional honour.

And no answer came. Fifteen days later, still waiting, 'It is very annoying,' she wrote, 'as the good effect of the early recognition of his services has thus been marred.'[12]

The telegraph wire had been broken in two or three places. By the time the wire reached Nasri island for onward transmission by steamer, the Sirdar had left in a hurry for the south.

18

THE DIPLOMAT OF FASHODA

KITCHENER HAD CARRIED sealed orders in Salisbury's own hand sewn into a jacket, to be opened after capturing Khartoum. He found that he was to head a flotilla south up the White Nile to find and warn off a French expedition under Commandant Marchand which had set out long ago from French West Africa to claim the Nile basin for France; but Salisbury wanted no corpses. And Hunter would ascend the Blue Nile to turn off any Abyssinian troops from Sudanese territory.

On the fifth day after the battle the Sirdar was still organizing the homeward dispatch of the British brigades when one of Gordon's old 'penny steamer' gunboats, captured by the Mahdists in 1885, the *Tewfikieh*, came in from the south, having hastily hoisted a white flag. Her captain reported that some hated 'Turks' had installed themselves at Fashoda, five hundred miles upriver. After 'a scrimmage' (the bullet holes were plainly visible) the dervishes had retired and dispatched the gunboat to the Khalifa for reinforcements to destroy the 'Turks'. Wingate and the Sirdar realized that these 'Turks' were Marchand and his French.

Having no information about the strength of the French force at Fashoda and not knowing whether the escaped Khalifa had gathered a new army, Kitchener formed a strong expedition of two Sudanese battalions of six hundred men each, a company of the Cameron Highlanders and an Egyptian mountain battery to be conveyed by three gunboats and two stern-wheelers towing barges. At 7.30 a.m. on Saturday 10 September, while Queen Victoria's telegram was still stuck in the desert, the flotilla steamed away from

Omdurman, the Sirdar sailing in the stern-wheeler *Dal* with Wingate, Jimmy Watson, Cecil, Freddy Roberts and Malcolm Peak, who commanded the guns.

The voyage was a discovery for all the British officers. First the White Nile at its broadest, almost like a lake, then narrowing as they pushed against a strong current and wind for four days, tying up at night while soldiers were sent ashore to cut wood for the boilers and endure mosquitoes, flies and bees. They saw hippos and crocodiles and herds of hartebeest. On the fifth day, as the scenery began to change, they met groups of naked Dinkas who warned them of a dervish fort a few miles south. They approached in battle order and quickly overcame a defensive zariba guarded by another of Gordon's old gun-boats, the *Saffiyeh*, which Beatty riddled with shells and set briefly on fire so that Kitchener teased him afterwards: 'You dam' sailors can never see anything afloat without wishing to destroy it!'[1]

The banks were now lined with forest. On 17 September the flotilla reached the large Shilluk village of Kaka. A Shilluk sergeant was sent ashore to invite the chief to come aboard to meet the Sirdar. The chief was in his national dress of nothing, clothes being considered a sign of slavery, so the sergeant handed him a towel for his middle. But on seeing the Sirdar the chief pulled it off and wound it around his head as a mark of respect. All the not-ables then came aboard. The Sirdar was puzzled that they were being pre-sented in groups of seven, until told that there were only seven spare towels. He ordered that the rest should come as they were.[2]

That night, as Jimmy Watson recorded in his diary, 'large numbers of Shilluk warriors came down to us. Dances etc. Our bands played.'[3]

Fashoda lay fifty miles upriver. Kitchener had thought out very carefully how to ensure Marchand's removal without causing an incident that might even lead to war between Britain and France. Having lived in Brittany as a youth and served with the French Army, he knew the French mind. He sent off two Shilluk sergeants carrying a letter in elegant French addressed to the Commander of the European Expedition at Fashoda, to congratulate him on his magnificent feat of bringing his expedition so far across Africa. Kitchener announced the victory outside Omdurman and made plain that he was coming to re-establish the khedive's authority at Fashoda and everywhere else. He would arrive in two days.

The sergeants travelled Shilluk-style, but the French were astonished when two handsome Blacks in khaki drill and red tarboosh saluted smartly at the gate of 'Fort St-Louis' and handed in the letter. Marchand was also relieved, because natives had warned him that a force of 1,500 hostile dervishes was approaching in a flotilla of gunboats.[4]

The Sirdar wished to give Marchand time to reflect on his impossible position, and approached Fashoda only on the morning of 19 September, having given Horace Smith-Dorrien, commanding the troops, alternative orders for hostilities or peace. He kept the Cameron Highlanders out of sight and put on Egyptian uniform. Fashoda came into view on a spit of land surrounded by marshes, once a district capital but abandoned by the Khalifa. Kitchener and Wingate, on the upper deck of the *Dal*, could see the French flag flying from the old government buildings. A small steel boat approached. An enormous French flag flew at her stern, and a crew of Senegalese in smart red jerseys plied rough wooden paddles. When the boat drew alongside, a Senegalese sergeant came on board with a letter from 'the High Commissioner' of the Bahr-el-Ghazal province, polite and congratulatory but uncompromising.

The flotilla steamed in line astern into the narrow channel and anchored with every gun trained on the French post and every deck lined with the Sirdar's Black soldiers fully armed. Marchand and another officer in spotless white uniforms came on board and were conducted to the Sirdar as he stood with his staff on the upper deck. Saluting and bowing and exchanging compliments, Kitchener and Marchand spread out a map and began a negotiation that could lead their countries to war or peace. Both men immediately took to each other, Kitchener admiring Marchand's achievement as explorer, Marchand appreciating Kitchener's fluency in French, though he groped for words now and again. Of all officers in the British Army, Herbert Kitchener was best shaped for this moment of fragile diplomacy between serving soldiers.

Kitchener said he was authorized to state that the French presence was a direct violation of the rights of Egypt and Britain and that he must protest in strongest terms. Marchand replied that he had carried out his orders and must await further orders from France. Kitchener asked if Marchand would resist the re-establishment of Egyptian authority and pointed out that the Anglo-Egyptian force was much more powerful than the French, at which Marchand gave a deep bow of his head. Kitchener said he was 'very averse' to hostilities and begged Marchand to consider his decision most carefully. He added that he would be pleased to put a gunboat at his disposal to take the gallant explorers and their escort to Egypt.

Marchand said he was ready to die at his post.

After further discussion Kitchener proposed a face-saving compromise: he would hoist the Egyptian flag but both flags would fly together and Marchand's party remain until he received instructions from his government to withdraw. Would Monsieur Marchand resist the hoisting of the Egyptian flag? 'M. Marchand hesitated and then said that he could not resist the Egyptian flag being hoisted. I replied that my instructions were to hoist the flag and that I intended to do so.' Marchand's hesitation was caused by a 'terrible desire' to refuse, and die for the glory of France, but then he dared not take the responsibility for peace or war by himself.

Kitchener had prepared for resistance but now arranged for them to carry out the ceremony together.

Smith-Dorrien, watching the proceedings by field glasses from another gunboat, had mistaken Gallic gestures for anger and was mightily relieved when he saw 'golden liquid' being brought up and toasts exchanged. Kitchener never knew what a sacrifice Marchand and his companion made for France by drinking lukewarm whisky and soda.

'During these somewhat delicate proceedings,' wrote Kitchener, 'nothing could have exceeded the politeness and courtesy of the French officers,'[5] nor indeed of Kitchener. Both sides could now fraternize. Marchand admitted that they had expected to be wiped out by the dervishes. Kitchener was too polite to express his amazement that the French government should have attempted a vast undertaking with such a tiny force: he found seven French and fewer than two hundred Senegalese troops. Marchand had expected to meet another party coming by Abyssinia.

The Egyptian flag was hoisted at a mutually chosen mudbank on the only road to the interior, with bands and gun salutes. Kitchener and his staff returned Marchand's visit amid much hospitality and good wine. They also left newspapers that revealed to the French the scandals rocking their army and country over the Dreyfus case. Kitchener remarked as he left that 'your government won't back you'. When the French read the newspapers they wept.

Kitchener sailed farther south to place a strategic but unsalubrious post at a river junction, welcomed as liberators from the Arabs, then took the remainder of his force back towards Khartoum, carefully avoiding another contact with Marchand, whom he left a virtual prisoner, with swamps on two sides, guarded by a Sudanese battalion and shadowed by a gunboat commanded by young Walter Cowan, who went on to become an admiral and a baronet in the First World War and a commando in the Second, earning a bar to his 1898 DSO at the age of seventy-three.

Kitchener's 'chivalrous character and diplomatic gifts', as Lord Salisbury described them,[6] which would prove even more important in another sphere a few years later, had prevented the 'Fashoda Incident' becoming a *casus belli* in itself. Kitchener had no part in the high-level negotiations between Paris and London against a background of cross-Channel popular fury and news-paper warfare. By late October Marchand had become so upset by hearing nothing that he took a lift in one of the Sirdar's gunboats and arrived unexpectedly in Omdurman. Walter, in Herbert's absence, entertained him, expressing admiration and sympathy so that on leaving for Cairo 'Le Chef de la mission française en Afrique Centrale' wrote to say that he was 'très touché de votre opinion trop flatteuse sur la marche de la mission'.[7] `He sent his most profound respects to the Sirdar.

On 4 December Marchand arrived sadly back at Fashoda with the news that France had renounced all pretensions to the Nile Valley and that the expedition must withdraw, allowed to evacuate through Abyssinia as a sop to French pride. Marchand and one of his officers rose to be distinguished generals.

On leaving Fashoda on 20 September the Sirdar and his staff in the *Dal* sailed swiftly down the Nile, helped by a strong current. At the Shilluk village where they had watched the dancing they met Walter bringing up telegrams in the *Tewfikieh*, including Queen Victoria's dated 6 September:

> It is with feelings of admiration and thankfulness that I announce to you my intention of conferring a Peerage on you as a mark of my deep sense of the services you have rendered under such most difficult trying circum-stances. VRI[8]

Kitchener had not expected a peerage.[9] Roberts had received only a baronetcy for Kandahar; his peerage came later. Wolseley had been made a peer for Tel-el-Kebir, but he was commanding a larger, wholly British army and serving directly under the Crown. When Kitchener's staff talked of a peerage his inclination was to refuse on ground of poverty. Peerages, always hereditary except for Law Lords, were sparingly given and a newly created peer was expected to maintain appropriate style, yet Kitchener had little beyond his pay, although a Parliamentary grant was probable. The Queen's gracious words made refusal impossible. As Herbert read them Walter is supposed to have said, 'You had better take it as you'll never get another chance!' Herbert ordered champagne and they all drank 'success to "Khartoum of Aspall". I'm rather sorry he drops the Kitchener', Walter wrote to Carry, 'but as he says who knows where Lord Harris is Lord of . . .'[10] Harris's great-grandfather, conqueror of Tipu Sahib, had been gazetted as Baron Harris of Seringapatam and Mysore, but the family had long dropped the mouthful. Herbert also remarked in a letter which presumably he did not show Walter, that 'Kitchener is too horrible a name to put a Lord in front of'.[11]

'Lord Khartoum' had been the title they had all been using in confident expectation of the peerage, but in Britain Kitchener had become a household name, the focus of hero-worship and the pride of the empire: dropping it was impossible. He was created (1 November 1898) Baron Kitchener of Khartoum, of Aspall in the County of Suffolk, with remainder to the heirs male of his body.[12]

'K of K' was born.

Before leaving for Fashoda the Sirdar had given two orders: by the first, Walter Kitchener, using dervish prisoners and following a design already sketched by Herbert, began the new Khartoum, 'cutting roads through the mass of ruins and developing a real R.E. chess board pattern town. When roads are levelled and blocks marked out, the people now in Omdurman will be told to move over, and we shall have a flourishing town again', Walter told his brother Arthur.[13]

The second order caused a storm to blow around Herbert's head. The Mahdi's tomb had been damaged by gunfire, rather unnecessarily although a highly visible target. The structure was now dangerous. The Sirdar consulted Muslim officers from the Sudanese battalions. They regarded the Mahdi as a heretic and feared that his tomb might become a second Mecca, and advised that it be demolished. The tomb was the only large structure in Omdurman. If repaired, to continue dominating the skyline, the Mahdi would seem still to be dominant. Several influential citizens did not disagree, whether through fear or conviction.

The officers went further: they urged that the Mahdi's bones be thrown into the Nile. The iron railing was removed and the tomb opened. By Muslim burial custom the body had not been embalmed or placed in a coffin and had long since decomposed. Some Sudanese soldiers present who believed that the Mahdi had been taken to heaven were astonished to find a skeleton and cried out, 'By God, this was not the Mahdi after all he told us'. The bones, except the skull, were placed in a weighted box and dumped (probably at night) in the Nile.[14]

Kitchener told the Queen: 'When I returned from Fashoda the Mahdi's skull in a box was brought to me and I did not know what to do with it.' Some insensitive wag suggested making it into an inkpot, and the rumour lingered for years: a charming playlet, wholly fictitious, shows Kitchener presenting it to an alarmed Queen.[15] He thought of sending it to the Royal College of Surgeons.

Meanwhile 'Monkey' Gordon, as the only man who knew how to lay a circle of guncotton, had blown up the tomb and reduced it to rubble.[16]

Radicals in England were outraged. Even Churchill, in his *River War* the next year, did not hesitate to declare that 'to destroy what was sacred and holy to them was a wicked act, of which the true Christian, no less than the philosopher, must express his abhorrence.'[17] Churchill's editor, Frank Rhodes, who was wounded at Omdurman, publicly differed in a footnote, holding that the Sirdar's action was politically necessary, if done the wrong way. The controversy rumbled for months. Queen Victoria, although accepting her beloved Sirdar's need to destroy the tomb, felt that as to 'the destruction of the poor body of a man who whether he was very bad and cruel, after all was a *man* of a certain importance – that it savours in the Queen's opinion too much of the Middle Ages not to allow his remains to be buried in private in some spot where it would not be considered as of any importance politically or an object of superstition. The graves of our people have been respected and those of our foes should, in her opinion, also be.'[18]

When the Sirdar sent the skull in its box to Egypt with his baggage, suggesting burial in a military cemetery, Cromer wired to the Foreign Office: 'This is very unfortunate. It will never do to have burial here.' He wanted it sent back to Omdurman 'as quickly as possible'.[19] In the end it was buried secretly at Wadi Halfa.

Kitchener would have been wiser to have buried the whole skeleton in a remote unmarked and undiscoverable grave, for the skull haunted his reputation far into the next century. Once the generations had passed away which venerated him for the foundation of the fine government and peace, the Sudanese remembered Kitchener chiefly for the slaughter at Omdurman, the destruction of the tomb (since rebuilt) and the indignity done to the bones, whereas Gordon continued to be venerated as a saint.

19

THE MAGIC WAND

KITCHENER LANDED at Dover on 27 October. He was long overdue for leave and his eyes were giving trouble. Walter's wife Caroline (Carry) and their children still lived in Dover. When she had told Walter that she was much involved in plans for a civic reception, he was worried: 'You will all have been a bit disappointed at Dover I expect, as I am sure Herbert will just rush thro' – don't run away with the idea he's "têtetourner" (head turned, I can't spell it) if he is off hand, as he hates *tamashas* [shows] and behaves abominably, really thro' shyness' – and did not mind how much offence he gave.[1] But Herbert was at his most charming and gracious. When the ferry *Empress*, belching black smoke because of its speed, drew near the harbour, he was amazed to see every vantage point crammed by the largest crowd ever known there. At first they were silent, ignorantly expecting a magnificent uniform, not a tall gentleman in a 'grey tourist suit', standing with two others on the platform above the paddlewheel. But when the ferry docked and the dignitaries stepped forward and shook the Sirdar's hand, the crowd erupted in tremendous cheering.

At the civic luncheon the Sirdar praised his 'magnificent' troops, for if sparing with face-to-face thanks he was generous in dispatches, recommendations for honours, and in speeches. He spoke of his hopes for the Sudan, having suppressed his horror of functions for the sake of Gordon College:

> . . . The vast country has been opened to the civilising influence of commercial enterprise. I sincerely hope by the means of education and good

government we shall be able to raise the standard of life of the inhabitants of that country, and that in the place of persecution, tyranny, and fanaticism, we may establish the reign of prosperity and peace.[2]

He and Jimmy Watson then went by a special train of the London, Chatham and Dover Railway to its terminus at Victoria, where the scenes were extraordinary. The railway company had not expected such crowds of all classes who came to welcome the hero of Khartoum, the avenger of Gordon, the skilled diplomat of Fashoda (the crisis between France and Britain was at its height). Moreover, George Steevens's book, *With Kitchener to Khartoum*, had been rushed into print to be a runaway best seller, although annoying Queen Victoria for its rather inhuman portrait of the Sirdar as 'the Sudan machine'.[3] All London wanted to see him and engulfed the official party, which included Roberts, Wolseley and Evelyn Wood, and the two princes who had served with him in the Sudan. *The Times* commented: 'No incident of recent times, not even the arrival of Lord Beaconsfield and Lord Salisbury after the Berlin Conference, has elicited such a remarkable demonstration of popular feeling.'[4] Passengers in trains standing at other platforms even climbed to the roofs of carriages, while outside the station the crowd went wild when a hansom cab emerged and they had nearly unhitched the horse in order to drag the cab in triumph before realizing that the man inside was not the Sirdar.

Extracted with difficulty from the overexcited crowd, the Sirdar stayed one night at Pandeli Ralli's house in Belgrave Square and on the Friday evening went down to Hatfield with the Prime Minister and his nephew, A. J. Balfour, First Lord of the Treasury and Leader of the House of Commons. The Cranbornes, Lord Edward, who had carried home the Fashoda dispatch, and other Cecils made him feel at home, and Salisbury outlined his plans for the Sudan, with Kitchener at its head. On Sunday they all attended the parish church, where 'Fish' (Lord William) was rector and Kitchener could notice the old marquess dozing quietly through his son's sermon.

The night express to Scotland stopped at Hatfield to pick up the private saloon and sleeper which had been taken for Kitchener and Balfour. A royal carriage met them at Ballater for the drive to Balmoral Castle, where, directly after luncheon on Monday 31 October, the Queen, as she recorded in her journal, 'saw the Sirdar, Lord Kitchener, who only arrived in London a few days ago. he looked very well and bronzed, but had caught a bad cold.'[5]

The audience took place 'in a sort of bower of palm branches', as Herbert described it to Walter. Victoria was most gracious, even giving him the honour, allowed to Beaconsfield but never to Gladstone, of inviting him to sit down.

Herbert was amused to see tables littered with soda-water bottles and blotting paper, for in Khartoum they had picked roses from Gordon's garden. Walter had placed six roses in soda-water bottles filled with spirits, so that they should arrive fresh, expecting the Royal Household to break the bottles and make up the roses nicely with maidenhair fern before presenting them to the Queen. He had pressed others into blotting paper. The roses had been carried to Balmoral by Lieutenant-Colonel C. G. C. Money of the Cameron Highlanders with the Sirdar's Omdurman (Battle of Khartoum) dispatch. The Household, however, had left the roses in the bottles and blotting paper, but the Queen was 'very pleased' with them. She talked of all that had passed 'and how well everything had gone off'. At dinner 'Lord Kitchener sat next to me, and was very agreeable, full of information, and Mr Balfour also made himself very pleasant'.[6]

Marie Mallet was again in waiting. She wrote to her husband:

Kitchener has conquered us almost as effectually as the Sudan. We were more or less prejudiced against him, but he is certainly a gentleman and can talk most intelligently on all subjects, he also has a sense of humour although of rather a grim order and there is no doubt he is a marvellous soldier; what he lacks is the softness so many strong men have hidden away under the roughest exterior, and there is that in his eye which makes me truly thankful I am neither his wife nor his A.D.C.[7]

She was not allowed to penetrate to the softness, kept rigorously in check; nor did she know how the the wound and his bad sight gave him the eye of a basilisk.

Next day he walked in the grounds with a courtier and laboured at the speech he must make at the City of London's banquet in his honour. Balfour tried to help, but their styles were different and Balfour's 'far too mild and aesthetic'. Ponsonby, the Queen's Private Secretary, found Balfour lying in an armchair dictating a speech 'but whenever he said anything Kitchener contradicted him' and later rewrote Balfour's speech in his own style. Balfour, knowing the plan for the new Sudan, observed him closely, recognizing his boundless courage and resolution but wondering if he could adapt himself to different and larger problems. And 'He seems to have a profound contempt for every soldier except himself, which, though not an amiable trait, does not make me think less of his brains'.[8]

Kitchener bemoaned to Mrs Mallet that he would sooner fight a dozen battles than make a single speech. He went back to London and that night received a standing ovation as he entered his host's box at the Gaiety Theatre. Next morning at a splendid ceremony he received the Freedom of the City of London with a rather tasteless sword of honour, its hilt encrusted with dia/monds and figures of Justice, Britannia and the British Lion. In the evening the Lord Mayor gave a great banquet in his honour at the Mansion House which Sir George Arthur, present as a liveryman, voted 'a roaring success', writing to a friend three days later:

The Sirdar paid a fine – and evidently heartfelt – tribute to the Agent/General [Cromer] and fine, and equally genuine, tributes were paid by all the speakers to him: – to his diplomacy and economy no less than to his mil/itary organization and strategy. The Prime Minister must have been supremely happy on this occasion. Not only was he the chief witness to the great ovation given to the man whom he had backed in every way and whose career he was one of the first to foresee, but he could seize the occa/sion to announce the prospective French retirement from the Nile, and to associate that prudent and amiable step with Kitchener's tact and concilia/tory methods.[9]

The French ambassador had informed Salisbury that very afternoon that Marchand had been ordered to retire. The crisis was over. Salisbury's announcement brought prolonged cheering and clapping.

The Queen wired Kitchener her approval of his speech and hoped his cold was better. He wired back that he was greatly honoured by her approval. His cold was better, and he was 'much gratified at the splendid reception given him in the City'.[10] George Arthur, however, commented that 'K. has probably suffered more from the hero/worship he has had to put up with these last days than from the heat and dust, toil and trouble, which have been his lot during these past years'.[11] Arthur was right; Kitchener was tempted to bolt back to the Sudan after one week[12] but stood the hero/worship for the sake of his dream for the Sudan.

At Cambridge he received an honorary degree, staying at Christ's College lodge with the Master, his Kitchener cousin Thomas Day, to whom he had given his stamp collection many years ago.[13] Here and at Edinburgh and at numerous functions in London his theme was that 'those who have conquered are called upon to civilize. The work interrupted since the death of Gordon must be resumed.' They must establish a good administration, give justice, organize a police force, but government could not afford to provide education: this must be given by the people of Britain. In a letter to *The Times* he appealed for the very considerable sum (for 1898) of £100,000: £10,000 to set up a Gordon Memorial College and £90,000 as endowment.[14] His vision was for a college of higher education eventually, despite critics who asserted that primary schooling to provide clerks and minor officials was enough; but Sudanese boys must first be taught to read and write. 'How Gordon would have rejoiced', the Sirdar told his Edinburgh audience, 'had he known that by his death the blessing of education would be given to the people that he loved and among whom he died'.[15]

The war correspondents back from the Sudan, who had been the first to hear of the scheme, encouraged their papers to publicize it, and the Sirdar used his skills of persuasion. The Rothschilds gave a luncheon for him; he first secured a promise from Sir Ernest Cassell and another banker to match the sum given by his host; when Lord Kitchener arrived at the luncheon he announced playfully that he would not stay unless Rothschild promised a really handsome cheque, which he was thus able to treble.

Lord Edward Cecil, still his ADC before leaving for South Africa, worked with him at the Ralli house in Belgrave Square and recalled later that Kitchener was

a dangerous man to go and see in London, as, quite regardless of the fact that you had other things to do, he seized you and set you to work on whatever he thought you could do efficiently. Few — I was going to say no one, and I am not sure it is not nearer the truth — dared refuse: and the result was that the house was always full of the most heterogenerous elements, grumbling over their servitude, but often, if they had any sense of humour, amused at the situation. A very proper friend of mine spent his time in burning, after seeing there was nothing important in them, the mass of love-letters which descended on Kitchener, and which would have offended him. He placed women on a far higher level than is usual in these days, and it really hurt him to hear or see anything which touched this ideal. Another very sensitive man of great natural politeness [probably George Arthur] spent his time in interviewing the most intimidating people, such as multi-millionaires, corporations, big banks, and firms, to obtain from them contributions to the Gordon College. He used to come back in the evening, looking as if he had been at a disturbed mass meeting, and gloomily wonder what Kitchener would say to the result.[16]

But the richest nation on earth responded. Kitchener caught the mood of the hour, the glow still lingering from Queen Victoria's Diamond Jubilee, of pride that Britain was called to lead and civilize. The Christian conscience of the nation was it its strongest after two generations when the Christian ethic had become predominant in Britain, whatever a man's or woman's personal faith or lack of it. And even those whose conscience had disapproved of the slaughter could share 'the white man's burden'.

The money came. A hundred thousand pounds was subscribed, including £40,000 from the nation by a cheque signed with a flourish by Victoria R.I and two of her Lords of the Treasury.

20

REBUILDING A NATION

KITCHENER ARRIVED BACK at Khartoum on 28 December 1898, a week before he was due, to find that the troops had suffered severely from malaria and the exertions of campaigning against the Khalifa's remaining forces up the Blue Nile, on the Abyssinian border and far away up the White Nile. The Khalifa himself had reappeared about 150 miles south of Khartoum. Intelligence suggested that he had been badly received and was robbing and looting.[1]

Most of the Sirdar's senior officers were now acting as governors of his vast new domain. He therefore summoned Walter, whose deafness and lack of Arabic made him unsuitable as a provincial governor. Walter had been downriver and disembarked at Khartoum just in time to receive the message. He crossed to Omdurman. 'Herbert had crowds of work [*sic*] and natives on hand, but about 12 he came out of his office tent and said "Well I'm glad you turned up, you nearly lost your chance as after 12 o'clock I was going to appoint someone else. You are to go and catch the Khalifa,"' taking a compact force of an Egyptian and a Sudanese battalion, 100 of the Camel Corps and some 400 'Friendlies' a total of about 1,100, with 4 guns. 'I was never so astonished in my life', wrote the delighted Walter to his wife, asking for her prayers and telling her not to worry. 'I've had as good a training under Herbert as any man ever had, and I know he trusts me to bring all through satisfactorily. He doesn't make mistakes often. He has given me some real good hints' (on how Walter's Kordofan Field Force could defeat and capture the Khalifa).[2] But, the Sirdar told the Queen, 'owing to the difficulty of the country I am not very confident in their being able to do so'.[3]

The new Khartoum had already begun under the direction of Walter as city governor, with George Gorringe and his sapper officers. Two thousand dervish prisoners were clearing the rubble of the old city and laying out Kitchener's own town plan of a rectangular grid of avenues crossed by streets, as in ancient Alexandria and much like many American cities, although he had never seen one. Kitchener also planned diagonal streets, to ensure the swift suppression of riot. The result suggested a city designed like the Union Jack but this was unintentional.[4] Kitchener insisted that the palace should be rebuilt swiftly as a sign that the British had come to stay. Since Gordon's palace had been thoroughly looted, Kitchener ordered Wingate to 'loot like blazes' to recover its old glories.

Cromer arrived to lay the foundation stone of Gordon Memorial College on 4 January 1899 on behalf of Queen Victoria. A fortnight later the Convention was signed which created, by right of conquest, the Anglo-Egyptian Sudan, a condominium that was neither British nor Egyptian but in effect a trusteeship, new to international law. By creating a new state, Salisbury and Cromer prevented interference by the Commissioners of the Egyptian Debt, or by the legal privileges of foreign nationals.[5]

Kitchener was appointed first governor-general, remaining Sirdar of the Egyptian Army.

Cromer told the Sudanese notables to look neither to the khedive nor to himself but to Kitchener alone. Cromer, however, had intended Kitchener to be his henchman, not to spend more than £100 without his authority. Kitchener refused and Salisbury supported him, but by the terms of the Convention his position was subordinate to the Agent-General in Cairo, even as the Viceroy of India, for all his grandeur, was subordinate to the Secretary of State for India in London.

Cromer did not understand Kitchener any more than he had understood Gordon. He gave the Sirdar all credits for the reconquest, was deeply touched by his sensitive visit of condolence on the death of Lady Cromer and assured him: 'You will always find in me a true friend.'[6] But with his formal instruc-tions he wrote privately: 'Pray encourage your subordinates to speak up and to tell you when they do not agree with you. They are all far too much inclined to be frightened of you.'[7] Cromer evidently had never heard that during the campaign the Sirdar had lived with his staff rather than apart with his ADCs and had encouraged discussion when in the mood. Girouard's cheek, Watson's stories and laughter, Rawlinson's frankness were beyond Cromer's comprehension. Possibly he had listened to disgruntled or rejected officers from the fringe.

He thought 'My Sirdar terribly bureaucratic' when in fact Kitchener still considered regulations to be for the guidance of fools. Cromer decided that the Sirdar could not see the difference between governing a country and com-manding a regiment, whereas the War Office would have nervously removed any colonel who gave such free scope to his officers. Scattered across the vast country, they were already doing their unfettered best to bring peace and prosperity, settle land claims, reopen caravan and river routes and restore the rule of law. As Kitchener told the Queen on 21 January: 'The administration of the country is gradually being formed and I hope before long we may get affairs into some order.'[8]

All was still 'hand to mouth', as one of his officers put it, 'and every paper that is not absolutely urgent gets chucked aside to be dealt with later. There are only two typewriting machines with the whole force here . . . The office accommodation is inferior in every way . . . One is besieged by petitioners at every turn.'[9] When the Sirdar was absent from Omdurman, 'all is in chaos', wrote the officer he left in charge at Omdurman. 'He bottles up all reports etc. I am acting for him here but know nothing of the irons he had in the fire.'[10] Kitchener, however, rejected Cromer's charge of secretiveness, telling Wingate in Cairo that everything of consequence was telegraphed down: Cromer must be imagining things that had not occurred.[11]

The Sirdar and Jimmy Watson had left Omdurman in the gunboat *Dal* with a small escort to sail up the Blue Nile to inspect garrisons. They took a medical officer, J. W. Jennings, DSO, to advise on the health of the troops and their newly built barracks. They watched crocodiles and hippos, were grounded on a sandbank for nearly an hour and found the inhabitants every-where 'well disposed and very glad to see us'.[12]

During this voyage Kitchener completed a memorandum or directive to governors of the provinces and their district inspectors all of whom were British officers of the Egyptian Army, with Egyptian and some Sudanese officers under them. He issued it on his return to Omdurman. He thus stamped his ideals and personality on the new nation. Long after he had left, and indeed for all the fifty-five years of the Anglo-Egyptian Sudan until inde-pendence, this directive was the inspiration of those who governed. It also throws light on his own character.

Pointing out that the uprooting by the dervishes of the old system of government had given an opportunity for a new administration 'more in harmony with the requirements of the Sudan', he emphasized that it was not mainly to the laws and regulations which would be framed and published that 'we must look for the improvement and the good government of the country. The task before us all, and especially the Mudirs and Inspectors is to acquire the confidence of the people, to develop their resources, and to raise them to a higher level.'

The officers could do this only by being thoroughly in touch and knowing personally the principal men of their districts, showing them by friendly deal- ings and interest in their individual concerns 'that our object is to increase their prosperity'. Through them they would influence the whole population. He went on: 'Once it is thoroughly realised that our officers have at heart, not only the progress of the country generally, but also the prosperity of each individ- ual with whom they come into contact, their exhortations to industry and improvement will gain redoubled force.' Proclamations and circulars would have little effect. 'It is to the individual action of British officers, working inde- pendently but with a common purpose, on the individual natives whose con- fidence they have gained that we must look for the moral and industrial regeneration of the Sudan.'

His next point emphasized that 'truth is always expected' and must be well received whether pleasant or not. Behind his words lay the memory of working alone among the Arabs when Gordon was cut off in Khartoum, and the difficulty of learning the truth: 'By listening to outspoken opinions, when respectfully expressed, and checking liars and flatterers, we may hope in time to effect some improvement in this respect in the country.'

He next directed that the courts of law should inspire the people 'with absolute confidence that real justice is being meted out to them'. The administration should be strong, with no signs of weakness, and 'insubordi- nation' promptly and severely repressed; but 'a paternal spirit of correction for offences should be your aim', with clemency.

Kitchener's later points directed that religious feelings were not in any way to be interfered with and the Muhammadan religion respected. Town mosques would be rebuilt, but private mosques, shrines or other possible centres of fanaticism were not to be allowed. He said nothing about the pagan south where the animist tribes welcomed him as a liberator from Muslim tyranny and slave-trading, but he affirmed that 'Slavery is not recognized in the Sudan'. Willing service would not be investigated, but cruelty, or interference with liberty, would be sentenced severely.

The memorandum continued for several more pages of detailed instructions to mudirs (governors), inspectors (district officers) and mamurs (their
subordinates). Kitchener, from the recesses of his own deepest beliefs and
experiences, set forth the Victorian imperial tradition at its highest: a firm
paternal hand for the benefit of the ruled, not the rulers. All Sudanese would
'feel that an era of justice and kindly treatment has begun', in contrast to the
dervish rule that 'plundered and enslaved'.[13]

The country could not be fully pacified, nor hope to be prosperous, until the
Khalifa was captured or killed. Walter returned in February empty-handed.
His letter reporting failure had crossed one from Herbert ordering him to
abandon the chase and bring back his Kordofan Field Force. To his intense
humiliation, Walter had found the Khalifa reinforced and about to surround
him in a waterless desert. A battle would end in disaster: 'I don't believe that
one of us would have got away if I had stayed another hour where I was.'[14]
Had Walter been wiped out, Herbert would need to suppress a rising in
Kordofan. Herbert and Cromer both assured Walter that they approved of his
retreat.

In mid-February the Khalifa was reported to be advancing on Khartoum
just when the Duke of Connaught, Kitchener's Woolwich contemporary,
Prince Arthur, now a distinguished general, was making a holiday visit with
his duchess, the only visitors whom the Sirdar allowed up. They rode around
the Omdurman battlefield, still offensive to sight and smell, saw the staircase
where Gordon had fallen, took tea in Gordon's garden and the duke
inspected a parade of nine thousand Egyptian and Sudanese troops, many of
whom were recruits filling the vacancies caused by disease. They were
scarcely ready to fight. The apparent (but false) danger from the Khalifa
made an excuse to bundle the Connaughts downriver after twenty-four
hours.[15]

During these early months the problems fell one after another, and though
outwardly impassive, as always, Kitchener could be depressed. After another
nagging letter from Cromer he wrote to Wingate, who was stationed in Cairo,
to send up supplies and manpower:

> I am rather sick and low so I will not bother you. I can quite see there is no
> confidence in my work.
>
> I have been bothered out of my life about this refugee question, everyone

asking what they are to do with these destitute individuals. They have nothing here to live on except charity, and grain is very dear and scarce.[16]

He wired to Cromer that he had 20,000 jabbering women and no use for them.

Another bother arose from religion. The Austrian Roman Catholic fathers had returned from Egypt to restart their school. The surviving Copts and Greeks had their clergy, but the Anglican bishop in Jerusalem, Blyth, was already pressing for a suffragan bishopric in Khartoum, although, as Cromer remarked, providing means for the confirmation of naked Shilluk savages from the south 'seems to me a little premature'.[17]

Then the military railway at last reached 'Khartoum North', its intended terminus on the opposite bank of the Nile, and out stepped a Nottinghamshire vicar who had been selected by the Church Missionary Society as their first representative in the new Sudan, Llewellyn Gwynne. Although he never knew it he was a distant cousin of General Gordon. In his thirties, he had somehow slipped through the Sirdar's restriction on visitors and Bishop Blyth's dislike of the CMS.

He was soon summoned by the Sirdar, now using an office on the ground floor of the rebuilding palace, approached across planks and debris. Gwynne asked when he could start his missionary work. Lord Kitchener replied that no such work might start: the Egyptians had spread a rumour that the British had reconquered the Sudan in order to convert Muhammadans to Christianity. The rumour had 'greatly disturbed the people and the new government must do all in its power to reassure them'. Gwynne explained that he wanted to work only among the pagan or animist tribes in the south. Kitchener said he was inclined to approve, once the south had been fully brought under administrative control. Even then, Lord Cromer wanted to discourage proselytizing which might offend Muhammadans: the Indian Mutiny had been sparked by similar false rumours.

'What harm can I do?' asked Gwynne. 'I can't stir up any trouble among the natives as I don't know any Arabic.'

'I know your sort,' replied Kitchener. 'You'll soon pick up enough Arabic to make yourself understood. What you can do, is to look after the spiritual needs of the British officers and non-commissioned officers attached to the Egyptian Army in various parts of the Sudan; there are plenty of heathen among them!'[18] Kitchener knew them well and if a sergeant or corporal were leaving the Sudan in broken health he might well be summoned by the Sirdar and depart with a fistful of Egyptian pound coins or English sovereigns, given with muttered remarks as if the Sirdar's left hand must not know what his right hand had done.[19]

Gwynne left the palace to begin a notable chaplaincy, continued alongside an even more notable missionary and episcopal ministry. Kitchener's appreciation led him, sixteen years later, to put Bishop Gwynne in command of all the British chaplains on the Western Front.

A missionary could be disposed of quickly. Far more worrying was the Sudan's financial dependence on Cairo until the country's revenue and production should flow strongly. The new financial adviser to the khedive and holder of the purse strings of Egypt was the thirty-eight-year-old Eldon Gorst who had been his predecessor's deputy, much trusted by Cromer but soon loathed by Kitchener. 'Gorst', exclaimed Kitchener to Wingate, 'is the meanest little brute I ever met, professes all sorts of help and then leaves you in the lurch. We will have as little as we can to do with him. Am very sorry Cromer backs him up as he is not and never has been straight.' Kitchener claimed that Gorst 'bagged' revenues from Dongola and the railways and the posts but never gave anything back. He tinkered with Egyptian army allowances, which did great harm, yet accused the Sirdar of diverting some of the army's pay to other purposes. Kitchener became exasperated with 'that little creature Gorst', as he called him in one furious letter to Wingate. Gorst and his people were leaving officers and men homeless and suffering while taking Sudanese money 'in their comfortable offices in Cairo. To my mind it is quite a scandal' which needed a question in the House of Commons. 'The troops did good service and this is all the consideration we get – just what one would expect from Damned mean civilians. *Yours disgustedly, K of K.*'[20]

Kitchener was working fourteen hours a day, wrestling not least with the famine conditions that were blighting the Omdurman region and up both the Blue and the White Nile. The root cause lay in the later Mahdist years, when many grain-growing areas reverted to scrub, but failure to finish off the Khalifa made shortages worse. Kitchener called a meeting of the leading merchants. When he stood up to speak, 'he pronounced Arabic as we pronounce it and understood it as we understand it'. He allowed a sharp discussion. Merchants complained that camels and boats which had brought grain had been requisitioned to bring building materials. When the youngest merchant asserted that the government had cornered the market, His Excellency 'thrust his hands behind his back and came quickly towards me until he stood in front of me and bent his head down a little to bring him face to face with me (for he was tall and I was short) and he said, "Is it the Government that is cornering the grain?"

'"Yes," I replied.

'"How so?" he asked.'

Babikr Bedi gave his reasons. The Sirdar shot back a question, then he announced that from that day the government would buy corn only from contractors appointed by the merchants. He also put a proposition that big foreign merchants should not be allowed to live in the Sudan: they could invest money and send goods, and the Sudanese would act as their agents, thus pursuing Kitchener's unfashionable aim that the country should be for its inhabitants, not for foreign exploiters. But the merchants disagreed. 'Uncle' Ibrahim Bey Kalil, in whose garden Gordon used to relax, who had survived the loss of all his property under the Khalifa, cried out, 'No, no, your Lordship! Better that the great mercantile houses come to us with their owners to work alongside us and we shall benefit from them.' After discussion Lord Kitchener said: 'As you will.'[21]

Kitchener would not allow private traders to travel to the south while it was still a region of military operations, yet no further expedition could be made against the Khalifa during the summer heat. Cromer thought this policy wrong, and a cause of the famine. When Kitchener came to see him in Cairo in late May, Cromer begged him to remember that he was a Christian ruler dealing with human beings, not blocks of wood. Kitchener resented the implication. Trade in the south would fall into the Khalifa's hands without ending the famine, which at least deprived him of local support. It also provided the government with cheap labour for all needs at Khartoum and Omdurman. Once again Cromer could not comprehend that Kitchener refused to allow sentiment to impede the Sudan's future. Cromer even told Salisbury (without explaining the context) that Kitchener had become 'especially bored with his own creation – the Gordon College – at which I am not at all surprised'.[22] College affairs were in limbo until the building was up, the staff formed and the first boy selected: towns such as Berber wanted to enrol far more than could be taken. Whatever had prompted Cromer's curious conclusion, it did an injustice to Kitchener, for whom the college was an intense and abiding interest to the end.

Kitchener left Cromer and Cairo for his summer's leave in England, saying he needed rest and 'had had about enough of the Sudan';[23] he even talked of service in India. Yet his mind was full of ideas for the Sudan; part of his purpose in going home was to select men who would meet his ideal.

He left a Sudan which was much like Khartoum itself at that moment: an excellent plan, much rubble, but some fine structures emerging.

PART THREE

Fighting for Peace

1900–1902

21

BOBS AND K

ON A SUMMER morning of 1899 at Taplow Court on the Thames, the eleven-year-old Julian Grenfell, home for the holidays from Summerfields Preparatory School, had got up long before breakfast

and on going downstairs found a gentleman whom I did not know at all. He asked me to come for a walk, and we went for over an hour. He found out that I was to be a soldier, and asked me what regiment I was going in for, and how I was getting on at school, and a great many other questions; he told me a great many things about the army, and yet he never mentioned himself at all, and I had not the least idea who he was. I enjoyed the walk very much indeed, and when afterwards I was told who he was I was not at all surprised.

Lord Kitchener had arrived late the evening before to stay with his friends, Willie and Etty Grenfell (later Lord and Lady Desborough). 'When I come here I feel like coming home. I have no home.'

Julian, who grew up to be a supreme athlete like his father and to be killed in action, with posthumous fame for his poem 'Into Battle', was writing down his memory three years later when at Eton. He continued about his new friend:

It was easy to see that he was no civilian; he looked a soldier from head to foot, and there was something about his manner that showed that he was no ordinary man, and yet he said nothing about himself or his own doings.

He spoke in a way that showed he meant what he said, and it was easy to see that he was used to being obeyed. I think that on seeing him for the first time one would feel an impulse to say 'That is a man who would never leave what he had once resolved upon till he finished it to his satisfaction.' I should think it would be impossible to find features on which self-restraint and tremendous will are more clearly marked.[1]

Kitchener was on a round of country-house visits, having gone first to Hatfield as usual. He specially enjoyed Welbeck, home of the Duke and Duchess of Portland, 'quite a wonderful place and everything so perfectly arranged'. He also crossed over to Ireland. While in Ulster he stayed at Mount Stewart with the Marquess of Londonderry, immensely rich from landown-ership and from Durham coal royalties, a former viceroy of Ireland and soon to join Salisbury's Cabinet.

This visit produces a mystery. The Londonderrys' elder son was away serving with the Household Cavalry but their younger son, nineteen-year-old Lord Charles, lay seriously ill. Kitchener's kindness to the boy and sympathy with his only sister, Lady Helen Vane-Tempest-Stewart, then aged twenty-three, led to a friendship. After he had left Mount Stewart she wrote to say that Charles was better. Kitchener in his reply from the Curragh Camp near Dublin wrote: 'I know how anxious you are about him.'[2] Charles died that October after Kitchener had returned to the Sudan. The correspondence con-tinued. He destroyed her letters with the rest of his private correspondence, but she kept his. They read like the letters of a kindly uncle (he was more than twice her age), not of a lover, but two years later, in September 1901, the future Queen Mary's aunt, Augusta, a Grand Duchess in Germany, remarked in the course of their regular correspondence: 'There is a story that Lord Kitchener, wanting to become fashionable, proposed to Lady H. St. Vane (*sic*) and was refused. I can't believe it . . .'[3]

One month after the Grand Duchess wrote, Lady Helen became engaged to young Lord Stavordale, future Earl of Ilchester and a noted historian, land-owner and patron of the arts. Kitchener in South Africa wished her 'every joy and though rather filled with envy of the lucky one I hope when I get home I may have the pleasure of seeing you again'.[4] The correspondence stopped.

If Kitchener had vague thoughts of founding a dynasty, the only daughter of a rich Tory nobleman would have been a suitable match. But the previous year one of his staff officers in South Africa, William Birdwood, had written to his wife: 'I don't think he will ever marry. I spoke to him about it one day and asked him when he was going to think of it! "Marry," he said, "Why I have never had time to think of it. I've always been too busy in Egypt and at work generally." I think', commented Birdwood, 'he would look on it as a sort of campaign which he regularly had to undertake and would require so many months set aside for hard work to get through it successfully!'[5]

Long after Kitchener's death the myth arose that he was homosexual. A new generation found it hard to believe that any male could be fulfilled unless sexually active. Because Kitchener never married and was affectionate towards his young personal staff officers (who all except one married later), he was retrospectively labelled homosexual regardless of evidence to the contrary, including the absence of any substantive rumours in his lifetime, although in the Sudan 'everything is known',[6] as Kitchener himself remarked.*

Any thoughts of matrimony would have faded because war clouds were gathering in South Africa. Apart from possible comments at Hatfield, Kitchener knew no more about the causes than any newspaper reader, but by that summer of 1899 two masterful men were on a collision course: Paul Kruger, President of the South African Republic (the Transvaal) and Sir Alfred Milner, the new High Commissioner for British South Africa and Governor of Cape Colony. When the Boer (Afrikaner) republics of the Transvaal and the Orange Free State had repudiated annexation and defeated a British force at Majuba in 1881, a convention was signed which left vague the question of suzerainty. The discovery of gold in the Transvaal in 1884, and the earlier discovery of diamonds in the Orange Free State, had transformed their economies and had brought in many Britons and Continentals, whom the Boers termed Uitlanders, and large numbers of Africans to work the mines. The mining companies and the Uitlanders were taxed but allowed no representation in the Volksraads, a grievance which had led to the disastrous Jameson Raid in 1896 when, backed by Cecil Rhodes and secretly by Joseph Chamberlain, the British Colonial Secretary, a scratch force of British and foreign volunteers led by Leander Starr Jameson attempted to invade the Transvaal and raise rebellion.

The Kaiser's telegram of congratulation to Kruger on their capture, and the increasing wealth from the mining taxes strengthened Kruger's vision of a

* Kitchener's sexual orientation is discussed at more length in Appendix 1.

South Africa entirely under Boer control. He imported arms. Milner's vision was for a South Africa wholly under the British flag.

Public opinion in Britain supported Milner and particularly deplored the harshness of Boer treatment of native Africans and the injustice inflicted on the heavily taxed Uitlanders. But a small and vocal group in Britain, the 'pro-Boers', saw Kruger and his burghers as brave rural farmers bullied by the British Empire.

Milner and Kruger conferred at Bloemfontein in June 1899 but found no compromise. Every sign pointed to war — a white man's war. Until its last months the dispossessed natives would be only the helots of the warriors. Boer and Briton alike would have been astounded that less than a century later the African majority would rule South Africa.[7]

As war looked more likely, Kitchener wanted to run it; indeed, when the editor of the Liberal *Westminster Gazette*, J. A. Spender, met him on the lawn at Lord Rosebery's house near Epsom that June, and Kitchener expounded his plan of campaign, 'It was perfectly clear that he both hoped and expected to have the conduct of the coming war. I remember being struck by the extreme frankness of this talk in the presence of a chance comer whom he was seeing for the first time.'[8]

Unknown to Kitchener, Queen Victoria pressed Lord Salisbury to name him 'to command the whole expedition', as she reminded the Prime Minister when disasters struck, 'but she was not listened to'. (Lord Salisbury tactfully replied that he had no recollection of being told of her recommendation.)[9] Sir Redvers Buller, much the senior, with considerable South African experience but defects of character which Kitchener had experienced in the Gordon Relief Expedition, was selected to lead the strong force to be sent should war look inevitable. Many, including Kitchener's former staff officer Rawlinson, believed that Buller would fail to win the swift victory expected by the public and that Lord Roberts, the greatest soldier of the day, would be sent for. Kitchener, eleven years younger, and Roberts had served in different conti-nents and did not know each other, for Roberts was commanding in Ireland when the Sirdar had returned briefly after Omdurman. Rawlinson, who had worked closely with both, brought them together in Dublin, where they reached an informal understanding that if Roberts were sent out to South Africa he would ask for Kitchener as second-in-command and chief staff officer.

Before he returned to the Sudan, the Sirdar received a charming commission from the Queen. He had already sat for von Angeli for the portrait she wanted, and now she asked whether, on his return to Egypt, 'he would be so kind as to procure a white female donkey for her'. Wolseley had sent a big and handsome male in 1882, named rather naughtily Tewfik after the khedive, which had sired several fine white donkeys, and now she would like an Egyptian female. The Sirdar obliged, and the Queen duly wrote that 'the donkey is in perfect health, having borne the long sea voyage very well. She is a remarkably big one and very handsome', and soon was gently pulling the Queen in her garden chair along the paths of Osborne.[10]

While the donkey was at sea the Sirdar resumed the government of the Sudan. Many of his River War officers had now left the Egyptian Army – for South Africa or India, including Hunter, MacDonald, Smith-Dorrien and Walter. Jimmy Watson, for his career's sake, had regretfully left Kitchener's side to be military secretary in Cairo.

The new state showed progress. In Khartoum Gordon College was going up, streets had been laid out, a hotel and two banks had opened, but the palace was still unfinished. At the Atbara the permanent bridge had been built in nine months. The Sirdar drove the last rivet, then steamed across the bridge in one of their biggest engines, breaking a silk rope while the troops fired a *feu de joie* and bands played. His Excellency had to make a speech.[11]

These last months in the Sudan were dominated by the need to hunt down the Khalifa. His followers were deserting, but he would not surrender. Kitchener led a hunt in Kordofan across open country where deer, giraffe and ostriches seemed tame, then into forest, where Khalifa eluded Sirdar. Late in October the Sirdar left the hunt to settle financial questions in Cairo. The dis-cussions went very smoothly, Kitchener told Lady Cranborne in one of his regular letters for the Hatfield circle. Lord Cromer was very nice and happy 'and gives me no trouble at all, such a blessing when one has one's hands full'.[12]

Kitchener cut short his time in Cairo and hurried south. To strengthen the prestige of Sir Reginald Wingate, whom he was determined should succeed him as governor-general, he placed the final operation in his hands. On 24 November, at the battle of Um Dibaykarat, the Khalifa was brought to bay and when all was lost died gamely, sitting with his lieutenants on their sheep-skins, facing Mecca: Queen Victoria admired the manner of his death, 'grand and fine'.[13]

By then the Boers had invaded Natal, and Buller had arrived with his army. Not knowing how the war would develop, Kitchener had asked the Cecils to lobby the War Office for a command. But in December Reuter's daily wire service brought to Khartoum the news of 'Black Week', one severe British reverse after another.

On 18 December a cypher telegram carried the call that Kitchener had expected since Black Week: Lord Roberts was appointed Commander-in-Chief and about to sail from Southampton. Kitchener was ordered to join him at Gibraltar..

'I had to get off sharp and travel fast to catch him at Gib', he told Lady Helen. 'I reached there in just a week from Khartoum and five hours before Lord Roberts arrived.'[14] At Cairo he was met by Jimmy Watson, released from his hated headquarters desk by a wire from the Sirdar who appointed him ADC again.

They sailed from Alexandria in the cruiser HMS *Isis* at midnight on 21 December and reached Malta through very heavy weather on Christmas Eve, continuing on Christmas Day, 'a fine bright day', in the faster HMS *Dido*. They arrived in pouring rain at Gibraltar on 26 December.[15] The liner *Dunottar Castle* put in at midnight carrying Roberts with various generals and colonels, including Percy Girouard to take over the railways.

The little sixty-seven-year-old field marshal and the tall forty-nine-year-old major-general had met only once, at their discussion in Ireland, but despite very different characters they bonded swiftly, helped by mutual grief for the valiant death, winning the VC by saving the guns at Colenso, of Freddy Roberts. Kitchener's affection and admiration for his former ADC touched Roberts, desolated by the death of his only son.

Among the letters that Roberts brought out for Kitchener was advice from an elderly Royal Engineer retired general, Sir John Stokes, whom he had known in Egypt. 'You have many well wishers in your old Corps', wrote Stokes, 'but there are probably not a few in the Army generally who are not so well disposed'. Stokes pointed out in a rambling way 'the danger when men who have held almost autocratic positions' are transferred to a staff appointment where they must subordinate themselves to the orders of another. 'In your case there is no question of reputation – that is made. Rather your reputation stands in your way: some of it by your very personality may be the anticipatory cause of friction'.[16]

Stokes's fears were groundless. Kitchener allowed no friction: Roberts was one of the very few senior officers he admired without reservation. As the

Dunottar Castle speeded south, the white hair and heavy white moustache of the one and the brown hair and famous moustache of the other were frequently seen bent over maps and papers as Roberts unfolded his plan to turn the tide of war. Kitchener wrote to Lady Helen while the ship lay briefly at Madeira:

> We shall have a pretty hard time to get things right at the Cape, as it seems things have got a good deal mixed up but Ld Roberts is the right man and when we have got things square I hope we shall be able to show the Boers a somewhat different war game to that they have been having lately.[17]

Soon after they had landed at Cape Town on 10 January 1900 there was a little incident that lights up the contrast in character. A newly arrived battalion, still on board ship, learned that they were to disembark and entrain for the front, and that Lord Roberts and Lord Kitchener would inspect them very soon on the quay. A young volunteer officer formed up his troop in time, only to realize that he had left his gloves and stick on deck. As he rushed back up the gangway his helmet fell into the slimy water, to be retrieved by a ship's cook with a marlin spike which made a hole in the crown. He shoved the dripping helmet on his head and stood rigidly at attention at the front of his men, ignoring sniggers from behind.

> The C-in-C was going through the inspection as quickly as possible, and walked down the ranks without comment until he came opposite me; then he stopped and a crinkle crept round his eyes as he said: 'Ah, I see you have been in the wars already, Sir,' and he passed on. I remember Lord Kitchener's face: it was perfectly expressionless; not so, however, the face of the Colonel and our Adjutant, both of whom I thought were going to have fits.[18]

Roberts and Kitchener spent nearly a month at the Cape laying the foundations of the new strategy. Instead of a three-pronged advance on the Boer heartlands, Roberts concentrated all available forces for a single thrust to the north, aiming to defeat General Cronje's invasion of Cape Colony, relieve Kimberley which De Wet besieged, and then move across swiftly to capture the Orange Free State capital, Bloemfontein.

Until Roberts's arrival in South Africa the British had mostly used infantry and thus were confined to the neighbourhood of railway lines. Roberts turned several battalions into mounted infantry to make them more mobile (when they had learned to ride) and raised two regiments of irregular horse – Roberts's Horse and Kitchener's Horse – from the sons of Cape farmers, born to the saddle, Uitlanders exiled from the Rand, and the young men flocking in from Canada, Australia and New Zealand, including Millie's second son, James Parker, aged twenty-six. He joined Kitchener's Horse and was killed in action three months later.

Roberts also changed the time-honoured system in which each regiment had its own transport of horse- and ox-drawn vehicles (motor cars had not yet been seen in South Africa) which he considered wasteful, and put them all together to be used where required. Kitchener carried through Roberts's reform with enthusiasm and took the blame when the new transport system, at first a major element of success, proved later to be unworkable and earned him a title among indignant colonels: K of Chaos.

Kitchener harried and pushed and rode roughshod over feelings and objections. Whereas the great German general von Moltke thought the organization of Kitchener's Nile expedition the finest in recent military history,[19] Kitchener thought the War Office's organization for South Africa so poor, and rent by petty jealousies and refusals, that 'if we had worked the Sudan campaign like this we should never have reached Dongola – most of us would be in prison at Omdurman or dead by now! Lord Roberts is splendid.'[20]

Roberts and Kitchener left Cape Town incognito on 6 February 1900. Two days later they arrived at Modder Camp, 600 miles north, where 37,000 men, 12,000 horses and 22,000 transport animals had been concentrated secretly. Roberts then took Cronje by surprise with a swift flanking movement away from the railway in broiling late summer heat. By 15 February French had relieved Kimberley, and Cronje lay trapped on the banks of the Modder river. Roberts fell ill with a severe chill. Kitchener had the future of the war in his hands.

22

THE BATTLE
THAT WENT WRONG

THE MODDER RIVER flowed strongly below sloping banks. The surrounding hilly veldt was treeless. Close to the river grew mimosa trees and scrub. Cronje's laager of four thousand men, with guns and carts, women and some children, lay in a confined space at a drift (ford) east of the small town of Paardeberg and plainly visible from the higher ground. In high summer the fast-flowing river did not cover its sandy flood plain, so Cronje, unknown to Kitchener, had dug a trench system with clear views of the veldt: he even had made a two-mile-long communication trench for his burghers to move, out of sight, from one strongpoint to another. He had placed sharpshooters in the outer scrub but was short of ammunition because Kitchener had caught many of his wagons (sending back to Roberts 'a bottle of Cronje's best champagne' with the list of captured equipment).[1]

By dawn on Sunday 18 February 1900, two of Roberts's infantry divisions with a brigade of mounted infantry, totalling some 15,000 men, were investing Cronje's laager, while to the north-west stood Major-General John French's cavalry and guns. They had ridden back hard after relieving Kimberley, and their horses were exhausted: French could stop Cronje escaping but could not take part in an assault. The senior divisional commander was a tall Catholic bachelor Irishman Thomas Kelly-Kenny, ten years older than Kitchener. As he held the local rank of lieutenant-general he had assumed he would command in Roberts's absence since Kitchener was only a major-general.[2] He was therefore not pleased when handed a note from Roberts: 'Please consider that Lord Kitchener is with you for the purpose of communicating to you my orders',[3] especially as Kitchener made plain that Roberts had given him a free hand to conduct the battle. Kitchener's plan was to assault the laager, whereas Kelly-Kenny had intended to invest, bombard and starve it.

Kitchener knew that speed was essential before Cronje could break out or be relieved. He therefore planned for simultaneous assaults from all directions, both sides of the river, after a sharp bombardment. He may have expected (although he never mentioned the comparison) a repeat of the battle of the Atbara – an overwhelming advance on a battered enemy in a confined space beside a river, some grievous casualties followed by swift and total victory. He would have been wise to recall the words of Queen Victoria in her letter of good wishes and 'great confidence' when he was appointed: 'It must however be borne in mind', the little old lady told her famous general, 'that this is a very different kind of warfare to the Indian and Egyptian. The Boers are a horrid brutal people, but are skilled in European fighting and well armed.'[4]

Kitchener stood on a well-defended kopje, soon to be known as Kitchener's Kopje, looking down at the Modder river. His divisional and brigade commanders had precise orders, and Kitchener had impressed on Colonel O. C. Hannay, commanding the Mounted Infantry, his key role: to cross the Modder upstream, creep up as close to the laager as possible and rush it, supported by T. E. Stephenson's 18th Brigade from the other side of the river, while MacDonald and Smith-Dorrien, veterans of the River War, put in an attack from the opposite direction.

Kitchener took out his watch and said to Jimmy Watson: 'It is now seven o'clock. We shall be in the laager by half past ten.'[5]

The guns opened. Soon he could see Cronje's carts and tents in flames. Then the divisions advanced across the open veldt. Kitchener sent a heliograph message to Roberts: 'It must be complete surrender.'

But everything started to go wrong. As the British lines advanced, man after man dropped, hit by accurate fire from smokeless rifles. Kitchener saw the converging divisions, one after another, falter then stop, and because Roberts had given him no proper staff he was unable to co-ordinate the battle quickly as the situation changed. Half-past ten passed and the advance had become hardly a crawl. The river ran tantalizingly fresh a few hundred yards away, but accurate Boer fire denied it to men who were lying or moving in the hot summer sun, their thirst maddening, the Highlanders' kilted legs roasting (MacDonald had urged some days before that the kilt should be replaced by trews).[6]

Then Stephenson and Hannay, on the northern flank, suddenly turned their men away from the direction of the laager: Boer snipers, approaching the battlefield from elsewhere undetected, were causing havoc. Kitchener sent furious messages, believing that these casualties should be accepted and nothing should impede the main advance. But the impetus was lost.

At about half-past one he rode down from Kitchener's Kopje to regroup the divisions and inch them forward. An hour later a staff officer (whether acting on a direct order or believing that he interpreted Kitchener's wishes is uncertain) withdrew the experienced troops on the kopje and sent them to reinforce the crippled advance below. He replaced them by men of Kitchener's Horse, untried in battle, to hold the most important feature of the field, which Kelly-Kenny had recognized as the key to victory, even if Kitchener did not.

All that dreadful Sunday afternoon under the blazing sun the casualties mounted on both sides. The British suffered more dead and wounded in that one battle of Paardeberg than in any single action of the South African war, and more than the combined Anglo-Egyptian losses of the entire River War.[7]

While the battle continued below, still undecided, with gallant charges which pushed back the Boers but could not reach the laager, a disaster occurred on Kitchener's Kopje at about five o'clock. De Wet, having abandoned his siege of Kimberley when French broke through, had ridden hard with three hundred men and several guns to aid Cronje. Undetected, he had crossed the Modder river higher up and galloped behind the British and up to the kopje, surprising the inexperienced young troops, who put up a poor fight and then surrendered. De Wet seized the whole south-west ridge and trained his guns. The first shells fell on the hospital tents, causing panic and misery to the wounded and seriously endangering the morale of Kelly-Kenny, who was about to visit them but never did.

With darkness nor far away, Kitchener believed that one more co-ordinated attack would overwhelm the laager despite De Wet's attack on his rear. If more soldiers were killed and wounded, the price must be paid. Kitchener was not reckless with lives, hence the low casualty rate in the River War, but he would not allow sentiment or harrowing sights to deflect duty.

He sent a strong message to Hannay:

The time has come for a final effort. All troops have been warned that the laager must be rushed at all costs. Try and carry Stephenson's brigade on with you. But if they cannot go the mounted infantry should do it. Gallop up if necessary and fire into the laager.[8]

Some said afterwards that this message to Hannay was dishonest because all troops had not been warned; but in the fog and din of war Kitchener may have believed that his intention had been conveyed, or he may have meant that the order to rush the laager had been in force since morning, although Kelly-Kenny had refused to renew the attack. Hannay took the message as a reflection on his courage and honour. He made no attempt to co-ordinate with Stephenson's brigade but collected some fifty men and rushed forward in the spirit of the charge of the Light Brigade, to die under a hail of bullets.

Night fell and the battle died down, with Cronje unable to escape but Kitchener frustrated. He determined to renew the attack on Cronje the next morning despite failing to dislodge De Wet from the south-west ridge. At ten o'clock on the Monday morning Roberts arrived, recovered from his chill, and resumed command. His first instinct was to agree with Kitchener, but Cronje sent a white flag and asked for an armistice to bury his dead. He also wanted British doctors to treat his wounded. Roberts refused, and Cronje politely breathed defiance. Much of Monday passed in negotiation. On Tuesday evening Jimmy Watson recorded laconically: 'Situation unchanged and not very pleasant.'[9] Roberts had wanted to renew the assault but first called a council of war. Kitchener pressed for assault. Smith-Dorrien urged they remain quietly in their lines until Cronje surrendered. Roberts accepted Smith-Dorrien's advice, to Kitchener's dismay. As Smith-Dorrien was mounting his horse, before Roberts had issued any orders to confirm his decision, Kitchener went up to him 'saying that if I would attack them at once I would be a made man'. Smith-Dorrien smiled and replied that Kitchener knew his views and that he would attack only if ordered.

By Wednesday morning De Wet's rifle and gunfire from the kopje and ridge and the continued failure to dislodge him had so affected Roberts that in confidential discussion with Kelly-Kenny he contemplated withdrawal, a move that would have been disastrous. That afternoon the cavalry under Brigadier-General Broadwood, another River War veteran, with Watson at his side,[10] drove De Wet from the kopje, although some claimed afterwards that De Wet was already evacuating the position by his own decision. Roberts dropped all thought of retirement and settled down to starve Cronje into surrender.

Roberts's mind was now on capturing the Free State capital, Bloemfontein, by swift moves afterwards. He needed the co-ordination of his columns operating to the east, and the opening of the railway line. He ordered Kitchener to ride across country to ensure this, and he left the battlefield with Watson at half-past four on the afternoon of Thursday. He was not therefore present the following Tuesday (the nineteenth anniversary of the Boer victory at Majuba) when Cronje surrendered to Roberts and went into captivity with four thousand fighting men, the first great British victory of the war.

By then the Modder river had become so polluted by dead horses and oxen and the filth of the siege, yet so tempting to thirsty British soldiers, that it was the direct cause of a serious outbreak of enteric fever which claimed more British lives in the weeks to come than would have been lost had Roberts renewed the assault at once.

Kitchener was heavily and justly criticized (except by Roberts) for his tactics and handling of the battle of Paardeberg, but his instinct was sound.

During the next three months, as the hot summer turned to the South African autumn, Roberts used Kitchener more as second-in-command than Chief of Staff. He sent him wherever trouble arose, such as the rising of the Cape Dutch which might have grown into a dangerous rebellion had not Kitchener crushed it by a sledgehammer blow after riding with mounted troops forty miles in one day.

Kitchener would have preferred a cut-and-dried campaign like his advance on Omdurman. The flavour of the war is well caught by a letter that Kitchener wrote to the Grenfell boys, Julian and Billy, during Roberts's advance on Pretoria, in reply to theirs

> . . . which caught me up on the march here, and I read them while our guns were pounding away at the Boers, who were sitting on some hills trying to prevent our advance. However, they soon cleared out, and ran before we could get round them. I wish we could have caught some of their guns, but they are remarkably quick at getting them away, and we have only been able to take one Maxim up to the present.
>
> Sooner or later we are bound to catch them, but they may give a lot of trouble. The Boers are not like the Soudanese who stood up for a fair fight, they are always running away on their little ponies. We make the prisoners we take march on foot, which they do not like at all . . .[11]

Actions often had to be fought far from the main line of advance. Boers could be effective soldiers one day and apparently innocent farmers the next. Writing regularly to the Queen, Kitchener told her of British troops being fired on by Boers holding up white flags. 'On one occasion they put the white flag up over some farm buildings and when a squadron rode up they fired on them at close range. It is very sad but it is a good deal the fault of our men for not taking proper precautions.'[12] Sometimes he was discouraged by casualties and deaths from enteric and other setbacks. 'I hope the authorities at home keep their hair on', he wrote to Lady Cranborne, 'and if they want a victim to sacrifice, I am always at their disposal'.[13]

He told the Queen that Lord Roberts was 'the most delightful chief to work under',[14] but her Assistant Private Secretary, Arthur Bigge, received an illuminating letter from a fellow gunner, Colonel James Grierson, fortyone years old, who had lately joined Roberts's staff as quartermastergeneral. Grierson had wide experience and had published books on military affairs. 'I don't think somehow that Kitchener is quite in the proper place as Chief of Staff,' he wrote.

> In the first place, he is too big a man for it, and having held an independent command, finds it hard to be only chief staff officer to another. Secondly, he is accustomed to absolute autocracy and to everything being done according to his own method. Now his own method is to do everything himself, which works with 25,000 troops along a river, but does not work with 200,000 scattered over half a continent. He has only been a few days at Headquarters since I joined.

Both Roberts and Kitchener tended to do things 'off their own bat', which made difficulties for those who had to carry out their orders. 'The best man in the world can't do everything by rule of thumb.'[15] For his part, Kitchener felt that the army were looking on the war 'too much like a game of polo with intervals for afternoon tea'.[16]

Nevertheless by the end of May a flying column had relieved Mafeking (the news sent London wild – 'Maffiking') and Roberts had captured Johannesburg and all the gold mines intact. Kitchener believed that the Boers were tired of war, but no one liked to be the first to give in. On 7 June 1900 the British Army entered the Transvaal capital, Pretoria. As at Bloemfontein, Roberts ran up his wife's small silk Union Jack above the President's house.

Kitchener wrote, that very day: 'in another fortnight, or three weeks we may have peace.'[17]

At the formal entry into Pretoria as the Cameron Highlanders marched past the saluting base, a young officer noticed that Lord Kitchener, standing beside Roberts, concentrated his gaze on the men's boots. The War Office had sent out too many which failed the rigours of marching across the veldt. The Camerons' boots looked good. 'He had known the battalion in Egypt', noted Craig Brown in his diary that day, 'so had evidently made a mental note of their marching powers, for he sent us off on the trek again the very next day'.[18] To Kitchener's satisfaction many of his Sudan troops and senior officers were serving in South Africa. Major-General Sir Archibald Hunter, KCB, as he now was, had been second-in-command in Ladysmith during the siege. He had led a daring night raid to silence guns that were bombarding the town from a height. After the Relief of Ladysmith he secured a great victory by the surrender of a Boer Army at Brandwater Basin. Lord Edward Cecil was with Baden-Powell at Mafeking; Hector Macdonald commanded the Highland Brigade under Roberts and Kitchener.

While the Camerons marched east to take part in the action that culminated in the battle of Diamond Hill, Kitchener was sent south down the railway to deal with De Wet. The Boer generals Botha and de la Rey had opened negotiations for surrender by sending Botha's wife under flag of truce to arrange a meeting, but Christian De Wet had embarked on a series of guerrilla raids on British communications. His string of successes banished thoughts of surrender, which gave way to a hope that if the Boers continued the war, Germany or another great power would come to their aid. Capturing guns, ammunition and supplies, De Wet seriously embarrassed Roberts's campaign. And on 12 June 1900 De Wet nearly brought Kitchener's career to a stop.

Kitchener's headquarters saloon was coupled to a train carrying troops and railway repair men. At each station he alighted to hustle the officials in charge of strengthening the line and repairing bridges.[19] Having reinforced and reorganized the scattered detachments along the railway, he was returning towards Pretoria and had bivouacked with his staff in tents a few yards from his train which stood at Heibron Road station guarded by an infantry company. He was sleeping partially undressed when Jimmy Watson shook him awake: De Wet and his men had ridden in under cover of darkness, had surprised and overwhelmed part of the protecting company and were rounding them up as prisoners, unaware what a quarry lay on the other side of the line. Kitchener, Watson and their orderlies ran to the train, unstabled horses and rode for their lives some miles across the veldt in the moonlight to the safety of a yeomanry camp. By a curious chance of war the British just missed taking Kruger pris/ oner near Diamond Hill at almost the same time as the Boers missed Kitchener at Heibron Road.

Roberts had proclaimed an amnesty for any Boer (except leaders) who would surrender and many did, some even changing sides; but the guerrilla war dragged on. Roberts also proclaimed on 16 June that wherever Boers broke up the railway, severed telegraph lines or wrecked bridges and embankments, the homesteads in the immediate neighbourhood would be burned down: De Wet's own farm near Roodewal, where he had captured a large supply convoy, was set on fire that very morning. Roberts also organized camps for the women and children made homeless. Thus the policy of scorched earth and camps which would blacken Kitchener's memory originated with Roberts: Kitchener, with his instinctive concern for the welfare of women, at first opposed Roberts's plan.

Despite bloodshed and misery continuing, the end of the war still appeared to be close. Roberts and Kitchener both looked to their futures. Roberts had been informed that he would succeed Wolseley as Commander/in/Chief of the British Army and that Kitchener would succeed him in South Africa. After that, Kitchener had set his heart on India as Commander/in/Chief. This most important and influential post normally went to an officer with Indian experience, but Lord Curzon, the viceroy, wanted the glamour of Kitchener's name and his powers of organization.[20] Roberts, who had spent forty/one years in India, pressed Kitchener's appointment on the Secretary of State for War, Lord Lansdowne, a former viceroy.[21] On 29 September Lansdowne wrote to Arthur Bigge, Queen Victoria's Assistant Private Secretary:

Roberts who knows the Indian army, if anyone does, and who also knows Kitchener has strongly recommended us to send him to India. I was at first opposed to the idea, fearing that Kitchener's inexperience of the country and hardness of disposition might lead him into trouble. Roberts I think held this view at first but he tells me that Kitchener has improved immensely and has got over any little failings of manner which he may have possessed and that he, Roberts, considers him far better qualified for this most important post than any other candidate.[22]

Queen Victoria, however, felt 'most strongly' against Kitchener's appointment. She said that she had the greatest admiration and regard for him and did not want him placed where he might fail. He had not perhaps the right gifts for dealing with native armies – and that his appointment 'might lead to serious consequences detrimental to her rule in India and also to Lord Kitchener's own career in which the Queen takes a very great interest'.[23] And to pass over more senior generals with long Indian experience would cause great resentment.

She urged instead that his 'remarkable qualities as an organizer' would be of great value at the War Office. This was the other option that Lansdowne had put to the Queen. 'Kitchener would be very valuable here', he wrote from his desk in Pall Mall. 'He is a man of independent views and great courage, and the public believes in him.' He would inspire confidence in the new regime under Roberts.[24] The point had already been put forcibly to Bigge by a knowledgeable correspondent:

He is an ideal man to carry out a policy of reform in the Army at home. And however much fond he may be of smart people etc I think he is one of the few men who would ignore the immense social pressure and opposition that will be formed and brought against any reform that touches the comfort of the office. I mean, that entails an office working after lunch, for that is what it amounts to.[25]

Kitchener was 'quite frightened' when he heard rumours that he might be sent to the War Office. 'I could do no good there and would sooner sweep a crossing.' If not India he should be given the Sudan again. Otherwise, he told Lady Cranborne, he had better try civil employment.[26]

He had a thorough contempt for the War Office, its regulations, red tape and leisurely ways. Once, in the Sudan, he had joked that he would like to start a new War Office with a small staff of selected officers and proceed to issue orders by telegram and telephone, and 'it would probably be three months before the old War Office realized that he had taken over control of the Army'.[27]

For the moment his future was clear. He would tie up loose ends and bring, as he thought, a quick peace. On 12 October 1900, some six weeks before Roberts handed over, Kitchener wrote to the Queen: 'Madame, I feel sure Your Majesty will be pleased to hear that the war is almost over. Although there are still several bodies of the enemy in the field they can do very little harm now, and are running short of ammunition.'[28]

He would have been horrified to know that the end was more than eighteen months away. Had the politicians let him have his way he would have brought an honourable peace to the Boers in less than four months from the date of his letter.

23

1901: PEACE ABORTED

KITCHENER WOULD NEED to increase his staff, and asked Buller in the Natal to send a suitable officer. Buller chose William Birdwood, a Bengal Lancer aged thirty-five who had seen action in frontier wars in India and was mentioned in dispatches five times during the South African war. Roberts approved, wanting to advance Birdwood's career.

Birdwood presented himself in Pretoria with considerable misgiving, but on 16 October 1900 he wrote to his wife, 'My own, very darling dear Jenny Jane', in India: 'He was most awfully nice and after all one has heard of his being such a brute, I was quite astonished how very nice and easy he was to get on with.' Kitchener made him Deputy Assistant Adjutant-General and 'gave me no time to answer anything or think of anything but plunged into it at once'.[1]

Birdwood first had to work out a reorganization of troops on the lines of communication, doing it in Kitchener's dining-room. K (as he was generally known in the army) came in to speak with him several times a day. 'I am quite astonished', Birdwood wrote to Jenny Jane, 'how well I get on with him and I find him most awfully nice to work for'. When Kitchener took him on his afternoon rides, Birdwood noticed how he would deliberately look the other way to avoid returning salutes, which annoyed Birdwood as he knew it was unpopular, but 'He really is, what people I think don't give him credit for, very shy indeed and hates new people about him (so I don't know how I have ever got to know him so well)'.[2]

Not long after Birdwood had joined the staff Lady Roberts told him that she had happened to mention his wife to Kitchener, who nearly bounded out of his chair with a shout of 'What! Birdwood married! married!!' She said she had never seen him so excited and it was just as if a bombshell had fallen on him. I was most awfully amused for it sounded as if he looked on my little Jenny Jane as an ogress! Lady Roberts finished up by saying, 'I told him you would be far more useful to him as a married man than as a bachelor, on which we had a great argument, as I have always maintained that a good soldier is only improved by marrying!'[3]

Kitchener, perhaps not realizing that Jenny Jane was far away in India, had feared that she would be a distraction. When he came to know her in India he was charmed, and grew very fond of their children. Once, at a viceregal garden party, a sudden loud noise frightened five-year-old Christopher, who ran at once to Kitchener and held his hand tight. Kitchener told a cousin years afterwards that it was the proudest moment of his life.[4]

Kitchener also selected, as another ADC, a twenty-nine-year-old cavalry-man who had recently won the Victoria Cross: Francis Aylmer Maxwell of the 18th Bengal Cavalry. Frank Maxwell, while adjutant of the volunteer Roberts's Horse, had saved the guns at Sanna's Post when the Boers had sur-prised a forward column during the advance on Pretoria. Maxwell came from a military family, and his five brothers were all serving. In India he had been recommended for a VC in the Chitral campaign. His was a delightful person-ality with charm and perfect manners and a great sense of humour. As he looked very youthful, Kitchener nicknamed him 'the Brat'. The Brat was to be a vital member of Kitchener's 'family' for many years to come.

Lord and Lady Roberts left Pretoria for England at the end of November 1900, having delayed their departure until one of their daughters recovered from enteric. Kitchener took command of the 230,000 British and Imperial troops in South Africa and was promoted lieutenant-general, with temporary rank of full general.

He had a new master in Whitehall as Lord Salisbury, who had been con-firmed in power by the 'khaki election', no longer wanted to carry the Foreign Office with the premiership and handed it to Lord Lansdowne. Lansdowne was replaced at the War Office by St John Brodrick, six years younger than Kitchener, and heir to Viscount Midleton, who owned estates in Ireland and Surrey. Kitchener and Brodrick worked harmoniously in South Africa and later in Indian affairs, perhaps partly because Brodrick was not a dominant personality.

Kitchener had not been long in command when his strongest supporter, Queen Victoria, died in January 1901, aged over eighty-two. Subject and sovereign had been drawn even closer in her last months through mutual grief at the death in Pretoria of her grandson, his former staff officer, Prince Christian Victor, a fine soldier who had survived battles in India, the Sudan and South Africa, only to die of enteric following malaria. 'The Queen knows', she wrote, 'how fond Lord Kitchener was of our darling Christian Victor, who was much attached to Lord Kitchener'. She spoke of the great loss to the army and the country, and conveyed the thanks of her broken-hearted daughter to Lord Kitchener 'for all his kindness to him. The Queen feels much upset and shaken by this event and the loss of her grandson who was very useful to her, and at whose birth she was present. The war drags on, which is very trying.'[5]

Grief and anxiety sapped her strength. During January she fell ill. Princess Beatrice told Kitchener that on the day before she died, when hardly conscious of her surroundings, she suddenly asked, '"What news is there from Lord Kitchener? What has been happening in S. Africa?" Her whole mind was wrapped up in her soldiers fighting for her.'[6]

Their fighting seemed to bring victory no nearer. The army had rightly expected that Kitchener would prosecute the war with more vigour than Roberts in his final months, but as Kitchener wrote to Lady Cranborne: 'The country is so vast out here that the troops we have are all swallowed up.' So many were holding towns, guarding bridges and railways that he had too few 'to act vigorously against these roving Boers'.[7]

Sir Alfred Milner, the High Commissioner, had put up ideas on the policy to follow 'to put an end to this tiresome war, or brigandage, or whatever you like to call it'.[8] Milner and Kitchener, outwardly friendly, distrusted one another. Milner thought Kitchener in too much of a hurry, while Kitchener deplored Milner's aim of unconditional surrender: Kitchener aimed for a negotiated peace leading to a new South Africa in which the qualities displayed by the Boers would be harnessed in a free association within the British Empire.[9] But first he must convince them militarily that guerrilla warfare could end only in defeat. 'I puzzle my brain', he wrote to Lady Cranborne in January, 'to find out some way of finishing but without much result';[10] and a few days later, writing about personal finances to Arthur Renshaw, who had invested for him the Parliamentary grant given for Omdurman, he closed: 'I am so full of work that I am sure you will excuse a scrawl like this. I wish

I could finish up this war and get out of the country but I do not see at present much signs of the boers giving in for some time. Anyway we will all do our best.'[11]

Some in the army thought Kitchener not much interested in strategy,[12] but early in 1901 he conceived the strategy of the drive and the blockhouses: General French's cavalry swept through eastern Transvaal to round up roving commandos, using the blockhouses (built to guard the railways) as stoppers, rather as beaters in a grouse shoot drive the birds against butts. The 'bag' was disappointing, but Kitchener soon had evidence that 'our drive sweeping the high veldt has changed the idea of the boers and made them far more peace fully inclined than they were a few days ago'.[13] On 22 February Mrs Louis Botha, wife of the Transvaal commandant general, appeared in Pretoria with a letter desiring that he and Kitchener should meet 'with the view of bringing the war to an end'.

Kitchener agreed at once and wrote excitedly to Brodrick that a personal meeting 'may end the war if we are prepared not to be too hard on the boers ... It will be good policy for the future of this country to treat them fairly well and I hope I may be allowed to do away with anything humiliating to them in the surrender if it comes off.'[14]

Kitchener arranged that they should meet six days later at Middleburg, north east of Pretoria, in a countryside of rolling downs of grassland and 'a most glorious climate', as the Brat wrote home. 'One feels as fit as a lark, and the rest and change is doing K a lot of good.' Before Botha's final acceptance of the rendezvous Kitchener 'with his usual impatience was beginning to fidget but is now quiet again',[15] and went for a good ride.

At 8.30 a.m. on Thursday 28 February Watson rode out and met Botha and four others about a mile and half beyond Gun Hill Post. They were back by 10 a.m. at the requisitioned house where Kitchener was staying. Botha made a good impression: heavily set but with a pleasing expression and a quiet manner. While the ADCs entertained the Boer staff ('Quite good fellows ... much chaff was bandied'), the two leaders were closeted by them selves.[16]

Botha had brought ten points for discussion, and hoped for some form of independence to be allowed if the Boers laid down arms. Kitchener, knowing the home government's mind, ruled that out, but Botha's other points seemed capable of adjustment, although Kitchener found him greatly opposed to any vote being given to African natives: Kitchener then suggested that this should wait until representative government was restored to the former republics; Botha agreed. Some historians, long after, attacked Kitchener for this compromise. But his primary aim was to create a stable, united nation, rising from an early peace. Moreover, not many of his own countrymen were interested in votes for natives. His thinking was ahead of his time.

Kitchener offered generous terms, including acceptance of their legal debts and a large sum for the rebuilding and restocking of farms. He agreed to an amnesty for acts of war, even for the Boers in the Cape and Natal, who had taken up arms and therefore were rebels against the Crown, since Botha could not desert them to be severely punished, although agreeing that they should lose the vote. Kitchener's conclusion was that if the home government wished to end the war, he did not see any difficulty. Botha spoke of Boer and Briton being friends again, and hoped to bring his Free State allies round to accept the terms.

The luncheon between sessions, with both staffs present, was somewhat heavy but cheery. Before Watson escorted the Boers away in the evening, Kitchener allowed a group picture to be taken despite his dislike of being photographed. But when, later, he discovered that the Boers circulated the photograph as proof that Botha had captured Kitchener, he ordered that the plate and all copies that could be found (except his own) should be destroyed.[17]

Kitchener cabled to Brodrick and to Milner, for forwarding to Chamberlain as Colonial Secretary, with great optimism. But Milner stiffened the terms and specially objected to any amnesty for Cape and Natal rebels. Kitchener 'did all in my power to urge Milner to change his views, which on this subject seem to me very narrow'[18] and vindictive. Chamberlain backed Milner and even rebuked Kitchener in Parliament.

Kitchener was exasperated. 'We are now carrying the war on to put 2–300 Dutchmen in prison at the end of it. It seems to me absurd and wrong, and I wonder the Chancellor of the Exchequer did not have a fit!'[19] 'I was amazed the Govt were not more anxious for peace', he wrote to Lady Cranborne, but remembering she was the Prime Minister's daughter-in-law he added tactfully: 'Of course there are some reasons for it, I do not understand or know of, probably political.'[20]

In England the rising Radical, David Lloyd George, a leader of the 'pro-Boers', contrasted Kitchener and Chamberlain: 'There was a soldier who knew what war meant; he strove to make peace. There was another man, who strolled among his orchids 6,000 miles from the deadly bark of the Mauser rifle. He stopped Kitchener's peace!'[21] It would have been well, eighteen years later in 1919, had Lloyd George recalled his words when he forced through a vindictive peace, which Kitchener, had he lived, would have made a 'peace of reconciliation'.

The guerrilla war resumed with increased bitterness and atrocities on both sides. If a commando captured British soldiers, they would strip them (needing their clothes and boots) and send them naked and bleeding to find their way back, then take advantage of their uniforms: when a squadron of Colonel Douglas Haig's 17th Lancers was cut up at Elands River Poort (during Smuts's invasion of Cape Colony) they had held fire until too late because the men approaching were wearing British khaki.

With the roving Boers using homesteads on the veldt for supply cover and camouflage, Kitchener was forced to burn farms, the policy he had opposed under Roberts. 'It is a horrid war', he wrote in April. 'No straight fighting. I wish we could get it over but I have done all I can and do not see how it is to end except by utter exhaustion on the part of the Boers.' And again, in June, he commented to the Cecils: 'There is no pleasure in destroying a country and catching the inhabitants and yet there is no other way of bringing irreconcilʹ ables to book.' He admired their tenacity and recognized that they were fightʹ ing for their independence, which the British government would never grant. Thus the war must continue, and on 21 June he told Lady Cranborne: 'I hope if they have anyone who can do the work better they will send him – it is not fair on the Army if anyone else could bring matters to a nearer end.'[22] But the government had every confidence. Moreover, when Milner left for home on leave in May they approved Kitchener's appointment as Acting High Commissioner.

Milner arrived in London to an effusive official welcome and a peerage. He had an audience with King Edward VII, who apparently spoke somewhat disʹ paragingly of Kitchener, probably echoing Lord Esher, who despised his uncouth face and had heard that no one who worked with him liked him.[23] Milner, after reflection, sent a long letter to the king's Private Secretary to correct the 'rather unfair impression' left on His Majesty's mind.

'. . . No doubt', wrote Milner, 'Kitchener is not a genial man and is a hard taskmaster. On the other hand I do not think he is slow to recognize good work. I remember his saying more than once that he wished it was easier to *reward men promptly* when they had done anything specially distinguished.' He would be most pleased at the king's recent special awards.

'Another very strong point is his enormous energy and power of work. In this respect I do not think I have ever met his equal. No doubt the weak point is the enormous number of different operations which he has to control, and there is *a tendency* to control them too much.' Milner welcomed Kitchener's recent grant of more operational independence to Sir John French in the Cape and hoped he would allow wider discretion to column commanders as the Boer formations broke up.

> But when every deduction is made, there is a great source of strength in Kitchener's grasp and driving power and iron constitution for work . . . He is doing a terribly heavy bit of work with splendid zeal and devotion, and the least I can do, who have seen him at it, is not to allow this side of the case to be forgotten.[24]

And another 'side of the case' was shown by a letter that Kitchener had received when the Egyptian Army reclaimed Jimmy Watson. Their farewells had been typically British – a last game of billiards and scarcely a word. Watson wrote from Durban when his ship was about to sail:

> I wanted to say so much. Even now it's difficult. But my 'home' has been with you so long and I do want you to know how awfully sorry I am to leave it, and to thank you very very much for all you have done for me. I hate going more than I can say. Goodbye again, I shall always look back on these five years as the best and happiest I've ever had.[25]

24

I WISH
I COULD SEE THE END

KITCHENER WAS NOW both political and military ruler of South Africa. He soon found himself at the centre of a storm.

The burning of farms made women, children and the elderly destitute unless the authorities took action. Lord Roberts had formed 'camps for refuge' and 'government laagers' for refugees, especially Boer families who had surrendered (the 'hands-uppers') and were in danger of reprisals from the 'bitter-enders'. Kitchener made these laagers the pattern for accommodating the increasing number of Boers brought in from the veldt as the scorched earth policy took hold. Families who had lived in isolation, miles from their neighbours, were concentrated in camps hurriedly sited and laid out, which became known as concentration camps. The motive was humanitarian and the term had none of the sinister meaning and purpose which it was to acquire in Nazi Germany. But the army had no experience of interning large numbers of civilians, and the Boer women no experience of living in communities. They continued their usual habits of hygiene which mattered little on isolated farms but were disastrous in camps. As Kitchener wrote, 'the doctor's reports of the dirt and filth that these boer ladies from the wilds revel in are very unpleasant reading'.[1] He thought the inmates better off than in their homes or than the British refugees in Boer hands.

Sickness was followed by epidemics and a rising death rate, especially among children. Newspaper reports produced unease, then outrage, in England, especially after a committee, formed by some who opposed the war, had sent out Miss Emily Hobhouse, middle-aged daughter of the late

Archdeacon of Bodmin in Cornwall.[2] Her brief was to lessen distress, and she had been given permission to visit the camps. She was appalled . On return to England she stirred the national conscience, but mixed her humanitarian mission with pro-Boer politics, speaking of the Cabinet and Kitchener as the enemy. *The Times* attacked her, but the Liberal leader Campbell-Bannerman, in a phrase that became famous, said the war was being carried on by 'methods of barbarism'.

Kitchener, as supreme in South Africa, cannot escape some of the blame for deaths, which he did not foresee – or intend, as Boer propaganda claimed. He should have sent to England for experienced civilian administrators, not rely on harassed servicemen and medical officers. He visited camps[3] but too hurriedly to realize the growing problem until the statistics became alarming. He would probably have acted more swiftly had Miss Hobhouse not seemed to be encouraging the enemy. When she returned to South Africa she unwisely held a conference in her liner in Cape Town harbour with Cape women who were known to be hoping for a Boer victory. Kitchener forbade her to land. She went home and took out an action against him in the courts. 'I shall prob-ably be put in prison on arrival in England, I suppose',[4] he joked to Lady Cranborne when he wrote to her on New Year's Day 1902.

By then the death rate was falling dramatically. The government, respond-ing to Opposition furore and public unease, had sent out a commission headed by a noted social worker and patriot, Mrs Henry (later Dame Millicent) Fawcett, widow of a blind MP. The commission toured the camps and made many wise recommendations, including the sending out of nurses from home.

But the bitterness ran deep, and Kitchener would be remembered among the Afrikaner people as the creator of concentration camps and 'murderer of children', and not for the enlightened peace he brought, at the last, despite the politicians.

'The boers are growing very weak', wrote Kitchener to Arthur Renshaw on 5 July 1901. 'The constant drain of killed, wounded and prisoners is telling on them but they won't chuck it hoping for something to turn up. They very rarely now let us get within 4 miles of them except at night and they are gener-ally off when we are 20 miles away. We have to ride 40 or sometimes 50 miles to catch them.'[5] The 'we' referred to his columns, but he visited them when-ever he could get away from Pretoria. Sometimes his carriages for staff and Cameron Highlander bodyguard, with horse wagon, would be attached to a troop train. If, when he stepped down at a station, an officer should snap him with his Kodak, the film would be promptly confiscated by an ADC. More often the C-in-C travelled in his own special train which would stop overnight in a well-guarded siding. Next morning the Chief would be ready when the Brat was still washing his teeth. The Brat sent home a vivid description:

> Everything is at high pressure; at 7.15 we were off at a gallop and visited two small columns and two large ones. Quite unofficial visits, the commanders being unwarned almost invariably being found in their blan-kets having a well-earned sleep. No one is turned out but K. just rides through the lines looking at the horses and speaking to any one who happens to be about. Fifteen to twenty mile canter, mostly through herds of lowing cattle, brought us back to the station at 10. Breakfast and an hour up the line we again disembarked, and galloped out to see more columns, the farthest being about seven miles out. Here we found the New Zealanders, who had put up a very fine fight with De Wet's lot who had broken through some three nights before. K. made them a little speech which pleased them mightily, and so on to the next.[6]

The Boer commandos had become skilled at breaking through, blowing up bridges, ambushing trains or patrols, descending on isolated depots and disappearing again. Kitchener's mind ranged continually on ways in which to end the war. Boer men and boys, captured in the field, were sent to St Helena (where Cronje languished) and to Ceylon, India and Bermuda, a total of 25,000.[7] In a long and reasoned letter to Brodrick, Kitchener even explored the possibility of sending into permanent exile in the Dutch East Indies or Fiji all Boer families who would not accept British rule: the idea was summarily rejected.[8] Despite this absurdity Kitchener's policies as High Commissioner were enlightened, using both carrot and stick. Although the former South African Republic was now the British Colony of the Transvaal, and the Orange Free State the Orange River Colony, he did not treat the burghers as rebels but as combatants. He could be ruthless with Cape rebels, born under the Crown, and Boers captured wearing British uniform might be shot without trial, but Sir Richard Solomon, the Cape lawyer who had become Attorney-General of Transvaal colony, noticed how frequently Kitchener commuted death sentences imposed by courts martial or civil. In one case he was so moved by a letter from a condemned man's father that he went through the papers himself instead of relying on official advice, and commuted. 'He is not a cruel man or hard', Solomon concluded, 'but may behave as such to hide his softer side'.[9] Kitchener approved French's public execution of a group of Cape rebels caught with a Boer commando, for which the Cabinet rebuked him, but he did not reprieve two Australian lieutenants who had allegedly ordered their men to murder twelve prisoners of war.[10]

Five Australians and one English officer had been court-martialled for the multiple murder. The execution of only Morant and Handcock caused an outcry in Australia. Friends of Morant, who was the illegitimate son of a British admiral, contended that the court-martial had been a farce, that the Boers, including a reverend predikant, had not been shot in cold blood but in a raid that went wrong, and that the predikant was a spy. After Kitchener had signed the death warrants he disappeared on tour, removing himself from any attempt to secure reprieves. Morant's friends accused Kitchener of dishonourable conduct. The case remains contentious, a fertile field for fiction and film.

To rule as well as to command was wearying, and Kitchener must answer the flow of telegrams from the Colonial Office and the War Office, both harried by a vocal opposition. 'I saw Herbert early in July', wrote Walter, now a major-general operating in the bush country of eastern Transvaal, to their cousin Johnny Monins on 21 August, 'He was showing signs of overwork and worry, but I cheered him up a bit.' Walter gave him evidence from the field of 'quite wonderful progress' towards winning the war, and of the splendid spirit of the troops. 'Of course', added Walter, 'in Pretoria he does not see the change as we do on trek'.[11] Walter admired and liked the Boers as he pitted his wits against theirs.

General Walter Kitchener was in for a surprise. Far away in England his devoted wife, unable to throw off her lassitude and weakness although only thirty-seven, consulted a Harley Street specialist. He told Carry that the pernicious anaemia contracted in India was at an advanced stage, that there was no cure (the cure would not be discovered for another twenty years) and she had just a few months to live. Determined to see Walter again before she died, she secured a berth on a troopship without telling him, put the children in the care of her unmarried sister Hetty Fenton, arrived in Cape Town and rejoiced Walter's heart by a wire.

Caroline Kitchener was a woman who loved to help others and everyone loved to help her. Colonel Fife of the High Commissioner's staff arranged for her to go north with the officer carrying Herbert's mail. Seeing how weak she looked Fife provided a nurse to escort her. The railway journey of three days and two nights through Cape Colony and across the devastated Orange River Colony where Boer guerrillas and British columns were operating was a sad experience for Carry: 'it was dreadful to see the dead cattle and sheep.' As the train passed each blockhouse the soldiers would come to the line for books and papers and luxuries to be thrown to them.

At Johannesburg she stayed at Heath's Hotel where she could sit on the veranda and the proprietor took her for drives. On 2 October she wrote to eleven-year-old Hal at his prep. school in England: 'Uncle Herbert came here yesterday and we had a grand lunch together and he was very kind and nice.' Herbert arranged for the best beef to be sent in, to help keep up her strength.

On Sunday 13 October at early church the matron of St Mary's hospital, Miss Lloyd, noticed Carry's prematurely grey hair and 'sweet face' and invited her to tea to see over the hospital. She came on the Monday with flowers and picture books for the wards but feeling poorly. Miss Lloyd and Mrs Kitchener became friends. A week later Carry asked the matron for two special favours: Might she have a private room at the hospital but not be treated as an invalid? And please not to tell the two generals, her husband and her brother-in-law.

She moved in, and 'all grew to love her for her sweet ways,' wrote the matron. Matron summoned Dr Pearce who said he had never seen anyone so anaemic. Evidently, despite Carry's wishes, the commander-in-chief was told, for next she wrote to Hal: 'My dear old Hal, Joy. Joy. Joy. Daddy and I are both coming home and we shall have it for Christmas. O won't that be lovely. Kind Uncle Herbert is giving him three months' leave as soon as ever he comes off his trek chasing Botha.'

But the disease was gaining hold despite all the nourishment and even a primitive (and highly dangerous) blood transfusion. Then came a wire from Walter: he was arriving that night. Carry brightened, with a look of intense joy. He came, and stayed in her room, doing all he could for her comfort, but to his great distress he was too deaf, and her voice too weak, to hear much of what she said. The matron, writing to Miss Fenton afterwards, said she never knew anyone so devoted as the general was to his wife. 'All our generals are heroes but one seldom meets such a perfect man and husband'.

Early on Saturday morning Carry seemed worse. The specialist, Dr Davis, came and warned she had only twenty-four hours to live. Walter suggested another blood transfusion and gave five ounces, which was injected into her

Wingate interrogates Mahmud.
A posed photograph by Captain Loch four months after the battle of the Atbara

'Friendlies' at Berber, ready for action

Bringing up gunboat sections

Bringing up the troops: early morning toilet beside the train

The Union Jack and the Egyptian flag fly out

A Lancer and a Grenadier hold Gordon's telescope

Father Brindle, DSO,
the best loved man in the Expedition

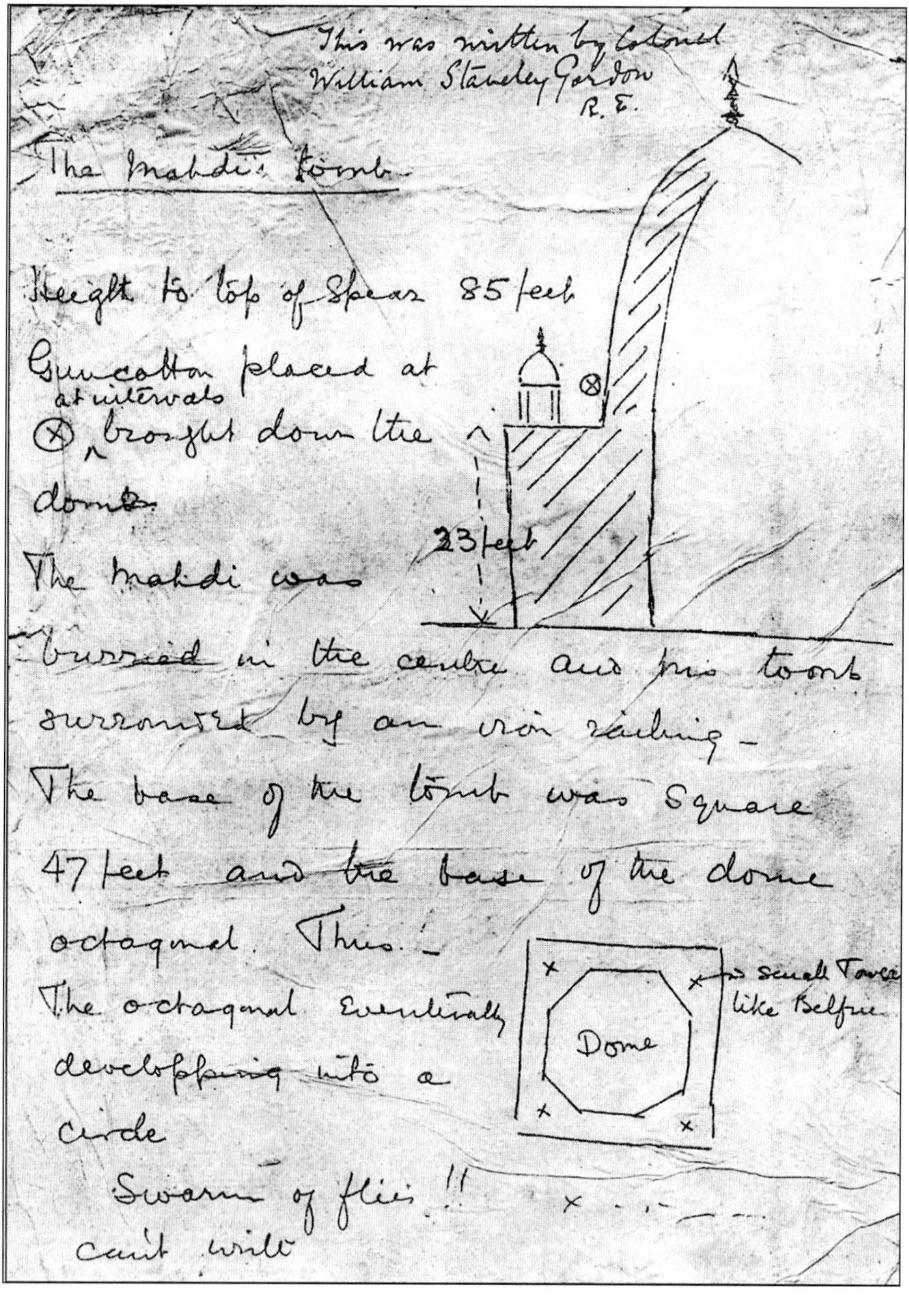

This was written by Colonel
William Stanley Gordon
R.E.

The Mahdi's tomb

Height to top of Spear 85 feet

Guncotton placed at
at intervals
⊗ brought down the
dome.

The Mahdi was

buried in the centre and his tomb
surrounded by an iron railing —
The base of the tomb was square
47 feet and the base of the dome
octagonal. Thus —
The octagonal Eventually
developping into a
circle
    Swarm of flies!!
can't write

23 feet

Dome

small Tower
like Belfrie

'Monkey' Gordon's own sketch of his plans before demolishing the Mahdi's tomb

by Heinrich von Angeli
Queen Victoria commissioned the portrait 'which she thinks very like & a very fine picture'

Walter, the youngest brother
(Lieutenant-General Sir Walter
Kitchener, KCB, 1858–1912)
Painted when Governor of
Bermuda, by Jongiers, 1910. He
greatly admired Herbert yet could
laugh at him

His wife Caroline ('Carry')
née Fenton
Her hair is prematurely grey from
pernicious anaemia. She died in
South Africa, November 1901,
aged thirty-seven

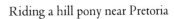

Col. Henderson   Van Velden   Major Watson   M Fraser   Major Maxwell   H. De Jager
De Wet.   Genl Louis Botha   Lord Kitchener   Col Hamilton

The abortive peace conference of 28 February 1901.
The British government repudiated Kitchener's generous terms.
The Boers used this photograph to 'prove' they had captured Kitchener!

With his ADC Frank Maxwell, VC,
'The Brat'

Riding a hill pony near Pretoria

period of years with 3 per cent interest. No foreigner or
ebel will be entitled to the benefit of this Clause.

Signed at Pretoria this thirty first day of May in the
Year of Our Lord One Thousand Nine Hundred and Two.

Kitchener's copy of the last page of
the Peace Treaty [which ended the
War,] with Melrose House where it
was signed

arm. That evening the chaplain brought them Holy Communion with the matron and Carry's special nurse receiving the Sacrament too. Very early on Sunday morning, a smile on her face, Carry died in Walter's arms.

Herbert sent him home on leave to the children. 'Poor boy he is much knocked out by his wife's death.'[12]

On 14 August Kitchener and his staff came down from Pretoria to Pietermaritzburg in Natal for a ceremonial parade to honour the heir to the throne and Princess May, now Duke and Duchess of Cornwall and York, soon to be Prince and Princess of Wales. They were on their way home after inaugurating the Commonwealth of Australia. The Duke of York had first met Kitchener in the summer of 1899 in London, when seated next to him at a dinner of fifty men given by the rich Sir James Blyth in Portland Place.[13] The thirty-four-year-old Duke had invited him to ride in Rotten Row and they became friends, so far as allowed by the wide social gap between royalty and subject.

At Pietermaritzburg the duke pinned some fifty Distinguished Service Orders on gallant breasts and nine Victoria Crosses, including the Brat's, with the citations read in full. Then came a marvellous spectacle when two hundred Zulu chiefs in full war paint advanced slowly in a semicircle, singing a deep-throated battle song, until they stopped before the duke with a thunderous *Bayete!* repeated three times. 'No cheer one has ever heard', the Brat told his mother, 'had the depth, power, and volume of this royal salute, and I would go a long way to hear it again'.[14]

After the loyal address and an inspection, the duke had 'a most interesting talk' with Kitchener at Government House. 'I thought him looking remark-ably fit and well', the duke told the king, 'and he has grown fat', (Kitchener thought the duke looked rather thin.) Kitchener, in great spirits, asked the duke to tell the king that his 180,000 fighting men were in splendid condition and working hard; blockhouses guarded thousands of miles of railway lines at 1,600-yard intervals; 839 Boers had been captured or killed that past week and they must also be getting short of horses. He was directing from head-quarters no fewer than 61 separate columns. He then rushed back to Pretoria delighted with a gold cigarette case and photographs from the Yorks, who returned to Durban and their ship.[15]

The numerous columns, and the peculiar nature of the South African war, caused cavalrymen to rise faster in their profession, and thus to high command in the Great War, including household names such as Field Marshals French, Haig, Allenby and Byng. The future Viscount Byng of Vimy had a curious personal link with Kitchener. Back in 1890, when 'Pandeli Tom' Ralli had commissioned the famous Herkomer full-length portrait of his great friend Herbert Kitchener Pasha, aged forty (now in the National Portrait Gallery), he also commissioned a smaller Herkomer to hang near it, of his young niece Evelyn Moreton, whose father was Master of Ceremonies at Court: Ralli fondly hoped that the two would marry

No evidence exists that either showed interest in the other. In 1899 Evelyn fell in love with Major John Byng of the 10th Hussars, who went off to the South African war without declaring himself. In 1901 a column commander, he wrote from the veldt asking if she would marry him. She replied by wire: 'Yes, come home immediately. *Evelyn.*' She handed it in at Aldershot near her home. When the telegram reached the army post office in Pretoria and a clerk saw its Aldershot origin and the name *Evelyn*, he jumped to the conclusion that Sir Evelyn Wood, Adjutant-General, was urgently recalling Colonel Byng. The clerk gave an entirely unwarranted top priority to the wire and thus speeded a happy engagement.[16]

Lord Milner landed again at Cape Town on 27 August. With him, also back from leave, came Neville Lyttleton, who had commanded the British brigade at Omdurman and had distinguished himself in South Africa. He was ordered to Pretoria. When he reported to Kitchener he found him in obvious grief because Seymour Vandeleur, one of the most promising of the younger lieutenant-colonels, a good friend at Omdurman and in South Africa, had just been killed defending a train of refugees, ambushed by an Irishman and his gang which both sides looked on as brigands. 'The tears stood in Kitchener's eyes', noted Lyttleton. 'Indeed, on occasions such as this he often showed a real tenderness of heart. At other times he might appear ruthless, but this would be where a question of efficiency was involved.'[17]

The war dragged on. The young Jan Smuts with a small Transvaal commando was causing mild havoc in Cape Colony and had been joined by many Cape Dutch rebels. Transvaalers and Cape rebels alike scorned Kitchener's proclamation threatening banishment for all burghers in arms after 15 September. Milner and the home government had altered the draft in such a way that all but a few Boers ignored it.[18] Then, two British columns suffered minor defeats. Kitchener wrote to Lady Cranborne on 20 September:

Just a scrawl at the end of a hard day's work. I wish I could see the end of it all but when one has done all one can somebody goes and gives one away by losing guns. It is most ///////// you can put in the proper expression. How I wish it was over, I am getting quite worn out but I mean to see it through if the authorities think I am competent.

He enclosed for the Hatfield circle a funny sketch he had doodled of a yeomanry trooper running away.[19]

He could moan to the Cranbornes but to his staff the Chief kept his composure. That very day his senior ADC, Raymond Marker, commented to his sister Gertie that these unexpected and unnecessary reverses were very hard on Lord K, for whom he was very sorry. Marker added: 'He is always wonderfully even minded over everything and never "murmurs" in any way. At the most merely says — I do wish people would use a little common sense.'[20]

Raymond Marker, always known as Conk, had been adjutant of the 1st Battalion Coldstream Guards in the field when Kitchener invited him to be Jimmy Watson's successor. Birdwood reckoned him 'a *real* good fellow . . . one of the very best one could ever hope to meet, and so able'.[21] He was a Devonian, heir to a fine estate, and had been ADC to the Viceroy, Lord Curzon. Conk guessed rightly that he had been chosen partly to be pumped about India, though Kitchener's appointment as the next Commander-in-Chief was not yet official. Kitchener would ask questions as they rode, and Conk sent for a Hindustani grammar as Kitchener wanted to learn that hybrid of Hindi and Urdu which the Indian Army used. But first they must win the war. Conk wished that the politicians at home, who had never met a fighting Boer or understood the country, would give the Chief a free hand.[22]

The Chief, though he did not show it, was becoming discouraged and depressed. The Boers were 'utter fools' not to give in. He was not fighting a proper war, with pitched battles and front lines, but must catch or kill every man. And people at home were losing patience: the English papers 'help the enemy to keep up their spirits by the hope that we shall get tired and give it up'.[23] On 19 October Roberts tactfully asked, at the Cabinet's request, whether Kitchener would like a rest, lest his health give way and he be lost to future service. Roberts would come back and relieve him. Kitchener, conscious of rumours that he was to be replaced, replied that if he retained their confidence he wanted to see it through. 'I only fear that there may be something I have not done to hasten the end, and that someone else might do it better. You know I do not want any incentive to do what is possible to finish. I think I hate the country, the people, the whole thing, more every day.'[24] Milner was privately disappointed that he would stay, because it was impossible 'to guide a military dictator of very strong views and strong character'.[25]

Roberts offered, and Kitchener gladly accepted, to send back to South Africa Lieutenant-General (acting) Sir Ian Hamilton to be Chief of Staff so that Kitchener be less tied to Pretoria.

A Gordon Highlander three years younger than Kitchener, 'Johnny' Hamilton had served mostly in India, although he had managed, when on leave, to take part in the Gordon Relief, where they had first met. In South Africa he had been a survivor of the Majuba defeat in the First Boer War and in the present war had been recommended for the Victoria Cross when in command of a brigade. (The War Office refused to award it to so senior an officer.) He had returned home with Roberts, to whom he was very close, as Military Secretary.

Hamilton arrived at Pretoria on 1 December.[26] By then Kitchener had made four fresh moves.

He extended the blockhouses and connected them by barbed wire and telegraph lines to divide the veldt into vast paddocks which could be swept clean of Boers unable to escape. The land eventually was scarred temporarily by no fewer than 8,000 blockhouses covering 3,700 miles, guarded by 50,000 white soldiers and 16,000 armed African.[27]

He raised two regiments from among the surrendered Boers who were prepared to fight their compatriots in order to end the war more quickly. The National Scouts (Transvaal) and the Orange River Volunteers played a part far more important than their military contribution by gradually convincing the fighting burghers that if peace did not come soon the Afrikaner nation would cease to be one 'volk'.

He changed his policy on the concentration camps. The columns stopped bringing in civilians when an area was cleared. He allowed many in the camps to leave. Thus the Boer commandos were encumbered again with women and children.

He armed native Africans, not only for their protection but as combatants, thus worrying the Boer leaders that the Africans whom they had traditionally mistreated might become a danger after the war.

These four moves marked the beginning of the end.

25

1902: 'WE ARE GOOD FRIENDS NOW'

JOHNNY HAMILTON TOOK up residence, along with Hubert Hamilton (Military Secretary, no relation, known as 'Hammy') and the ADCs at the Commander-in-Chief's residence, Melrose House, a large Renaissance-style mansion built by a prosperous general dealer of English descent, George Jesse Heys, who had leased it furnished to Roberts, the principal furniture being mostly reproduction Chippendale and Sheraton. Conveniently near the railway station and with a large garden, it was probably particularly attractive to Roberts in the South African winter because it had electricity and, very unusually, central heating operated by steam, with a system of ventilation for summer.[1] Kitchener took over Roberts's Indian servants and police but brought in a company of his favourite Cameron Highlanders as bodyguard.

At about 5.30 a.m. Kitchener and Hamilton would emerge from their bed-rooms in dressing gowns, unshaven. Hubert and the ADC on duty had already deciphered and arranged the telegrams that had poured in from fifty or sixty column commanders or elsewhere, putting aside, until later, those unconnected with operations. The two generals would then crawl over the maps laid on the dining-room floor, with telegrams and little red flags in their hands, until they knew every position, problem, opportunity or need.

Kitchener would then dictate to the two Hamiltons orders for each of the fifty or more column commanders. The orders were mostly explicit and terse: 'Halt', 'March', 'Attack', 'Make for such-a-place and entrain'. He had all the details in his head and had been thinking out the next moves, even in his sleep.

He did not use the normal method, outlining his wishes but leaving details to the staff or to the discretion of commanders, except for French; he did it all himself, sometimes against their better judgement. Haig complained that Smuts would never have slipped across the Orange River to begin his dam-aging raid through Cape Colony had not an order from Kitchener caused a ford to be left unguarded.

After the operational telegrams, the two generals disappeared to shave and dress before breakfast with the personal staff and then, for Kitchener, a morning of interviews with departmental heads of the General Staff and of the military government of the Transvaal and the Orange River Colony. Kitchener specially detested the Adjutant-General's questions, which he con-sidered the trivia of military life, and at last handed him over to Johnny Hamilton. Since the Adjutant-General had relished his right of audience with the Commander-in-Chief and hated Hamilton, Johnny thought 'this inspiration sprang from one of K's strongest motives, a love of mischief'.[2] The one caller whom he really enjoyed was his director of intelligence, Major David Henderson. Ten years later Henderson became the army's first director of aeronautics; his enthusiasm for flying may well have sprung from the reflec-tion that had aeroplanes been invented earlier the Boer guerrillas would have been spotted and suppressed (unless they had shot down the primitive aero-planes).

Last came the representatives of the press. Kitchener knew he should humour them but disliked imparting information since newspapers tended to inflate skirmishes into battles and unfortunate incidents into atrocities, and might always unintentionally help the enemy. The press tended therefore to present 'This commander-in-chief of ours as a cold, exacting, unsympathetic figure, much more given to jumping down your throat then to patting you on the back', as one lieutenant-colonel put it, only to find on being sent to brief him that 'for twenty minutes or so I found myself enjoying the pleasantest interview with a much senior officer than I had ever had in my life. He listened to my exposition . . . occasionally interjected a question or criticism . . . but seemed not in the least displeased when I stuck to my own view. When he dis-missed me he spoke in a particularly friendly way, and my experience of him on this occasion was nothing short of a revelation.'[3]

Hubert Hamilton commented to the colonel that the Chief was in one of his good moods. 'You might not always find him so tame.'

After the day's interviews and correspondence, the Chief always went for a ride, with Johnny Hamilton or Birdwood or one of the ADCs. The whole personal staff would dine with Kitchener before a game of billiards and then, for K, more work, often far into the night. Six of the nine who sat around the dining-table in Melrose House would be killed in the next war. All were devoted to the Chief. Johnny Hamilton, near him in age, perhaps regarded him with admiration tinged with affectionate exasperation rather than with the intense devotion of the younger men. When the serious-minded Hubert Hamilton was killed as a divisional general in October 1914, leaving a wife and small children, his sister, Lady Allendale, told Kitchener that his last talk on leave before they parted 'was chiefly about you, so quiet and intense. The devotion to his chief, of course. The sure appreciation based on the experience of years. And there was more than all this. I think he loved like George Colley loved Lord Wolseley long ago.'[4] Colley, the general killed at Majuba, had been her first husband.

But the brightest spark in the mess was 'the Brat', Frank Maxwell. He quickly got Kitchener's measure:

> K is not the purposely rough-mannered, impolite person those who have never even seen him suppose. He is awfully shy, and until he knows any one his manners — except to ladies — are certainly not engaging. He really feels nice things, but to put tongue to them, except in very intimate society, he would rather die . . . I suppose most Englishmen loathe any sort of gush, display of sentiment. K is unfortunately endowed with ten times most people's share of this virtue, with the result that it is almost a vice to him.[5]

Maxwell was a man of intense virility, one of six brothers in the army, a fine polo-player and shot as well as a first-rate soldier who wore the VC and the DSO. He was always cheerful and humorous and had a quiet, deep Christian faith. Kitchener treated him as a son. If the Chief were wrapped in gloom, with his facial disfigurement more like a scowl than ever, the Brat could coax him out of it. Sir Ian Hamilton recalled how, like the young David in the Bible, the Brat could 'play the harp to our Saul without ever once striking a note of discord'. He could say what he liked to K, 'and the more cheeky the better it went down. Often we all trembled, but the awful scowl melted always into a chuckle and the javelin was never hurled.'[6]

The Brat and Marker got up a polo team on a new ground laid out by another ADC, Ferdy Stanley, Lord Derby's son, 'much assisted by Lord K

with hints and advice. He takes a keen interest in polo.'[7] He played occasionally, but because of his bad eyesight his team would generally lose.

The Brat kept his parents amused with many stories of his Chief, such as
that of the starlings.

The Chief always liked to have dogs around and was fond of horses, but
he had not been known as a bird-lover until one morning, early, Frank
Maxwell entered the room to find him in his dressing gown, hair unbrushed,
darting about the room trying to catch two young starlings that had fallen
down the chimney.

> We caught them after a heated chase, and deposited the poor little beggars
> in the wire pigeon-house in the garden. Then there was much fuss all day
> about their food and the good man would leave his important duties every
> half hour to see if I had given them meat or procured succulent worms, and
> bustle in and say they were starving. It was no use pointing out they hadn't
> learnt to eat by themselves yet or that the pigeons wolfed any food put in for
> the infants. The poor parents were in great distress, flying round and round
> the cage, but at length got bold and fed the little things through the wire,
> which interested the Commander-in-Chief so much that the operations in
> South Africa received no attention most of the remainder of that day.

Next morning the Chief noticed a third young starling flying around in the
garden and ordered the Brat to catch it. Since protests of inability were always
lost on K of K, the Brat sneaked out of breakfast, took the four-foot-high sham
stork from the hall, placed it in the cage and lost himself. 'The joke came off
A1. He was fairly drawn, laughed much, said I was an impertinent beast, and
hasn't murmured a word about catching any more third birds.' During the day
the C-in-C would frequently leave the war to visit the cage, chirping at the
birds or trying out his new-learned Hindustani phrases.

One bird died. The other grew up, but, when Kitchener was away on tour,
it escaped. Hubert Hamilton was thrown into gloom and eventually decided
that the awful news should be broken by telegram. The Brat composed and
sent: 'C-in-C.'s humming bird after being fed by a Highlander this morning
broke cover and took to the open. Diligent search instituted. Biped still at
large. My. Secy. desolate. ADC in tears. Army sympathises.'

When the Chief returned he hurried through two days' telegrams, summoned ADCs, servants and orderlies, and rushed about the garden, several

times falling into wet flowerbeds, until lunch, which he ate dishevelled, remarking, 'I've never been so fond of that bird as since it's been loose'. It was eventually captured in the chimney of a neighbouring house, minus its tail. The Chief could again be seen in leisure moments spouting Hindustani at a starling.[8]

The most perceptive study of Kitchener's personality at this time comes from a letter written by Conk Marker to his sister on 17 January 1902. He had been on tour with the Chief, including inspection of a concentration camp, where they found conditions now satisfactory and the male internees eager to per- suade the remaining Boer leaders to come in from the veldt to make peace. Conk had told Gertie that the blockhouse lines in the Orange River Colony might soon end the careers of De Wet and Steyn, and he went on:

> It has been a very great pleasure to read the appreciation of Ld. K in the recent speeches of Ld. Rosebery and Mr Chamberlain. Six months ago I felt that the Government did not in the least appreciate his gigantic work, but I think now they are beginning to get a glimmering of what a great man they have got out here. In this age of self-advertisement there was always a danger that Ld. K with his absolute contempt for anything of the kind, and his refusal to surround himself with people who attract attention, would not be appreciated at his real value, but I think the country recognizes him now.
>   The more I see of him the more devoted I get to him. He is always the same – never irritable – in spite of all his trials, and always making the best of things however much he may be interfered with. As Chamberlain said, to praise him is almost an impertinence.[9]

A comment by Kitchener to Arthur Renshaw, at the end of a letter concern- ing investments, sums up his feelings more succinctly than his detailed letters to Brodrick or Roberts. 'It is a horrid nuisance', he wrote on 26 January 1902, 'these Boers will not give up. They have no chance of success and very little hope but like Banditti they can still hop down on any weak column that is not looking out and our people *will* go to sleep if they do not see an enemy. Most annoying.'[10]

But on the day before he wrote, the Dutch government, in touch with the Boer exiles including Kruger, offered to mediate. Lord Lansdowne refused: terms of peace must be discussed by the commanders on the field. Kitchener received the correspondence on 4 March after two successful drives in the Orange River Colony, although De Wet once again evaded capture. He sent it immediately, as instructed, to Schalk Burger, Acting President since Kruger's departure for Europe, of the South African Republic. In Boer eyes the Crown Colony of the Transvaal did not exist.

Kitchener waited for Burger's reply. Then a most alarming telegram came: Major-General Lord Methuen had been defeated, wounded and captured with most of his men at Tweebosch in the Western Transvaal by de la Rey. Kitchener was devastated. Methuen was handed back very soon, but this defeat at such a critical moment 'floored poor old K more than anything else during the campaign, and he didn't appear at five meals', as the Brat wrote home. The Chief continued to work from his room, for he gave orders and wrote a long letter to Roberts, but he was distraught at the prospect of the Boers now fighting on: army reform at home would be delayed, more money would drain from the exchequer, the United Kingdom almost denuded of troops, Germany and Russia encouraged to scorn British strength. Moreover the king's coronation and Kitchener's own departure for India would be delayed. At last, after forty-eight hours, he appeared for breakfast. He remarked that he believed his nerves had all gone to pieces. Ian Hamilton had detected that though Kitchener was 'impassive as a rock in appearance, he was really a bundle of sensitive and highly-strung nerves kept under control 999 hours out of 1,000 by an iron will'. A very sound breakfast, the Brat told his father on 16 March, 'was the end of the slump in his spirits, and he is, and has been, as right as possible since'.[11]

Vice-President Burger was too much a realist to be deceived by an unexpected local victory. His reply stated that he would like to offer terms of peace but must first confer with President Steyn (Orange Free State). Kitchener was not optimistic because Steyn and his commandant-general De Wet were more bellicose than the Transvaalers. Before they hunted for Steyn under British safe-conduct, Kitchener made sure that Burger, Botha and their small party were brought to see him as they passed through Pretoria. They gave nothing away at Melrose House but were deliberately treated as honoured negotiators, not defeated suppliants. Kitchener even arranged that the wife and daughter of one of them, 'tubby little Krogh', should be in the garden to greet him; at a later meeting Botha introduced his ten-year-old son.[12]

Thus began thirty days of negotiations, Boer with Boer, Boer with Kitchener and Milner; and, in effect, Kitchener against Milner.

Twenty years later, in 1922, three years after the Peace of Versailles which Kitchener had not lived to influence, Sir Ian Hamilton was unveiling a war memorial in Scotland. 'How is it', he asked, his rhetoric not masking the fundamental truth,

that the Boer War put an end to the feuds, race hatreds, bankruptcies, dis-orders and bloodshed which had paralysed South African progress for a generation, whilst the Great War has on the contrary inflicted race hatred, bankruptcy and murder over the best part of the old world from Ireland in the West to the Near East . . . ? I'll tell you why it is; it is because our Politicians entirely ignored the ideals of those to whom we have raised this memorial by making a vindictive instead of a generous peace . . . it was only by fighting those rulers for half a year that Lord Kitchener forced them to make a good peace in South Africa. Indeed, so few seem to realise it now that I feel it my duty, as Lord Kitchener's Chief Staff Officer that was, to keep the fact in being, alive. Lord Kitchener forced them to make a good peace in South Africa. For six months Lord Kitchener fought the politi-cians who wanted to make a vindictive peace, an 'unconditional surrender' peace as they called it, a peace which would above all things humiliate and wound the feelings of the conquered. They were death on this, I promise you. Well, Kitchener fought them fairly with one hand whilst he fought the Boers with the other, — and he beat them both. He beat them and made his own peace; a generous soldierly peace. He lent the Boers money; he rebuilt their farms; he rebuilt their dams; he re-stocked their farms. He always said; 'We must not lose one moment setting business on its legs again, otherwise South Africa will be ruined and many of us with it.' What has been the result? The war lasted three years; South Africa was more completely ruined than Central Europe; hate was stronger than it is in Germany:— and yet, within one year South Africa was smiling and so were we.[13]

Kitchener's magnanimity was neither merely pragmatic nor a cynical ploy but arose from the deepest recesses of his heart, informed by his Christian faith.

On 12 April twelve Boer leaders representing both republics conferred with Kitchener at Melrose House. On the first day, by order of the Cabinet in London, Milner was excluded: Hubert Hamilton was present as a witness because Sir Ian was in the Western Transvaal commanding five columns in a drive planned in great secrecy: Kitchener explained the scheme on the ground to the column commanders, including Walter. The drive had ended the day before with a crushing Boer defeat at Rooiwal, where Commandant Potgieter died in a gallant, impossible charge.

At the Pretoria meeting on the next day, when Kitchener showed surprise that the Boers should ask for independence, and President Steyn interjected that the people must not lose their self-respect, Kitchener replied that there could be no loss of self-respect for men who had fought so bravely.

He advised them to accept the British terms and bargain later for self-government. Hubert Hamilton told the Brat that 'K did the business extraordinarily well, they were all afraid of him and respected him tremendously'. The two presidents had tea with him the next day, Sunday, and on the Monday Milner arrived and terms continued to be hammered out. Milner complained that Kitchener, though 'extremely adroit', did not care how much he gave away, even willing to name a date for self-government;[14] Milner was still manoeuvring for unconditional surrender. Kitchener told Lady Cranborne that the Boers had 'a deadly loathing for Milner which makes it difficult at times as he realizes how much they detest him'.[15]

While waiting for the Cabinet's reply to the terms agreed, the ADCs took the Boer leaders to watch them play polo, which was much admired, Milner and Kitchener both coming too. The Cabinet sent a good reply, and on Friday 18 April the Boers left Pretoria to put the terms to the commandos in the field, which would take three weeks at least. Kitchener gave safe-conducts for delegates but firmly refused an armistice. Drives maintained the pressure to early May.

On 15 May sixty Boer delegates met under British protection in a large marquee at the border town of Vereeniging, where the railway crosses the Orange River from the former Free State into the Transvaal, about sixty miles south-east of Pretoria. Through his director of intelligence (Henderson) Kitchener kept abreast of the debate: Botha speaking strongly for peace as the only alternative to the ruin of the Afrikaner nation; de la Rey, with all the prestige of his defeat of Methuen, stunning the delegates by his conversion to peace, 'lest the door be bolted in our faces'. The conference would not accept the terms as they stood. They therefore appointed a commission of four, led by Botha, to negotiate further at Pretoria. For two days British and Boer wrestled verbally at Melrose House. At one point, when General De Wet became so obdurate that Milner was a about to break off negotiations (and resume his campaign for unconditional surrender), Kitchener cannily suggested that the military members withdraw and leave the lawyers to work out the point – and thus removed De Wet from the discussion. At another critical moment Kitchener drew Smuts aside in the open air and confidentially gave his personal opinion that in two years the Conservative government would fall and the Liberals come in. The Boers had been deeply touched by the Liberals' sympathy over the camps, and believed that the Liberals would be more willing to hasten self-government. Kitchener's intervention was decisive. 'That', said Smuts afterwards, 'accomplished the peace'.[16]

Smuts, thirty-two years old that week, had been born in Cape Colony and worked with Cecil Rhodes until transferring his allegiance to Kruger after the Jameson Raid. He had been a brilliant commando leader but now was ardent for reconciliation. Thus Botha, Smuts and de la Rey out-argued De Wet and won over the wavering Hertzog.

The commission returned to the Assembly of the People at Vereeniging and presented the ten articles 'to terminate the present hostilities'. The Boers would agree to lay down arms and become subjects of King Edward VII. No one would be prosecuted or sued except for criminal acts contrary to the usages of war. Dutch would continue to be taught where desired and used in administration and law alongside English. Civil government would replace military 'at the earliest possible date' leading up to self-government. However, 'the question of granting the Franchise to Natives will not be decided until after the introduction of Self-Government'. Kitchener had striven for a franchise at once, since otherwise it might be postponed indefinitely, but had to concede the point.

The most generous clauses came last: no levy would be imposed to defray the costs of the war, in stark contrast to the vindictive reparations that Versailles would impose on the defeated; and the British government would give the then very considerable sum of three million pounds sterling, together with loans, to aid reconstruction.

The delegates took the terms back to Vereeniging. They were debated long and hard until the late afternoon of Saturday 31 May 1902, when the Assembly agreed to the treaty by fifty-four votes to six, in a resolution that amounted to acceptance under protest, with side-swipes at British barbarity.

The result was wired to Pretoria at 3.30 p.m. with a request that it be kept secret until signed, and not signed until the Monday. Kitchener and Milner rejected delay: the treaty must be signed that night.

[211]

Burger, Botha and eight others were 'bundled into a train', as Frank Maxwell put it, brought up to Melrose House at 10.30 p.m. and taken to the dining-room, which the patent steam heating made warm on that autumn night of 31 May 1902. They asked to be left alone to reread the typed document and were given three minutes. Then Kitchener and Milner came in and sat at the head of the heavy dining-table (which now bears a plaque) with the six Transvaalers on one side, next to Milner, the four Free Staters on the other, next to Kitchener.

Four copies — one for the king, one each for the archives at Pretoria and Bloemfontein, and one for Kitchener — lay on the table, of a four-page document merely headed *Army Headquarters, South Africa*. Acting President Burger signed first, the Boers signing on the left of the last page, Kitchener and Milner on the right.

A stunned silence followed. Milner sat impassive. As the Boer leaders rose to leave, Kitchener went round giving each a handshake and saying, 'We are good friends now'.[17]

26

LOOKING FORWARD

CONGRATULATORY TELEGRAMS and letters poured in. 'Perhaps', wrote one friend, 'the greatest thing about it, is the way in which you have succeeded in conquering deep seated animosities and making the end radiant with the spirit of conciliation and goodwill.'[1]

Six days after the signing Kitchener received a telegram from the Prime Minister offering him a viscountcy. He accepted gratefully and asked if the patent of this peerage might include a special remainder to his two nephews in succession (if the elder had no male heir). Kitchener backed his request by a telegram to Salisbury's long-serving Private Secretary, Schomberg MacDonnell, who had also fought in South Africa in the early months of the Boer War and would be killed on the Western Front thirteen years later. Kitchener's telegram caused amusement at Downing Street, for after thanking MacDonnell for his congratulations he wired: 'Arrange if you can what I asked Lord Salisbury as I do not want at all in order to keep title in family to have to take a permanent encumbrance.'[2]

Salisbury minuted in red ink, in his now shaky handwriting, 'Does he mean a wife?' MacDonnell minuted back: 'The "encumbrance" to which K alludes is certainly a wife!'

In sending on the request to King Edward's Private Secretary, MacDonnell wondered whether, until Kitchener 'reaches an age when his celibacy seems more assured it might cause inconvenience to give remainder to his nephews'? He added that Lord Salisbury regarded Kitchener as 'a confirmed celibate' and that since both Wolseley and Roberts had peerages with special remainders to daughters it would be a gracious act for the king to bestow a similar favour.[3]

The College of Arms objected that a generation could not be skipped: in default of sons or daughters of his own, the peerage must go in succession to brothers and their male offspring. Schomberg wired to Kitchener for details and was given the names of Chevallier and his son Henry (Toby), who was nearly twenty-four and in the Navy, and Walter, whose only son, another Henry (Hal), was nearly twelve. 'I have one other brother between the two, Arthur Buck Kitchener, but as he is not in the Service, and is not likely to have children, I think he might possibly be omitted unless there is any legal desirability for putting him in.'[4] They were on affectionate terms but Arthur had married, in 1898, a middle-aged spinster, Edith Paterson from Melbourne, a novelist and spiritualist who held seances at Waihemo Grange before they left New Zealand for England. If Chevallier and his son should be dead, Herbert had no wish for the peerage conferred for military achievement to stick on a civilian before Walter could have it. However, Arthur was the first of the brothers to die, in 1907, followed by his widow in 1908.

The peerage was gazetted, with the special remainder omitting Arthur, as Viscount Kitchener of Khartoum, and of the Vaal in the Colony of the Transvaal, and of Aspall in the county of Suffolk.[5] Kitchener was even more grateful to be promoted to full general in the army 'as it completes the series of my ranks from Captain on, having all been obtained by brevet for active service'.[6]

On Sunday 8 June Kitchener attended early Holy Communion celebrated by the Archbishop of Cape Town who had reached Pretoria in the middle of the night. Then followed a great peace parade of more than five thousand men, eleven bands, all Pretoria church choirs and one from Johannesburg, one archbishop, two bishops and parsons from all denominations. The Chief decorated nurses and nine VCs and a Thanksgiving Service then followed. Nine days later the Chamber of Mines and Commerce gave a great banquet to Milner and Kitchener. All differences were forgotten. 'Milner made an A.1 speech, *most* generous to K.', recorded Frank Maxwell in his diary. 'K. made an even better one and did it splendidly. Everybody, delighted – a most successful evening.' The following day Kitchener spoke at Johannesburg, ending with a resounding tribute to his late enemies.

Three days later he and his staff left Pretoria through streets lined with troops presenting guard as his carriage passed. Arms of Honour were drawn up at each station the train steamed through , and at Kroonstadt came a typical K. incident.

His train had stopped. At the opposite platform stood a train full of troops going north to the front for routine guard duties. Recognizing his carriage, they began to shout, 'We want the Chief! We want K!' Kitchener looked embarrassed and shy and remained seated. A senior staff officer said, 'Don't mind, Sir, these are only the troops shouting'. But the Brat, with sure instinct, dashed up to the Chief. 'These men want to see you, Sir! We are going home. They are going back.' And on the instant Lord Kitchener went out with Maxwell and along the troop train, receiving a great ovation.[7]

Kitchener sailed from Cape Town after a resounding civic farewell. No doubt he had trophies and booty in his baggage like any victorious general, but he had not yet seen a magnificent gift from a South African.

Sammy Marks was a Jewish industrialist of great wealth and wide interests from agriculture to coal mining: his company had founded Vereeniging to exploit coal seams. Before the War he had commissioned from Europe a great bronze statue of Kruger, who chose a young sculptor, Anton van Wouw who went to Italy to supervise the casting by Francisco Bruno. Using Neapolitan fishermen as models van Wouw also sculpted four supporting figures representing Voortrekkers in typical attitudes. He had intended to present the whole group to the city of Pretoria. The statues had arrived in packing cases at Lourenço Marques harbour in Portuguese East Africa, where they stayed throughout the war. In June 1900 Marks had encouraged the start of the guerrilla war, but by February 1901 he was active in promoting Botha's peace talks. The longer the war continued, the more he deplored the refusal of Kruger in Europe to advise the Boer leaders in South Africa to accept that the war was lost and to make peace. He transferred his admiration from Kruger to Kitchener. After the signing of the peace he approached him and offered the four Voortrekker figures as a free and personal gift: Kruger should be erected in Pretoria in due time but without the magnificence conveyed by the supporting statues.

Kitchener accepted and arranged for them to be shipped from Lourenço Marques to England. Two could form part of a Royal Engineers South African War Memorial at Chatham and two would grace his park when he bought an estate: he had received another Parliamentary grant which Renshaw would invest wisely. Through Renshaw he had already made on abortive enquiry from Pretoria about Rothley Temple, since the man who had bought it from Harry Parker, when he and Millie had returned to New Zealand, had apparently left the district.[8] The Parkers were no longer well off. Herbert had brought one son into the Egyptian Army and had paid for a daughter's educa-tion at Cambridge.

The statues reached Chatham during 1902 and were placed at temporary sites. When Kitchener bought the Broome estate in 1910 he chose two, which were erected in 1913; the other two he gave to the Royal Engineers to form part of their memorial. The government of the new Union of South Africa had tentatively asked for the statues, but no action was taken because they were not loot but a gift to Kitchener from their rightful owner.

By then, opponents of Kitchener in his controversy with Curzon in India had spread the rumour that he had removed 'statues of Kruger and other famous Boers from public squares in Bloemfontein and Pretoria'. This libel crept into biographies, although the true facts were easily obtainable and the figures had never been unpacked from their cases until they reached Chatham.

In 1921, five years after Kitchener's death, his nephew Viscount Broome, who had inherited Broome Park, visited South Africa with his wife, saw the Kruger statue in Pretoria (erected in 1913) and met General Smuts. Lord Broome consulted the Royal Engineers and together they decided to present their statues to the city of Pretoria. The Colonial Office arranged transport to the Union. Years later, after her husband's death, Lady Broome visited Pretoria and saw them at the four corners of the Kruger Memorial 'and rec-ognized our dear old lead [sic] friends from Broome'.[9]

Kitchener landed at Southampton on Saturday 12 July 1902 to a tremendous civic and popular welcome. He had sailed from Cape Town on SS *Orotava* with French, Ian Hamilton, Rawlinson and his personal staff. His beloved Cameron Highlanders had arrived too late at Cape Town to sail with him. Their ship later passed his at sea. He had *Orotava*'s captain signal to ask for their transfer, but wireless telegraphy was still a few years in the future and the lamp signal went unnoticed. When he found them drawn up on the quay at Southampton with other troops, his great smile of pleasure was caught by a photographer using the new fast film, to become almost the only public photo-graph of Kitchener with a smile.

After the mayor's address he boarded a decorated train with the generals and staff. The engine carried a great K on its front; its journey was among the first public events to be recorded on film. People crowded the platforms at every station passed. At Basingstoke the special train stopped for another mayoral address, then was diverted from the usual boat-train route to arrive at a beflagged Paddington Station at ten minutes to two. The Prince of Wales and his uncle the Duke of Connaught went on board to greet Kitchener and the other two generals 'all looking very fit and well'. More royalty, and Lord Roberts, were on the platform. When K of K saw the Mayor of Paddington, he asked, 'How is the dam?', for Sir John Aird was head of the civil engineering company building the Aswan Dam, made feasible by the victory of Omdurman, now nearly four years ago. While Sir John read his mayoral address Kitchener fidgeted.

Then came the drive through London. The Prince of Wales wrote in his diary: 'He got a tremendous reception from thousands of people, the whole route from Paddington to St. James was lined with troops including the Indians, and Colonials who looked splendid.' They were still in London awaiting the coronation, postponed by the king's appendicitis operation: the stands along the processional route were freely used by the public. Both Birdwood and Rawlinson caught a glimpse of the wives they had not seen for three years. As the procession passed Buckingham Palace, not yet refaced with grey Portland stone, Queen Alexandra, the Princess of Wales and other royal ladies watched from the centre window.[10]

For Kitchener, hating fuss, this magnificent reception was a sore trial. He looked grim as he tried to suppress emotions that might cause him to burst into tears. George Arthur wrote two days later to his friend in Paris that he expected that at heart K 'really appreciated the warmth of it but unfortunately he is constitutionally unable to show that he enjoys anything like a noisy welcome'.[11]

At St James's Palace the Prince of Wales was host at a luncheon for fifty in honour of the returned victors. Then the Duke of Connaught took Kitchener up the Mall to Buckingham Palace for an audience of the king, lying in bed. To mark his coronation King Edward had founded the Order of Merit, an honour without title, to be limited as originally constituted to six generals, six admirals and twelve civilians chosen for their contribution to science, literature or the arts. The king fished the insignia from behind his pillow and delighted Kitchener by saying that he was the first to be invested.[12]

The next three months were spent partly in London on official work, such as completing his dispatches, testifying before the commission on the war, consulting with the India Office, and forming his staff as Commander-in-Chief, India, to include Birdie, Conk, the Brat and other devoted men; partly in country-house visiting; and, too frequently for his taste, enduring public occasions in his honour.

While in London he lived as before at Pandeli Ralli's house in Belgrave Square, along with the Herkomer portraits. If he walked out he was recognized and mobbed,[13] but he rode on Rotten Row, once with the Prince of Wales whose horse that day, to mutual amusement, was K of K,[14] and several times with Arthur Renshaw, discussing K's portfolio. Renshaw had recently married at the age of forty-eight. He and his brother had gone fishing in Ireland where both fell in love with the red-headed barmaid at their inn, only to discover that she was Lady Winifred Clements, sister of the young local landowner, the Earl of Leitrim, who was away at the war. Arthur won her, and when their son Tom was born Kitchener gladly stood godfather by proxy and took much interest in his godson. Like her husband Winifred became a great friend. Herbert Kitchener could relax with her sense of humour and uninhibited Irish ways and appreciate her wise head. He would bring their children presents and play trains on the floor with Tom. Lady Winifred grew to know the real Kitchener and was a doughty defender of his reputation until the end of her long life.

That summer of 1902 Walter and Herbert stayed at their mother's ancestral home, the moated manor at Aspall in Suffolk: the oriental rug that K gave to his Chevallier cousins was still on the floor in the last years of the century.[15] K stayed at Hatfield, as on every leave. The old marquess was ageing and had resigned the premiership the day before Kitchener had landed; his nephew, A. J. Balfour, had succeeded him. Kitchener stayed again with the Grenfells at Taplow Court. Julian, now fourteen, was home on Long Leave and wrote down his impressions on his return to Eton: Lord Kitchener looked just the same except more sunburned.

> When I asked him about South Africa he told me without the slightest 'swagger' or self-praise; in fact, I think modesty is one of his greatest qualities: he said he was very glad to get back to England again . . . Whatever was going on he seemed to pay the greatest attention to it, even if it was not of the slightest importance. He saw me catch a pike once, which got into a deep bed of weeds and took a very long time to land, and proposed that we should get up early next morning and see

if we could have any luck. The next morning there was a high wind and frequent showers of rain, an ideal day for fishing, but one when most people would prefer to be in bed. He was dressed before the time, and came to my room when I was still in bed. We managed to land two nice fish that morning, and Lord Kitchener seemed very pleased; while he could not help laughing as he just slipped the landing-net under the biggest we had yet seen and it gave a sharp turn, made a frantic push and broke the line.

'Lord Kitchener', added Julian inconsequentially, 'cannot stand two things – state dinners and being photographed.

'I think it would be very hard to find a man in whom there is so much will and so much ability to carry it into execution, and who in addition is so modest, so interested, and so clever and amusing.'[16]

Julian Grenfell was Kitchener's page at the delayed coronation in August. Shortly afterwards Lord Kitchener presented the Boer leaders Botha, De Wet and de la Rey to the king at Cowes at the time of the Coronation Naval Review. They had come over hoping to increase the indemnity promised in the treaty. The Prince of Wales wrote to his wife with unintended snobbery: 'They seemed quite decent sort of people but distinctly common, but were very civil and nice. They wore frock coats and high hats!'[17] Kitchener did all he could to make the Boers welcome, and they received much applause from the crowds.

After the coronation and the review he visited several great houses, such as Wynyards, Welbeck and Knowsley, then at the height of their glory, with scores of well-fed indoor and outdoor servants, their ducal or noble masters the centre of the political and social life of their counties. The strongly hierarchal structure of the English class system still had twelve years to run before the Great War brought great changes.

Earl and Countess Cowper invited him to Wrest, their curious Italianate villa up a long avenue in a beautiful Bedfordshire landscape. The old earl, a Knight of the Garter, was a great-uncle of Etty Grenfell and a cousin of Alice Cranborne. In the large house party which included the new Prime Minister, was a diarist, Adolphus Liddell, a middle-aged bachelor barrister in the Lord Chancellor's office who knew everyone and was asked everywhere. He liked to study in detail those he had not met before, and he noted in his diary at Wrest: Lord Kitchener the lion.

He has a curious face, something of the bulldog and something of the man of intellect, a long upper lip and huge moustache, which makes his strong chin look quite small. The whole skull is massive, and the bones of the brow are singularly prominent, so much so that in profile the upper part of the forehead seems to recede, though in full face the brow is wide. In repose there is rather a rough, heavy look about him, but his face lightens up strongly when he smiles, as is often the case with big men. His eyes are clear and alert, and his figure strong and youthful. He never held the floor, and did not talk much unless questioned, when he answered generally from a stock of platitudes about the war, which he seemed to keep for fashionable consumption.[18]

The lion went to Balmoral. 'We had a deer drive to-day', he wrote to Arthur Renshaw. 'The three first drives were blank and at the fourth and last I got a stag, the only one shot – not a bad beast. I hit him twice first in the chest at about 200 yards, then at 150 yards right in the centre of forehead which floored him. I like stalking better.' He added that Balfour was taking him to stay at his home in the Lowlands next day and that the king was wonderfully well.[9]

Interspersed with these delights were the sore trials of public dinners and presentations, including a Sword of Honour from South Africa. If a livery company or city fathers wished to give him their freedom he would bargain. He did not want the usual ornate gold casket of elaborate design, which would spend its days in the bank. He asked for gold cups, or saltcellars or other collec-tions to grace his table in India. The man who had won the Sudan by calcu-lating every penny wanted value for fame. This bargaining caused considerable ill feeling and grumbles about greed. Moreover he hated making speeches: he would get Ian Hamilton to draft them, then learn them by heart. If, as on one occasion, the gift was different from what he had been led to expect, and his prepared speech useless, he bowed, said Mr Joseph Chamberlain being more eloquent should speak at once, and sat down.

At Sheffield he was about to be presented with a magnificent service of silver plate before a distinguished gathering. Hamilton, beside him recalled:

We were all up on the platform 'on view'. So also were the plates. The applause had died away and now we were only waiting awkwardly for an aged duke to bring himself to the moment when he would begin his speech. K was very nervous but kept encouraging himself by looking at the plate.

'What do you suppose one of those plates would weigh?' he whispered to me.

'Half a pound,' I hazarded.

'Great Scot, man!' he exclaimed. 'They weigh three pounds if they weigh an ounce. Pick one up and see.'

I was seated next the plates and so I took one up delicately between fore-finger and thumb and had just balanced it when, in one flash, a shout of laughter shook the hall to its foundation. The people simply rocked with laughter. No one on the platform knew what had happened except the two of us and, if I was blushing, K was as red as a beetroot! He simply could not understand that anyone should think our close and obvious interest in the face-value of the gift was either amusing or in any way out of place.[20]

In October Kitchener slipped away from Victoria Station, refusing the official farewell which was customary for Commanders-in-Chief designate, and crossed the Continent while the staff and baggage went round by sea. On Tuesday 27 October he was in Cairo, where he was met by Wingate, now Sirdar of the Egyptian Army and Governor-General of the Sudan. They journeyed south by river and rail to fulfil Kitchener's dream – the opening of Gordon Memorial College.

Lord Edward Cecil told his sister Alice: 'From the moment we started from Cairo K. informally but firmly annexed the Sudan.' 'Nigs' Cecil was amused in his sardonic way to see Wingate, his present master, deferring to Kitchener at every point as if he were still governor-general. They inspected the construction site of the Aswan dam, still far from completion, and they landed on Kitchener Island, where Kitchener directed young sapper officers in laying out the measurements of a house. Cecil was amazed, because accord-ing to Cairo gossip Kitchener had sold his island. He had indeed put it on the market when India was confirmed, and had accepted an offer from George Denison Faber (later Lord Wittenham), MP for York, a rich banker and sup-porter of grand opera and of the turf, who had recently given far more for the Derby favourite than his offer for Kitchener Island. But Faber had not paid up, querying this and that. In September Kitchener had thought the sale might not come off, and Faber had still not paid when Kitchener had left Cairo.

But instead of giving the facts, Kitchener's sense of mischief made him pull the puzzled Cecil's leg when he 'ventured to enquire', as he told Alice, 'how the general impression, which was shared by the would-be purchaser, had got about that he had sold his island'.

'There are three,' said K., 'and the one I sold is the small one lower down the river.' 'What, the black rock,' I most incautiously said (it is not 30 ft. square and has a solitary thorn bush on it). 'The smaller stony one,' corrected the Great Man. Curiosity overmastering my terror, I asked if the purchaser had understood this. 'Not at first,' said K. indulgently, 'but I explained it. Besides, he has a son in the Hussars.' The subject then dropped.' [Faber was childless.][21]

After they crossed the border into the Sudan, 'We have lived under a merciful despotism', recorded Cecil. 'Everyone in turn has had the errors of the last three years clearly but kindly explained to them ... "Ah, Kennedy, I thought I told you to build these houses two stories high." A hurried explanation. "Yes, a very great mistake. Quite spoilt, but they can be pulled down later." Such is the ordinary type of conversation I listen to.'

The ex-Sirdar's criticisms, however, were constructive. He told Reuter's correspondent of his pleasure at the progress. The mass of ruins of three years earlier had become a rapidly rising city with fine buildings, avenues of young trees and an immense future, under the skilful eye of Lieutenant M. R. Kennedy, one of the finest young engineers the corps had produced.[22]

Kitchener stayed at the palace, now complete. The ADC, Captain C. E. C. G. Charlton of the Royal Horse Artillery, 'had never met him before and had always heard that he was a silent, taciturn man. But on this occasion at least he was in great spirits and ready to chaff and joke with us junior officers.'[23]

He opened Gordon Memorial College in its new brick building with due ceremony on 8 November 1902. Cromer had found a young Scottish educationalist, James Currie (afterwards Sir James), who was not only the first principal of the college but director of education, steadily placing primary schools throughout the Sudan. Kitchener was impressed, saying the growth of education was 'a most essential factor in opening up the country'. In future years he read the annual reports and sent encouraging messages to Currie through Wingate. He aimed for higher education provided, he would write from India, that it avoided creating 'the dissatisfied educated class we suffer from here'.[24]

His hopes for a medical college were fulfilled by the Sudan's choice of his own memorial. Gordon truly avenged, Kitchener left Khartoum on 11 November 1902.

Back in Cairo, where he was fêted by the khedive, 'that beast Faber has at last paid up after giving us an enormous amount of bother'.[25] The sale of Kitchener Island seemed to draw a line under the African period of his life. Ahead lay India, with its imperial magnificence, its opportunity for much-needed reform, which would lead unexpectedly to the resounding dispute with the viceroy which turned into a personal quarrel, not of Kitchener's making. Afterwards would come years of achievement in India and beyond, followed by a disappointment which led to further opportunity to serve Egypt, especially its poor. And then the sudden and supreme moment when he was called to save England.

That would be fourteen years ahead. In Khartoum, this November 1902, a speech by an Egyptian kaimakan (lieutenant-colonel) at a dinner in Kitchener's honour at the Egyptian officers' club, offers a fitting coda to the Africa years. Despite the natural exuberance of the original Arabic, the colonel's declamation demonstrates Lord Kitchener's hold, at the age of fifty-two, on the people of the East.

Verily! To your Lordship's prowess the decisive conquest of the Sudan is attributed. What a splendid and experienced leader you are! And how crushing the glorious victories were! Yours is a name that will live as a white mark on the brow of time for ever.

O! Noble minded General, the great hero of South Africa! We will never forget your eminent name. It is engraved on our hearts for ever.

Your glorious deeds coupled with your wonderful fore-thought and admirable management whereby we marched into the tumult of battle and affronted the soldiers' glorious death under your gallant command, have gained for us the highest honour to which one can aspire – to be numbered amongst the gallant warriors.

Your Lordship, all that you have noticed of the vast improvements and the progress of Khartoum City and throughout the places you alighted at or passed by since entering the Sudan on your present visit are the outcome of your brilliant conquests, reflecting great glory and unlimited credit upon you. At last all your stupendous efforts have been crowned with success.

In South Africa you were as one horse against the field, and yet, with your unfailing energy and indomitable pluck, you conquered, and gained not only the credit of the whole British Nation, but also that of the whole civilized world.

How great is our joy to see you amongst us once more! May'st thou live long! O great and noble General! and enjoy life with felicity and prosperity.[26]

APPENDIX I

KITCHENER AND SEX

A theory gained acceptance after Kitchener's death that he was a homosexual. This became an accepted part of the later twentieth-century portrait, some times expanded to suggest that he had a 'taste' for boys.

The theory is destroyed by the contemporary evidence. It was not believed in his lifetime by any who knew him. *The Times* correspondent in Peking in 1909 was told by a British officer who had served in Egypt that Kitchener, 'like most officers in the Egyptian army', had a tendency to buggery, but this was guilt by association. Peter King's *The Viceroy's Fall* (1986) records second-hand gossip, recalled at least seventy-two years later, which would not be accepted as evidence by a court of law; but contemporary private diaries and letters give not the slightest support to the theory, rather the reverse.

The death of his mother when he was on the verge of puberty may have frozen or retarded Herbert's sexual development, yet at 'the Shop' he went to balls, though gauche and shy, and enjoyed the relaxed friendship of his fellow cadet's sisters and friends during the visit to Truro and danced happily with them. Then came the years of intense dedication to his profession in Palestine and Cyprus. Army officers of his time were not expected to marry until at least their late twenties, hence the row over Walter. Many officers may have taken the occasional prostitute, but Kitchener's strong morality and his spiritual experiences at Chatham and Aldershot would have kept him away from brothels even before he joined the Guild of the Holy Standard and pledged himself 'to be sober, upright and chaste'. Working among Arabs and Turks, he could not fail to be aware of sodomy (the word 'homosexual' had not been coined), but he would have agreed with St Paul's judgement against men who 'burned in their lust towards another'.

Kitchener's unofficial engagement at the age of thirty-three to Hermione Baker is another indication of a heterosexual character. Her death, coinciding with the pressures of the desert campaigns, seems to have turned him into a confirmed celibate, 'married' to his profession, sublimating any sexual urges into the intensities and ambitions of his career, apart from mild flirtations with such as Ellen Peel. As Birdwood noted, K. had no time for marriage.

In 1981 a retired medical major-general, the late Frank Richardson, who was respected for administrative rather than medical gifts, included Kitchener in his book, *Mars Without Venus: A Study of Some Homosexual Generals*. He suggested that Kitchener's passion for porcelain and his love of flower arranging were symptoms of homosexuality. Porcelain is not the preserve of homosexual collectors and as for flower arranging, the present writer knew a retired senior general of the Second World War, happily married with three sons and a daughter, who would come down to the village church on the day before a major festival, with his gardener loaded with flowers, and transform the chancel screen into a floral display of great beauty as an aid to Easter or Whitsun worship.

General Richardson insinuates a homosexual implication to the nickname of the creators of the Sudan Military Railway: Kitchener's 'band of boys'. To any contemporary in the Sudan that idea would have been ludicrous. 'The band of boys' label was attached to those sapper officers because they were so young for the job. Any 'boy' whom Kitchener saw on his frequent inspections of the desert line in the making would have been hard at work surrounded by Arab labourers and British NCOs.

Proponents of the homosexual theory also write of 'Kitchener's boys', referring to his ADCs and younger staff officers. Most of these were in their late twenties or older, and later married: the Chief had plenty of godchildren. In the Sudan and South Africa his personal staff were always hard at work in a close-knit team. And as Lord Edward Cecil noticed, K would not allow smutty stories at mess. It is a matter for admiration, not sexual inuendoes, that the stern general had such excellent and even affectionate relations with ADCs like Jimmy Watson and 'the Brat'.

The India period (in Volume 2, to come) is even less encouraging to the theory that Kitchener was homosexual or had a taste for boys. When Hector MacDonald was summoned home from Ceylon to answer allegations that he had been having sex with native boys, Kitchener wrote to Hunter: 'What a horrible thing this has been about MacDonald. I expect he went quite mad after leaving South Africa. Did you hear anything of the sort before about him? I never did.' That was hardly the reaction of a man affected by a similar sexual pull. And when, in the great quarrel, Curzon's allies spread every libel (such as heavy drinking) they never even hinted at what they would have called unnatural vice or sodomy – even one story half-confirmed would have wrecked Kitchener's career, yet in the gossipy society of Simla, where nothing could be hidden for long, no such story emerged.

General Richardson ends the essay with a comment that Lord Kitchener was drowned in HMS *Hampshire* with Colonel Oswald Fitzgerald with whom he had been *living openly* (author's italics) for over three years. To the reader of 1981 that phrase had only one meaning, and to use it to describe their profes-sional and human relationship during the Great War is offensive. Moreover, at York House 'Fitz', as Military Secretary, was not the only one living at close quarters with the field marshal, now Secretary of State for War in terrible times. His Private Secretary (civil), Sir George Arthur, had parked his beloved wife in the country so that he could be at Kitchener's side whenever needed, day or night. Arthur was a deeply religious man, as also were Fitz (who never married) and Kitchener himself.

Sir Philip Magnus concluded in chat with a friend (and hints at it in his book) that Kitchener was probably homosexually inclined but kept it so tightly controlled that it never had physical expression. No one can fully know another's intimate thoughts, but Kitchener's proposal of marriage to Lady Helen (if true) and his platonic friendships in later life with older women in India, Egypt and England, together with the social, legal, moral and religious attitudes of the period, all suggest strongly that Lord Kitchener was not homosexual.

In a letter to a young cousin who had announced her engagement to a Captain Preston, Kitchener wrote that he hoped to meet him before leaving England again. 'Not having been in the happy state you are in now I hardly know what the correct observation should be but I am quite sure Preston is not good enough for you and though I shall delight in your happiness I cannot help envying his good fortune.'

'Your affectionate cousin, Herbert.'

APPENDIX 2

KITCHENER'S MASONIC
APPOINTMENTS
1883–1902

Like King Edward VII, King George V and many senior officers, including Sir Reginald Wingate, Kitchener was a freemason.

1883	Initiated in La Concordia Lodge, No. 1226, Cairo (lodge erased in 1890). [Kitchener does not appear in the Grand Lodge Register under Lodge No. 1226, nor under No. 1355, which is given as his lodge when later a founder of Drury Lane Lodge, No. 2127. United Grand Lodge Grand Officers file states his initiation presumed to be in Star of the East Lodge, No. 1355, in 1883 or if not there in the Egyptian Grand Lodge or La Concordia, No. 1226.]
1885	Founder of Drury Lane Lodge, No. 2127, London.
2 November 1889	Joined Bulwer Lodge, No. 1068, Cairo (now meeting in London).
12 February 1890	Exalted in Bulwer Chapter, No. 1068, Cairo.
8 March 1890	Joined Grecia Lodge, No. 1105, Cairo. Worshipful Master, 1892.
15 November 1892	Joined Star of the East Chapter, No. 1355, Cairo. Most Excellent Zerubbabel (i.e. Head of Chapter), 1896.

1895	Founder and 'Honorary Worshipful Master' of the Fatieh Lodge (National Grand Lodge of Egypt).
5 April 1895	Past Senior Grand Warden of Egypt.
1896	Made 'Honorary Worshipful Master' of El Lataif Lodge.
c. 1896	Appointed Past Third Grand Principal of Grand Chapter of Egypt.
1897	Appointed Junior Grand Warden (Past Rank) United Grand Lodge of England (at special Queen Victoria Jubilee Celebration Meeting; Jubilee Medal in Grand Lodge Museum).
1897	Appointed Grand Scribe Nehemiah (Past Rank), Supreme Grand Chapter of England.
1898	Made honorary member of Lodge of Edinburgh, Mary's Chapel No. 1.
1899–1901	District Grand Master, Egypt and the Sudan.
7 November 1902	Joined Khartoum Lodge, No. 2877 (later made honorary member).
29 November 1902	Appointed District Grand Master, Punjab, India.

[Information kindly supplied by the Librarian of the United Grand Lodge of England, Freemasons' Hall, London)

Volume II

Saviour of the Nation

for

Emma, Julian and Peregrine

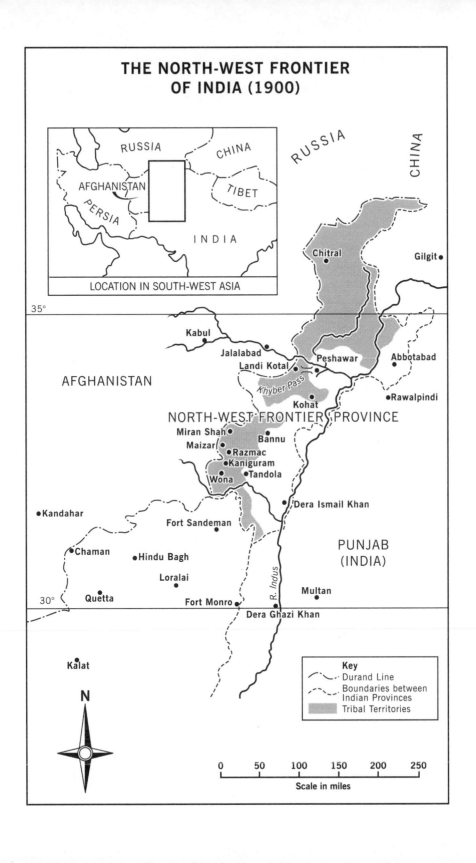

THE NORTH-WEST FRONTIER OF INDIA (1900)

RUSSIA
CHINA
AFGHANISTAN
TIBET
PERSIA
INDIA

LOCATION IN SOUTH-WEST ASIA

RUSSIA

CHINA

Chitral
Gilgit

35°

Kabul
Jalalabad
Landi Kotal
Peshawar
Abbotabad
Khyber Pass
Kohat
Rawalpindi

AFGHANISTAN

NORTH-WEST FRONTIER PROVINCE

Miran Shah
Maizar
Bannu
Razmac
Kaniguram
Wona
Tandola

Dera Ismail Khan

Kandahar

Fort Sandeman

Chaman
Hindu Bagh

PUNJAB
(INDIA)

Loralai

30°
Quetta
Fort Monro
R. Indus
Multan

Dera Ghazi Khan

Kalat

N

Key
— ·— Durand Line
— — — Boundaries between
Indian Provinces
▨ Tribal Territories

0   50   100   150   200   250

Scale in miles

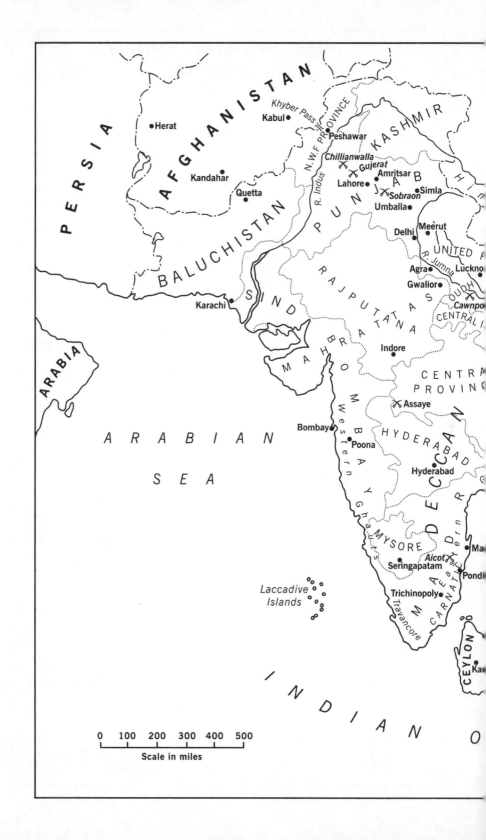

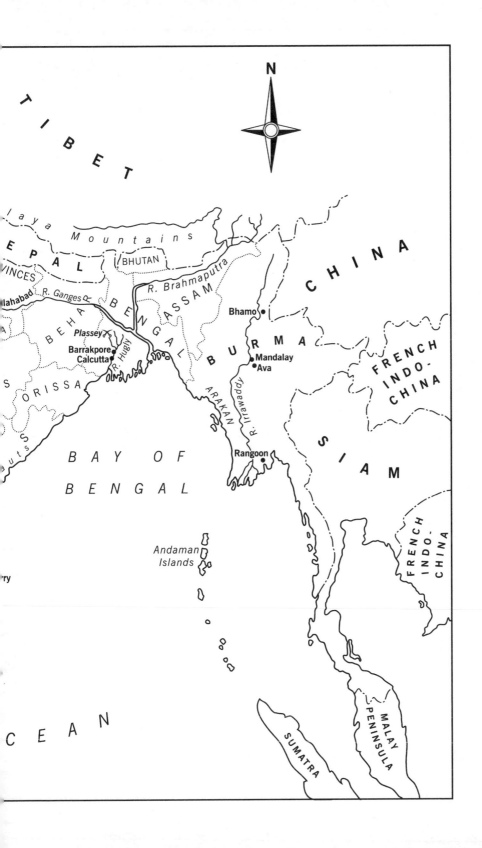

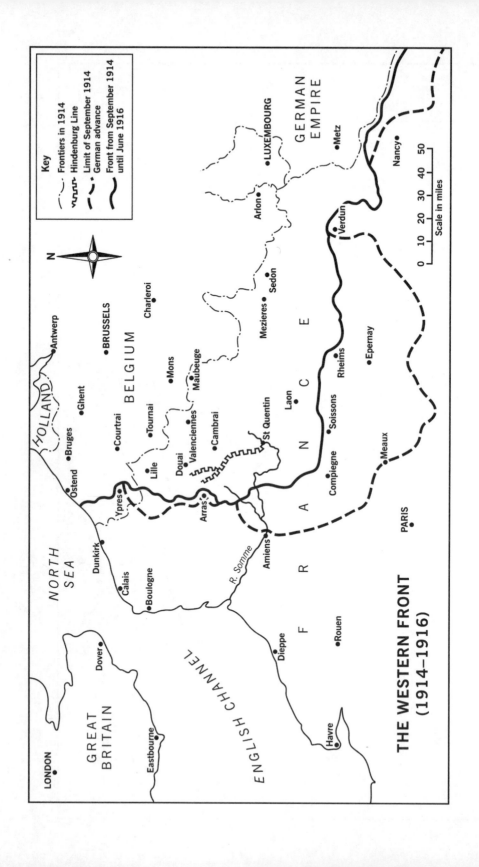

THE WESTERN FRONT (1914–1916)

Key
- Frontiers in 1914
- Hindenburg Line
- Limit of September 1914
- German advance
- Front from September 1914 until June 1916

N

Scale in miles
0 10 20 30 40 50

GREAT BRITAIN

LONDON

Dover

Eastbourne

NORTH SEA

ENGLISH CHANNEL

Dieppe

Rouen

Havre

HOLLAND

Antwerp

BRUSSELS

BELGIUM

Ghent

Bruges

Courtrai

Ostend

Dunkirk

Calais

Boulogne

Ypres

Arras

Amiens

R. Somme

Lille

Douai

Valenciennes

Cambrai

Tournai

Mons

Maubeuge

St Quentin

Laon

Soissons

Compiegne

Meaux

PARIS

Charleroi

Mezieres

Sedon

Arlon

LUXEMBOURG

Rheims

Epernay

Verdun

Nancy

Metz

GERMAN EMPIRE

F R A N C E

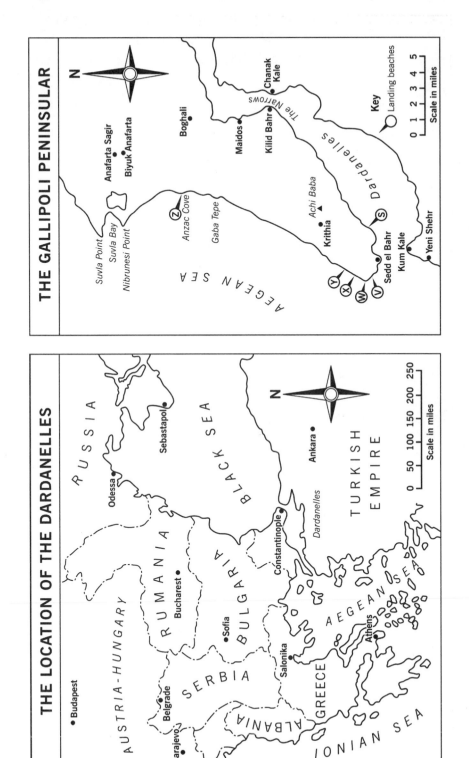

THE LOCATION OF THE DARDANELLES

AUSTRIA-HUNGARY

RUSSIA

• Budapest

• Sarajevo

Belgrade •

SERBIA

ALBANIA

RUMANIA

Bucharest •

• Odessa

BLACK SEA

Sebastopol •

• Sofia

BULGARIA

Salonika •

GREECE

Athens •

Constantinople •

Dardanelles

Ankara •

TURKISH EMPIRE

AEGEAN SEA

IONIAN SEA

N

Scale in miles

0   50   100   150   200   250

THE GALLIPOLI PENINSULAR

N

Suvla Point

Suvla Bay

Nibrunesi Point

AEGEAN SEA

Anzac Cove

Gaba Tepe

Ⓩ

Anafarta Sagir •

Biyuk Anafarta •

• Boghali

Achi Baba ▲

Krithia •

Ⓨ
Ⓧ
Ⓦ
Ⓥ

Sedd el Bahr •

Kum Kale

Ⓢ

Yeni Shehr •

Maidos •

Kilid Bahr •

The Narrows

Chanak Kale •

Dardanelles

Key

Ⓞ Landing beaches

Scale in miles

0 1 2 3 4 5

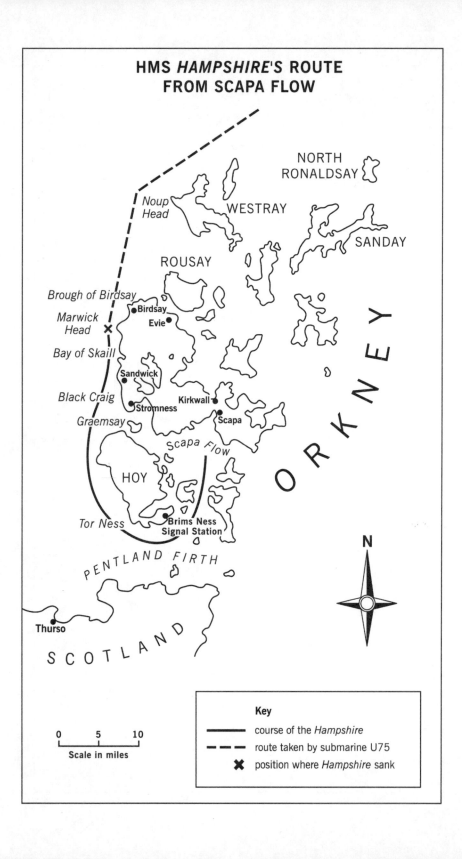

HMS *HAMPSHIRE'S* ROUTE
FROM SCAPA FLOW

NORTH
RONALDSAY

*Noup
Head*

WESTRAY

SANDAY

ROUSAY

Brough of Birdsay

Birdsay

*Marwick
Head* ✕

Evie

Bay of Skaill

O R K N E Y

Sandwick

Black Craig

Kirkwall

Stromness

Graemsay

Scapa

Scapa Flow

HOY

Tor Ness

Brims Ness
Signal Station

N

PENTLAND FIRTH

Thurso

S C O T L A N D

0   5   10
Scale in miles

Key

—————— course of the *Hampshire*

— — — — route taken by submarine U75

✕ position where *Hampshire* sank

PART ONE

Two Tigers

1902–1905

I

A CORDIAL WELCOME

IN THE BRIEF INTERVAL between his return to Cairo from opening
Gordon College in the Sudan and embarking at Suez for India, General
Viscount Kitchener of Khartoum wrote to his great friends the Cranbornes
at Hatfield, with whom he had corresponded for fourteen years. Lady
Cranborne had been worried because he had set off alone across France
and the Mediterranean while his staff went round by sea, but 'Your evident
want of confidence in my power of looking after myself,' he told her, 'was
not verified in the least, as I have managed perfectly and done all I intended
without a single mistake or losing my luggage once. I have been quite well
the whole time.' He added that the people of the Sudan had been glad to
see him, that his old chief, Lord Cromer, recently remarried, was very
much in love, while the Khedive of Egypt was being unfaithful to his
wife.[1]

Kitchener also wrote to Raymond ('Conk') Marker, who had gone
ahead to India to prepare, since he had previously served on the staff of the
Viceroy. After various instructions Kitchener concluded: 'My best salaams
to Lady Curzon and his Excellency. I am looking forward with great
pleasure to serving under him in India.'[2]

Curzon was about to enter the final year (as was supposed) of a brilliant
viceroyalty. Four years earlier George Curzon, then thirty-nine, had been
with Queen Victoria at Balmoral for his audience on appointment to India
when Kitchener's Omdurman dispatch arrived. The Queen could not find
her glasses; Curzon was commanded to read it aloud. Some weeks later he

wrote a note to welcome Kitchener home 'after your great exploits. It is a great thing that the nation should have heroes but a still greater that it should recognize them as such.'[3] They met briefly, and Curzon urged Kitchener to come to India as Commander-in-Chief at the next vacancy.

In the four years since, many barriers had been overcome: the doubts of the old Queen and the new King Edward and others;[4] and the long-drawn-out war in South Africa which detained Kitchener after the appointment was confirmed. Curzon had begun to fear that his viceroyalty would be nearly over, but Kitchener cut short the six months' leave to which he was entitled. He did not, however, follow Lady Curzon's advice to find a wife. He had no wish 'to take a permanent encumbrance'.[5]

The post of Commander-in-Chief would not be merely ceremonial and routine. Curzon wanted Kitchener to reform the army. 'I see absurd and uncontrolled expenditure,' he had written in his grandiloquent style. 'I observe a lack of method and system; I detect slackness and jobbery; and in some respects I lament a want of fibre and tone.'[6] Kitchener had learned in South Africa that the land forces of the Indian Empire, although valiant, were scattered around without clear shape or co-ordinated purpose. In England during his leave he had spent time with William Birdwood, one of the two Indian cavalrymen on his staff, who had organized his lines of communication troops and was coming out as his assistant military secretary. After Birdwood had described the situation, Kitchener exclaimed:

> You really have no *Indian* Army with esprit de corps as such. You have a large number of small armies — some very small — all jealous of one another, and each probably thinking itself superior to the rest. I want to see a real Indian Army . . . I want you to make me proposals to carry out my idea, and have them ready as soon after I reach India as possible.[7]

Furthermore, the Indian army and the British regiments serving in India were under a confused structure of higher command, a problem that was highlighted for Kitchener when his old subordinate, Sir Horace Smith-Dorrien, veteran of Omdurman and Paardeburg, suddenly arrived from India.

Smith-Dorrien was the Adjutant-General, second only to the

Commander-in-Chief. He told Kitchener how he had wanted to resign in despair at the confusion caused by the time-honoured system whereby the C-in-C's decisions in military matters could be vetoed by the junior general who was the Military Member of the Viceroy's Council. Smith-Dorrien's resignation was not accepted. Instead the outgoing C-in-C, Sir (Arthur) Power Palmer, sent him on special leave to brief Lord Kitchener. 'I shall never forget,' recalled Smith-Dorrien many years later, 'that masterful man's face as I read and explained to him case after case. He fairly gasped out, "Is this the sort of thing I have got to compete with?"'[8]

The Military Member, responsible for supply, transport and ordnance, was not comparable to the Secretary of State for War at home, who, as the civil head, was answerable to Parliament and had the last word, but viceroys were inclined to treat him as such. A proposal to abolish the Military Member might therefore spark a constitutional dispute, although the Commander-in-Chief also sat on the Council when military matters were discussed. Kitchener told friends that he would not quarrel with Curzon but exert his popularity and prestige on the next Viceroy if necessary. He discussed the proposed abolition with the Prime Minister, who promised general support to the idea, and with Lord Roberts, who disagreed; Roberts's forty-one years in India had ended ten years earlier. Kitchener assumed that abolition would be simple. He never dreamed of serious trouble, he later told his old brother-in-arms Archie Hunter, or he would never have come at all.[9] And he knew that Birdwood, going ahead on a troopship with his wife and children, would have a clear proposal ready when they met in India.

Birdwood was generally called 'Birdie'. Nicknames were common in the army at a time when gentlemen addressed each other by surnames, without prefix, unless relatives or intimate friends. Kitchener's devoted staff or 'family' was led by Colonel Hubert Hamilton, DSO, of the Queen's, a Burma, Omdurman and South African veteran aged forty-one, perhaps a little solemn but well liked. He was known as 'Hammy' ('Handsome Hammy' behind his back). Major Raymond Marker, DSO, of the Coldstream Guards, the senior ADC, aged thirty-five, was invariably 'Conk', and the second ADC was the delightful Major Frank Maxwell, VC, DSO, whom Kitchener had nicknamed 'the Brat' for his youthful looks. Like Birdie, he was a Bengal Lancer and was now aged thirty-one. The third ADC and the youngest, at nearly thirty, was Captain Victor

Brooke, DSO, of the 9th Lancers. He seems to have had no nickname unless, like his younger brother who grew up to be Field Marshal Lord Alanbrooke of the Second World War, he was 'Brookie'. All had distinguished themselves in the field before Kitchener invited them to his personal staff.

They were never known as 'Kitchener's Boys' or 'The Boys',[10] which would hardly have been appropriate when their ages ranged from forty-one to thirty. 'The Band of Boys' was the nickname given by the army to the young Royal Engineers officers in the Sudan who built Kitchener's 'impossible' desert railway in 1897. It was not used in India for his mature, battle-tried staff, a close-knit 'family' which would mean much to him in the unexpected struggle to come. Moreover, all five staff officers had served in India, which 'the Chief', as they always called him, had visited only once, on leave from Egypt when his brother Walter was stationed in Poona. Hammy had the Burma Medal, Birdie and the Brat had been in action on the North-West Frontier, where the Brat had been recommended for a Victoria Cross for the first time. Conk knew the corridors of power as a former ADC to the Governor of Ceylon and to the Viceroy, and Brooke had been serving in India with the 9th Lancers when they were ordered to South Africa. All lost their lives in the First World War.

Conk and Birdie had gone ahead. The Chief joined the Brat, Hammy and Brooke at Suez. They had brought the Chief's baggage from England, including liveries for Indian servants and much plate to grace his table, presented with the freedom of cities after he had made himself a little unpopular with civic fathers for objecting to traditional useless caskets. Southampton, however, remained obdurate but played up at last with 'a tremendous casket – must have cost £250 at least. Luckily it had 8 little gilt figures of soldiers which I rapidly removed and am having turned into salt cellars.'[11] Also in the liner's hold were crates of Kitchener's collection of ceramics, armour and curios which had been stored in Cairo during the South African war.

Kitchener was travelling towards the command he had wanted. As if to emphasize to himself that the future was all that mattered, the victor of Omdurman and peacemaker of South Africa reread his personal correspondence of the years that were past, tore up the letters, except those from his father, and threw them into the sea.

*

Kitchener landed at Bombay on 28 November 1902. The outgoing C-in-C greeted him with yet another case where the Military Member had vetoed an administrative decision, trivial in itself but symptomatic. Kitchener, of sterner stuff than Palmer, quietly reversed the veto.

He travelled upcountry in his special train, and at Bhurtpore, later to be famous for its bird sanctuary, he spent two days with the Viceroy and his American wife. 'He is very well and she is as beautiful as ever,' he told Lady Cranborne. 'They both gave me a very cordial welcome.'[12]

Curzon, nine years younger than Kitchener, was at the height of his fame and splendour as Viceroy. Although appointed so young, he had a wide knowledge of Asia from his early pioneering travels. In India he had effected reforms and was widely admired by all races and religions and also left an indelible mark by his restoration of the Taj Mahal and other monuments. At Eton, Oxford and in politics he was one of the most sparkling of his generation, though not without flaws, and lived up to his Oxford nickname of 'Superior Person'.* He was conscious that he was heir to Kedleston, the estate which had been held by Curzons in unbroken male descent since Norman times, and to an old peerage, while Kitchener was merely grandson of a tea merchant.

Sir Walter Lawrence, Curzon's Private Secretary, who had known him since Oxford, wrote long afterwards:

> There was a likeness between these two remarkable men. They both lived for work, and cared nothing for the susceptibilities of others. Neither could tolerate inefficiency nor be lenient to failure. Lord Curzon was the greater student and could work longer than Lord Kitchener. Both were equally impatient of criticism or opposition. Both loved pageantry, loved beautiful surroundings, and took an almost feminine interest in the details of domestic arrangements. Both were determined and acquisitive collectors, and both had an extreme reverence for rank. Lord Curzon loved debate and revelled in logical and masterly minutes. Lord Kitchener distrusted and despised all such official exercises . . . Both were great lovers of their country and devoted to duty. Many

* My name is George Nathaniel Curzon
  I am a most superior person,
  My cheek is pink, my hair is sleek,
  I dine at Blenheim once a week.

probably regarded them as hard, strong men; yet I saw Lord Kitchener in tears as he watched some old veterans of the Mutiny totter by at the Delhi Durbar; and I knew of a case where he had punished an offender harshly, and soon after had found him congenial work on better pay. From the old Balliol days to the time of his death, I knew how gentle and affectionate Lord Curzon could be when he was off duty.[13]

Both men were Christian believers, but whereas Curzon had a string of mistresses until his marriage to Mary Leiter, daughter of a self-made Chicago millionaire, Kitchener was chaste, even before he became a member of the Guild of the Holy Standard and pledged himself 'to be sober, upright and chaste'.[14] Curzon was outgoing, Kitchener painfully shy; both men were physically handicapped, Kitchener by poor sight and Curzon by curvature of the spine which gave him frequent pain.

'We had long, confidential and most friendly talks,' wrote Curzon after their discussion at Bhurtpore, 'and he greatly impressed me by his honesty, directness, frank common sense and combination of energy with power. I feel that at last I shall have a Commander-in-Chief worthy of the name and position.'[15] Kitchener knew of Curzon's unpopularity in the army, which blamed him personally for every fault of the system. Kitchener wanted a better system and even remarked that perhaps he might have made a mistake in not coming out as Military Member, a post he had once coveted as a suitable follow-on to his term as Sirdar of the Sudan, before the South African war changed the direction of his life. He outlined his plans. Curzon asked him to wait a little until he had seen the system at work. Kitchener had already decided to do so.[16]

Before they parted – Curzon to put finishing touches to the coming Coronation Durbar, Kitchener to umpire the manoeuvres – a charming incident gave much pleasure. Queen Victoria's Indian servants, who had been sent home by King Edward, joined Kitchener's household at their own request.[17] They had been impressed at Balmoral and Windsor by this magnificent Lord of War (*Jangi Lat*) who was now their own new *Jangi Lat Sahib* of India. He alone could be worthy to command those who had waited on their beloved Queen Empress.

Sir Power Palmer had left the planning of the manoeuvres to Smith-Dorrien, who was gratified that 'when Lord Kitchener arrived he told me to carry on'. Twenty-two thousand British and Indian soldiers as the northern army advanced from Umballa against a southern army of 14,000 defending Delhi, 120 miles away. Kitchener praised Smith-Dorrien for his scheme and the seventeen days of operations; but privately he was all the more certain that reforms were essential.[18]

During the manoeuvres he made a swift hundred-mile journey to Simla, the summer capital in the Himalayan foothills, to see the Commander-in-Chief's bungalow, Snowdon. Kitchener could never take over an official residence without wanting to make it grander. Snowdon was not dignified enough for the Lord of War who must entertain maharajahs and visiting generals, nor roomy enough for his staff to live comfortably under his roof, except for the married Birdie. Its chief rooms were not spacious enough to display his trophies and captured banners and his ever-growing collection of porcelain, nor could he give dinners worthy of his gold and silver plate, received with the freedom of British cities. And he detected, as a Royal Engineer, that Snowdon was structurally unsound.

Full of plans for Snowdon, he returned to the plains for the final days of the manoeuvres and the umpires' conference that followed. The two armies then went into camp together, ready for the great Delhi Durbar to proclaim the absent King Emperor, in effect his Indian coronation, although wags spoke of his 'Curzonization'.

The Durbar also celebrated the first twenty-five years of a united empire, formed by the patchwork of native states, large and small, which were self-governing under viceregal supervision ('the India of the Princes'), and British India, the provinces ruled directly through the Indian Civil Service, led by a comparatively small number of British. Whether magistrates or district officers, commissioners or governors, they fulfilled Queen Victoria's command, 'Be kind to my Indians', despite occasional lapses and that inbred sense of national superiority which was common to their times. In the words of Sir Walter Lawrence, who spent many years in the service: 'Their mission was clear; it was to secure the welfare of the millions, to prevent corruption and tyranny, to prevent and to fight famine, plague and pestilence, and to ensure that every Indian should have the free right to enjoy unmolested the rites and rules of his religion, his caste and his tribe.'[19] Forty-five years had passed since the Mutiny, which had affected only part of the subcontinent although shaking the whole. India had long been at peace except for occasional small wars on the North-West Frontier.

Hindu and Muslim, Buddhist and Christian lived together. Despite areas of deep poverty, the Indian Empire prospered. The Queen Empress had been venerated and her death deeply mourned. The opening reign of the new *Kaiser-i-Hind* evoked loyalty and hope across the Raj. Kitchener entered on his East Indies Command, as it was termed officially, at a propitious time, symbolized by the imminent Durbar.

2

POMP AND CIRCUMSTANCE

ON 29 DECEMBER 1902 His Excellency the Viceroy, accompanied by His Excellency the Commander-in-Chief and an array of maharajahs and princes, British governors and generals, went in state to Delhi railway station to welcome His Royal Highness the personal representative and brother of the King Emperor. The Duke of Connaught and his Duchess knew India well from his years of military service. Kitchener watched the Viceroy and the Duke and their ladies mount ornate howdahs on richly caparisoned elephants: the Curzons' elephant had gold circlets on its feet and had carried a previous Viceroy in 1877 to proclaim Queen Victoria Empress of India.

Kitchener then mounted his charger. Someone had made Curzon nervous by saying that Kitchener was such a bad rider that he might fall off.[1] Possibly this critic had watched Kitchener in Egypt some years back at polo, which he played badly because of poor eyesight. He had in fact won races in his youth, hunted with hounds and conducted three major battles from his white Arab.

Led by a squadron of turbaned Bengal Lancers, he and his staff rode at the head of the state entry into Delhi, a brilliantly colourful procession of 150 elephants, each with ceremonial escorts of mounted and marching troops, spearmen and macebearers, which wound slowly through the city by a circuitous route so that more thousands of Indians could enjoy the spectacle. The trappings of the elephants and their howdahs, the splendour of the uniforms or robes of those who sat in them, and the jewels sparkling

[249]

on maharajahs and rajahs made a magnificence 'the like of which even India, that land of pageantry, had never beheld', as an English journalist enthused.[2]

Three days later, on 1 January 1903, the King Emperor was proclaimed before a vast concourse in an amphitheatre specially built in Mogul style. When the Viceroy and the Duke had taken their places, 500 old men – Indian and British veterans of the Indian Mutiny – marched, limped and shuffled by the saluting base. Walter Lawrence saw Lord Kitchener's tears. Many others wept as they cheered and clapped. The veterans were followed into the arena by regiment after regiment, guns, cavalry and infantry, British and Indian, who formed up before the Viceroy, the Duke and Kitchener. The chief herald then read the Proclamation.

During the next day all manner of displays and entertainments filled the arena. The march past of retainers and household troops gave Kitchener a glimpse of India of the princes, including the Rao of Cutch's sword-and-buckler men marching on stilts, and the Gwaekwar of Baroda's guns of solid gold and silver, drawn by bullocks. On the Sunday, Kitchener was in a more familiar setting when the British troops and civilians attended a parade service on the polo ground. Their numbers were too great for a sermon to be preached, and the choirs sang through megaphones to lead the soldiers as they roared out familiar hymns. Curzon had vetoed 'Onward, Christian Soldiers' because of the line 'Crowns and thrones may perish . . .'.

They then marched back to their camps. The British and the Indian troops were camped all over the Plain of Delhi. Thus, the Durbar, so soon after Kitchener's arrival, enabled him to inspect in a week more regiments of varied races and traditions than a Commander-in-Chief would normally see in six months. He found an immediate rapport with Indian troops, just as he had with his Sudanese, but he relied on Birdwood to translate. He never mastered Urdu as he had Arabic. He was fluent in Arabic (with a Sudanese accent) because he had lived among Arabs, whereas his attempts to learn Urdu (often called Hindustani at that time) were limited by his scanty leisure time in South Africa and on the journey out.[3]

To Indian troops the new Lord of War looked a magnificent presence who surely must be the next Viceroy. To British officers and men who did not know him from the Sudan or South Africa, and to many who did, he seemed majestic but aloof. 'He certainly inspired awe,' as one officer recalled. 'Over six feet in height, square-headed and massive about the shoulders, his general aspect was striking, and the impression was heightened by the impassivity of his face from which a stranger could gather nothing.' The slight cast in his left eye 'increased the difficulty of judging his thoughts, though it is said that his intimate friends could form their own conclusions by watching that eye, in which the cast increased if he were troubled or annoyed'.[4] Army gossip did not realize that the glare of the deserts had, with his wound of 1888, already widened the cast and combined to give him the harsh, even cruel look that disappeared when he smiled.[5]

Kitchener had his own camp, not as big as the Viceroy's, which contained 2,774 people, but the tents had been transformed into palatial reception rooms and luxurious bedrooms for his guests. Among friends and relatives whom he had invited to India for the Durbar were Colonel Sir Henry Rawlinson, the future general who had been with Kitchener at the battles of the Atbara and Omdurman, and his wife. Rawlinson wrote in his diary: 'I have been immensely interested to see K in these new surroundings. He has taken to all the ceremonies like a duck to water, and looks a splendid figure of a man on his horse, on parade, or at a full-dress function in the evening. He is a perfect host, and takes endless pains to see that his guests are comfortable. It was a sight for sore eyes to see him footing it in the royal quadrille at the state ball,' held in the glorious Diwan-i-Am, the Hall of Public Audience in the palace of the Mogul emperors within the Red Fort, the room where the Peacock Throne once stood.

After the supper the Viceroy collected round him the most distinguished of his guests in the smaller Diwan-i-Khas, the Hall of Private Audience, with its exquisite inlays which Curzon had restored, and the famous inscription in Persian: 'If a paradise be on the face of the earth, it is this, it is this, it is this.' Electric lights brought out the beauty of the latticework.

Rawlinson wrote in his diary:

I shall never forget that sight. There were gathered together, Curzon with his lady in a lovely gold-embroidered dress, the Duke and Duchess of Connaught, the Duchesses of Portland and Marlborough, and a raja or two, and K, even in the midst of those splendid women and gorgeous Eastern potentates, was the most impressive figure of the lot. The competition has been severe, for Curzon does these things in the grand manner, but K keeps his end up well. The ladies of Delhi are full of apprehension, for they have never conceived of the possibility of a bachelor Commander-in-Chief, and they are wondering what will happen when they get to Simla. They need have no fears; K means to do them well, and I am sure he will.[6]

Another of Kitchener's guests at the Durbar, Lady Winifred Renshaw, recalled him as a delightful host who 'took a personal interest in everything, arranging the flowers and gold plate himself on the dinner table'.[7] She had come out with her husband, Arthur Renshaw, the old friend who for years had looked after Kitchener's investments, including the Parliamentary grants of £30,000 for the Sudan victory and £50,000 for the South African. Unfortunately, Lady Winifred caught measles.

On the Durbar's last day but one, Kitchener commanded a parade of 30,000 troops. The Viceroy took the salute with the royal Duke and Kitchener behind him, all on horseback. The parade was marred slightly by the incident of the 9th Lancers, Victor Brooke's regiment. Some weeks before Kitchener's arrival (with Brooke) an Indian cook had been accidentally killed, or possibly murdered, during misbehaviour by the lancers. A court of inquiry failed to identify the culprits. Curzon suspected a cover-up because the man had been 'merely' an Indian, and wrote a stinging rebuke to the local general which caused offence in the army. The outgoing C-in-C had punished the regiment and banned it from the Durbar. Curzon unwisely overruled him, saying that he needed all his cavalry, and Kitchener, equally insensitively, did not insist that his predecessor's decision should stand. When the 9th Lancers rode by the saluting base, some of the Indian spectators hissed, which brought a retaliatory outburst of cheering and clapping by the British in the stands, to the intense annoyance of Kitchener. 'I could see Lord Kitchener frowning, and ejaculating curses, as he sat upon his horse at the saluting point,' wrote Bampfylde Fuller, Commissioner of Assam.[8] Kitchener nearly turned in his saddle to order them to be quiet. The Viceroy ignored the interruption, to Kitchener's admiration.

That evening the two men had a further talk, Returning to his own camp, Kitchener told his guests at dinner (as recorded by Rawlinson in his diary) that 'in the course of conversation, Curzon remarked that there was only one thing in the review which he had regretted. "Yes," said K, "that business about the 9th Lancers was certainly in bad taste." "Oh," answered Curzon, "I was not thinking of that at all. What I felt was that in receiving all the salutes of those splendid troops I was doing what you should by right have done." Curzon must have chuckled at the opportunity K gave him, and the affair augurs well for their future relations.'[9] Curzon was either being disingenuous in flattery or Kitchener misunderstood him, for the Duke of Connaught would have taken the salute had not Curzon held the doubtful proposition that the Sovereign's Viceroy must not yield precedence except to his Sovereign.

The Durbar made Kitchener all the more eager to press ahead with reforms. 'He seems to think,' wrote Curzon to the Secretary of State in London a few days later, 'that the military government of India is to be conducted by concordat between him and me. Accordingly he comes and pours out to me all sorts of schemes to which he asks my consent. It is all so frank and honest and good tempered that one cannot meet these advances with a rebuff. Here and there I head him off or steer him into more orthodox channels. But of course as yet he does not know the ropes.'[10]

He was determined to learn them. As soon as the Durbar ended he left the magnificence of Delhi for the wilds of the North-West Frontier, exchanging massed formations of troops in full dress for small scattered outposts on unending active service. The accepted wisdom in London and Simla had long held that Russia might invade India through Afghanistan in a climax to the 'Great Game' played by agents, spies and diplomats as the Russian Empire expanded eastwards into central Asia. The Russians had not yet been humiliated by the Russo-Japanese War; the British had forgotten their own disastrous attempts to manipulate Afghanistan. Some seventy years later the Russians would meet disaster and disgrace in an Afghan civil war; but in 1903 the Russian threat seemed real. Kitchener therefore made the first of three tours of the terrain where attack might come. Curzon, however, despite urging Kitchener to look around before proposing reform, deplored his decision, fearing that the presence of the Commander-in-Chief on the Frontier, reported far and wide, might stir up the tribes, scare the Afghans and annoy the Russians.

Taking Birdwood, Hubert Hamilton and Sir Charles Egerton, the general commanding the Punjab Frontier force, the Chief went by rail and then by ferry across the Indus to Dera Ismail Khan. After inspecting the garrison, they travelled with an escort by tonga (fast pony cart) or on horseback into remote districts of Waziristan, often riding thirty miles in a day through valleys and over passes, 'real Frontier country this,' as Birdwood described it, 'with never a tree or blade of grass to relieve the barren hills and desolate expanses of rock and stone.' Hot by day, it could be intensely cold at night, and at Wana, a small town at 4,500 feet, the glass stood at zero even as the Chief, who hated cold, inspected the garrison. Outposts were manned by detachments from Indian regiments or the local militia. Since field telegraph wires would be stolen, the Chief's party could give little or no warning of his arrival. He was able to see conditions as they were, not scrubbed and polished. He learned of the hardships and dangers. British officers told of their love for the Frontier and its fanatical tribesmen. Both Egerton and Birdwood were veterans of recent uprisings and punitive expeditions, and at Saraghari Birdwood described in detail the stand of the tiny garrison of twenty-one Sikhs who had fought to the death in the uprising of September 1897, inflicting heavy casualties on a large tribal force until overwhelmed: Birdwood had been with the column that recaptured the post two days later. At Bannu, the gated town made famous by Sir Herbert Edwardes, the evangelical Christian who had achieved an extraordinary hold over the Muslim tribes, Kitchener presented new colours to the 3rd Sikhs, one of the smartest regiments of the Punjab Frontier Force, the 'Piffers'.[11]

They left the Frontier and travelled south-eastwards across the Indian Empire to Calcutta, then the capital and still beautiful despite the slums growing round its edges. He alighted to a public reception at Howrah railway terminus and was welcomed with much enthusiasm, as the carriages and escort trotted through commercial and residential streets to Fort William, the winter seat of the Viceroy and his government, in the beautiful public park, the Maiden, on the banks of the Hoogly river, eighty miles from the sea. Here, at the Chief's residence, Treasury Gate, 'he was to spend many happy winters', as Birdwood wrote long after.[12]

They had arrived just in time for Curzon's state ball in fancy dress to celebrate the centenary of Government House, which by a curious coincidence had been built by Lord Wellesley as a replica of the Curzon family's famous mansion at Kedleston in Derbyshire. Every guest wore uniform reproducing those of 1809. Curzon, in blue, represented his remote predecessor but slightly spoiled the effect by wearing the ribands and stars of the two Indian Orders of Knighthood which had not been instituted until many years later. Kitchener, in the scarlet of a full general of 1809, wore his Grand Cross of the Bath, but he, too, was a little wrong since the Order of the Bath had no grand cross before 1815.

Treasury Gate was a dreary building. Kitchener thought it poor quarters for the 'Lord of War' who ranked second to the Viceroy and must receive maharajahs.[13] He laid plans at once for expansion and improvement at government expense. For the present his 'family' was cramped but happy and well looked after. Together with Queen Victoria's servants and their British orderlies they had taken on Akbar Khan who had served General Lockhart, the Brat's late uncle, a former Commander-in-Chief. Akbar Khan was the *abdar* (literally water-carrier), who kept the wine and supervised the table servants. Lady Lockhart called him 'the best servant I ever knew anywhere', whether for formal dinners, picnics or campaigning.[14]

The Kitchener and Curzon staffs worked well together in the incessant round of interviews, visits, inspections and entertainments and were brought even closer when Conk Marker became engaged to Lady Curzon's sister, Marguerite ('Daisy') Leiter. They had known each other in the early years of Curzon' s viceroyalty when Conk had been one of his ADCs and Daisy had made long visits from Washington. The Leiters had come again for the Durbar, where Daisy and Conk fell in love. She was demonstrative almost beyond the conventions for engaged couples, and when the Leiters went home there was a most affectionate parting at the quayside.

These domestic details were merely the background to the accumulation of papers and decisions which awaited the Chief. Army headquarters was at Simla in the Himalayan foothills, the summer capital of the Raj. The headquarters staff could keep away from the heat of the plains all the year round, since most of their work was by telegram or mail. But the Military Member of the Viceroy's Council, Sir Edmond Elles, and the Adjutant-General, Sir Horace Smith-Dorrien, followed the Viceroy and Commander-in-Chief in their winter migration to Calcutta. Smith-Dorrien was preparing two minor military operations and a survey. He found Kitchener 'always in splendid form, so cheery and happy and such a pleasant chief to serve'. Like Kitchener, Smith-Dorrien hated writing minutes and would remind the Chief of his promise to release him to active command before too long: yet if he had been obliged to remain on the staff, 'I am sure I should have been perfectly happy with Lord Kitchener, for he was most interesting and instructive, and much less secretive than I had imagined. He discussed every sort of question openly with me and told me his views, always searching and far-reaching. He had a fascinating habit, when he was considering a question, of speaking his thoughts, arguing with himself all the pros and cons, then summing up and coming to a decision.'[15] This habit would annoy fellow members of the British Cabinet eleven or twelve years later.

Kitchener had now found, to his astonishment, that regiments, whether from the British Army or the Indian, were scattered 'higgledy-piggledy', as he put it,[16] around the subcontinent as if to hold India against the Indians, despite nearly half a century of civil peace since the Mutiny. He saw an army unprepared for any war fought with modern firearms: he would not like to lead it against a Russian invasion. Moreover, there was in effect no Indian army as such, only the armies of Bengal, Madras and Bombay, deriving from the three historical presidencies, and the Punjab Frontier Force, all with British officers.

In an emergency or to mount an expedition, a brigade would be cobbled together of British and Indian regiments who might never have trained together and might even despise or distrust each other as coming from the 'wrong' army.

For a start he proposed to renumber all regiments in single sequences. There would no longer be a '1st Bengal', '1st Bombay', '1st Madras' but only one '1st' for the cavalry and one for the foot. Each regiment should choose the name to follow its number so that traditions and historical associations would be preserved, and they could henceforth all be part of a single great Indian army.

Curzon was faintly amused. He thought Kitchener was tinkering. And the Military Department, under the Military Member of Council, put the proposal into a file. As Kitchener would soon tell Lord Roberts, 'the difficulty in getting anything done under the present system is simply enormous and quite heartbreaking.'[17]

3

'I WANT POWER TO DO GOOD'

THE COMMANDER-IN-CHIEF controlled operations and training but not supply, transport, ordnance or general organization. These were the exclusive province of the Military Member, who could veto, block or alter decisions of the C-in-C. Elles, the current Military Member, a gunner two years older than Kitchener, seemed pleasant enough, and his wife was regarded as a saint, but he was broadly content with the system, although when Adjutant-General he had often shaken his fist at the MM's department. Lord Roberts had told Kitchener that Elles was a clever fellow but had lacked initiative when troubles had broken out during his command on the Frontier.

Frustrated, Kitchener invited Walter Lawrence (the Private Secretary) to breakfast at Treasury Gate and brought out the section of Birdwood's scheme which showed how the post of Military Member might be abolished. Lawrence, with his great experience of India and love for its people, and already impressed that 'the most cordial relations existed between [Kitchener] and the Viceroy', liked the Indian army as it was, 'an old fashioned army for an old fashioned continent'. He advised Kitchener to wait until he had seen more of the country. Kitchener agreed and put the paper back in his pocket.[1]

A day or two later he raised the subject again with Curzon. He was finding that 'Curzon is all that one could wish and as kind as possible.'[2] He went to see him in the Viceroy's study, which overlooked the gardens and could be entered by a side door, avoiding the ceremonial front steps or using the dark passages beneath them.

The conversation was friendly. Finally, Kitchener said: 'What it comes to is this: a machine is handed over to the C. in C. for him to work by turning the handle but he must not interfere in any way with the defects in the complicated machinery. Why do you keep up such a farce?'

Curzon replied: 'If the C. in C. had anything to do with the machinery he would become too powerful. So to keep him down we take his power away and run another man as well. Between the two the civil elements get control.'

Curzon had put his finger on the root of the problem: his fear that civil power might cease to be supreme. The system was perhaps not logical, he admitted, but it worked very well.

Kitchener was astonished at such complacency. Back at Treasury Gate he was soon pouring out his heart to Lady Cranborne: 'As to power, I do not want more power outside the Army, but I do want power to do good in the Army. If I am incapable why appoint me, if I fail get rid of me, but why keep on a dead level of inefficiency or drift backwards because you won't trust the person you appoint to do good?' Initiative to do good was 'so choked that it ceases to be workable. Human nature again. I suppose one ought to be able to work, but there it is.' He filled sixteen sides on the defects of the Indian army and the difficulties of righting them under Dual Control.

A few weeks later Kitchener went back to the Frontier with Birdwood, travelling to Peshawar and on to the Afghan border through the famous Khyber Pass, which he was particularly keen to see; he had already deter-mined to order the building of a military railway, despite all the difficulties of the terrain, since this would be a Russian invasion route. Then they rode and walked through another tribal area, where every village presented the Chief with fine goats which he returned according to custom the next day 'with the request that they might be kept with their flocks till our next visit – both parties knowing full well that there was little likelihood of our return. But it would never have done to refuse the gifts outright!'[3]

Wherever he went the Chief inspected, rather speedily, the cantonments, forts and detachments which were strung about the country by history or tradition. Back in Calcutta in March he wrote: 'I feel quite frightened when I consider what has to be done or rather the amount that ought to be done and the poor means of doing it.'[4]

He wanted to reorganize his scattered forces into divisions and brigades which could be mobilized quickly into an all-India fighting army, to repulse an invader or go wherever the British Empire was threatened, leaving enough men to sustain the civil power. Some of his suggestions ran counter to long-received political wisdom, but Kitchener would not be put off. That month Curzon wrote to the Prime Minister's Private Secretary:

> Kitchener is mad keen about everything here. I never met so concen-trated a man. He uses an argument. You answer him. He repeats it. You give a second reply, even more cogent than the first. He repeats it again. You demolish him. He repeats it without alteration a third time. But he is as agreeable as he is obstinate, and everyone here likes him.[5]

Curzon thought him very self-centred, and although more urbane than in 1898 when they had first met, his language and his indifference to public opinion 'still retain their pristine frankness and charm'.[6] Curzon was in patronizing mood. When the Secretary of State, Lord George Hamilton, asked whether Kitchener would be good as the next Viceroy if Curzon's term was extended a further two years, he thought not: Kitchener's whole heart was in the army, he had no grasp of administration, he confused finance with arithmetic.[7] This last was a little unfair since Kitchener had reconquered the Sudan on a shoestring, spending less than the estimate. Lord Salisbury spoke only half in jest when he had told the Mansion House banquet in 1898 that if Kitchener had not been a great general he could have been a great Chancellor of the Exchequer.

That month of March 1903 brought unsavoury news about one of the most celebrated veterans of the Sudan, Major-General Sir Hector MacDonald, now commanding in Ceylon, whom Kitchener held to be the real hero of Omdurman. Lord Roberts, who had commissioned him from the ranks for outstanding courage in the Second Afghan War, had received 'terrible accusations' that MacDonald had seduced young native boys. Roberts was astonished that MacDonald failed to clear his name and summoned him back to London; unsatisfied with his explanations, Roberts ordered him to return to Ceylon and face a court martial.[8]

On 25 March Kitchener saw Curzon about convening four major-generals to try MacDonald 'should he present himself again in Ceylon'. According to Curzon, 'Kitchener with characteristic emphasis said he would like the brute (supposing him to be guilty of which we hear from

Ceylon that there is no doubt) to be shot.' Both men knew that sodomy was not a capital offence: in the highly unlikely event of a death sentence the Commander-in-Chief must commute it to imprisonment. Curzon thought that 'catamites' preferred 'Continental exile to the dubious amenities of one of His Majesty's gaols'.[9]

That very day MacDonald shot himself in a Paris hotel. Kitchener was disgusted by sodomy, as the law termed it, but whatever he said to Curzon he wrote in a different tone to Archie Hunter a few days later: 'What a horrible thing this has been about MacDonald. I expect he went quite mad after leaving South Africa. Did you hear anything of the sort before about him? I never did.'[10] And to Roberts: 'What a sad ending it has been to MacDonald. I never heard any rumour of the sort about him but Marker, who has just joined me from Simla, says there is some story at Belgaum of a similar nature: however, nothing is known, only gossip.'[11]

Kitchener soon was off again to the North-West Frontier with Birdie as guide, by train through the Baluchistan desert and the long, curving Bolan Pass between steep yellow sides, with the dry river below and the tribesmen, in red cloaks and large black turbans, walking their camel trains and flocks in the spring migration back to Afghanistan. The Chief came at last to Quetta, already famous as a political and military station, where he planned to place the Indian Staff College already forming in his mind.

After a field day they rode off into the western hills to investigate a possible site for a cavalry brigade, then round and back to the railway and up to a hill where they could look across the wide plain which the Afghan Frontier crossed, and almost to Kandahar. Back at the railway they sat at the front of the engine as it twisted through the Khojak tunnel, made by miners sent out from England. At Chaman on the Frontier they found a Baluchi regiment of the garrison in a state of worry because their colonel, Yate, had ridden across the Frontier when exercising his greyhounds. He had been arrested by Afghan soldiers and was not yet retrieved.

Chaman had railway stores, ready for a line to be laid into Afghanistan in the event of war. They rode back by the rough road over the Khojak Pass and above it for 'a lovely view of the snows of the distant Hindu Cush and the plateau of Toba', and so back to Quetta.

They separated, Birdwood going ahead to Simla while the Chief, with an ADC (probably Marker) and a small escort, made a remarkable journey up a long length of the North-West Frontier to the Khyber again, mostly on horseback. He explored every valley, noting where strategic railways should be laid, and arriving unexpectedly at the little garrisons, which put them on their toes yet encouraged them that they were not forgotten by the 'Lord of War'. Kitchener was exhilarated by the dry heat and barren countryside relieved by little patches of almonds in blossom and the red of the tamarisk bushes, yet his ride was a considerable feat for a man of nearly fifty-three and brought him thoroughly fit to Simla, which he reached by 24 April to find that his dog Bruce had died. Frank Maxwell, the Brat, had sat up all night with it before the end.[12]

4

'THE CURZONS HAVE BEEN VERY KIND'

THE NARROW-GAUGE petrol-driven railway would not be ready for another six months. Kitchener and Marker made the sixty-mile ride to Simla up the well-made and beautifully engineered Great Hindustan–Tibet road from the main-line railway at Kalka in the the plains, staying the night at a government rest-house.

Next morning they approached the ridge and its spurs where the rather English town sprawled at about 6,000 feet. They rode past the polo and cricket grounds and Annandale racecourse, the hospitals and schools and departmental offices, and glimpsed the native quarters. Clinging to the side of the ridge were the houses of government officials and richer Indians. At the top ran the main street, so narrow that only the two Excellencies and the Lieutenant-Governor of the Punjab might use their carriages. Others must ride, walk or take rickshaws drawn by coolies.

The high eastern end, known as Jakko, led to the even higher Observatory Hill occupied by Viceregal Lodge, some twenty years old. Built like a Victorian country house in mock-Elizabethan style, opulent rather than magnificent and not in the least Indian, it was set in wide and beautiful terraced gardens kept by forty gardeners, with glorious views of the Himalayan snows when clouds or mist allowed. Slightly below were Barnes Court, summer residence of the Lord Sahib of the Punjab, and Snowdon.

The government of India had admitted that Snowdon needed renovation. The Treasury had placed a sum at Kitchener's disposal. As in

Calcutta, he laid plans: he once remarked that he ought to have been an architect, not a soldier. He would create a residence worthy of the Lord of War; he would not be the only C-in-C to enjoy the improvements; indeed, he might not be around when they were finished if his army reforms were rejected.

He began minor reforms at once. The news of his arrival had spread swiftly, as news does in India, and officers were at their desks with unwonted punctuality. The head of Intelligence, Lieutenant-Colonel (later Brigadier-General) E. W. S. K. Maconchy, recalled in old age Kitchener's first visit:

> He just walked into my room at Army Headquarters, said 'Not much of a room' and walked out again. One had always heard of him as a dour man with whom it was difficult to work but I always found him the very opposite. He always knew what he wanted and meant to get it: but there was none of the 'Knock me down' manner adopted by many senior men. He would always talk over a question quietly and listen patiently to what one had to say as long as it was brief, but he never wavered from the main point. Minor difficulties in the way of what he wanted were for his staff to deal with, he would not be bothered with them, and he always seemed to take the 'long view' in any question that he touched.
>
> He impressed me, more than anyone I have ever met, as a man with a great mind and absolutely devoted to the service of his country regardless of all personal interests and ambitions. His methods were often unorthodox but he did not care how it was done as long as he could get his end. Action, not talk, was the key note of his character.[1]

Kitchener immediately formed an advisory council of the heads of all departments. At the first meeting, on 12 May, he told them that as he was a stranger to India they were to advise him. At each fortnightly meeting a different member, in turn, was to produce a measure for the improvement of the army, worked out practically and financially. 'You are not to confine yourselves to your own departments but to attack each other's branches. But no one is to resent anything you all say or do.'[2]

In a short time every sinecure was abolished. The first plans were laid for a staff college, with Curzon's warm approval, and a cavalry school.

The general reorganization of the army was put in train. And the writing of minutes was reduced. Army headquarters, like most departments of the Indian government, had lived by minutes, which circulated in red tape slowly, fattening as they went, until expiring into a file.

The fortnightly meetings 'worked splendidly', in Maconchy's view. Curzon was not so sure. 'Kitchener,' he told the Secretary of State on 7 May, 'abominates our files and departmental method of working. In fact he is just like a caged lion stalking to and fro and dashing its bruised and lacerated head against the bars.'[3] Thus, when Kitchener proposed that the reorganized army's brigades should be wholly British or wholly Indian instead of mixed, and that the Indian brigades must include native field artillery, Curzon told him that native batteries had been forbidden since the Mutiny, when they had turned their guns on the British. Without these guns and trained gunners the Mutiny would have been suppressed quickly. So his proposal was of 'vast and tremendous significance'. Curzon insisted that the plan be submitted by army headquarters to the Military Department, where Elles rejected it, strengthening Kitchener's dislike. When Elles produced a Governor-General's Order over Kitchener's name without consulting him and Curzon said he had every right to do so, Kitchener threatened to resign. The matter was resolved, but a week later Curzon supported Kitchener over an appointment and half expected Elles to resign. Curzon moaned to Lord George Hamilton:

I provide a Tom Tidler's ground on which these two turkey-cocks fight out their weekly contests each clamouring to get me on his side, and threatening me with resignation if I take the other. Moreover it is all so unnecessary and so stupid. If only Kitchener would show a little grace and tact things would go better. As it is I am the focus of a perpetual turmoil which I have done nothing to provoke, and of which I am a mortified but helpless spectator.[4]

He ascribed Kitchener's reforming zeal to his loneliness, with nothing to do at home but think out schemes, being unmarried and dependent on his personal staff, whom Curzon rated as young officers without experience, although Hubert Hamilton was only two and a half years younger than Curzon and all were well tried in battle, used to staff work and knew India. 'Kitchener,' wrote Curzon, 'stands aloof and alone, a molten mass

of devouring energy and burning ambitions without anybody to control or
guide it in the right direction. Now the Viceroy, as long as he is a personal
friend of this remarkable phenomenon, is the only man who can supply the
want.' Curzon was determined, he told Lord George, to do so and prevent
'such a stupid disaster as the loss of Kitchener's services',[5] not least because
the British public, for whom Kitchener could do no wrong, would blame
the Viceroy. Curzon, though a great reformer on the civil side, seems not
to have realized the depth of Kitchener's convictions. When Kitchener
offered a fresh draft of his plan to put the Military Department and army
headquarters in one building, with the Commander-in-Chief as unchal-
lenged head, Sir Edmond Elles rejected this sentence of his own extinction
point by point.

Curzon invited Kitchener to a friendly tête-à-tête dinner on 20 May.
'What is at the bottom of it all?' he asked. 'What do you object to?'
Curzon asserted that Kitchener had said he had nothing against the
Military Department, 'yet you want to destroy it. Where does the grievance
come in?' Kitchener, Curzon affirmed, lacked enough experience of the
system to judge it.

Kitchener, however, did not recount examples: he went for the
principle. He could not allow a subordinate to criticize or reject rather than
merely submit advice. 'You may be unable to understand it,' he said, 'for it
is all a matter of military feeling and military discipline.' For Curzon it
looked all a matter of civil against military control. If the post of Military
Member disappeared and the next Viceroy were ignorant of India 'and
probably less strong-willed than myself', Kitchener would be 'the ruler of
the country in all but name'.[6] Curzon failed to see that Kitchener did not
want power outside the army but to do good in the army.

The Viceroy offered concessions without yielding the main ground. The
Chief promised to postpone his proposals for a year.

The two Excellencies were viewing both principle and practice from
opposite points. Thus, when Curzon was contemplating a political
mission to Tibet and asked how many troops should protect it, Kitchener,
having not yet seen Kanchenjunga or the passes of the eastern Himalayas,
named far too high a figure for the terrain. His 'foolish answer' was
corrected by the Military Department, a proof to Curzon of its value. Yet
this incident was equally an argument for its abolition. Army headquarters
had not needed to plan operations in the north-east, so the staff were

ignorant of the facts. Had the Military Department been under the Chief's direct control he would have been correctly advised at once.

Curzon was on firmer ground when he passed on what Kitchener in schoolboy slang called 'rather a wigging' from the Secretary of State for writing about his plans for reform to Lord Roberts direct, not through the Viceroy. Kitchener replied humbly that he had been drawing on Lord Roberts's advice for years but henceforth would stand alone. He would have been more honest to refuse openly to limit a long-established private correspondence, perhaps quoting his maxim that had helped win the Sudan: 'Regulations are for the guidance of fools.' This would have horrified Curzon for whom correct procedures were more important even than national emergency. During the South African war Kitchener had once telegraphed direct to the C-in-C in India for more troops. Power Palmer selected them at once and they were about to sail when, Curzon boasted to his wife, 'I heard of it by accident and stopped the whole show in the twinkling of an eye.'[7]

Kitchener's promise to Curzon was empty. He sent a copy of his next memorandum to Roberts as before, merely adding a covering letter about the wigging. 'I do not know exactly what is meant, but no doubt one has to be circumspect where people are so touchy.' He added: 'P.S. It is very annoying, for I never thought I was a great letter writer!'[8]

He was also determined to continue his uninhibited private correspondence with Lady Cranborne, to share with her husband and Arthur Balfour, his first cousin, the Prime Minister. He urged her to be 'careful that *nothing* comes from me and that my name is never used. This is a very curious government and in some points seems to resemble the Khalifa in Omdurman.' Curzon's attempt to gag him had seemed 'rather petty where imperial interests are in the balance'.[9]

Lady Cranborne was kept in touch also by occasional letters from Kitchener's 'family'. Hubert Hamilton once described for her the Chief's methods: 'It is wonderful how he gets through his work – 3 or 4 hours a day does it all, and only 5 days a week; yet I think he does more than an ordinary man in a similar position working 8 or 10 hours for 6 days. He discards all detail on the one hand and, on the other, makes his staff work very hard, and very willingly, at all the bigger questions he takes up. He chucks ideas and projects at us anyhow and in no time, and then goes off'[10] – to improve the garden or pore over plans for new rooms at Snowdon.

Headquarters officers noticed that the family, 'whom he treated more as sons than ADCs adored him. He made them work however and they were quite unlike the ordinary gallivanting ADCs of popular fancy.'[11] Hammy Hamilton would do anything and go anywhere at any time except miss his polo.

The ADCs were the secret of Kitchener's rapid success as a host in the crowded social life of Simla. Where so many British families lived at close quarters, all with numerous faithful Indian servants, the balls, dinners, amateur theatricals and tennis parties followed fast. Viceregal Lodge even had an indoor tennis court so that play could continue during the monsoon rains. Kitchener would not play tennis because of his poor eyesight,[12] but he gave dinner parties. If the memsahibs had been alarmed at the prospect of a bachelor C-in-C, reputedly dour, his very first ball won them over. He supervised every detail. Guests who 'nervously looked for a rather stand-offish reception were almost startled by the friendly greeting and the evident desire that everybody should have a good time in his house'.[13] They marvelled at the display of Dervish and Boer banners and the richness of the gold cups presented with the freedoms of London and Ipswich, and other such rewards, and they dined off the silver soup and meat plates given by Sheffield at the ceremony where Kitchener had caused such amusement by trying to discover their weight.[14]

He must also entertain the numerous Indian princes who visited Simla and always called on the Chief. Most spoke English, but sometimes Birdie would be in attendance to interpret. One old-fashioned Sikh rajah with a long white beard asked through Birdie that next time he be presented to 'Lady Kitchener'. 'But there is no Lady Kitchener, and I am too old to marry.' The rajah earnestly assured him that this was certainly not so. He also added that if the Lord of War taught his soldiers to eat their dead enemies, such terror would be created that no army could stand against him.[15]

Kitchener found that 'Living is pretty expensive here, and balls and entertainment run away with one's money,' but he could recoup when he went off on tour.[16]

If, like Curzon, he disliked Simla society, he hid it well, yet after less than three weeks, when writing to Renshaw about investments, he added: 'I don't like this place at all, have had bad headache and can't sleep ever since I have been here – wish I was out of it again but am fixed now. All staff send their love.'[17]

Simla's climate was not as pleasant as that of hill stations founded later, and Kitchener may have been suffering from altitude. However, he leased a bungalow, Wildflower Hall, at Mahasu, 1,000 feet higher than Simla, at the top of a hill surrounded by pine trees, with a splendid view of the high Himalayas. There, he told Lady Cranborne, 'I spend my Saturday afternoons and Sundays. It is 5 miles away and makes a very pleasant retreat where I am able to do gardening and some improvements and have peace.'[18] Wildflower Hall was not in the least luxurious; he furnished it in camp fashion. The gardens were his love. He began to make rose gardens and terraces. He had a passion for removing hillocks and making fresh ones, altering angles and improving vistas, planting shrubs that would not grow fast enough, and transplanting forest trees at the wrong season so that they died. His next-door neighbour, Edward Buck, agent for Reuters and Associated Press, who lived at Northbank and was also an enthusiastic gardener, noticed that Kitchener would lose interest in a project when finished and start another. In addition to his *malis* (gardeners) he hired coolies for heavier work, and he once tried to make the table servants become gardeners between meals but they went on strike. Each weekend he took the Brat or Hammy or another of the family to relax by working like a coolie under his personal supervision. Buck said, 'The absolute devotion and love which his personal staff had for him was very remarkable.' Buck and Kitchener often rode out to Mahasu together, talking about shooting and gardening. Buck added: 'He never hesitated to annex – I use a mild term – flowers and shrubs from my little hill garden, but he gave me very little in return from either a gardening or a journalistic point of view.'[19]

On Sundays, church was an easy ride along the Great Hindustan–Tibet road, well cut and engineered, and generally dusty except in the rains. It passed close to Wildflower Hall and the Viceroy's alpine chalet, The Retreat, a little below at Mashobra. Just beyond the Sinfauli bazaar, a tunnel, about 200 yards long, had been hacked through solid rock by convict labour fifty years before. The tunnel was just wide enough for a rickshaw if foot passengers squeezed themselves against the white-washed rock. It was dark, lit by a few lanterns in the evenings, and coolies tended to shout to scare off evil spirits. The roof was supported by massive beams, and heavy beams ribbed the sides. No one noticed that these might be dangerous to a rider.

That summer of 1903 the Viceroy and the C/in/C deepened their friendship, although Kitchener was alarmed by the rumour that Curzon's term of office might be extended.

Curzon invited Kitchener to the charming viceregal camp in the green hills at Naldera above the monsoon rains. 'The Curzons both of them have been very kind and nice to me,' Kitchener told Lady Cranborne. 'When you write to them you might say how very much I appreciate it all, he is really a first rate Viceroy and we work together much better now, quite cordially in fact.'[20] Each thought the other had improved. Curzon told Lord George Hamilton that Kitchener had admitted he had thought the Viceroy was intent on wrecking his schemes. 'He now realizes his mistake and is aware that I am his best friend.'[21] And Kitchener wrote to Lady Cranborne a fortnight later: 'We are all very fit and I am getting on very well with Curzon. I think my having shown him there was an extreme point of endurance that might be reached has done much good.'[22]

Lady Curzon was always friendly. Kitchener was amused by her birthday present of 'two charming mustard pots, as she had suffered from my not having been able to give her mustard in a sufficiently beautiful pot',[23] despite all the gold on his table. They may also have been intended as atonement for an unfortunate incident at a viceregal ball. Lady Curzon had failed to check her traditionally small and select supper room or notice that no place was laid for the C/in/C. By the time she had rushed into the ballroom to apologize and bring him in, he had ordered his carriage and slipped away. Kitchener knew that seating was always by strict precedence in the Raj. There was even a book for every hostess to know precisely where to seat her guests from high to low. If, therefore, the C/in/C was not placed, some lesser mortal had the honour of the viceregal table, perhaps excitingly for the first time, and would have been sent off if the C/in/C had been retrieved. Rather than displace him, Kitchener disappeared: the discourtesy in not saying goodbye was preferable to unkindness, let the gossips say what they will.[24]

Lady Curzon was a staunch ally because, unknown to Kitchener, she was trying to persuade the Viceroy to refuse an extension of his term. With sure instinct she realized that though he would finish these five years in a blaze of glory, a further two might end in tears. Walter Lawrence, the Private Secretary, was also urging him not to 'tempt Providence by overstaying his time, and that a collision with Lord Kitchener was inevitable if he stayed on': two tigers in the same jungle. 'He laughed at my fears, and was confident that he could manage Lord Kitchener.'[25]

The extension was announced early in August, to follow exceptional leave at home. Kitchener rather hoped he, too, might get home leave, to state his case, for he felt 'perfectly hopeless' about the future. The present military system was 'almost impossible', with every suggestion blocked or carefully put away. Yet the Viceroy supported it. The Curzons were very kind, the weather delightful and everything beautifully green, 'but I feel no pleasure in life while the service suffers'. Was he not wasting his time? Could he afford 'to go on taking responsibility for an effete service which when war comes must be shown up?'[26] On 6 August he sent Lady Cranborne three bound manuscript volumes containing a long imaginary story of a Russian invasion of India and the chaos which would follow. He called it his War Game or *Kriegspiel*, to be kept most private, seen only by the Cranbornes and Balfour, with a shortened version for Roberts. Whether they were in Kitchener's own hand or prepared on his instruc-tions by two officers at army headquarters is unclear as the volumes are lost. In a letter to Balfour he admits that some of it may be exaggerated, 'but as I was writing my impression of India I thought it advisable to bring out as vividly as possible our position under the present system of Military Administration'.[27] In the covering letter to Lady Cranborne he discussed his future, even suggesting that they might arrange to bring Cromer back from Egypt into the Cabinet and give Kitchener his post, ruler of Egypt in all but name and overlord of the Sudan: 'that is what I should really like.' Or he might take a year or two of rest or travel. 'Though I rather like India it is too heartbreaking to go on seeing inefficiency rampant and fostered in every way.' They might find C-in-Cs who will 'shut their eyes tight and let things go on but I cannot and as the Viceroy likes the present system there is no doubt I ought to clear out'.[28]

Hubert Hamilton, writing to Lady Cranborne three days later, thought Curzon, though an admirable Viceroy, 'dangerously ambitious for himself because of self *rather* than as God's agent for the good of his country. So different from Lord K who never thinks of himself or how things may affect him personally.'[29]

And if Curzon and Kitchener were different, so were Mary Curzon and Alice Cranborne, the other *grande dame* in Kitchener's life at this time, though far away. Both were beautiful and gracious, but Mary was insecure. However many dollars her very rich father had, Simla and Calcutta society never quite forgot that she was a shopkeeper's daughter, whereas Alice Cranborne, daughter of an earl and married to the Marquess of Salisbury's heir, moved utterly unconscious that she belonged to one of the great political and landed families of England.

Mary knew that her husband could be fickle sexually, though devoted to her. Alice was supremely happy in her family life even if her husband was a little dull. And Alice had sons, while Mary was all too aware that she had failed to produce an heir.

Mary saw Kitchener solely in relation to George Curzon. Alice supported 'my dear Sirdar' or 'K' for his own sake, and he could trust her as he could never trust Mary.[30]

5

EXPLORING THE PASSES

IN LATE AUGUST the Chief and five of his staff were climbing high into the Karakorams through the ancient kingdom of Hunza, perhaps the most superb scenery of the Himalayas, with great peaks towering above the terraced fields and small villages. Kitchener was determined to see the high passes through which an enemy might seek to invade India, so they were marching by pony, foot and yak towards the point where the Russian Empire lay nearest to the Indian.

They had started from Srinagar, where Birdie had made sure that Kitchener wore his frock coat for his audience with the Maharajah of Jammu and Kashmir, Pertab Singh, a stickler for etiquette; the frock coat was posted back to Simla the next day.[1] Then, with ample camp and escort, they crossed the Wala lake and rode over two easy passes into the land dominated by the splendour of Nanga Parbat. At each town, deep in the mountains, the Chief inspected the Kashmiri troops and wrote a memorandum about the defences. At one he was handed a telegram from England, forwarded by Simla: the great Lord Salisbury was seriously ill. They sent a wire to Hatfield for news and rather marvelled to receive a reply twenty-four hours later at their next stop, forgetting, perhaps, the Chief's 'clear the line' priority. Lord Salisbury, Kitchener's earliest and strongest patron, died on 22 August. Jem and Alice Cranborne became the 4th Marquess and Marchioness of Salisbury. Kitchener's letter of condolence from Gilgit on 26 August told the new Lady Salisbury of the passes and forests they had passed through and of the 'most glorious and brilliant colours' of the wild flowers.[2] The way became steeper. They had to dismount and ascend a steep winding hill track (a *pari*) going up and down for five miles. 'Very high at times,' Birdie noted in his diary for 29 August, 'and the Chief had a man pulling him by each arm (such men are like goats on the side of a precipice) and another holding on to his belt and shoving him up, or holding him back when going downhill! One really steep rock-face crossed by cracks in rocks and several built-up stair-cases and zigzags on wooden pegs along the face of the *pari* – in places only a log of wood to be crossed lengthways. We made only 14 miles.'[3] Kitchener had never been a hill climber nor much of a walker. He said later that he did not mind the rope bridges but his legs 'got frightfully tired of the continual pull up and down again', especially when it was a matter of 'pulling oneself up and down precipices and crossing glaciers melting all the time'.[4] Their guides had led them across the Batir glacier, where one of their animals fell into a crevasse. Birdie, watching the Chief, thought it 'rather amazing how, at the age of 53, he tackled all this'.

They came down to the last village, its approaches strongly guarded on both sides, and then climbed up and over the 16,000-foot Mintakha Pass and thus into China, where the Pamirs open into a huge, rolling grassy plain, with black tents of nomads surrounded by their herds of yaks, sheep, goats and even two-humped camels. The party descended a thousand feet and bivouacked by a stream: their baggage train had taken a lower route so they had only small tents in the bitter cold, but next morning a friendly Chinese official, who had been expecting them, called with unlimited milk and cream.[5]

Next day they rode across the plain, in Chinese territory, crossed the Kalik Pass into India again and found their light camp pitched in treeless country, again very cold.

During the next month, on this thoroughly organized tour, they explored all the main passes, enjoying wonderful views. Their strategic reconnaissance of possible battlefields was also a holiday, away from desks and minutes. 'We have had a delightful and very interesting tour so far,' Kitchener told Renshaw when replying to a query about investments.[6] He had been moving too fast for shooting but let Victor and the Brat go off, catching the rest up at night with some good heads. The most exciting and stiffest ordeal was the crossing of the Darkot glacier and pass on the way over to the town of Yasin. The approach path was too steep for ponies.

The Rajah of Poonch had lent them riding mules which tended towards the outer edge above the precipice, testing a rider's nerves. They camped at 12,500 feet in bitter cold. 'Kitchener detested the cold,' records Birdwood, 'but no discomfort could ever dissuade him from seeing what he had set out to see – not even when it took us $3\frac{1}{4}$ hours to cross the seven-mile Darkot glacier, and that during a 20-mile march.' They started at 6 a.m. riding ponies to the edge of the glacier, where they breakfasted. They then mounted yaks, which the Brat thought 'the queerest animal one ever threw a leg across', and ascended the glacier. 'Easy going at first,' wrote the Brat in his diary that night, 'but later deep snow which would not bear the yaks' weight; four miles to the pass, where Yasin people met us in snowstorm, then two miles down glacier on south side with some nasty little crevasses to negotiate; then five miles down, very steep, to Rowat, where Amir Ali had a repast for us in a warm climate. Yaks are great animals, enormously strong, and steam along like snow ploughs – nose to ground, licking up snow all the way. Fine snow fell most of the way.'[7]

Warm again in camp that night, they could all be heard singing, even the Chief, 'The yak's the mount for me' in parody of a popular song.

Next day they descended to Yasin and promptly challenged the governor (*mehtar*) to polo. In the peaceful well-ordered valleys that they had passed through on their travels, where the people dressed in Mongol style with hats over the ears and thick, long coats above trousers, every village played polo, which possibly originated centuries earlier in this region. The Mehtar of Yasin accepted the challenge: he had a good team. The British Political Agent and Kitchener both agreed to join to make seven a side instead of the usual four. Kitchener had not played since Egypt. He was provided with a hill pony almost too small so that his legs nearly touched the ground as they processed to the field, led by a band, the two dignitaries each having two grooms holding their mounts while 'the opposite side performed feats of horsemanship all the way, galloping madly about the plain, jumping walls, etc. This they told us was to get their ponies' blood up for the tournay.

'The game was started by the Governor galloping from his goal to half-way down the ground, ball in hand; arrived half-way he flung the ball in air and going top speed, hit it a rare crack down towards our goal; then we went at it hammer and tongs, and had great fun.' The Chief enjoyed himself although, with too short a stick, and defective eyes, he did not hit the ball very often. Good hits were marked by 'a blaring crescendo from the band and wild yells from both players and onlookers'. Kitchener's team lost, but was excused the local custom whereby the losers danced before the victors while the band plays.[8]

Next day they returned to Gilgit. As they had already been through passes of the Hindu Kush, including a short time in Afghan territory, Kitchener could be well pleased: 'I have been round all these passes leading into India and am now on my way back to Simla.'[9] The final stages of his two-month tour of some 1,600 miles took them some way down the River Indus on skin rafts. 'Negotiating the rapids was great fun', thanks to the skill of the boatmen. Leaving Kashmir by the Babusar Pass they re-entered British India and descended the Khagan valley, lovely with wild mulberries, fig trees and vines, and majestic forests above. They reached the railhead and cantonment at Abbotabad on 16 October, all very fit and happy.

Their baggage included quite a few heads, among them one that elated the Chief. High in the Hindu Kush he had seen markhors, the elusive wild goat which, Conk Marker told his sister, 'he will call "macaw" to the astonishment of the public'.[10] When he had returned to Gilgit he had found that their trek had been so smooth that he had some days in hand for shooting. They paired off in different directions. The Chief, determined to bag a 'macaw', took Conk, an excellent shot. Conk knew that the Chief was a poor shot because the cast in one eye prevented both eyes focusing together.

Led by a local *shikhari* (hunter), they set off up a steep valley or nullah until in due time a markhor was in Kitchener's sights within range of his rifle. He fired. A split second later Conk fired, most probably, for when the head was cured and mounted and proudly put up at the drawing room end of the hall at Snowdon with the inscription *Shot by Lord Kitchener, Damot Nullah Cashmir 9 October 1903*, Hubert Hamilton joked to Conk, by then in London, 'Most people believe what they read in print!!!'[11]

Some way back, before the polo match, the Chief was being difficult, 'what we call the "poisoned pup" state', as Frank Maxwell told his parents. The Brat had a way of getting him out of it and making him 'feel, I really think, rather ashamed of his behaviour during the previous three days – a good thing for him to feel now and then. This sounds very egotistical, but it seems such a pity a big man like he is should make an idiot of himself, and instead of being corrected, or shown that he is doing so, to have people, if not encouraging it, at any rate acquiescing in it. So I generally tell him one way or another. He is extraordinarily good about it, and never rounds on one, as I think most mortals would.'[12]

The Brat did not, perhaps, know, although Conk did, that Kitchener was 'in throes of uncertainty', whether Balfour might be about to summon him back to England as Secretary of State for War. They had learned as they passed through Chitral in the North-West Frontier Province that resignations over tariff reform and free trade were breaking up the Cabinet. Balfour must bring in new blood. Kitchener, as he once said, would rather sweep crossings than go to the War Office, whether as Secretary of State or as the Quartermaster-General, who at that time was the professional head under the Commander-in-Chief. The awful prospect made him irritable.

At Gilgit, where they stayed with the Political Agent, Kitchener read the list of Balfour's Cabinet changes and knew that he was safe. 'What exciting times you have been having in England,' he wrote to Arthur Renshaw, 'the break up of a great party and formation of new groups. I wonder how it will all pan out . . . I rather pity the the W.O. under Arnold Forster – poor Lord Bobs.

'Mrs Adair tells me my godson is like me – you will have to make a soldier of him.'[13]

Arnold-Forster, a grandson of Arnold of Rugby, succeeded St John Brodrick, who moved to the India Office. Kitchener had a poor opinion of Brodrick, but they had worked together from opposite ends of the cable between London and Pretoria during the South African war. Kitchener had hopes that Brodrick would be sympathetic to army reform although one of Curzon's oldest friends.

Reaching Simla on 23 October, Kitchener threw himself again into the plans for reorganization and redistribution. His headquarters staff had been working out details during his absence, but loose ends needed tying. At one meeting of the council Colonel Maconchy fought hard to retain the name Punjab Frontier Force ('the Piffers'). 'As I seemed to be alone against the rest Kitchener told me to wait and see him afterwards. This I did and he was most sympathetic', but pointed out that as the North-West Frontier had now been separated from the Punjab he was removing 'Punjab' from the title, and in doing so was following advice of his predecessor. Maconchy was flabbergasted at hearing this. 'I stuck to my guns until at last Kitchener came up to me and took me by my coat button, shook me and said "Look here, you are too persistent, go away!!" The Piffers lost the word "Punjab" but Kitchener left us with the words "Frontier Force" against the wishes of the whole of the rest of the Heads of Departments in Simla.' Maconchy liked to think that his persistence may have influenced the decision.[14]

Kitchener's scheme would create fighting divisions and cavalry brigades, positioned to reinforce the North-West Frontier quickly and throw back an invader. Enough troops would be retained for internal security throughout India, and the rest would form a field army and at least two divisions could be sent out of India to defend other parts of the British Empire. As Birdwood wrote long after (and he was in a position to know): 'I shudder to think what would have happened on the outbreak of war in 1914 had not Kitchener's reforms been in force.' India was able to send troops to the Western Front and Mesopotamia, 'each brigade and its staff proceeding complete from its peace-time station: all without a hitch. Under the pre-Kitchener system, nothing short of chaos must have resulted from such an effort.'[15]

But when Kitchener submitted his completed scheme of reorganization to the government of India on 4 November 1903, he had no certainty of its acceptance. And he was convinced that under Dual Control it would fail. He had promised Curzon not to attack Dual Control for a year; therefore his scheme had to assume its continued existence. Thus, as he wrote to Lady Salisbury a week later, 'I have an army without any means of feeding, mounting or supplying it. For this I have to trust to a totally distinct and separate department of Government which is, I firmly believe, very inefficient, and certainly knows nothing of the requirements of war. When war comes disaster must follow, and then I suppose the soldiers will be blamed.'[16] He wrote much the same to Brodrick as the new Secretary of State, adding: 'Curzon, however, will not take the matter up and the responsibility must rest with him. I have been doing my best under very difficult circumstances to make some improvement in the Indian Army.'[17]

He was struggling also to get the best men. He brought Douglas Haig back to India as Inspector (head) of Cavalry, rejecting complaints that Colonel Haig was too junior. And in asking Brodrick to obtain for him a particularly intellectual major he wrote: 'Personally I have never been able to work without good tools and I have therefore always looked on appoint-ments to the HQ staff as of supreme importance . . . I am not over-burdened with a thinking staff and now that I have found a man I hope and trust you will help me to get him transferred.'[18]

With the scheme submitted and the structural improvements to Snowdon waiting to start and winter coming on, the Chief was looking forward to leaving Simla. He would inspect troops and stations in northern India and then attend the manoeuvres before going down to Calcutta.

But on Sunday afternoon, 15 November 1903, everything changed.

6

DISASTER IN A TUNNEL

ON SATURDAY 14 NOVEMBER 1903 Hubert Hamilton and Frank Maxwell went down from Simla to check arrangements, expecting to rejoin the Chief as he passed through Ambala on the Monday. After church on the Sunday, Conk Marker asked at lunch whether the Chief would be riding out to Wildflower Hall that afternoon, but he was not so inclined, having given the *malis* their winter orders two days earlier.

Later in the afternoon he changed his mind and ordered one of the horses he had brought from South Africa, not his charger but a mare, which was very quiet and safe in the hills. He decided to ride to Wildflower and back for exercise. A former C-in-C's Military Secretary had ruled that 'His Excellency must never be unaccompanied', but Kitchener ignored rules and rode alone that Sunday afternoon, out along the road, through the short Mashobra tunnel and up to Wildflower, where he stayed only a quarter of an hour. On the way home he was halfway through the narrow, badly lighted tunnel when his mare shied violently sideways from a passing coolie and collided with a supporting beam. The toe of Kitchener's blucher boot became wedged between the beam and the tunnel wall, forcing the fixed spur on the heel into the horse's flank. The sudden pain made her spring forward and round. Kitchener's left leg, held fast by the toe, was twisted until it could twist no more; both bones snapped above the ankle. All was over in seconds.

The mare stood still. Kitchener, in great pain, managed to slide to the ground, where he lay in the dark shouting for help. The few coolies in earshot fled, frightened of being accused of attacking the Jangi Lat. After five or ten minutes, as Hubert Hamilton told Lord Roberts, 'an empty rickshaw came along from Mashobra direction, and poor Ld. K holding on all the time to the blucher boot which contained his broken leg and suffering frightful pain managed to get lifted into the rickshaw.' A little later a European, Mr Jenn, came up in another rickshaw with some coolies whom he ordered to run ahead to Snowdon, where Birdwood alerted the doctors, seized a blanket and a bottle of brandy and met the Chief half a mile off. It was now six in the evening. An army doctor, Lieutenant-Colonel A. E. Tate, and a young civil surgeon, Dr Green, put him under chloroform for an hour and set the leg, strapping it in splints. By eight o'clock he was in bed, reasonably comfortable. Unfortunately, they set the leg badly, though 'quite satisfied' when they checked it two days later. Current medical practice dictated that he must lie in bed with the leg in splints for three weeks before it could be put in plaster of Paris.

Hamilton and Maxwell returned immediately to Simla. The pain subsided after two days. Hamilton wrote to Lord Roberts on the third day: 'I think he is getting reconciled to his fate, certainly he is as good as possible about it and never grumbled though he must feel the restraint terribly; he reads a lot, and yesterday we began playing bridge with him.'[1]

The Simla authorities were aghast at this thousand-to-one accident. The tunnel was soon almost doubled in width, whitewashed regularly and given electric lights.

The Curzons and Sir Edmond and Lady Elles had already left for Calcutta, but with army headquarters and other government departments remaining in Simla all year, and Mr Nicolls, the chaplain of All Saints, Kitchener had as many visitors as he wanted. 'Here I am tied by the leg and in a most unholy frame of mind,' he wrote to Lady Salisbury eleven days after the accident.[2] It was most annoying that he must miss the manoeuvres. The three weeks in splints should have ended on 6 December, but the famous surgeon Sir Frederick Treves was on a world tour and came up from Bombay on that day. Treves had saved King Edward's life by removing his appendix and was a skilful manipulator but not an orthopaedic surgeon. He changed the position of the splints but did not question the setting.[3]

Treves ordered another week in bed. Kitchener's morale sank. 'I am still on my back with my leg tied up, it is frightfully boring and unpleasant,' he told Renshaw. He called it 'rather a dismal time'; he was wishing the wretched thing had never belonged to him, he told Lady Salisbury.[4] He became 'very unsociable'. The Brat wrote to his mother an amusing account of this low point in his Chief's recovery:

> He couldn't read, nor play bridge, and lay and moped all day. He never allows any one to do anything for him, and has steadily from the first refused to be read aloud to. However, he has caved in in this regard at last, and finds he rather likes it. Three days ago I found him at about 5 p.m. looking grievously sorry for himself and without a kick in him. Following is the dialogue, accurately described, which ensued:
>
> 'Bridge to-night, sir?' in the most objectionably cheerful voice. Answer from bed, hardly audible, 'Oh dear, no.' 'That's a pity; aren't you feeling quite up to the mark?' Reply, a groan. 'Here's the paper, would you like to read it?' Deep sigh, and, 'I can't possibly.' 'All right, I'll just read you out some of it, shall I?' 'No, don't bother.' And so the paper was read through, accompanied by heavy sighs from the bed.
>
> That finished, dialogue begins again. 'Paper is finished; what book are you reading, sir?' Feebly, 'I don't know.' 'Oh yes; I expect it's this one, is it?' 'No, I don't think so.' 'Which one then?' No answer. 'Oh I know; you were reading "Gough's Life". How far have you got in it?' 'I don' t know,' and a groan. 'All right then, as you haven't finished it, I'll read the last chapter, which will make certain of not going over same ground.' Then, however, seeing there was no way out of it, he let out where he was in the book, and we soon got to work. Moans, frequent at first, gave place to short exclamations on anything that interested him in the book, and he never suggested a stop till more than two hours afterwards, when I had to go and change for dinner . . .[5]

On 15 December the Chief was allowed up and recovered his spirits. He went down to his study where a day bed had been prepared. 'He looks pretty well. Played bridge and Victor read to him afterwards.' Next day he announced he would go to Calcutta in four days. The Brat thought it too soon 'and very nearly had a row with him'.[6] On 17 December the leg was X-rayed; unaccountably the poor setting was not recognized before they put it in plaster of Paris . The Curzons had thoughtfully sent up the luxurious viceregal train to Kalka, the lower terminus of the just-opened mountain railway, and it took Kitchener to Calcutta and so to Treasury Gate, where he was carried round the new rooms and his other improvements, completed during his long absence. Soon after Christmas and New Year Frank Maxwell could note in his diary: 'K going about on crutches in a most enterprising way.'[7] His cousins and close friends John and Edith Monins and her sister were staying before touring India, 'and it is very pleasant having them', Kitchener wrote to another cousin. Monins enjoyed reminiscing about being with Kitchener in Cyprus long ago, and he was one of the very few with whom the shy general would talk freely of the simple faith which meant much to both.[8]

The misery of splints followed by plaster of Paris and crutches had taken their toll. 'Laid up like this I find I can hardly do any work at all,' he wrote on 30 December. 'I do not know why it is but the brain refuses to do anything.'[9] Then the English mail came in, and he was much heartened by a private letter from the Prime Minister behind Curzon's back. 'My own personal conviction,' wrote Balfour, 'is (at least as at present advised) that the existing division of attributes between the Commander-in-Chief and the Military Member of the Council is quite indefensible . . . I cannot say how thankful I am that we have got you, in this critical and in some respects transitional period, as our military adviser and guide to the problems of Indian Defence.'[10]

Soon it was quite like old times with Curzon keeping the peace between Commander-in-Chief and Military Member. 'The former,' wrote Curzon to Brodrick in London, 'most unreasonably and unjustly dislikes and despises the latter and writes most unfairly about him and his schemes in the departmental notes. He wants to break and destroy the Military Department and thinks, I fancy, that the best way to do it is to force Elles to resign. This would be a great misfortune.'[11]

Meanwhile, his 'family' suffered an unexpected blow. The new year of 1904 had begun well with the Brat winning a popular winter paperchase on his splendid horse, English Lord. But the third week of January brought shattering news for Conk Marker: Daisy Leiter, Lady Curzon's sister, jilted him by post. They had been engaged for a year, and he was very much in love. Ever since their emotional farewell in March she had written regularly, scribbling a few lines daily and sealing them up on mail day. And to add insult to injury she said she would marry Eustace Crawley, whom the army nicknamed 'Useless' Crawley, a hard-riding, flirtatious fellow known to be deep in debt. She had fallen for him when hunting in the Shires.

Marker was devastated. Hamilton had 'never seen anyone so completely knocked out'.[12] Lady Curzon, who had now sailed for home, had warned Kitchener on their last drive together that there might be difficulties, but he had felt that Marker's belief in Daisy's affections was too full to come to grief.[13] Marker still believed in her; if he could see her, all would be well. Kitchener immediately opened a way. Conk Marker was on the list of officers qualified for employment on the staff but had never attended the Staff College at Camberley.[14] The Chief had four nominations in hand for officers from India and gave one to Marker, who booked an immediate passage home. He could also act unofficially as the Chief's eyes and ears, both while passing through Staff College and wherever posted afterwards. Kitchener's close-knit 'family' were astonished at Daisy's change of heart, for not only had she been very demonstrative during their engagement but Conk was 'a *real* good fellow . . . one of the very best one could hope to meet'.[15] Hubert Hamilton was inclined to blame Lady Curzon. He believed that at the time of the Durbar she had eyed Lord Kitchener himself for Daisy and then opposed her own choice of Conk, though the Curzons later agreed to the engagement if her father approved.[16] Lady Curzon was not too popular with the two households. Conk had thought her 'absolutely unlike' her sister and her mother, 'for her knack of being disagreeable to the staff does not seem to have diminished, though she has always been like honey to me'.[17]

Marker now begged Kitchener to ask Lady Curzon to help him reclaim Daisy, which he did, although thinking that the sudden jilt was for the best: 'Nothing less would have opened his infatuated eyes.'[18] No evidence exists that Kitchener hinted to his staff that the Curzons may have persuaded Daisy to throw over Conk, but the incident drove a potentially dangerous wedge between the two camps. It also gave Marker, after Staff College, an unexpectedly useful opportunity to help the Chief to whom he was devoted.

But he failed with Daisy. She threw over 'Useless' Crawley (who may have been a decoy to ditch Conk), and at the end of the year married another viceregal ADC, the 19th Earl of Suffolk and Berkshire. In 1940 their eldest son, the 20th Earl, won a posthumous George Cross for disarming thirty-five unexploded bombs in the London Blitz before the thirty-sixth killed him.

After Marker had left for England, the Chief took the others on a tour of inspection to southern India, having been promoted from crutches and plaster to a stick. At Secunderabad, the garrison town near Hyderabad where the fabulously rich Muslim Nizam reigned over a mainly Hindu state, a young garrison engineer. E. W. C. Sandes, was warned the previous afternoon that as the C-in-C would be unable to mount his charger in the normal way the sappers must solve the problem. Sandes set two carpenters to make a small table as a high mounting-block with a hinged ladder and had it ready for the parade. Sandes stood by the table nervously because he shared the widespread opinion of those who knew Kitchener only from afar that he was 'hard and unsympathetic, impervious to sentiment and pity'. Kitchener hobbled from his carriage and up the ladder. 'Nothing, however, would induce the charger to approach the table, and, with K's popular reputation in mind, my heart sank into my boots. The horse circled round and round the table and K pivoted to watch it. Never was I more agreeably surprised than when he smiled, made some jocular remark, descended the ladder and was hoisted on to the charger by his staff.' Later, inspecting the hospital, the C-in-C wanted to know the cause of some strange marks on the stone-flagged floor of the verandah. Neither the brigadier-general nor the brigade-major could answer. The Royal Engineer was pushed to the front:

'What are these marks?' said K, looking at me with one eye and not quite at me with the other, which I found very disconcerting. 'Weather, Sir,' I replied promptly, knowing that some reply must be given at once though I had no more idea of the cause than he. 'Ah,' said K and passed on apparently satisfied.

Sandes' guess was correct, but his chief memory of the incident was his relief when swallowed up in the crowd again: despite Kitchener's geniality that morning, Sandes still supposed him to be 'severity personified'.[19]

Kitchener and his staff were back in Calcutta by 9 March when Frank Maxwell wrote to Lady Salisbury (the Chief liked them to keep her in touch) that the leg was getting well slowly. He would have more incentive if he were a polo player, or shot regularly, but the tour had helped, as he had to use the leg more. He rode morning and afternoon and exercised on a fixed dummy bicycle on the verandah. He had massage and did gymnastics. 'His spirits are "top hole" and he is exceedingly nice in every way.'[20] A week later the Chief went out to watch English Lord jumping perfectly to win for Frank the Calcutta Paperchase Cup. But the leg continued to give trouble. As late as eight months after the accident, despite massage and the fixed bicycle, he complained that it had put years on to his life and might never be quite well. 'However it is no good desponding . . . I still hope to eventually make it right.'[21]

Eventually, he walked without a noticeable limp, but from time to time the leg gave him pain. Years later he decided to have it reset, having heard of a brilliant surgeon in Germany. He planned to go there during his summer leave (from Egypt) in 1914. Providentially, he cancelled after a second opinion warned him that the operation might bring gangrene and lead to amputation; otherwise Lord Kitchener might have been caught in Germany at the outbreak of war.

7

ASSAULTING DUAL CONTROL

CURZON SAILED for England on 30 April 1904. By then Kitchener had reached Simla after another whirlwind tour of inspection. 'We go full steam ahead without stopping to draw breath anywhere,' Hubert Hamilton had told Conk Marker, now at the Staff College in Camberley: 'Less than 23 days and goodness knows how many thousand miles and 3 tigers',[1] the tiger shoot being arranged by the Maharajah of Gwalior and his Mahratta commander-in-chief, whose moustache outgunned Kitchener's.

At Simla the rains had already begun and the new rooms at Snowdon were not finished. Overseeing the alterations, planning further improvements and gardening at Wildflower Hall were Kitchener's chief interests while the Military Department slowly digested the schemes he had sent them: they were 'gorged to repletion', in Hamilton's phrase. 'I am sure people at home do not realize, even if they care to, how hopelessly K's hands are tied out here,' Hamilton remarked to Marker, who had reported a helpful conversation with the Prime Minister, 'but some of them will if we keep rubbing it in, and I am sure your conversations have done much good in that direction.'[2]

The Chief and his staff missed the scintillating atmosphere of Curzon's viceregal court. The acting Viceroy, Lord Ampthill (Governor of Madras), was only thirty-five, an outstanding oarsman at Oxford but now an old head on young shoulders. He was popular, although inclined to be pompous and a little condescending: he was convinced that Kitchener's staff lacked Indian experience, yet Hubert Hamilton had been

[286]

campaigning in Burma when Ampthill was still at Eton. They found his first ball dull: Kitchener stayed for two dances with an effort and then left. He could be rude when bored or shy. He would stand at the entrance to a ballroom, unsmiling so that the scar of his war wound and the cast in his eye made him appear to scowl. When ladies in their much-buttoned elbow-length gloves were brought up to be introduced, he would give them two fingers and a few banal remarks.

In his own home he was different, always the excellent and interested host. 'Thanks to K's constant supervision and inexhaustible stock of ideas'[3] the new, splendid dining room was ready for the Peace Dinner on 31 May to celebrate the second anniversary of the signing of the peace treaty at Melrose House in Pretoria. Thirty-seven senior veterans of the South African war sat down at a central table and four small ones, having passed through the hall where Dervish and Boer banners hung proudly to remind them of past glories. A few days later Kitchener gave a big dinner for the Viceroy and his wife, daughter of an English earl, who was much liked as a 'real lady': Simla society could never quite forgive Mary Curzon for being American. Mary had given birth in London to their third daughter but was suffering ill health. She wrote friendly letters to Kitchener which do not survive.

The Chief gave a little tea party for selected lady friends, without their husbands, writing the notes of invitation himself and receiving his guests in the middle of a thunderstorm and, after tea, showing them the wonders of the new Snowdon, as yet incomplete. Whether entertaining officers' wives became a habit is unknown. Perhaps he wanted to honour the husbands without being bored by them, but he liked the company of ladies in early middle age who, being married, would not flirt. In June he gave a great ball. '600 people came,' he told Lady Salisbury, 'and I wondered where they would all go. However, though it was a bit of a crush for a time it all went off very well. I gave them a good sit down supper so they went away happy.'[4]

Meanwhile, he renewed his attack on Dual Control, for in mid-May the year's wait which he had promised Curzon was over.[5]

When his intentions became known he was opposed by senior officers retired to England and roundly criticized by medium-rank officers throughout India who held positions in the overweight secretariat spawned by the Military Department. These had comfortable jobs and spent much time securing posts for their friends. In the opinion of General Sir O'Moore Creagh, now Adjutant-General and eventually Commander-in-Chief himself, 'Lord Kitchener made a mistake in not tackling this octopus at once, for to effect any reforms without being hampered by the Military Department was out of the question.' Creagh suspected that Kitchener had hesitated through motives of delicacy, since the system had the strong support of Curzon to whom he owed his position,[6] a view later confirmed by Kitchener himself to Valentine Chirol of *The Times*.[7]

With Curzon away, Kitchener did not propose outright abolition of the Military Department but that it should hand over the control of supply and transport to army headquarters. Ampthill regarded this as the thin end of the wedge which would lead to the union of the executive and adminis-trative branches, which he deplored, whereas Kitchener, desperately keen, continually referred to it on every possible occasion even, Ampthill complained, when discussing diseases of camels.[8]

Meanwhile, Kitchener had sent a memorandum on his larger scheme for abolition to Balfour secretly through Lady Salisbury. Balfour replied through the Salisburys that because it came secretly he was unable to use much of Kitchener's information and that he was trying to find, through Roberts, an official or semi-official channel for Kitchener to use.[9] The memorandum found its way, perhaps by the underhand action of someone in Balfour's office who was hostile to Kitchener, into a pile of papers given to Curzon in London before he attended the Imperial Defence Committee. Curzon was indignant. As he had still been in office the memo should have come through him. Balfour mollified him hastily. Meanwhile, Brodrick sent a copy secretly to Ampthill, who replied that Kitchener was not quite playing the game. Ampthill would have called foul even more loudly had he known that Brodrick had written direct to Kitchener asking him to tell of his troubles privately: Brodrick admitted that as Secretary of State he should have written through the Viceroy, but 'while the cat's awa' . . .'[10] Kitchener therefore sent a long, reasoned reply setting out his case.[11]

Opinion in London was divided. Roberts continued his friendly opposition. Sir George Clarke, a former Royal Engineer and colonial governor well skilled in secretariat matters, who had been a member of the Esher Committee which led to the creation of a General Staff to replace the office of Commander-in-Chief at home, was also opposed at first, but after long talks with Colonel H. Mullaly, whom Kitchener had sent home to assist the Imperial Defence Committee, Clarke switched to Kitchener's view. Clarke was unprejudiced, knowledgeable and deeply committed to army reform. His switch was a strong endorsement and costly to Clarke, for Curzon never forgave him. Clarke believed that six years later Curzon blocked his likely promotion from Governor of Bengal to Viceroy.

Kitchener disliked the Esher reforms but rather wished 'we had an Esher Committee out here. It would be a violent remedy, but nothing less than that would I am sure get the Indian carriage out of the old ruts leading to defeat and disaster.'[12] Balfour and Brodrick suggested such a commission for India when they conferred with Curzon in London on 4 August. Curzon agreed reluctantly to the transfer of supply and transport but was adamant for Dual Control and against a commission. Balfour and Brodrick were increasingly in favour of Kitchener's view. They would have been kinder therefore to stop Curzon's return to India, using the excuse of both Curzons' ill health, rather than to send him back, only to undermine his position, especially as he was willing to resign.

Curzon was the only barrier against a reform which Kitchener desperately needed. He wrote to Conk Marker, still a student at Staff College but moving freely in the political drawing rooms where so much was settled in Edwardian England:

> I am pretty sick of the present state of affairs. The Mily Member is the real C-in-C, I am merely his suggestor [*sic*] and as to getting things done, it is almost hopeless. If my redistribution scheme is accepted at home I feel quite sure it will be wrecked out here by the interference of the Mily Dept in every detail. Peg away at this whenever you get the chance.[13]

As O'Moore Creagh commented, 'There cannot be two different authorities giving advice to a government.'[14] Kitchener would have been willing to have a deputy if leadership of the whole organization was considered too much for one man: 'A deputy should play up to his chief and can be trusted by him. An independent Military Member plays up for himself and would not be intensely grieved at seeing the other military chief coming to grief.'[15]

He had two examples about that time, when Elles was able to score off

Kitchener at Council. In both cases Kitchener's mistakes would not have occurred had the Military Department been his own and not that of a rival.[16] Elles himself said there was nothing personal in their dispute: he would retire willingly, firing a parting shot that who the gods would destroy they first make mad. And there is no evidence that Kitchener hated Elles.[17] When Lady Elles died that autumn, his sympathy would have been as strong as that of all Simla as they buried the best-loved woman of the station, whose good deeds were proverbial. Both Elles and Kitchener were Christian believers who found difficulty in expressing their deepest convictions or they might have found a compromise.

Kitchener was in two minds. He was ready to resign. He remarked to Lady Salisbury that 'my time in the Army is nearly up' in a letter dated 4 August 1904 – precisely ten years before the outbreak of the war in which he would give his finest service to army and nation. Against this desire to resign was his belief that the Indian army could be made great if he were allowed to reform it: to that end he tried to ignore pinpricks and frustrations, not very successfully. 'I wish,' he wrote to her, 'I had been created so that I could look on useless delays and multiplication of work with perfect equanimity but then I am afraid I was not built that way, worse luck.'[18] He had put up a scheme for British privates and NCOs of good character to be allowed a furlough to their homes in Britain once in their seven years' overseas service, at their own expense: it would be an inducement to save money and lead steady lives. Elles objected that he could not spare the men. Kitchener withdrew the scheme rather than face another argument. The Military Department, not army headquarters, had the Viceroy's ear. It made decisions and gave orders to the C-in-C 'from which he is supposed to have no appeal'. It often misrepresented his views. Kitchener would then raise the matter in Council and generally won, 'but after what labour'.[19]

At last his patience snapped. Elles issued a troop movement order in his name without consulting him and in conflict with his plans. When Ampthill supported Elles, Kitchener cabled London that he was resigning his command and retiring from the army. His cable caused consternation. The Cabinet ordered Ampthill to back down. Kitchener withdrew his resignation. Only a few were aware of the crisis, but it cleared the air. 'I knew I was right by the feeling of intense relief when it was over,' Kitchener wrote to Lady Salisbury. 'I felt quite a young man again instead of a worried preoccupied old cripple.'[20] By the same mail Frank Maxwell commented to her that the Chief 'was often thought impatient and impetuous and so in a way he is – but never when patience and moderation are the elements of success'.[21]

The Brat had been away at another hill station to take his Staff College examinations. On return ('the staff exams effort rather knocked him,' commented Hammy Hamilton)[22] he was much amused when on the illness of the coachman, Sergeant Verney, he dressed up in Verney's livery 'and drove K in brougham to Masonic banquet. He never noticed it.' Next day the Brat put on the coachman's livery again over his concealed mess kit, drove the Chief to the Masonic ball, 'went to the ball, and afterwards drove K back again in Verney's kit'.[23] Freemasonry flourished in Simla, and the annual Masonic ball at the town hall was always a great event in the season, with the Viceroy and his wife received with full Masonic honours.[24] Kitchener had been installed as District Grand Master of the Punjab soon after arrival in India. He joined the long-established Himalayan Brotherhood Lodge and in 1903 was a founder of Kitchener Lodge.

The Chief, now very fit despite his leg, then took his staff for a short tour up the great Hindustan–Tibet road into the glorious upper Sutlej valley and several hill states of the high Himalayas, led by Birdie. He inspected yet another possible (though unlikely) entry point for a Russian invasion, and would have gone on into Tibet but Ampthill was too dependent on him to allow a longer absence. It would be Frank Maxwell's last tour with his Chief, for on 22 October he recorded: 'Wire from Conk: "Many congrats," so evidently the list is out and I have got nomination for Staff College. Arranged to sail on November 2nd, and nearly had to give it up because Victor going away to Afghanistan, leaving only Reggie with K.' Victor Brooke was to represent Kitchener on the diplomatic mission to settle a dispute between India and the Amir of Afghanistan. Reggie Barnes, 10th Hussars, the new ADC, was a link with Gordon of Khartoum, being the son of Prebendary Barnes of Exeter who had been his close friend.

However, recorded Frank, 'K awfully kind, as usual, and insists on my going.'[25]

A new player now came backstage. Lieutenant-Colonel (retired) Charles à Court Repington, at present writing for both *The Times* and the *Westminster Gazette*, was about to take up appointment as military correspondent of *The Times*, the most influential newspaper of the day.[26] He had already written brilliant articles analysing the Russo-Japanese War.

As Major Charles à Court (he changed his name on inheriting an estate) he had been an able staff officer in the British division at the Atbara and Omdurman battles. He had also been carrying on an affair with the young wife of the much older Sir William Garstin, chief engineer of the Egyptian government, although à Court had long been married and had one daughter. He was somewhat notorious in the army as a womanizer, but in Mary Garstin he had found the love of his life, yet continuing sexual peccadillos from time to time. Garstin was busy with plans for the Aswan Dam and at first ignored the affair. When Mrs Repington discovered that her husband, on leave from Egypt, had spent a 'honeymoon' in London with Lady Garstin, the uproar endangered his career. To save it, he signed a solemn undertaking never to see her again; Mary signed a similar paper. On a flimsy excuse, he broke his word. Sir William sued his wife for divorce, naming Repington as co-respondent.

The Victorian and Edwardian army held that any co-respondent in a successful divorce case had been disgraced by conduct unbecoming to an officer and a gentleman. If he did not 'send in his papers' (i.e. resign his commission) he might be informed that Her Majesty had no further use for his services. Repington, who was disgraced also for breaking his solemn word, sent in his papers and took to his pen. His articles were anonymous, like all serious journalism of the day, but quickly won him a considerable reputation. (He could not regularize his matrimonial position as his wife refused a divorce. Lady Garstin changed her name to Repington and they lived happily as man and wife until his death.)

Kitchener, with his high view of women, thought Repington had behaved dishonourably and was an unsavoury character whatever his military merits. On the divorce being listed, Kitchener, as his former commander, is said to have written him an angry and threatening letter.[27]

When the dispute over the Military Member became a chief topic in London clubs and drawing rooms, Repington studied the facts and became an enthusiastic supporter of Kitchener's scheme, not for personal reasons (he had known Curzon since Eton) but from conviction that Kitchener was right. He was also 'quite sure that Curzon will never let go control of the Army he exercises through the Military Member and that K will never get a free hand so long as that pernicious system endures'. Repington was aware that the retired generals and ex-governors, whom he called 'the East Coast Rajahs', were 'red hot in favour of preserving the Military Member, whom they consider, no doubt rightly, the palladium of all their monopolies and interests'. And the older men 'are all so infernally jealous of K'.[28]

Repington therefore wrote to Conk Marker in England a letter that Conk passed to Hubert Hamilton in Simla offering to come out to India and write up the Dual Control controversy from Kitchener's viewpoint. Hamilton, knowing the Chief's opinion of Repington, chose his moment carefully. He first read aloud a Reuters' telegram reporting a speech by Lord Rosebery, the former Liberal Prime Minister, which supported Kitchener's view and did not, this time, annoyingly refer to him as 'our Hercules of the Himalayas'. While the Chief purred, Hamilton produced the Repington correspondence.

'K was rather funny and nice, ' Hamilton told Conk. 'His first instinct was to shy at Repington – that is natural, but I pointed out the great impor-tance of the question and R's power for good or bad. Then he came round and hit upon the Mullaly idea' – that Repington should talk with the colonel whom Kitchener had loaned to the Imperial Defence Committee. Colonel Mullaly's anonymous article of 1902 in the *Contemporary* against Dual Control had spurred Kitchener to bring him out to India as staff memorandum writer; no one knew the subject better. Kitchener's view was that Repington could get all he wanted without coming to India.

Kitchener explained to Hamilton that while the matter was still under discussion he could not himself resort to the press in any way. 'Of course the thing is known more or less,' he continued, 'and can be discussed in the press and elsewhere, but people must get what material they can for discussion from others – I cannot give it. Curzon knows that I am prac-tically the only one who understands that he alone is the real obstacle, and if the reform I consider essential is blocked why then I resign. I cannot go to the press over this, or in the meantime to fight my cause. It would not be right.'

Hamilton agreed but commented to Marker cryptically: 'It always amuses me when he pauses to do "what would not be right"!'[29] – thus detecting a whiff of the common political hypocrisy of the time, that a principal must not demean himself by talking to the press but may do so through a trusty mouthpiece.

The ploy worked. Before returning to India, Mullaly briefed Repington. *The Times* became strongly pro-Kitchener in its military correspondence. The foreign editor, Valentine Chirol, was the friend and ardent supporter of Curzon but had no control over the military correspondent, who frequently upstaged him because Hamilton would wire to Marker who would confidentially brief Repington. When Chirol on his next visit to India asked Kitchener why he had used a man he had censured, he replied that when driven to fight he could not afford to be too squeamish.[30]

Kitchener was fast approaching a moral dilemma: might actions which he would consider dishonourable in private affairs between gentlemen be acceptable when the public interest and the defence of the Empire were at stake? Before Omdurman he had deliberately deceived the Dervish hordes, poised to destroy him by a night assault; he infiltrated friendlies whose lies and false information made them wait all night and advance only at daylight, to Kitchener's advantage. Might he apply similar tactics to a political issue of gravest importance? Through Lady Salisbury he was sending the Prime Minister information that officially should reach him only through the Viceroy. If official channels were blocked by prejudice, was it intrigue if Kitchener used private lines that a long-established friendship had opened? Was he unscrupulous to use Repington? 'K doesn't like him at all and would prefer to have nothing to do with him,' wrote Hamilton when congratulating Marker on organizing the man while keeping him at arm's length from the Chief. He added: 'so strange to find his qualities don't appeal to K'[31] – presumably a reference to Repington's ruthlessness in achieving his aims and his contempt for public opinion.

The weather in the Himalayas was now delightful, but the close-knit 'family' would soon be scattered when the Chief set off on his autumn tour ('if he doesn't break a leg in the meantime', as Hammy wrote to Conk).[32] Birdie stayed in Simla as Assistant Adjutant-General, with Victor Brooke remaining a few days before departing for Afghanistan. The others travelled together the short distance to Umballa, where they said goodbye to Frank Maxwell with typically British lack of emotion as he set off for England and the Staff College. At Bombay he received a letter from Victor which evokes the atmosphere of the Chief's family: 'I feel horribly down in my luck tonight, dear old boy,' Victor wrote, 'and cannot bear the thought that you are really gone and that all our happy times together are over, probably never to come again . . . I am sure you cannot know, Frank, how fond I am of you (for, for some reason or other one somehow always tries to hide one's feelings). You have always been a standing example to me of all the qualities that I most admire (but sadly lack) and I *do* thank you for the good and deep influence you have had over me ever since I first got to know you.'[33]

And when Hubert Hamilton received Frank's letter of farewell from Bombay he replied in similar vein, adding that though they had sometimes clashed over small things he had never felt uneasy over the bigger questions 'in which we have been so closely associated for the past 4 years with such satisfaction to myself and I hope to the benefit of our Chief, whose welfare has always been our great common interest, and will continue to be tho' we cannot always be so closely associated with him as we have been'.[34]

The Chief, Hamilton and Barnes went down to Karachi and across India to Calcutta, inspecting regiments and garrisons. As Hamilton commented later, 'All inspections (except of old china) bore the Chief intensely and he gets through them with indecent haste.'[35]

He was also looking for a new ADC and inspected several possibles. The only good one was Captain Oswald FitzGerald of the 18th Bengal Lancers, Frank Maxwell's regiment. The Chief objected that two ADCs from one regiment might seem favouritism, but Hamilton thought this a 'silly objection'. 'I tell him the real point is to have the man he wants and not care a d⁄⁄⁄ where he comes from,' he wrote to Maxwell. 'Don't you agree? Then K started the idea of having a VC. I suppose he thought he would be like you! . . . I am in great hopes that it will end in our having FitzG. in spite of such an almost insuperable objection.'[36]

Thus, hesitatingly, began a connection that would endure until FitzGerald and Kitchener drowned in the loss of HMS *Hampshire* nearly twelve years later. Sir George Arthur wrote in his memoirs of 'Fitz' or 'Ossy' FitzGerald, 'who had rooted himself perhaps deeper than anyone else in K's affections, to whom K opened all his heart and from whom no secret, official or private, was at any time hid'.[37]

He also took on another VC, hoping he would be as good as the Brat, commenting to Marker: 'Love to Frank and Rawley. I am rather lonely without F and V. You can tell him I have taken on FitzGerald and a rather nice boy from the Guides called Wylly.'[38]

Before these two joined the staff, Kitchener and Hamilton made another tour after a short time in Calcutta. They went through Bengal and Assam and over the Naga mountains into Burma, which Kitchener quickly appre-ciated for its great natural beauty and its friendly people. They travelled by cross-country marches, the Chief always for going further unless his leg stopped him ('he never thinks of the poor coolies and ponies').[39] By train and river steamer they finally reached Rangoon after 'a very interesting tour'[40] and returned to Calcutta in December by sea.

By then, Curzon was back, alone.

8

'BITTER AND UNSCRUPULOUS ENEMIES'

'CURZON LOOKS and talks somewhat depressed as if he had been somewhat unfairly treated by the divinity and had great cause to complain – perhaps he has.'[1] Curzon was lonely: Mary was ill in England. He had many matters to wind up before retiring at the end of April, according to his original intention. The grass widower and the bachelor spent Christmas together at Barrackpore, the viceregal country retreat up the Hooghly river and visited the battlefield of Plassey (1757). In the first days of 1905 Kitchener found Curzon more cheerful and less aggressive and changing his mind about early retirement.[2]

Curzon was, however, adamantly against the abolition of Dual Control. Kitchener had submitted his detailed proposals to the Viceroy in a minute, dated 1 January 1905, describing why and how the Military Department should be abolished to make the Indian army effective in the event of war. Curzon told him he would reject them. 'I regard K's proposals as a positive menace to the State,' he told Mary. 'He proposes to set up the C-in-C as an absolute military autocrat in our administration. The scheme if accepted would collapse within a year of his leaving India. I do not see why we should revolutionize our constitution to humour him.'[3] He told her that Kitchener was sticking at absolutely nothing and showing personal antagonism and spite against Elles. But Kitchener told Birdwood a few weeks later that 'Elles is pretty personal in his remarks and shows himself very hostile to me.'[4]

Kitchener admitted in a letter to Mary Curzon that her husband would probably win. 'Poor Army! Poor soldiers! I do think it is hard that they should be sent to fight the battles of the empire all unprepared and without leaders to guide them. It is next door to wholesale murder. Well, it cannot be helped, and I shall at least have the comforting thought that I have done all I could for them, so I am starting my packing-up.' The packing may have been imaginary at that stage, but after a further conversation with Curzon he wrote to Birdwood in Simla: 'How is Snowdon getting on? I feel it is somewhat doubtful if I shall see it again as the Viceroy backs up the Mil[itar]y Dept and I have told him unless something is done I intend to go.' If Curzon saw the Military Member's Department as the equivalent of the War Office at home under its civilian political head, Kitchener and his staff saw it as an inefficient and costly duplication of army headquarters. They suspected that Curzon liked having a buffer between himself and commanders-in-chief who might be over-mighty or eccentric. It gave him the opportunity to meddle in military details. Above all, its abolition would result in an infringement of his prerogative; Kitchener commented sarcastically: 'Perish the Empire rather than allow such sacrilege to be perpetrated',[5] a view of Curzon disputed by his friends.

To save the Empire Kitchener broke the rules. The final decision would not rest with the Council in Calcutta but with the Cabinet in London. He expected 'a good deal of opposition in the Council by those who are more or less pledged to no change'. If the Council voted down his proposals the Cabinet might never see them. He therefore sent to Lady Salisbury, marked *Quite Private*, two copies of his official memorandum of 1 January. He asked her, unless she thought she had best not do so, to show them, before the Cabinet met, to Austen Chamberlain and the two Lyttletons. Hugh Arnold-Forster, who had succeeded Brodrick as War Minister, had already seen the gist of the proposals, months earlier, in response to his personal request to Kitchener, but as yet had made no comment. Lady Salisbury must not, however, tell Brodrick, presumably because he might be embarrassed to receive privately a document that should reach him only officially. Brodrick soon knew of these secret channels and approved. Long after both protagonists were dead he reflected in his memoirs that Kitchener was putting his career into the melting pot; had he communicated with the Cabinet only officially he must depend on a sick and overstrained Viceroy who could include or omit information at will, and the home government must decide the case blindfold, 'though it involve the removal from the Army of our most distinguished combatant soldier'.[6]

While the copies of the memorandum were at sea in the homeward mail, Hubert Hamilton spotted an exciting item in a Calcutta newspaper, the *Englishman*. A wire dated London 13 January reported that Major R. J. Marker had been appointed Assistant Private Secretary to the Secretary of State for War from 1 January 1905. He was in fact to be full Private Secretary (Military), his first appointment on passing out of Staff College. Hamilton wrote to him enthusiastically: 'We can only think you know it won't be for long, and you see the opportunity for peeping behind the scenes for K. Otherwise we don't believe it!'[7] Conk Marker's letter describing how he got the post is lost. Kitchener's surprise suggests that he had no hand in it, but Arnold-Forster may have welcomed someone close to Kitchener, who immediately wrote to Conk to wire freely but privately, paying the charges which the Chief would refund; the telegrams would thus be secret. He forgot, however, that the Viceroy had the legal right to inspect any wire received in India from any source. Some months later, at the height of the Curzon–Kitchener quarrel, an Indian produced a whole sheaf of Kitchener's private wires, both received and sent. Curzon refused to look at them.

Marker's appointment was good news; the next mail brought plenty less welcome. Repington's first articles (in the *Westminster Gazette*) were good yet contained 'some bad mistakes'. Items in other papers and a letter from Rawlinson, now commandant of the Staff College, revealed that a press and whispering campaign had begun, presumably inspired by officers on leave or retired who supported Curzon and the Military Department: Kitchener, they said, was 'greatly changed recently, has become apathetic, has lost his energy, and drinks much more than he *ought* to'. 'Rawley writes that they say at home I drink too much and have generally gone to the dogs,' he told Birdwood in Simla. 'I did not know I had such unscrupulous enemies. It is rather disquieting.' After Birdie's sympathetic reply, he added: 'I knew you would be annoyed at the low brutes at home. It is the curse of the army to have such men.'[8]

On 12 January he wrote:

My dear Lady Salisbury, It is rather a miserable result of one's work to find that one has formed bitter and unscrupulous enemies who do not hesitate to stab one in the back in the most disparaging way. I cannot think what I have done to cause such lies to be circulated about me at home or how any officer can be so malicious. On the other hand I have many good friends, yourself for example, so I ought not to complain.[9]

He was 'much touched' to receive 'a kind and sympathetic letter' from the new editor of the *Standard*, a London newspaper. H. A. Gwynne had been on Kitchener's Dongola campaign as Reuters' correspondent when thirty years old and later their head man in the South African war. Kitchener replied that he knew he had some unscrupulous enemies at home, 'I really do not know why . . . Now as I never vary what I eat and drink, I apparently must be according to them in a continual state of apathetic booze.'[10]

One lie was never even whispered. The very slightest suspicion of a homosexual tendency would have been seized upon, but in Simla, where, as in the Sudan, every secret was soon known, no one ever suggested it.

The idea that Kitchener was lazy may have started with officers of the Military Department at Simla who looked out of their windows and noticed his comings and goings at army headquarters but knew nothing of his immense energy in the short hours inside or of the work done at home. The drink canard could have been sparked by the tendency of his face to go purple under strong sun rather than red, the more usual colour of Englishmen in the East before suncreams became efficient.

Kitchener was certainly not a teetotaller. Edward Buck of Reuters whom he liked as a neighbour and fellow gardener but would not help as a journalist by offering titbits, had an amusing story of a shoot as guests, with Maxwell and Brooke, of a hill rajah near Simla when the Chief was still recovering from the accident; he had to be carried in a palanquin over the steeper ground. Buck knew the Chief was a very keen but by no means reliable shot.

After a hard and tiring morning we all sat down to lunch on the hill side in an uncommonly hot and stuffy valley. I remember very well how Lord Kitchener enjoyed a remarkably generous modicum of bottled beer on that occasion, and how later on when the *kitmatgar* [table servant] produced a particularly large glass of port and handed it to the Commander-in-Chief, Maxwell frowned at me heavily, and I ejaculated 'Good Lord.' 'What's the matter?' said Lord Kitchener. 'Surely Sir,' I said, 'You're not going to drink port in this heat and after all that beer.' 'Why not?' growled the Chief. 'Well you'll not hit any more birds if you do,' I rejoined. And a minute afterwards, evidently very annoyed, he said gruffly – 'Damn, *lejao*' [take it away] to the servant, and Frank Maxwell murmured 'Well done.'

An hour or so later the beaters were again at work and we were all lining the side of a difficult and precipitous *khud* [valley]. I was a little below Lord Kitchener, when there was a cry of *ata* [coming] from the beaters and a fine old cock *kalege* [pheasant] came swinging at a tremendous speed down the steep hill side. 'Bang', and the bird crashed down some thirty yards below me, clean killed by a shot from the Chief. A minute or two later a small *karkar* [barking deer] tore down through the scrub in front of the Chief at some 80 yards. Lord Kitchener picked up his rifle and toppled it over with a really splendid shot. I have seen many hundreds of successful shots in the Himalayas but never two finer ones than those Lord Kitchener happened to make on that occasion. Then came his voice roaring down down the *nullah* [ravine]. 'Buck, are you there?' Yes Sir,' I shouted in return. 'Did you see those two shots?' cried an exultant voice. I shouted again, 'Rather, splendid shots both of them.' 'Why the something, something, didn't you let me drink my port?' was all I got in reply, and by the camp fire in the evening I was asked the same question more than once, and was assured that the port wouldn't have made the slightest difference to the shooting![11]

Frank Maxwell, now back in England, working hard at Staff College and enjoying the hunting, had worried lest his old Chief had heard of the 'rumours (all lies) of his apathy and drunkenness' and been upset. Frank was relieved to receive a letter signed 'Your drunken friend, K'.[12] Kitchener, however, was somewhat bothered that the lies might have reached the King, since Lord Roberts appeared to believe them. Hamilton told Marker, half-jokingly, that Frank had been appointed agent in the matter 'owing to his facilities for approaching Kings and Queens',[13] possibly a reference to the Brat having famously fallen in love, from a distance, with Princess May when Prince George (now Prince of Wales) had pinned the Victoria Cross on his chest at the Pietermaritzburg investiture. Frank may have had relatives at court, for he discovered that the tale-bearer to the King was General Kelly-Kenny, who had been angry when Roberts had placed Kitchener over him at the Battle of Paardeberg (1900) and angry, with good reason, at Kitchener's handling of the battle.

The Brat somehow put the truth into the royal ear. As Kelly-Kenny left England immediately in the suite of the Duke of Connaught, who was travelling to Japan by way of Egypt, the Brat made the Chief and Hamilton roar with laughter by implying that Kelly-Kenny had fled to the Nile to escape the wrath of the King.

Curzon helped by writing to the King in his letter of 25 January: 'Lord Kitchener is beginning to walk much better and frequently spends a weekend with the Viceroy at Barrackpore. He is very much annoyed at some lying stories of his being inert, indifferent to business, and even taking to intemperance (!) which he says are being circulated about him at home, and which he thinks may have reached Your Majesty's ears. Of course they are a preposterous invention.'[14] Even as late as December 1906 the Chief told Frank Maxwell: 'I still get letters from old ladies at home begging me to give up my drinking habits. What disgusting people there are at home going on spreading such lies.'[15] By then he was convinced that the Curzons themselves had been partly responsible, whether through George Curzon's regular private letters to Chirol of *The Times* or Mary's gossip at home. Certainly George had written disparagingly to Mary of 'this wayward and impossible man' who had been shocked when George had upset his plans by returning.[16]

'I cannot enter into details,' wrote Hamilton to Marker on 1 February, 'but the Viceroy is being nasty and is evidently preparing to put K in the wrong if it comes to his resignation. Knowing the Viceroy's cleverness you will understand how very careful K has to be, and you know this is not his inclination. He likes to talk and to be dodgy and to play the ostrich – all without meaning any harm but all decidedly inconvenient weaknesses at a time like this.' Curzon let it be thought that the case of Dual Control would be taken in Council on 10 February and that all the other members would support him. Council's decision would be wired home. Then (as Frank Maxwell had already discovered from a talk with Brodrick) a commission would be sent out to report, 'so that on its composition,' Hamilton commented, 'very much, practically all, depends'. (The plan for a commission, however, was abandoned.) Curzon knew that Kitchener wanted to resign if the final decision went against him so was urging him to stay and, in effect, eat humble pie. Hamilton told Marker that 'K is very fit and in capital spirits except for a short time this morning when he was writhing under Curzon's bullying, and thought that even to succeed Milner would be better than this!!!' Lord Milner had announced his retirement as High Commissioner in South Africa.[17]

Kitchener had come back from Curzon's office grumbling, 'Here is all this wrangling while we are on the brink of war at any moment, and preparation for this goes to the winds.' The negotiations in Kabul were going badly, and both London and Calcutta expected the Amir of Afghanistan to aid a Russian invasion of India to offset their defeat by the Japanese in the Far East, and that the railway they were building to their Afghan border had no other aim.

The Viceroy next wrote a memorandum disputing Kitchener's Dual Control proposals but would not show it to him. Then Elles let slip that the case was postponed until 2 March. Kitchener felt he was being played with and that his only hope was to ensure that the Cabinet knew the facts. 'I hate all this secrecy in dealing with what is after all a national question,' he told Lady Salisbury on 8 February, and eight days later he wrote again of Curzon's 'rather absurd' fear that without a Military Member he would have no one to advise him if the C-in-C went to war, whereas Kitchener would leave him a good general. He thought it had not occurred to Curzon that 'It might be more important to win the war than to advise the Viceroy. I feel it is almost lèse majesté to suggest this.' Kitchener only wanted to field the army with a fair chance of success. 'If I get this I get all I want.'[18]

Meanwhile his fears were renewed that if the tottering Unionist government fell, the Liberals might want him home as Secretary of State for War. 'There is nothing that would be more distasteful to him,' Hamilton commented, 'though he might feel it is his duty to try what he could for the Army if the conditions were possible.' But he would make his Indian reforms a precondition.[19]

Relations between Viceroy and Commander-in-Chief were becoming strained though outwardly courteous and friendly. Curzon had been 'rather unpleasant' again about Kitchener's writing to Roberts, although Lord Bobs was on Curzon's side in the controversy. Curzon knew nothing of the correspondence with Lady Salisbury, to whom Kitchener complained that Curzon was a past master at turning things into unpleasant meanings and 'ought to have been a lawyer'[20] – or an actor. When the Council met and the case was postponed again, Hamilton, in the secretaries' seats behind the members, saw Curzon put on a consummate act of surprise that the C-in-C had not seen the memorandum that the others had received.[21]

The tension eased somewhat when Lady Curzon arrived back in Calcutta to an official welcome, a service of thanksgiving for her restored health, and general rejoicing. She took Kitchener for drives, and when he showed the Treasury Gate improvements and his latest acquisitions of porcelain she was much amused when he pointed out a space left for the yellow and rose crackley bottles which he said her mother (another porcelain enthusiast) had promised him. She assured him these were promised to herself. He insisted. She and George had a good laugh at 'his greed';[22] he was indeed a highly acquisitive collector, not always with discrimination. Mr Tong, the Chinese envoy for Tibetan affairs and a great expert on porcelain, came to luncheon or tea from time to time and 'played havoc', dismissing proudly treasured pieces while giving sound advice.[23]

The visits of the envoy of the Chinese Emperor may have suggested a comparison, for at about this time Kitchener began to feel that Curzon found it hard to see the distinction between a viceroy and an emperor and thought of his India as almost an independent entity ruled by himself: 'in a very clever man this idiosyncrasy is a very strange development . . . He and the Amir of Afghanistan have much in common.'[24] The British Cabinet were rather reaching the same conclusion: that their Viceroy was behaving as if India were a separate and not always friendly power.

To save the British Empire from this quasi-emperor the Commander-in-Chief was forced to work behind his back. But Kitchener did not seek the support of the British press – the press offered it. Repington of *The Times* wrote again to suggest he receive a weekly letter from the staff. His 'rather objectionable' tone implied 'I can make or mar you: you choose.' Hamilton told Marker: 'I don't think K took it too badly, but what he really dislikes is the individual. He hates having anything to do with a man who has behaved as he has, and his first inclination was not to answer. He has now written quite a nice put-off, and has told Repington he has no objection to Birdwood answering any questions he may wish to put . . . Repington must make the best of this and need not expect to hear again from K.'[25]

More embarrassment came when H. A. Gwynne of the *Standard* plunged into the breach. Kitchener had privately asked each of the generals commanding districts or divisions (except Barrow of Peshawar, a strong Curzon supporter) to comment on the gist of his official minute on abolishing Dual Control. He believed he had the right to ask them, although Curzon disagreed. Eight, including his brother Walter, had replied that the Chief's case was unanswerable. Only Smith-Dorrien, who had first alerted him to the need for reform, had replied cautiously, worried that abolition of the Military Member might place too great a burden on a Commander-in-Chief.[26] Kitchener had sent Gwynne a summary of their replies, to be published only if he had to resign; otherwise the summary was to be kept strictly confidential. Kitchener therefore received 'an awful shock' when Reuters wired to India an article in the *Standard* which summarized the generals' views. Hamilton immediately wired Marker to keep the press quiet and told him that Gwynne 'was only allowed to know what he does to provide for the contingency of resignation and was in the meantime to make no use whatever of his knowledge. Press people are always dangerous.'

Curzon was shocked also by the wire-service report. Away on a shooting trip, he wired 'to extract a denial from K. He did not get much change out of him and said he would mention the matter in Council, which he did, and here again K defeated him.' 'Please tell Gwynne, discreetly,' wrote Hamilton to Marker, 'that K has been obliged to disclaim him and the *Standard* altogether, and that if he is to help in any way the greatest caution is necessary.'[27]

Curzon later demanded to see what the generals had written but Kitchener refused, fearing that if the decision on Dual Control went against him their careers might be harmed. One general, Sir Alfred Gaselee, of Boxer Rising fame, claimed that he disagreed with the Chief but dared not say so.

On 10 March 1905 Kitchener's case against the Military Department came at last before the small group of men, all British, who ruled India's millions. 'Whatever happens, the way is well prepared,'[28] wrote Hamilton the day before. Regardless of correct official procedures, niceties of conduct between gentlemen, or between a Commander-in-Chief and his superior, the Viceroy, Kitchener had sent off privately on 8 March to General Stedman, the Military Member in the India Office at home, a long and detailed paper refuting the Viceroy's memorandum point by point.[29] Kitchener believed, probably rightly, that if he had placed this before the Viceroy's Council it would not be forwarded as it stood without endless delay and argument, with disaster if a war broke out in the meantime. For him the action was not a matter of being dishonourable or honourable but of wise strategy in the face of misguided obduracy. As at Omdurman, he must outmanoeuvre the enemy or leave the field. To Renshaw he had written: 'I'm having a bit of a row with Curzon. It is quite possible I may leave India before long as he will not give in.'[30] And to Rex Wingate in Khartoum: 'I am having rather a row here with the Mily Dept – they are quite impossible with an ass at their head. I do not know how it will go but I have the whole army behind me.'[31]

The men who ruled India met in the Council Chamber in the west wing of Government House, remote from the endless noise of the Calcutta streets. Kitchener described the scene slightly naughtily to Birdwood:

> The case was taken in Council on 10th and went off well I think. I said a few words and then Elles made a long hesitating speech justifying himself in everything. The Viceroy then said what a beast I was to attack a pure white angel like Elles and rallied the Council to him. They all agreed Elles was much ill-used by the brutal C-in-C. I said nothing nothing [sic] so they had an order in Council to say they rejected my proposal (2) they thought Elles had fully justified himself (3) that the case should now be referred to the S of S [Secretary of State]. I dissented from 1 & 2 and this was recorded and all was over.
>
> I merely shrugged my shoulders and said 3 to 1 is long odds . . . I want all officers to be proud of the Indian Army and you cannot be proud of a bad show.[32]

Curzon wrote a covering dispatch for the Secretary of State. Kitchener considered that parts of it were misleading. Curzon agreed to rewrite and it left at last for London, with the Council's resolutions and Kitchener's dissenting minute, on 23 March. 'The papers have at last gone home and I shall try and forget it for a month.'[33] 'K has some breathing space at last,' Hammy Hamilton told Conk Marker. 'He has never been able to get away from the beastly thing for 3 months.'[34]

Nor could he quite get away from it yet. On 29 March, after Curzon in his Budget speech had announced that the Commander-in-Chief's scheme for the redistribution of troops had been accepted and that the heavy cost would be recouped within a few years, they were conferring privately when Curzon complained of Kitchener's determination to resign if his other major reform, the abolition of the Military Department, were rejected. Curzon, who knew that Balfour and the Cabinet were scared of the British public's reaction should their hero resign, said this threat weighted the scales unfairly. Kitchener replied that Curzon could square the scales by 'throwing in your own resignation as a counterbalance'. Curzon was annoyed. That evening, therefore, Kitchener expected a frosty meal when he took General Sir Ian Hamilton (Johnny), newly arrived on his way home from observing the Russo-Japanese War (with a present of vases for Kitchener), to dinner with the Viceroy. Curzon came in late and in a bad temper, but he asked about the war and Johnny held forth, to Curzon's fascination. 'Your jabber was just the stuff to give him,' said Kitchener afterwards.[35] He took the ebullient little Scotsman, who had been his Chief Staff Officer in the last six months of the South African war, to the manoeuvres in western India a few days later in the C-in-C's special train before sending him off via Bombay, with Douglas Haig and Victor Brooke.

Meanwhile, far away in England, the Brat had an opportunity to help, for during Lord Derby's house party at Knowsley for the Grand National he found himself placed opposite the King in the immense dining room 'and was called by name and bowed to'. Next day, after the races, 'while waiting for dinner the King spoke to me, asking about K v Curzon', and about Frank's career. The King sent word later how much he had enjoyed the conversation.[36]

Lord Derby's heir, Lord Stanley, gave Frank an even better opening a few weeks later. The tubby, genial Eddie Stanley, now just forty years old and in the Cabinet as postmaster-general, had been close friends with Kitchener since South Africa. He arranged a small dinner party in a private room at the House of Commons for Maxwell, Marker and Rawlinson, to brief the Prime Minister, who charmed Frank. The conversation was general until the servants left, then over coffee, liqueurs and cigars 'questions, answers, comments bandied across the table like so many shuttlecocks'. Balfour had begun by saying he was generally convinced that their side was correct but wanted justifying details. 'He finished by saying he had no idea that the case was so strong as he now saw it to be.'[37]

And at about that time one of the cleverest unofficial summaries of the dispute was being written by Sir George Arthur, who had known Kitchener since the Gordon Relief expedition, in a letter of 18 April 1905 to a friend who worked in Paris:

> There seems to be something like a battle-royal going on between the Viceroy and the Commander-in-Chief in India; as both are very strong men, the fight must be fairly fierce and will probably be fought to a finish. I suppose the India Office will be the referee. Kitchener complains that under the system of dual control, the Viceroy is guided in military matters, not by the soldier who is responsible for the efficiency of the army but by the Military Member who is at the Viceroy's elbow. Theoretically, I believe the Military Member may be a civilian, but in practice he is always a soldier and actually is independent of the C-in-C in matters of food, clothing and transport. Of course there are two sides to every question, but the situation seems anomalous, and Kitchener apparently votes it to be intolerable. Curzon, of course, talks shrilly about the supremacy of the Civil power, which is unquestionable and which no good soldier would dispute: he hints at the possibility of a military autocracy, he believes all eminent ex-officials are on his side . . .
>
> But I gather that what Lord K claims is simply that in all military affairs the C-in-C shall have direct access to – and the last word with – the Viceroy, and that his proposals shall not run the chance of being shelved by a middleman who is in fact a rival official, or of being minuted on by some junior officer who happens to be in that official's department.[38]

On 4 April a severe and widespread earthquake occurred in north-western India, killing 15,000 people, including 470 Gurkha soldiers at Dhamsala, the hill station where Frank Maxwell had taken his staff exam. At Simla Lady Curzon and her baby had a narrow escape from a falling chimney at Viceregal Lodge. Snowdon and Wildflower Hall were untouched. Shocks continued for several days, followed soon by an outbreak of plague in another part of India claiming 57,000 lives.

Kitchener was touring and inspecting and paying courtesy calls on maharajahs such as at Jaipur, 'a very pleasant tour'. He was also able to stay a night at his brother Walter's headquarters near Lahore for the fifteenth birthday of his nephew Hal, to whom he was devoted. The younger daughter was going home while the elder, Madge, now sixteen, stayed to keep house for her widower father. Kitchener then went 'to earth-quake country to cheer them up a bit'.[39]

He arrived at Simla with his personal staff on 8 May to find a 'double-barrelled summons' from Curzon, who was in bed with a recurrence of his spinal trouble and a bad leg. Kitchener took Birdwood, who had remained in Simla, while the others played polo without much success: the Chief had given up hope that they would win their matches. Curzon's temper had been cruelly reported as 'peevish', probably the result of shock following the earthquakes and Mary's narrow escape. He looked seedy, Kitchener told Hammy Hamilton. 'He whined pitiably about the press,' Hamilton reported to Marker, 'but K was ready and would take no notice of it.'[40] Although the English-language press in India remained favourable to the Viceroy, the London papers, as they emerged from the mail, looked increasingly on Kitchener's side. Curzon had told his father not to believe them: Kitchener was getting more of what he asked for than any C-in-C before him – but not, Curzon failed to point out, the major reform he sought.

If Curzon's almost-weekly private letters to Chirol of *The Times*, and the more general weekly articles by his former Private Secretary were being annoyingly upstaged by Repington, Kitchener also had his worries with the press. The *Standard* appeared to have seen his confidential memorandum to Stedman. Only after careful study, and letters from Marker and another insider, could Hamilton conclude that the writer showed no more knowledge than could be gleaned from Mullaly's 1902 anonymous article in the *Contemporary Review* which had shaped Kitchener's views, or perhaps his own earliest note of February 1903: 'Though the article in the *Standard* may give suspicion of being inspired, there are absolutely no grounds for this.'[41] He finally convinced the Chief that neither Stedman nor Marker had let him down.

That night Lady Curzon gave a farewell dance for Colonel Baring and his wife, who were leaving the staff for home. The Chief had thrown off the touch of fever which had caused him to cut her dinner party, writing a charming note of apology afterwards: 'I was really bad and could only keep my head on my shoulders by holding it with both hands so I went to bed instead of dining with you.'[42] At the dance she tried to discover what he knew about how things were going in the case, but he told her nothing except that the Secretary of the Imperial Defence Committee, Sir George Clarke, entirely agreed with him.[43] Mary said she expected a compromise as Balfour liked compromises. But Kitchener knew no more than the Curzons. While on tour he had written: 'Lord Bobs is I hear working hard against me and has got a party of old Indians with him. It is quite impossible to say how things will go. I should say an even toss up.'[44] Frank Maxwell reported that Eddie Stanley thought it was all right, while another 'equally important personage unnamed thinks it will certainly go against you'. Kitchener commented that Curzon and Elles 'think they are winning hands down'.[45]

As a distraction, the Chief had the excitement of seeing the great changes at Snowdon, though not quite finished. 'You never saw such a pandemonium as Snowdon,' wrote Hamilton. 'Armies of workmen in all directions – the noise and confusion is too much even for K though he loves strolling round, supervising all, and he'll have occupation for two months.' Hammy described the new wings upstairs, the new library below, 'and the whole front is completely altered. Stone-faced below and Elizabethan-suburban above.'[46] 'An infernal din all day,' wrote Kitchener. He owed the Secretary of State a letter 'but this frightful noise puts every thought out of one's head'.[47] Only from six in the evening until half-past seven in the morning was there peace.

Snowdon and the garden at Wildflower were indeed 'a perfect godsend' in this month of waiting at Simla where routine business was quickly dispatched but no long-term plans could be made. In England matters moved faster than Kitchener could have hoped. Brodrick set up a committee, chaired by himself, early in May to consider the Viceroy's dispatch and Kitchener's dissenting minute. By 24 May he could place most of the committee's report before the Cabinet. He assured the King that the committee had laboured earnestly to avoid the resignation of either Curzon or Kitchener. Curzon himself feared that the Cabinet would be more afraid of losing Kitchener.

On 30 May the Cabinet made its decision. Next morning Marker hurried out of the Guards Club and sent a wire to Simla.[48]

9

THE QUARREL

'DECISION AS FOLLOWS . . .' As Hamilton deciphered Marker's wire to the Chief he was excited. The Military Member was to disappear, replaced by a member of Council for Finance and Stores who might be a civilian, or a soldier below the rank of major-general who would not proceed to higher command. Almost all the military departments were to be handed over to the C-in-C, who would have direct access to the Viceroy and be his sole military adviser. HQ staff organization was to be 'practically as suggested by you'.[1]

'K is very very happy today, I wish you could see him,'[2] wrote Hamilton to Marker next morning, a glorious first of June indeed, and also Ascension Day. The Chief wrote a delighted letter of thanks to Lady Salisbury, asking her to convey his thanks to Balfour. That night the Curzons happened to be coming to dinner. Hamilton studied their faces and was sure they knew nothing: no one at the India Office had had the courtesy or perhaps the courage to wire a summary of the dispatch which Brodrick had put into the mail.

During the three weeks it was being carried through the Mediterranean and the Suez Canal and onwards, Kitchener's staff were in a state of euphoria. The decision had opened a new era. Had it gone against him and he had been obliged to resign, the army would have followed a downward path to disaster. 'Now there is hope. The decision is far more than one for the C-in-C against the Military Member or for K against Curzon, or for the Home Govt against the present constitution of the G[overnment] of

I[ndia]. Whether the Cabinet realise this or not it is a decision for the Soldier against the Civilian – one which recognises for the first time the paramountcy of the Soldier in military matters and in the control of the Army – at least that is what it must come to, for they have actually recognised it here in India by giving K control.'[3] Out of context his words might seem to cele, brate a return to the Cromwellian military autocracy that Curzon had been fearing, but Hamilton was writing to a brother officer as loyal to the Crown as himself: neither had the slightest doubt that the army was the tool and not the master of constitutional government.

When Brodrick's dispatch arrived at Simla on 19 June the euphoria somewhat dispersed: the decision was not an outright victory for Kitchener but a compromise. As Brodrick told the King, he had 'laboured very earnestly to bring the views of conflicting authorities into accord', to ensure a workable proposal 'and to avoid the resignation of the Viceroy or Lord Kitchener'.[4] Instead of a subordinate officer for finance and stores, as Marker's wire stated, a Military Supply Member would be appointed. In several other ways the dispatch differed from Marker's wire, but letters from Lady Salisbury and General Stedman emphasized that in essence Kitchener had 'got what he wanted'. The Military Department would cease to exist, the Commander-in-Chief would no longer be vetoed or delayed by a subor-dinate officer. The new arrangement was well described by Brodrick to Lord Cromer in Egypt, who had advised him to reject Kitchener's views:

> We propose, while giving the Commander-in-Chief a freer hand on purely military matters, to keep up the financial and political check through the Military Supply Member, who will be equally at the elbow of the Viceroy, as he is now, but who will not be able to raise discus-sions on purely military points extending over very many months, and often obscuring the real issue.
>
> I hope you will consider this a fair compromise. It is not adopted merely to make the path easy for Kitchener, or to avoid wounding the Viceroy by removing the Military Member; but it is a genuine expression of the view, in which both Lord Roberts and White, who were at first widely apart, finally concurred.[5]

Sir George White, like Roberts, was a former C-in-C, India. They had both pressed the Cabinet to ensure that the Military Supply Member should be familiar with the attitudes and needs of the native army, since Kitchener had made errors from inexperience.

Although disappointed that he would not have a free hand, Kitchener wrote to Marker: 'Never mind, we will make the best of it and make it a success in spite of all Curzon can do to wreck it.'[6] Curzon sent no word for several days, until a note that he was consulting Council members and offering a time when he and Kitchener might meet at The Retreat. The next Sunday, 25 June, the day after his fifty-fifth birthday, Kitchener rode the short distance down from Wildflower.

Aware that the wording and style of Brodrick's dispatch might have left Curzon humiliated, and mindful of Eddie Stanley's tip to 'let him down easy', Kitchener entered the first-floor study, with its fine mountain views, assuming that Curzon's choice lay between resignation, which at that point might harm the British government, or acceptance of the dispatch as a whole. He was therefore surprised when Curzon opened the discussion by announcing that he would leave India next Saturday unless certain modifications were made. He listed four points. Kitchener reckoned they were unimportant, indeed puerile, and that if the Viceroy wired his requests to London the Secretary of State would accept them to save Curzon's face. Then Curzon went on to insist that the title 'Military Department' be retained. Kitchener objected strongly, for with its old title its old pretensions would never cease. Curzon would not give way and again threatened to leave India the following Saturday. 'It would of course have been very stupid of him but he was quite capable of doing so.'[7] Kitchener grew desperate as he strove to conciliate the Viceroy and prevent a crisis, to stop Curzon resigning yet preserve the vital core of the dispatch for which he had struggled so long. He felt he had a pistol held to his head which he really believed to be loaded, as Curzon was very much upset at the terms of the dispatch and his loss of prestige, and 'I suppose I was rather excited by the discussion. I was prancing up and down his room, talking to him very straight on the subject. I told him if he insisted on the title everyone would know what he meant by it, and that he did not intend to loyally carry out the decision of the Government.'[8] Suddenly Curzon flopped on to a sofa, his shoulders apparently shaken by sobs, and gave way about the title. Kitchener was so surprised and pleased that he volun-teered to 'associate myself with him in obtaining his puerile requests', and in any action if they were refused. He acted on impulse 'out of pity for the man when he is down';[9] for underneath the stern, often brusque exterior Kitchener had (in the words of Sir Frederick Milner, 'the soldiers' friend', who had personal reason to know) 'a heart as tender as his will was strong', and as Rawly said, "He was a much kinder man than he ever dared admit, even to himself, though he sometimes let his tongue run away with him in conversation.'[10]

The discussion ended with Kitchener promising to send Beauchamp Duff (Adjutant-General) to Curzon next day to settle the terms of a telegram to Brodrick. None was drafted on the spot.

Kitchener left the room. No sooner had he gone downstairs than he wished he had bitten off his tongue. By impulsively offering to stand with Curzon he might seem to have betrayed his friends who had worked so hard. Moreover, he had thrown himself into Curzon's hands, 'never a wise proceeding', as Hamilton commented to Marker, continuing:

> I think K has conceded practically nothing that was not given in the dispatch, but I feel his position is not as strong as it was, and Curzon will not fail to turn every little point to K's disadvantage. This is where K is disappointing – he is too impetuous and gets carried away when he ought to walk warily, as he well knows how unscrupulous Curzon is – really K is no match for him when it comes to talking.[11]

Next day came the first sign of the damage that might be done by his 'slip of tongue' in offering to associate himself with Curzon. General Duff reported the substance of his meeting to draft the telegram, but when Kitchener next saw the Viceroy he came back to Snowdon saying that Curzon had 'lied like a fiend' in his account of the interview with Duff.[12] Kitchener would have been wise to demand a sight of the telegram, which Curzon sent to Balfour, bypassing Brodrick.

In a more pleasant interlude that same day, Mary Curzon wrote Kitchener a friendly if belated birthday letter announcing a gift of silver candlesticks and asking for the home address of the Brat as she was sending him pictures of Naldera Camp, which he used to like so much.[13] The poor Brat, Frank Maxwell, was, however, on sick leave from the Staff College with a bad knee and ticking in his head, headaches and wobbling eyes. He was undergoing a rest cure in Harley Street in the hospitable home of the widow of the distinguished judge Lord St Helier: six weeks in bed, a regime of massage, 'twelve to thirteen glasses of milk a day, besides huge meals; three pipes allowed; no letters, but once a week Mother writing news to nurse'. Frank's amusement was occasionally to use a peashooter from his third-floor window at the top hats passing below.[14]

While the Brad languished in Harley Street, Balfour in Downing Street was astonished to receive a telegram from Simla, the original having apparently been signed by both Curzon and Kitchener, which stated that both were agreed that the scheme proposed in the dispatch would be mischievous if not unworkable unless modified in important particulars. Five modifications were stated, including retaining the name of the Military Member and Military Department. Balfour's reaction was that Kitchener had betrayed his friends who had worked so hard for them. Brodrick asked Eddie Stanley to wire Kitchener: had he accepted such great and serious modifications? Kitchener wired back, explaining why he had agreed to let Curzon use his name, adding: 'I know nothing of Viceroy's telegram beyond bare conditions.' He also drafted an official answer, but Curzon would not wire it to London but asked Kitchener to see him next morning. They had a critical but friendly discussion for an hour and a half. While they talked, the Prime Minister's reply to Curzon arrived and Kitchener was relieved to learn that Balfour and Brodrick 'were delighted that V and K had been able to agree', but Curzon was galled that they pointed out the emptiness of his modifications; he explained to Kitchener their great importance. After Kitchener had left, Curzon sent a long wire to the Prime Minister in their joint names but did not show it to Kitchener, who therefore had no opportunity to soften the phrase 'are in absolute agreement', or know that this phrase, which did not represent his true position, would again be read in London as if he had signed the original telegram with his own hand; it made other points that Kitchener would have disputed had he seen them.[15]

On 6 July Curzon wrote to King Edward a rambling letter of twelve pages asserting that Kitchener supported him against the home government,[16] and next day he addressed the Viceroy's Council. To Kitchener as he listened, Curzon's words could bear no other meaning than that an ignorant home government had attempted to foist an impossible scheme on the enlightened government of which Curzon was the head, and that after a hard struggle he had forced them to accept certain modifications which entirely changed the character of the scheme that he was now prepared to accept. Kitchener noticed the blank look on his colleagues' faces as Curzon listed the modifications, and one of them remarked afterwards that it was all very satisfactory 'but why ever did we sign the despatch supporting the old system?' Hamilton commented to Marker that the Viceroy was quite impossible 'and really India would get on much better without him'. Meanwhile, everything was rather hung up 'and if we are to work out the new system with Elles you can imagine the difficulties and wrangling there will be. It seems such a pity,' he added, that they always seemed to make a mess of things, inevitable where person-ality was stronger than patriotism.[17]

Curzon next issued a Gazette that the Viceroy and Commander-in-Chief were in absolute agreement, and this brought a blaze of laudatory comment in the Calcutta press, for the *Times of India* was firmly in Curzon's camp although he personally made few direct contacts with journalists. The following day the Viceroy received Brodrick's official wire accepting the modifications. Hamilton commented that 'if K now puts his back to the wall and stands no more nonsense he will be all right. But he will have to fight and will have to be thoroughly alert, active and unbending. He must adhere absolutely to the terms of the despatch and insist in every detail on the strictest interpretation of its spirit.'[18]

This looked all the more necessary when army headquarters received the file discussing the proposals for giving effect to the new scheme. The comments of the Viceroy, his advisers and the Military Department looked 'so hostile to the changes ordered as to leave no doubt', in Hamilton's view, 'as to their intentions to wreck the scheme or at least render it unworkable'.[19]

On 18 July Curzon addressed the Legislative Council, composed of the Viceroy's Council together with (British) officials nominated by the provinces and a few Indians elected by provincial legislatures. He stated that the government of India had received 'with regret' the British government's instructions to introduce a new form of military adminis-tration, contrary to their almost unanimous advice. He criticized the tone of the dispatch. Then he announced that he and his advisers had effected 'the removal of some of its apparent anomalies' and had 'very considerably strengthened the guarantees for civil supervision and control'. He did not mention that two days earlier Kitchener had once again 'entirely repudiated' any notion of imposing a military autocracy.[20]

The meetings of the Council were open to the press. Reuters' correspondent wired to London a summary which reasonably gave an impression that the government of India had regretted the British government's action and had insisted on vital changes; in effect, the Viceroy had assumed the role of a head of state negotiating with Britain.

Balfour and Brodrick were astounded, demanded the full text and reacted with outrage at the 'unconstitutional nature' of the Viceroy's remarks. Brodrick told the King that as these could not be vindicated against Parliamentary attack, 'it has been impossible to overlook altogether the outburst of the 18th inst.'[21] However, the Cabinet decided not to censure Curzon.

By now the mail from India had come. Brodrick could report to the King that Kitchener was never shown the telegram in which Curzon 'alleges they were in agreement', and that their accounts of their interviews 'differ very much'.[22] Balfour put it far more strongly, with exasperation, in his letter to the King of the same date, 25 July:

> The statements which Lord Curzon and Lord Kitchener have at various times made upon the parts they have respectively taken in respect of the reform of the Indian military department are absolutely irreconcilable: and the allegations contained in Lord Curzon's communication to Your Majesty are in flat contradiction to Lord Kitchener's account of the same transaction. This is deplorable: and neither of these eminent men can be said to emerge from the controversy with any credit whatever. But as they *have* come to a working agreement, and as this agreement leaves untouched the essence of the proposals which, largely in consequence of Lord Kitchener's views, the Government have pressed upon the Viceroy, it seemed to the Cabinet that the 'least said soonest mended', and they therefore resolved not to make more bad blood even by the most legitimate condemnation of the tone which the Viceroy has thought fit to adopt in his recent utterances.[23]

In Simla, however, bad blood between 'these eminent men' was flowing more strongly. They battled over who should replace Elles to be the first holder of the new office of Military Supply Member.

Curzon wanted Major-General Sir Edmund Barrow, a former Secretary of the Military Department. In 1903 Curzon had written: 'I have never worked with any military officer with greater satisfaction or parted from him with greater regret.'[24] He had fallen ill and had to return to England immediately after appointment to command the Peshawar district. Kitchener had ordered his place to be kept open. 'I fear Lady Barrow must be very anxious about you,' he wrote 'and I sympathize very sincerely with you both in this trouble.'[25] The doctors cured him and he was soon back in India. Eighteen months younger than Kitchener, who regarded him highly as a soldier, he was steeped in the attitudes of the Military Department, and so devoted to Curzon that when Kitchener had consulted the generals about the new scheme he had ignored Barrow since his comments were predictable. If he became Military Supply Member the scheme might be fashioned to Curzon's wishes rather than in the spirit of the dispatch.

When Curzon named him, Kitchener expressed doubt, then protested. Curzon insisted later that Kitchener had agreed to Barrow. Barrow had come to Simla early in July on his way to home leave in Britain. Curzon told him that he was submitting his name to the Secretary of State, and Barrow accepted. In an account he wrote for Curzon three months later Barrow said that Kitchener had seen him immediately on arrival and given him a distinct impression that he was happy to work with him, and hoped he would start at once as he could not work with Elles. Kitchener could be garrulous when not giving precise instructions; his habit of thinking aloud, stating the options before choosing one of them, may have left Barrow with a confused view of his attitude. And if London appointed Barrow, Kitchener was bound to make the best of it; this did not necessarily imply agreement with the choice.

The more Kitchener contemplated Barrow, the more he saw Dual Control appearing under another name, and his every wish subjected to criticism by Barrow, who would have the Viceroy's ear. Hamilton wrote to Marker at the War Office on 12 July: 'I am afraid K has not been altogether alive to the dangers of the situation, and was carried away by pleasure at his apparent victory and the new prospects it opened up. He should at once have fixed on Barrow as his own Chief of Staff and thus denied him to the Viceroy.' Hamilton wanted 'you people at home' to realize (and Marker underlined the words when he read them) *that the Viceroy is doing his best to make the scheme unworkable, and that K is to some extent playing into his hands* – not intentionally of course, but simply in his desire to be conciliatory and to make no difficulties for those at home who have done so much for him.'[26] Barrow sailed to England believing he would return as Military Supply Member, but Kitchener had let Brodrick know his opposition.

As to Hamilton's idea that Barrow take the new appointment of Chief of Staff, Kitchener liked it at first, except for the disappointment of the Adjutant-General, Beauchamp Duff ('a clever little man and we get on well together'),[27] who would be the natural choice for the new post. But he cooled rapidly as he thought about Barrow's special relationship with Curzon, and on 3 August he wrote to Marker: 'More row! I do hate them – but for goodness sake don't let me have Barrow as C of S. I could not trust him [next two words illegible]. You know how openly I speak sometimes.' He would rather have Barrow outside his office than inside. 'I would never be able to sleep on both ears.'[28]

By then the home mail had brought the astonished and disappointed reaction of Kitchener's friends to Curzon's wire reporting the interview of 30 June. As Kitchener was still not aware of Curzon's treachery, he was upset and went around muttering that he would give £500 if he could have wiped out his agreeing to associate himself with the Viceroy, and he was hardly comforted when Hamilton reminded him that the friends at home had subsequently wired their later understanding.

The dispute was mounting towards a climax. Kitchener had wired to Brodrick a minute setting out in detail a strict interpretation of the modifications to which he had agreed in accordance with the spirit of the dispatch. The next day, 3 August, Curzon wrote to a former member of his Council, his Balliol contemporary Clinton Dawkins: 'Kitchener is kicking over the traces everywhere and is giving the Depts a taste of his quality as the coming dictator. If I am here I can keep him in control but I can only have a strong capable soldier like Barrow to help me.' He would resign if Barrow was not appointed.[29]

Two days later, Saturday 5 August, the Bishop of Lahore, the redoubtable Valpy French, who went on to be Bishop of Calcutta and Metropolitan, was to lunch at Wildflower Hall. He was touring his wide diocese and would be preaching at All Saints, Simla, on the Sunday: he had lunched at Snowdon on a previous visit. That morning a telegram arrived at Viceregal Lodge from London: Barrow would not be appointed Military Supply Member – the Viceroy must consult with Kitchener and recommend another. Kitchener had just ridden out to display the wonders of Wildflower to the Bishop when the Viceroy's secretary telephoned Hamilton and said that Curzon wanted to see the Chief at once. Hamilton explained the position, but Curzon would brook no delay: Kitchener must come at once and could lunch at Viceregal Lodge. Hamilton telephoned Wildflower. An angry Kitchener left the Bishop and his other guests with an ADC and rode back through the now-widened and safe tunnel. 'I met K as he came in at 1.30,' Hamilton told Marker. 'He was furious (quite the right frame of mind for him when he is going to see the V) swore he would do nothing to help the V and would not lunch there.'[30]

He found Curzon as angry as himself. They stormed at each other as Curzon said he would have no one but Barrow and insisted that Kitchener had agreed to the appointment. Kitchener denied it and insisted that he had never wavered from his original protest. Curzon called him a liar, although not yet to his face. 'Used as I am to Kitchener's complete indifference to truth,' he wrote to Ampthill a few days later, 'I was somewhat shocked and surprised.' Whenever Kitchener contested Curzon's memory, Curzon held that he was lying. Each man recorded entirely different versions of this angry interview. According to Curzon, Kitchener suggested General Egerton as Military Supply Member and Curzon had laughed out loud because Egerton was 'an elderly caricature'. 'Why not take him as your Chief of Staff?' 'Oh, no, I don't want a duffer.' But Egerton, two years older than Kitchener, had been distinguished on active service in India and abroad, and on returning to England was appointed to the India Council and promoted to field marshal. As for 'duffer', Kitchener may have said, 'I want Duff.' And he could hardly have suggested Egerton for Military Supply Member when, all along, he wanted General Scott and said so. Curzon thought Scott a placid dummy. 'What if he criticizes you?' The idea of Scott criticizing, rather than offering dissenting advice, tickled Kitchener's latent sense of mischief. 'Criticize me?' he cried. 'Scott criticize me? I should resign at once!' Curzon took the joke seriously and solemnly reported it to Ampthill.[31]

Curzon undoubtedly said he would resign if Barrow were not appointed. Kitchener this time would not help him. He had worked hard to stop him resigning but now believed that the home government wanted Curzon to go. Whatever his undoubted past achievements, he had strayed from the Cabinet's line over Tibet and Afghanistan; they had accepted his advice to partition Bengal and were now dismayed by the wave of protest from both Hindus and Muslims. The quarrel over the Military Member had further soured relations, which now had reached an impasse.

Kitchener could hardly have brought the Bishop with him but that lunchtime interview needed a wise reconciler. If either Curzon or Kitchener had come from a Church tradition which was accustomed to extempore prayer they might have humbly prayed over their differences, for each of these two essentially simple and honourable public servants was convinced that the other was a liar. As Colonel Maconchy of Army Intelligence, who was General Scott's son-in-law, afterwards commented: 'Unfortunately feelings ran high, tempers were lost and the affair developed into a personal quarrel with accusations and insinuations on both sides.'[32] Some said that Kitchener had lived so long among Arabs that he had an oriental view of truth, but those who had worked with him in the Sudan, or under his inspiration after he had left, were certain that he was guided personally by the principle he had laid down for their guidance, that 'truth is always expected', and that opinions must be well received, whether pleasant or not, and liars and flatterers checked.[33]

Kitchener ended the interview by saying he would have General Scott and no one else. He left the room, refused Mary Curzon's plea to stay to lunch, and rode back to Snowdon. His temper had cooled, for he knew now that he had won and was convinced that Curzon had deliberately nominated Barrow in order to wreck the scheme. He wolfed some lunch and left at once lest Mary send a note begging him to return. He rode back to the Bishop.[34]

That night another home mail came up to Simla. At breakfast on Sunday morning Kitchener opened a letter from Eddie Stanley 'telling me what misrepresentations the Viceroy has been making in secret telegrams about my views. I *was* angry. I always thought his misrepresentations were about the so-called modifications and it never occurred to me that he could have told such unwarrantable lies about my views of the whole scheme. I think,' Kitchener told Lady Salisbury, 'I shall catch him out with direct proof that he was wilfully misrepresenting me before long. I do not now believe a word he says and I hope neither you nor any of my friends will do so in the future.'[35] Kitchener regretted more than ever his 'gross mistake' of 30 June in allowing Curzon to associate his name in the wire which he would not let him see. As Brodrick told the King's Private Secretary,

Curzon on three or four separate occasions had used Kitchener's name in support of propositions that he had never agreed to, including the assertion that the proposals were 'mischievous and unworkable' when he had said they would work.[36]

On reading Stanley's letter, Kitchener's first inclination was to jump on his horse, ride straight to Viceregal Lodge 'and ask Curzon what the D he meant'. Bishop to preach or not, he was not going to sit simmering in church in the next pew to the Viceroy. Hamilton rode out in the afternoon and found him still most indignant.[37] And he did not believe, that Sunday, that Curzon would resign: he supposed they must hobble on until the original agreed date for Curzon's retirement next April.

But one week later Curzon submitted his resignation over the refusal to appoint Barrow. The government accepted it, together with Curzon's request that he should stay until November to greet the Prince and Princess of Wales. Kitchener believed that Curzon was foolish to resign over Barrow: had he resigned over the dispatch he might have brought down the Unionist government, which, although a Tory, apparently he wanted to do. 'What a fool he has been,' Kitchener wrote on 24 August after seeing the telegrams, 'and his last attack on me is I think as foolish as anything else. It must come out that he has wilfully entirely misrepresented my proposals for an ignoble purpose *viz* in order to maliciously lead people to think that I have acted as disloyally as he has with regard to the S of S's orders.'[38]

Relations were now frigid but correct. As the Curzons had planned a holiday in Kashmir and Kitchener in Kulu, they need hardly meet before Kitchener left on his autumn tour of inspections. He had already travelled 32,350 miles on his tours.[39] Then Curzon took an extraordinary step and (as Kitchener afterwards thought) brought about a deliberate rupture 'so as to be better able to abuse me later when he gets home'.[40]

10

THE INSULT

THE CAUSE was trivial. Back in July General Scott had submitted a note showing how the then Ordnance Department could be redistributed between army headquarters and the new Supply Department under Kitchener's scheme, but he had not mentioned the numbers of officers involved. Kitchener had minuted in the margin: 'I think we could accept the Director-General of Ordnance's suggestion.' When the file was passed back, the Military Department wanted the numbers and Scott wrote a second note which passed through the Chief's office, unmarked, at the bottom of a large file on another matter. Kitchener did not therefore see that Scott had given a higher proportion of officers to army headquarters, under the Chief's direct control, than he himself had intended.

When the correspondence was 'printed up' for the Viceroy a few weeks later (typing was expensive and copiers not invented), the two notes had somehow come together as if one, and Curzon pounced on this apparent extension of the Chief's power – forty-four officers compared with twenty-five – endorsed by his note of approval. In reply, Kitchener explained that the numbers were not as he had intended and that he had not seen them when he had minuted his approval. The Viceroy challenged this. Kitchener immediately wrote to Scott on 26 August: 'The Viceroy has stated that I saw the numbers of officers affected by your proposal of the 25 July.' He asked when the numbers were added and ordered a 'searching enquiry' as to why General Scott's second note was not drawn to his attention.[1]

On learning the facts, Kitchener sent a renewed explanation to Curzon and thought no more about it until he received, to his astonishment, a letter from Curzon on 28 August rejecting his explanation and claiming that he had made enquiries and found that the sheet containing the figures '*was included in the file sent to you, and was marked with a green slip, to which your attention was especially drawn*'.[2] Possibly he had relied on gossip at the Military Department that the file had been seen going to the Chief's room with a green slip – but attached to an entirely different paper.

Kitchener was astounded. Curzon was calling him a liar, impugning his honour to a degree which a lifelong civilian perhaps could not fathom. The code of honour in the Edwardian army was strict. An officer caught lying in a serious matter would be ostracized by his mess, and might even be told to send in his papers. In earlier times an officer accused by another of lying ('given the lie direct') would be expected to challenge him to a duel or forfeit his personal honour. 'The Viceroy has grossly insulted me by giving me the lie direct in the last letter in the enclosed correspondence,' Kitchener wrote to Marker. 'I think his friends in England ought to be warned of the sort of man he is, it may result in his not being quite as popular when he reaches home.

'Of course everyone knows out here that I never saw the paper, it was hid away in a big Mily Dept file and it was through no carelessness of mind that I did not see it. I shall have nothing further to do with him until he goes. I should like to call him out and rid the world of such a ///////. In the old days I suppose I should have done so.'[3] And to Lady Salisbury, in a long letter, he wrote that a Viceroy should not be allowed to insult his subordinates at his will and pleasure. 'I certainly thought it was impossible in this century . . . It is very unpleasant to have to do with such a man who evidently does not know what it is to be a gentleman.' Curzon had been treating him disgracefully, 'and this insult quite puts the rest in the shade'. He told her he was going away on tour 'to be clear of the whole thing. It all seems so low and disgusting.'[4]

Curzon seemed oblivious – indeed, almost hilarious – writing to Barrow that same day: 'When my reply came out I believe that the scene at AHQ baffled description. Corpses littered the ground and the indignant protagonist has now retired to Kulu to the great relief of his surroundings – to work off his mortification in solitude and silence.'[5] When Curzon was finally and officially persuaded that the Chief had never seen the figures, he merely said, 'Oh, I see now that is doubtless how it happened' but took no steps to withdraw his letter or apologize.[6]

Kitchener therefore believed that Curzon intended on reaching England to make 'a violent attack on me and on my administration of the Army in revenge for his recent defeat . . . I do not think from our recent experience he will be hampered by any strict regard for the truth in such matters . . . he can never believe he can make a mistake.'[7] Arthur Balfour deplored that his two old friends were calling each other liars. When Curzon published eleven modifications to the new scheme, claiming that they had been agreed with army headquarters, and Kitchener repudiated them as misrepresenting his views, Curzon again called him a liar in a letter to Chirol of *The Times*, adding, 'One of my difficulties has been that I have been dealing with a man who has not a regard for truth, and who has been pursuing in the background a campaign of which I am only gradually beginning to learn the ramifications',[8] forgetting perhaps that Chirol himself was 'pursuing a campaign' for Curzon.

A week later, on 21 September, the day when Kitchener was writing to Brodrick that Curzon was unhampered by any strict regard for truth, Mary Curzon wrote to General Barrow in England a violent attack, running to more than twelve sides of Viceregal Lodge writing paper, on that 'clay idol' Kitchener and 'this dreadful gang at Simla'. Mary Curzon was unswervingly, delightfully partisan for her George. Whatever the Cabinet thought, Kitchener had lied if George said so, and 'it is nothing short of a public scandal to blame the man who has been sacrificed in order to keep a halo on the despot in the drama!'[9]

She was even more outspoken in letters to her mother. 'England thinks him a hero. I know him to be a liar.'

While Kitchener was carrying out his tours of inspection, thankful to be avoiding the farewell balls and banquets, she wrote: 'Lord Kitchener had to clear out as he is absolutely abhorred by everyone, and he is wandering about in the heat of the plains . . . His prestige is shattered in India and he has lied so that he is a pricked bubble and no one respects him and in the army he is detested because of his intrigues and his methods.'[10] Disgruntled officers in the Military Department and the pro-Curzon *Times of India* might assure her so, but Kitchener knew that the army as a whole was behind him.

Mary then wrote begging Kitchener to return to Simla for the final departure. He thought it not very pleasant to shake hands with a man who had called him a liar, but reflected that he would be saying goodbye to the Viceroy of India rather than to George Nathaniel Curzon.

And thus, on a late October day, with Simla and the distant high Himalayas at their best, Kitchener stood like a ramrod surrounded by his staff. Since the Curzons had rightly been popular in Simla, the farewell on the viceregal lawn was emotional, with many weeping. Curzon and Kitchener shook hands in silence. Mary said one word, 'Goodbye', and passed on and 'never spoke to him again'. As the carriage moved away with the crowd cheering, Kitchener raised his white helmet and stood like a sphinx.

Both men would have been astonished had they known that less than ten years later they would be walking together from Curzon's house to Downing Street for the widower Curzon's first attendance as a Cabinet minister. The Secretary of State for War had called for him in a deliberate gesture of reconciliation.

Commander-in-Chief, India
The *Jang I Lat Sahib* (Lord of War), 1903

With The Personal Staff, 1903

From left to right: Brookie, Hammy, The Chief, Birdie, Conk and the Brat
(Brooke, Hamilton, K., Birdwood, Marker, Maxwell)

Frank Maxwell and his Bride,
Charlotte Osborne

Left: Fitz (Oswald Fitzgerald)
Right: Birdie (William Birdwood)

Lady Salisbury (with Lord David Cecil), Kitchener's confidante,
and secret link with the Prime Minister

Snowdon, Simla, after Kitchener's restoration

The fatal tunnel on the road between Wildflower Hall and Simla

Lord Curzon

Sir Edmund Elles (in old age)

St John Brodrick (afterwards Earl of Midleton)

Lord Kitchener.   Sir George Clarke.   General Sir O'Moore Creagh.

"THE THREE MUSKETEERS," GANESHKIND, SEPTEMBER 9, 1909.

Kitchener and his Successor with Sir George Clarke,
Governor of Bombay

The Tall and the Short: Kitchener inspects future heroes of Gallipoli, Dunedin,
New Zealand, 1910

Kitchener at Mona Vale Camp, Tasmania, 1910

On the quarter-deck of
HMS *Drake*, combined fleet
manoeuvres off Scotland, 1910,
snapped by Sub-Lieutenant
Lesley Creery-Hill

Kitchener and Wingate
escort George V at Port
Sudan, 1912

PART TWO

The Years Between

1905–1914

I I

INDIA WITH MINTO

THE NEW VICEROY, the Scottish Earl of Minto, who was a few years older than Kitchener, had ridden five times in the Grand National and broken his neck in a fall but survived. While in the Scots Guards he had served on Lord Roberts's staff in Afghanistan and also briefly in Egypt, and had lately been governor-general of Canada. Kitchener had met him only once, but it would be 'a great relief to have Minto to deal with as anyway he is a gentleman'. Within a few weeks of Minto's arrival in Calcutta Kitchener was writing: 'He is very nice and quite different to [*sic*] what I used to have to deal with when I went to Government House.'[1]

Minto wrote home to the Secretary of State that he had been warned against Kitchener:

> . . . that he is over-bearing, self-seeking, and difficult to deal with. One can only speak of people as one finds them, and all I can say is that I find him very broad-minded, very ready to see both sides of a question, and perfectly easy to deal with . . . Of course he has strong opinions, and no doubt is inclined to speak of them, but so far I have found him perfectly ready to look at this from different points of view.

Minto quickly rejected Curzon's view of Kitchener's ambition, that he aimed at military autocracy and intended to minimize constitutional safeguards. On the contrary, Kitchener had been 'perfectly straightforward with me . . . and anxious to recognize all constitutional requirements'.[2]

'K gets on extremely well with the Mintos,' wrote Conk Marker to his sister after he had returned to India when Hubert Hamilton went home, 'and altogether things are most cheery now — very different from the late regime.'[3] And the Chief wrote later to Frank Maxwell in England: 'The Viceroy is first rate and we get on capitally.'[4] Conk had 'found the Chief looking wonderfully well and in the best of spirits, naturally very pleased at having got his way but not in the least bit exultant over his victory'.[5]

The new Viceroy was a strong influence in ensuring that the reforms were not reversed when Balfour's Unionist government was defeated in December and the Liberals came in. The new Secretary of State, John Morley, a pacifist at heart who would resign from the Cabinet in 1914 because he believed that Britain should stay neutral, took time to decide whether to confirm or cancel his predecessor's decision for army reform. Kitchener had 'an agitating wait', especially as Curzon and his supporters tried to influence Morley. Kitchener heard of 'disgraceful lies . . . circulated about me at home'.[6] In February 1906 Kitchener gathered that Morley was taking a sensible view and had 'found out that Curzon's yarns are not to be trusted. I thought he would in time, but just at first things looked rather shaky.'[7] Repington of *The Times* helped to clear Morley's mind, and by 1 March thought he was 'coming round to Lord K very fast and growing more and more suspicious of Lord C and all his works'.[8]

Kitchener found an even more exalted ally than the Viceroy. The Prince and Princess of Wales (the future George v and Queen Mary) began a six-month tour of the Indian Empire and took a special interest in the army, especially the native regiments. After their return to England, Repington told Marker that 'Lord K has made a very important conquest in the Prince of Wales who has come home with unbounded admiration for him and his work and is slowly conquering the disaffected elements here.'[9] A highly personal attack by Curzon in a letter to *The Times* and a strongly adverse article by his friend Chirol, who had toured India, did not affect the Cabinet's decision on Dual Control.

Morley confirmed the new system which, Kitchener wrote in late May, 'is working splendidly and I think everyone out here now only wonders why it was opposed'. A fortnight later he added: 'My office is working capitally and the Viceroy knows more than ever Curzon did of what is really going on in the Army. None of the awful things that Curzon foretold has happened.' Less than a year later a dispatch was signed by the whole Council 'stating that the new system was a complete success and an immense improvement'.[10]

A deep friendship was forged with Prince George which was to be important to the nation eight years later when, as King, he would be both supporter and confidant to Kitchener as War Minister in the crisis of 1914.

In 1906 Kitchener wrote to Arthur Bigge, the Prince's Private Secretary (afterwards Lord Stamfordham):

I should like to tell you how deeply grateful I am to your master for the kind support he has always given me. HRH has helped me enormously and I hope before I leave India I shall have justified his confidence in me by proving that the new system is a vast improvement on the old and is one that will make the Indian Army not only efficient, but also a happy service.

Another part of that letter throws further light on Kitchener's character. In thanking Bigge for his personal kindness, he wrote:

As you know there is nothing I like better than hearing frankly what people think. It gives me the chance of considering whether I have made a mistake by acting too hurriedly on wrong information or through faulty deductions or whether what I have done has been misunderstood or is being incorrectly interpreted. Well I am not good at expressing my feelings so you must take it as said.[11]

The Prince's own remarks were an encouragement. 'I have always,' he wrote to Kitchener, 'taken such a keen interest in you and all the splendid work you have done for our great Empire.' He believed the new scheme would be 'to the great benefit of the Army and to the safety of the Empire'.[12]

The royal tour brought much interest and enjoyment. Kitchener pretended to be thankful that Frank Maxwell, the Brat, was away because the Princess of Wales 'seems to improve in looks each time I have seen her. I was quite glad the Brat was not there to fall in love again as he assuredly would have done'[13] — another reference to Frank being bowled over by

Princess May in South Africa when he received his VC from Prince George.

For manoeuvres, parades and camps Kitchener had taken over a plain near Rawalpindi. The Princess recorded in her diary their arrival at 'Lord K's beautiful camp where Capt. FitzGerald met me and showed me our charming tents.'[14] After the Prince had returned from watching the manoeuvres Kitchener laid on a review of 55,516 troops, British and Indian, including 16 cavalry regiments, 146 guns and even the Mule Corps with their carts. Colonel Maconchy thought the great review 'perhaps the most magnificent spectacle I ever saw . . . Kitchener, always with a "big" idea in his head, had conceived the plan of the infantry marching past by divisions with brigades in mass . . . It was perfectly done and anyone who has not seen it cannot conceive the impression produced by thousands of men moving in silence in a solid mass.'[15] The day ended with a torchlight tattoo with fifty-two massed bands.

Later in the royal tour Kitchener entertained the Prince and Princess at Treasury Gate. 'At Calcutta,' wrote the Princess to her brother Alge, 'we had a most agreeable dinner with Lord Kitchener who has such a nice house in the Fort which he has arranged quite charmingly. He has a very good collection of Oriental China and the whole house is arranged with taste, he does it all himself, and the dinner was one of the nicest I have ever been at.'[16] Whether the future Queen Mary admired any piece of oriental China so much that her host asked for the honour of presenting it to her is not known, but she and Kitchener both acquired a reputation for expecting to be given pieces by less exalted collectors. On the other hand, when a man named Renwick wished to give him a valuable porcelain plate, Kitchener wanted to buy it 'as he has already taken so much trouble. You can arrange so not to hurt his feelings,' he told Birdwood.[17]

Stories about Kitchener's acquisitiveness were numerous, probably mostly apocryphal. Thus, a rajah with a fine palace invited the visiting Commander-in-Chief to choose a souvenir. Kitchener pointed to a sabre of steel and ivory. 'Alas,' said the rajah, 'I cannot give you that, as it has belonged to my family for hundreds of years.' When the rajah came to Treasury Gate and Kitchener in his turn offered a souvenir, he pointed to an oriental vase, but Kitchener said it was an heirloom and he could not part with it. A year or two later the rajah came again and, so the story went, Kitchener gave him the vase, having substituted a fake. The rajah sent the sabre. That, too, was a fake made in Birmingham. Years later Lloyd George picked up gossip that Kitchener 'has a little habit of appro-priating articles which take his fancy – he has no scruples whatever' – a charge probably arising from his skill in begging or buying when a host was too well wined to resist.[18]

Kitchener's collections included a little booty from the Sudan and South Africa, legitimate by the standards of the day, and many presents from sheikhs and rajahs. Oriental ceramics were his main collecting interest but he had Egyptian, Greek and Roman antiquities and articles from Turkey and Persia. One of his chief relaxations was to arrange or rearrange his treasures.[9]

The smooth working of the reforms gave Kitchener plenty of time not only for extensive official tours but for his social duties especially as he rose early for desk work before breakfast, At Simla he had to give two balls every season; so many officials and their wives and high-caste Indians must be invited by the Commander-in-Chief that he could not get them all in together. One season he decided that a ball should include a cotillon, which is danced by ladies in short dresses. He sent to Paris for the dresses and favours but missed the ball through an attack of a malarial fever. As Birdwood, now his Military Secretary recalled,

> He became really sorry for himself on the rare occasions when he fell ill. I shall always remember finding him in bed with his cap and spectacles on, and a thick dressing-gown round his shoulders – and with all the windows shut because Peter, his Madrassi servant, had said he must keep the flies out! And he whispered to me, 'Better send for Walter. He would like to be here at the end . . .' I could do nothing but laugh at his pessimism, and assure him that he would soon be himself again – as he was, with no need to summon his brother.[20]

Snowdon was now transformed. On entering the large ante-room a visitor first saw, on an easel, a portrait of General Gordon, Kitchener's hero, in Chinese mandarin's robes, a copy of the portrait in the officers' mess at Chatham. Busts of Caesar and Alexander stood nearby, perhaps to encourage comparisons. The banners captured from Dervish and Boer hung from a gallery, and its staircase featured an arm of Kruger's presidential chair. Chinese vases and plates were tastefully arranged round the room and also in the drawing room beyond, which was white and gold with light grey-blue silk panels, 'and a specially beautiful Japanese picture painted on silk, calculated to make any one break the tenth commandment', in the words of the celebrated letter-writer Lady Wilson.[21] The plaster ceiling was a replica of one at Hatfield. Kitchener told Lady Salisbury that it 'was made here in the house by Indian workmen. No European but myself had anything to do with it. I think you would like it . . . When I have finished here I think I shall set up as a house decorator in New York.'[22]

The gardens at Snowdon and Wildflower Hall were his special delights, always being altered as fresh ideas came. Oswald FitzGerald ('Ossy', or more generally 'Fitz') became an expert on roses, but before his time Walter Lawrence, on his early-morning ride, saw two ADCs scrambling down a bank from a high official's garden carrying rare rose bushes. Lawrence pointed out that these were the private property of someone on leave in England. The ADCs said that was the point: while he was away they could grace the Chief's garden.[23]

Kitchener could be ingenious with gardens. At Fort William he had invited 1,500 guests to a garden party, but the Treasury Gate lawn was too small. He hired 800 Calcutta coolies to transform the Fort ditch. They levelled the sand, laid walks of pounded bricks, sowed the surrounding area with mustard and cress, well watered, then brought in cartloads of flowers, shrubs and palms. By the time of the party the new 'lawn' looked as if it had been there for years.[24]

The ADCs were a vital support to Kitchener's official and social duties and acted as family for an otherwise lonely bachelor. Conk Marker would return to England on promotion after a year. On 2 July 1906 Frank Maxwell, the Brat, now passed Staff College and, recovered in health, received a letter from the Chief inviting him to return as senior ADC. He accepted by return. But he had just fallen in love with Charlotte Osborne, a girl he had first met when she stayed in Simla for some months with her married sister, Jane Hamilton. Frank persuaded himself that he could hold off for the Chief's remaining year of office (not knowing it would be extended) but love overwhelmed him and he became engaged to Charlotte on 13 July 1906, the 'one spot in my happiness' being that he would break 'my compact with Lord K'. But as Hubert Hamilton wrote, 'K will feel it, but when he has recovered from his own disappointment he will welcome your happiness', especially as he knew the bride.

Kitchener wrote: 'My dear Frank, your news certainly startled me as I had no idea you were thinking of matrimony – I am indeed very glad to think you are quite happy' and would have long years of happiness, 'for I think you have chosen right well and are a very lucky fellow to find that your love is returned by so charming and sensible a lady.' Frank had worried that he was deserting Kitchener since he believed, rightly, that he could say things for the Chief's good that others could not, and this was echoed by Kitchener when he wrote: 'Of course I am sorry not to have you back on the staff but do not think of that for a moment. I hope we may arrange to have you both not too far off so that you can come round and bully me at times as of old.'

Frank and Char, as he called her, were married on 22 December. Kitchener insisted that he was best man – Hubert Hamilton was only his proxy. Hubert was ordered to buy the bouquet, encircled with a gold bangle inscribed K of K, who in due course was godfather to their first-born, Rachel Nina.[25]

Frank's special relationship with the chief was gradually filled by Oswald FitzGerald, 'one of the very best of fellows who ever breathed in this world', in Birdwood's estimation, and held in deep affection by all who knew him.[26] Son of Colonel Sir Charles FitzGerald, late of the Indian Political Service, he was less extrovert than the Brat but just as efficient, devout, modest and selfless. He became Kitchener's principal helper and closest friend.

Freemasonry, then widely and uncritically accepted, especially among royalty and the military, continued to be important to Kitchener, now District Grand Master of the Punjab. He enjoyed the rituals and wearing the insignia, jewel and apron, and took seriously the words of the prayer to 'the Great Architect of the Universe' that a Mason 'may the better be enabled to unfold the beauties of true godliness, to the honour and glory of Thy Holy Name'. Kitchener believed strongly in the divinity of Christ but accepted that Freemasonry welcomed men of all religions and that the Masonic attitude was in tune with the gospels: 'to measure our actions by the rule of rectitude, square our conduct by the principles of morality, and guide our inclinations, and even our thoughts, within the compass of propriety. Hence we learn to be meek, humble and resigned; to be faithful to our God, our Country, and our Laws; to drop a tear of sympathy over the failings of a Brother; and to pour the healing balm of consolation into the bosom of the afflicted.'[27]

In 1907 he took part in an extraordinary Masonic occasion which had an influence on history.

The Amir of Afghanistan, Habibullah Khan, aged thirty-four, who was now friendly to Britain, came on a state visit to India. He had been much impressed during frontier negotiations by Sir Henry McMahon, a rigorous Freemason, and astonished him by asking to be admitted to the Craft, saying he had long set his heart on this. Convinced of the Amir's sincerity, McMahon realized that all three degrees must be given in one ceremony and kept secret from the Amir's staff. Kitchener sent a telegram to the Duke of Connaught, as Grand Master, who agreed to waive the usual regulations. The secretary of the exclusive Concordia Lodge in Calcutta took round summons to a special meeting. The Amir, who had already been to Treasury Gate with all his entourage for a state dinner, told them they would not be needed, as he wished 'as a great compliment to his friend Lord Kitchener' to dine with him alone. After dinner Kitchener, McMahon and the Amir drove unobserved to the Masonic Hall. The Amir had shown knowledge of operative Masonry, but McMahon could learn no reason for his wish to be a Mason except that he had been impressed by Masons whom he had met.

When the Lodge was opened, Lord Kitchener proposed the Amir as a candidate for initiation. The ballot was unanimous, and the ceremonies began, prolonged because the Amir insisted that McMahon translate all into Persian and explain every step, and because Kitchener gave an overlong address on the meaning of Freemasonry. The Amir took the oaths on the Koran. By the end of the evening he had been initiated into the first degree, passed into the second and raised to the third.

On his last night in Calcutta the Amir dined again with his equerries and the Chief's staff and refused to leave. He played the piano, he talked, he wept, he even took a rest on a sofa. Kitchener had to send a message to the railway station to stand down the guard of honour. Finally, in the small hours, he led the Amir by the hand to his car and the special train carried him to Bombay.

When, weeks later, Afghans discovered that the Amir had become a Freemason, he summoned the angry Mullahs, told them he was proud to be one and threatened to cut off the heads of any who complained. And

McMahon was always convinced that the Amir's Freemasonry was an important factor in his keeping the Frontier quiet throughout the Great War, thus freeing British and Indian troops for war service abroad.[28] Trouble began again only after his assassination in 1919.

In 1907 the home government extended Kitchener's tenure for two years, giving him more time to establish his reforms, and in 1909 gave him the entire system he had fought for by abolishing the post of Military Supply Member on the Viceroy's Council. The Commander-in-Chief was now directly responsible for all matters concerning the army in India. They had abolished it to save money, but failed to provide funds for him to establish senior deputies.

Kitchener had already achieved much. The Staff College he had founded was flourishing and had been moved to Quetta. He had created Northern and Southern Armies, intended to act swiftly to confront invasion or to put down internal disorder, or to provide troops for trouble spots beyond the borders of India. But his new creation needed time and money to become more than an outline or good intention. As Sir Charles Monro, a later C-in-C, wrote in 1916, 'Lord Kitchener laid the foundation stones of a sound system but was hampered by want of money from proceeding as far as he desired.'[29] Monro was writing after the disaster to the Indian army in Mesopotamia which was being blamed on Kitchener's system, yet Monro had no doubts: 'We now want to follow his policy,' he wrote. The failures came because it was not fully in place by the outbreak of war in 1914. Kitchener found continually that new barracks, cantonments or hospitals could not be built because the Indian Treasury refused money; nor could the medical and transport services be expanded.

Lord Morley, as Secretary of State, thought Kitchener was keeping too much in his own hands; but Minto denied this: 'K has been a tremendous decentralizer,' he wrote; his divisional system had removed so much work from army headquarters that 'K has little to do', and left his work early, to Minto's approval, and had time for touring.[30] Birdwood, however, was certain that Kitchener's instinct was to centralize. Writing to Lord Midleton (St John Brodrick) soon after Kitchener's death, he said that 'seventeen years of close touch with him gave me an insight into his character and enabled me to understand it as far as his reserved and somewhat sphinxlike attitude would allow. He was a man of great conceptions, but his power lay in his imposing personality and I have never met anyone who could get more out of his subordinates than he; but he had the fatal defect of over-centralization' or his success would have been even more striking. He failed to organize a complete chain of responsibility. However, in Birdwood's experience 'it is very unusual to find highly organizing power and great personal driving power combined in one and the same individual . . . and in spite of his apparently selfish nature I know that he had one of the kindest of hearts, and under his cold exterior there was a fund of real sympathy and even affection.'[31]

Birdwood went with Kitchener on all his tours, including an impressive visit to Nepal, then an almost closed land. The King was treated as a divinity without executive powers, which were wielded by hereditary maharajahs as prime ministers, who were always friendly to Britain and provided large numbers of the legendary Gurkha soldiers for the Indian army but had not allowed them to continue as reservists after they returned to Nepal. Kitchener and his Adjutant-General now persuaded the maharajah prime minister to agree to the formation of reserves. By command of Edward VII he invested him with the sword and rank of a British general.

Kitchener took a particular interest in the Gurkhas, as in all native regiments: little annoyed him more than the libel that he despised or ignored them. 'The lies about my treatment of the native officers and men out here,' he wrote to Rex (Reginald) Wingate in the Sudan, 'are *too* absurd for words but my opponents will do anything to blacken my character and have no regard for the truth.'[32] He did what he could to improve their conditions of service, and recognized his importance to them as their personal head and protector. 'I have the greatest admiration and affection for the native troops; they are splendid men, devoted to the service, and I hope they may never be led away by agitators',[33] for Curzon's mistaken division of Bengal had increased what to the Raj was sedition but to the growing number of educated 'agitators' was a hankering for independence. Kitchener was convinced that the poorer masses of the nation liked and believed in British rule, as just and sympathetic, and that they would be ruined by its abolition. He was grateful that the sepoys rejected attempts to subvert their loyalty to the King Emperor.

Kitchener was equally concerned for the wellbeing of British troops.

He ordered improvements in hygiene which reduced death and sickness lists significantly. He established convalescent depots. And he was only too aware of the temptations and problems of service in a hot country far from home. He urged commanding officers to keep men well employed and interested in their duties and to 'foster a love for games and outdoor exercise of all sorts' and check excessive drinking. Venereal disease was an even greater problem: Kitchener had tried from his first arrival to combat its spread in the army. British public opinion had long ago suppressed the practice of maintaining prostitutes for the use of soldiers, who therefore were tempted to native brothels. Kitchener kept close touch with chaplains and medical officers, and then decided that a personal appeal from the Commander-in-Chief might strengthen resistance to temptation. He drafted a long memorandum, overlong for the ordinary ranker, to be placed in every soldier's paybook. The heart of the message might have seemed risible three generations later, or even counterproduc-tive, but in the early years of the twentieth century it struck a chord: 'Remember the better influences of life. What would your mothers, your sisters, and your friends at home think of you if they saw you in hospital, degraded by this cause?'[34]

The great Swedish explorer of central Asia and the Himalayas, Sven Hedin, emerged from Tibet to Simla. Kitchener had met him in Calcutta in Curzon's day and on a previous visit to Simla. This time Hedin first saw Kitchener at the Mintos' ball – a magnificent figure, taller than the rest, standing very upright, in scarlet uniform with a fortune of diamonds in the orders he wore on his breast. When the Mintos left for the higher hills, Kitchener invited Hedin to move to Snowdon for the last five days of his visit.

Hedin found him a delightful host who personally chose the flowers for his room and books about Tibet for his bedside table. Hedin was intrigued that before a dinner party Kitchener supervised the laying of the table 'and inspected it as critically as if it were a battle-formation', moving every spoon or glass until all was rigidly in line.

Hedin enjoyed the bachelor life at Snowdon, themselves and two ADCs, with billiards in the evenings and Kitchener, so impassive at the ball, laughing a lot. They went for walks along the Tibet road, exchanging experiences and opinions. When Hedin expressed surprise that the

Commander-in-Chief could give up a week to entertain a guest, Kitchener replied that his experts did the work. Hedin thought him a man of contrasts: he could shoot down thousands of Dervishes yet fuss about his pet poodle. Looking at the portrait of Gordon, Hedin reflected that Gordon was to Kitchener what Livingstone was to Stanley. Without Gordon, Kitchener would have been a general but not world-famous. Kitchener was frank in his disdain for politicians and dislike of being dependent on them: most of the instructions he received from London in the River War were impracticable and 'entirely silly'.

One evening Kitchener remarked (as he had to others) that he was greatly surprised not to have been given the Nobel Peace Prize since he had brought peace to the Sudan and to South Africa. 'In our time I have done more for peace than any one else but I have yet to see a peace prize.'

'Yes, but how did you free the Sudan?' asked Hedin.

He had already noticed that Kitchener sometimes made outrageous remarks which he meant in a jocular sense, so Hedin did not take it at face value when Kitchener, instead of a reasoned exposition of the River War, mimicked the critics whose libels had disgusted him after Omdurman: 'With dum-dum bullets I exterminated the whole male population of the Sudan! Since then it is quiet and still and total peace prevails.'

Hedin said that Nobel had intended the prize for those who helped peace by brotherhood and reconciliation, not through bloodshed. The adjudicators had never considered the Sudan.

'That is unjust,' replied Kitchener. 'No one can deny that I achieved a permanent peace in the Sudan, and that justifies the award of a peace prize.'

Hedin retorted that the British Empire was a different world from that which Nobel (who had made his fortune from explosives) wished to create. Kitchener understood, but claimed that Nobel was a dreamer who 'did not understand what our empire has achieved for all people'.[35]

A curious footnote to this conversation came five years later in 1914 when Sven Hedin turned bitterly anti-British and accompanied the Germans invading neutral Belgium as they bombarded, burned and plundered, and shot civilians, while Kitchener was working day and night to save Belgium, France and Britain.

For the moment, Hedin had enjoyed British hospitality. Kitchener took him to the station in the smart two-wheel gig that he drove furiously:

Birdie thought him the worst 'whip' in the world, having never been trained. Sentries would cower in their boxes when they saw the C-in-C hurtling towards them. On this Sunday morning he scattered the people meandering out of church as he yelled, 'Keep out of the way!'

When Kitchener's own time came to leave India, he was aghast at the Cabinet's choice of successor: General Sir Garrett O'Moore Creagh, VC, whom he liked as a 'very amiable and amusing Irishman' but found 'undoubtedly second rate'. The reforms needed five more years 'of capable handling other than mine, to render the working of the machine stable and permanent, and to bring in at the present juncture a well-meaning but rash and hot-headed manager would be disastrous', Kitchener wrote to Bigge in an unavailing hope that he might persuade the Cabinet not to appoint Creagh. Creagh, an Indian army man with little experience of administration, had been Military Secretary to Morley at the India Office. Kitchener suspected, rightly, that Morley wanted to rein back the reforms and make finance the dominant factor. The appointment of Creagh would entirely discourage officers who were striving after professional efficiency.[36] His pleas were unavailing, with disastrous consequences seven years later in 1916 which, ironically, were blamed on Kitchener.

After his final tours and the winter in Calcutta, Kitchener came again to Simla in April 1909. 'Back again in my old haunts for the last time,' he wrote to Lady Salisbury, 'the house and garden look charming and I shall be rather sorry to turn out and leave them to my successors.'[37]

The summer went all too quickly. In August he learned that he would be promoted to Field Marshal from the date of vacating his command. Then came the round of farewell banquets and speeches, which he generally made others write. He would read the speech and when he expected applause he would pause and look over the top of his spectacles until it came. His final speech at the Viceroy's farewell dinner on 3 September was a little marred because Beauchamp Duff gave him a text which included an affecting passage lifted from Curzon's farewell at Bombay, to the amusement of Simla and the fury of Curzon when he read it in *The Times*.

At midday on 6 September, with two ADCs, he left Simla in a motor through guards of honour and a crowd of people on the ridge who cheered him lustily. Minto was sorry to see him go. He had always been loyal, he told Bigge, ending his letter: 'Anyhow he is a big man with big ideas — a shocking bad speaker — a great deal of "the old soldier" about him — would steal the roses out of our garden and that sort of thing! — but he and I became great friends and I am really fond of him.'[38]

12

WORLD TOUR

THE JOURNEY by rail to Bombay was like a triumph, with guards of honour, parades and farewell banquets at military stations and princely states. The experience made Kitchener hope all the more for the fulfilment of a long held dream: that he should be the next Viceroy of India when Minto's term ended in November 1910.

But the government had put a shadow on the new Field Marshal's path. Haldane, Secretary of State for War, had asked him to take up, after as long a leave as he wished, the nearly new Mediterranean Command, vacated by the Duke of Connaught, who had found it uncongenial and superfluous. Kitchener cabled to Haldane declining, only to receive a personal telegram from the King saying that he attached great importance to Kitchener's acceptance. Kitchener wired back that His Majesty's wishes were commands to him; he had refused but would place himself in the King's hands. The King, after reading the reasons for his refusal, sent another personal telegram saying that he was anxious for Kitchener's acceptance, if only for a short period. Kitchener therefore wired Haldane accepting. As he remarked, 'When they played the King card I was done.' The one consolation, he wrote to Wingate in Khartoum, was that 'It will be most pleasant and interesting to be again associated with the Egyptian Army and so many of my old friends.'[1]

With the home government's permission he had accepted an invitation from Australia and New Zealand to advise on defence and army affairs. He went first to the Far East, with Fitz and Victor Brooke, by Singapore,

Hong Kong and Shanghai. At Peking he was given an unprecedented honour for a foreigner when the imperial guard turned out. The regent of the boy emperor (who would lose his throne in the revolution three years later) honoured him further by presentations of porcelain, knowing of Kitchener's hobby through the Chinese representative at Simla and Calcutta. At the imperial reception in the Forbidden City, trays of little treasures were offered for his choice without anywhere to put them. Kitchener put them in his pockets and in those of Fitz and Brooke, to the horror of the representative of *The Times*, who assumed the Field Marshal was behaving like a petty thief.

Rawlinson, newly promoted to major-general, joined him at Peking to explore the battlefields of the Russo-Japanese War in Manchuria. They saw part of the vast system of defensive trenches which the Russians had unavailingly dug around Mukden; neither of them guessed that trench warfare would involve them both in Europe. At Mukden they were taken to see the emperor's best porcelain in conditions of strict security. The regent had invited Kitchener to choose four specimens of valuable 'peach-bloom' china from a treasury of a hundred and fifty pieces. The party were conducted under armed guard through a labyrinth of passages to a room so badly lit and thick with dust that Kitchener had to trust to luck more than knowledge and was delighted to be told by experts later that he had picked four vases of finest quality.

Reaching Japan on his holiday, Kitchener and his party saw the army manoeuvres and were treated as personal guests of the emperor, with such a programme of feasts that Brooke's waistline suffered. The counsellor at the British embassy, Horace Rumbold, who had known Kitchener in Egypt, was not overawed by his 'curious mixture of the brutal soldier and an enthusiastic collector of china, swords, etc., always with an eye open to the main chance'. Rumbold's wife was even more unflattering: 'He is most unattractive and unhuman, just like a big overpowering machine, and so common and underbred looking. He takes all he can and gives nothing in return.'

The ambassador had to push him to make a handsome return for a handsome present, rather than a signed photograph, a contrast to his care in choosing presents for his staff in India. 'Then,' added Ethel Rumbold, 'he is always in a hurry to move on and gets up abruptly before an entertainment is over and says good-bye without hardly any polite phrases.'

And at a farewell party he refused, unsurprisingly, to allow a geisha girl to sit on his knee. He left Japan, so Rumbold heard, with twenty-five cases 'of porcelain, etc.'.[2]

After an enjoyable cruise by way of Java and Indonesian islands (then ruled by the Dutch) he reached Australia, appropriately at Darwin, since he had recognized a possible future danger from Japan, with its expanding population and imperial ambitions. He found Darwin's defences and communications unsatisfactory.

He sailed on to Brisbane, where he received a rapturous welcome that was to be repeated wherever he went in Australia. His visit 'caused a tremendous amount of excitement', runs part of an unsigned, undated document from Australia among the Kitchener Papers. 'He was the greatest Englishman that had ever visited the country; his personality and reputation appealed to the Australian people.' If he had accepted half their invitations 'he would have eaten about twenty square meals a day and made a corresponding number of speeches. For the time being Australia went Kitchener mad.'[3] He was remembered 'with love and pride'.[4]

Kitchener worked hard, inspecting and discussing, and prepared the Kitchener Report issued early in 1910. Building on the contemporary volunteer militia and somewhat nebulous plans which had been embodied in the Defence Act of 1909 but not yet in operation, he drew up a manageable scheme for compulsory part-time training for all males between the ages of twelve and twenty-five, to provide a wartime army of 80,000 for defence and a mobile striking force within the Commonwealth of Australia. He inspired the creation of the Royal Military College at Duntroon, opened in June 1911, and recommended that it be formed on the lines of West Point (which he had not yet seen) rather than Sandhurst. He also insisted on a war railway council to facilitate mobilization. Without his Report and the Act, which embodied his recommendations, the Australian Imperial Force which did such matchless service on Gallipoli and in France in 1914–18 would not have been raised in time.[5]

He achieved similar results in New Zealand. He was now alone. Both Brooke and Ossy FitzGerald had been recalled to India, leaving Kitchener sad at losing 'my last connection with my happy Simla family . . . I must say I feel rather lonely without a companion after being so many years surrounded by my boys who always looked after me so well and were such friends,' he wrote to Lady Salisbury.[6]

At Dunedin in South Island the first person to greet him as the train drew into the station, where the mayoral reception party waited and huge crowds thronged the streets outside, was his sister Millie Parker, whom he had not seen for years. He had given generously to her Parker offspring, financing one of the daughters through Cambridge, who then annoyed him by becoming a suffragette. Millie herself somewhat displeased him by giving a gushing press interview about her famous brother. At Dunedin the review and manoeuvres of cadets became a 'wretched fiasco' when 10,000 rapturous spectators milled around a smiling, genial Kitchener, so that he never reached the ranks of Boer War veterans and the cadet companies had been pushed out of line by the crowds. The march past was a farce. Then the Field Marshal left by car from one exit while the Prime Minister left by another; they met in the saddling enclosure, where they were rushed by ten small boys, wildly cheering.[7]

Kitchener returned to Britain through North America and arrived, after nearly eight years' absence, on 26 April 1910. Two days later Edward VII, just back from Biarritz, received him in audience to present his Field Marshal's baton. As they talked, the King mentioned the Mediterranean Command and astonished Kitchener by saying: 'I would not accept that appointment if I was you. It's a damned one.'

'But Your Majesty wished me to do so! Have I your leave to refuse it now?' 'Yes.' Kitchener was so overjoyed that he forgot to pick up the baton and had to retrieve it surreptitiously from the King's study.

Haldane had just announced the appointment and was most upset at the refusal, saying Kitchener was treating the government shamefully. Kitchener retorted that it was Haldane who had treated him badly by bringing in the King. Haldane pointed out that the King was a constitutional monarch, at which Kitchener said: 'Should HM change his mind I'll know it's not his wish but that of the Cabinet.' On the spur of the moment Kitchener suggested Johnny Hamilton, who went happily off to Malta.[8]

Then followed the greatest — and most providential — disappointment: he was refused the viceroyalty.

He had been widely tipped for the post. Roberts, who knew India and Kitchener so well, had 'gladly supported the suggestion' but later felt that it would be 'better for the country to have you nearer home', perhaps in Egypt. Haldane found the King 'eager to have Kitchener in India. When Haldane explained why Lord Morley, as Secretary of State, wanted Sir Charles Hardinge, a former ambassador who was now permanent head of the Foreign Office, the King was not convinced but said he would wait until Kitchener returned.'[9]

Kitchener's arrival, as Morley wrote to Minto that evening, set up a 'tremendous clatter which may possibly swell. "The greatest man in the Empire – what are you going to do with him? Strong man – that's what we want!" He came to see me on his arrival. I was a good deal astonished, for I had expected a silent, stiff, moody hero. Behold, he was the most cheerful and cordial and outspoken of men, and he hammered away loud and strong, with free gestures and high tones. He used the warmest language, as to which I was in no need of any emphasis, about yourself; it was very agreeable to hear, you may be certain . . .'

Nothing was said on either side about his returning to India, but when Kitchener dined that night alone with Haldane (before the King's permission to refuse the Mediterranean) he 'expressed his *firm* expectation with perfect frankness'. Dining next night at Morley's house, with Haldane and Esher, he became so garrulous that after he left Morley remarked that he should never be Viceroy – according to Esher; but Morley had not made up his mind, especially as he knew that the Prime Minister, Asquith, favoured Kitchener, and the King was hot for him. Morley promised the King to turn over all the arguments afresh.[10]

The King went to Sandringham, caught a bronchial infection and returned to London sick, although still working at his papers. The Queen was summoned back from Corfu, the Prime Minister from a cruise. On 6 May, aged only sixty-eight, the King died. Kitchener was one of the friends of the King whom Queen Alexandra led gently by the arm into the bedroom to see the dead monarch: Kitchener had never felt more shy, but his kindness and sympathy drew them together.[11]

Kitchener always believed that he would have become Viceroy and governor-general had the King lived.

As it was, when the funeral was over and the eight visiting Kings had departed, Morley set out in a strictly confidential printed submission dated 5 June 1910 the factors for and against.

He first asked whether Kitchener would 'make an efficient Governor-

General' and answered that he saw 'no reason whatever to doubt that the answer to this question ought to be affirmative', continuing:

> I believe that he would follow the instructions of the Secretary of State with military fidelity. He would have the eye of a soldier for facts and forces around him. He has the virtues of the economist, sorely needed in India. He has a natural instinct for making a good business of civil administration. Finally he has shown marked gifts in managing and composing difficult positions, at Fashoda, for instance, in South Africa, and in Australia. This striking personality would make itself felt in a perfectly wholesome way throughout the army of civil functionaries.

Morley doubted whether Kitchener would be popular with civil or with military functionaries; and indeed ten days after the memorandum was signed Minto was writing to Bigge that he heard on all sides opinions against, 'and yet I myself know what an entirely different person K is to what his public assume him to be', and favoured the appointment.[12]

Morley in his memorandum next asked what effect the appointment would have on Indian public opinion. Shortly after Kitchener had left, the Liberal government had introduced long-planned reforms that gave Indians a greater say in their affairs and opened new avenues for expression. 'Any step that would jar, estrange, shock or startle . . . would be a wanton courting of mischief.' The office of governor-general had only once been held by a soldier; it was essentially a civilian post. Therefore 'the selection for this post of the soldier of most conspicuous fame now in active service, would be regarded as a loud proclamation of the military basis of British rule in India.' Morley had always recognized this military basis. 'But to appoint for the first time the most famous soldier you can find to be the chief agent of His Majesty, is to hoist the signal flag of military power before India and the world.'

Were India on the verge of insurrection, the appointment of Kitchener would be wise, and it would be welcomed by those who had opposed the new liberalization, but with the experiment newly launched, the sending out of a soldier Viceroy would be regarded by Indian educated opinion as a step of 'sinister significance', especially following the outpouring of loyalty and attachment to the Crown that had just been seen at the death of King Edward and the accession of King George: 'a very sensitive people might not regard the immediate appointment of a famous bearer of the sword as a gracious reply to the their affectionate salutations.'

And finally, it had long been the practice to send out 'a fresh mind, trained in public business and national affairs, but without special Indian experience'.[13]

Kitchener was deeply disappointed. Unable to peer four years into the future to see how his absence in India would have been disastrous for the nation, he felt almost that he had no future. He went off to Ireland.

On 22 June, two days before his sixtieth birthday, he wrote to Maxwell in Australia from Glengarriff:

Old Morley would not have me for India at any price and the Mediterranean command was mere bunkum so I am at a loose end with nothing to do. I could not stand London where I must either appear to be cap in hand to this Govt or join Ld Bobs and Charlie Beresford and criticize the military powers that be which I do not consider a sound course, so I have bolted to the country of my birth and am doing some touring and trying to learn how to enjoy doing nothing.

He added a PS: 'I feel a bit sick at times at the result of one's work but that will pass when I can settle down to something. You are such an old friend I can tell you what no one knows or sees. The iron went in pretty deep.'[14]

He was determined not to accept the War Office under the present government. He would like Cromer's old post as Agent-General in Egypt if it became vacant or the embassy at Constantinople. Or he might take up an invitation to return to China to advise on modernizing their army.[15] Meanwhile he accepted an invitation from Winston Churchill, First Lord of the Admiralty, to the naval manoeuvres off the west coast of Scotland, an important episode because the two men became friends on HMS *Drake*. Twelve years earlier Kitchener as Sirdar had been annoyed when young Churchill gate-crashed, in effect, the Battle of Omdurman; and angry after the battle when he supported the libels that Kitchener had ordered the slaughter of Dervish wounded, or given them no medical help, or prevented their families from removing them, all false accusations.[16] When Kitchener was in India he wrote of him as 'that bounder'.[17] But now he recognized him as a man who cared deeply about the defence of the realm and could inspire the navy and his Cabinet colleagues.

Kitchener went country-house visiting, including his old haunts: Hatfield with the Salisburys and Taplow Court with the Desboroughs. Lord Desborough later recalled his five-year-old daughter Imogen, Kitchener's goddaughter, 'meeting us, as we came in for tea from a walk, outside the tea room (she was, I may say, his god-daughter), and she immediately said to the great Lord Kitchener, "Don't go in there, they are making such a *chatter*; come up and have tea with me," and up he went right to the top of the house, with his lame leg, and sat down with Imogen and her nurse and had a long talk.'

Desborough noticed that 'children accepted him as a natural friend.'[18] Lady Winifred Renshaw was not surprised when one day, coming back to the flat above Constitution Arch which Arthur then rented from the Crown, she found Kitchener on the floor helping young Tom, his godson, to lay out the model train system he had just bought him.

On the other hand he was rather embarrassed, staying with his cousins John and Edith Monins at Ringwould in Kent, to wake up one morning to find little Bridget saying her prayers at his bedside. Smaller children were often taught to say their prayers aloud at their mother's knee, but Bridget had decided that her mother was getting a little bored with the daily ritual, so she went to the spare room. She recalled when aged over ninety, 'Kneeling down beside his bed to say my prayers. Nanny traced me and I was told what a naughty girl I was. I remember *vividly*, replying: "Well, Cousin Herbert is my godfather and I thought he'd like to 'hear' me" – the agonized man retreating under the blankets!'[19]

Kitchener's main interest in the summer of 1910 was to find a country estate that would be his summer home, with a house that he could love and cherish as another man would his wife; to house and display his treasures and to be the seat of the Kitchener dynasty, like Marlborough's Blenheim or Wellington's Stratfield Saye on a smaller scale, to be carried on after his death by his eldest brother's son Henry, always known as Toby. Toby was a naval officer and not yet married. Kitchener put in a bid for Parham in Sussex but a South African millionaire outbid him. The Birdwoods arrived from India, and Birdie generously gave up some of his leave to drive his old Chief about the countryside, without early success. On 26 August they left London at 7.30 a.m. by train for Canterbury, and motored by hired car some seven miles to view Broome Park in the parish of Barham, in a valley just off the Dover road: Dover lay seven miles further. Birdie described Broome in his diary as having 'a nice old red brick Jacobean part in 476 acres of Park and I think Lord K will buy it if he can get it for £1500 or under. It will take another 1000 to do up.'[20]

Kitchener was enchanted. Broome had been put on the market by Sir Percy Dixwell-Oxenden, an elderly baronet who had lost much of his money. Built in the reign of Charles 1 by his Dixwell ancestors, the Oxendens of Deane had inherited the house in about 1753. Sir Percy had handed over much of the land to his son but could not afford to maintain the mansion, which was mortgaged to the hilt. Kitchener immediately made an offer.

'I have bought a house in Kent six miles from Canterbury,' he wrote from Balmoral in September to Frank Maxwell, now military secretary to a governor in Australia, when congratulating him on the birth of his daughter Rachel. 'It is rather a big place and will want a lot of doing up but as I have nothing else to do it will interest me enormously to make it a nice abode. I hope I shall see you and your wife there some day; lots of work in the garden for you to do.'[21]

The Oxendens dragged out the negotiations. The sale had not been completed when Kitchener left England in November. Determined not to endure an English winter, he had arranged a tour in the Sudan and East Africa to shoot and to find somewhere to spend future winters. FitzGerald would join the big game hunt, on leave from India, and Kitchener's nephew Toby, on short leave from the Mediterranean Fleet. Toby, a naval lieutenant, then aged thirty-two, would be his heir. When Lord Salisbury had offered a viscountcy in 1902, Kitchener had asked if the succession might pass direct to Toby in order to keep it in the family without his having to 'take a permanent encumbrance'. Salisbury had minuted on the telegram: 'Does he mean a wife?' But this was not allowed. It must pass to Toby's father.[22]

Kitchener travelled out by Vienna and Constantinople, alone except for his soldier-servant, to Cairo, where Toby joined him. Writing ahead to Wingate in Khartoum, he ended: 'I *shall* be glad to see the Sudan again and all old friends. Everyone has been very nice here.'[23] As Toby's leave was short, Kitchener took him for a shooting trip up the Blue Nile from Khartoum. He had not known his nephew well until now. Toby was very much a sailor, with bluff naval humour but great vitality, and simple at heart, a hard worker and thus a worthy heir.

At Khartoum, where Kitchener had a great reception from Sudanese, Egyptians and British, they stayed in the rebuilt palace with the Wingates. One of the guests at a New Year dinner was Violet Asquith, the Prime Minister's twenty-three-year-old daughter whose brother Arthur had joined the Sudan political service. She disliked Toby at first, then fell a little in love with him, but he knew she was mourning for her fiancé, killed in a motor smash. Violet was introduced to the Field Marshal. She wrote in her diary: 'He looks *most* impressive & just as he should − a grim iron conqueror − 8 ft high bright red coat square jaw − inaccessible martial eye. Casting about for a conversational opening fatuity I hit upon the most apposite thing I could have said − by praising the s-shaped staircase − which he made & is *much* prouder of than the Battle of Omdurman. He unbent considerably at this . . .' Next day she watched the New Year procession and thought him splendid on a white horse, 'looking very grim and victorious'.[24]

Kitchener was pleasantly astonished at the progress of the Sudan, especially the irrigation schemes and the rebuilt Khartoum and the Gordon Memorial College. He promised to raise funds for a cathedral. Toby left for Malta. Kitchener and Fitz and a former ADC, MacMurdo, travelled up the White Nile in a luxurious steamer placed at his disposal, passing Fashoda (which had been renamed), where Kitchener could recall his diplomatic triumph over the French. They saw vast amounts of game on the plains, and shot elephants, buffalo, hippo and six kind of antelope, for these were the days before big game hunters abandoned their guns for cameras.

They reached British East Africa (Kenya) overland and were met by a Royal Engineer officer, Major Humphrey Leggatt, who had been seconded to the protectorate government to help develop the higher, temperate parts of the country through white settlers, according to the accepted colonial practice of the times. Leggatt, who later became a distinguished figure in Kenya's history, and knighted, acted as their host, arranging the shooting and then the search for a property. While in the Sudan Kitchener had thought of buying a concession in almost-empty land near the Abyssinian border, to hunt game in the winters, but he abandoned the idea in favour of taking up land in Kenya in partnership with the other three: the colonial government offered settlers wide stretches free, under strict rules for agriculture and the protection of the Africans. The governor at Nairobi was Kitchener's old friend and subordinate, Sir Percy Girouard, the Canadian who as a young sapper officer had built Kitchener's 'impossible' desert railway, the key to the success of the River War.[25] He was only too ready to oblige his old Chief and to stretch the rules on residency in order to secure the prestige and investment he would bring. Kitchener, Fitz and MacMurdo would be absentee settlers, while Leggatt ran the property. It happened that one tribe, the Nandis of Muhuroni on the southern end of the Highlands, had been punished for raiding and robbery by being confined to a reserve: their forfeited hunting and grazing lands, mostly of scrub and wild animals, were available for development of suitable crops. Kitchener would have a home away from English winters and all the interest of developing the land for the people. Thus he acquired the 9,000-acre Songhor estates in partnership.[26]

While in East Africa Kitchener received orders from the new King, George V, to command the troops at his coronation in June, and also to bear the sword of state in the Abbey. He arrived home to good news. At 1.34 p.m. on 6 April 1911 he handed in a telegram at the post office off the Haymarket, addressed to his cousins: 'Monins, Ringwould, Walmer: *Broome is mine.* Herbert.'[27] He had bought it for £1400, with woodland, after much bargaining. Eighteen days later he was writing to Conk Marker: 'Broome was simply delightful, trees coming out, birds singing, flowers everywhere.' He had gone down with Fitz. The resident steward or agent, Walter Western, had put them up in the steward's house.[28]

He set to work at once, commissioning Detmar Blow, an architect in his early forties. A disciple of Ruskin, he had designed a hunting lodge in France for the Duke of Westminster and had a flourishing private practice. As a start, Kitchener pulled down features that were not in accord with the house's Jacobean origin, built a new gate lodge in Dutch clinker bricks and ordered the principal rooms to be made higher by doing away with an entire storey.

He could only rush down at weekends, the weeks being filled with the military preparations for the coronation. As visitors from all over the world began to pour into London, Kitchener had many social engagements. Lady Salisbury bravely invited Kitchener and Curzon to the same luncheon party at Arlington House, two icebergs passing in the night, it was said.

On the coronation day, 22 June, Kitchener was up very early to check on the procession troops. He then toured the route in a little car, driven by an officer, to check on all units lining the streets, and that crowd barriers were in place: a rather unpopular innovation which he had prescribed lest popular enthusiasm get out of hand. He then put on full dress for the Abbey. He had chosen his godson Herbert Horatio (Tom) Renshaw as page: 'Tom better practise carrying swords – if I drop the beastly thing he will have to carry it,' he joked to Tom's father.[29]

When the great ceremony was over and Kitchener, with Birdwood (an ADC to the King) and young Tom, had returned to his rooms at Whitehall Court, he found that the valuable jewel of his Grand Cross of the Star of India was missing from its place on the sash. Birdie telephoned the police in case it had been picked up and not fallen into a drain. He recalled:

Presently, we went into our rooms to change, and a moment later Kitchener shouted: 'Here, Birdie, come at once. There's something awful in my boot.' He was, of course, wearing the high Field Marshal's boots, of which a flap stands out clear of the leg, and in a flash I saw what had happened. His GCSI jewel had disappeared down his boot when he started to pull it off! The question was then, how to recover it; and he was not at all pleased when I produced a razor wherewith to spoil his beautiful new boots. However, the operation was performed satisfactorily. As someone said afterwards, 'No one but Kitchener would have had such luck!' That, by the way, bears out what Lord Salisbury had said when selecting him, over the heads of his seniors, to command the Sudan expedition – 'Kitchener has luck.'[30]

13

PORTRAIT OF A PHARAOH

'Coming in cruiser. Have special train awaiting me.' . . . 'Central platform of Cairo railway station to be carpeted. Royal entrance to be open. British officials to attend in top hats and frock coats.' The general manager of Egyptian State Railways, Brigadier-General Blakeney, was delighted by the telegrams. He had been one of the 'band of boys' who had built Kitchener's desert railway and was a veteran of Omdurman and the Boer War. Robert Blakeney rejoiced that His Britannic Majesty's new representative in Egypt, Viscount Kitchener, would begin his 'reign' with a flourish.

The British agent and consul-general held an extraordinary position. Technically he was merely one of the diplomatic representatives accredited to the Khedive of Egypt, himself a vassal of the Ottoman Sultan in Constantinople. Practically, since the time of Lord Cromer, he was the *de facto* ruler of Egypt, supported by a British Army of Occupation. The Khedive and his Prime Minister and Legislative Assembly could do little that was not in accord with the British agent's policy, and the permanent heads of departments were mostly British. Cromer had been followed by Sir Eldon Gorst, who governed with a looser hand like a self-effacing civil servant rather than a potentate. He had allowed the economy to slip and nationalist agitation to increase and British prestige to be weakened. Back in England, Cromer was alarmed. When Gorst fell ill, and by the coronation summer of 1911 was plainly unable to retain office, Cromer urged the Foreign Secretary, Sir Edward Grey, to appoint Kitchener. Two days before the coronation, Kitchener received a handwritten note from Grey that the King approved very cordially, 'and the arrangement is one which has evidently given him much pleasure'.[1]

On the evening of 28 September 1911, precisely one minute before schedule, the special train drew into the station. The red-carpeted platform was packed with all the dignitaries of Cairo, religious and diplomatic, Egyptian Cabinet ministers and British officials, senior army officers of both armies, and heads of the great commercial houses. Outside, such a large crowd had gathered that officials were nervous. A serious strike had taken place a few weeks earlier, and when Kitchener's appointment had been announced the nationalist press had run inflammatory articles about 'the Butcher of Khartoum'.

The train stopped opposite the royal exit. 'Soon,' in Blakeney's words, 'a tall figure was seen, towering above the heads of the crowd, while arms clashed and the Guards' band played the national anthem. Though dressed in a grey frock-coat and top-hat Kitchener was martial as ever. He inspected the Guards of Honour, made himself most charming to the officers, was courteous but rather frigid to the high dignitaries, and walked down the ranks, greeting old friends and subordinates. We followed close on his heels until he emerged from the building and paused at the top of the baize-covered steps before descending to the Agency carriage. For a moment, our hearts stood still. Then came a wild yell of delight from the populace. They closed in and followed the carriage, cheering, yelling, and clapping hands, the whole way to the Agency. Kitchener, with his matchless knowledge of Oriental mentality, had struck the right note.'[2]

One of those at the station drove hurriedly by backstreets to arrive at the Agency first. Ronald Storrs, Oriental Secretary, was some weeks short of his thirtieth birthday. He knew that Gorst and Kitchener had been on bad terms because Gorst, then in charge of finance, had grudged every penny during the River War and the reconstruction of the Sudan. As Gorst's man, Storrs had hardly expected to keep his job. But Kitchener summed him up as one who honestly spoke his mind to help his Chief. From their first encounter in the gloomy study of the Agency, records Storrs, 'followed three years of such happiness, interest and responsibility as no gratitude could repay . . . where he trusted, he trusted absolutely'. And Storrs soon became used to Kitchener's ways. When he warned his Chief that a number of British officials might be tendering their resignations, either from old dislike or to forestall compulsory retirement, Kitchener 'significantly tapped a drawer in his desk and said: "You'd better go down to the Club and let it be generally known that I've always kept printed acceptance forms for resignations, only requiring the name to be added to become effective." I duly circulated this news and need hardly say that, for whatever reason, not one single resignation was submitted. Next day, curious to see how the forms ran, I opened the drawer, and found it to contain a box of cigars.'[3]

Ronald Storrs had met Kitchener only twice before, at social occasions, but several of the officials now working with him had known him well, especially Lord Edward Cecil, his ADC during the River War and now deputy head of finance. He found Kitchener 'a genial man of the world, laughing at matters which would have irritated him profoundly in '96'. Cecil had disliked him at first in the Dongola campaign but came to appreciate him and respect him. They were meeting almost every day at the Agency. Cecil became devoted, although never unaware of 'the oddities and contrasts of his character'. Kitchener was always devising some new improvement, and the sense of hurry could be stimulating but tiring. In middle age, Cecil observed, he still had the vitality of a young man, which made him tend to take personal control of details best left to subordinates, who might find themselves left to pick up pieces[4] – a Kitchener characteristic which was to be notable in the Great War.

Another Sudan and South Africa companion now in Egypt was Jimmy Watson, for so many years his senior ADC. Watson, like Cecil, marked how Kitchener's horizon had widened; he was always developing and imbibing new ideas, always learning 'and never had to learn the same lesson twice'. If he found himself ignorant, he looked around for a man who could inform or explain.[5] He had, however, so Storrs found, a disconcerting habit of occasionally deriding 'with merciless wit' an opinion he had invited, only to bring it up as his own next day, 'or he would gravely propound fantastically improbable choices of action, solely for the purpose (and sometimes for the malicious pleasure) of observing whether – and how – they were countered'.[6]

Jimmy Watson had the unenviable post of equerry to His Highness the Khedive Abbas Hilmi II, helping to keep him out of mischief. Years earlier, when Kitchener was Sirdar, the Khedive had deliberately insulted him in an episode which backfired to the Khedive's hurt. He was honourably nationalist but devious and unreliable and too much involved in corruption: Kitchener once remarked that the undiluted truth 'would wash H. H. off his throne'.[7] The intricacies and gyrations of Egyptian politics consumed many days and hours for the British agent and his chancery, but the details fade into history. Kitchener's chief concern was to better the lot of the poor. As Cecil wrote after his death, 'He was naturally and ever on the side of the weak and the oppressed. No one was perhaps in a sense more dictatorial, but no one was more truly just or had more reverence for the rights of his poorer fellows. The oppression of the fellaheen, and the way in which the half-civilised upper classes of Egypt regard them as little better than animals, stirred Lord Kitchener to the depths of his character. I often used to wonder what the feelings of some of the pashas would have been if they could have seen his real opinion of them in his face,'[8] instead of sphinx-like courtesy.

He reverted at once to the open-door custom of oriental rulers, generally receiving in the beautiful garden which ran down to the Nile. Anyone, however poor or lowly, might seek audience or send in a petition: 'His Excellency The Lord Kichiner [sic],' reads one petition with an Arabic signature but no doubt written in the English of a professional scribe. 'Our lovable Lord, where is justice? Justice should be where you are. I beg my Lord to pass over my case. Long Live Lord Kichner [sic]!! Your Obedient servant . . .'[9]

A special correspondent wrote for the *Morning Post*:

> Everybody may go to him; he finds time for everyone; and to every visitor of his, be he English or native, he invariably says: 'My task is to better the condition of the poor and to introduce into Egypt as a whole as many improvements as are compatible with the natural conditions of the country, as given by God, and with the character of the people which cannot be altered, either in a day or in a generation.[10]

His greatest achievement for the fellahin (peasantry) was to pass the Act popularly known as the Five Feddan Law, a feddan being approximately an acre. Previously, a creditor could seize all a debtor's goods and land, leaving him destitute. As a young officer in the Egyptian army, Kitchener had been concerned at the grinding poverty of debt-ridden fellahin and had conceived a scheme whereby fellas should be entitled by law to keep a small portion of land, and all implements, however high the debts. He had put his idea to the authorities in vain. During his Indian days he had been attracted by schemes in the Punjab to meet this problem, and now he forced through, against the outcries of moneylenders, great landowners and businessmen, the Five Feddan Law: no agricultural holding of fewer than five feddan might be mortgaged or a debtor's agricultural implements removed. The fellahin were not particularly grateful at the time, grumbling that the Law interfered with the right of every Egyptian to dispose of his property as he liked, but twenty years later it had become an important feature of Egyptian agriculture. The cultivators were more content with another Kitchener reform which stopped the immemorial robbery of cotton growers by middlemen. He set up government offices of information so that a fella could know the correct market price and not be dependent on the lies of purchasers. And beside the information booths he set up savings bank branches, but these never caught on.

Irrigation, drainage, public health, education, measures to reduce infant mortality, 'All these you will notice,' wrote FitzGerald to Sir George Arthur in England in May 1912 after touring with Kitchener, 'are primarily for the benefit of the lowest – the fallahin. K has accomplished this and consequently has incalculably raised British prestige.' He had even, claimed Fitz, reconciled the Coptic Christians and the Muslims who 'now work peacefully alongside one another'. Touring was 'tiring work for the Chief but conducive to good results. Great activity in reforms every-where. Schools being built, cotton markets established etc etc and every-where where they have not got them they are shouting for drains.'[11]

Kitchener, records Storrs, 'was considered the real friend of the Fellah, and none that saw will ever forget his gazing from his railway coach in deep contentment upon the green illimitable wealth of the Delta. He actively liked meeting, talking and laughing with Egyptians, who in spite of the habitual sternness of his expression never said of him, as of some of his compatriots, that the Englishman's face is *mubawwiz* – sullen or overcast. He had a personal and life-long knowledge of places and of families,'[12] and a particular concern for women and children. He asked Bonte Elgood, wife of one of his former staff officers who now held a senior post in a ministry, to set up a school for midwives. He organized its finance and ordered provincial governors to send two women each for six months.

Bonte Elgood (*née* Amos) remembered, as a little child, the then Major Kitchener coming to Shepheards Hotel to see his fiancée, Hermione Baker, as she lay dying, but Bonte never mentioned the memory on the Elgoods' frequent visits to the Agency. Her training school proved such a success that when, five years later, some forty Egyptian notables raised a sum of money in Kitchener's memory, they asked that it be used to help women, leading to the opening of the Kitchener Memorial Hospital for Women.[13]

Kitchener's tours brought him great pleasure, and he seemed a different man on tour from the stern taskmaster giving brusque instructions in his office. Colonel André von Dumreicher, a German who held a senior post in the Ministry of the Interior (his family had been in Egypt for many generations) and was married to the niece of General Archie Hunter, Kitchener's second in command in the River War, had many extra responsibilities in suppressing the smuggling of arms during the war between Turkey and Italy, but he often accompanied Kitchener on his tours in the desert away from the Delta and the Nile. He had a delightful memory of Kitchener's easy rapport with the Beduin. Although Kitchener's Arabic was good if colloquial, one chief asked in English: '"Lordi Kitchner, why you not married?"

'"Be quiet, Mulazim Mohammed Ahmed!"

'"It would be nice to have little Kitchners running around."

'"Will you be *silent*, Mulazim Mohammed Ahmed," says the Chief, pretending to be angry.'[14]

The residence at the British agency in Cairo was soon receiving the treatment Kitchener had given to Snowdon in Simla and Treasury Gate in Calcutta. The doorkeepers (cavases) were put into splendid Turkish-style liveries. He disguised the ugliness of the drawing room by making it a showcase for his ever-expanding collection of porcelain, Byzantine icons and miscellaneous treasures. He turned the unfurnished ballroom into a state reception room, with Chippendale mirrors and brocade hangings. He extracted from the Office of Works in London the money to build a new ballroom. He bought statues and stone capitals for the garden and drive, intending them later for Broome, and when invited to inspect the renovated Ghezireh Palace Hotel he only consented to be photographed with the manager if he were given the two marble lions that were relics of its days as a Khedival palace. Nothing was safe from his eye: British colleagues learned to hide treasures before he came, lest they disappear into his pocket and a cheque arrive next day. His great relaxation was to visit the bazaars and antique shops, where he was well known from his years as Sirdar. Storrs found it 'pleasant to see and to share his happiness. The years fell from his shoulders, his expression concentrated with the intentness of an eager and prehensile child. On his return to the Agency, he almost ran up the steps to undo his parcel, and to ring for one or more of the staff to approve the purchases.'[15]

As in viceregal lodges or government houses of the British Empire, the agency entertained a constant flow of visitors, especially as Cairo was a favourite winter resort of Europeans. In addition to relations and old friends and their young people — Salisburys, Portlands, Desboroughs — came guests received as proconsul duty, as Storrs would mention in letters to his parents: 'Prince George of Saxony, his fiercely mustachioed sister, his Bourbon wife and her not unattractive sister, Maria Immalata, with their unsurpassably tedious suite, at dinner.'[16] When the Mediterranean Fleet put into Alexandria with Prince Albert, the future George VI, then a midshipman, 'K's first ball in the new ballroom went off well enough. Little Prince A, an odd mixture of extreme timidity and considerable freedom of speech, was much liked.'[17]

Prince Albert's parents came through the Suez Canal on their way to the coronation tour in India. When the Khedive and Kitchener attended on them in state at Port Said, in their liner the *Medina*, King George made a gesture that was widely applauded throughout the Middle East. A very ancient ex-Grand Vizier of the Ottoman Empire, Kiamil Pasha, had been expelled by the so-called Young Turks after their revolution and arrived in Cairo. The Khedive ignored him, but Kitchener, who had known him when both were consuls in Anatolia,[18] at once called on him at his hotel and brought him along to meet the King, for he had been always a warm friend to England. When a group photograph was arranged on deck, with chairs for the King and Queen, the rest to stand, the King refused to sit but placed the venerable ex-Grand Vizier in his chair and stood between the Khedive and Kitchener, who towered over them all.

Kitchener was much amused when entering the royal sitting room after an important ceremony and 'heard the Q say to the K "George, you *are* a fool." She had put a signed photograph into his hand for a departing monarch and he had carelessly omitted to give it.'[19] As Sybil Graham, the

Queen's former maid of honour who had married Ronnie Graham, a senior official, commented to Queen Mary when describing the success of the ball for the navy: 'Lord Kitchener inspires great awe in everybody here, and few people get to know him well enough to realize how human he is.'[20] This was echoed by another of Queen Mary's friends visiting Egypt, who told her that Kitchener 'is a wonderful success out here. Everybody likes him, and besides he is respected and feared, a combination very necessary to the land of Egypt.'[21]

When the King and Queen were returning from India, Kitchener and Wingate, governor-general of the Sudan and Sirdar of the Egyptian army, arranged a great Durbar and review at Port Sudan, the new port on the Red Sea, built mainly for the export of cotton. All the tribes sent their principal sheikhs and the King presented a coronation medal to each. Kitchener then went by a newly built railway to inspect the cotton-growing areas where once had been little but scrub. The British agent-general, by constitution of the Anglo-Egyptian Sudan, was the governor-general's superior, as Cromer had been to Kitchener, who was now delighted with the progress. His system of government had proved successful in establishing peace and prosperity. Wingate kept him closely informed. He took a special interest in Gordon College. When the rich American banker Pierpont Morgan passed through Cairo with a party of ten, Kitchener told Rex Wingate to touch him for a substantial donation. When the pharmaceutical magnate Wellcome withdrew his support from the Medical Research Laboratory, Kitchener hunted for a substitute: his ambition was to see a medical school as part of an enlarged Gordon College. And he took great trouble to find a worthy successor to Sir James Currie, Gordon's first warden.[22]

He had a secret hope that one day the borders of the Sudan would be pushed into the mountains of turbulent Abyssinia (Ethiopia) to secure a protectorate over Lake Tana, from which the Blue Nile flows, essential (with the White Nile) for irrigation in the Sudan and Egypt. More practically, he foresaw the collapse of the Ottoman Empire, though not its manner, and welcomed Sharif Feisal, the eldest son of Sharif Hussein, the vassal ruler of Mecca and the Hejaz, hoping secretly to encourage their desire to throw off the yoke of Constantinople, the first moves in what became the Arab Revolt. Meanwhile he must remain officially strictly neutral.

In 1912 his sister Millie and her husband Harry Parker came to Egypt on their way from New Zealand to England. Their son, Alfred Chevallier Parker, was Governor of Sinai and later chief of police. They stayed with Herbert, then went up the Nile. Harry fell ill and died. Herbert did what he could for Millie but he had never been close to Harry. A much deeper grief came with an unexpected telegram from Bermuda: his brother Walter had died of appendicitis after a mismanaged operation. Lieutenant-General Sir Walter Kitchener had been appointed Governor of Bermuda two years earlier. Walter, Kitchener's much younger brother, was his companion in arms during the Omdurman campaign, South Africa and in India, and whereas he had drifted somewhat from Chevallier, the brother next to him in age, and Arthur had already died, the only civilian of the three, Walter's sudden death hurt deeply. Fitz and Storrs realized how deep was the grief, but the usual impassive sphinx-like face was shown to the public. Walter's wife had died during the Anglo-Boer War. His unmarried daughter, Madge, had been doing the work normally done by a governor's wife. Walter's only son, Hal, had entered Sandhurst, but the Chevallier hered- itary deafness, which had afflicted Walter but passed over Herbert, caused him to leave without a commission and he entered McGill University in Canada to study mining engineering. When Walter died, Uncle Herbert paid Hal's fees. In 1914 Hal joined up and was in the first wave of Canadian troops to come to England, and entered the Royal Flying Corps.[23]

Another death in 1912 throws light on Kitchener's character. The Duke of Fife, husband of King George's sister, the Princess Royal, died suddenly at Assuan on the Nile. When the coffin was in a chapel at All Saints' Church in Cairo while arrangements were made for its journey to Scotland, Kitchener sent fresh flowers from his garden each day. He knew also that a mutual friend, Sir Frederick Milner, was on his way by sea to join the Fifes. Kitchener told the consul at Port Said to meet Milner's ship and hand him a letter breaking the news 'and I shall never forget,' wrote Milner four years later, 'his thoughtful kindness when I reached his house.' Milner had done much for army welfare, was a Member of Parliament until the sudden onset of severe deafness compelled retirement in those days before electronic hearing-aids. 'Of all my many men friends,' he wrote of Kitchener, 'I know of none from whom I received more sympathy and kindness, especially in regard to the infirmity which has done so much to wreck my life. He was always doing little things to show his sympathy with me.'[24]

Milner naturally came to know the chaplain of All Saints' Church, the Reverend J. H. Molesworth, who told him 'he could never sufficiently appreciate the help and kindness he received from Lord Kitchener'. After Kitchener's death, Molesworth wrote a memorial pamphlet, *A Soldier of God*, telling how the coming of Kitchener brought a moral change in the English community; how he insisted that although the Muslim Friday was the official day of rest, no Christian should be prevented from attending Sunday worship; how he revived the custom of being preceded by runners in livery as he drove to church himself, to emphasize its importance. 'We never doubted that beneath that stern exterior beat a true and warm heart. His relations with the poor peasantry of Egypt were touchingly beautiful, and the feeling of regard was reciprocal. They had free access to him and they knew that their grievances and difficulties would fall on sympathetic ears. "I am here to administer Egypt for the Egyptians, not for the English,"' he would say to Molyneaux, who specially noted his rescue of a substantial charitable fund for the poor which the Khedive and his cronies had diverted to their own use.

Kitchener would never speak openly about his own faith, unlike his hero Gordon but like his early patron Salisbury; both Molesworth and Bishop Llewellyn Gwynne of Khartoum, who had known him since 1898, were certain that he was 'an earnest believer' with a reverence for all things sacred.[25] Lord Edward Cecil, however, wrote with much amusement to his wife in England: 'K is very comic. He presided over the church committee yesterday. It was done in his best robber baron style. I nearly died of suppressed laughter at the faces of the committee when he explained how he proposed to raise money. It ran along the edge of the criminal law the whole time.'[26] Cecil's sardonic humour invaded his letters, but he and Molyneaux recognized that Kitchener's life was rooted in the will of God. Long service in the deserts and among Orthodox and Coptic Christians had transmuted the Anglican sacramental zeal of his early manhood; and he respected Islam without compromising his loyalty to Christ. In George Arthur's enigmatic words, 'Christianity was to him not an attitude but an atmosphere.'

During the hot summer, the senior British officials invariably took some home leave, and the politics and economics of Egypt seemed to flow quietly while they were all away. Kitchener would look forward to Broome, 'where his heart is turning ever',[27] and in Cairo would open at once any letter from his agent Western or his cousin Flo Marc who was looking out for antique furniture, pictures and stained glass, and their correspondence was his delight. As soon as he was back in England and official business disposed of in London, he would hurry down to Broome, always filled with workmen raising the hall roof, pulling down partitions, laying floors. 'My accommodation is very rough,' he warned Rex Wingate when inviting him for a night so that they could discuss the Sudan.[28] He was also playing around with the landscape in the manner of Capability Brown.

When he made visits to country houses such as the Portlands' Welbeck he would notice interesting chairs or cabinets or pictures and then commission copies, so that Broome was beginning to be a potpourri. It was also 'eating money', which may explain why the scale of his necessary entertaining in Cairo, according to Cecil, began to be somewhat mean.

At the start of his leave in 1913 he opened the 'Old English Fete' in the beautiful grounds of the rectory at Barham, Broome's village, to raise money to repair the church organ. He was received by the thirty-strong troop of Boy Scouts under his own agent, Walter Western, as scoutmaster, and two Scout buglers from Canterbury. The rector, the Reverend F. R. Mercer, made a pompous speech of welcome, and Viscount Kitchener expressed his pleasure at meeting his neighbours 'and thanking them for the very kind manner in which they had received him (applause)'. He had made it a rule never to accept invitations to open bazaars, 'but that rule could not apply to his home. Three cheers were given at the close of the speech.'[29]

As his leave of 1914 approached, he could look back on two and a half years of highly successful proconsulship, almost universally popular, even when he suppressed a newspaper for sedition: the one attempt on his life by a well-known nationalist agitator had failed, thanks to the quick action of FitzGerald. Kitchener had ruled almost as a modern pharaoh: when he rescued a long-hidden ancient Egpytian statue of Ramses II and raised it to a prominent position in one of his street-widening schemes, *Punch* joked: 'There is no petty jealousy about K of K.'[30]

The responsibility, however, as *de facto* ruler of millions, sometimes weighed on him so heavily that occasionally, when alone with Storrs or Fitz, he felt almost crushed. In May 1914, shortly before his leave, during a Cabinet crisis in Cairo, he suffered almost a nervous breakdown, as Cecil wrote to his wife ('of course don't breathe a word about it') on 6 May: 'Lord K was, as you know, very overworked and worried during the winter [although Fitz had thought him in excellent health and spirits][31] and he became as the spring drew on more and more irritable and difficult to deal with.' The Khedive was being impossible and wanted to dismiss the Prime Minister, Mohammed Said, who after trying to please both the Khedive and Kitchener had come over to the British side, 'which made the Khedive loathe him more than ever'. Kitchener was about to have an audience with His Highness, and Cecil found him 'very nervous and depressed as he always is before he sees H. H. for some unknown reason', all the more odd because the Khedive, when receiving Kitchener, generally looked as if he expected him to produce a death warrant signed by Sir Edward Grey. This time Kitchener told Cecil he did not know what he could say if the Khedive wanted to dismiss Mohammed Said. 'I was very much astonished but of course replied that after all the Khedive had to do as he was told.' When Kitchener returned from the palace and sent for Cecil, 'I found him in what I can only call a state of collapse. He told me the Khedive *insisted on a change and though K had argued with him for two hours he could not convince him:* and he did not know what to do.' The Khedive wished to refer to the British govern‐ment through Kitchener and 'K had already drafted a telegram to London which was a complete surrender saying that perhaps the Khedive was right and proposing the change. We had a most awful row and I told him this was ruin and destruction, that it would be a fearful blow at British prestige, that ministers would no longer trust us . . . He was furious, or rather helpless and cross.' They fought it out for an hour, and Kitchener agreed to modify his telegram.

As the crisis developed, Cecil told his wife that K was:

> . . . hopelessly weak and for some reason funks the Khedive. I suppose it is health and he has had what is called a nervous breakdown but it puzzles me and worries me . . . I don't feel as if there was solid ground under my feet. I should just as much have expected the Nile to run south as for him to behave like this.
>
> Of course he hates me now rather but that cannot be helped and my only comfort is that in August if all goes well I propose to go over to

Broome and tell him the truth in love. It is no good doing it now as he cannot hear it.[32]

The storm blew over and Kitchener recovered his nerve. When he arrived in London on leave, the King received him in audience and recorded in his diary: 'I had a long talk with him about Egypt & the Khedive who is behaving abominably & intriguing against us.'

The King added: 'I have just made K of K an earl.'[33] Fitz had written in May to Arthur to ask if the government was going to recommend the Chief for a Birthday Honour. 'It would please him enormously and repay him for some of the hard time he has put in here.'[34] Before he left Cairo on 18 June he learned that he was to be created an earl.

On the ship crossing the Mediterranean he announced that he would take the title Earl of Broome. Fitz and Storrs replied that this was impossible. Not only was there already a Lord Brougham, pronounced 'Broom', but the nation would never let the name Kitchener disappear.

He was gazetted as Earl Kitchener of Khartoum and of Broome – still K of K, with his greatest days to come.

PART THREE

The Guns of August

1914–1915

14

INTO THE BREACH

On 27 July 1914 Kitchener wrote from Pandeli Ralli's house in Belgrave Square to Birdwood in India. Birdie was now Adjutant-General and thus second in command to Sir Beauchamp Duff, now Commander-in-Chief. 'We are having quite exciting times here,' Kitchener wrote. 'Every chance of war all round on the continent and civil war in Ireland.' He had been rather on the rush and had found little time for Broome, which he had first seen with Birdie and liked more and more. His great ambition was still to be Viceroy of India and he was to stay with the Secretary of State, Lord Crewe, the next week, but a general election was due in 1915 before the viceroyalty would become vacant: Kitchener thought the Liberals would probably be defeated 'and as regards the others George Nathaniel will do his utmost and will I have little doubt great weight and probably succeed in preventing my being offered the place. It is all in the lap of the Gods.'[1] He pressed his case when lunching with the King at Buckingham Palace.

Later that same day, scribbling a note to cousin Flo about a Chinese fire screen for Broome ('no sage green lacquer for me') he added that things 'look very like a European war. I hope we may get through somehow as otherwise I may have to go back to Cairo in a hurry.'[2] Next day Austria declared war on Serbia. As Germany moved closer to war with France and Russia, Kitchener had discussions with Winston Churchill, First Lord of the Admiralty, on the defence of the Suez Canal and Egypt. Churchill had kept the fleet concentrated after a recent royal review, and thus ready for possible hostilities, but at luncheon at Admiralty House

Kitchener agreed with him that if Germany demanded passage through southern Belgium the Belgians would probably protest but not resist.[3] Asquith's Cabinet was divided as to whether England need be drawn in. Kitchener believed that if they did not stand with France they would lose all influence in Europe; also that Germany would use high explosive, opening a new and more devastating form of warfare.

The luncheon left Kitchener worried that in the event of war the Prime Minister might hold him back from Egypt to give general advice, for Asquith had kept the War Office in his own hands since March and now had asked Lord Chancellor Haldane to act as his deputy; Haldane, when War Minister, had created the Territorial Army and done much to prepare for the limited war which was all that the French and British staffs expected.

Kitchener had no wish to hang around and had always resisted moves to draft him to the War Office: he would rather be a crossing-sweeper, he used to say. He was therefore relieved when the Foreign Office instructed all who were on leave to return to their posts. But when his old Sudan comrades, Maxwell and Rawlinson, now generals, called on him to say goodbye they urged that England needed him: by providence or good fortune he was not abroad and must not go. And the newspapers were taking up, ever more loudly, the cry that Kitchener was the only war leader the nation could trust.

On the morning of Saturday 1 August, Kitchener drafted a proclamation to be issued in Egypt if war broke out before he could reach Cairo. Leaving Ossy FitzGerald to keep contact with Downing Street he then motored down to Broome 'for a last look round'.[4]

By the time he arrived, since Ralli's chauffeur kept to the 20 m.p.h. speed limit, the craftsmen in the house and the gardeners had knocked off their Saturday work. He wandered around and then, since his agent Western's house, where he always stayed, had no telephone, he went by car to the village. Barham post office was one of the many which displayed a blue plaque: 'You may telephone from here.' He placed a trunk call to London. When it came on the line he heard that no message had come from Downing Street, for the Cabinet were still debating whether to support France or stay neutral.

On Bank Holiday Monday morning, 3 August, when many Britons ignored the crisis to show that they still loved to be beside the seaside,

Kitchener drove the short distance to Dover and boarded the cross-Channel steamer. Ronald Storrs, summoned by wire from his father's deanery at Rochester, arrived to find Kitchener 'striding alone up and down the deck. "Tell the captain to start" he kept saying. I reminded him of the boat-train, but he fretted, dreading to be held back at the last moment in an advisory capacity, with functions unspecified. After fifteen difficult minutes the boat-train came in, bearing FitzGerald with a message from the Prime Minister instructing Kitchener to remain.'[5] Asquith had also tried to reach him through the village post office. Lord Edward Cecil had come on the boat-train too, but he, Storrs and FitzGerald had difficulty in persuading their Chief to leave the ferry and return to Belgrave Square, where he found a note from Asquith: 'I am very sorry to interrupt your journey today . . . But with matters in their present critical position I was anxious that you should not get beyond the reach of personal consultation and assistance.'[6]

The next twenty-four hours were miserable for Kitchener. While German troops invaded Belgium, and patriotic crowds converged on Buckingham Palace to cheer the King, Kitchener could get no word beyond a verbal request to stay because if war were declared the Prime Minister would want to see him alone before a council of war convened the next day. Kitchener was bewildered and angry, feeling that the Cabinet were making a fool of him, that he must be allowed to go or be given a proper appointment. A leading editor told him that if he were allowed to go, and Haldane with his (wrongly) supposed German sympathies became War Minister again, the entire press would erupt against the government. Then Johnny Hamilton (Sir Ian) called straight from seeing Haldane, who now favoured Kitchener's appointment.

At 6.30 on the evening of 4 August, with less than five hours before the British ultimatum would expire, Lord Milner came to Belgrave Square, certain that Kitchener was the best possible choice for the War Office. He found him with Wingate and Pandeli Ralli, and Lord Lovat coming in a few minutes later. He urged that Kitchener demand to see Asquith that evening and force his hand.

Asquith received him between 7 and 8 p.m. Neither left notes of their discussion but Kitchener made plain that he wished to return to Egypt: if he must stay, he must be placed in full authority as Secretary of State for War. Nothing was settled that night, for the Foreign Secretary was saying that he could not spare Kitchener from Cairo. Churchill, Crewe and now Haldane were urging Asquith to bring him in, yet several other ministers were nervous at the prospect of a serving soldier in the Cabinet.

Next morning, 5 August, with Britain now at war, Kitchener went back to Downing Street. Asquith formally offered him the post. He accepted, reluctantly and as his duty, on the understanding that he entered the Cabinet as a non-party, non-political soldier for the duration of the war. His Cairo post would be kept open. His ministerial salary would be paid in addition to his Field Marshal's pay and he would receive an allowance for expenses.

Back in Belgrave Square, FitzGerald, Wingate, Storrs, Cecil and their host Pandeli Ralli had waited in the front room. The telephone rang, and they rejoiced. When the news broke, a wave of rejoicing and trust swept the nation. Here was their national hero, untouched by scandal or failure, renowned for his indomitable will. His long years abroad had kept him aloof from the bitter political disputes of the recent past. His physique enhanced the rock-like impression of his character and the element of mystery increased his hold on the people. As F. S. Oliver was to write a year later in his celebrated book, *Ordeal by Battle*:

> No appointment could have produced a better effect upon the hearts of the British people and upon those of their Allies. The nation felt – if we may use so homely an image in this connection – that Lord Kitchener was holding its hand confidently and reassuringly in one of his, while with the other he had the whole race of politicians firmly by the scruff, and would see to it that there was no nonsense or trouble in that quarter.[7]

Kitchener remarked to Percy Girouard over breakfast at Belgrave Square the very next morning: 'May God preserve me from the politicians.'[8]

That afternoon Kitchener attended the ad hoc council of war in Downing Street. He had not yet received the seals of office but was treated as already Secretary of State for War. The Prime Minister took the chair. Round the Cabinet table sat Sir Edward Grey (Foreign Secretary), Winston Churchill (First Lord of the Admiralty) and Haldane, with the aged Lord Roberts, together with Field Marshal Sir John French, who had been appointed Commander-in-Chief of the British Expeditionary Force (BEF), and several senior generals.

For a nation entering what would become its greatest war to date, the proceedings were haphazard. Sir John French claimed years later that he had earlier urged Kitchener to become C-in-C with himself as chief of staff, while General Sir Douglas Haig believed that French was unsuitable for the supreme command, as he told the King a few days later. Haig's disquiet increased when French suggested that the BEF should be sent to Antwerp in Belgium rather than to France, but after debate the council rejected this and thus saved their troops from probable disaster. Anglo-French staff talks before the war had settled that the British should concen-trate at Mauberge, close to the Belgian frontier. At the council Kitchener objected. They could be outflanked by a German sweep through northern Belgium. He urged concentration at Amiens, seventy miles further back. His argument was tentatively accepted, pending allied agreement.

Kitchener then astonished the others, except Haig, by saying that the war would last three years. They were convinced it would be over by Christmas. The politicians believed that no European nation could afford a long war: faced with financial ruin, they would come to terms. The generals other than Haig were sure that the large French army, mainly of conscripts, and the small BEF, all volunteers but highly professional, would swiftly stop the Germans and win the war.

Kitchener's certainty that the war would be long was no sudden hunch but settled conviction. In South Africa he had frequently told his staff, when lecturing them about politics, that an Anglo-German conflict was inevitable and would be long; and in India a future German general on his travels in 1908 to 1909, who took up a private introduction, was deeply impressed by the clearness of Kitchener's outlook 'regarding the future of Europe':

He spoke with the greatest firmness of conviction in telling me that in his opinion war between England and Germany had become inevitable – not because of any vital antagonism between the two nations, but because of the weakness and indecision of leading statesmen on both sides – that an Anglo-German war, whoever else participated, would last at least three years, and finally that there would be no victory at all, both countries being bound to lose most of their influence in world affairs, especially in the Pacific area, the only possible winners being the U.S.A. and Japan.[9]

At the council of war Kitchener did not expound his conviction but further astonished them by announcing that to defeat Germany he must raise a vast new army, turning Britain from a predominantly maritime power into a military nation. To win the war he needed a million men, including 100,000 at once. Each division of the BEF must leave behind enough officers and NCOs to train the recruits.

Haig agreed, reading out a memorandum he had brought up from Aldershot. But Major-General Henry Wilson was contemptuous, although too junior to voice his contempt. Wilson, the opinionated Irishman and anti-Home Ruler, outwardly genial but inwardly cantan-kerous, had done the detailed planning for the mobilization, sea transport and concentration of the BEF. He was a fluent French speaker, like Kitchener, and the friend of Joffre, the French C-in-C, and had no doubts of a swift French victory if the entire strength of the BEF was at Joffre's disposal. He was appalled by Kitchener's plan to hold back officers and men.

Kitchener returned to Belgrave Square. Next morning, 6 August, Ronald Storrs arrived early, as instructed. Kitchener appointed him Personal Private Secretary, handed him two baskets of letters and ordered him to settle details of two proffered loans, of a residence and of a Rolls-Royce. Storrs mildly asked if the Chief had arranged with the Foreign Office to release their Oriental Secretary from Egypt and transfer him to the War Office. The Chief told him to do it himself.

At 10 a.m., in morning dress, Kitchener entered the recently built new War Office in Whitehall, climbed the wide staircase which, years later, would be dominated by a bronze bust of himself, and entered the Secretary of State's enormous room to meet the heads of departments, civil and military, including the Principal Private Secretary, Herbert Creedy. To all of them Kitchener repeated: 'We have no army!'

From that moment the War Office changed tempo. Traditionally so slow and sleepy that Kitchener used to joke that if he set up a rival estab-lishment in another part of London the War Office would not notice for weeks, it now moved, as it were, at the double. Even dignified messengers, mostly retired sergeants, were seen to run when the Secretary of State wanted someone in a hurry. The Chief of the Imperial General Staff, Sir Charles Douglas, was efficient but no genius (and soon to die); all the best senior officers had been allocated to the BEF. Kitchener had already had a long discussion with Haig, and they were of like mind except on one question, but he could not hold him back from taking into battle the troops he had trained. Johnny Hamilton could have resumed his Boer War task at Kitchener's right hand. Instead, fearing a German invasion, or rather a disruptive raid, Kitchener appointed him that morning to organize a 'Central Force' to resist it; he would be close at hand to consult.

Kitchener swiftly drew all the reins into his own hands, becoming in effect his own chief of staff, treating the generals around him as executives rather than advisers and not always ensuring coordination. At the age of sixty-four years and two months, his physical and mental powers were not diminished, whatever some might claim afterwards, and the comparatively easy years in Egypt enabled him to summon up fresh reserves of energy. He was uninhibited by his lack of close knowledge of British industries and politics, caused by long years of duty abroad. He would meet the country's urgent need unbothered by doubts as he set about raising the first hundred thousand.

Shortly before the outbreak of war, the director of recruiting, foreseeing the need to replace casualties in the BEF, had commissioned Caxton Publications, who produced a somewhat turgid call to all unmarried young men to enlist. Headed *Your King and Country Need You*, and ending *Join the Army To-day*, it had appeared in a prominent place in the news pages of all daily papers (except one that opposed the war) on the previous day. Kitchener strengthened the layout and wording and with a sure instinct made it personal: 'An addition of 100,000 men to His Majesty's Regular Army is immediately necessary in the present grave National Emergency. LORD KITCHENER is confident that this appeal will be at once responded to by all those who have the safety of the Empire at heart . . . ' Since constitutional practice forbade the use of the King's name and Kitchener had used his own, he insisted that the appeal should end with, *God Save the King*.[10]

The poster that would become so famous would not emerge for another month, but men were already hurrying to enlist. Their numbers included many unemployed or crossed in love or in financial trouble, or drawn by a spirit of adventure or by the supposed romance of war, ignorant of the horror to come; yet the majority were genuinely spurred by the country's need.

At 1.15 King George v held a meeting of his Privy Council at Buckingham Palace. Asquith gave up the seals of the War Office. Kitchener was sworn in as a Privy Councillor and received the seals of office from the King, as the King recorded in his diary in the first of forty-seven wartime entries when 'Kitchener came to see me' or they met at inspections or functions.[11] The council of war met again late in the afternoon and covered much the same ground.

Kitchener returned to Belgrave Square. At about 8 p.m. Ronald Storrs arrived and was sent upstairs where he found his Chief stripped to the waist at his china basin, washing away while four men sat on cane chairs behind him: three French generals and Walter Long, Wiltshire landowner and former (and future) Cabinet minister who had nearly become Tory leader. A white tie, boiled shirt, and evening tail coat were laid out on the bed, and Kitchener's faithful man Henry Segar hovered in the background as his master interrogated the generals and Walter Long about manpower. Long, who had cancelled a dinner engagement on the sudden summons to Belgrave Square, never forgot the vivid impression made on him that evening by 'that splendid specimen of the British race', who had just received the seals of office at such a time of crisis yet was as 'cool and collected as if nothing at all had happened. His questions were clear and concise and his decision unhesitating on the numbers of men he would require.'[12]

When Storrs appeared, the Chief took him into the passage. Storrs reported that the residence and the Rolls-Royce were fixed, but then 'with a heavy heart' told him that the permanent head of the Foreign Office had briskly ordered him to return to Egypt at once. Kitchener had already heard this disappointing news. They said goodbye and as Storrs went down the stairs Kitchener leaned over the banisters and called out, 'Good luck.' Storrs never saw him again.[13]

Kitchener returned to his bedroom and continued the discussion. Long felt a strong confidence in him that he was the right man at the right place.

When Kitchener had dressed and Henry Segar had adjusted the tail coat, they all went downstairs. The War Office clerk in attendance asked, 'Have you got your Cabinet keys, sir?' Kitchener looked blank. 'Cabinet keys?

No, of course I haven't got any keys.' There was a strained silence, for Walter Long knew from his days in office that a minister's keys to his red boxes were a sacred trust. Then Ossy FitzGerald said quietly, 'It's all right. I took the keys. I have them.' Then they found they had not enough change for a taxi; the banks had been ordered to stay shut after the Bank Holiday to prevent a run on gold sovereigns, so change was hard to come by. Eventually they borrowed from Walter Long and the French generals and entered the taxi that Segar had called up from the nearby cab rank.[14]

The dinner was a meeting of the Other Club, a dining club founded by Winston Churchill and F. E. Smith, political opponents and great friends. Distinguished men were members regardless of party. The club had not dined together since the Marconi scandal which had nearly destroyed Lloyd George and Rufus Isaacs, then Attorney-General and now Lord Chief Justice, who had dishonourably used their official positions to make a profit. The large attendance included three future Prime Ministers. Kitchener, a founding-member, was invited to take the chair with Churchill opposite. During the evening F. E. Smith, the leading advocate of the day, agreed to leave his practice and head the press bureau at the War Office. During a long conversation with Smith and another diner, Sir George Riddell, the lawyer who was chairman of the *News of the World*, which he had lifted from its rather unsavoury past to be an influential Sunday paper with a large circulation, Kitchener asked Riddell to advise on censorship and to secure the cooperation of the press.

Next morning the three met in Kitchener's room at the War Office, joined by Colonel Jack Seely, who had been War Minister until he had resigned in March over the Curragh incident, when senior officers had threatened to refuse orders to march against Ulster Protestants, and Sir Reginald Brade, the Permanent Under-Secretary of State. Riddell recorded in his diary that in the course of their discussion Kitchener said: 'We must make the English people understand that we are at war, and that war is not pap. At the present moment they do not understand the situation. They ought to act as if we were at war, and give up playing and watching games. War is the game at the moment, and as I have said, war is not pap,'[15] – a sentiment in tune with Kipling's famous line about 'flannelled fools at the wicket or muddied oafs at the goals'.

Next, Colonel T. E. Hickman, MP, was brought in. Hickman had been second in command to the thirty-eight-year-old Kitchener Pasha at the disastrous Battle of Hardub in eastern Sudan twenty-eight years before and had taken over when Kitchener was wounded. He was now president of the British League for the Defence of Ulster. Kitchener said: 'I want the Ulster Volunteers.' Hickman suggested he meet the Ulster Unionist leader, Sir Edward Carson, and his lieutenant, James Craig, both members of Parliament, and left at once to set up their meeting. Carson and Craig had raised and illegally armed 16,000 Protestants, ready to oppose Home Rule by force and fight the smaller body of Irish Volunteers (Roman Catholics) raised in the south by John Redmond. Redmond had already announced in the House of Commons that his men were at the disposal of the Empire, and Kitchener had spoken to him: 'Get me 5,000 men and I will thank you. Get me 10,000 and I will take off my hat to you.'[16]

Kitchener had watched from the sidelines as Ireland had moved to the brink of civil war. Irish-born, with an Irish boyhood but no Irish blood, he had watched with some exasperation. Confronted now by the Ulster leaders, his love of reconciliation and his latent sense of mischief made him say to Carson, 'If I had been on a platform with you and Redmond I should have knocked your heads together!' But when he saw that Carson took this seriously he turned at once to business. They willingly agreed to bring in Ulster Volunteers en masse, if they had not already enlisted or returned to the Colours if reservists. Kitchener promised that they should keep the names of their battalions and wear the Red Hand of Ulster in their caps. Craig went at once to the clothing firm which had supplied khaki to the Ulster Volunteers and ordered another 10,000 outfits.[17] In due time the 36th Ulster Division covered itself in glory.

Fitz now brought in a man whom Kitchener specially wanted to see: Sir George Arthur, the dapper little baronet whom he had first met, then a subaltern in the Life Guards, on the Gordon Relief expedition when they had ridden together across the desert.[18] Although ten years younger, Arthur had become a friend, not as close as Renshaw, Ralli or Lord Derby, and on returning to the army during the South African war he had served for a time on Kitchener's staff. He was a great favourite in society; it was typical that when Fitz had telephoned to the little house in Old Windsor that Arthur and his wife had taken for the summer of 1914, to give him early news of Kitchener's appointment, he had to trace him to the apartment in Windsor Castle where the Arthurs were dining with Queen Victoria's granddaughter, Princess Alice, and her husband, Queen Mary's brother, afterwards the Athlones.

Arthur loved balls and plays and was a devout High Churchman who saw Christianity much as Kitchener but was more zealous in churchgoing. He had written a history of the Household Cavalry and was well used to handling papers – and handling people: he had tact and courtesy as well as knowing everyone who mattered. Therefore when Kitchener could not have Storrs his mind went at once to George Arthur, who early next morning received a 'rather laconic message', telephoned by Segar after his master had left:

> that Lord Kitchener would like me to 'look in' at the War Office. In the corridor outside his room one found a long line of people waiting, some fondly hoping, some rather excitedly trying, to get a word with the man whose name was on every lip; he saw me at once and suggested one might be able to 'give a hand to Fitz'. Three days later, without any circumlocution, came word I had been 'put down for' Personal Private Secretary, Fitz – who, of course, remained as Personal Military Secretary – adding that I should be expected to live in the house in Carlton Gardens which Lady Wantage had placed at Lord K's disposal.[19]

The Arthurs had a large house in The Boltons in South Kensington, but his devoted wife, whom he had married sixteen years before (as a widow; they had no children), gladly made the sacrifice that so many wives were making in August 1914.

Arthur, as a civilian, was subordinate to Herbert Creedy, the civil servant who had been Principal Private Secretary since 1911. Creedy's first request to Arthur was to find a pen with which Kitchener could sign his name for reproduction on all official printed papers. Arthur brought one to Kitchener. The pen refused to write. Arthur produced another, with the same result.

'Dear me,' murmured Kitchener. 'What a War Office. Not a scrap of army and no pen that will write!'[20]

15

THE CONTEMPTIBLES

NUMBER 2 Carlton Gardens was one of the finest smaller mansions in London, built by Nash in 1828 on the terrace above St James's Park when he pulled down Carlton House on the orders of George IV. Number 2 stood semi-detached, with Marlborough House to the west; a lawn, the little that remained of the gardens, lay to the east. The principal rooms were light and airy and had splendid views across the Mall and the park to the Victoria Tower of the Houses of Parliament. Public steps led down to the park, to where the statue of George VI would be placed half a century later.

The house had been leased from the Crown by Samuel Loyd, Lord Overstone, founder of the London and Westminster Bank and said to be the richest man in England. His daughter Harriet had inherited it. Her late husband, Colonel Robert Loyd-Lindsay VC, created Lord Wantage, had been a great supporter of the Volunteer Movement, founder of the British Red Cross and also a prominent Freemason. Lady Wantage, aged seventy-seven, offered to lend the house, with domestic staff, to Kitchener for six months while he looked for a London home. Segar brought over his things and he took up residence, finding a fine drawing room with a bow window, a study and a large bedroom and rooms for Fitz and George Arthur. An additional delight, since no one imagined air raids, was Lord Overstone's collection, including porcelain, to be admired, examined, and perhaps coveted. When Kitchener wrote to thank Lady Wantage and say that everything was comfortable, she replied: 'Your task is indeed a heavy one, but the heart of the nation is with you.' Later he paid her a formal call at the house of her husband's great-nephew, the Earl of Crawford and Balcarres, in Cavendish Square, where she was staying with his mother; Crawford, although in his forties, had enlisted as a private with the RAMC. George Arthur was much intrigued by Kitchener's flattery in apparently letting Lady Wantage into secrets while giving nothing away.[1]

When Kitchener attended his first meeting of the Cabinet Asquith had sat him on his immediate right, thus according him precedence. The empty fireplace and the portrait of Walpole were behind him, the Corinthian pillars away to his right, and the windows to his front, looking over the garden wall to Horse Guards Parade and the Admiralty. With twenty-two men seated at the rectangular table, not yet boat-shaped, the comparatively small room seemed crowded. Sir Edward Grey, Lloyd George and Winston Churchill were opposite. Several faces were hardly known to him, but he trusted implicitly the wily lawyer who was Prime Minister.

Asquith had told his young confidante, Venetia Stanley, that Kitchener's appointment was hazardous but the best in the circumstances. Margot Asquith claimed in her memoirs that she was one of the very few who disagreed with it, basing her objections rather absurdly on memories and gossip of twenty years before, when as a young unmarried woman she had wintered in Cairo with her father before the River War. Colonel Kitchener was Sirdar and came several times to see her. He was not popular, a little underbred, arrogant but not vain; 'but he is either very stupid or very clever and never gives himself away'.[2]

Asquith had written to Venetia that it 'will be amusing' to see how Kitchener got on in the Cabinet. The Cabinet in August 1914 was one of the most intellectual. Yet at once they were in awe of him. In this grave crisis he was their only expert: Winston had seen fighting, including Omdurman, but he had never commanded large bodies of troops. Moreover, Kitchener possessed the heart of the nation in a way that none of his colleagues could claim. And they were almost hypnotized at first by his clear blue eyes, finding it almost impossible to look away when he spoke. The slight cast in the left eye was not obvious, nor did they know about the war wound and the burning by the desert sun which had affected the eyes. They did not realize that one eye followed another (the reason he had never played ball games) and because of the squint they were often unsure who he was addressing.[3]

At Cabinet, Asquith turned at once to Kitchener, who expressed again his conviction that the war would last at least three years. Therefore they would lose it if they did not discard the pre-war plan, which provided for an Expeditionary Force of some 150,000 men to fight in France; the Territorial Army kept for home defence; and the regimental Reserves and the Special Reserve to replace casualties at the front and keep up numbers in India and the colonies. Instead, he said, Britain must produce an army large enough to count in a European war. He had a new plan, 'rough hewn in my mind' but not yet worked out in detail: to raise and train a vast number of divisions so that at the start of the third year of the war, when their allies were faltering and the enemy reaching exhaustion, Kitchener would have large forces, fresh and fully equipped and trained, to take the field and win the war. He admitted that his idea ran contrary to European military wisdom, which held that armies could be expanded within limits during a war but not created, apart from raw recruits being rushed into battle to do or die. Kitchener felt there might be some justice in this view, but 'I had to take the risk and embark on . . . a gigantic experiment'.[4] He must raise a million men at once.

The Cabinet were sceptical. That the war would last three years 'seemed to most of us unlikely if not incredible'. Grey remarked to a colleague as they walked away that he believed the war would be over before a million men could be trained and equipped but as this belief might be wrong they should all agree to what Kitchener wanted,[5] as indeed they did. They also confirmed Amiens, far back, as the place of concentration — to Kitchener's relief.

Kitchener prepared formal instructions to the Commander-in-Chief, which Asquith thought 'quite good'.[6] Sir John was to support and assist the French army in preventing or repelling a German invasion and restoring the neutrality of Belgium. While all courage, discipline and skill should be displayed, 'greatest care must be exercised towards a minimum of losses and wastage'. In a key passage he warned Sir John not to allow the French command to expose his little army in forward movements unsupported by large formations of their own: the BEF was the ally, not the servant, of the French army, and Kitchener was determined not to let British soldiers die merely to save French lives. Before any such risk, Sir John must consult him and take government instructions. In effect,

General Joffre, the French C-in-C, was warned that he was not supreme commander on the Western Front, although obviously the BEF would conform where possible to his plans.[7]

The BEF began to cross the Channel on 9 August, to strict press silence and in safety from German warships thanks to the Royal Navy and the dispositions made by Churchill and the First Sea Lord, Prince Louis of Battenberg. The troops were read a rousing message from the King. They were all given a sheet of paper from Lord Kitchener 'to be considered by each soldier as confidential, and to be kept in his Active Service Pay Book'.

Both messages (and the instructions to Sir John) were drafted by George Arthur[8] after Kitchener had said what he wanted. He corrected them and inserted fresh thoughts in pencil. His personal message to the troops, accepted as thoroughly apt even by those who might flout it, throws light on the British character in 1914 and discloses Kitchener's high moral view of a soldier's duty:

> You are ordered abroad as a soldier of the King to help our French comrades against the invasion of a common enemy, you have to perform a task which will need your courage, your energy, your patience. Remember that the honour of the British Army depends upon your individual conduct. It will be your duty not only to set an example of discipline and perfect steadiness under fire, but also to maintain the most friendly relations with those whom you are helping in this struggle.

He reminded them that they would be serving in a friendly country, and each man could do his own country no better service than by showing himself 'in the true character of a British soldier'.

'Be invariably courteous, considerate, and kind. Never do anything likely to injure or destroy property, and always look upon looting as a disgraceful act. You are sure to meet with a welcome and to be trusted; and your conduct must justify that welcome and that trust. Your duty cannot be done unless your health is sound. So keep constantly on your guard against any excesses.'

He ended with words that might horrify the civil liberties lobby of a later age but showed the splendour of his chivalry and that of his troops:

In this new experience you may find temptations both in wine and women. You must entirely resist both temptations, and while treating all women with perfect courtesy, you should avoid any intimacy.

Do your duty bravely.

Fear God.

Honour the King.

Kitchener, Field Marshal.[9]

On Wednesday 12 August, eight days after the declaration of war, Kitchener suffered a setback. Sir John French brought to the War Office three French officers who had arrived from Joffre's headquarters that morning. He was accompanied by Archie Murray, his chief of staff, and Henry Wilson. They all argued strongly for concentrating the BEF at the place originally agreed, Mauberge, near the Belgian frontier, and not at Amiens, as Kitchener had persuaded the Cabinet. Kitchener remained very sure that to put the little army at Mauberge would lead to swift retreat, costly in lives and ammunition at the very start of the war.

No one opposed him more than Henry Wilson. Kitchener had mistrusted and disliked Wilson since the South African war when, after his return to England with Roberts, he had refused Kitchener's request to come back to the Cape and help him. The dislike was mutual. Wilson wrote in his diary that evening that he and the others 'wrangled with K for 3 hours. K wanted to go to Amiens, and he was incapable of understanding the delays and difficulties of making such a change, nor the cowardice of it, nor the fact that either in French victory or defeat we would be equally useless. He still thinks the Germans are coming north of the Meuse in great force and will swamp us before we concentrate'[10] – which they nearly did. Kitchener could hardly have seen the Schlieffen Plan, the basis of the Germans' strategy, but he knew their minds. Moreover he had little faith in Joffre's belief that his immediate gallant offensive into the lost province of Lorraine would draw off German invaders from the north, opening the way for a decisive counterattack. And indeed the French advance was thrown back speedily with such high waste of life that the casualty figures were suppressed.

As the argument continued, Kitchener was handicapped by his weakness in oral exposition. He failed to convince the others of his certainty of a German sweep through northern Belgium; the Belgians were defending their frontier forts with great courage, but if these fell, that sweep must follow.

After three hours of debate, six against one, Kitchener said that he and Sir John must lay the case before the Prime Minister. Asquith agreed with the majority, 'not knowing anything at all about it', as Wilson tartly commented in his diary.

Asquith's decision left Kitchener, if he were to save the BEF from an inevitable costly retreat from Mons, with only one resource: to offer his resignation. Asquith, scared that this would provoke popular fury and bring down his government, might agree to Amiens after all. No evidence exists that Kitchener contemplated resignation; the raising of the new armies was his overriding concern. He returned to the War Office with a heavy heart.

Next day, on one of his rare wartime social occasions, he dined with his old friend and fellow Mason the Duke of Portland and his Duchess at their London house in Grosvenor Square. Another guest and even older friend, Lady Salisbury, wrote that very night to her husband: 'I have just come from dining at the Portlands with K. He was ridiculously like himself to look at; and in conversation. I should guess on the whole appearance that he is in good spirits but of course he is always a mystery.' She reported that he was 'very much surprised and pleased' that the BEF had got across the Channel in secrecy. The newspapers had kept their promise to say nothing. He told her he had insisted that the troops should have three days after arrival in France to shape down 'and find each other and get comfortable. There is always something unexpectedly human about K.'

She also reported that he was very much puzzled about what to do about the Territorials. 'It really is worrying him a great deal and rightly so.'[11] Haig and Haldane had pressed him to make the Territorial Army (their own creation) the framework for his first 100,000, to expand rather than create anew, but he was not convinced.

Most Territorials had enlisted for Home Defence only and had the legal right to drop out at the end of their term of service. Kitchener had immediately announced that battalions might volunteer for overseas service, but in the days when he must make up his mind the response was not encouraging although later it would prove excellent. The Territorial Army was under-strength. Many units were neither fully trained nor able to train new recruits efficiently. He took seriously the possibility of a German raid on the east or north-east coast, and if the Territorial Army was split between those who defended the realm and those who trained recruits, he would never get his first 100,000 ready in time. Moreover, this 'Town Clerks Army', as he called it, had been raised on a county basis with much of the direction in the hands of county magnates who might resent or deflect War Office orders. He was also influenced by a somewhat unhappy memory of the volunteer Imperial Yeomanry coming out to South Africa half-trained; and more distantly of French citizen-soldiers in the closing weeks of the Franco-Prussian War.

In its brief existence the Territorial Army had never caught the imagination of the nation. 'Join the Territorials' was scarcely an inspiring cry, yet men were hurrying to join the regular army in response to his personal appeal. He would therefore form his new battalions, already popularly known as Kitchener's Army, round historic regiments steeped in history and tradition under the unfettered control of the War Office.

Many regretted his decision and the debate has not ended, with historians arguing on both sides.[12]

Kitchener rejected the third option: conscription or compulsory service, such as Lord Roberts had preached for years and most European countries practised. No Liberal Cabinet would have accepted it in 1914, even if a fair system could have been organized in time. Margot Asquith, who had quickly come to appreciate the new Secretary of State, even if she made snide remarks behind his back, later wrote that in this matter

> Lord Kitchener's judgment amounted to genius. No ordinary man would have foreseen that had we attempted to apply Conscription a day earlier than we did we should have checked the enthusiasm that brought masses of men of their own free will into our army; that industrial troubles must have broken out all over the country, and that we should have transported sulky soldiers to France instead of men inspired by a great faith. In this he showed moral imagination of a rare order.[13]

They were pouring into the recruiting centres, especially as Kitchener had announced that those who joined up together could serve together — the origin of the 'Pals' Battalions', which seemed a fine idea but, many months later, led to whole villages or streets mourning their boys killed in the same action.

Drill halls, church halls and schools were summoned into use where recruits could feed and sleep before being sent to barracks or canvas camps. Rifles and khaki for uniforms ran short; many men trained for the first weeks in their own clothes and drilled with broomsticks. Asquith, visiting Aldershot on a Sunday when they were off duty, saw most of them as a rabble swanning around in 'East End costume'.

On 15 August King George wrote to his uncle, the Duke of Connaught, governor-general of Canada, that 'Kitchener has . . . already done wonders and everyone has confidence in him.' The King explained Kitchener's scheme and that he was raising another 100,000 men and expected to send many more in future because the war would last a long time. 'The spirit in the country is splendid, it has never been like this before, everyone is ready to help in any way he can and the recruits are pouring in by thousands a day . . . Kitchener will not allow any to go to the front until they are properly trained. I think he is right, a European war is not like the Boer war.'[14]

Kitchener had found the man to train them into an army. His long-ago second in command in the River War, Sir Archibald Hunter, was the senior general on the active list, but he had been placed on half-pay after an unfortunate episode as Governor of Gibraltar. The proud inhabitants had complained that when he tried to force through some needed reforms he had treated them as if Sudanese natives. The British government effectively dismissed him. By then he was married, late in life, to the widow of a Scottish peer: Kitchener and Hunter, years earlier, had wagered each other that whoever first married would pay the other £100. Kitchener, back from India, was his best man. In the vestry after the signing of the register, Archie Hunter solemnly handed over £100.

In August 1914 he and his wife were living on the Ayrshire coast. On 9 August he wrote to Kitchener: 'I live in hopes of your giving me a command . . . am ready to go anywhere and do anything at a moment's notice.' He was coming to London the next night.

He was too senior to fit into the command structure of the BEF and Kitchener had not replied when Hunter wrote on arrival in London: 'To be a bother to you is the last thing I want to be. But do give me some work to do . . .'

Kitchener appointed him to command a newly formed division on Salisbury Plain, having already named Sir Horace Smith-Dorrien, another comrade from the Sudan and India, to organize the Aldershot Training Centre. Then General Grierson, commander of one of the BEF's two Army Corps, a fine soldier, apparently fit and energetic but rather apoplectic, dropped dead in a train in France. Sir John asked for Herbert Plumer, who had won fame chasing De Wet, but both Asquith and Kitchener believed that Smith-Dorrien was more suitable, although French disliked him.

Kitchener thereupon gave Smith-Dorrien's vital Aldershot command to Archie Hunter, who wrote at once: 'Let me thank you very cordially for the appointment. I shall do my very best.' And Archie Hunter, though pining for a command at the front, turned the rabble into a superb fighting force.[15]

Smith-Dorrien went to France. Within a few days his skill and powers of leadership would help avert the disaster that Kitchener had foreseen. For, as Arthur related in his memoirs, 'although "I told you so" never fell from his lips, his worst fears were being realized'.[16]

16

AVERTING DEFEAT

LATE IN THE EVENING OF 23 August, as Churchill related:

> I had a talk with Lord Kitchener. We knew the main battle had been joined and that our men had been fighting all day; but he had received no news. He was darkly hopeful. The map was produced. The dense massing of German divisions west of the Belgian Meuse and curling round the left flank of the Anglo-French line was visible as a broad effect. So was the pivot of Namur, in front of which this whole vast turning movement seemed precariously to be hinged. He had in his mind a great French counterstroke – a thrust at the shoulder, as it were, of the long, straining, encircling arm which should lop it off or cripple it fatally. He said of the Germans 'They are running a grave risk. No one can set limits to what a well-disciplined army can do; but if the French were able to cut in here,' he made a vigorous arrow N.W. from Namur, 'the Germans might easily have a Sedan of their own on a larger scale.' . . . We went anxiously but hopefully to our slumbers.[1]

The BEF had moved swiftly from the Channel ports by train and then by road. The infantry battalions marched in fours, through sunshine and much rain, singing a mixed repertoire drawn from music-hall ditties, popular hymns and 'It's a Long Way to Tipperary', the song written and composed a year earlier. At every village they were welcomed rapturously by the women and the elderly and the children, and even more when they

THE GUNS OF AUGUST

crossed into Belgium. By 22 August the BEF, as Kitchener knew from French's telegrams, had reached the Mons–Condé Canal 'on a line roughly east and west through Mons', and were digging in on the left of the larger French forces, in their distinctive and all too visible dark blue, ready to repel the invader. All next day, while Kitchener waited for telegrams and the British nation knew nothing because Joffre had begged Kitchener to exclude war correspondents, the BEF's rifle fire was so fast and disciplined that the Germans were convinced they faced machine-guns, They were unable to advance. The Battle of Mons was becoming a victory for the British Army. Night fell. 'The attack was renewed after dark, but we held our ground tenaciously.' Then, suddenly, the BEF found themselves in utmost danger.

Early next morning Churchill was sitting up in bed at Admiralty House at 7 a.m. working at his Cabinet boxes, when the door opened 'and Lord Kitchener appeared. These were the days before he took to uniform, and my recollection is that he had a bowler hat on his head, which he took off with a hand which also held a slip of paper. He paused in the doorway and I knew in a flash and before ever he spoke that the event had gone wrong. Though his manner was quite calm, his face was different. I had the subconscious feeling that it was distorted and discoloured as if it had been punched with a fist. His eyes rolled more than ever. His voice, too, was hoarse. He looked gigantic. "Bad news" he said heavily and laid the slip of paper on my bed,' a telegram from Sir John French.

French informed Kitchener that he had just received a message from General Lanrezac, commander of the 5th French Army on the BEF's right, reporting that the fort of Namur (thought to be virtually impregnable without a long siege) had fallen, that his own troops had been driven back and that he had withdrawn to a line some miles further back. He had thus, without prior consultation or warning, left the British unsupported, exposed and in danger of encirclement.

The BEF had no option except a retirement, which, Sir John's telegram continued, 'is being carried out now. It will prove a difficult operation, if the enemy remain in contact. I remember your precise instructions as to method and direction of retirement if necessity arises. I think that immediate attention should be directed to defence of Havre. Will keep you fully informed.'

Kitchener and Churchill were aghast at French's implications, that his retreat might turn into a rout, that Dunkirk, Calais and Boulogne might fall and the BEF depend on the longer sea route to Le Havre. Churchill's account continues: 'I forget much of what passed between us. But the apparition of Kitchener *Agonistes* in my doorway will dwell with me as long as I live. It was like seeing old John Bull on the rack!'[2]

Kitchener had 'cursed and swore', so he told Asquith,[3] when he had first read Sir John's telegram, for if the French had not insisted, against his own better judgement, on the forward position the Germans would have found the BEF ready near Amiens to throw them back when they were exhausted by a swift advance, at the end of a long line of communication, and vulnerable to a French counteroffensive on their flank.

But Churchill and Kitchener need not have feared that the BEF's withdrawal might become a rout. The courage, discipline and profession-alism of the highly trained regular army turned the retreat from Mons into one of its most glorious episodes. Like the evacuation from Dunkirk nearly twenty-six years later, it became a moral victory for those who were engaged. But each day the casualties were heavy – in Smith-Dorrien's gallant, controversial but vitally important stand at Le Câteau the British lost more in dead, wounded and missing than at the Battle of Waterloo. Kitchener personally had lost two of his former staff 'family': Victor Brooke of the 9th Lancers had been stricken with appendicitis on arrival in France and died on active service; 'Conk' Marker of the Coldstream, now a colonel on the staff, had been killed by a shell. And apart from personal grief, their old Chief recognized that many, of all arms, who would have been generals and colonels and sergeant-majors when his new armies took the field were gone already.

News of the retreat caused consternation in Downing Street. All that afternoon of 24 August they waited to hear whether the BEF had been cut off. Mrs Asquith recorded in her diary an absurd episode. After an inter-rupted dinner, for which they did not change into evening dress or dinner jacket, the Asquiths and several secretaries and three dinner guests sat in an upstairs sitting room in desultory, nervous conversation, their thoughts away in France. Cabinet Ministers walked in unannounced for news. Then Asquith's private secretary, Eric Drummond, returned from making enquiries.

'They say, Sir,' he said, 'a despatch has arrived and is being deciphered in the War Office.' Margot's account continues:

On hearing this Henry left us and went down to the Cabinet room. I followed him and stood at the top of the stair watching anxious Ministers, and groups of officials waiting and talking in the corridor, while Eric ran back to the War Office. I joined Henry, whom I found alone; I sat in silence while he ran through a mass of papers.

Eric Drummond told us on his return that the deciphered message had gone to Lord Kitchener, but that no one knew where he was, or what was in the telegram. At this Henry looked furiously angry: the door opened and various officials came into the room.

Everyone spoke at the same time:

'Why was a bed and bath put into the War Office if K doesn't sleep there?'

'I hear he was dining with Arthur Balfour,' someone said, at which someone else exclaimed:

'I doubt if he or anyone else could keep Arthur up after 11 o'clock.'

A voice of more authority suggested that as Lady Wantage had lent Kitchener her house we should telephone to him there; at which Eric Drummond went into the other room and took up the telephone, some of us following:

'Hullo!! . . . Hullo!!! . . . I am the Prime Minister's Secretary. Who are you? . . . Yes . . . yes . . . the butler? . . . all right . . . tell Lord Kitchener the Prime Minister wants to see the message from General French at once. Hullo!!! . . . Hullo!!!! *Do you hear? . . . At once* . . . What??? . . .

'Oh!! Damn! He's not the butler, and he's gone away.'

Henry was still alone and in a state of exasperation when I returned to him. He rang the bell and said: 'Tell them to find Lord Kitchener at once; this mustn't happen again — I must have the despatch *at once*; do you *hear*?'

Messengers and secretaries went off in all directions, while we waited in silence for what seemed an eternity of time. The door opened at last and Sir William Tyrrell rushed in, hot and breathless, with the telegram: 'Loss of over 2,000 men. Fighting since Saturday the 22nd [*sic*], but all in line again.'

The communications were still open, and the British Army had not been cut off. Thank God. It was 4 a.m. when we went to bed.[4]

They had, in fact, fussed themselves unnecessarily, since Kitchener would have been round at once if he had needed action by the Prime Minister.

Next morning at 7.30 Kitchener sent to the King, through Lord Stamfordham, the gist of the telegram. Because their French allies had retired again, the BEF had to conform. 'In spite of some hard marching and fighting,' Kitchener added, 'British force in best of spirits . . . I do not like these retirements.' He feared that unless Joffre could take the offensive the British left flank could be badly turned by a German thrust 'before we can act effectively'. He also told the King that one of the divisions, which had been held in England against a possible German raid, had joined French.[5]

That afternoon Kitchener had to make his maiden speech in the House of Lords. Asquith found him very nervous as he went over the speech beforehand, but their lordships allowed him to read most of it from a prepared statement, contrary to normal usage of their House. As one peer recorded: 'It was rather a dramatic occasion . . . He received general cheers throughout.'[6]

As the fighting retreat continued, through a countryside being smashed by gunfire and troop movements, but not yet a wilderness of mud and shell-holes, Sir John kept Kitchener informed by telegrams. On 27 August he sent a five-page typed account and situation report, received next day by King's Messenger. When Kitchener turned the last page he found a postscript in purple ink. First French assured him that the remarks in the letter about strengths and losses were inserted for the Cabinet's benefit since Kitchener already knew. Then French added words of appreciation, almost of affection, which make his attitude to Kitchener only five days later more extraordinary:

We all feel here that we are absolutely safe in your hands and we have the most unbounded trust in your support and help. I repeat what I have said to you before 'Thank God you are there' and I mean it! You are the one man I have always looked up to and believed in as a soldier and I rejoice to be serving under you again. I am deeply touched by the kind tone of your telegram to me — it reminds me of all your kindness and friendly attitude in the vicissitudes of South Africa.[7]

The next day's telegrams suggested that the situation was improving after a French counterattack. Kitchener was therefore shocked to receive a message from the general in charge of communications in France that he had heard from General Headquarters (GHQ) that the Commander-in-Chief had decided to make a definite, prolonged retreat. Kitchener wired at once to Sir John for clarification. Early next morning a long reply included the ominous words that Joffre, who had secured a local victory but was retiring again, had been told plainly that in the present condition of the BEF 'I shall be absolutely unable to remain in the front line as he has now begun his retirement. I have decided to begin my retirement tomorrow in the morning behind the Seine in a south-westerly direction west of Paris. This means marching for some eight days without fatiguing the troops at a considerable distance from the enemy.' He must reorganize and refit but had 'no idea of making any prolonged and definite retreat'. Yet he was leaving the line.[8]

'What does he mean?' asked George Arthur when they had read the telegram. 'Mean?' replied Kitchener. 'It means that French is off. He has had enough of it.'[9]

Kitchener saw the consequence clearly. French would lose touch with Joffre, the Germans would drive a wedge between the allied armies and cause a disaster. Paris might fall. The war might be lost. France would be betrayed. Britain disgraced.

He telegraphed his surprise, asked the C-in-C to consider the consequences. The Cabinet meeting that morning debated the matter hotly but endorsed, almost unanimously, Kitchener's certainty that keeping unbroken contact with the French was paramount. At Asquith's request he telegraphed Sir John again: 'The Government are exceedingly anxious', lest the proposed retirement would prevent close cooperation. 'They are waiting for an answer . . . and have all possible confidence in your troops and yourself.' A further telegram urged French not to break away.

All afternoon, while carrying on with needed business, Kitchener waited. The Foreign Secretary, Grey, sent across an appeal from President Poincaré that French should not withdraw: Poincaré enclosed a copy of Joffre's own appeal to French. Kitchener sent George Arthur to the Foreign Office with proposals should French prove obdurate.

In the evening Kitchener left the War Office, calling on Winston Churchill at Admiralty House on the way home to keep him informed, all the more important because he was a close friend of French. At Carlton Gardens, after dinner, Kitchener worked on papers with Fitz and Arthur, waiting for French's answer. Shortly before midnight the telephone rang: the War Office had received a telegram from French, in code as always. Kitchener ordered it to be given him by telephone at once, word for word as decoded.

Arthur held the receiver on its long cord to his ear, writing the words down as they came through and calling out each phrase to the Chief.

In a long statement French reported that he did not think his force could withstand a strong attack from even one German army corps. He blamed his allies for retiring, but if he tried to save them he would 'run the risk of absolute disaster'. His next words were ominous, referring to the losses at Le Câteau: 'I do not think you understand the shattered condition of the Second Army Corps, and how it paralyses my power of offence.' If he could refit, and when further reinforcements arrived from England, he would have 'a self-contained and efficient army capable of acting with telling effect'. He asked Kitchener to trust him 'to watch the situation and act according to circumstances'[10] — independently of his allies was the unspoken implication.

Kitchener decided that he must go to France at once and insist on the Cabinet's wishes face to face. While Arthur ordered a special train to be ready, Kitchener went to Downing Street, where the Prime Minister came downstairs with two Cabinet Ministers who had been dining with the Asquiths (probably to play bridge). Winston, alerted by telephone by Arthur, came in, Lloyd George soon after. Swayed especially by President Poincaré's appeal, they decided on behalf of the whole Cabinet that Kitchener must indeed go to France without delay, in total secrecy, to unravel the situation and 'if necessary put the fear of God into them all'. Winston promised a fast light cruiser from Dover. Kitchener left Downing Street to collect his kit and to change into uniform.

The time was now about 1.30 on the first morning of September. Lloyd George remarked that Kitchener was 'a plucky old boy'. Asquith joked, 'Well, I'm nearly twice his age and I would think nothing of it!' He was actually nine years younger. Churchill commented that Kitchener had told him he was feeling very tired, 'but he is a piece of hard stuff'.[11] Asquith wrote later that day to Venetia Stanley: 'He is a real old sportsman when an emergency appears.'[12]

Half an hour later Kitchener walked into Sir Edward Grey's bedroom in the house near his own, and woke the Foreign Secretary, who must be informed. A few minutes later he left in a taxicab for Charing Cross Station, enjoining George Arthur to tell no one except the Principal Private Secretary, the Permanent Under-Secretary and the King.

During the next thirty-six hours, so Arthur commented in his memoirs, 'to preserve the secret of the hurried historical journey, I told more innocent fibs than in all the rest of my life'.[13]

Kitchener travelled alone, which he disliked. Had he taken Fitz, a rumour might have spread that they had gone to salvage remnants of a defeated BEF, and that might cause a stock-market panic or a run on the pound, especially as a defeatist and inaccurate article about the retreat had slipped through censorship and appeared in *The Times*.

He wore his Field Marshal's khaki service-dress. In these early months of hostilities he and other officers at the War Office were still working in their usual plain clothes according to long-established tradition in peace and war. British officers, unlike Continentals, had only worn uniform when on parade, picquet duty, exercises or operations, while other ranks had worn it always, in barracks and in the streets or parks, to the admiration of nursemaids when it was scarlet. As soon as sufficient khaki cloth became available, and tiresome women were beginning to present white feathers to any male of military age not wearing it, Kitchener decreed that all ranks wear uniform at all times.

He chose khaki for this hurried visit to France because he wanted to inspect and cheer the troops in the battlefield after he and French had conferred. And at the back of his mind, so George Arthur believed, was the thought that if French refused his plea, or order, to keep the BEF in the line, he might need to relieve him of his command and take over temporarily until the Cabinet appointed a successor.[14]

He did not foresee any problem in coming to France in uniform.

He had wired French to name a meeting place but could not take the shortest route because the Germans straddled the Calais–Paris railway. The longer voyage to Le Havre gave opportunity for a brief sleep on the cruiser. He reached Paris and the elegant British embassy on the rue du Faubourg St-Honoré to learn from the British Ambassador that the C-in-C would shortly arrive and that Sir John had asked the French Prime Minister, Viviani, and the new Minister of War, Alexandre Millerand, to join their conference, together with several senior French officers and the Ambassador himself.

Kitchener had not intended a conference but a tête-à-tête.

Sir John entered the room (probably the 'throne room' or the large dining room) apparently irritated and resentful. As discussion began, General Huguet, head of France's Military Mission with the BEF, noticed the contrast between the two British Field Marshals, the tall Kitchener, 'calm, balanced, reflective, master of himself, conscious of the great task he had come to perform: the little French sour, impetuous, with congested face, sullen and ill-tempered in expression. The one really looked the man and leader he was while the other looked on the contrary like nothing but a spoiled child upon whom fortune had smiled prodigiously but who, the day she left him, seemed abandoned and forlorn',[15] which was a little unfair since French had come straight from the battle-front after nine days of heavy fighting, much bloodshed and heavy responsibility.

French immediately complained that Kitchener had come in uniform, implying that as the senior Field Marshal he was French's superior and not simply a Cabinet Minister. Only five days before, French had written to Kitchener that he was the one soldier he had always looked up to and believed in, and 'I rejoice to be serving under you again.' Yet now he was treating him as a civilian politician and complaining of interference. When Kitchener said he intended to visit the troops in the field, French objected, apparently believing that his own dignity and prestige would be harmed but subconsciously afraid that his two corps commanders would inevitably disclose his shortcomings and near panic at times in the retreat, although at other times he was splendid.

French made such a fuss, and was backed by the Ambassador, the long-established seventy-year-old Sir Francis Bertie, that Kitchener agreed not to go. Thus a great opportunity was lost. For the troops, tired but in great spirits, sensing that they were superior to their enemy but forced back by the failures of their allies, would have been excited and heartened to see their own popular C-in-C walking side by side with Britain's national hero. Far from Sir John being diminished, they would have assumed that

Kitchener had come over specially to congratulate their C-in-C and themselves. And Kitchener was deprived of an opportunity to witness what this war was like.

Kitchener had a curious innocence. Just as in India he had expected lusty young British soldiers to stay away from brothels because he begged them to remember their mothers, so he assumed that Sir John would never put his self-esteem before winning the war.

In the embassy the discussion on the main point, whether the BEF should drop out of the line to refit, was getting nowhere. At last Kitchener asked French to come to a private room where they could talk alone. What passed between them can never be known accurately. Kitchener did not reveal it, anxious not to belittle the man who had such great responsibility, even if he had suffered a spasm of defeatism; and French's account in his immediate post-war memoir, *1914*, was generally held to be untrustworthy: he did not even mention the true reason for Kitchener's hurried visit.

Whatever was said, Sir John agreed to stay in line with the French armies and to conform to Joffre's movements, while being cautious not to allow his own flanks to be unsupported. Kitchener telegraphed the Cabinet with this news, sending French a copy with a minute that he was sure this represented their agreement but in any case 'please consider it an instruction'. In his acknowledgement, French wrote: 'I fully understand your instructions.'

As soon as Kitchener had returned to London and French to GHQ, French's resentment boiled over, writing to Churchill only three days later: 'I can't understand what brought Kitchener to Paris . . . Kitchener's visit was most unfortunate . . . I do beg you, my dear Friend, to . . . stop this *interference* with field operations. Kitchener *knows nothing* about European warfare. Of course he's a fine organiser but he never was and never will be a commander in the field . . . '[16] This from the man who had written to Kitchener the previous week that he was the one man he had always looked up to and believed in as a soldier, and, 'Thank God you are there, and I mean it!'

Whether Churchill showed this letter to Kitchener or not, nothing mattered except that French did not break ranks with his allies and was thus available when Joffre seized upon a German error of strategy and, on 5 September, launched the brilliant offensive known as the Battle of the Marne. The BEF fought with great gallantry and effect, and the Germans were thrown back thirty miles. Without Kitchener's intervention four days earlier this would not have happened.

As the German retreat began, F. E. Smith, as head of the Press Bureau, brought to Kitchener in his room at the War Office a draft communiqué which described the Battle of the Marne as 'an important success'. Kitchener shook his head, scratched out the phrase and wrote, 'decisive victory'. Smith and George Arthur both asked if he really meant to write such a sweeping statement.

Kitchener replied: ' The Germans have been routed in what I think will be the decisive battle of the war.[17]

17

'AN ENORMOUS ASSET'

London Opinion, a popular weekly of the day, was about to go to press with the issue dated 5 September when the editor rejected the front cover. He commissioned Alfred Leete, a black-and-white artist, to design something topical – fast. Recruiting being the great topic of the day, Leete drew very quickly the head of Lord Kitchener in his Field Marshal's cap, full face as seen in the illustrated papers. To the left he drew a large gloved hand with the index finger pointing at the reader, and, underneath, the words: YOUR COUNTRY NEEDS YOU, the YOU being drawn very large.

Leete drew Kitchener's eyes as clear, with no hint of the cast, and the moustache was fuller and darker than in life, but the very simplicity of the design brought the message home to hundreds as they stopped at newsstands in streets and railway stations. All that week, readers asked for reproductions. The editor offered the Kitchener picture on postcards. The War Office requested permission to use it. By the end of the month it was on posters all over the country with various texts emphasizing the message. Leete's drawing with the stern face and the pointing finger became the most famous picture of the Great War. Adapted, parodied, reproduced in dozens of ways, it made Kitchener's face one of the best known of the twentieth century, and the poster itself was voted the century's most influential.[1]

By the time it was first published Kitchener had already received his first 100,000 but did not announce this lest potential recruits were discouraged from joining up: he needed millions. The flow had slackened a little, partly because the system was being choked. Leo Amery, MP, representing the Parliamentary Committee set up to extend recruiting, and Rawlinson, briefly Director of Recruiting at the War Office before being given command of a new division in France, toured the south-west of England in an attempt to sort out confusions; many men who had taken the oath were being sent home to await orders, but others were still being enlisted. The Army Council wanted to check the flow, but Kitchener replied to the Master General of the Ordnance, von Donop: 'I have held up my finger and the men are flocking to me in thousands. How can I now hold up my hand and tell them to go back?' And when Sir Charles Harris, the rather deaf civilian Head of the Financial Department, suggested raising the minimum measurements for height and chest, Kitchener drew him to the window and pointed to workmen erecting a lamppost. 'You ask me to slack off recruiting. The British public has taken charge, and if you or I get in the way we shall be hanged on the lamppost those men are putting up!' Harris said he would take the risk. On 11 September the War Office announced the higher physical qualifications, the flow eased and some 10,000 men previously accepted were discharged as too small. (Later, Kitchener was intrigued by a suggestion from the Liverpool area that 'Bantam Battalions' should be formed of smaller men; he agreed, and they did good service.)

Harris had looked remarkably unmoved by the lamppost threat and some days afterwards Kitchener asked him why. Harris replied that he had noticed that the men were erecting an electric light standard, not a gas lamppost, and it would stand sheer without the high crossbar so neither of them could be hanged 'à la lanterne'. Kitchener smiled.[2]

Each day Kitchener would arrive at the War Office at precisely 9 a.m. having been driven in the borrowed Rolls from Carlton Gardens. Very occasionally he would walk the much shorter distance down the steps, across St James's Park and through the Horse Guards arch. After 9 September, when he ordered uniform to be worn in the War Office, he would wear his Field Marshal's blue undress, keeping khaki service dress for visits to troops.

The morning was spent dictating orders and in interviews. As on campaigns and at Simla, he proceeded by what a casual observer might think a semi-organized chaos. He knew what could be left to others but frequently worked on matters that his War Office staff could have done for him, or gave orders to the wrong man. When officers moaned, the Quartermaster-General told them that it was the Chief's way and any muddle could be sorted out afterwards by himself or another departmental head. Some of the less senior were too frightened of him to offer advice or information, and thus he was left with gaps in knowledge. He was indeed brusque with those who were muddled or did not carry out orders, though he never raised his voice; but as one dugout general commented, 'certain of his subordinates seem never to have discovered that he was in reality the very reverse of unapproachable and harsh.'[3]

At lunchtime, when the generals and colonels walked or drove to their clubs, Kitchener would eat a cold collation sent across from Carlton Gardens in a napkin. He then smoked a cigar. Brade, the Permanent Under-Secretary, said that 'while he is smoking this he is most amenable to any request. He is very approachable and interviews a constant stream of all sorts.' When the cigar made him too amenable he took to disappearing for fifteen minutes into George Arthur's little room, not to be disturbed on any matter while he smoked a rather special Havana.[4]

To one request he was not amenable. The young Edward, Prince of Wales, just twenty years old and already showing the blend of charm and self-centredness which was to mark his life, was an ensign in the Grenadier Guards, stationed in London and often calling on George Arthur at the War Office. 'With the face of a child he possessed nerves of steel and the heart of a lion,' thought Arthur. When the Prince's battalion was ordered to France early in September and he was told to remain behind, he pleaded with Kitchener. The Prince pointed out that with spare brothers his death in action would not matter. Kitchener took time to explain that his death might not matter, but 'I cannot risk your being captured.' Writing to tell Arthur of the 'terrible moment' when he saw the battalion march off, the Prince added: ' It was very kind of Lord K to give me that long interview, and I must say he stated his views most clearly,' and promised (and kept the promise) that the Prince should go out as soon as the line became stable. In his diary, however, the Prince called him a great fat bloated man, a rough customer but mighty strong and just the man to boss the politicians.[5]

Some 200 letters a day were reaching the War Office addressed personally to Lord Kitchener. One of King Edward's daughters, Princess Louise, wrote to encourage him: 'The country looks up to you, not only as their wise councillor [*sic*] but as their friend.' She added rather wild advice about German prisoners and naturalized Germans.[6] The King's Private Secretary wrote to say that 'it is not at all advisable that Queen Alexandra should get any news which is to be treated as secret.' He suggested any news about to be released should be sent to her 'shortly beforehand';[7] presumably she could not keep her mouth shut and, being very deaf, spoke in a loud voice. She read the letters, written by Arthur, twice and then burned them with her own hand.[8]

Most of the letters to Kitchener were from the public. It was rumoured by October that 2,000 envelopes had piled up, unopened. The director of the Victoria and Albert Museum offered to send his now underworked educational staff to help, but the War Office refused; possibly the rumour was false. The personal secretaries could filter out love-struck females and cranks, and do their sympathetic and practical best for the stream of pathetic enquiries from high and low about officers and men who were missing in action. The Chief had to be shown an embarrassing request from his old friend, the eccentric Lady Sackville, for a safe staff job for her husband, Lord Sackville: when he answered in his own hand that he could make no exception for an individual officer, she wrote back asking him to exempt the carpenters on the Knole estate. His reply was polite and evasive.[9]

A letter to 'Dear good Lord Kitchener' from three children in Lancashire came with a photograph of one of them on an old pony, 'which we are very afraid may be taken for your army! Please *spare her!*' They had given two others, and three of the family were 'now fighting for you in the Navy. Mother and all will do anything for you but *do, do please* let us keep old Betty . . . '

They asked for official word '*quickly*' and signed off as 'Your troubled little Britishers, P. L. and Freda Hewlett'. Freda received a typed reply almost by return, signed by Creedy: 'Lord Kitchener asks me to say . . . that if you will show the enclosed note to anyone who asks about your pony he thinks it will be left to you quite safely.'[10]

The note enclosed is not extant but those who penetrated beyond Kitchener's rather cold exterior and extreme shyness knew his kind heart. Thus, an Oxford scientist who had closed his laboratory on joining up wrote to Kitchener that the old soldier commissionaire had been refused a long-service pension because no former commanding officer was alive to endorse his application. Kitchener interviewed the man, studied his papers, then took him on at the War Office and made sure the pension was granted. [11]

He discovered that André von Dumreicher, who had served him well as a high official in Egypt but was a German national, had not only been dismissed but interned. His wife, May, who was a niece of General Hunter but under the then law had lost her British citizenship on marriage, had come back to Britain a few weeks before the war for the birth of Hugo; André had followed on his summer leave. The whole family were interned and her mother's twin brother, General Sir Archie Hunter, did nothing to help. Kitchener ordered their release.*[12]

As for Sir Rudolf von Slatin, who was on leave from the Sudan in his Austrian homeland at the outbreak of war, Kitchener sent a message through a neutral country that if he would come to Britain and join his old friends in the defence of the Empire he would obtain him a peerage. Von Slatin replied that loyalty to his own Emperor must come first: he must not leave Austria. Kitchener therefore made certain that von Slatin's pension would be paid throughout the war.[13]

Beside the great issues of manpower, munitions and strategy came lesser problems. The Director-General of Army Medical Services was Sir Arthur Sloggett, who had been Kitchener's senior medical officer on the Dongola campaign and badly wounded at Omdurman, a humorous man with a taste for risqué stories. He was vain and irritable, if kindly. Kitchener had ordered him to ensure that all casualties from gunshot wounds in the BEF were treated at once with antiseptic inoculation against tetanus. When many wounded died, Kitchener discovered that Sloggett had not fully passed on the order. He dismissed him for incompetence and disobedience, and discoursed to Asquith at great length and 'with much vehemence' on the shortcomings of the medical arrangements. Kitchener summoned back Sloggett's predecessor, Sir Alfred Keogh, rector of Imperial College and working as head of St John's in France, and gave him exceptional powers. He established an excellent service. Sloggett fell ill, then went to France as director of medical services on the Western Front and chief commissioner of the Red Cross and St John's. He redeemed himself by gallant work for the remainder of the war.[14]

* After Kitchener's death they were re-interned!

Too many hospitals in Boulogne, however, were organized by unqual-
ified society ladies at their own expense, one reason why Kitchener would
never receive ladies at the War Office: he knew that every duchess or
countess would want his personal advice or aid to set up a hospital (or
obtain favours for a relative). These amateur hospitals and their high-born
matrons were adding to the general medical muddle that Keogh was
putting right. The muddle had first been brought to Kitchener's attention
by J. A. Spender, the leading Liberal editor. Later he seized upon Spender
at a small dinner party, told him the problem of the amateurs and said:
'You have got to go over there and tell them to go . . . I mean it quite
seriously.' And Spender went, an example, he noted, 'of Kitchener's
peculiar power of compelling people to do all sorts of things which they
had no intention of doing'.[15]

Like the physicians, the padres brought problems, though unwittingly.
Before the war the Chaplain-General had worked out a scheme for
mobilization, but the Adjutant-General had not included it in the War
Book, so that when sixty-five chaplains went to France with the BEF they
found no official provision for their rations, accommodation or transport,
although senior officers from Sir John French downwards were highly
appreciative of their work, especially during the retreat. Most of the padres
were Anglican yet by chance of seniority the principal chaplain was an
Ulster Presbyterian.

Back home, scores of clergy offered themselves to the Chaplain-General,
some without their bishops' leave. Since nearly every parish in 1914
England had its own parson and many were of military age, he had no
shortage of volunteers. The Chaplain-General since 1901, Bishop John
Taylor Smith, a former colonial bishop who had been personally selected
by Edward VII, was a stalwart evangelical, deeply spiritual, yet very
popular with the old professional army for his humour and pithy talks. On
5 October, the leading Anglo-Catholic layman, Lord Halifax (father of
the future Viceroy and Foreign Secretary), complained to Kitchener that
the Chaplain-General was not giving Anglo-Catholic clergy a fair chance
of being accepted, probably because some applicants trained to help the
dying by prayers and sacraments, were tongue-tied if Taylor Smith
examined them about bringing wounded men to personal faith in Christ.
Taylor Smith, however, asserted that churchmanship weighed little against
ability to help the men of the new army.[16]

Kitchener did not then interfere, but one new temporary chaplain, already in France, was to be of great assistance to him at the height of the war. Sixteen years earlier, Llewellyn Gwynne had broken red tape to arrive as a missionary in Khartoum soon after the Battle of Omdurman. Kitchener sent him to minister to 'heathen' British troops until the animist southern Sudan was open, where he had a great ministry and became Bishop of Khartoum.[17]

Gwynne was on leave in England in August 1914. As an honorary chaplain to the forces (in the Sudan) he at once offered himself to the Adjutant-General and went to France. 'I am placing myself so entirely under the orders of the chaplain-general,' he wrote to the Archbishop of Canterbury, 'that even my mustache has to be sacrificed at his command.' He was not due back in the Sudan until November. 'Please God the War will be over before then.'[18]

Along with decisions on physicians and padres, Kitchener had to decide about the press. He had tolerated war correspondents in the Sudan and South Africa, but in 1914 Joffre had begged that they be kept back at base. The 'defeatist' dispatch in *The Times* and the growing disquiet among the public, starved of hard news and prey to rumours, convinced Churchill, F. E. Smith and Kitchener that the newspapers must be fed with authentic articles by a trustworthy and knowledgeable writer. At Winston's suggestion Kitchener chose Ernest Swinton, a sapper major who had won the DSO in South Africa and would win fame in the future as the progenitor of armoured tanks. Swinton had written stimulating and amusing tracts on tactics and was a historian. Kitchener sent for him and, friendly but brief, ordered him to write anonymous articles about the operations in France, have them censored at GHQ and sent direct to him.

Swinton left for France at once, but on arriving at GHQ, now advancing, he found that Sir John French, whose 'nerves were plainly on edge . . . imagined I had been sent out by Lord Kitchener to keep a watch upon his actions'. This mystified Swinton, since he knew nothing of the Paris meeting or French's bitterness towards Kitchener.

I was able to compare the attitude of the two men, and felt that the distrust of which I had just had evidence was not mutual. In contrast with Sir John, Lord Kitchener had been so calm. It is true that he was farther from the scene of action and could afford to be more detached; but it is doubtful whether the strain on him was less than that on the commander in the field, though he took it differently. Each was carrying an immense and special load of responsibility in a crisis that was a supreme test for all.[19]

The mood at GHQ was buoyant after the Germans had been thrown back thirty miles in the Battle of the Marne. Henry Wilson even believed that the Allies would be back at the Belgian frontier in a fortnight. When Henry Rawlinson passed through on his way to take command of his division, he found Wilson certain that one big effort would finish the war by Christmas and 'furious with K for keeping officers at home to nurse his ridiculous armies'. Rawlinson disagreed; fresh from the War Office he considered that 'K is an enormous asset. In the future he will be yet more valuable, for he has the confidence of the nation, and can do pretty well what he likes. I think the war will go on till the 'K' armies are fit to take the field.'[20]

The talk was of a bold plan to move the BEF from the Aisne to Flanders, to block any German race for the Channel ports. London buses had been requisitioned to take infantry battalions by road, beyond the range of German guns.

Before the move was complete, Kitchener had to take a quick decision in the middle of the night.

In the late evening of 2 October, at about 10.15 p.m., while Kitchener was reading Foreign Office telegrams, the Foreign Secretary came round unexpectedly to Carlton Gardens. Grey showed Kitchener an alarming telegram from Sir Francis Villiers, the British Minister to Belgium.

King Albert and his government had left Brussels before its capture and were now, like the Minister, with the Belgian army defending Antwerp, the great port up the Scheldt, already under bombardment from new giant howitzers. Kitchener believed strongly that Antwerp must be saved for as long as possible: its fall would endanger the Channel ports, whereas in allied hands it could threaten the Germans' flank and compel them to divert troops from their main front in France. He had sent a representative to encourage and advise the Belgians and was planning to dispatch Rawlinson's division to reinforce the defenders.

The Minister's telegram shattered hopes. It announced that acting on unanimous advice, the King, with the Queen, would withdraw his gallant but battered army to Ostend, starting the next day. 'It is said,' Sir Francis continued, 'the town will hold out for five or six days but it seems most unlikely that when the Court and Government are gone resistance will be so much prolonged.'[21]

Grey and Kitchener were certain they must stop the King and army leaving prematurely and give them new heart. Every day that Antwerp held out would buy time for the BEF to complete its movement from the Aisne, after the allied victory on the Marne, to Flanders, where it would protect the ports and prevent a fresh attempt on Paris.

They could not consult Asquith: he was making a recruiting speech in Cardiff. Winston Churchill had just left for Dover to visit his naval brigade in Dunkirk. They decided to bring him back. And thus, about twenty miles out of London, Churchill found his one-carriage special slow down, stop at a wayside station in Kent, and then reverse all the way back to Victoria without any explanation. At Victoria a staff officer told a puzzled Winston to go at once to Carlton Gardens, where he found Grey and his Private Secretary with Kitchener and the First Sea Lord. They showed him the telegram. He offered to go to Antwerp himself. He believed (wrongly) that only one big gun was knocking out the forts. If two allied divisions could drive away the gun's supporting troops, Antwerp could be saved. After discussing the possibilities Kitchener agreed, and Winston, soon after midnight, rejoined his special train, which steamed back into the Kentish countryside while heartening telegrams were sent to the Belgians urging no decision until he arrived.

The defence of Antwerp is Winston's saga rather than Kitchener's. Kitchener backed him fully, dispatching a relief force under Rawlinson and securing promises from the French, which were not fulfilled. When Asquith read out Winston's famous telegram offering to resign as First Lord and take over the defence of Antwerp, and the Cabinet burst into laughter, Kitchener alone was silent. He minuted on the telegram that he was prepared to make Churchill a local lieutenant-general. To Asquith, Churchill was merely a major in the Oxfordshire Yeomanry, but Kitchener knew his worth.

Churchill's offer was refused. He was ordered to return but he stayed, and his presence, and those units of Kitchener's relief force which got through in time, strengthened the defence. Had not Sir John French suspected (though he denied this) that Kitchener was aiming for a second front under his direct command, Joffre might have been more zealous in supporting the Belgians. The fighting was fierce but increasingly hopeless. Kitchener kept in touch through George Arthur, who spent his days at the Central Telegraph Office 'where telephone conversations with the beleaguered city were carried on under truly difficult conditions. Personally I could not hear a word or make myself heard, so a P.O. official was called in, sworn to secrecy, and shut up with myself in a padded room, conducive to profuse perspiration, to receive the cheerless news.'[22]

Churchill, Rawlinson, the British and Belgian troops withdrew when all hope had gone. The city fell on 9 October. They had prolonged the defence by five days.

Churchill was criticized in the press for what many believed was a wild dash to win personal glory. Kitchener stayed silent, as his position demanded, but he was certain that the press were wrong.

18

NOTHING TO FIGHT WITH

THE GERMANS pressed forward, intending to occupy the featureless flat lands of Flanders which would win them the Channel ports. The BEF, their move from Aisne to the northern flank of the French almost complete, advanced into the countryside beyond Ypres. In these preliminaries to the great First Battle of Ypres, Kitchener lost one of the closest of his 'family': Major-General Hubert Hamilton, the 'Hammy' who had worked so faithfully at his side in South Africa and India. Hamilton commanded a division in the 2nd Corps. On 14 October, as they advanced slowly under sporadic gunfire, he was standing conversing with regimental or staff officers 'with the quiet nonchalance which was characteristic of him'. A shrapnel shell burst above and a splinter struck him on the temple, killing him instantly. They buried him that night in a village churchyard. The German guns opened up and the group of weary officers around the grave could hardly hear the padre's words 'for the whiz and crash of shells'.

'He was a grand commander, beloved by his men,' wrote Conan Doyle in his history of the 1914 campaign, 'and destined for the highest had he lived.'[1] His sister, Lady Allendale, replying to Kitchener's letter of condolence, wrote that their last talk together had been 'chiefly about you, so quiet and intense. The devotion to his chief, of course. The sure appreciation based on the experience of years. And there was more than all this. I think he loved like George Colley loved Lord Wolseley long ago.' Colley, her first husband, was the general killed at Majuba, previously Wolseley's military secretary.[2]

Hubert Hamilton had been invaluable to his Chief in their great struggle for army reform in India. Had he lived a little longer he would have seen one vital fruit of their victory over Curzon – the arrival of Indian troops in Flanders. Birdwood wrote in his memoirs: 'I shudder to think what would have happened on the outbreak of war in 1914 had not Kitchener's reforms been in force.' As military secretary to the government of India, 'Birdie' was at the centre of the mobilization of the Indian army in August 1914. Kitchener had immediately asked for his services at his side in London, but Beauchamp Duff wisely did not let him go. As each order came from Kitchener to send divisions abroad – to Egypt, to East Africa, to France – the brigades went from their peacetime stations 'without a hitch. Under the pre-Kitchener system, nothing short of chaos must have resulted from such an effort.'[3] It was only later, when the divisions sent to Mesopotamia pressed ahead towards Baghdad, against Kitchener's advice to the Cabinet, that the failure to complete the reforms (after 1905) led to disaster, allowing Curzon and his friends to damn them.

At Ypres the German offensive that began five days after Hubert Hamilton's death nearly succeeded, despite the disciplined firepower of the BEF and the skill of the French in thwarting a massive attack by German cavalry. Casualties on both sides were heavy, but the Germans had brought up new formations including student battalions. Towns and villages, slagheaps and pastures were scenes of fierce fighting, with the pressure steadily mounting against the Allies. On 1 November an anxious, indeed upset Kitchener went over to Dunkirk for secret talks with President Poincaré, Joffre and his deputy, Foch. 'Well, so we are beaten!' were his first words, according to Foch. Foch assured him they were not, but detailed the heavy allied losses. The French begged him to send out many more men. He had already telephoned the War Office to send five Territorial battalions which he could spare from home defence, since a German descent on East Anglia now seemed less likely and could be destroyed by the Royal Navy, but he would not send any from the half-trained New Armies. He refused to respond to French panic by abandoning his conviction that only fully trained and equipped divisions should go. He told Joffre and Foch, 'On 1 July 1915 you will have one million trained British soldiers in France. Before that date you will have practically none.' The French spoke up together that they did not ask for a million but some of these men at once. He replied: 'Before that date, do not count on anything.'

The disappointed Foch was, however, struck 'by the accuracy of his conceptions in what concerned the war'.[4] Kitchener also remarked that if the Allies were not happy with Sir John French he might replace him with Sir Ian Hamilton. The President and Joffre replied that they got on well with Sir John. Foch mentioned the remark to Henry Wilson who, ever the mischief-maker, told Sir John that Kitchener had proposed to dismiss him and that the French generals saved him. Sir John sent a furious telegram to Asquith.[5]

The Indian troops had arrived in time. The balance slowly turned to the Allies' advantage. On 11 November the aged Lord Roberts, their beloved former Chief, crossed the Channel to visit them. He toured the areas of the still-fluid front while the Germans were making their last effort to break the line, but he caught a chill and died on 14 November within sound of the guns.

He was given an elaborate military funeral at St Paul's Cathedral which caused Kitchener to remark that he would not want a grand military funeral for himself but to be buried quietly in Barham churchyard, a place of peace and tranquillity.[6] The funeral also concentrated his mind on the problem of the Indian sick and wounded. Large numbers of Muslim, Hindu and Buddhist soldiers were still in hospital ships (Roberts had visited them) because no hospitals in England had the facilities to handle the special arrangements for food, water and accommodation demanded by Caste and Religion Rules

Kitchener sent that very day for Sir Walter Lawrence, Curzon's former Private Secretary, who had later arranged the Indian tour of the Prince and Princess of Wales in Minto's first months. Kitchener appointed him his personal Commissioner to advise and keep him informed. Lawrence promptly secured the Royal Pavilion at Brighton, with its oriental atmosphere, and set up hospitals there and on the Sussex Downs.[7]

Lord Roberts had been the first Colonel of the Irish Guards, formed in 1900, an obvious choice as he came from a long-established Anglo-Irish family. Kitchener had been born in Ireland because his English parents had moved there shortly before; his parents had taken the family to Switzerland before Herbert's thirteenth birthday. He never thought of himself as Irish. However, shortly after George v's visit to the troops in the Ypres Salient the King appointed Kitchener as the second Colonel of the Irish Guards. Kitchener immediately sent telegrams to the battalions:

'How proud I am to be associated with so gallant a regiment. My warmest greetings and best wishes to you all!' The Irish Guards in reply greatly appreciated 'the honour conferred on them by H.M. the King and are proud to have such a distinguished soldier as Colonel of the Regiment'.[8]

At the height of the First Battle of Ypres Kitchener received an American steel king at the War Office for a vital, brief discussion.

Ten years earlier Kitchener had written: 'Soldiers must always be ready to lay down their lives for the Empire, but in my humble opinion it is the bounden duty of the Govt. to so administer, equip, and put them in the field, as to ensure the least possible slaughter of their men.'[9] On taking up office he was amazed by what he called the 'criminal neglect'[10] of the government to equip the army with arms and ammunition and all else needed. Asquith retorted that they had prepared enough for the limited war they expected. Kitchener would murmur to his friends, 'No one can say my colleagues in the Cabinet are not courageous; they have no Army and they declared war against the mightiest military nation in the world.' And one night at Carlton Gardens after a particularly nerve-wracking day he cried, 'Did they remember when they went headlong into a war like this that they were without an army, and without any preparation to equip one?'[11]

He then received a cable from Charles W. Schwab, who had created the Bethlehem Steel Corporation, America's second largest, which had rolled the structural steel that made skyscrapers possible. Schwab's sympathies in neutral America were firmly with the Allies and, although Bethlehem in Pennsylvania was the chief centre of the pacifist Moravian Brethren, he now offered Kitchener to turn out quantities of rifles and millions of bullets. Kitchener replied with a request that he come to London urgently to settle contracts.

Schwab took passage on the liner *Olympic*, which, near the coast of Ireland, went to the aid of the dreadnought HMS *Audacious* which had struck a mine, and rescued the crew while passengers took photographs. As *Audacious* was the first capital ship to be lost, Churchill, backed by Kitchener, persuaded the Cabinet to keep the news secret for as long as possible. The *Olympic* was therefore held at anchor offshore for a week. Schwab alone was allowed to land at a small fishing village, the captain knowing him as a prominent American and accepting his plea that he must reach Kitchener. Schwab secured an ancient taxi that drove him at an exorbitant price the seventy-five miles to the ferry, where he found he had left his passport on the liner. The ferry captain scented a German spy and refused to break the rule: no passport, no passage. Schwab urged him to send a telegram to Kitchener. The captain laughed. After heated discussion he agreed to send a wire but placed Schwab under arrest; unless a War Office telegram met them at Liverpool, Schwab would be handed over to the police and sent to the Tower of London.

Kitchener replied to the wire and complimented the captain for breaking a rule intelligently. Schwab failed to hire a special train and had to take the express.

His interview with Kitchener was as brief as the journey had been long. Rifles and bullets were agreed. 'Can you make a million shells?' 'Yes!' 'How long will it take?' 'Ten months.' 'Can you make guns?' 'Yes.' 'What else can you make?'

Schwab told him briefly. Kitchener asked about prices and agreed to a war profit for Bethlehem Steel provided that Schwab contracted not to sell control of the corporation for five years. 'This is not going to be a short war', and Kitchener did not want some pro-German shipping the rifles and bullets, guns and shells to Germany. 'Have the papers drawn and I will sign them,' said Schwab.

He bowed himself out, crossed Whitehall and sold submarines to Winston.[12]

Unfortunately, the rifles were not delivered by April 1915 as promised. Broken promises abroad and in the British Isles dogged Kitchener and the Master-General of the Ordnance, von Donop, an efficient and patriotic gunner despite his name. Moreover, as Kitchener admitted, he had himself weakened the munitions industry by allowing skilled workers to enlist in the first weeks of the war. By the time the recruiting posters told them not to apply, many had escaped from mill and mine to the comparative freedom of the barrack square. Kitchener arranged later for skilled men to be released to essential production lines while remaining in the army, available if needed.

As the fighting intensified, the demand for munitions increased inexorably. Kitchener also made good the heavy losses of the Belgian army. Then, on a cold winter's morning, when both the fireplaces in the Chief's room were kept well stoked (for he hated cold and had not endured an

English winter for thirty years), the senior French-speaking colonel who served as liaison officer between the French and British high commands suddenly arrived at the War Office with an urgent plea from Joffre. Much of the industrial area of north-east France lay in German hands or was badly damaged. The French army was running dangerously short of munitions and equipment needed to beat back the next German offensive. Joffre begged Kitchener to supply all he could of a long list which the colonel brought, and asked for an answer within hours. Kitchener sent for his appropriate officials and for the head of the French technical mission in London, the Marquis de Chasseloup Laubat; they had already had long conversations and Laubat was impressed by 'his common sense, his will and his sincerity'.

Kitchener had the liaison colonel tell the marquis the facts, and explained that he could not meet all the needs but would do everything possible. Dropping other work, he 'studied the question on all sides', wrote the marquis, continuing:

and examined every kind of possible combination and arrangement. At the end of the afternoon of that very same day he was able to make up his mind as to what he could and could not do. Then took place a scene which I can never forget.

The day is falling and the large room is in semi-darkness. The Secretary of State for War dismisses everybody except the British colonel and myself; he has put on his large spectacles and is sitting down before his desk, where all the requisite papers lie in front of him; the British officer and myself stand motionless. In the deep silence one can only hear the faint sound produced by the papers which Kitchener's hands turn over. Then he orders me to sit down at the right-hand corner of his desk and carefully note what he has decided to do for the French: I obey. A long pause and a deep silence which nothing disturbs: the Secretary of State for War has ceased turning over his papers.

Kitchener then slowly dictates the ('alas, too short') list of the things he can give Joffre. Another pause and another deep silence.

Kitchener again tells me to write: I note the extraordinary and unprece-dented facilities and powers with which he entrusts me in order to render every possible help to the army of my people defending their native soil. Kitchener takes off his spectacles. A third pause and deep silence.

The Secretary of State for War leans back in his chair and remains motionless as if buried in his thoughts. Then suddenly in a deep and half-strangled voice, as if he were suffering agonies of pain, he slowly addresses the British officer with these following words and short sentences which still ring in my ears and between which were great silences, as if he were gasping for breath: 'Tell Joffre . . . tell my friend Joffre . . . that I am very sorry . . . so very sorry that I can do no more.'

As I have finished writing down what he dictated I turn round and gaze at him; and to my intense astonishment I see that Field Marshal Earl Kitchener actually has tears in his eyes, because he is 'so very sorry that he can do no more'.

He catches my look and, as if he was ashamed of himself and of what he seems to consider a weakness, he quickly puts back his spectacles.

From that moment my feelings towards him greatly changed: up to that time I had already admired his fine intellectual and moral qualities; but from that instant I also felt for him a deep affection, which, with a kind of instinct, Kitchener at once discovered and trusted, though I never said a word about it. And after that evening we shook hands when we parted in a different way from any we had done before.[13]

Kitchener's burdens of mobilizing industry, directing strategy, protecting the Empire and raising vast numbers of troops were made heavier by meetings of the Cabinet and the Cabinet's War Committee. He enjoyed gathering colleagues round him while he explained from a map the latest positions of the troops, but he was not happy at the Cabinet table. Expounding a case to those who did not understand war or the army, arguing with men equal in status but each with a departmental axe to grind was frustrating. Some thought of him as a lighthouse which flashed with brilliance now and then. His task was made more difficult by his curious eyes. Jack Pease, then President of the Board of Education, noted that in discussion the Cabinet never quite knew who Kitchener was addressing, or looking at: 'one eye seemed to be following the other and was apparently incapable of concentrating his attention on any particular person.' Often two colleagues would answer at the same time. Pease only discovered the reason when he happened to meet General Sir Lovick Friend, who as a young officer had helped Kitchener to rebuild Khartoum. Kitchener had mentioned to Friend that the cast in the left eye prevented the eyes working together, so that he was never able to compete with men or boys at any game. Pease was astonished to hear of this long-ago confession because Kitchener never admitted any defect whatever in public and 'to this self-confidence may be attributed the public's great trust in him'.[14]

Kitchener much disliked providing military information at Cabinet. 'My colleagues,' he explained to Asquith, 'tell military secrets to their wives, all except Lloyd George, who tells them to other people's wives', or more likely to his mistress and secretary, Frances Stevenson, who at least was discreet. Kitchener never realized that Asquith himself was regularly breaching the Official Secrets Act by providing a running commentary to Venetia Stanley. At one time, when Lloyd George was demanding detailed information about the supply of shells, Kitchener appealed to Asquith: 'Must I answer?' Asquith said that Cabinet members were entitled to know. 'Very well,' replied Kitchener, 'I will answer – next month.'

He was particularly irritated when Lloyd George lapsed into Welsh. Kitchener would suspect conspiracy against himself. One day he was being pressed by Lloyd George and the Financial Secretary, Edwin Montagu, younger son of the Jewish banker Lord Swaythling. These two retired to a corner for a whispered consultation. Kitchener said in a loud voice to his neighbour: 'Good heavens! That fellow George speaks Yiddish too!'[15] 'The little Welshman is peppery, but he means to win the War, which is what matters,' Kitchener would remark to his friends.[16] Arguments continued. Lloyd George complained that Nonconformists were insulted at recruiting offices. Kitchener objected to Lloyd George's desire that words of command be given in Welsh, although even in the Indian amy, with its confusion of tongues, the words of command were in English.

On 28 October 1914 the two had what Asquith described as 'a royal row' over Welsh recruiting and a Welsh Army Corps. Kitchener had told Asquith that no purely Welsh regiment was to be trusted: they were wild and insubordinate, an opinion that Lloyd George strongly rejected. 'They came to very high words, and it looked as if either or both of them would resign.' Kitchener indeed said he would, at which Asquith remarked mildly: 'that's not practical.' He thought Kitchener most to blame: 'he was clumsy and and noisy.'[17]

That afternoon General Rawlinson arrived in London on a duty visit and had a long talk with his old Chief. 'He had had a stormy Cabinet meeting, and was rather down on his luck in consequence, but I tried to cheer him up. He talked about resigning, and seemed very angry with some of his colleagues in the Government. What was the cause of the disagreement I did not discover.'[18] But in the evening Kitchener decided that Lloyd George was right in principle (though very wrong in the commanders he nominated for appointment). Two days later Lloyd George commented to Riddell:

> Look here! Kitchener is a big man. Nothing small and petty about him. Yesterday he sent for me. He said, 'I have thought over what you said. There is a good deal of justification for these complaints. Tell me exactly what you want.' I said, 'That, that, that, and that!' K wrote an appropriate order against each item. He really acted extraordinarily well.[19]

Lloyd George wrote to Kitchener: 'I feel I must thank you for the whole hearted and generous manner in which you met me this afternoon over the Welsh Army Corps and recognized the national susceptibilities of the Welsh people.'[20] And a few months later a new regiment joined the Household Brigade: the Welsh Guards.

Wrestling with the Cabinet depressed Kitchener. He would unburden himself to Ossy FitzGerald. Fitz was a friend of J. A. Spender, the Liberal editor, for whom Fitz was 'a man greatly beloved and respected', and when Fitz begged Spender to call on his way home from the *Westminster Gazette*, 'nearly always it was the same tale — some tangle between Kitchener and the politicians in which the latter seemed to have behaved very incomprehensibly, if not downright wickedly. Kitchener could not and never would understand these strange animals, the politicians. They were inquisitive and meddling, and wanted to know things which no soldier with any military instinct could be expected to communicate to twenty-three other people with whom he was not intimately acquainted.'

Having heard something of the other side, Spender advised that Kitchener should not evade and parry his colleagues' questions or give them figures and estimates which concealed the truth, even if technically accurate, but should state frankly that in wartime certain matters must not be revealed, even orally to the Cabinet. Privately, Spender thought

Kitchener rather an oriental politician himself, seeking to win his way by being equal or superior in political devices to the others round the table. Spender admired Kitchener's absolute trust in Asquith as 'a solid rock amid shifting sands'.

Spender never sought interviews with Kitchener, believing that his aloofness from the press was a valuable part of his public character; but one evening as 1914 drew to a close they had a talk, 'when he painted the situation in black colours and earnestly impressed on me that cheerfulness ought not to be encouraged. His parting words were, "Oh, how I wish I could go to bed to-night and not wake up till it's all over!" '[21]

Whatever his difficulties, nothing could alter the certainty that nearly a million men were under arms already, volunteers who were turning into professionals. Kitchener inspected formations when time allowed, even when many were still parading and exercising in plain clothes. By January 1915 enough divisions were fully equipped for Kitchener to order extensive reviews to encourage the French Minister of War, Alexandre Millerand, a leading lawyer with white hair and a black moustache. French Cabinet Ministers had been worried that as fox-hunting and pheasant-shooting continued in England the war was not being taken seriously.

Unfortunately, heavy snow fell the day before his visit. The snow turned to slush in lower ground but Kitchener and Millerand were delayed as they drove down from London to Epsom Downs, although the drive gave the opportunity for serious discussions (in French) which would continue during the inspections and conclude at a working dinner in Carlton Gardens with Asquith, Grey and Lloyd George. ('Will you see the dinner is good?' the Chief had said to Arthur.)[22]

By the time the two War Ministers had inspected many formations in the snow of Epsom their programme was running late and the road could not be taken at speed to Aldershot, where 40,000 troops were drawn up on Laffans Plain. Some had marched ten miles in bitter wintry weather and then had to wait more than an hour in the slush. 'At long last,' recalls Colonel Hugh Sinclair, 'a cortege of motor cars arrived. Lord Kitchener, M Millerand and their Staffs got out and started walking up the road in front of us, as we presented arms. They passed in earnest conversation and neither of them turned their heads in our direction! A chill ran through the ranks, colder than anything caused by the snow. To have come so far, in such discomfort, not even to be looked at, or our salute acknowledged, depressed the most enthusiastic, and made us feel exceedingly small.'[23] Further off another brigade waited. The great men alighted opposite one battalion and then drove off. A young officer wrote that night to his mother: 'It seems a rotten thing to say, but I think K behaved rather rottenly . . . They might at least have driven or ridden quickly along the whole length of the line.'[24]

A much happier inspection came on a sunny day in the following spring when Kitchener went to Salisbury Plain to review newly formed divisions. A retired 'dugout' general now commanding the artillery of one of the divisions watched with Kitchener as splendidly horsed batteries trotted past the saluting base in excellent order — former shop assistants, grooms and factory workers presenting a fine appearance after several months' training on the Plain. 'The Field Marshal, as pleased as a schoolboy, was delighted and as I stood alongside of him said, "We've done it, we've done it, they said we could make Infantry but could not make Artillery, and yet we have done it all ourselves, we have trained the men, made the guns and the harness, and bought the horses. We've done it!"'[25]

The war would be won, whatever disasters might lie ahead. As Haig wrote after all was over: 'Who can doubt now that but for this man and his work Germany would have been victorious?' And Ludendorff, who with Hindenburg nearly was victorious, had no doubts:

Lord Kitchener . . . created armies out of next to nothing, trained and equipped them. Through his genius alone England developed side by side with France into an opponent capable of meeting Germany on even terms, whereby the position on the front in France in 1915 was so seriously changed to Germany's disadvantage.[26]

The Field Marshal, 1910. Note the stars of six orders of knighthood
(the Garter still to come) and the Order of Merit

With General Joffre

Far left:
Sir John French
and Asquith

Left:
Sir William Robertson

LORD KITCHENER SAYS:-

'MEN, MATERIALS & MONEY ARE THE IMMEDIATE NECESSITIES. ......

DOES THE CALL OF DUTY FIND NO RESPONSE IN YOU UNTIL REINFORCED — LET US RATHER SAY SUPERSEDED — BY THE CALL OF COMPULSION?'

Lord Kitchener, Speaking at Guildhall, July 9th 1915

ENLIST TO-DAY.

Kitchener welcomes the wounded to Broome

Broome Park

The Nephews

Toby (Lieut-Commander
H.F.C. Kitchener, afterwards
Viscount Broome, Chevallier's son)

Hal (Captain H.H. Kitchener,
R.F.C., Walter's son)

In Gallipoli: Kitchener, with Birdwood, greets the French C-in-C

Kitchener greets Jimmy Watson, for many years his ADC

I believe it is arranged for me to go on Sunday — might I have a look at the fleet 'en passant' & see Jellicoe. I should not have more than about an hour

r 20 —

Writing his own 'death warrant'. The note pushed across
the Cabinet table

The last snapshot, annotated and signed by Jellicoe

Col. Fitzgerald. Jellicoe, Lord Kitchener. Capt Dyer.

Jellicoe

The last photo taken of "K of K", on board H.M.S. "Iron Duke" at Scapa Flow on 5th June 1916, about 1 hour before Lord Kitchener embarked on H.M.S. "Hampshire".

The Memorial Chapel of All Souls, St Paul's Cathedral

Edward Prince of Wales unveils the statue on Horse Guards Parade,
June 1926

PART FOUR

War on Two Fronts

1915–1916

19

DARDANELLES DILEMMA

'I DON'T KNOW what is to be done. This isn't war!' complained Kitchener in the last weeks of 1914.[1] The Western Front had fossilized into trench warfare. From Calais to the Swiss border the Germans and the Allies faced each other from elaborate networks of trenches which became more sophisticated and impregnable with each week, yet for the ordinary soldiers and officers were a world of mud, discomfort and danger. Bombardments and raids across no man's land inflicted daily tallies of death and wounds without any noticeable effect on the outcome of the war, while telegraph boys throughout the British Isles delivered the yellow envelopes which brought grief for wives or parents. To Kitchener, war was movement, or painstaking advance followed by fierce, decisive battle. He must find the answer to this strange stalemate.

On 20 December Sir John French crossed the Channel. Kitchener met him at Folkestone and they motored to Walmer Castle, which had been lent to Asquith by the Lord Warden of the Cinque Ports, for a meeting with the Prime Minister to be kept secret from the public. Asquith's daughter Violet was thrilled to see them. She wrote to her close friend Rupert Brooke, the poet, serving with one of her brothers in the naval division, that French and Kitchener 'furnished the sharpest contrast imaginable'. Looking no further than outward form and manner, she named Kitchener as 'the biggest ruffian' and French 'the smallest (in stature I mean) gentleman ever born'. She found French amazingly optimistic, 'much more than either Father or K'.[2]

French, whose recurrent optimism frequently disturbed Kitchener, thought they were now fighting old men and boys and that a sudden German collapse might end the war in the spring. Kitchener had no such illusions. Although he was sure that the war would be decided on the Western Front, he wanted to relieve the pressure by attacking elsewhere. His Cabinet colleagues had several suggestions, but many observers outside the Cabinet, such as Lord Milner, felt that apart from Kitchener none of the men at the head of affairs was 'equal to the job. That is one depressing reflection.'[3]

Churchill favoured a landing on the German island of Borkum off the coast of Holland, and from there an invasion of Schleswig-Holstein. He and French also wanted divisions to land at Dunkirk and advance up the coast, helped by the navy, to retake Ostend and Zeebrugge before the Germans could turn them into submarine bases. Kitchener rejected this scheme because his New Armies were not ready and Sir John would require many more guns than were available. Churchill's interference in military matters annoyed Kitchener: Asquith had to persuade him not to send off a sarcastic letter to Churchill suggesting he take over the War Office and let Jacky Fisher become First Lord of the Admiralty. The colourful Lord Fisher, creator of the dreadnoughts, had returned to be First Sea Lord after public opinion had unjustly hounded Prince Louis of Battenberg from office.[4]

Lloyd George tried his hand at strategy by suggesting bold moves in the Balkans, either by making a base at Salonika, if neutral Greece permitted, or by landing on the Dalmatian coast of the Adriatic, which would mean engineering a second line along the railway through the mountains and enlarging tunnels before enough troops could link up with the Serbs. Kitchener himself preferred an attack on the Turks, who had sided with Germany.

When he had concentrated a sufficient force in Egypt he wanted to land at Alexandretta on the Gulf of Iskenderun in the eastern Mediterranean, where the Anatolian coast turns south to meet the Syrian. An allied invasion would soon cut the railways to Baghdad and Palestine and paralyse the Ottoman Empire, since any Turkish counterattack would be frustrated by unfinished tunnels through the mountains. HMS *Doris* had carried out a raid on Alexandretta in which the Turkish garrison had obligingly blown up their guns with explosives given by

Doris, thus spreading an unfortunate impression that the Turks were easy to beat. Kitchener's instinct had recognized where sea power allowed a blow to be struck with the least effort and deadliest effect. The local population was largely Christian Armenian and would have risen against their Turkish oppressors to help the invaders. As General Sir Gerald Ellison, then a senior staff officer, wrote after the war: 'Had the Alexandretta scheme been adhered to and carried through with the whole might of India, Australia, and New Zealand behind it, together with moderate assistance from home, Turkish resistance would almost certainly have collapsed before the end of 1915,'[5] without the costly campaigns of Mesopotamia and the Dardanelles.

Churchill had already suggested a joint naval and military attack up the Dardanelles towards Constantinople when discussing the defence of Egypt, but Kitchener was too short of troops for a vast enterprise. Then, on 2 January 1915, the Foreign Office received an appeal from the Grand Duke Nicholas, the Russian Commander-in-Chief in the Caucasus, for a demonstration to relieve pressure on his troops in eastern Anatolia and to stop the Turks moving reinforcements up the Dardanelles to the Black Sea. On 13 January 1915 the Cabinet's recently formed War Committee met in the Cabinet Room at noon to discuss the twin questions of the stalemate in the West and the Grand Duke in the East, although news had since come of his winning a great victory.

Asquith placed French on his left and Balfour, who had been invited to represent the Unionist Opposition when the Committee was formed, on his right. Beyond French sat Kitchener; Asquith noted with approval that the two Field Marshals were 'polite and almost mealy-mouthed to each other' when putting forward their opposing views on the New Armies. French urged that these should be mingled with the old units; Kitchener that this would dissipate their esprit de corps. They should fight as they trained, in their own divisions. The subject was postponed.

Beyond Kitchener sat Fisher with Winston next to him and a former First Sea Lord, Sir Arthur Wilson, on Winston's left. Crewe (India), Grey and Lloyd George completed the table except for the secretary, Colonel Maurice Hankey. When they adjourned for lunch at 2 p.m. the various options had been discussed intensely without conclusion, except that French deplored any transfer of troops from the Western Front. He believed the war could be won that year by a massive offensive.

[427]

The coal fire had been well stoked when they returned. The winter afternoon wore on, the blinds were drawn, the air was heavy. They did not smoke during meetings of the Cabinet or War Committee but several probably longed for their cigars as they concentrated on the prolonged discussion. The table was littered with papers and discarded notes.

Suddenly Winston Churchill announced that he had received a telegram from Admiral Carden of the Mediterranean Fleet proposing a naval attack on the Dardanelles. Carden had worked out that after a preliminary bombardment of the forts at the entrance, the navy could clear the minefields and sail through the Dardanelles, outgunning the Turkish batteries. 'The whole atmosphere changed,' noted Colonel Hankey. 'Fatigue was forgotten', as the Committee turned in imagination from the dreary slogging match of the Western Front to a vision of the Royal Navy led by *Queen Elizabeth*, the newest battleship, steaming up to Constantinople, destroying the two German cruisers lurking there, and precipitating a coup d'état in the Allies' favour.

Churchill, seconded by Balfour, swayed the Committee. Since no troops were required, Kitchener agreed. But Fisher remained ominously silent.[6]

A few days before this dramatic meeting Kitchener had suffered an annoying pinprick from his old antagonist Lord Curzon, who attacked him from the Opposition benches of the House of Lords.

George Nathaniel (Earl Curzon of Keddleston since 1911) was deputizing for Lord Lansdowne, the Opposition leader, when Kitchener read a statement to the House. Curzon complained to Tory peers privately that Kitchener read out platitudes that the Liberal press called an inspired oration, and stayed for only one speech, Curzon's, into which he injected an occasional curt affirmative or negative. Then he marched out, leaving the debate to colleagues who affected to know nothing or hid behind Kitchener's authority. Curzon's speech lasted an hour. He spoke of the problems of an Opposition who gave unstinting support without being informed of what was happening, who stayed silent 'where speech was tempting and criticism would have been easy'. Lord Sandhurst, the genial and popular Lord Chamberlain, noted in his diary that Curzon 'was thoroughly out of sympathy with his audience and was very coldly supported, hardly a cheer'. Two weeks later Sandhurst heard a story that 'K was furious with Curzon's speech on January 6, and told George

Arthur, his Private Secretary, to go to the Carlton and stick up that the Kaiser had given him the Iron Cross.'[7]

It may have been Lord Sandhurst who at this time, as Lord Chamberlain, instigated a gracious act of the King towards Kitchener.

Lady Wantage's six-month loan of Carlton Gardens was about to end, although she was not pressing for its immediate return in mid-January. Kitchener and his personal secretaries had been too busy to house-hunt and would soon be homeless. The Comptroller of the Lord Chamberlain's Office, Douglas Dawson, wrote to the Keeper of the Privy Purse, 'Fritz' Ponsonby, suggesting that the north-west part of St James's Palace, known as York House, should be lent to Kitchener. York House had been the residence of the King and Queen as Duke and Duchess of York from their marriage in 1893 until they became Prince and Princess of Wales. It had been used since August 1914 by the Prince of Wales's National Fund for the Relief of the Poor. The Lord Chamberlain's office nearby would prefer the fund's workers to go elsewhere.

Ponsonby agreed that the fund should go but raised objections to offering York House to Kitchener, especially that it would create a precedent – his successor would expect to have it. Dawson disagreed. These were abnormal times and 'K is an abnormal Minister of War. At the moment of the greatest crisis the British Empire has ever faced this man steps into the breach, gives up his job in Egypt *and his official residence*, and takes the helm at the W.O. to see us through the trouble and *to drop it immediately the trouble is over.*'

Dawson pointed out that Kitchener 'hates and despises politicians of all creeds' and was apart from party. The offer could never be construed as a precedent. Kitchener knew nothing of the proposal, and as to his having enough salary to rent somewhere, 'the money aspect never entered my head. My only thought in this matter was that this man at such a crisis is worthy of honour, and that a gracious offer by the King of this house under the circumstances would not only be appreciated by K but by everyone who knew of it.'[8]

Lord Stamfordham, the King's Private Secretary, agreed that the offer would be a recognition of what Kitchener had done and was doing and enable him to live close to his work and to Buckingham Palace; 'it would give H.M. another opportunity of rendering personal help in this time of war and would I expect be generally appreciated as an act of grace and favour to an *individual*.' If Kitchener died or the war ended and he retired (probably to be the next Viceroy) his successor would have no possible claim. The King's offer would be a gracious and popular act and need create no precedent, 'for the conditions will, please God! never arise again'.[9]

Kitchener accepted, sight unseen, and with George Arthur and Ossy FitzGerald moved into York House during February, leaving all details to Arthur, not even choosing his bedroom or knowing which servants were provided by the Lord Chamberlain's department and which hired by Arthur. The house was a little dark after the delights of Carlton Gardens, the main rooms facing north up St James's Street. The pictures were dull and the furniture uninteresting; when French statesmen were coming to dinner Arthur borrowed some fine pieces for the hall. The King and Queen soon came to tea and enjoyed being taken by Kitchener round the rooms they knew so well.[10]

On 28 January the War Council again discussed the Dardanelles. Kitchener had learned from FitzGerald that Lord Fisher (they were close friends) was unhappy at attempting to force the straits and take the Gallipoli peninsula by naval power alone. Kitchener did not know that Fisher had written letters of resignation to Asquith and Churchill which they refused to accept, or that the three had conferred in the Prime Minister's study immediately before the War Council, when Fisher had apparently agreed to withdraw his resignation and accept the plan. But as the Council began to discuss it, Fisher left his chair. Kitchener was immediately alert, while the others perhaps assumed that the First Sea Lord wanted the lavatory. Kitchener drew him towards a window and asked his intentions. Fisher replied that he was leaving the meeting and proposed to resign. In a hurried, whispered consultation, Kitchener pointed out that Fisher was the only dissentient and must abide by the Prime Minister's decision. 'Look at me where I am – I am not going. You ought to stick to the thing.' Eventually, Fisher resumed his seat.[11] No one asked him why he was unhappy.

Kitchener stressed that the naval operation was vital; its success would be equal to a successful campaign by the New Armies: if a failure, it could be broken off. Later that day the Council and its sub-committee discussed how to help Serbia, likely to be attacked by strong Austro-Hungarian forces. Kitchener agreed that once sufficient troops were available they should go to Salonika in Greece, then a cooperative neutral, and might persuade both Greece and Bulgaria to join the Allies as well as strengthening the Serbs; but he insisted that to send too few would be disastrous and that he had none to spare, an assertion that Churchill never fully accepted.

Henry Rawlinson came over from France next day (to discuss experiments in firepower) and Kitchener opened his heart to his old friend. 'Lord K sent for me,' Rawly wrote on 31 January, 'and I had a long and intimate talk with him. He unfolded to me his thoughts and ideas as to the future conduct of the war.' These were much too confidential for a diary, but Rawly was in 'full concurrence with many of the proposals which he has in view. These cannot mature for six weeks or two months, at least, and must largely depend upon what the enemy may do in the meantime. The one thing certain is that, before considering these projects, we must see that the line in France and Flanders is absolutely secure against German attack. Upon this we are agreed.' Kitchener was well aware that the Germans might withdraw troops from the Russian Front to mount powerful offensives against the French or British, such as those which were nearly victorious at Verdun later and against the British 5th Army in March 1918. In 1915 the Allies might have been still too weak in men and ammunition to withstand them.

> Lord K was most communicative . . . I have never seen him in better health and spirits; but he gets very tired in the evening after a hard day's work. He has had immense difficulties to contend with, which have not been made easier by the leader of the Expeditionary Force; but he resents nothing, has kept his temper under the most trying conditions, and is too broad-minded to allow these petty differences to make any alteration in his attitude towards those who have given him every provocation.[12]

While Rawlinson listened to Kitchener in London, the Turks were emerging from the Sinai Desert to attack the Suez Canal and invade Egypt. During three days in early February they were thrown back from the canal with heavy loss, confirming Kitchener's unfortunate belief that Turkish troops were easy to beat. Their defeat removed the threat to Egypt and released for operations elsewhere the fine troops in training there – the

Australian and New Zealand Army Corps, the Anzacs. As a direct result of Kitchener's advisory visit in 1910, 30,000 young men of splendid physique, courage and independence had sailed to the war zone.

By an inspired choice Kitchener had asked for Birdwood, now Adjutant-General in India, to command them. Beauchamp Duff released him but did not choose an adequate successor, undermining an essential element of the Kitchener reforms: that in wartime the Commander-in-Chief of India should be in the field, appointing a senior general to advise the Viceroy at Simla or Calcutta. Duff stayed at the Viceroy's side when the difficulties began in Mesopotamia and thus contributed to disaster.

Fisher withdrew his objections to the Dardanelles plan and went in 'the whole hog, *totus porcus*'. Knowing this, Kitchener had an uncharacteristic fit of wishful thinking. On 16 February he sent for one of his War Office Intelligence staff, Captain Wyndham Deedes, who knew the Dardanelles. Deedes, younger son of a landowner in Kent, had an unusual background. A spiritually minded bachelor, he had been seconded to the Turkish police and after commanding them throughout Tripolitania until it was ceded to Italy he had been stationed at Smyrna, where he had done much to relieve refugees. The Dardanelles and Gallipoli were not far away. Kitchener asked Deedes whether the navy could take the Gallipoli peninsula without calling on the army. Deedes replied that the operation was fundamentally unsound. He began to explain, but Kitchener interrupted him angrily, told him he did not know what he was talking about and ended the interview. Nine months later, at the Dardanelles, Kitchener sought him out from among the staff officers and apologized.[13]

The navy bombarded and destroyed the outer forts of the Dardanelles from positions well out to sea, beyond the range of Turkish guns. Churchill immediately issued a triumphant communiqué which caused a sensation in Constantinople and throughout the East. Kitchener was aghast. Had Churchill kept quiet, the Turks would have been left guessing. Instead, the publicity had committed the Allies; there could be no going back. If the fleet could not get through the straits unaided, the army would have to 'see the business through', as Kitchener told the War Council. A defeat in the Orient would be very serious.

Kitchener was being slowly sucked towards committing the army to an operation that might become a drain on its resources rather than a speedy coup of strategic importance. Britain had only two divisions left of the old regular army, the 28th and 29th, formed of battalions that had been serving in India and had been recalled. Churchill wanted the 29th Division of 19,000 men to be sent at once to the Mediterranean to be on call. Kitchener had agreed at first, but Russian defeats and the importunities of Sir John French decided him to keep it as a reserve for the Western Front. Churchill put his case strongly but claimed afterwards that he was powerless against the overwhelming presence of Kitchener. He said in his evidence to the Dardanelles Commission after Kitchener's death, with some exaggeration because he was shifting the blame:

> Scarcely anyone ever ventured to argue with him in Council. Respect for the man, sympathy for him in his immense labours, confidence in his professional judgment, and the belief that he had plans deeper and wider than any we could see, silenced misgivings and disputes, whether in the Council or at the War Office. All-powerful, imperturbable, reserved, he dominated absolutely our counsels at this time.[14]

If the fully trained 29th was not available, Birdwood's Anzacs, though still training, were at hand and eager. Kitchener chose Birdwood to command the whole expedition, not only his 30,000 Anzacs but the Naval Division (11,000) and the 19,000 promised by France. He ordered him to take staff to the Dodecanese Islands, which the neutral Greeks had placed at the Allies' disposal as base and harbour, and personally reconnoitre the Dardanelles on a naval ship in case landings proved necessary. Kitchener intended the troops for operations after the navy had forced the straits and caused the fall of Constantinople.

Birdwood was overjoyed. Steaming across the Mediterranean in HMS *Minerva*, he wrote in pencil on 3 March:

> My dear old Chief, I cannot tell you how deeply grateful and touched I do feel by the confidence you have placed in me in giving me this command. I am really almost overwhelmed in my feelings as of course I well realize that no one but you would ever have done such a thing with so many senior men to be provided for. I know you must have found it difficult to ride out their claims. I can only promise in return that I am [? ready] and will do my very best to work for success . . .[15]

[433]

Before Kitchener received Birdie's letter he had been obliged to place a full general in command because the Russians promised a force to join in (a promise never fulfilled) and the 29th Division would be sent after all. He chose Sir Ian Hamilton. Birdwood's command would be limited to the Anzacs. Birdwood accepted the disappointment gallantly. On return to Egypt, however, he reported his conviction that the navy could not get through alone, and suggested the best landing places for supporting troops; but under Hamilton his detailed staff work went to waste. And at the War Office the Director of Military Operations did not dig out the pre-war reports of the British Military Attaché at Constantinople, who had studied the ground, to place them before Kitchener. In contrast to the exhaustive and lengthy preparations for the Normandy landings a quarter of a century later, the Dardanelles operation was planned in a hurry. The commission that examined its failure, after Kitchener's death, blamed him for lack of consultation, but his surviving Personal Secretary rejected this and gathered comments to the contrary, that he consulted all the time. Yet he seldom held planning sessions, as distinct from taking advice from individual experts.

Kitchener summoned Hamilton on 12 March. They had been meeting almost daily and Kitchener had not mentioned the Dardanelles. When Johnny Hamilton opened the door and walked up to the desk, Kitchener went on writing 'like a graven image'. Then he looked up and said in a matter-of-fact tone: 'We are sending a military force to support the fleet now at the Dardanelles and you are to have command.' He resumed writing. At last he looked up and said, ' Well?'

Hamilton, accepting gratefully, said: 'We have done this sort of thing before, Lord K . . .' He promised to do his best and started to ask questions. 'K frowned; shrugged his shoulders; I thought he was going to be impatient.' His answers were curt at first, but soon Hamilton could hardly get in a word.

Kitchener may have deliberately deflated Hamilton, whom he knew to be cocky, lest he take on a hazardous operation with too much self-confidence, but it was Hamilton who suggested changing the name from 'Constantinople Expeditionary Force' as too optimistic to 'Dardanelles Expeditionary Force'. When he called next day to say goodbye, Kitchener said that he hoped Hamilton would not have to land at all, but, if he did, the powerful fleet at his back would be a decisive factor in choosing the place to land. Kitchener had chosen Hamilton's chief of staff, Walter Braithwaite. Braithwaite sensibly suggested that an efficient air force was essential. Kitchener, according to Hamilton, 'turned on him with flashing spectacles and rent him with the words, "*Not one!*"'[16]

Lord Fisher still hoped that the Expeditionary Force would be used at Alexandretta, Kitchener's own first choice. The day before Hamilton was appointed, Fisher wrote in his peculiar style to Kitchener: '"*What has been won by the sword will be given up by the pen*"!

'We must put up a stiff fight for Alexandretta. The politicians both sides (Balfour the worst!) want to pander to the French!

'But as you rightly said, if the French are properly approached and made to realize *what we have done for them!*' they would, he wrote, let the British occupy Syria, traditionally a French sphere of interest. Fisher coveted Alexandretta as the harbour for a canal he wanted across to the Persian Gulf to bring oil for the navy's new oil-burners.[17]

Events drew the Force instead to Gallipoli. On 18 March the navy began its operation to force the Dardanelles. Admiral Carden had collapsed and been replaced by De Robeck, who led the mighty armada into the narrows. At first all went well, but a French battleship blew up and was lost with almost all hands. Other casualties caused De Robeck to waver and withdraw. The Turks believed that the fleet would return next day and reach the Sea of Marmara. But the fleet did not return. On 19 March Hamilton told Kitchener that he doubted the fleet could carry on and that 'the soldiers would have to do the trick'; and next day, reluctantly, that it would have to be 'a deliberate and progressive military operation'.

Kitchener replied: 'You know my views.' The Dardanelles must be forced, and if large military operations were necessary to clear the way 'they must be carried through'. Hamilton regarded this as a 'peremptory instruction . . . to take the Peninsula'.[18]

20

CONSPIRACY

A<small>T A CABINET</small> on 4 March 1915 Kitchener proposed legislation to increase the labour force for munitions. He wanted 32,000 men from factories which were not contributing to war supplies to be put to work on shells. He was backed by Lloyd George and, although one or two Ministers preferred voluntary effort, the Cabinet decided that a scheme should be drafted.

A week later Sir John French launched a surprise attack from the British trenches which captured the ruined village of Neuve Chapelle but failed to break through beyond the German front lines. He had been very secretive about his plans and explained them only at the last minute by sending his Private Secretary, Brinsley FitzGerald (a stockbroker in civil life). War Office staff were shocked that no senior staff officer had come. Arthur asked a little nervously whether Kitchener wanted a sharp answer to the conscious or unconscious slight. 'Oh no,' he chuckled, 'I might wire French, "Many thanks for sending FitzGerald but just now I have no money to invest."'[1]

Neuve Chapelle was costly in lives on both sides but also in ammunition. Rawlinson wrote that one division's failure to follow up the initial surprise had lost them total victory; together with poor communications between commanders. French blamed shortage of shells, although more ammunition was spent in the three-day battle than in the whole Boer War. Kitchener told French that he had wasted ammunition, using twice the number of shells he had advised the War Office that he would need.

Nearly 8,000 men were killed, wounded or missing, 'but it isn't the men I mind,' Kitchener remarked according to Lloyd George, and speaking pragmatically rather than callously. 'I can replace the men at once, but I can't replace the shells so easily.'[2] Kitchener was never callous in his heart about the human cost; ten months later, on the night when he feared many were dying in the evacuation of Gallipoli, he could not sleep for agonizing. But in strategic discussions he must be pragmatic. He could replace the men because in 'Kitchener's armies' all ranks were raring to go. Hunter wrote to him on 16 March: 'I do wish you could come down for an hour or two, just come on to the Ranges and pat one or two of them on the back by saying "It won't be long" or "Your chance will come soon." It would spread like wildfire and keep them perfectly happy.'[3]

'More shells' became the great cry of the spring of 1915, at home and in the trenches. Arthur Lee, of Chequers, the gunner MP whom Kitchener had used on various missions, saw the slaughter at Neuve Chapelle and rushed back 'to try to impress upon Kitchener the tragic consequences of hurling men's bodies against uncut wire entanglements and batteries of machine guns. He received this very ill and, almost before I could complete my story, burst out into a tirade against what he called the "preposterous waste of ammunition" which had been indulged in before and during the battle and the hopelessness of keeping the Army supplied with munitions if they were to be "squandered in such reckless fashion".' When Lee refuse to name the artillery general responsible, 'he flared up again. "Do you mean to tell me it has come to this; that the British soldier cannot be relied upon to advance and attack with the bayonet unless the enemy has first been battered into a state of insensibility?"'[4]

Lee sought out Lloyd George as the only Minister who could stand up to Kitchener. Lloyd George flared up, too, saying he would never rest content until they had 'enough shells to rain on the enemy for forty days and forty nights and all the machine guns they can use as well' – the attitude which was to lure 19,000 men to their deaths on the first day of the Somme.

Lloyd George's enthusiasm was somewhat ironic since his pre-war economies had prevented a greater stock being ready in 1914; whereas Kitchener had placed orders in the first few months of the war which were based on serving an army of over one million men in the field, using 2,500 firms in Britain and Ireland. He had, however, contributed to the shortage because his call, 'Your country needs you', did not exclude munitions workers. Thousands joined up, weakening the factories: contracts were not fulfilled on time. The trade unions were retaining pre-war labour restrictions and allowing strikes, as Kitchener pointed out in one of his rare speeches to the House of Lords (he had rehearsed the speech to both Asquith and Lloyd George, declaiming in a parade-ground voice, yet rather mumbling when he read it from his place in the House).[5]

Lloyd George met trade union leaders and put them in a better mind. He was also aware that absenteeism caused by drunkenness was seriously affecting output. He favoured prohibition, but the Cabinet baulked at such an unpopular move. Licensing laws were passed which lasted the rest of the century. Lloyd George persuaded the King to take the pledge for himself and his Household for the duration of the war, hoping that his example would be widely followed by rich and poor, especially munitions workers. Kitchener, in duty bound, followed the King's lead, rather to the detriment of his temper, according to Violet Asquith.[6] He had always been moderate and had kept a dry mess during the River War, but like the King he missed his glass of wine at meals: he reduced his table to seltzer water and ginger ale and adhered to his pledge strictly, though becoming aware that Lloyd George did not. Churchill was honest and refused the pledge.

Kitchener was also aware that Lloyd George had a muddled view of the complexities of munitions manufacture, especially of high explosive, which trench warfare demanded in large quantities. Yet ordnance factories could not prepare the tooling for high-explosive shells without creating a shortage of shells for shrapnel. Kitchener and his Master General of the Ordnance, von Donop, had worked hard and were only too aware of not producing enough, but the policy of rush and hustle which Lloyd George urged on the War Office and Cabinet could be disastrous. Von Donop had rejected a fast-track manufacture of guns by the French and was not surprised that many of their guns blew up when fired.

Asquith tried various compromises to satisfy both Lloyd George and Kitchener, who agreed to a Munitions Committee under Lloyd George. This soon led to a dramatic confrontation in Cabinet. Kitchener arrived very obviously perturbed. He at once abused Lloyd George for compromising the safety of soldiers by disclosing to his Munitions Committee the figures of the armies in the field or at home which Kitchener had given to the Cabinet in strict confidence. If this went on he would resign. Lloyd George retorted that without these figures the committee could not plan. The Cabinet quickly lapsed into a general quarrel, Winston supporting Lloyd George and being aggressive and tactless, while the Foreign Secretary championed Kitchener, and the Home Secretary gloated over the imminent shipwreck of the Munitions Committee, which he hated. As tempers rose, Asquith noted that Lloyd George let slip 'some most injurious and wounding innuendos which K will be more than human to forget'.[7] Then came an incident that was still vivid to Winston Churchill twenty-five years later when he was again First Lord of the Admiralty early in the Second World War and was reminiscing about Kitchener to fellow members of the dining club Grillions. (Winston's memory confused the subject of the dispute with that of the previous October over the Welsh division.) Lord Crawford recorded Churchill's story in his diary: Kitchener, said Churchill:

realised that he was failing to make out his case – he glared angrily to one side and the other; his fiery bloodshot eye made no impression on Lloyd George who was really zealous in his cause. Suddenly Kitchener got up, walked behind Asquith's chair towards the door and the Cabinet was horrified to realise that he was about to retire – from the room, from the government, and that a terrible crisis was impending. Kitchener stalked the last few paces to the door, slowly, sombrely, until to his surprise and everybody else's, Jack Pease, whom nobody had noticed, was in front of him, and stood with the folding doors behind him, with his arms widely extended to either side ('with a sickly grinning grin on his face' as Churchill added). Kitchener found his exit barred. 'You can't leave the cabinet room,' said Pease two or three times. 'You can't leave the cabinet room,' and then Kitchener with the slow subconscious movements of the somnambulist, moved silently back to his seat.[8]

Asquith wrote to Venetia Stanley that night that Kitchener came out of it best, clumsy and tactless in expression as he often was. The give and take of Cabinet discussion and comradeship was unnatural to one who all his life was used to give or take orders, Asquith commented, but 'He was really moved to-day, though I am sure he would not have persisted in resignation, and showed in the end a largeness of mind and temper which I greatly admire.'

Next morning, Saturday, Asquith went down to Walmer Castle and at teatime Kitchener arrived unexpectedly, having motored over from Broome. 'He spoke quite nicely and quietly about the incidents of the last Cabinet',[9] and back in London the next week he asked Lloyd George to call, was 'most pleasant', and they found a compromise.

At Walmer Kitchener told Asquith about the passage of troops towards the Dardanelles and referred to a meeting with Sir John French three days earlier. Asquith was going to Newcastle to address munitions workers, and Kitchener had already written him a note, that French 'told me I could let you know that with the present supply of ammunitions he will have as much as his troops will be able to use on the next push'.[10] At Walmer Kitchener said he was not only supplying their own troops but giving explosive (TNT) to the French.

When Asquith made his speech at Newcastle he expanded Kitchener's assurance about 'the next push' to declaim that no army had ever entered upon or been maintained during a campaign with better or more adequate equipment and that there was not a word of truth in the statement that troops were being crippled or hampered 'by our failure to provide the necessary ammunition'. The speech was seized upon by the press as an untruthful boast: soldiers on leave had spread wide the knowledge that shells were in short supply .

Two days after the Newcastle speech the Germans fired poison gas shells into the British trenches, having noticed that the Hague Convention only referred to gas bombs dropped from the air. The poison gas caused grievous loss. When Kitchener received President Wilson's representative, Colonel House, he 'spoke with much bitterness concerning the German mode of warfare, and said no one could have made him believe in advance that they would have struck below the belt in the way in which they have. He thought it was imperative that the Allies should use asphyxiating gases in order to hold their own.' He also told House that if America came in it would shorten the war enormously 'and save an infinite number of lives on both sides'.[11]

Far away in the Dardanelles, Hamilton and Birdwood landed their first troops on the Gallipoli beaches, supported by the navy. The Turks and their German advisers were ready. At first Kitchener was buoyed by the news and sure of a breakthrough. But despite much gallantry the British,

Anzacs and French failed to win the heights and soon were in a stalemate on the beaches and narrow areas below the hills, always under fire. By 8 May the British and Anzacs had incurred nearly 20,000 casualties. Then, on the evening of 12 May, Lord Fisher told Kitchener that he was withdrawing the *Queen Elizabeth*, the most powerful ship afloat. Kitchener went across to the Admiralty. He felt betrayed, since he had committed the army to help the navy force the Dardanelles. Fisher said he would resign if the *Queen Elizabeth* were left there. Kitchener got up from the table and left. Early next morning he summoned his Director of Operations, General Callwell, told him of his objections 'and that he was to accompany him to a meeting at the Admiralty . . . "They've rammed that ship down my throat," said he in effect. "Churchill told me in the first place that she would knock all the Dardanelles batteries into smithereens, firing from goodness knows where. He afterwards told me that she would make every' thing all right for the troops as they landed, and after they landed. And now, without 'with your leave or by your leave' old Fisher says he won't let her stop out there." '[12] The Chief seemed resentful at the way in which he had been treated, but when Callwell advised, probably wrongly, that the great ship might make little difference Kitchener accepted Fisher's decision without another scene.

He sent Hamilton reinforcements but would have withdrawn the entire expedition were it not that British prestige would be seriously damaged in Egypt and the Muslim world and throughout India.

On 14 May *The Times* printed a strong attack on the War Office for the shortage of shells. An assault on Aubers Ridge had failed. According to *The Times'* military correspondent, 'the want of an unlimited supply of high explosive was a fatal bar to our success.' The anonymous military correspondent was Colonel Repington, Kitchener's long-ago supporter in the Indian controversy but now allied to Sir John French, his very old friend. When Kitchener heard that Repington was writing from French's headquarters, despite the ban on correspondents, he reproached Sir John mildly, only to receive answer that Repington was there in a private capacity. Kitchener soon became aware that Sir John had encouraged or even inspired Repington's attack.

Behind Repington was Lord Northcliffe, the owner of *The Times* and the *Daily Mail*, who, as Alfred Harmsworth, had been the founder of the penny press. Already inflated with the self-importance that would lead to megalomania and premature death, he was so incensed by Kitchener's ban on correspondents going to the front that an interview at the War Office ended with Kitchener ringing for an aide to eject him. Northcliffe's hatred increased when his nephew, Lucas King, was killed in action: 'Kitchener murdered him!'

While Northcliffe stoked 'the Shells Scandal' by editorials, a separate crisis brewed. The morning after *The Times* article, Lord Fisher deserted (as Asquith saw it) the Admiralty, saying he could no longer work with Churchill, whom he blamed for the Dardanelles. Since Fisher was the darling of the Tories and they loathed Churchill, not least because he had once been one of them, Asquith realized that his Liberal government was in danger. He did not have a majority over all other parties, and the choice lay between a breakdown of the wartime political truce, followed by defeat, or a coalition. On 17 May he asked Bonar Law, the Unionist leader, to call on him.

Throughout the manoeuvrings and the flurries of the next week, so much described and analysed in histories, memoirs and biographies, Kitchener stood almost aloof, although not impassive. On the morning of 19 May he asked Lord Esher, an invaluable mediator, counsellor and encourager, to call at the War Office. He explained his anxiety that Lloyd George wanted the War Office. Esher made inquiries and that evening wrote from 2 Tilney Street (the house where he had first heard Kitchener's name from Gordon nearly forty years before):

> My dear Lord K, there *is* something, from what Harcourt told me just now, in the rumours about Lloyd George.
>
> It seems that the Harmsworth Press plot is to get him to the WO if they cannot get him to 10 Downing Street.
>
> It seems to me incredible but there may be something underlying the press reports.
>
> I hope that under *no* circumstances you would relinquish the Secretaryship of State . . . The essence of the only conditions under which we *may* (by no means certain!) possibly win this war, is that the reins should be firmly held in one hand.

Kitchener underlined *one* as he read.[13]

Lloyd George sent Asquith a letter claiming that Kitchener had lied about munitions, and describing how high-explosive shells were made, but his facts were wrong on both subjects.

The King, to protect Kitchener, suggested to Asquith, through Lord Stamfordham, that the responsibility for munitions should be separated from the War Office, an idea already in Asquith's mind.

Kitchener became certain of French's disloyalty and intriguing, but since Asquith was not minded to relieve him of the command, Kitchener stilled the agitation for French's removal and sent Esher to France to bring him to a better mind. Esher wrote back to Ossy FitzGerald that 'the little man is so fashed by troubles that have been brought upon him by his infernal friends, that he is trying to get the whole episode off his mind.'[14] Esher made suggestions for better relations. He added to FitzGerald: 'Lord K's dignity and self-restraint have been wonderful.'

French had realized almost too late that high-explosive shells were now needed more than shrapnel and should have come over to place the facts before Asquith and Kitchener. As Lord Birkenhead (F. E. Smith) wrote later, 'If he realized them imperfectly and tardily (as he certainly did) how could a more complete, or an earlier, realization be expected from Lord Kitchener? Nothing in Lord Kitchener's career was greater than the serene and noble composure with which he endured a Press campaign against himself, instigated by his subordinate, and incredibly wounding to his dignity.'[15] Kitchener said he was ready to black French's boots if it would help win the war.

Northcliffe's *Daily Mail* now made an unrestrained attack in the issue of 21 May headlined THE SHELL SCANDAL: LORD KITCHENER'S TRAGIC BLUNDER. The article blamed him for the shell shortage and urged his dismissal. The article backfired. It produced a massive surge of public support for Kitchener. Copies of *The Times* and the *Daily Mail* were ceremonially burned on the steps of the Stock Exchange. Several London clubs refused to carry the *Mail*, and its circulation fell dramatically. A deputation of senior officers called on Kitchener at the War Office to beg to be allowed to publish a refutation (serving officers were not permitted to write to the press without permission). Kitchener thanked them but refused their offer.

From the Western Front Rawlinson wrote to FitzGerald on 24 May:

This attack on K is perfectly monstrous, and has raised us out here to a pitch of fury. It is a diabolical plot, the ins and outs of which you probably know much better than I do; but what I like least about it is that it should come on top of Repington's visit out here, and his article on the H.E. shell.

The true cause of our failures is that our tactics have been faulty, and that we have misconceived the strength and resisting power of the enemy. To turn round and say that the casualties have been due to the want of H.E. shells for the 18-pounders is a perversion of the truth. Feeling out here is one of intense disgust at the initiation of a Press attack when all should be working in combination against the enemy.[16]

Meanwhile, the Cabinet crisis had reached its climax. Asquith cunningly ensured that instead of a true coalition, as in 1940, the chief offices remained with Liberals except for the Admiralty, where Balfour replaced Churchill, who remained in the Cabinet in a minor post.

Lloyd George was given the new Ministry of Munitions, taking all production matters away from the War Office. Kitchener urged his staff to cooperate loyally. For the next eleven months every shell, bullet and gun came from orders given, as George Arthur wrote, 'by a rather unkindly abused War Office. So on an April [1916] morning on the way to Whitehall, Kitchener could take his cigar from his mouth and murmur to me, "Lloyd George fired off his first shell yesterday."'[17]

Kitchener remained Secretary of State for War. Asquith had toyed with removing him or setting up an unworkable joint-secretaryship, but the outpouring of public support had made him impregnable. A few days later Asquith wrote to Kitchener that he had advised the King to give him the Order of the Garter in the Birthday Honours, adding: 'After these many months of association in times of stress and trial, it is a great pleasure to me to couple with this announcement the assurance of my profound gratitude and unabated confidence.'[18]

On reading the letter Kitchener chuckled. 'I suppose for the future if I want anything, I have only got to get French to write me up!'[19]

21

TWO TRIUMPHS

ON THE MORNING of 25 May when Churchill was waiting at the Admiralty to hand over to Balfour, Kitchener walked into the room. 'He spoke very kindly of our work together.' Churchill surmised that Kitchener had no idea how narrowly he had escaped the same fate (not so narrow, because of his indispensable prestige), but he never forgot Kitchener's next words. As he got up to go, 'he turned and said in the impressive and almost majestic manner which was natural to him, "Well, there is one thing at any rate they cannot take from you. The Fleet was ready."'

In the months ahead Churchill would often oppose and criticize. 'But I cannot forget,' he would write in *The World Crisis*, 'the rugged kindness and warm-hearted courtesy which led him to pay me this visit.' After the Second World War the only time he mentioned Kitchener in the hearing of his daughter Mary was to recall this visit and those parting words.[1]

Two days later Kitchener went from York House to Carlton House Terrace to escort Lord Curzon to his first Cabinet meeting, 'as an act of respect, friendship and reconciliation'.[2]

Later that day he heard that Julian Grenfell, soldier and poet ('Into Battle') had died of wounds. Kitchener broke down, the only time in the war that he had to leave his desk for an hour or so to recover. In his letter of sympathy to Lord Desborough, Kitchener recalled Julian's boyhood and how they had fished together at Taplow and how he had helped guide and encourage his career in the regular army. He concluded: 'We all wish

sometimes that the trumpet would sound for us, but we have to stick it out
and do our very best until the release comes. I only wish that I could do
more, or rather that what I do was better work.'[3] Kitchener had no doubts
of the Resurrection. When Julian's brother Billy was killed in action two
months later, Mrs Asquith was speaking of the brothers' deaths, during
dinner in Downing Street, and said to Kitchener that she 'longed for one
glimpse of God's purpose – if only a gleam of hope as to our sure immor-
tality. The expression on Lord Kitchener's face was one of puzzled
kindness, and he handed me the port.' To hide her emotion he turned
abruptly away and began a general conversation on a different subject.[4]

Kitchener found the Coalition Cabinet even more uncongenial than the
Liberal. He never felt comradeship with either, nor attempted to get to
know colleagues he did not need to work with. 'I don't remember his
name but he has got curly hair,' he would remark to a War Office general
about a junior Cabinet Minister. He regarded Asquith as his only true
friend among them. Bonar Law, the Unionist leader, born in New
Brunswick, brought up by aunts in Glasgow, where he made his fortune,
disliked Kitchener, partly because he regarded him as a Tory whose
willingness to serve in 1914 had propped up the Liberal government which
Law had hoped to displace. Balfour, who had been so helpful in 1905,
acknowledged that Kitchener had great personality but decided, 'He
knows nothing. Does nothing right.'[5]

Curzon could not forget India. Some months after he had joined the
Cabinet he was visited by the Archbishop of Canterbury when confined to
bed. The Archbishop learned that Curzon regarded Kitchener as 'totally
devoid of imagination or vision, and therefore it is only within very narrow
limits that he would respect K's opinion. All this,' the Archbishop
commented shrewdly, 'has of course to be taken in conjunction with the
known disputation in India between Curzon and K'; Randall Davidson
remembered, if Curzon did not, Kitchener's clear and decisive vision at the
outbreak of war. On another occasion the Archbishop noted that Curzon
'distrusts K except for his value as the hero of the man in the street whose
confidence in the Government is kept up by the infallible K. One
discounts all this, knowing Curzon's old hostility to K.'[6]

By now Kitchener was a engaged in a war on two fronts, one overseas
against the Germans, the other in Downing Street against his Cabinet

colleagues. As the war dragged on between triumph and disaster in France, the Dardanelles and in far-flung corners where British or Indian troops had seized German colonies, every policy decision had to be defended against enemies at home.

Lord Birkenhead (F. E. Smith) wrote later that 'No living soldier could have made a tenth as much out of the actual situation as Kitchener made. That he did not make more was the fault of the system, and the system is inherent in government by democracy, which adapts itself strangely and laboriously to the policy of war.' Smith had been profoundly impressed when head of the Press Bureau before going to France. When he joined the Coalition as Solicitor-General he noted that Kitchener was beginning to be disillusioned and 'pathetically conscious that his prestige, after labours so incredible and achievements so vast, had none the less begun to wane'.[7]

Then came two personal triumphs. Early in July 1915 the political and military leaders of France and Great Britain met at Calais to discuss future strategy, especially as divisions of the second New Army were arriving in France. Sir John French and Joffre wanted another offensive in the summer. Kitchener wanted to hold back until 1916, when their numbers and arms would be overwhelming. Lord Esher wrote to Fitz next day: 'I heard Lord K was extraordinarily good. He fairly astonished them all — his futile English colleagues and all the French.'[8] In an otherwise disparaging book Esher described Calais as

for Lord K a meteoric moment. He seemed to be freshened up by contact with the French, whose language, of all the English present, he alone spoke tersely and well. He was calm and deliberate without inconsistency in the propositions he brought forward. He put the best construction upon everything that was said, and, while stating in convincing argument the military objections to a premature offensive and the reason for urging a halt until the spring, he appeared to appre-ciate more clearly than any of his colleagues, and to state more clearly than the French themselves, the political motives indissolubly bound up with the psychology of the French armies and people, which outweighed the purely military argument for delay. On that occasion he proved himself in discussion resourceful, bold, and candid.[9]

After Calais he made a quick visit to Haig's 1st Army which, Haig wrote to Fitz, 'gave an infinite amount of pleasure to all ranks in the Army, and we all hope he will soon repeat it and stay longer'.[10] Returning to England, he was due to speak at a great recruiting meeting chaired by the Lord Mayor of London in the Guildhall; volunteering had slackened off and an agitation was brewing for conscription.

On the morning of the meeting, so Arthur wrote to a friend in Paris two days later:

> he happened to look out of the window half an hour before he started and could not make out what the huge crowd was waiting for, and was genuinely surprised when told that they were waiting for him. All the route was lined with cheering people, and the reception at the Guildhall itself was tremendous; it was if everyone were determined to show the utter trust vested in him.[11]

'My dear Lord K,' wrote Esher, 'The meeting seems to have been a great success and your personal triumph at the Guildhall only second to what you secured at Calais. I wish that appreciation by our people of all you have achieved would suffice to beat the Germans!'[12]

The only other speakers were Carson and Lord Derby, who had done much for recruiting in Lancashire and was appointed that October as Director-General of Recruiting and devised the Derby Plan, which both Asquith and Kitchener hoped would postpone conscription that might lead to industrial unrest. Meanwhile, a National Registration Act was passed in July to create a census of manpower resources, but this provoked the Northcliffe press to shout louder for immediate conscription of able-bodied males for war service. Margot Asquith wrote to Kitchener in mid-August:

> Let me warn you as I know *for a fact* what is happening, Northcliffe, George Curzon & co are running this campaign for conscription to put you in a hole. You must show pluck & beat them. It is for *you* to say to the Prime Minister *when* you want conscription & you will get it so why should you & Henry be jockeyed into it by Northcliffe & Curzon? . . . Don't let Curzon score, he is an untrustworthy fool. You have been weak over Northcliffe as I have told you before.[13]

Kitchener had asked the other papers not to abuse Northcliffe or his press, but Esher told him that unless he asserted himself it would go hard for him, and the political gentlemen who abused him behind his back would get the better of him. 'In that case the Entente will collapse and we shall finally be beaten.'[14] But Kitchener would not lift a hand against Northcliffe. As Laubat the Frenchman noticed, 'He rendered full justice to efforts which he considered honest and well meant . . . But perhaps the strongest and finest characteristic of Kitchener's mind was his love of truth and his sincerity: he had for lies and for liars an unbounded contempt, a deep hatred, and a kind of real physical repulsion . . . Kitchener was in the highest sense of the word a Christian gentleman who trusted gentlemen only.'[15]

He remained to the end very shy, and therefore could be brusque with those he did not know, and slow to confide. He was also diffident about himself. He surprised his old friend Derby by exclaiming, 'I wish you could tell me what I am doing wrong.' When Derby demurred he went on: 'I feel there is something I ought to be doing. There is something more I ought to do for the country. I am doing all that I can and yet I feel that I am still leaving much undone.'[16] He said much the same to Esher, who saw tears in his eyes.

Despite his frequent sudden decisions by instinct he could take his time to decide a question. A head of department in the new Ministry of Munitions wanted his agreement to exempt certain workers from call-up. In a straight and friendly interview Kitchener listened, then walked up and down his room explaining the difficulties as he argued the case with himself. Then he said, 'I agree that what you ask should be done', and the interview closed.[17]

Now sixty-five, he was visibly ageing. One senior officer on Haig's staff noted during an official visit that 'He carried his load easily enough, so far as one can judge',[18] but General Murray, on returning from France to be vice-chief of the General Staff, thought that he tired as a week wore on. Unwisely he took no leave: the times were too urgent; and unlike Asquith with his bridge and Lloyd George with his golf he had no hobbies except his beloved collection and Broome. In the early weeks of the war he would not go down, but his secretaries persuaded him. He would drive with Fitz or Arthur to be there by Saturday noon. According to Arthur they never slept in the house but lodged at the long-suffering agent, Western. Family tradition, however, holds that Kitchener slept in his own rooms once the

[449]

workmen went. Western, a former sapper warrant-officer, was expert on drains and elevations, while Fitz was an expert on roses, and Edith Monins might drive over in the dog cart to advise about furniture and pictures since Flo Marc was too far away. Sometimes a party of wounded would enjoy the grounds at Kitchener's invitation, but most weekends he would forget the war until Sunday evening when, back in York House, the red boxes were waiting to be opened by Fitz or Arthur as he would never turn a key. The telegrams and papers gave no rest; but Broome had rejuvenated him.

That July one problem was settled which was important for morale. The Archbishop wanted more chaplains on the Western Front because the Kitchener Armies (as he and everyone called them) were beginning to go over in increasing numbers: one chaplain to 4,000 men was the norm. Further complications arose from the Deputy Chaplain-General in charge being Presbyterian, while most chaplains were Anglican, and some of them disliked the Chaplain-General as too evangelical. Archbishop Davidson, wanting a bishop in charge at the front, suggested an advisory committee. Kitchener warmly agreed and proposed his old and fervently Anglican friend Lord Salisbury to chair it. As a result, towards the end of July 1915 Kitchener summoned Bishop Gwynne of Khartoum, who had joined the BEF while on leave (and shaved off his moustache). An ordinary chaplain, he was one of the best-loved men on the Western Front. Kitchener told him he was to be Anglican Deputy Chaplain-General and invited him to discuss the work over dinner at York House, where Gwynne said that if he must leave his battalions he would prefer to return to Sudan. 'Bishop,' replied Kitchener, 'you are now in uniform and under my orders for the duration of the war. If I order you to go to Timbuctoo that is where you will have to go. Afterwards you ought to go back to the Sudan but now you must obey me.'

Kitchener had already told the Chaplain-General that he had appointed a bishop for the Western Front. Taylor Smith asked who had been chosen, and when Kitchener replied, 'Gwynne', Taylor Smith exclaimed: 'Sir, this is an answer to prayer!'[19] Dr Simms, the Presbyterian, remained Principal Chaplain for all other denominations.

In August, when the BEF and the French were preparing for their next offensive, Kitchener paid an official visit to Haig's 1st Army. Haig urged conscription. Kitchener replied that his call for volunteers at the beginning of the war had produced better men. He would do nothing until the National Register was ready. Charteris, Haig's head of Intelligence, thought Kitchener was coming round to conscription. After luncheon Kitchener spent two hours in Charteris' office. When discussing the general situation Kitchener said the next offensive must be 'pressed to the uttermost, even though we suffered very heavy casualties'. In contrast to the French, who were exuberantly optimistic that Germany was on the verge of cracking, Kitchener did not think the next offensive would be decisive. He talked, noted Charteris in his diary, 'about what would have to be done next summer. But he has no doubt at all about the ultimate result. K is always impressive, but I think this time he was more impressive than usual. *It is ten thousand pities that he is not in supreme control at home.* He would know what to do, and would do it. I am sure the country would accept from him far more stringent orders and laws than from any of the politicians, whom they have been taught to criticize from their earliest youth.'[20]

22

THE END IN GALLIPOLI

AFTER TEA ON 6 October 1915 'Kitchener came to see me', recorded the King in his diary. 'He was rather low about things in general and wanted to resign. I told him of course I wouldn't allow him to do such a thing & that I had every confidence in him.'[1]

He had reason to be gloomy. The offensive at Loos on the Western Front had failed to make a breakthrough despite heavy losses. Both sides were using poison gas and decimating a generation by throwing their young men at the other's wire and guns. On the Gallipoli peninsula an offensive from Anzac cove had not captured the heights, despite the courage and death toll of Australians and New Zealanders, and a fresh landing at Sulva Bay had not been exploited. In neutral Greece the pro-Allied Prime Minister, Venizelos, had allowed an Anglo-French force to land at Salonika, expecting to pass through Greek territory to aid the Serbs. Venizelos intended Greece to join the Allies, but the Greek King, Queen Alexandra's nephew, dismissed him and installed a ministry that leaned towards his brother-in-law the Kaiser.

Two days after Kitchener's audience at Buckingham Palace an Austro-German offensive captured Belgrade, and in another three days Bulgaria, wooed by both sides, declared war on the Allies. Only in Mesopotamia had there been progress, and this was against Kitchener's advice. The Indian army had successfully occupied the oil ports at the head of the Persian Gulf, and Kitchener urged they go no further up the rivers unless they were sure they could capture and hold Baghdad, which he seriously doubted at their present strength and organization. But the Cabinet and the government of India had rejected his advice (which was also Curzon's). General Nixon had ordered Major-General Townshend, formerly one of Kitchener's staff officers at Simla, to advance, and at first all was well.

At home Kitchener could register a small success. Labour troubles among munitions workers and a falling off in recruiting had led Arthur Henderson, the only Labour member of the Coalition Cabinet (and a future Foreign Secretary), to invite Asquith and Kitchener to place the position candidly before trade union leaders. Lord Kitchener's statement, 'like all his utterances, was terse, somewhat formal, and totally devoid of any kind of oratorical appeal', Henderson recorded.

> It was received with respect, but respect was soon absorbed in a far more cordial and human feeling, when in the give-and-take of conversation and discussion which followed the audience became aware of the good humour, homely sense and frank comradeship which underlay the more formidable qualities of the great soldier. In half an hour, I believe there was not a single man among those to whom he was speaking who had not conceived for him a warm personal affection . . . He was no less delighted with the warmth and goodwill with which it was received.[2]

He believed the trade unions and the country were not yet ready for conscription. He had brought in three million volunteers. Thirty-five divisions were now operating across the world on fronts and expeditions and in garrisons, and another thirty-five were being formed. After the severe casualties at Loos, nine Cabinet Ministers, convinced that only conscription could keep the divisions up to strength, urged Kitchener to force Asquith's hand by asking for it. Asquith wrote hurriedly to Kitchener that the real object of Lloyd George and Curzon was to oust him and that 'so long as you and I stand together, we carry the whole country with us. Otherwise the deluge.'[3]

In a final attempt to postpone conscription, Kitchener and his old friend Lord Derby, now Director-General of Recruiting at his invitation, promoted the Derby Plan whereby all men between the ages of eighteen and forty-one should be persuaded (not compelled) to attest their willingness to serve if called upon. The Prime Minister then announced that the unmarried would be called up first, a pledge made without consulting Derby, who was much abused for it. He and Kitchener worked on for the voluntary system although both believed that conscription must come. Derby had long appreciated Kitchener as 'a very faithful friend, always searching for the good qualities of those who served him, rather than trying to detect their faults . . . Only those who knew him well really understood him.'[4]

The overriding worry of these autumn months of 1915 came from the Dardanelles, whether victory was still possible or whether the expedition should be withdrawn.

Sir Ian Hamilton was much loved by his embattled troops and, unlike Sir John French, he trusted Kitchener. Back in June he had written thanking him 'with all my heart for your constant great kindness and sympathy as shown in your cables and messages to this country. Believe me, whatever happens hereafter, I shall never forget the wonderful, unwavering support you have given us throughout. My constant prayer is that I may be permitted to prove myself worthy of it.'[5]

Later Hamilton believed that if Kitchener had not diverted high explosive and heavy guns to France they would have captured the heights and won the peninsula, but his dispatches remained highly optimistic, even after Bulgaria entered the war, giving Germans' munitions unhindered access to the Dardanelles. Hamilton's optimism now exasperated his own staff, who conspired to place the true position before Asquith, by-passing Kitchener, to his annoyance. The Cabinet, including Kitchener, lost faith in Hamilton and recalled him on 16 October. On 20 October Kitchener ordered General Sir Charles Monro to leave France and take over at Gallipoli, and to assess the prospects. Birdwood would act as Commander-in-Chief until Monro's arrival. Kitchener was vehemently against evacuation because of the loss of life it might involve and the devastating effect on attitudes and loyalties in India and Egypt. Monro's first cable, within hours of arriving at the Expeditionary Force's island base, contained no views either way. In reply Kitchener ordered him to send his report as soon as possible on the main issue, 'leaving or staying'. Monro cabled back that leaving was inevitable.

Meanwhile, in London Asquith was under increasing pressure from Lloyd George, Curzon and Balfour with their determination to oust Kitchener and run the war in their own way. Asquith knew that his government might fall if the public saw Kitchener as dismissed. Casting round for a way to ease the pressure, he suggested that Kitchener go out to the Dardanelles and personally assess whether the Expeditionary Force should leave or stay. Asquith would take the War Office temporarily. He half-hoped Kitchener would decide to stay on in the Mediterranean theatre, thus vacating the War Office. The opportunity of sending him to India as Viceroy had passed as a new Viceroy had been appointed. Kitchener would be too old when the next vacancy came, so he would probably be content, when the war was won, with a dukedom and some money.[6]

Kitchener agreed to go to the Dardanelles. He sent a long cipher telegram to Birdwood, not to Monro, telling him that he was coming and was against evacuation. Since Monro wanted that, Kitchener ordered Birdwood to take over the command: Monro would go to Salonika. Birdwood was to make a fresh landing on the northern coast of Gallipoli.

Birdwood was horrified. Although he knew from their long friendship the difficulty of changing his old Chief's mind, he bravely replied that a fresh landing was impossible and begged him to think again about Monro, whom he had asked for an honest answer. Birdwood suppressed the telegram and awaited Kitchener's arrival.

Kitchener left London worried and depressed, although between an audience with the King and leaving York House for the station he spent a happy quarter of an hour absorbed in designing and drawing a cabinet for some of his best china at Broome. In Paris he was still depressed, and Esher saw tears in his eyes as Fitz read to him, as he stood with his back to the fire in a little room in the embassy, letters of support and affection from War Office colleagues who, he guessed, suspected that he might not return to them.[7] But when he left Paris his spirits revived. 'He is delighted at being away from London,' wrote FitzGerald to Lady Salisbury on 9 November. 'He hates the atmosphere there in which he has to work and the criticism and lack of support of his colleagues, who are always putting all the work and all the blame which should really be accepted by the Cabinet, on his shoulders.'[8]

On arriving at the Expedition's base on Mudros he greeted Birdwood, who had not seen him since the coronation, with such warmth that Birdwood was touched, remembering him as very undemonstrative. Birdwood found him quite unchanged since 1911, and very fit and well and active.

After full discussions with Monro and others, Birdwood took him to the Anzac beach and battle area. No word had been given that he was coming but, as the official Australian press representative saw:

> by the time Lord Kitchener had reached the end of the pier the men were tumbling like rabbits out of every dug-out on the hillside, jumping over obstacles and making straight for the beach. Australians do not cheer readily, but as Lord Kitchener, accompanied by Generals Birdwood and Maxwell and others, passed the crowd along the beach, the men spontaneously called for cheers and gave them again and again. It was purely a soldier's welcome.
>
> Lord Kitchener many times turned to the men. 'His Majesty the King has asked me to tell you how splendidly he thinks you have done,' he said. 'You have done excellently well. Better,' he added, 'even than I thought you would.'
>
> Without any pause Lord Kitchener went straight up the steepest road in the Anzac area direct from the beach to the highest point in the old Anzac area, and in less than ten minutes one could see the tall figure stalking by the side of the little figure which all Anzac knows so well, right at the top of the steep ascent. Most persons arrive at that summit breathless, but Lord Kitchener went straight up without a halt. He went through the front firing trench on the neck where the Light Horse had charged. The troops could scarcely be restrained from cheering him, although the Turks in places were within twenty yards, and the Anzac Staff had some moments of considerable anxiety at certain awkward corners all too visible to the Turkish snipers.[9]

As he stood at this high vantage point and looked around he put his hand on Birdwood's arm: 'Thank God, Birdie, I came to see this for myself. You were quite right. I had no idea of the difficulties you were up against. I think you have all done wonders.'[10]

After visiting the beaches and much discussion with the generals and brief journeys to Athens and Salonika, where the French commander of the Anglo-French force did not impress him, Kitchener came slowly round to evacuation, although remaining curiously distant towards General Monro, who had first urged it. The navy had dashed any hope of another attempt to force the Dardanelles; the Turks on Gallipoli were likely to grow stronger with direct German help through Bulgaria; Egypt was in danger of another Turkish assault through Sinai, helped by the Senussi in the Western Desert; and in Mesopotamia General Townshend had been defeated in a battle outside Baghdad and was withdrawing to Kut.

When he returned home Kitchener finally recommended to the Cabinet a complete withdrawal in two stages. Birdwood had assured him that losses should be less than he feared, if the weather held and the Turks did not discover the plan, but on the night chosen for withdrawal, when he was one of the very few in England who knew what was impending, Kitchener spent the two nights of the first evacuation pacing up and down his room at York House, sleepless, in mental agony, as he saw in imagination thousands drowning and wounded and perhaps many caught by the Turks. When the telegram arrived, stating complete success without a single casualty, he shared Birdwood's relief and gratitude to Providence, especially as a great storm blew up the next night. That morning of the telegram, Sir Mark Sykes, the young MP who was negotiating the secret Sykes-Picot agreement for carving up the Ottoman Empire, came to report:

> Kitchener, after talking for a little said, 'I have a dreadful headache and can hardly keep awake; the fact is I have not slept for two nights at all; I was thinking of those poor men evacuating at Suvla; I made sure they would mostly be killed or drowned – I never have felt so anxious, and I never felt so relieved.'[11]

He was down at Broome on the afternoon after the final evacuation. The Barham postmaster brought up a telegram: 'Second operation even more successful than the first.' He said not a word but his 'eyes were eloquent of a great content'.[12]

23

PARTNERSHIP FOR VICTORY

Kᴉᴛᴄʜᴇɴᴇʀ ʜᴀᴅ ᴀʀʀɪᴠᴇᴅ back in London early on 30 November. At the War Office he learned that in his absence Asquith had removed the Ordnance Department and placed it under the authority of the Minister of Munitions. This convinced Kitchener that he should resign. He had been leaning towards resignation, but his old friend Rennell Rodd, his host in Rome during the return journey, had dissuaded him.

He went at once to Downing Street. Asquith refused to accept his resignation, urging that Kitchener's duty was to remain at his post because the King, the army and the public trusted him as they trusted no other. Asquith broke the news that Kitchener would no longer control strategy, and that the Imperial General Staff, which he had allowed to become ineffective, had been reconstituted by Order in Council so that the decision could not be reversed. Asquith had asked General Sir William (Wully) Robertson to move from chief of staff in France to Chief of the Imperial General Staff. Robertson was in London considering whether to accept, and on what conditions, and had been awaiting Kitchener's return. Faced with these humiliations, Kitchener again insisted he must resign, and again Asquith persuaded him that his duty to the King and country demanded that he stay at his post.

Asquith's daughter Violet was being married to his secretary, Maurice Bonham-Carter, at St Margaret's, Westminster, that afternoon. Kitchener's arrival at the church caused a sensation, since most of the large and smart

[458]

congregation thought him still in Italy. He was one of those who signed the register.

Kitchener had Wully Robertson to dine alone with him that evening at York House. Kitchener pressed him to accept the post. Robertson had been afraid that Kitchener, the centralizer, would be impossible to work with. Kitchener said: 'I am not the K they think I am.' And Robertson, who had never had opportunity to know him well, soon saw that his own view of him was wrong:

> He referred quite frankly to the unenviable reputation he had acquired, and asked me not to believe it for it was not true, and he assured me that I might rest satisfied that no action of his would endanger our working smoothly together. I was much impressed by his outspoken manner, and felt that I was in the presence of a man whose character was totally different from what I had been led to suppose; but I still thought it would be best for both of us, and for the country, if before finally deciding we came to a definite understanding, in writing, on the particular points regarding which I was in doubt.[1]

William Robertson had risen from the ranks, highly unusual in his gener-ation, especially as he had earned his commission by professional skill and competence, not as a reward for valour. He had not been a 'gentleman ranker' but a Lincolnshire cottager's son who had begun as a footman at the local manor and enlisted in the Lancers at seventeen. In 1914 he won great respect and gratitude as Quartermaster-General to the British Expeditionary Force, keeping it fed and equipped through the retreat from Mons and after, before becoming chief of staff. He was unassuming and gentle but forthright and straight.

Robertson went back to France and began composing a long memorandum. He was still working on it on 5 December when he attended an allied conference at Calais, where he was impressed by Kitchener's handling of the French, persuading them by threat of resig-nation to withdraw the Anglo-French force that was cooped up uselessly in Salonika; a decision reversed by the Chamber of Deputies. But Robertson's memorandum, dated two days later, would have reduced Kitchener to little more than a shopkeeper and recruiting poster. As Curzon remarked when Asquith showed him a copy, he would have been left commanding only Sir George Arthur and Colonel FitzGerald. Nevertheless, Kitchener recommended Asquith to accept it and wrote to Robertson that it would be impossible to remain in office without any executive work; that as the troops would not now be withdrawn from Salonika he would be leaving office and had suggested Derby as his successor. 'I may still be a member of the War Council though not as S of S. In that case you may rely on me to always do my best to support you in carrying out the difficult task you will have before you.'[2]

This letter reached Robertson at General Headquarters at St-Omer at about 7 p.m. on the evening of 7 December. To Robertson, 'This example of patriotism and subordination of self was the more striking as coming from a man of his standing in the Empire and with his record of service, and I had not a moment's hesitation as to the right thing to do.' First, he dashed off a letter to Wigram at Buckingham Palace urging that the King should not let Kitchener resign. Then, knowing that Kitchener would be passing through Calais that night on his way to Paris, Robertson drove after dinner to meet him. 'He greeted me very cordially, albeit a little sadly, I thought, and with an air of disappoint-ment. I came at once to the point and said that whatever happened I would not hear of his leaving the War Office, since there was no one who could fill the position which he held in the country, and I begged him to discuss with me the paragraphs in the memorandum to which he objected.'[3] As the train was soon leaving, Kitchener suggested that Robertson jump in.

They discussed all the way to Paris and late into the night at the Crillon Hotel. After breakfast they resumed. Esher came in, finding Robertson in his shirtsleeves lying on a sofa, pipe in mouth, and Kitchener at the table with a sheet of paper before him. Esher helped resolve some of the issues between these two men who were totally disinterested, wanting only to win the war. The memorandum was amended to the satisfaction of both.

Asquith remarked to Henry Wilson that he looked forward with amusement 'to the clash of K and Robertson', a remark that Wilson thought showed up Asquith as a perfectly callous man of no principle. But there was no clash, Robertson writing afterwards:

During the time we worked together, Lord Kitchener would sometimes refer to the memorandum as 'our bargain', and would ask his personal staff whether he was carrying his part of it out, thus showing a genuine desire to make everything go smoothly. For myself I never had occasion to give it another thought, and I shall always regret that the unfounded gossip to which I have alluded caused me to misjudge him, even though temporarily, and so add to the cares and anxieties he was then carrying, alone and unaided save by those loyal friends who really knew and appreciated him.[4]

Robertson took office as CIGS on 23 December 1915. His task, and Kitchener's, was made easier because Sir John French had gone at last. He had lost the confidence of the King, and of Asquith and Kitchener, but they had been reluctant to move him. Asquith offered him a peerage and a new post as Commander-in-Chief in the United Kingdom. Before accepting, Sir John made a last attempt to destroy Kitchener by hinting broadly that to be successful the new post would require a new War Secretary, but Asquith ignored the hint. Sir Douglas Haig took over command of the British Expeditionary Force. Haig, Robertson and Kitchener formed a partnership which, had it not been cut short by death, might have brought victory sooner.

Early in February Kitchener made another visit with FitzGerald to Haig's headquarters. 'He looked very worn and old and tired,' recorded Charteris, 'and was sombre and gloomy all the evening.' He went to bed immediately after dinner. Next morning he was 'quite himself', going into all matters concerning the campaign, emphasizing, that 'you *will not* break through' the German line. They might bend it and press it and kill Germans, but the end would come when the German people, rather than their armies, gave up.[5] He was against attempting a massive offensive for the present. He then went out among rear formations and into the trenches. After a three-day visit he was a different man, Adolphus Duke of Teck, Haig's military secretary, told the King, and had received a great reception from all the troops he saw.[6]

The change that came over him in those days in France and Flanders seems symbolic. The politicians, engulfed in controversies that preceded the Conscription Act, wearied him with their amateur strategies and demands for swift results. Haig told Charteris that 'K is being very heavily attacked at home in the Cabinet, and that although Robertson and K are working together excellently, the hostile element headed by Lloyd George may succeed in getting rid of him. Curzon is apparently siding with Lloyd George, while Asquith is backing K. The real thing that matters is what the nation thinks. I feel sure they would stand by and for K against any or all of the politicians.'[7]

Whenever he went among the soldiers his spirits revived, as Rawlinson saw when Kitchener visited his part of the front on 30 March, emphasizing again that they must resist French pleas for a big offensive to relieve pressure on Verdun, although accepting that the British could not do nothing while the French suffered great losses. 'K himself was looking very fit, far better than he did last year,' recorded Rawlinson. 'K, D. H. and Wully are making an excellent team, as I knew they would. Wully is doing first-class. In fact, the military side is working so well now that I hear some of the politicians are saying it is a military dictatorship!'[8]

Kitchener's strategy was to wait until all the divisions of the New Armies were ready and fully trained; but the pleas of the French prevailed with Robertson and Haig, who prepared for a great offensive on the Somme.

For Kitchener, every month that passed without throwing the troops away at a heavily fortified line would make final victory more certain, especially as Britain was now perfecting its secret weapon, soon to be known as the tank. When Kitchener had first been offered, in August 1914, the idea of adapting a cumbrous caterpillar-tracked farm vehicle, first seen in 1902, into an armoured fighting vehicle, he was dismissive because the campaign was then a war of movement and a slow, large and unwieldy machine would be destroyed by gunfire. Churchill at the Admiralty had been more far-seeing and encouraged the idea of 'landships'. The stalemate of trench warfare changed Kitchener's attitude, and he appointed a committee. One year later he was able to demand a field trial, and in February he went to Lord Salisbury's park at Hatfield and watched a prototype being put through its paces. Far too many dignitaries had been invited. Kitchener, deeply impressed, left the trial early with the deliberate intention of suggesting he had lost interest; he realized that these 'tanks' could win the war but if they were talked about, the Germans would hear. He ordered a hundred.[9]

He also encouraged the expansion of the Royal Flying Corps, then part of the army; unlike many, he believed that aeroplanes could be used to bomb troops and supplies, not merely for reconnaissance or to shoot down zeppelins raiding London.

Although he never took any full leave, he could relax whenever he managed a short weekend at Broome. Toby was now in a shore job before being posted to the Aegean as captain of a monitor, and he often drove down with his uncle and either FitzGerald or Arthur. Toby left a vivid picture. Uncle Herbert spoke little during the drive.

> Once at Broome, no other thought would enter his head, and the day would be spent laying out the garden, or designing for the inside of the house. The smallest details, such as the coming out of a copper beech, or the right position for a piece of china, gave him great pleasure.
>
> When working in the garden at Broome, we used to refer to Broome as the Great Pyramid, which joke he quite liked. Everybody has to work, either driving in pegs, or being at the movable end of a tape measure, while he worked out his ideas. If after some time you stopped at all, he would come and try to do it himself, or, in some other pleasant way, flick you along.
>
> His opinion of people in general was that they did not realize the amount of work in a thing. He would take infinite pains to get a right effect and, when finished, they would say – 'How splendid! Why can't I do that?'
>
> He never read during the day, and would be quite happy sitting in the garden without talking, but I always fancied he liked to have somebody with him.

Occasionally he read a Stanley Weyman or similar novel in the evening, or back numbers of *Country Life*, or studied pictures of Italian gardens. 'After supper he would, perhaps, talk about his work: he looked at things most simply, and put himself on no high level. He only looked upon his power as depending upon his finding out the right thing to do.

'Sometimes at this time I would tell him of my ship life, and he was a most sympathetic listener, provided you talked at the right time.'[10]

Back at York House he could relax on the few occasions when he gave a dinner party for friends. In April 1916 Frank Maxwell, 'the Brat', with Charlotte and their two little daughters, returned from India. Frank had at last persuaded the Viceroy to release him from his personal staff and was on his way to the Western Front, where he was killed in action during 1917 as a brigadier-general. On 27 April Kitchener gave a dinner party for the Maxwells, although he could not forget that in Mesopotamia General Townshend, besieged in Kut, was on the verge of surrender.

He invited the Derbys, Lady Salisbury and the Duchess of Portland, together with Arthur and Fitz, Sir William and Lady Robertson and the Birdwoods. Birdie, briefly on leave, had brought the Anzac division to France, and had been touched by the warmth of his dear old Chief's handshake when receiving him at the first Anzac Day memorial service in Westminster Abbey two days earlier. Winifred Portland, on leave from running a hospital in France, wrote next day: 'What fun it was last night & how I loved my only dinner party – I just had to write & tell you!! The House looked so nice with your glorious flowers and I liked both my dinner neighbours immensely!

'It was *delightful* seeing you again – & altogether I felt like a child out for a holiday . . .'[11]

But all too soon it was back to the war for all of them. Kitchener had written early in 1916 to Asquith: 'I feel very strongly that unless we make every effort this year we may either lose the war or drift into a most dangerous peace for this country.'[12] A negotiated stalemate peace would lead to another war in seven years.

Kitchener had saved England in 1914 and had laid the foundations of victory, but the war had become bitter, as he revealed to two emissaries of President Wilson in March 1916, urging them that America break off diplomatic relations with Germany, which would shorten the war. He sought to convince them that no permanent peace would come in Europe 'except as a result of some effective arrangement between Great Britain and the United States'.

As he said goodbye to the Americans, Kitchener seemed to be seeing the past conflicts of his life in a rosy memory compared with the present. Mr Forbes and Mr Strong reported to President Wilson:

Lord Kitchener spoke very bitterly of the German atrocities, their duplicity and their thoroughly underhand manner of conducting the war. He characterized their policy as foul play of the most dastardly sort; in comparison he said the Dervishes, the Boers and the Turks, with all of whom he had conducted warfare, were gentlemen; that they fought each with their code of honor. He told us that the Turkish soldiers refused to do the dirty underhand things ordered by their German officers. He said that after fighting with any of the others he was glad to be friends with them; that he would shake the hand of his enemy, and made special mention in a most complimentary manner of General Smuts, who is commanding a campaign under his orders now, and with whom he had fought over an important part of a continent; but he said that he never wanted to shake hands with a German foe.[13]

Yet, as he would tell Lord Derby one month later, once they had been victorious the Allies must not make a vindictive peace but a peace of reconciliation.

PART FIVE

June 1916

24

JOURNEY TO RUSSIA?

On Sunday morning 14 May, down at Windsor, George V was puzzled to receive a telegram forwarded by the War Office: 'For H.M. the King, from the Emperor of Russia:— "I think that Lord Kitchener's visit to Russia would be most useful and important. Nicholas."'

Stamfordham wrote at once to Kitchener to ask if he could throw light on this as the King 'never sent any telegram to the Emperor of Russia and this . . . is the first he has heard of your suggested visit to Russia!' Kitchener explained, a little ingenuously, that the idea of his going there to work out about Russian purchases of munitions (and to inject some moral support) had been discussed at the War Committee but nothing was yet decided. Apparently, the Russian Ambassador, hearing about this unofficially, had telegraphed Petrograd 'as I have also received an invitation through him'. Asquith wanted to settle the matter next day.[1] When a Cabinet mission was first discussed and Kitchener wanted to lead it, Lloyd George was to be in the party as Minister of Munitions but Asquith needed him in Dublin to help settle the after-math of the Easter Rising; had he sailed, history would have been different.

Kitchener never expected Russia to make a major contribution to victory, but their defeat or withdrawal in the East would seriously damage the Allies on the Western Front. Prince Youssoupoff, father of the prince who, a few months later, killed the monk Rasputin for his evil influence on the Tsarina, had been most impressed on his recent visit to London by

Kitchener's knowledge of Russian affairs and his fears for Russia's future. Youssoupoff admired his 'fine penetrating intellect . . . even more than his commanding presence'.

Prince Felix, the son, later believed that the Tsarina told Rasputin of Kitchener's coming and that Rasputin, in his cups, spilled the secret to German spies.[2] Rumours that Kitchener might come were circulating in Petrograd.[3] But when the German submarine U.75 (under Lieutenant-Commander Kurt Beitzen) left Kiel to sow mines off the Orkney Islands, further north than any submarine had sown them, the German naval command knew nothing of Kitchener's plans: the mines, like the many laid by surface ships, were intended to sink or hinder ships of Sir John Jellicoe's Grand Fleet based on Scapa Flow, since the German High Seas Fleet was preparing to put to sea.

On 26 May, with Cabinet approval, Kitchener crossed Whitehall from the War Office to the Admiralty and personally asked the chief of naval war staff, the newly knighted Vice-Admiral Sir Henry Oliver (a future admiral of the fleet and centenarian) to arrange his journey. Oliver, with no knowledge of U.75, selected embarkation from Scapa Flow, the nearest British anchorage to Archangel, and on 26 May, five days before the Battle of Jutland, he telegraphed to Jellicoe asking him to supply a ship. Jellicoe chose the armoured cruiser HMS *Hampshire*.

U.75 arrived in Orkney waters from the north, out of wireless contact with German naval headquarters, and early on 29 May, undisturbed, laid twenty-two mines close inshore between the Brough of Birsay and Marwick Head, a route not normally used by capital ships: Beitzen is believed to have mistaken Marwick Head for the headland overlooking Hoy Sound. Jellicoe had no intention of sending Kitchener by that route.

Kitchener welcomed his secret Russian journey. The smooth partnership with Wully Robertson allowed him the time; with his technical colleagues he might strengthen and stiffen the Emperor and his armies; it would be a rest, as he told his old friend and trustee Arthur Renshaw when they lunched alone together on 31 May.[4] And Kitchener looked forward to a respite from the jealousies and ignorance of politicians. He knew that many wished to be rid of him. A censure motion had been put down on the House of Commons order paper for that very evening. Major-General Sir Ivor Herbert would move that the salary of the Secretary of State for War be reduced by £100 – the traditional means of opening a censure debate on an individual minister.

The previous evening Asquith had called on one of his regular *confidantes*, Lady Scott, the sculptor, widow of the Antarctic explorer. Asquith was dismissive of Kitchener, saying in answer to her question that he was going to Russia to talk munitions and finance and occupy his leisure – 'he's abdicated'. He was going to be abused in the House, and Asquith supposed he must defend him, 'but upon my word I don't know what I shall say, he's such a liar'. He complained that Kitchener was tortuous in speech and 'repeats himself so horribly'.[5] Kitchener, who trusted and admired Asquith, would have been surprised; trust might have turned to contempt; but he never knew, even as he never knew that Asquith had told military secrets regularly to Venetia Stanley, although he may have suspected, hence the 'lies', which to Kitchener were deceptions of war.

But Asquith was superb in the debate. Herbert's motion followed a long speech from Colonel Winston Churchill on a theme that would be one of his favourites when Prime Minister in the Second World War: the imbalance between the troops at the front and the far greater number who were behind the lines. Herbert's speech charged Kitchener with making himself effectively Commander-in-Chief at the outbreak of war: the members of the Army Council were 'held in an iron grasp by one personality'. He had ignored industrial resources and would not bring in national service although 'in the very first week of the war I urged the formation of a national register'. Kitchener had proceeded by a series of makeshifts.

The Prime Minister rose and praised Kitchener in a brief, brilliant oration which brought repeated cheers from all sides. He told the House 'with utmost sincerity and earnestness that I think the army, the country and the Empire are under a debt which cannot be measured in words for the services Lord Kitchener has rendered since the beginning of the war'. As he sat down his Coalition partner, Bonar Law, whispered to him: 'That was a great speech, but how after it shall we ever get rid of him?'[6]

Asquith was followed by a bad-tempered speech by the Liberal Sir Arthur Markham, an ironmaster and colliery owner and supporter of Lloyd George. His main charge was based on a false belief that Kitchener had not ordered enough machine-guns until the Prime Minister went to

France and saw the deficiencies. In effect, Markham charged Kitchener, as the next speaker, Sir Mark Sykes, retorted, 'with being incompetent, obstinate and wholly lacking in brains'. Markham's speech, said Sykes, shakes the confidence of the Allies, for whom Kitchener's name is a name to conjure with. Then another speaker claimed that his 'deficiencies are so great and the inefficiencies so apparent' that he ought to be removed. The sense of the House, however, was plainly against the motion. Kitchener's Under-Secretary of State, little Jack Tennant (Margot Asquith's brother), whom Markham had called 'the butt of the House . . . for the stupidities of Lord Kitchener', then sprang a surprise. He announced that on the Friday, 2 June, Kitchener would address as many Members as cared to come. 'Will he answer questions?' cried Markham. Tennant said yes. 'Then we'll be there!'

As the House of Commons debated, the Battle of Jutland was fought, with heavy losses of ships and men on both sides; but the German High Seas Fleet never ventured out again. U.75 passed through the debris and wrecks of the battle on her passage home and had an alarming experience while on the surface. The cover of the ventilation shaft accidentally slammed shut. Frantic efforts to open it from above and below failed at first; the crew inside would soon suffocate in the diesel fumes and the engines stop for lack of air. The submarine would be captured by British ships salvaging in the battle area; the log would be discovered and thus the whereabouts of the mines off the Orkneys. But the captain and engineer opened the cover in time and U.75 reached Kiel.

The day after the battle Kitchener passed a pencilled note across the Cabinet table to the First Lord, Balfour, during a War Committee meeting: 'I believe it is arranged for me to go on Sunday. Might I have a look at the fleet en passant and see Jellicoe. I should not have more than about an hour or so.' The First Lord presumably nodded an affirmative, as he did not write on the note. Previously, Kitchener had expected to board the *Hampshire* in Thurso Bay and proceed at once to the open seas.

That Thursday evening, and thus three days before leaving for Russia, Kitchener dined alone with Lord Derby. As Derby later wrote, Kitchener confided in him more than in most people. Derby asked him about his future 'and he told me that he was not looking forward to any future', a

remark of totally unconscious irony, for he did not disclose any premo-
nition.

Derby recorded:

> There was only one thing that he really hoped to live for, and that was to
> be one of the English delegates when Peace was made. I asked him
> whether, saying that, he had any strong views that he would want to put
> forward and he said he had one very strong one, and that was, whatever
> happened, not to take away one country's territory and give it to another.
> It only meant a running sore and provocation for a war of revenge to get
> back the ground so lost. He was most emphatic about that . . .

Derby replied that surely he would not apply this to France's two 'lost
provinces' taken by Germany in 1871? 'Yes, I should. I think if you take
Alsace and Lorraine away from Germany and give them to France there
will be a war of revenge.' Nor would he take away Germany's colonies:
they provided a safety valve: if they had colonies they would not want to
engage in war for new territory.

As in South Africa, so in Europe. Kitchener longed to see the war end
in a peace of reconciliation, not in the vindictive humiliation of the enemy.
As he said more than once to George Arthur, even when the war was
going badly, 'I have no fear whatever about winning the War, what I fear
greatly is that we may make a bad peace . . . Here I think I might be of
some use' – even were he not still in the government. He knew the Cabinet
wanted to be rid of him, but he did not mean to leave without a struggle.
He gave Derby, not then in office, a private code to telegraph him in
Russia any matters that might be of use on his return. 'He had a great faith
in Asquith,' Derby records. 'He was devoted to him and liked him very
much indeed just as much as he cordially disliked Lloyd George. They
had absolutely nothing in common.'[8]

Next morning, Friday 2 June, in his usual blue undress uniform of a
Field Marshal, with Wully Robertson beside him and Lord Derby at
hand, he met some 200 MPs, so many that the event originally planned
for the War Office took place in a large committee room of the House of
Commons.

Kitchener had wanted such a meeting for some time, regretting that as a peer he could never explain matters or face questioning in the chamber or the lobbies. He felt the time was ripe with the censure motion defeated, and with his officials he had taken much trouble preparing. When Mark Sykes saw him the previous day 'he was very keen on making a very friendly opening to his speech. I begged him not to be too conciliatory, because I assured him he had the majority on his side.'[9]

The deputy speaker, J. H. Whitley, was voted into the chair. He said that this was as a secret session, that no notes might be taken and that questions should be related to the present and future, thus ruling out sterile argument about past activities of the War Office. Kitchener emphasized that any questions must relate to administration and not to operations, for reasons of security, but he would welcome them.

He hit the right note from the start. Knowing he had a good brief he threw off his usual shyness and secretiveness. Rather charmingly, he reminded Members that his previous work in life had not been of a kind 'to make me into a ready debater, nor to prepare me for the various turns and twists of argument'. He was dealing with facts, and he knew that any criti-cisms would be made 'solely for the purpose of advancing the cause we all have at heart'.

He read his long statement very quickly, which led to some mishear-ings,[10] but as he described his certainty in August 1914 that he must raise a vast new army, and went on to show the huge task that the War Office faced in finding equipment and munitions, from nearly two million suits of clothes and half a million horses, to millions of rounds and thousands of guns, the MPs realized as never before what had been achieved. Cheers could be heard when he said: 'Owing to the extraor-dinary zeal and loyalty of my subordinates, and the immense adapt-ability and enthusiasm of the people, this colossal task was accomplished.'

He paid a general compliment to Lloyd George as Minister of Munitions: 'He and I have ever been in loyal cooperation and from the day he took charge there has not been a single cause of friction between us.' When Kitchener revealed that earlier, in October 1914, he had ordered two million rifles from America and that not one had been delivered by April 1916, and only 480 since, the statement 'caused a considerable flutter in the room', so Markham told Lloyd George, away in Dublin. Kitchener said nothing of the American munitions that had been sunk when the liner

Lusitania had been torpedoed, since it had been officially an innocent passenger ship.

He next 'easily answered' the criticism (which had been the heart of Sir Ivor Herbert's censure) that the War Office did not immediately bring in conscription in 1914. He pointed out that 'a social change . . . running counter to most ancient traditions of the British people' was for the Cabinet, not himself, to decide. He had publicly foreshadowed the eventual possibility as early as 25 August 1914, and gave his opinion that compulsion had come at the right moment, 'as a Military necessity and for no other reason'.

After Lord Derby had read a long statement from the Quartermaster-General rebutting Winston Churchill's complaint of too many troops behind the lines, Kitchener resumed, pointing out that because they had kept so many in ancillary services the breakdowns suffered in previous wars had been avoided: men had been fed, their health kept up, the wounded treated.

Kitchener answered questions frankly and pleasantly. The King had worried that Kitchener would be heckled and get flustered, but Members were by now wholly on his side, and rejoiced when he assured one questioner, who had asked 'whether the Germans could break our lines', that 'it was quite impossible for them to do so'. But when Markham asked if he would explain 'how we were going to break their lines . . . he did not reply', not surprisingly, with the Somme offensive only a month away.

A Labour Member proposed, in warm terms, a vote of thanks to the War Secretary for his clear statement, which had removed their honest doubts, and for the way in which he had delivered it and answered their questions. Sir Ivor Herbert, the chief censurer, himself seconded it. It was passed with prolonged applause.

Kitchener was 'in the highest spirits at the show having gone off so well', Mark Sykes saw immediately afterwards,[11] and he 'came back to York House under an unmistakable glow of satisfaction',[12] as Sir George Arthur recorded. The initiative had been regained. The combination of Kitchener and Robertson looked impregnable.

25

'A SPLENDID END'

THAT EVENING Kitchener had a farewell audience with the King and afterwards went to the Private Secretary's room. Lord Stamfordham found him 'full of life, and keen at the prospect of his visit to Russia'.[1] He then went to Downing Street, where he and Asquith talked alone for a long time. On the way down from the Prime Minister's study he looked into Mrs Asquith's sitting room: 'He told me,' recorded Margot, 'he was delighted to be going to Russia, that he had had enough of the British Ministers, and only regretted leaving one man, and that was my husband. I looked at his tall, distinguished figure and vigorous face, and taking both his hands in mind, bade him God-speed.'[2] At the bottom of the stairs, walking towards the front door, he chanced to meet Elizabeth, Asquith and Margot's daughter, not quite twenty. 'We laughed and chaffed a little,' runs her memory, and she congratulated him on his success with the MPs. 'He was purring like a Persian cat, delighted by a success on unfamiliar territory. Then, suddenly going serious, he said to me: "I haven't made many friends in my new walk of life. And if I were to die to-morrow your father is the only man I would count on to be loyal to my memory."

'I said, "Nonsense," and he said, "Good-bye."'[3]

When he left Downing Street the Russian visit had suddenly become doubtful. Kitchener's representative, General Hanbury-Williams, had telegraphed that the Russian Finance Minister wished it postponed because he would be starting for France. Kitchener had telegraphed back that postponement was impossible and he could see the Finance Minister while in Petrograd, then visit somewhere on the Eastern Front, then return via Moscow, all within a week. But he wondered whether they now did not really want him, in which case he would not come: Hanbury-Williams must discover the truth. The general went immediately to the Tsar who, as the Autocrat, had the last word. The Tsar vigorously reaffirmed his invitation as of benefit to both countries. The answer did not reach Kitchener until the Saturday afternoon.[4]

By then he was at Broome. After a morning at the War Office he had driven down with Fitz and Toby, who was on leave before taking over his first command, a monitor in the Mediterranean Fleet. Kitchener had invited his cousin Edith Monins to tea (Toby was courting her eldest daughter, Adela), and she drove over from Ringwould in a small pony cart with her youngest daughter, thirteen-year-old Bridget, Kitchener's goddaughter. They all had tea in the Italian garden, except Fitz, gone to Eastbourne to say goodbye to his sister Mrs May. As they chatted, Kitchener suddenly said: 'Edith, dear, I've got to go away.'

'Have you, Herbert? *Where* are you going?'

'*My dear Edith*, I'm not allowed to tell you. I'm going away — these *damned* politicians!' Bridget had never heard the word before, as her father never swore. After a little, Cousin Herbert got up and walked her mother off to the kitchen garden, to get out of the child's earshot. Bridget aimed her box camera and snapped them.[5]

Next morning Fitz and Kitchener went to the early Holy Communion at Barham church, according to their usual custom, and spent a short morning in the house and garden. The furniture, chosen with cousin Flo's help, was gradually filling the rooms. The sunken rose garden, Fitz's particular creation, looked as if it would be at its best after the return from Russia. Less than a week later Toby would be placing a spray of Fitz's roses on his grave.

For the grass square at the centre of the garden Kitchener had designed an elaborate fountain, a bust of Pan with nymphs and dolphins. At the corners of the square would stand four pairs of cherubs, wrestling, running, embracing, dancing, after the *amorini* at Melbourne in Derbyshire. He had commissioned the sculptor John Haughton Bonnor to make clay models; Bonnor had remarked gallantly when Kitchener showed his design: 'Without flattering you, sir, it is as good as any architect's design.' During the winter of 1915–16 Kitchener had slipped down to the Bonnors' workshop in Chiswick for an hour on several Sundays. Bonnor died young, but forty-four years later his widow could write:

> My memory of his visits (up to the elbows in clay) in the making of these models is a delightful one, and the one sentence that runs in my head, remembering the discussions that arose in the workshop *re* material, decoration etc. was, 'What Bonnor says, goes', from Lord Kitchener.

Shortly before leaving for Russia he had telephoned the Bonnors and they had set up the models of the fountain and the cherubs in their workshop so that he could see the whole design, which he liked. He asked the probable cost. Without committing himself Bonnor named a figure which was about the same as a year's salary of the Secretary of State for War.

'Kitchener shook his head,' remembered Baroness Bonnor, 'and peered over his peculiar glasses and said: "I can't manage this now or they will say 'Nero fiddled . . .' but after the War, if the Nation want to give me anything, it will be very nice to have this scheme to put up before them."'[6]

Before they left Broome, Major Humphrey Leggett, the third partner with Fitz and Kitchener in the Songhor estate, the Kenya lands granted in 1911, came briefly. Leggett was attached to the Belgian War Office throughout the war but maintained close contact with East Africa by mail and cable, and he needed his partners' approval for a plan to raise much-needed capital for development by floating a private company, unaware that in less than thirty-six hours he would be sole owner.

They left for London in the early afternoon. The weather was breaking and a north-east wind blowing hard, but they drove extra fast – well over the 20 m.p.h. speed limit – and skidded more than once: as Kitchener put it, 'We seemed to waltz all the way up.'[7] They went straight to the War Office, where George Arthur had some papers for the Chief's signature. Fitz went on to York House to see the Chief's papers and luggage and his own into the official car, but Buckingham Palace protocol had stopped him taking medals and orders to distribute in Russia.

Kitchener had tea alone with George Arthur, inviting him to come in the car to the station. 'The talk was easy, and K was not at all perturbed by a rising wind which augured a rough sea, but a little disappointed to find the passage from Scapa to Archangel would take longer than he expected;

he was very anxious to be back within three weeks,' in case the Cabinet were up to mischief, especially against von Donop, the Master General of the Ordnance. In the car Kitchener particularly enjoined Arthur to see that Ronald Storrs received his CMG.

At King's Cross a special coach had been attached to the Scottish express. Creedy had come to see the party off: Kitchener and Fitzgerald; Sir Frederick Donaldson, Technical Adviser to the Ministry of Munitions, and his assistant, Leslie Robertson; Brigadier-General Wilfred Ellershaw, a senior staff officer at the War Office; Hugh O'Beirne, counsellor at the Petrograd embassy; a young interpreter, Second-Lieutenant R. D. Macpherson from the Cameron Highlanders; three servants and Kitchener's personal detective, McLaughlin, who came because George Arthur did not trust Russian protection for his Chief. Then O'Beirne, who was responsible for the party's cipher clerk, found him missing, having gone with the essential cipher book to the wrong station. If they held the express until the clerk was retrieved the timetables all the way from London to Edinburgh would be disrupted. O'Beirne must follow by a special and join them in Scotland.

Kitchener had boarded the train at once, as he always did to avoid being stared at. Then, very unusually, he appeared on the platform again and said 'very quietly – and a little sadly' to Arthur, 'Look after things while I am away.' 'Thereupon,' records Arthur, 'as if unable to explain to himself the impulse which had prompted him to have a last word, he quickly resumed his seat and looked away out of the window until the train started.'[8]

Next morning, Monday 5 June, as the train wound its way through the Highlands of Scotland and along lochs and shores, the last division of the Kitchener Armies, raised before conscription in answer to his call, crossed to France, a coincidence which afterwards seemed to have some symbolism.

Towards midday, Kitchener and his party arrived at Thurso and embarked in the destroyer HMS *Oak* at Scrabster pier. They made the crossing of Pentland Firth in pouring rain with a strong north-easterly gale, slightly moderated by their being in the lee of the Orkneys.

Sir John Jellicoe, who only a few days before had been in battle, welcomed them as they were piped aboard his flagship *Iron Duke*. As he recalled a few weeks later:

Lord Kitchener was in excellent spirits on arriving, and looked very well. The men were intensely interested in his visit as soon as they realized who he was, and showed their interest by clapping as he came over the side. His visit had of course been kept entirely secret, so that it was not until he was recognized that the fact of his presence became known.

Jellicoe had invited the flag officers of his fleet to luncheon, and they described the tactics and events of the recent Battle of Jutland. Kitchener briefed Jellicoe on the military situation, spoke of his pleasure in going to Russia and said he must be back in Britain as soon as the two voyages and the week's visit would allow.

They went round the vast battleship. Kitchener watched drills, entered turrets and was shown the techniques of the wireless telegraph room. He was greeted wherever he went with spontaneous ovations. The ratings on the mess decks fore and aft were paraded for his inspection. 'There were no speeches, just a slow walk past us,' recalled one rating long afterwards. 'My impression of the great man on that one occasion was of a gentle man in uniform with not a care in the world, whose humorous grey eyes looked at each one of us in passing as one might look on a child one has been pleased to meet, he so old in war, we so young.'[9]

The north-easterly gale had now worsened. Jellicoe was in some quandary. The route he had planned for Kitchener, sailing north-east from Scapa Flow into the open sea, was endangered because the extreme force of the gale into which his designated cruiser HMS *Hampshire* must head would prevent the escorting destroyers keeping up with her to check for submarines. The best alternative route, through the Pentland Firth westward to Cape Wrath and then north, was compromised by a report of an enemy submarine, later found to be false, and because the storm prevented the minesweepers making certain that they had swept and destroyed every mine.

Kitchener not wanting to wait until the gale moderated, Jellicoe consulted his experts and ordered the *Hampshire* to take a third route, rarely used by warships but frequently by fleet colliers and storeships: through the Pentland Firth and then north, close to the western coast of the Orkneys. As he reported to the Admiralty two days later:

I had selected this route because during the day a heavy north-easterly gale was blowing, and the western route gave promise of shelter and a better opportunity for destroyers to screen the *Hampshire* against submarine attack. This route was in constant use by mercantile auxiliaries for a very considerable time after the minefield west of the Pentland Firth had been laid by the enemy, and I considered it perfectly safe.[10]

He knew nothing of the activities of U.75, whose mines were the first to be laid by submarine in the area, but they might not have been fatal had Jellicoe's chief meteorologist remembered that when the storm centre of a north-easterly cyclonic storm had passed, it would be followed by an even fiercer north-western gale, violently sweeping the seas towards the coast. The *Hampshire* would be between the storm and a lee shore of rocks and jagged cliffs.[11]

Kitchener and his party left Jellicoe's flagship at 4 p.m. in torrential rain, transferring to HMS *Hampshire* on a drifter (small trawler) as the sea was too rough for the Admiral's pinnace. They had to be hoisted aboard. Captain H. J. Savill welcomed them. HMS *Hampshire* (10,850 tons) was less than eleven years old. She had four funnels and with her coal-burning reciprocity engines could reach 23 knots. Kitchener had sailed in her once before, in 1912, when he had crossed from Alexandria to Malta to confer with Asquith and Churchill, cruising in the Admiralty yacht. The *Hampshire* had also come to his attention in 1914 when she had carried the German naval prisoners captured when the raider *Emden* had been cornered and destroyed in the Cocos Islands. She had recently been refitted and taken part in the Jutland battle, though not hit. She carried a crew of 650.

According to custom, Captain Savill made over his cabin to Kitchener, and at 4.45 *Hampshire* slipped from her buoy, sailed out of Scapa Flow and an hour later met her two escorting destroyers. The gale was shifting, and increased in violence as the cruiser and the two destroyers turned north. The destroyers were unable to keep up in the teeth of the gale. In such heavy seas the risk of meeting a submarine was negligible. Captain Savill ordered the destroyers to return to base. *Hampshire* continued alone on a course about one and a half miles off the western coast of the Mainland (Pomona) of Orkney, with battened-down hatches, pitching steeply in the huge waves: had she been able to sail smoothly she might have passed harmlessly over U.75's mines. But, as one of the few survivors said, 'The ship was in the teeth of the most terrific gale of my experience.'

Kitchener, a good sailor, was relaxing in his cabin. Some in the

Admiralty afterwards surmised that Savill brought the ship closer in so that Kitchener should eat his dinner in quieter seas, but this is doubtful since he was off a lee shore. The crew off watch were eating their suppers.

On the shore, near Marwick Head, a boy of sixteen named Fraser was working in his father's garden at about 7.50 p.m. despite the cold and high wind, for the rain had stopped and three hours of daylight remained. 'My father called me. "If you want to see a battleship going by come and look!" We noticed there were no destroyers. We watched.

'We saw a small cloud of black smoke at water-line under the bridge. Then came a sheet of flame and yellow smoke from under the forward gun turret and all round it. But we heard nothing – the storm was too loud.

'The captain turned her to starboard and my father said, "He's going to beach her. That'll be all right." Then she stopped and the wind blew her back on to her previous course.'[12]

On board the *Hampshire* they heard an explosion. The ship lurched to starboard, electric power failed, all lights went out, the ship was unable to steer, and water gushed into vacant spaces. Captain Savill saw at once that the ship would go down and gave the order, *Abandon Ship*. Evacuation procedures followed immediately without panic as the hundreds of men moved to their stations.

Kitchener did not put on his khaki greatcoat but went into the corridor and towards the companionway. As a survivor heard, a gunnery officer called out, 'Make way for Lord Kitchener.' He came out on the quarter-deck, joined by FitzGerald, Ellershaw and young Macpherson. The cold, which Kitchener always loathed, was intense. He looked impassive. Boats were being lowered, only to be dashed against the side. The captain's galley was swung on to port side davits and Captain Savill called on Lord Kitchener to get into the boat, but either he did not hear or decided that such an action was useless (and indeed no boat made shore, only two of the Carley floats, the rest capsized by the enormous waves or thrown on the rocks). Many on the rafts died of exposure.

Kitchener was last seen by a survivor pacing the quarterdeck, talking with the other three: 'he gave no outward sign of nervousness.' The previous year in his letter of condolence to Lord Desborough he had spoken of his longing sometimes that the trumpet would soon sound for him, but he could not have conceived that it would happen like this.

Some ten minutes after the explosion, in that roaring sea, the stern suddenly lifted, the ship almost somersaulted, and went down into forty fathoms. If Kitchener was not killed outright by falling debris, or his lungs crushed by pressure, he could not have survived the water or cold more than for a few moments.

Because the ship sank in daylight near the shore several Orcadians saw the disaster. The postmistress at Birsay sent a telegram to the authorities; crofters with carts, and military with motor cars converged on the scene; and Jellicoe ordered ships, hoping against hope that the vessel in distress was not the *Hampshire*. Orcadians complained that military refusal to let civilians near a naval wreck, and naval hesitation in ordering out the civil lifeboat prevented many more being saved: only twelve reached the rockbound shore alive out of more than six hundred. Many were able to leave the ship only to be drowned, or killed by the intense cold; an earlier arrival of the destroyers, or more crofters being allowed down to the rocks of the Bay of Skail would have made little difference.

FitzGerald's body was one of the first to be lifted off by a destroyer: he therefore received a full military funeral in his home town of Eastbourne. Kitchener's body was never found.

On *Iron Duke* that night, having ordered many destroyers and yachts to the scene, Jellicoe waited in intense anxiety. When HMS *Unity* reported that she had passed through wreckage and floating bodies, Petty Officer Kingswell, in charge of the wireless telegraph room, who had proudly shown Kitchener around only twelve hours before, telephoned the Admiral, who came down in a topcoat over his pyjamas and sat in the petty officer's chair waiting, knowing that his ships were crossing and recrossing the scene to rescue whom they could. A wireless message came, confirming that the wreckage and bodies were from the *Hampshire*. Kingswell handed it to the Admiral. Jellicoe 'buried his face in his hands and rested head and shoulders on the desk in front of him, his whole body convulsed with sobs'.

EPILOGUE

WHILE A GRIEF-STRICKEN King George V was completing his inspection at Felixstowe and Queen Mary writing her sad note at Buckingham Palace, and Birdie in France reeled from Creedy's advance telegram, Sir Ian Hamilton was arriving at Winston Churchill's house in Cromwell Road. The government had agreed to lay the Gallipoli papers on the table, and Churchill had picked out a number which he believed would lay the blame on Kitchener, not on themselves. While Hamilton's motor went back for his wife and some friends, all invited to lunch by Clemmie Churchill, he and Winston pored over the papers in the downstairs study.

Suddenly they heard someone in the street crying out Kitchener's name. Winston threw up the window and they saw a newsvendor of 'wild and uncouth aspect' with a pile of evening papers over his arm, shouting, 'Kitchener drowned! No survivors!'

They looked at one another 'with a wild surmise'. 'Johnny' Hamilton felt stunned, and sad, and feared quite wrongly that it was he who had put the idea of going to Russia into Kitchener's head. 'Fitz gone too — it was awful.' When they went into the dining room, where Clemmie had quite a number of guests, Winston signed to everyone to be seated and then solemnly quoted, 'Fortunate was he in the moment of his death!'[1]

The dining room incident on that June day was a first token of the way Kitchener's reputation would be tossed up and down in memoirs and histories and personal reflections. A few nights later at Downing Street, Asquith said to Jack Pease, after remarking that no one had felt

Kitchener's death more, and he had cried all night: 'The world will never know as we know, Jack, of his limitations. It was most tragic, but his reputation and abilities for all time will be placed far higher than a true appreciation. It is well that it should be so.'[2] Yet little more than a year later, thrown out of power and unhappy with Lloyd George's leadership, Asquith 'Spoke much, and very highly, of Kitchener' when dining with one of the senior staff officers during a visit to Haig's headquarters in France.[3]

Lord Esher showed the same swing. Five years later he wrote *The Tragedy of Lord Kitchener*, which belittled him and was heavily criticized for inaccuracies and misjudgements by F. E. Smith and Winston Churchill, yet two days after the news of Kitchener's death Esher wrote to Lord Stamfordham: 'It is difficult to understand why we are being so heavily afflicted by the hand of Providence.' Esher had been lunching alone in Paris with the French statesman Briand.

He felt the blow quite as much as any of K's colleagues who will shed crocodile tears. You know my *real* feeling for K and I resent the secret satisfaction of those who depreciated and tried to trip him up. His faults were obvious. But his supreme merit was, that by night or day, since August 1914, he never had but one thought – how to win the war. The worry of it gave him sleepless nights, and wore him out by day.

No one who cared for him could regret the manner of his death, though not the season. It has sealed his fame, and will leave him, for all time, the legendary hero of this war.

Poor dear Fitz. Much as I liked him I am glad to think that he accompanied his friend and master into the land where cavillers and detractors are not crowned with glory and decorated with ribbons.

Esher added that the King, in his grief, had the supreme satisfaction of feeling that 'he *never wavered* in the support he gave to K, or allowed himself to be swayed by the jealousies and ineptitudes of K's colleagues.'[4]

The King wrote to his uncle, the Duke of Connaught, Governor-General of Canada, that Kitchener's tragic death was 'a terrible blow to me, as besides being a personal friend of 30 years' standing, I had the greatest admiration for him and absolute confidence in his judgement. I shall miss him terribly and his guiding hand . . .' The King's letter crossed one of deep sympathy from Connaught, who had known Kitchener since they were cadets at Woolwich and had always liked him. Connaught suggested that Kitchener's raising so great an army by voluntary enlistment was 'unique in the history of the world'.[5]

A stunned British public could hardly believe that he was gone. When the placards went up and the newsboys were shouting, people tumbled off buses to seize papers. Every rumour that he was saved would bring a cheer, then disappointment and anger that it was false. Though blinds were drawn, in the traditional token of mourning, and shops and stores shut, many believed that he was a prisoner, or kidnapped, or was hiding away to reappear at Britain's moment of greatest danger. Legends grew: that he had been murdered – the IRA had planted a bomb while the ship was refitting at Belfast which apparently had escaped detection for weeks and stayed inert through all the gunfire of Jutland. Mrs Asquith even received anonymous letters accusing her or her husband of murdering him. An ex-Boer, now German, spy claimed later, in perhaps the silliest story, that he had smuggled himself on to Kitchener's train and signalled to a U-boat from Thurso, which then picked up the spy and torpedoed the *Hampshire*, although the logs captured in 1945 prove that no U-boat was in Orkney waters that day.[6]

The rumours would have ended much sooner had the Admiralty released a detailed account quickly. Millie Parker, Kitchener's widowed sister, who had heard the news while at a charity bazaar in Essex and refused for weeks, like many, to believe her brother was really gone, wrote on 18 July: 'I personally have no hope and the reports are very trying entirely owing to our being given no information as to where the fault lay or the cause of the disaster.'[7]

When all hope was gone, Kitchener's death became, in the words of Walter Page, the American Ambassador, to President Wilson, 'an extraordinary stimulus to the war-spirit of the whole English nation. You could almost see the grim determination rise in their minds as you see the hot sun raise the mercury in a thermometer.'[8]

On the Western Front in France the troops felt the same bewilderment and shock at Kitchener's death. Haig, who ironically got the news first from an intercepted German wireless message, said 'How shall we get on without him?' Rawlinson, commanding a corps, felt numbed by the news: 'Another of my beloved old Chiefs gone!' Rawlinson wrote in his diary:

> He has been a great friend and a great example to me, and I shall miss him after the war is over more than I care to think. He was one of the great landmarks of my life, a source from which one could not help receiving many and valuable inspirations. He had a personality in which one could confide one's most secret thoughts without risk of having one's confidence abused.[9]

Rawlinson was comforted by the thought that 'K had completed his task of raising the new armies', but wished he could have lived to have seen them fighting in the coming battle, 'for I feel sure they would have made him proud of them'. Indeed; yet perhaps it was a mercy that he did not live to learn that no fewer than 19,000 British soldiers died on the first day of the Battle of the Somme on 1 July 1916 less than one month after his death. Haig's Intelligence Department had failed to discover that the Germans had built huge underground bunkers so that the days of intense bombardment were unavailing and the massed advancing British troops, expecting a walkover, were mown down by machine-guns. Had Kitchener been alive he might have ordered Haig to call off the battle rather than continue to slaughter the flower of the new armies for little gain.

As the war dragged on, the fashionable immediate view (especially in the Cabinet) that Kitchener's work was done, that he was fortunate in the moment of his death and could safely be missed, looked increasingly threadbare. Haig in his post-war personal report to the King made a significant remark that he was 'supported while Kitchener lived'.[10] In March 1917 the King's Assistant Private Secretary, Sir Clive Wigram, receiving 'a charming portrait of the dear old Chief, to whom I was devoted', wrote: 'How different everything would be now, and how happy the Army would be to feel his influence at the top.'[11] And when in February 1918 Rawlinson complained of drift in the directing of the war, and that Lloyd George was *not* the great statesman they needed, he exclaimed: 'We want K back – we shall feel the want of him more and more as time goes on.'[12] Haig himself afterwards wrote that perhaps victory could have come sooner 'if he had been with us to the end'.[13]

When that end came he was more than ever missed. Even had he not survived in the Cabinet once Lloyd George became Prime Minister, his prestige might have brought him into the counsels of the peacemakers, where he would have forced them to face the dangers of making a vindic-tive peace instead of the peace of reconciliation that he had outlined to Lord Derby a week before his death. He would certainly have supported John Maynard Keynes and Robert Brand as they wrestled, in vain, to demon-strate the economic consequences of the peace being dictated by Lloyd George, Clemenceau and President Wilson. Kitchener with his fluent French might have calmed Clemenceau's resentments, and with his huge prestige in America, might have overturned Wilson's ignorant prejudices about Europe, thus preventing the disaster of a second world war.

As Edward, Prince of Wales, said when unveiling Kitchener's statue on Horse Guards Parade ten years after his death: 'It will always be within just surmise that had the span of his life been but a little extended the forger of the great weapon of war would have been a great architect of peace.'

Statues and monuments were raised in Britain and overseas. The Sudan founded the Kitchener Memorial Medical School, thus fulfilling one of his dreams for Gordon College. In Cairo the Anglican cathedral of All Saints, already planned, became his memorial. In London the Lord Kitchener National Memorial Fund, under the presidency of Queen Alexandra, was hugely subscribed, and thus Kitchener Scholarships became a feature of the twentieth century and into the next.*

Nine years after his death a Kitchener memorial chapel was dedicated in St Paul's Cathedral. A life-sized effigy in white marble by Sir William Reid Dick lies on a sarcophagus. Opposite stands a marble pietà (the Virgin holding the crucified body of Christ before his burial and Resurrection) also by Reid Dick. The Roll of Honour of the Royal Engineers stands nearby. Each year on the Sunday nearest 5 June, attended by family and scholars, a service is held in the chapel or in a larger chapel nearby.

It echoes the great memorial service in the cathedral on 15 June 1916, delayed a few days in case his body was washed up, allowing a funeral. In a remarkable, perhaps unique, tribute, brief services were held simultane-ously at two-mile intervals behind the line of the Western Front and at the various headquarters further back, still within sound of the guns.

*For details see Appendix.

The St Paul's service formed a fitting climax, not least because in contrast to the ornate military ritual of Lord Roberts' funeral it was simple.

The King and Queen drove to St Paul's in an open carriage with a sovereign's escort of Life Guards in khaki. The King found the service 'most impressive. Mama and all the family were there, all the Govt., Ambassadors and ministers and thousands of soldiers. There were large crowds in the streets,' despite a hard northern wind in that arctic June.[14] Queen Alexandra, her lady-in-waiting noticed, was most upset, for she had the greatest regard and admiration and he was 'always so nice to her'.[15]

Kitchener's elder brother, the new earl, was abroad. Toby, now Viscount Broome, led the family, with the visibly disconsolate George Arthur and Kitchener's closest friends, the Derbys and the Salisburys. Alice Salisbury had written, 'For himself I cannot grieve; it is a splendid end to that magnificent life but . . . for his personal friends the loss is absolutely overwhelming and irreparable.'[16]

The service[17] began with the hymn 'Abide With Me'. For Sudan veterans it inevitably brought back memories of that memorial service for Gordon in the ruins of his palace which had reduced Kitchener to tears. Two appropriate psalms followed, 'Out of the deep have I called unto Thee, O Lord', and the twenty-third psalm, 'The Lord is my shepherd'. The lesson, the last portion of 1 Corinthians 15, seemed specially apposite in those days of sudden death:

> We shall all be changed, in a moment, in the twinkling of an eye, at the last trump: for the trumpet shall sound, and the dead shall be raised incorruptible. . . . Death is swallowed up in victory . . . Thanks be to God which giveth us the victory through our Lord Jesus Christ. Therefore, my beloved brethren, be ye steadfast, unmovable, always abounding in the work of the Lord . . .

The Dead March was played and the choir then sang the Liturgy of St Chrysostom, to the Kieff Chant, in tribute to the Russian connection and Kitchener's contacts with the Orthodox Church in his Cyprus days.

After the responses and prayers from the Burial Service, the congregation joined in 'For All the Saints'. The rousing Vaughan Williams tune which would become so familiar had only been published ten years and was not yet in cathedral use: they sang to Barnby's somewhat gloomy yet emotional tune. Brigadier-General John Charteris, representing Haig and his headquarters, was 'soon lost in the beauty and solemnity of the service. One did not, could not, think, one simply *felt*. It was utter peace . . . It was only . . . when the "Last Post" rang out that one realized one was there to mark the passing of a great man, from a great work well done, into eternity.'[18]

Yet perhaps the final words may be those of Sir Frederick Milner, the 'soldiers' friend', who wrote four days later: 'He will live in history amongst the greatest of Great Britain's sons, but it is well that the world should know that this straight, true, stern man had a heart as tender as his will was strong.'[19]

APPENDIX

THE LORD KITCHENER NATIONAL
MEMORIAL FUND

Not quite a month after Kitchener's death a Memorial Fund was established by the Lord Mayor of London. Within two years the Fund was worth a massive £500,000 (around £12,000,000 in modern terms), a Royal Charter had been granted and Queen Alexandra had become the patron.

The money was put immediately to good use by giving relief to casualties of war, both financially, in the form of grants, and practically, supplying artificial limbs and equipment for the disabled. Two important memorials to Lord Kitchener were also supported with the Fund: the Kitchener Memorial was created in the Chapel of All Souls, St Paul's Cathedral, and a generous grant was made to the Kitchener Memorial Medical School at the University of Khartoum.

When the government started to take financial responsibility for the disabled the Fund was used to enable soldiers, whose education had been broken by serving on active duty, to resume their studies by way of Kitchener Scholarships. Later, these scholarships were offered to the sons of men who had served, who had been offered places at university. This became the Fund's principal function: the award of Kitchener University Scholarships to school-leavers going on to study at university. The two main requirements for qualifying candidates are:

a) they must have served in the armed forces and be under the age of 30 or must have one parent who is serving or has served in the armed forces.

b) they must possess a good school record and potential for future development.

Up to the Second World War these awards were often the sole means of enabling young men to embark on higher education. Thus, in 1923 Lindsay Phillips, the future chairman of the Fund who, long after, interviewed the elderly surviving witnesses of the sinking of HMS *Hampshire*, won an Exhibition to

Gonville and Caius College, Cambridge, worth £40 p.a. His father, a Post Office supervisor who had served in the war, could not afford to put up more than £40 p.a. The Fund awarded Lindsay £150 p.a. for four years, thus providing him with £236 p.a. the then minimum on which an undergraduate could survive, paying university and college fees and living expenses.

After the Second World War and the coming of government grants, available to any student wishing to enter further education, the Kitchener Scholarships began to function rather as supplements to the grants, in that they enabled students to buy books or materials, participate in field trips during holidays or to join the societies offered by the colleges.

In 1985 girls became eligible to apply for Kitchener Scholarships. Towards the end of the twentieth century changes in the sytem of undergraduate financing by the universities and the state meant that Kitchener Scholarships took on a renewed significance, very similar to the importance of the Scholarships awarded in the early years of the Fund.

In the late 1970s the Council of the Fund found another important area of real need in the field of management training; more specifically in the training of mature young men and women graduates for important posts in British business at home and abroad. Awards in this field are permitted by the Fund's original Charter, which authorized: 'Travelling Scholarships . . . to enable persons who have completed their degree course . . . to study at home or abroad, with special reference to the promotion of trade and industry.'

Wise investing and the generosity of former scholars and others gave the Fund continued strength. In 1980 the Council awarded its first Kitchener European Scholarships towards the cost of a one-year course leading to a higher degree in Business Administration (MBA). The European Institute of Business Administration at Fontainebleau was chosen so that students would be able to benefit from mixing with 'those from other business environments, particularly European'. The scheme was an immediate success.

Candidates, both male and female, must have service connections, as for the undergraduate Scholarships, and require a strong recommendation from their employers or associates. They must have been accepted for an advanced business course and satisfy the Fund that they possess the necessary character and potential ability to benefit British business at home and abroad.

The Kitchener Scholars' Association, formed in 1921 by the first Scholars, helps past and present Scholars to maintain contact and mutual encouragement, and to keep bright the memory and ideals of Lord Kitchener. Each generation of the Kitchener family have been closely associated with the Memorial Fund and the Scholars' Association.

(Based on material kindly supplied by the Fund.)

REFERENCES AND NOTES
TO VOLUME I

MANUSCRIPT SOURCES

ABBREVIATIONS

CK   Charles Kitchener Papers
Earl K   3rd Earl Kitchener Papers
KP   Kitchener Papers, Public Record Office
NAM   National Army Museum
RA   Royal Archives
RE   Royal Engineers Archives
SAD   Sudan Archive, University of Durham
Own Words   *Kitchener in His Own Words* by J. B. Rye and Horace G. Groser
Kitchener is referred to as K throughout References and Notes

KITCHENER FAMILY COLLECTIONS

Kitchener Papers, Public Record Office. PRO 30.57. Deposited by 3rd Earl Kitchener 1958–59, catalogued 1980.

124 files, some very extensive: files 1–25 cover 1850–1902; files 26–85 cover 1902/3–1916; files 86–124 are Sir George Arthur's collection of Kitchener biographical material (letters, memoranda, etc.).

The Kitchener letters to St John Brodrick, afterwards Earl of Midleton, have been incorporated in the Kitchener Papers from the Midleton Papers.

3rd Earl Papers. Manuscripts and press cuttings, etc. remaining in the personal possession of 3rd Earl Kitchener, including Arthur Kitchener's letters to their father.

Charles Kitchener Papers, collected by the late Charles Kitchener and owned by the Hon. Mrs Charles Kitchener, including K's correspondence with Arthur Renshaw, Mrs Alexander Marc ('Cousin Flo') and others.

Hall Papers. Letters of Major-General Sir Walter Kitchener to his wife and brothers Chevallier and Arthur, letters of K to his father and to his brother Arthur.

Owned by Sir Walter Kitchener's granddaughter, Mrs Peter Hall.

Parker Papers. Letters of K to his sister Millie, Mrs Harry Parker. Owned by her great-granddaughter, Mrs Harriet King.

ROYAL ARCHIVES

Journals of Queen Victoria, King George V when Duke of York and Prince of Wales, and his wife, the future Queen Mary.

Letters to and from Queen Victoria, King Edward VII and King George V, Queen Mary, their Private Secretaries and other members of the Royal Households.

OTHER MANUSCRIPT COLLECTIONS

Biddulph Papers of General Sir Robert Biddulph. Royal Artillery Institute, Woolwich.

Birdwood Papers. Letters and Diary of William Birdwood, afterwards Field Marshal Lord Birdwood. National Army Museum.

Craig-Brown Diary. Imperial War Museum.

Gainford Papers. Diaries and notes of the Rt. Hon. Jack Pease, 1st Lord Gainford. Nuffield College, Oxford.

Gordon Papers. British Library.

Guild of St Helena Archives.

Hamilton Papers. Papers of General Sir Ian Hamilton. Liddell Hart Centre, Kings College, London.

Hatfield Manuscripts. K to Lady Cranborne, later Lady Salisbury, wife of 4th Marquess. Correspondence of 3rd Marquess. Diary of Lord Edward Cecil. Owned by the Marquess of Salisbury, Hatfield House.

Ilchester Papers. Letters of K to Lady Helen Vane-Tempest-Stewart, afterwards Countess of Ilchester. British Library.

Magnus Papers. Papers of Sir Philip Magnus-Allcroft, Bt., relating to his biography of K. Owned by Sir Philip's nephew, Mr Charles Sebag-Montefiore.

Methuen Papers. Letters of K to General Lord Methuen. Wiltshire Record Office.

Marker Papers. Letters of Colonel Raymond Marker to his family. National Army Museum.

Letters of K to Marker, and related papers. British Library.

National Army Museum Archives. Collections as noted, plus miscellaneous items.

Public Record Office. Cromer Papers; Foreign Office Papers.

Rawlinson. Diary of Major Sir William Rawlinson, Bt., afterwards General Lord Rawlinson of Trent. National Army Museum.

Royal Engineers Archives, including K's Confidential Reports and miscellaneous items concerning him.

Stucley Papers. Diary of Colonel Humphrey Stucley, owned by Sir Hugh Stucley, Bt.

Watson. Diary of Major James Watson. National Army Museum.

Wingate Papers, including his diaries, official journal, letters from K. Sudan Archive, University of Durham Library.

Woodliffe Papers. Items about K collected by Mr Allan Woodliffe.

<hr />

NUMBERED NOTES AND REFERENCES

1 Mrs Marc (cousin Flo, daughter of Emma Day, née Kitchener) to her son Alexander Marc, 7 November 1916. CK.

2 Information from John Chevallier Guild, present owner. See also the *Dictionary of National Biography* for Fanny's father, and Parry-Jones, *The Trade in Lunacy*, 1972.

3 Information on Lieutenant-Colonel Kitchener's army career kindly supplied by the Worcestershire Regiment Museum and the Royal Norfolk Regimental Museum, based on Hart's Annual Army Lists and Regimental Histories.

4 Letter to *The Times*, 1850, reprinted in Webster, *Ireland Considered for a Field of Investment or Residence*, pp. 14–15.

5 Ibid.

6 J. Anthony Gaughan, *The Knights of Glin*, pp. 120–21, and *Listowel and Its Vicinity*, pp. 315–16; Magnus, pp. 4–6. For a fuller study, see Royale, *The Kitchener Enigma*, pp. 7–15. Royale is the only K biographer to have explored his Irish

boyhood. The 29th Knight of Glin, Desmond FitzGerald, FSA, believes that Ballygoghlan had probably been part of the Glin estate and that his ancestor, when the tenant went bankrupt, preferred to sell the freehold to Colonel Kitchener rather than seek another tenant.

7 Sharpe MS. KP, 93, GA3, 11b. Mrs Sharpe's maiden and Christian names are not known. She may have married a Mr Sharpe or been given in later years a cour-tesy 'Mrs'.

8 Ibid., and later quotes in this chapter unless otherwsie identified.

9 Not *foul* language, as in Magnus, p. 4. Walter Kitchener's daughter Madge, who had provided her late father's memories, rebuked Magnus for his mis-take. Madge Kitchener to Sir Philip Magnus, 13 November 1958. Magnus papers.

10 From the first verse of 'From Every Stormy Wind that Blows' by Hugh Stowell (1799–1865).

11 Magnus, p. 6, quoting unspecified (and subsequently unidentified) 'family infor-mation'. Field Punishment No. 1 was abolished in 1923.

12 F. E. Kitchener (1838–1915) contributed the Rugby memoir to the composite two-volume official biography of Frederick Temple, afterwards Bishop of Exeter and Archbishop of Canterbury.

13 Magnus, p. 6, not giving any authority for the statement.

14 Royale, *op. cit.* p.14, from information supplied by the Savage family, owners of Crotta in 1910. The house was demolished in 1921.

15 Ibid., p. 12, quoting B. Beatty, *Kerry Memories*, p. 26.

16 C. E. Gourley, *They Walked Beside the River Shannon*, p. 21, quoted in Gaughan, op. cit., *Listowel and Its Vicinity*, p. 317.

Chapter 2: No Cricket at the Shop

1 In the Parker Papers.

2 Letters from the widow of a successor to Bennett state that K replied to her that it was not he but a brother who had been at the school. Another hand writes on the letter: 'It was Herbert.' KP, 91, GA2, 36, 37.

3 Royale, *op. cit.* pp. 19–20, giving details from the official report.

4 Arthur, *Life*, vol. 1, pp. 6–7.

5 Major-General Sir Lovick B. Friend, remarks to J. A. Pease (a member of Asquith's Cabinet, afterwards Lord Gainford). Gainford MS 42, f. 78. (T/S autobiography, Chapter 4.) Nuffield College, Oxford.

6 Henry Nevinson, quoted in John Fisher, *That Miss Hobhouse*, p. 115; J. A. Pease comment, Gainford MS, op. cit., f. 79.

7 MS Reminiscences (dictated 1926). RA, Add 15.8452; Duke of Connaught to KG V, 8 June 1916. RA, GV A A 42/41.

8 K to Millie, 26 July 1868. Parker Papers.

9 Société d'Émulation des Côtes-du-Nord, *Bulletins et Memoires*, Tome XCI, 1963, p. 127.

10 K to Millie, 31 May [1869]. Parker Papers.

11 K to Augusta Gordon, 16 October 1885. BL Add Mss 51300, f. 156. The early acquaintance between Gordon and Kitchener is not documented, but their meeting first at Sir Henry's home is a reasonable conjecture were it not for Gordon's comment of 1877 (below). For Gordon's story, see the present writer's *Gordon: The Man Behind the Legend* (1993).

12 Colonel Gordon to – Mason, 15 January 1877. NAM.

Chapter 3: Heart and Soul

1 Arthur *Life*, vol. 1, p. 8n.

2 As Magnus asserts, pp. 8–9.

3 The French honoured his intention to serve in battle. In 1913 the Minister of War sent Field Marshal Earl Kitchener the campaign medal, writing that France had not forgotten the Woolwich cadet 'who at a sad hour of our history did not hesi-tate to offer his services and to fight under our flag'. Arthur, *Life*, vol. 1, p. 10 (in the original French).

4 Arthur, *Life*, vol. 1, pp. 10–11. The duke's remark is as Arthur remembered K telling the story. Lord Esher (*The Tragedy of Lord Kitchener*, p. 193) reports a differ-ent version but, as his memory of K's oral reminiscence is faulty in other details, it is not reliable.

5 K to Millie, 26 May [1871]. Parker Papers.

6 Ibid.

7 Details from K to Millie, 26 May [1871], 18 August and 1 December [1872]. Parker Papers.

8 Arthur, *Life*, vol. 1, pp. 5–6. The comments by Col. R. H. Williams, RE, were given orally at Dorchester to H. N. Hill, whose covering letters of 27 and 30 January 1917 to Arthur are KP 91, GA z, 41–2. The notes themselves are not extant.

9 Ibid.

10 16 October 1873. RE, M485.

11 Williams, MS cit., quoted in Arthur, pp. 12–13.

12 Perhaps K's nearest to preaching was his admonition, 'And now Millie you must always remember your awful responsibility in the bringing up of a boy who will eventually in the course of nature be a man, and you must try and inculcate good

things etc etc'. But then he felt embarrassed and ended, 'I thought I was writing a sermon'. K to Millie, 26 May [1871]. Parker Papers.

13 Chevallier family tradition.

14 K to Millie, 3 December 1873. Parker Papers. There is no documentary evidence that Colonel Kitchener blocked this by refusing funds (as in Magnus, p. 11). K would have gone at public expense.

15 K to Millie, 7 March '1874' (misdated for 1875, from Jerusalem). Parker Papers.

16 K to Millie, 18 March 1874. Parker Papers.

17 M. E. Monier, *Dinan: Mille Ans D'Histoire*, Mayenne, 1977, p. 554. Kawara (d. 1928) received the Croix de Chevalier de la Légion d'Honneor.

18 K to Millie, 22 December 1874. Parker Papers.

Chapter 4: 'The Footsteps of our Lord'

1 *Morning Post*, 20 June 1916, letter from A.S.C.

2 K to Millie, 22 December 1874. Parker Papers. Royale (p. 30) has K flirting with her but the MS does not support this.

3 Ibid. The following quotes and details are also from that letter to Millie, or the next dated 7 March 1875.

4 Information from Wellcome Institute of the History of Medicine.

5 K to Millie, 7 March 1875. Parker Papers. Punctuation supplied.

6 Conder, *Tent Work in Palestine*, vol. 2, p. 103.

7 Clermont Ganneau, quoted in Arthur, *Life*, vol. 1, p. 23n.

8 Kitchener argued for Khurbet Minieh, but Tell Hum was positively identified in 1905 and excavated and reconstructed from 1968.

9 Conder, *Tent Work*, vol. 2, pp. 195–9; Arthur, *Life*, vol. 1, pp. 17–18; *Own Words*, p. 32.

10 Arthur *Life*, vol. 1, p. 21 (from the Palestine Exploration Fund archives). The book, obtainable only from the Fund, had a small sale. No copy is in the British Library.

11 *The Sentry*, July 1916. The other quote is from an undated article (*c.* 1910) by the Reverend F. Penny (Archives of the Guild of St Helena). The guild flourished under the patronage of bishops and generals and founded Soldiers' Institutes in garrison towns at home and abroad. The Anglo-Catholic emphasis of its leaders became rather marked, until the chaplain-general who succeeded Edghill in 1903 (Bishop Taylor Smith, an Evangelical) withdrew his patronage and gave it to the Church of England Men's Society. The guild declined and was wound up in 1921, but its sister organization, the Guild of St Helena, founded in 1879 by Malet's wife, flourishes as a services charity. (Information kindly supplied by the secretaries.)

The (Evangelical) Officers' Christian Union (formerly Prayer Union) antedated the Guild of the Holy Standard, which in turn predated the non-denominational Soldiers' Christian Association (1887), still flourishing after amalgamation with the older Scripture Readers Association (1838) as the Soldiers' and Airmen's Scripture Readers Association (see Ian Dobbie, *Sovereign Service*, 1988).

12 In *The Tragedy of Lord Kitchener*, p. 7, Lord Esher says that he first heard the name of K when Gordon eulogized him, and the date of that conversation must be December 1882. The last time that Gordon and K were in the same country before that time was New Year 1877.

13 K to 'My dear Miss Hutchinson' (evidently middle-aged or elderly), 5 May 1877. Parker Papers.

14 K to Millie, 6 June 1877. Parker Papers.

15 K to Millie, 4 September 1877. Parker Papers.

16 For a good summary, see Samuel Daiches, *Lord Kitchener and His Work in Palestine*. Daiches was a Jewish scholar.

17 Walter Besant, *Twenty-One Years' Work in the Holy Land*, p. 127. Quoted Royale, *op. cit.*, p. 37.

18 The two were Edmund O'Donovan (killed with Hicks Pasha in 1883) and Frank Scudamore, later with K in the Sudan. Frank Scudamore, *A Sheaf of Memories*, pp. 93–4.

19 Walter Kitchener to Amy Fenton, 14 January 1878. Hall Papers. Written from the Curragh Camp near Dublin, where he was staying with the newly married Chevallier. Magnus, p. 22, wrongly names the recipient as 'Walter's young wife', i.e. Caroline ('Carry') Fenton. They married in November 1884. Amy, Hetty and Carry were daughters of Colonel Kitchener's great friend, Major Charles Fenton, late 9th Foot.

Chapter 5: Cyprus Survey

1 K to Thomas Clement Cobbold, CB, MP, 11 September 1878. Copy (by Guy Cobbold) in Magnus Papers.

2 Salisbury to K, 13 Septmeber 1878. No. 53, Cyprus Correspondence 1878–9, vol. 1, pp. 66–7 (in Biddulph Papers, RA Institute); Walter Kitchener to Amy Fenton, 3 September 1878. Hall Papers.

3 Walter Kitchener to Hetty Fenton, 4 June 1878. Hall Papers. Magnus names the wrong sister and interpolates a smell of incense and an exotic brand of tea without manuscript authority. A later writer then discusses whether these (mythical) features were symptoms of homosexuality!

4 K to Millie, 2 Oct 1878. Parker Papers.

5 K to Salisbury, 27 Nov 1878. Cyprus, No. 223.

6 K to Millie, 2 February 1879. Parker Papers.

7 K to Salisbury, 16 May 1879. Cyprus, vol. 2, pp. 7–8; Arthur, *Not Worth Reading*, p. 99.

8 K to Colonel Kitchener, 21 Aug 1879. Hall Papers.

9 K to Millie, 6 September 1879. Parker Papers.

10 Arthur *Life*, vol. 1, pp. 37–8.

11 K to Millie, 12 November 1879. Parker Papers.

12 Ibid., 22 March 1880.

13 Biddulph to Lord Kimberley (Foreign Secretary), 7 July 1881. *Annual Blue Book for 1880.*

14 K to Millie, 18 April 1880. Parker Papers.

15 Arthur, *Life*, vol. 1, p. 42n, quoting an unnamed friend.

16 Biddulph's letter of 7 July 1881, op. cit.

17 Memorandum by K in 1885, printed in Arthur, *Life*, vol. 1, pp. 44–6.

18 K to Millie, 2 August 1880. Parker Papers.

19 Arthur Kitchener, with one page by K, to Colonel Kitchener, 28 September 1880. Earl K.

20 Arthur Kitchener to Colonel Kitchener, 12 July 1882. Earl K. Arthur wrote immense reports to the colonel on every aspect of the Waihemo run's affairs.

21 Arthur, *Life*, vol. 1, p. 42. The colleague, unnamed, may have been (Sir) Charles King-Harman.

22 *Cyprus Herald*, 22 March 1882.

23 K to Arthur Kitchener, 19 March 1881. Earl K.

24 K to Millie, 2 July 1881. Parker Papers.

25 Colonel Kitchener to K, undated. From Sir George Arthur's notes of letters from father to son which were lost or destroyed after 1920.

26 K to Arthur Kitchener, 19 March 1881. Earl K.

27 Arthur Kitchener to Colonel Kitchener, 1 October 1883. Earl K.

28 Colonel Kitchener to K, undated. KP, 98, GA3/13.

Chapter 6: Arabi and After

1 Biddulph family tradition, per Miss Constance Biddulph, granddaughter of Sir Robert. Sir Charles King-Harman (1851–1939) married his daughter in 1888 and was Governor of Cyprus 1904–11.

2 Tulloch, Sir A. B., *Recollections of Forty Years' Service*, p. 264.

3 Frank Scudamore, *A Sheaf of Memories*, p. 96.

4 K to Colonel Falk-Warren, 28 August 1884. *The Times*, 19 August 1932, the letter having been sent by Falk-Warren's son.

5 Colonel Kitchener to Arthur Kitchener, 7 August [1882]. Hall Papers. Because he was unattached and not in uniform he was refused the campaign medal, though recommended for both army and navy campaign medals.

6 K to Biddulph, 2 August 1882, KP, 30/57/1/A5. Biddulph gave this letter to K's family after K's death, two years before his own.

7 Arthur *Life*, vol. 1, p. 49n; Colonel Kitchener to Arthur Kitchener, MS cit.

8 K to Arthur Kitchener, 20 September 1882. Hall Papers.

9 Confidential Report, July 1882. RE, M495.

10 Biddulph family tradition.

11 See the farewell testimonial from the Archbishop, 4 March 1883, quoted in *Own Words*, pp. 76–7.

12 Pollock, *Gordon*, p. 266; Esher, *The Tragedy of Lord Kitchener*. Brett became the 2nd Viscount Esher and a close friend of Kitchener's but rather betrayed him posthumously by his strange book.

13 KP, 1 A 8–9.

14 John Macdonald, *Daily News*, 30 January 1883, quoted with another version in *Own Words*, pp. 71–6.

15 K to Millie, 21 January 1883. Parker Papers.

16 Ibid., 22 March 1883.

17 Arthur Kitchener to Colonel Kitchener, 1 May 1881. Earl K.

18 Arthur, *Life*, vol. 1, p. 50n.

19 K to Millie, 13 March and 1 April 1883. Parker Papers.

20 Ibid., 25 August 1883.

21 A. E. Linney, *Kitchener and the Five Kitchener Lodges*, Transactions of the Bolton Masonic Research Society, 1970. His appointments are listed in Appendix 2.

22 Arthur (*Life*, vol. 1, p. 53) quotes K in a letter of October 1883 to Besant of the PEF as saying he had not been home for five years. He could not have forgotten his home leave of 1881, with the uproar over Walter, so this is probably a transcribing slip at PEF.

23 Arthur, *Life*, vol. 1, p. 55. The letter probably came from Wood, as K's superior, on the instructions of Baring. The original is not in KP.

24 Hon. Secretary of PEF to Arthur, 3 March 1917. KP, 91.48. Tinted spectacles (probably by Zeiss of Jena) were still fairly unusual.

Chapter 7: Blood Brothers on the Desert

1 Quoted in Arthur, *Life*, vol. 1, p. 60. La Terrière's comments are not in KP.

2 Letters to Sir Philip Magnus-Allcroft from Valentine Baker's niece, Mrs Agatha Turning, 31 October 1957, and great-nephew, Robin Bailey, 27 August and 20

November 1957; and from Mrs Bonte Sheldon Elgood, 1959 (T/S copy). Magnus Papers. Also Chevallier family information. Edith Cobbold, a second cousin, married Fanny Kitchener's nephew, John Monins. Edith was a close friend of K's, and her daughter married Toby, his heir, after K's death.

3 K to Colonel Kitchener, 20 March 1884. Parker Papers.

4 K to Colonel Kitchener, 25 March 1884. Parker Papers.

5 K to Millie, 10 April 1884. Parker Papers.

6 Ibid.

7 Mrs Bonte Shelton Elgood to Magnus, 1959. T/S copy. KP, 102 PA 24.

8 Robin Bailey to Magnus, 27 August 1957 (Bailey was a nephew of Annie, who married General Sir Elliott Wood); Mrs Agatha Turning (Lady Wood's sister) to Magnus, 31 October 1957. Magnus Papers. Their mother, Mrs Bourne, was Valentine Baker's sister.

9 Robin Bailey heard about the locket in K's lifetime, when staying with Sir Samuel Baker's widow before 1914. Mrs Turning believed it was later handed to the Dean of St Paul's (Inge) but was unable to discover whether it is actually in the sarcophagus beneath K's effigy. Magnus Papers, MSS cit.

10 K to Colonel Kitchener, 14 May 1884. Parker Papers.

11 K to Millie, 11 July 1884. Parker Papers.

12 Arthur, Life, vol. 1, p. 73. Lieutenant-General Sir Frederick Stephenson to Military Secretary, War Office, 1 September 1884. RE, M495.

14 K to Millie, 4 April 1885. Parker Papers.

15 Arthur, Life, vol. 1, p. 99.

Chapter 8: Lifeline to Gordon

1 Sir Ronald Storrs, *Orientations*, p. 133.

2 K to Millie, 25 April 1885. Parker Papers. He was criticizing Hake's *Life of Gordon* (1884), which she had sent him.

3 Sir George Arthur, *Not Worth Reading*, p. 117; Sir Ronald Storrs, *Orientations*, p. 133; Lord Edward Cecil, *Leisure of an Egyptian Official*, p. 192.

4 H. Seymour to Sir Henry Ponsonby, 24 August 1884. RA Add A12/2216.

5 Arthur, *Life*, vol.1, pp. 74-5. KP, 4, D9-10. Lieutenant-General Sir Frederick Stephenson to Military Secretary, War Office, 1 September 1884. RE, M495.5.

6 See telegrams in KP, 4. D.

7 K to Millie, 4 October 1884. Copy in another hand in Parker Papers; KP, 4.D.22(a).

8 Arthur, *Life*, vol. 1, p. 88; K to P. Ralli, 12 January 1885. KP, 5, E12. Printed Arthur, *Life*, vol. 1, pp. 90-93, slightly edited.

9 K to Ralli, MS cit. (12 January 1885).

10 See précis of telegrams 24 August to 11 October 1884. KP, D225, 226.

11 K to Ralli. MS cit.

12 K to Colonel Kitchener, 1 December 1884. Parker Papers.

13 Ibid. 24 November 1884. Hall Papers.

14 Colonel Sir Charles Wilson to K, 10 November 1884. KP, 4, D158. As K did not file the cypher, these telegrams were decoded only in 1959 by the PRO and were not available to Magnus.

15 *The Journals of Major-General C. G. Gordon, CB at Khartoum*, ed. A. Egmont Hake, pp. 360, 362 and 363.

16 K to Colonel Kitchener, 1 December 1884, MS cit.

17 K to Millie, 12 December 1884. Parker Papers.

18 Lieutenant-General Sir Frederick Stephenson to Military Secretary, War Office, 1 September 1884. RE, M495.

19 K to Colonel Kitchener, 26 December 1884. Hall Papers.

20 Adrian Preston, *In Relief of Gordon: Lord Wolseley's Campaign Journal*, p. 108.

21 Preston, op. cit., p. 129.

22 The Bishop of Plymouth (RC) to Arthur, 22 March 1925. KP, 91, P174.

23 Brindle must have told it often, as the versions given by Sir Evelyn Wood, in *From Midshipman to Field Marshal* (vol. 2, p. 174), and Frank Scudamore are slightly different.

24 Sir George Arthur, *Not Worth Reading*, pp. 116 and 117.

25 K to Colonel Kitchener, 17 March 1885. Arthur, *Life*, vol. 1, p. 105 (original MS missing).

Chapter 9: His Excellency

1 Arthur, *Not Worth Reading*, pp. 119–20.

2 Wolseley to Queen Victoria, 5 May 1885. RA O.26/12. Sir Charles Wilson's opinion was also to be asked. Wolseley consented, while pointing out that, as both officers were on the staff of the army he commanded, the request was irregular.

3 K to Colonel Kitchener, 16 February 1885. Hall Papers. K to E. A. Floyer (head of telegraphs), 17 March 1885. RE, 5001.4/3 (ES41).

4 Diary of Colonel Willoughby Verner. *The Nineteenth and After*, August 1916, p. 289.

5 It would have been at this time that an incident could have occurred but is probably apocryphal. According to a Canadian war correspondent writing fourteen years later, Kitchener disguised himself as an Arab prisoner and spent a night in the guard tent, where he overheard details of a plot to murder Wolseley and others.

Next day he was nearly murdered himself when the ringleader recognized him as he sat in full uniform with Wolseley, trying the case. The man jumped on Kitchener and nearly throttled him before being overpowered. The story is improbable, if only because such a memorable incident finds no mention in Wolseley's day-by-day journal. (See Charles Lewis Shaw, *Canadian Magazine*, March 1899.)

6 K to E. A. Floyer, 24 May 1885. RE, 5001.41/5 (E.S.41).

7 Arthur, *Life*, vol. 1, p. 105. Original not in KP.

8 Kitchener's *Notes on the Fall of Khartoum* is printed in Arthur, *Life*, vol. 1, pp. 116–24.

9 Lord Desborough's address at the Canadian Red Cross Hospital, Cliveden, 10 June 1916.

10 K to Colonel Kitchener, 3 July [1885]. Hall Papers.

11 K to E. A. Floyer, 6 September [1885]. RE, 5001.41.2 (E.S.41).

12 Magnus's assertion (p. 69) that K pulled 'every string within reach' is not supported by contemporary evidence. He also misdates the appointment.

13 K to Millie, 11 January 1886. Parker Papers.

14 This was Charles Watson, RE, who as a young officer had served in Equatoria under Gordon, whom he admired tremendously. Watson, personally brave, had a distinguished later career in survey, etc. and was knighted.

15 K to Arthur Kitchener, 5 November 1886. Hall Papers.

16 K to Millie, 7 September 1887. Parker Papers.

17 Abd Allahi Muhammad Turshain, Khalifat al-Mahdi (1846–99). His earlier victories had been a principal factor in the Mahdi's success. See Richard Hill, *A Biographical Dictionary of the Sudan*, 2nd edn.

18 K to *The Times*, 9 January 1888; K to Major-General Sir F. Grenfell, 1 January 1889. Quoted in *Own Words*, pp. 87 and 100–101.

19 K to Grenfell, 6 February 1887, quoted in *Own Words*, p. 95.

20 Sir Francis Grenfell to ? Salisbury, 31 December 1888. Copy in RA 0.27/44.

21 Fox's letter is quoted in *Own Words*, p. 98.

22 Baring to Sir P. Anderson (Permanent Under-Secretary), 24 March 1888. PRO, FO.633.5, p. 199.

23 K to E. A. Floyer, 31 December 1886. RE, 5001.41.6.ES.41. Magnus, p. 73.

24 K to Arthur Kitchener, 5 November 1886. Hall Papers.

25 Colonel Kitchener to K, 5 November 1886. Hall Papers. Undated letters quoted in Sir George Arthur's summary of letters no longer extant. KP, 93 GA 3.13.

26 A. B. M. Shakespear Bey to Millie, 19 January 1888. Galbraith's account is 24 January and McMurdo's (below) 10 February. McMurdo had replaced Peel. Parker Papers.

27 Wolseley to K, 3 February 1888. KP, 5.E.44.

28 K to Millie, 17 March 1888. Parker Papers.

29 Sir Henry Ponsonby (HM's Private Secretary) to the Duke of Cambridge, 21 March 1888. RA, E.63/29.

30 K to Millie, 1 May 1888. Parker Papers.

31 Grenfell to War Office, 19 February 1888. RE, 5001.

Chapter 10: Sirdar

1 Lord Edward Cecil, *Leisure of an Egyptian Official*, p. 183.

2 K to Arthur Kitchener, 13 August [1888]. Hall Papers.

3 Ibid., 4 September 1888. Hall Papers (and next quote, re grouse).

4 K to Millie, 24 July 1889. Parker Papers.

5 RE, ME 5001. Grenfell's response to the printed list of personal qualities was: 1. *Judgement*: Good, 2. *Tact*: Fair, 3. *Temper*: Good. 4. *Self-reliance*: Great. 5. *Power of Commanding Respect*: Sufficient.

6 K told this *c.* 1912 to Sir Maurice Amos, who told it to Stephen J. Gordon. Letter from S. J. Gordon to Magnus, 7 November 1958. Magnus Papers.

7 K to Millie, 14 January 1891, Parker Papers.

8 K to Millie, 12 February 1892. Parker Papers.

9 Cecil, op. cit., p. 184.

10 Martin Gilbert, *Sir Horace Rumbold*, p. 18.

11 Frank Scudamore, *A Sheaf of Memories*, p. 104.

12 Betty Askwith, A Victorian Young Lady, 1978, pp. 136–9.

13 For further details, see the list of Kitchener's Masonic appointments in Appendix 2. He was District Grand Master of Egypt and the Sudan 1899–1901.

14 K to Lady Cranborne, 9 November 1889. Hatfield MSS.

15 K to Millie, 4 October 1889. Parker Papers.

16 K to Millie, 14 January 1891 and 12 February 1892. Parker Papers.

17 Margot Asquith, *More Memories*, pp. 121–2.

18 Wingate Diary of the Inspection 13–23 January 1894. Wingate Papers, SAD. Original: 102.4.1–45. Copy in W's hand: 179.4.110–127. John Marlowe, *Cromer in Egypt*, pp. 173–7; Arthur *Life*, vol. 1, pp. 181–3; KP have nothing; Magnus, pp. 83–9. Magnus wrongly says the incident was hushed up; it was fully reported in the British press. His view of the incident's effect on K is questionable.

19 K to Edith Chevallier (afterwards Preston), 23 February 1894. CK.

20 K to Arthur Kitchener, 19 August 1894. Hall Papers.

21 Ibid. Letters 33–41 in Hall Papers.

22 K to Wingate, 2 August 1894. SAD, 256.1.249.

23 Marlowe, op. cit., pp. 200–201.

24 Walter Kitchener to his wife, 9 April 1896. Hall Papers.

25 Arthur, *Life*, vol. 1, p. 187; Scudamore, op. cit., p. 99. No copy of the telegram is in KP.

Chapter 11: *Advance up the Nile*

1 Arthur, *Life*, vol. 1, pp. 187–8. The best modern account of the campaigns of 1896–8 is in Henry Keown-Boyd, *A Good Dusting: The Sudan Campaigns 1883–1899*. The classic contemporary account is Winston Churchill's *The River War*, 1899. For a Sudanese history, see I. H. Zulfo, *Karari*.

2 The French and Russian Commissioners voted against but were outvoted by the British, Italian, German and Austrian. The money was therefore advanced, but the two dissenters sued the Egyptian government for its return on the ground that the decision should have been unanimous. See Marlowe, *Cromer in Egypt*, p. 203.

3 KP, 12. K 8 and 9.

4 Marlowe, op. cit., p. 202; KP, 11, J 1–9. The telegrams from the War Office to Knowles were shown to K only when the command was settled in his favour. Wingate's remark to his son that K was 'worried to death about his own position' (Sir Ronald Wingate to Magnus, 5 March 1956. Magnus Papers) referred to a later episode, in 1897.

5 MS memories of Major-General Sir Nevill Maskelyne Smyth, VC. KP, 93, GA 12. p. 1; Arthur, *Life*, vol. 1, pp. 193–4; Sir Victor Mallet, ed., *Life with Queen Victoria*, p. 100.

6 E. W. C. Sandes, *The Royal Engineers in Egypt and the Sudan*, p. 174.

7 Scudamore, op. cit., p. 95.

8 Cromer to Salisbury, 15 March 1896. Hatfield MSS, A/109. Quoted in Marlowe, op. cit., p. 206.

9 Lord Edward Cecil, op. cit., pp. 183–4; Arthur, *Not Worth Reading*, p. 80; Kenneth Rose, *The Later Cecils*, pp. 193–6.

10 For Watson, see Repington, *Vestigia*, p. 156ff, and *Roll of Honour* of 60th Rifles, 1942, pp. 105–6. The Cecil diary, unpublished, is in Hatfield MSS.

11 For Hunter, see Duncan H. Doolittle, *A Soldier's Hero: The Life of General Sir Archibald Hunter*, p. 80, and Archie Hunter, *Kitchener's Sword-Arm*. For Wingate, see Sir Ronald Wingate, *Wingate of the Sudan*.

12 A man commissioned from the ranks was usually sent to another regiment, except for ex-regimental sergeant-majors who became 'captains and quartermasters'. For MacDonald, see Royale, *Death Before Dishonour*.

13 Scudamore, op. cit., p. 138.

14 Before modern suncreams English faces in the tropics tended to burn red rather than brown under their obligatory sun-helmets.

15 Wingate, op. cit., p. 106.

16 Doolittle, op. cit., p. 80.

17 Slatin to Queen Victoria, 26 June 1896. *Letters of Queen Victoria*, Third Series, vol. 3, pp. 51–2.

18 Cromer to Sir Francis Knollys (Private Secretary to the Prince of Wales), 20 June 1896. RA, W 49/62.

19 Doolittle, op. cit., p. 80.

20 But see St Luke's Gospel, Chapter 17, Verse 9.

21 Hunter, op. cit., p. 51.

22 N. M. Smyth, VC, MS cit., p. 5. KP, 93 GA 3.12.

Chapter 12: Dongola 1896

1 It was said that the doctors were terrified of Kitchener and did not dare to demand more supplies.

2 A. G. C. Liddell, *Notes from the Life of an Ordinary Mortal*, p. 335.

3 K to Edith Cobbold, afterwards Mrs John Monins, as quoted by her to her grandson Charles Kitchener on his confirmation, 26 November [1936]. CK.

4 N. M. Smyth, VC, MS cit., p. 3.

5 Cecil, op. cit., p. 187.

6 W. E. Bailey was later Assistant Adjutant-General, Egyptian Army, and retired after the First World War as a major in the British Army; he died in 1934. Keown-Boyd, *Soldiers of the Nile*, p. 25.

7 Cecil, op. cit., pp. 185–8.

8 Cecil, op. cit., p. 187.

9 Hunter to George Hunter, 31 August 1896, quoted in Hunter, op. cit., pp. 53–4.

10 Hunter, op. cit., p. 53, quoting Cecil's diary about Hunter's 'murder' dispatch, and p. 52, describing Hunter's letter. This is not in KP. Possibly the dispatch mentioned by Cecil was in fact the letter.

11 N. M. Smyth, VC, MS cit., p. 2.

12 Ibid. See also Arthur, *Life*, vol. 1, p. 199.

13 Magnus, p. 99.

14 Cecil, op. cit., p. 190.

15 N. M., Smyth, MS cit., p. 2.

16 The reason was not generally known until Zulfo found evidence in the 1970s. See Zulfo, op. cit., p. 66.

17 *The Sudan Campaign* 1886–1899, by 'An Officer' (i.e. H. L. Pritchard, RE), p. 70.

18 *Letters of Queen Victoria*, Thid Series, vol. 3, p. 80.

Chapter 13: The Impossible Railway

1 Promotion proposed by the Secretary of State for War, 24 September 1896. RE, M495.

2 Victor Mallet, ed., *Life with Queen Victoria*, p. 99. The quotation from Marie Mallet below is from p. 100.

3 Queen Victoria's Journal, 16 November 1896. RA QVJ of E. W. C. Sandes, *Kitchener the Man*, RE Journal, December 1943, p. 230.

4 The dissenting French and Russian Commissioners had appealed to the Mixed Tribunal on the ground that the decision should have been unanimous. The tribunal found in their favour.

5 Magnus, pp. 102–103, quoting Hatfield MSS.

6 Doolittle, op. cit., p. 152.

7 E. W. C. Sandes, *The Royal Engineers in Egypt and the Sudan*, p. 233; Arthur, *Life*, vol. 1, p. 208, quoting 'a staff officer'.

8 Sandes, op. cit., p. 226.

9 The story of the construction of the SMR is told in Sandes, op. cit., Chapter 9.

10 RE 5001 (Miscellaneous Papers).

11 Sandes, op. cit., p. 222.

12 Doolittle, op. cit., p. 113. Kipling's 'Recessional' appeared shortly after. Both officers would have been astonished that within a century 'our pomp of yesterday Is One with Nineveh and Tyre'.

13 Watson Diary. NAM, RC 8412–4–6.

14 Ibid., 12 July 1897.

15 N. M. Smyth, VC, MS cit., p. 5. Ibrahim not only captured Berber but lived to be received by King George V in London in 1919.

16 The British officers killed at Omdurman on 2 September 1898 were serving with the British brigades.

17 K to Arthur Renshaw, 29 September 1897. CK.

18 N. M. Smyth, VC, MS cit., pp. 7 and 8; Keown-Boyd, op. cit., p. 61.

19 Sir Ronald Wingate to Magnus, 5 March 1956. Magnus Papers.

20 Arthur, *Life*, vol. 1, p. 217.

21 Sir Ronald Wingate, MS cit.

22 Grenfell Diary, 12 October 1897. Typed copy in KP, 10.I. p. 4.

23 Watson Diary, 16 October 1897.

24 Quoted in Sandes, op. cit., p. 204n.

25 Quoted in Magnus, p. 110. The Cromer–Salisbury correspondence of this time is well set out in Magnus, pp. 110 ff.

26 MS cit. Arthur bowdlerized 'cross' to 'ill'!

27 Watson Diary, 6–11 November 1897.

28 Grenfell Diary, 18 November 1897, MS cit.

29 K to Renshaw, 9 December 1897. CK.

30 Wingate Diary, 31 December 1897. SAD, 102/1/7.

31 Ibid., 5 January 1898.

32 Ibid., 14 January 1898.

33 Colonel F. W. Rhodes, Royal Dragoons, was a distinguished soldier but had been placed on the retired list for involvement in the Jameson Raid. He was restored for his services at Omdurman, where he was wounded. Kitchener scarcely knew him before 1898, but they became warm friends. He was welcomed as a member of the Sirdar's own headquarters mess. He distinguished himself in the South African war.

34 Ibid., 5 February 1898.

35 Walter Kitchener to his wife, 3 and 6 February 1898. Hall Papers.

36 Wingate Diary, 5 February 1898, MS cit. Cromer made a similar remark to Salisbury. A joke had the deaf Walter Kitchener going to sleep in his tent in a full camp and waking up next morning to find all gone.

37 F. Maurice, The Life of General Lord Rawlinson, pp. 31–2. With regard to the 'growling', when Cromer had assured Salisbury in February that K's eyesight and general health were 'not poor as reported', he added: 'The other soldiers are so fanatically jealous that they would welcome any excuse to get him away.' Cromer to Salisbury, 5 February 1898. Hatfield MSS, quoted Magnus, p. 119.

38 The phrase K used to (Sir) Ronald Storrs when describing it. Ronald Storrs, Orientations, p. 134.

Chapter 14: Crux of a Career

1 Rawlinson Diary, 19 March 1898. NAM. Charles à Court Repington, Vestigia, p. 167. He and his father changed their name from à Court to Repington in 1903 on inheriting an estate.

2 Walter Kitchener to Arthur Kitchener, 20 April, completed 6 May 1898. Hall Papers.

3 Repington, op. cit., p. 165.

4 Walter Kitchener to Arthur Kitchener, MS cit. K would say: 'Regulations are for the guidance of fools'.

5 Repington, op. cit., p. 128, printing a letter he (then à Court) wrote shortly after the battle of the Atbara.

6 Sir Ronald Storrs, *Orientations*, p. 134.

7 Wolseley to K, 14 April 1898. KP, 10.I.5. K's wire to Cromer (not in KP) is in Magnus, pp. 119–20.

8 Repington, op. cit., p. 161. A slightly different version is given by Lord Esher to Lord Knollys, quoting Charles à Court (later Repington), 9 August 1903. RA W 38/110.

9 Churchill, *The River War*, vol. 1, pp. 144–5.

10 Repington, op. cit., p. 33.

11 Walter Kitchener to Arthur Kitchener, MS cit.

12 Repington, op. cit., p. 117.

13 Walter Kitchener to his wife, 14 April 1898. Hall Papers. Magnus (p. 121) inter-polates, without MS authority, 'and rebuking men for wasting ammunition in that way', thus turning K's act of mercy into one of economy!

14 Walter Kitchener to his wife, 14 April 1898; Repington (à Court), op. cit., pp. 159–60. Charles à Court Repington, writing twenty years later, says that he per-suaded a reluctant K to come and address the men, but Walter, writing only six days after the battle, gives no indication of this and implies that their coming up at that moment was a coincidence. But there may have been a conversation outside Walter's range of hearing.

15 Arthur, *Life*, vol. 1, p. 228.

16 Repington, op. cit., p. 162.

17 Bennett Burleigh, *Sirdar and Khalifa*, p. 248. Burleigh was an eyewitness of the incident; I. H. Zulfo, *Karari*, p. 80; Arthur, *Life*, vol. 1, p. 228.

18 Noble Frankland, *Witness of a Century*, p. 213. The same phenomenon was noted in 1942 in the Western Desert campaign by the chaplain of the Queen's Bays when, after Alamein, they reached the site of their defeat seven months earlier at Msus. He could identify by facial features several bodies of officers and men found in smashed tanks. John Pollock, *Fear No Foe: A Brother's Story*, 1992, p. 134.

19 Maurice, *Rawlinson*, p. 34. Some critics blamed Kitchener because financial strin-gency had reduced the number of medical officers in the expedition.

20 Walter Kitchener to Arthur Kitchener, MS cit.

21 G. W. Steevens *With Kitchener to Khartoum*, p. 166.

22 Bennet Burleigh, op. cit., p. 269. Walter Kitchener's sketch is in his letter to his wife, 12 April 1898. Hall Papers.

23 The chains, halter, whipping, etc. as imagined by Magnus (p. 122) may have arisen from his misinterpreting Steevens. The Magnus version, and more lurid radio broadcast based on it by Christopher Sykes, so distressed a former head of Gordon Memorial College, N. R. Udal, that he protested to the BBC

Chairman and wrote to the 3rd Lord Kitchener to say that during his twenty-four years' service in the Sudan, 1906–30, 'I am quite sure I should have heard of it if it had been true, and it seems to me in complete variance with your great-uncle's treatment of the Sudanese, by whom he was universally venerated when I was there'. N. Robin Udal to Lord Kitchener, 5 March 1960; also 19 March. Earl K.

Magnus is not reliable on the Atbara battle and its aftermath. He seems to have slanted his account to support his claim that K was brutal: e.g. he writes that K won it 'at a cost of 583 casualties which to a general reader implies *deaths*, a vast exaggeration of the 71 actually killed on the Anglo-Egyptian side. When one of K's surviving friends read Magnus and told the Earl of Dunmore, VC, who as Lord Fincastle had served on his staff in Dongola, that a writer had portrayed K as brutal, he exclaimed: 'Kitchener brutal? Ridiculous!' Lady Winifred Renshaw to Magnus, 6 March 1961. Magnus Papers.

Lord Dunmore told Lady Winifred that he 'liked K very much' and was disappointed that the War Office refused him permission to be an ADC in the Omdurman campaign because he was on the Indian establishment. Lady W. Renshaw to Charles Kitchener, 1965. Note in CK.

24 Repington, op. cit., p. 111.

25 K to Wolseley, 6 October 1898 (referring to the Atbara). KP, 10, I 9.

26 N. M. Smyth, VC, MS cit., p. 6.

Chapter 15: Approach March

1 MS Recollections of Major Humphrey St Leger Stucley (1877–1914), 1910. Stucley Papers.

2 Ibid.

3 Walter Kitchener to Chevallier Kitchener, 16 September 1898. Hall Papers.

4 Repington, op. cit., p. 164.

5 Sandes, op. cit., p. 220.

6 H. Keown-Boyd, *Soldiers of the Nile*, p. 170; Repington, op. cit., p. 159; [George Arthur], *Some Letters of A Man of No Importance*.

7 RA, GV.cc.47/218. See also George Arthur, *Not Worth Reading*, pp. 168–9.

8 Randolph S. Churchill, *Winston S. Churchill Companion*, vol. 1, p. 971.

9 See, e.g., Doolittle, op. cit., p. 151.

10 K's verbal message to the *Daily Mail* correspondent with him in South Africa on hearing of Steevens's death at Ladysmith aged thirty-one. *Daily Mail*, 25 January 1900. Quoted in *Own Words*, p. 161. I have been unable to find a source for the 'drunken swabs' story before Magnus, who gives no authority for it but is often

quoted. Philip Ziegler has kindly told me that in his *Omdurman* he relied on Magnus for this story and K's relations with the press.

11 *The Times*, 2 December 1898. Quoted in *Own Words*, p. 130n.

12 Walter Kitchener to his wife, 22 August 1898. Hall Papers.

13 Ibid.

14 Walter Kitchener to Chevallier Kitchener, 16 September 1898. Hall Papers.

15 The general reader will find a good account of the battle in *Omdurman* by Philip Ziegler and in Henry Keown-Boyd, *A Good Dusting*. The account given in E. W. C. Sandes, *The Royal Engineers in Egypt and the Sudan*, though necessarily limited in scope, is excellent. There are numerous eyewitness accounts by journalists and officers. Zulfo's *Karari* describes it from a Sudanese standpoint. References for quoted MS sources are given in the next chapter.

Chapter 16: Omdurman

1 Doolittle, op. cit., p. 169.

2 Quotations from Walter Kitchener are taken from the following letters: to his wife, 4, 11 and 16 September 1898; to his brother Chevallier, 16 September; to his brother Arthur, begun 23 September, continued 1 October 1898. Hall Papers.

3 Doolittle, op. cit., p. 171.

4 Rawlinson, op. cit., pp. 38–9.

5 Stucley MS.

6 Quoted Ziegler, op. cit., p. 144.

7 Colonel David Francis Lewis (1855–1927). On retirement after the First World War he became military correspondent of *The Times*.

8 MacDonald to General Knowles, date unknown as first page of MS missing, but between 8 and 22 October 1898. Woodliffe Papers.

9 (General Sir) John Grenfell Maxwell (1859–1929). He put down the Easter Rising in Dublin, 1916.

10 Sandes, op. cit., p. 268.

11 MacDonald to Knowles, MS cit.

12 'A good dusting': Churchill, *The River War*, II, p. 162.

13 Stucley MS.

14 Ernest Bennett in the *Contemporary Review*, taken up by C. P. Scott in Parliament. K's official rebuttal is in *Own Words*, p. 155. See Randolph S. Churchill, *Winston Spencer Churchill*, vol. 1, p. 424; Army and Navy Gazette, 25 March 1899.

15 Scudamore, op. cit., p. 208.

16 Stucley MS.

17 Doolittle, op. cit., p. 173.
18 Scudamore, op. cit., pp. 214–15.
19 Stucley MS; Scudamore, op. cit., p. 217.
20 Magnus, p. 131, probably based on a Grenadier traditional story.

Chapter 17: 'Heroic Soul Whose Memory We Honour'

1 Memorandum by Wingate, 3 March 1899.
2 K to Cromer, 1 February 1899. Cromer Papers, PRO, 30.51.14, M 11 R2.
3 Walter Kitchener to his wife, 11 September 1898; Cecil, op. cit., p. 192. Cecil, writing twenty years later, forgot that Walter had been with them.
4 Walter Kitchener, ibid.
5 Brindle gave the paper to Rawlinson, who pasted it into his diary (now in NAM). It is reproduced facsimile in Maurice's *Life of Rawlinson*, pp. 40–41.

   K tried to get a knighthood for Brindle, but this was ruled out as inappropriate for a chaplain. He received a third bar to his DSO. After retirement from the army he became Bishop of Nottingham and died within a few days of K.
6 Maurice, op. cit., p. 42; Prince Francis of Teck to Duchess of York, begun 31 August 1898, completed after the battle. RA GV.cc.52.363. Unfortunately his handwriting on very thin paper is nearly indecipherable.
7 Repington, op. cit., pp. 170–71.
8 Scudamore, op. cit., p. 221.
9 RA, QVJ, 5 September 1898.
10 Arthur, *Life*, vol. 1, p. 245, is in error in writing that the telegram announcing the peerage was received and given out at the close of the memorial service.
11 *Letters of Queen Victoria*, Third Series, vol. 3, p. 275.
12 Ibid., pp. 283–4.

Chapter 18: The Diplomat of Fashoda

1 Smith-Dorrien, *Memories of Forty-Eight Years' Service*, pp. 121–9.
2 Sandes, op. cit., p. 280.
3 Watson Diary, 17 September 1898. NAM.
4 See Thomas Pakenham, *The Scramble for Africa*; Patricia Wright, *Fashoda*; Darrell Bates, *The Fashoda Incident 1898*.
5 Kitchener's dispatch, dated 30 September, is quoted in *Own Words*, pp. 133–9.
6 At the Lord Mayor's state luncheon to K, 4 November 1898.
7 J. B. Marchand to Walter Kitchener, 28 November 1898. Hall Papers.

8 RA, O 30/59.

9 K to his chousin, Mrs Emma Day, 7 October 1898. CK.

10 Walter Kitchener to his wife, 23 September 1898. Hall Papers.

11 Arthur, *Life*, vol. 1, p. 245. Probably to Arthur Renshaw, possibly to Sir George Arthur himself. Both MSS correspondences are lost.

12 K's title standardized the spelling as Khart*oum*. Previously it had been more usually spelt Khart*um*, which is a closer transliteration of the Arabic. K realized that English people would probably in ignorance pronounce Khartum to rhyme with tum⁄tum (which was Society's nickname for the Prince of Wales!).

The Kitcheners, like many rising families in the nineteenth century, were using arms which had not been matriculated at the College of Arms and therefore were not legal until Francis Kitchener, the headmaster, petitioned for them in 1899 after the new peer's arms had been matriculated, using their traditional achievement: in lay terms, a coat of three bustards within a saltire; a crest of a stag's head pierced by an arrow; and the family motto, *Thorough*. Lord K chose two camels for supporters, suggested by Walter (as a joke, he told his wife, 1 January 1899); he replaced one with a gnu (wildebeest) when raised to a viscountcy for his services in South Africa.

13 Walter Kitchener to Arthur Kitchener, 1 October 1898. Hall Papers.

14 Details from K's letter to Queen Victoria. *Letters of Queen Victoria*, Third Series, vol. 3, pp. 352–53.

The probability that the box was weighted is deduced from Cromer's convic⁄tion that no bones were kept as souvenirs.

15 Laurence Housman in *Victoria Regina*. The sketch was not included in the stage version of 1937.

16 W. S. Gordon's plan of the tomb is in possession of his grandson, Mr David Gordon.

17 Churchill, *The River War*, vol. 2, p. 214.

18 Queen Victoria to K, 24 March 1899. KP, II. T/S copy in RA Add V.18. See *Letters of Queen Victoria*, Third Series, vol. 3, pp. 353–4.

19 Cromer to Salisbury, Quoted M. W. Daly, *Empire on the Nile*, p. 6.

Chapter 19: The Magic Wand

1 Walter Kitchener to his wife, 10 and 16 November 1898. Hall Papers.

2 *The Dover Express*, 28 October 1898.

3 Mallet, op. cit., p. 142.

4 *The Times*, 28 October 1898.

5 RA QVJ, 22 November 1898 (and quote below).

6 Walter Kitchener to his wife, RA QVJ 31 October 1898.

7 Mallet, op. cit., p. 147.

8 Jane Ridley, ed., *The Letters of Arthur Balfour and Lady Elcho*, 1992, p. 156.

9 [Arthur] *Some Letters . . .*, op. cit., p. 67.

10 Telegram of 5 November 1898. *Letters of Queen Victoria*, Third Series, Vol. 3, p. 309.

11 [Arthur] *Some Letters . . .*, pp. 66–7.

12 Walter Kitchener to his wife, 1 January 1899. Hall Papers.

13 Mrs Florence Marc (neé Day) to her son, 7 November 1916. CK.

14 K's letter to *The Times*, 30 November 1898.

15 Edinburgh, 29 November 1898. *Own Words*, p. 143.

16 Cecil, op. cit., pp. 192–3.

Chapter 20: Rebuilding a Nation

1 K to Queen Victoria, 29 December 1898. RA O 31/39.

2 Walter Kitchener to his wife, 1 January 1899. Hall Papers.

3 K to Queen Victoria, as above.

4 Sandes, op. cit.

5 See J. S. R. Duncan, *The Sudan: A Record of Achievement*, 1932 and Sir Harold MacMichael, *The Sudan*. Both had served in the Sudan. Also M. W. Daly, *Empire on the Nile*.

6 Cromer to K, 19 October 1898. KP, 14, M1 pp. 35–7.

7 Cromer to K, 19 January 1899. KP, M3 pp. 14.42.

8 K to Queen Victoria, 21 January 1899. RA O 31/52.

9 Quoted in Daly, op. cit., p. 30.

10 Ibid.

11 K to Wingate, ND. Wingate Papers, 269.2.34.

12 K to Queen Victoria, 21 January 1899. RA, 031.52. See Watson Diary, MS cit., 8–21 January 1899.

13 The Memorandum to Mudirs, printed in Parliamentary Papers, Egypt, 1900, Number 1, pp. 55 ff., is reproduced in *Own Words*, pp. 145–54. The chief part is printed in J. S. F. Duncan, op. cit., pp. 85–7, and MacMichael, op. cit., pp. 74–6.

14 Walter Kitchener to his wife, 7 February 1899. Hall Papers.

15 Noble Frankland, *Witness of a Century*, pp. 212–13; Watson Diary, MS cit., 20–25 February 1899.

16 K to Wingate, 6 February 1899. Wingate Papers, 269.2.19.

17 Cromer to Salisbury, 2 February 1899. Cromer Papers, PRO Letter 308.

18 Quoted in H. C. Jackson, *Pastor on the Nile*, pp. 20–21. See also E. M. Edmonds to George Arthur, 28 September 1916. KP, 91.62.

19 Scudamore, op. cit., p. 94.

20 K to Wingate, 1 February 1899. Wingate Papers, 269.2.1. See also Ibid., 7 April (269.4.23). Cromer remarked to Salisbury (18 February) that K was 'such a terrible hand at quarrelling with everyone, except himself', but it was only with Gorst, and some bullying of his own financial officer, O'Leary, sandwiched between them.

21 Babikr Bedi, *Memoirs*, vol. 2, pp. 82–3.

22 Cromer to Salisbury, 19 May 1899. Hatfield MSS.

23 Ibid.

Chapter 21: Bobs and K

1 Typed copy sent by Viscountess Gage (Julian's sister) to Magnus. Magnus Papers. The boy's account is also quoted in Lord Desborough's address, *Lord Kitchener as I Know Him*, 11 June 1916 (where also is K's remark about home). KP, 119.

2 K to Lady Helen V-T-Stewart, ND. Ilchester Papers, BL Add Mss 51370, f.163.

3 The Grand Duchess of Mecklenburg to the Duchess of Cornwall and York, 27 August 1901 (Princess of Wales from November). RA GV CC 2929.

4 K to Lady Helen, 4 October 1901. BL Add Mss 51370, f. 170.

5 W. R. Birdwood (afterwards Field Marshal Lord Birdwood) to his wife, October 1900. NAM, 6707.19.236.

6 K to Wingate. N.D. [1899] Wingate Papers, 269.2.34.

7 For a full and most readable account of the origin and course of the South African war, see Thomas Pakenham, *The Boer War*.

8 J. A. Spender, *Life, Journalism and Politics*, 1927, p. 61. Spender, then aged thirty-eight, had bicycled down to the Durdans for an hour or two with Rosebery. K happened to be staying and Spender was introduced, Rosebery warning him that he might be 'eaten alive' as his *Westminster Gazette* had led the agitation over the Mahdi's skull, etc. But K seemed entirely unaware of the connection.

9 Queen Victoria to Salisbury, 10 February 1900. RA, P.6.88 (copy); Salisbury to Queen Victoria, 12 February 1900. *Letters of Queen Victoria*, Third Series, vol. 3, p. 486.

10 Queen Victoria to K, 24 July and 17 November 1899, 29 June 1900. KP, 16.R4(a), 5(c), 7(a); K to Queen Victoria, 25 July 1899. RA, O.31.76.

11 K to Lady Cranborne, 30 August 1899. Hatfield MSS.

12 K to Lady Cranborne, 6 November 1899. Hatfield MSS.

13 Queen Victoria to K, 22 December 1900. KP, 16.R.5.

14 K to Lady Helen V-T-Stewart, 28 December [1899]. BL Add Mss 51370, f. 165.

15 Watson Diary, 21–6 December 1899. NAM.

16 Lieutenant-General Sir John Stokes to K, 22 December 1899. KP, 17. S2. Stokes had known Gordon well and was vice-chairman of the Suez Canal Company.

17 K to Lady Helen, MS cit.

18 E. A. Baines, quoted in David James, *Lord Roberts*, p. 362.

19 Dudley Sommer, *Haldane of Cloan*, p. 182.

20 K to Pandeli Ralli. Arthur, *Life*, vol. 1, p. 275.

Chapter 22: The Battle that Went Wrong

1 K to Roberts, 16 February 1900. KP, 17 S5(b).

2 Kitchener had been promoted major-general before Kelly-Kenny and was therefore technically senior although carrying lower rank in South Africa.

3 Arthur, *Life*, vol. 1, p. 280. For a vivid and detailed account of the battle of Paardeberg, 18 February 1900, see Pakenham, *The Boer War*, pp. 332–40.

4 Queen Victoria to K, 22 December 1899. KP, 16 R.5(a).

5 Quoted in Pakenham, op. cit., p. 335.

6 Major-General H. A. MacDonald to K, 30 January 1900. KP, 17. S4.

7 Three hundred and three killed at Paardeberg; Anglo-Egyptian killed or died of wounds 1896–8, approximately two hundred and sixty.

8 Quoted from the Official History by Pakenham, op. cit., p. 338.

9 Watson Diary, 20 February 1900. MS cit.

10 Ibid., 22 February 1900.

11 K to Julian and Billy Grenfell, Kronstadt, 13 May 1900. Typed copy by their sister, Viscountess Gage. Magnus Papers.

12 K to Queen Victoria, 14 May 1900. RA P9 73. The father of a friend of the present writer was wounded in this way and carried a bullet in his body until his death aged eighty-three.

13 K to Lady Cranborne, 16 March [1900]. Hatfield MSS.

14 K to Queen Victoria, 4 March 1900. RA, p. 7.38.

15 Colonel J. M. Grierson to Arthur Bigge, 14 March 1900. RA P7 172a. Grierson rose to be a lieutenant-general. In August 1914, shortly after landing in France in command of an army corps, he died of a heart attack in a railway train. Smith-Dorrien took his place.

16 K to Lady Cranborne, 29 April 1900. Hatfield MSS.

17 Ibid., 7 June 1900.

18 Diary of Lieutenant Craig-Brown, 5 June 1900. 1 AM 92.23.2. EC.B.2.2 (photostat copy).

19 Ibid.

20 'Lord Curzon is evidently anxious to have you as Commander-in-Chief.' Roberts to K, 28 February 1901, after returning home. KP, 20. f. 6.

21 Roberts to Lansdowne, 19 September 1900. RA, p. 13.76 (copy).

22 Marquess of Lansdowne to Sir Arthur Bigge, 29 September 1900. RA W 16/78.

23 Bigge to Lansdowne, 29 September 1900 (copy). RA W 16/72. Other remarks paraphrased from RA, W 16/86, Notes by Sir Frederick Ponsonby, HM's Private Secretary, to Bigge, 4 October 1900, of the Queen's detailed comments to be passed to Lansdowne.

24 Lansdowne to Bigge, MS cit.

25 Sir A. Davidson to Bigge, 28 August 1900. RA P 12/76.

26 K to Lady Cranborne, 5 November 1900. Hatfield MSS.

27 In conversation with N. M. Smyth, VC, in the Sudan, Smyth, VC, *Reminiscences*. KP, T/S cit.

28 K to Queen Victoria, 12 October 1900. RA P 14/27.

Chapter 23: 1901: Peace Aborted

1 Birdwood to his wife, 10 October 1900. NAM, 6707.19.4, f. 230.

2 Ibid., ND, 1901. f. 238.

3 Ibid., 23 October 1900. f. 132. In his MS notes to Arthur and in his autobiography *Khaki and Gown*, Birdwood described this incident as if he had been present, but the contemporary letter is conclusive.

4 Lord Birdwood, *Khaki and Gown*, p. 118.

5 Queen Victoria to K, 16 November 1900. KP, 16.R.23.

6 Princess Beatrice to K, 8 February 1901. KP, 104 PA 5.14.

7 K to Lady Cranborne, 5 November 1900. Hatfield MSS.

8 Sir A. Milner to K, 31 October 1900. KP, 17.S.7.

9 Sir George Arthur, *Not Worth Reading*, p. 98.

10 K to Lady Cranborne, 11 January 1901. Hatfield MSS.

11 K to Arthur Renshaw, 26 January 1901. Copy in CK.

12 Viscount Esher to Lord Knollys, quoting J. G. Ewart, 10 October 1906. RA W 40/62.

13 K to Brodrick, 22 February 1901. KP, 22.Y.26.

14 Ibid.

15 Charlotte Maxwell, *Frank Maxwell, VC*, 1921, p. 79.

16 Watson Diary, 28 February 1901; Maxwell, op. cit., p.79.

17 K family tradition.

18 K to Brodrick, 22 March 1901. KP. 22, Y33.

19 Ibid.

20 K to Lady Cranborne, 8 March 1901. Hatfield MSS.

21 Rayne Kruger, *Good-bye Dolly Gray*, p. 413.

22 K to Lady Cranborne, 15 April, 7 June and 21 June 1901. Hatfield MSS.

23 Viscount Esher, *Journals and Letters*, vol. 1, p. 238.

24 Lord Milner to Sir Francis Knollys (Lord Knollys from 1902), 30 June 1901. RA, W.60. 126.

25 Watson to K, 12 April 1901. KP, 17. S.13.

Chapter 24: 'I wish I could see the End'

1 K to Lady Cranborne, 2 August [1901]. Hatfield MSS.

2 See John Fisher, *That Miss Hobhouse*.

3 K's letters to Brodrick and to Lady Cranborne, and Maxwell's and Raymond Marker's (see below) to their parents mention visits.

4 K to Lady Cranborne, 1 January 1902. Hatfield MSS.

5 K to Arthur Renshaw, 5 July [1901]. CK.

6 Maxwell, op. cit., p. 94.

7 Colin Benbow, *Boer P.O.W.s in Bermuda*, passim.

8 K to Brodrick, 21 June 1901. KP, 22.Y.63. An unprejudiced reading of the original does not support the assertion by Magnus (p. 185) that K 'fulminated'.

9 Adolphus G. C. Liddell, *Notes from the Life of an Ordinary Mortal*, p. 337. He heard Solomon say this in November 1902 at a small London dinner party which included the new Prime Minister, Balfour.

10 Pakenham, op. cit., p. 539. Five Australians and one English officer had been court-martialled for multiple murder. The execution of only Morant and Handcock caused an outcry in Australia.

11 Walter Kitchener to J. Monins, 21 August 1901. KP, 17 S.20.

12 Caroline Kitchener died 3 November 1901; Caroline to Hal Kitchener, 2, 23 October 1901; Miss Lloyd to Miss Fenton, 6 November 1901. Hall Papers; K to Renshaw, 13 November 1901, CK.

13 The duke's Diary, 9 June 1899. RA, GvD.

14 Maxwell, op. cit., p. 88.

15 RA GVA1 9/35, copy ('My letter to Papa'); GVD, 14 August 1901; K to King Edward, 16 August 1901. W 60/130; Bigge to King Edward [1 September 1901]. W 6/70; Maxwell, op. cit., p. 89.

16 Byng family tradition, per Mr Julian Byng. Evelyn's father, Sir Richard Moreton, was a younger brother of the 3rd Earl of Ducie, who was Lord-Lieutenant of Gloucestershire for fifty-four years.

17 Sir Neville Lyttleton, *Eighty Years' Soldiering*, p. 257.

18 See K to Brodrick, 2 August 1901. KP, 22.Y.79.

19 K to Lady Cranborne, 20 September 1901. Hatfield MSS.

20 Major Marker to his sister, 20 September 1901. Marker Papers. NAM, 6803.4.4.f. 26.

21 Birdwood to K (after Marker's death in action in 1914), 13 January 1915. KP, 61.WL1.

22 Marker to his sister, 17 and 25 May 1901. MS cit., ff. 20, 21.

23 K to Lady Cranborne, 18 October and 23 November 1901. Hatfield MSS. K to Arthur Renshaw, 13 November 1901. CK. See also K to General Lord Methuen, 20 November 1901. Methuen Papers, Wiltshire Record Office.

24 Roberts to K ('Secret'), 19 October 1901. KP, 20.0.43; K to Roberts, ND (draft of telegram in reply to above). KP, 21.P.1; see also telegram 5 November, p. 3.

25 Milner to Chamberlain, quoted in G. H. L. Le May, *British Supremacy in South Africa, 1899–1907*, p. 121.

26 Not October, as Hamilton writes in *The Commander*, p. 100. His memory in old age was faulty on this point, but his chapter on Kitchener, partly used also in his autobiography, is excellent.

27 Pakenham, op. cit., p. 537.

Chapter 25: 'We are Good Friends Now'

1 See the guidebook to Melrose House, Pretoria; the house is open to the public.

2 See Ian Hamilton, *The Commander*, p. 102.

3 C. E. Caldwell, *Confessions of a Dug Out*, p. 43.

4 Lady Allendale to K, 31 October 1914. KP, 108 PA 8.2

5 Maxwell to his father, 13 September 1901. *Frank Maxwell*, op. cit., p. 93.

6 Sir Ian Hamilton, op. cit., p. 107. See 1 Samuel, Chapter 16, Verses 22 and 23; Chapter 18, Verses 10 and 11.

7 Marker to his sister, 18 October 1901. MSS cit., f. 29.

8 *Maxwell*, op. cit., pp. 81–2, 86–7. This occurred shortly after the Botha talks.

9 Marker to his sister, 17 January 1902. MSS cit., f. 31.

10 K to Renshaw, 26 January 1902. CK.

11 Arthur, *Life*, vol. 2, p. 73n; *Maxwell*, op. cit., pp. 95–6.

12 *Maxwell*, op. cit., pp. 96, 98 and 100 for quotes re peace negotiations.

13 Sir Ian Hamilton, 29 July 1922. Speech when unveiling Kilmadock War Memorial, Doune. Hamilton Papers, 39.12.45. Liddell Hart Centre, King's College, London.

14 Quoted Le May, op. cit., p. 138.

15 K to Lady Cranborne, 20 April 1902. Hatfield MSS.

16 Smuts's remark was to Sir George Arthur. Arthur, *Not Worth Reading*, p. 98.
17 K's copy of the Treaty of Vereeniging is in Earl K.

Chapter 26: Looking Forward

1 Sir Rennell Rodd to K, 7 June 1902. KP, 17.S.22. Rodd (afterwards Lord Rennell), diplomatist, scholar and poet, had been in charge of the Cairo Agency at the time of Fashoda and now was First Secretary in the embassy at Rome.
2 K to the Hon. (Sir) Schomberg MacDonnell, 5 June 1901. Hatfield MSS.
3 Schomberg to Sir Francis Knollys, 9 June 1901. Hatfield MSS.
4 K to MacDonnell, 11 June 1902. Hatfield MSS.
5 *London Gazette*, 28 July 1902. Salisbury had supposed K would want to be 'of Khartoum and of Vereeniging'. Birdwood, according to his not always very reliable recollections in old age, thought the omission of Arthur was an oversight and offered to put it right, but K said, 'He is not a soldier, Birdie. Leave it alone', so that Birdwood thought his attitude cavalier and that he was not fond of Arthur, quite wrongly.
6 K to Lord Roberts, 8 June 1902. KP, 17.S.25.
7 [Charlotte Maxwell], *I am Ready*, privately printed 1955, pp. 50, 11.
8 K to Renshaw, 29 July 1901. CK.
9 Both Magnus, p. 191, and Royale, p. 189, repeat this libel as if true. The facts are in the MS correspondence in RE, being 22 letters dated 11 January 1903 to 21 July 1914 (SA 61, 93), together with a typed summary. Also the supplement to the *RE Journal* for February 1921. An undated MS note from Lady Broome to Magnus after reading his book, and another typed note by her dated December 1977, both in CK, give the facts about the return of the statues to Pretoria. See also Standard Encylopaedia of South Africa, p. 474.
10 Prince of Wales Diary, 12 July 1902 (and quotation above). RA GVD. Princess of Wales Diary, 12 July 1902. RA QMD. cc68. 18. p. 193.
11 [Sir George Arthur], 14 July 1902, *Some Letters . . .*, p. 155.
12 Rawlinson, op. cit., p. 79.
13 K to Renshaw, ND, 'Thursday' (July 1902). CK.
14 RA GVD, 13 August 1902.
15 Aspall Visitors Book for 1902. John Chevallier-Guild and his mother showed the rug to the author.
16 Memo by Julian Grenfell, 1902; typed copy by his sister Viscountess Gage. Magnus Papers.
17 Prince of Wales to Princess of Wales, 17 August 1902. RA, Geo V. cc 3.32.

18 A. G. C. Liddell, *Notes from the Life of An Ordinary Mortal*, p. 334 (diary entry for 2 August 1902).

19 K to Renshaw, Thursday (19 September 1902). CK.

20 Sir Ian Hamilton, op. cit., pp. 115–16.

21 Kenneth Rose, *The Later Cecils*, pp. 203–204 (and next quote); K to Renshaw, 21 February, 10 May, 24 September and 19 October 1902. CK.

22 *The Times*, 12 November 1902; Sandes, op. cit., pp. 475–6.

23 C. E. C. G. Charlton, *A Soldier's Story*, p. 59.

24 *The Times*, 12 November 1902; K to Wingate, 15 November 1907 and 24 December 1908. Wingate Papers.

25 K to Renshaw, 18 November 1902. CK.

26 Speech by Kaimakan Mohmud Bey Husai, Khartoum, 7 November 1902. Translation T/S, KP, 36. JJ: 2.

REFERENCES AND NOTES
TO VOLUME II

MANUSCRIPT SOURCES

ABBREVIATIONS

BL   British Library
CK   Charles Kitchener Papers
Earl K   3rd Earl Kitchener Papers
KP   Kitchener Papers, Public Record Office
KRO   *Kitchener: The Road to Omdurman* (the first volume of this work)
NAM   National Army Museum
NWR   *Not Worth Reading* by Sir George Arthur
OIOL   Oriental and India Office Library (Department of British Library)
RA   Royal Archives
RE   Royal Engineers Archives
Kitchener is referred to as K throughout References and Notes

KITCHENER FAMILY COLLECTIONS

Kitchener Papers, Public Record Office. PRO 30.57. Deposited by 3rd Earl Kitchener 1958–59, catalogued 1980.

124 files, some very extensive: files 1–25 cover 1850–1902; files 26–85 cover 1902/3–1916; files 86–124 are Sir George Arthur's collection of Kitchener biographical material (letters, memoranda, etc.).

The Kitchener letters to St John Brodrick, afterwards Earl of Midleton, have been incorporated in the Kitchener Papers from the Midleton Papers.

3rd Earl Papers. Manuscripts and press cuttings, etc. remaining in the personal possession of 3rd Earl Kitchener.

Charles Kitchener Papers, collected by the late Charles Kitchener and owned by the Hon. Mrs Charles Kitchener, including K's correspondence with Arthur Renshaw, Mrs Alexander Marc ('Cousin Flo') and others.

Hall Papers. Papers of Major-General Sir Walker Kitchener, his daughter and son. Owned by Sir Walter Kitchener's granddaughter, Mrs Peter Hall.

Parker Papers. Letters of K to his sister Millie, Mrs Harry Parker. Owned by her great-granddaughter, Mrs Harriet King.

ROYAL ARCHIVES

Journals of King George v when Duke of York, Prince of Wales and King, and Queen Mary.

Letters to and from King Edward VII and Queen Alexandra, King George v and Queen Mary, their Private Secretaries and other members of the Royal Family and Royal Households.

OTHER MANUSCRIPT COLLECTIONS

Asquith Papers. Bodleian Library.

British Library, Additional Manuscripts: Ilchester Papers; Marker Papers (part).

British Library, Oriental and India Office Library: Ampthill Papers (2nd Lord); *Barrow Papers* (General Sir Edmund); *Birdwood Papers* (later Field Marshall Lord); *Curzon Papers; Lady Curzon Papers*.

Cecil Papers (Lord Edward). Bodleian Library.

Gainford Papers. Diaries and notes of the Rt Hon. Jack Pease, 1st Lord Gainford. Nuffield College, Oxford.

Imperial War Museum. Papers of H. W. Gwynne; Miscellaneous.

Inge Papers. Diaries of Dean W. R. Inge of St Paul's and his wife. Magdalene College, Cambridge.

Hamilton Papers. Papers of General Sir Ian Hamilton. Liddell Hart Centre, King's College, London.

Hatfield Manuscripts. K to Lady Cranborne, later Lady Salisbury, wife of 4th Marquess, and other correspondence. Owned by the Marquess of Salisbury, Hatfield House.

Ilchester Papers. Letters of K to Lady Helen Vane-Tempest-Stewart, afterwards Countess of Ilchester. British Library.

Lambeth Palace Archives. Archbishop Davidson Papers; Bishop Blyth Papers.

Lloyd George Papers. House of Lords Record Office.

Magnus Papers. Papers of Sir Philip Magnus-Allcroft, Bt, relating to his biography of K. Owned by Sir Philip's nephew, Mr Charles Sebag-Montefiore.

Marker Papers. Letters of Colonel Hubert Hamilton to Colonel Raymond Marker. Letters of Marker to his sister. National Army Museum.

Midleton Papers. Sir John Brodrick, later Viscount and Earl of Midleton. Public Record Office.

National Army Museum Archives. Birdwood Diary; Maxwell Diary; collections as noted, plus miscellaneous items.

Royal Engineers Archives.

Storrs Papers. Sir Ronald Storrs. Pembroke College, Cambridge.

Wilson (President Woodrow) Papers. National Archives, Washington.

Wingate Papers. General Sir Reginald Wingate. Sudan Archive, University of Durham Library.

Chapter 1: A Cordial Welcome

1 K to Lady Cranborne, 15 November 1902. Hatfield MSS.

2 K to Major R. J. Marker, 26 October 1902. Marker Papers, BL Add MSS 522 76 B. 5.18.

3 Curzon to K, 29 October 1898. Royal Engineers Archives, ES. 42.

4 See KRO, pp. 184–5.

5 See KRO, pp. 213–14.

6 Curzon to K, 21 August 1900 (but not sent until later). KP, 26.Z1.

7 Lord Birdwood, *Khaki and Gown*, 1942, p. 141.

8 Smith-Dorrien, Sir Horace, *Memories of Forty-Eight Years' Service*, 1925, p. 314.

9 Report of a conversation in Bombay on 22 June 1905 between Lovat Fraser, editor of *The Times of India*, and Hunter. In a memorandum from Fraser to Curzon, 26 January 1908. CP, 111.411. See Archie Hunter, *Kitchener's Sword-Arm*, 1996, p. 195.

10 As in Peter King in *The Fall of the Viceroy*, 1985. He uses this term frequently but without contemporary authority. It gives a misleading impression. For background to the staff, see KRO, pp. 188 (Maxwell), 170–71 (Birdwood), 201 (Marker), 203 (Hamilton); and many other references.

11 K to Marker, 18 October 1902. Marker Papers (BL), Add MSS 52276A, f.11. I have supplied punctuation, as is often necessary with K.

12 K to Lady Cranborne, 10 December 1902. Hatfield MSS.

13 Sir Walter Lawrence, *The India We Served*, 1928, p. 249; for Curzon, see David Gilmour, *Curzon*, 1994.

14 See KRO, pp. 36–7.

15 Curzon to Lord George Hamilton (Secretary of State for India), 3 December 1902, Curzon Papers, 111/162.

16 Maurice, *Life of Lord Rawlinson of Trent*, 1928, p. 80.

17 K to Lady Cranborne, 10 December 1902. Hatfield MSS.

18 Smith-Dorrien, op. cit., p. 315; Maurice, op. cit., p. 80.

19 Sir Walter Lawrence, op. cit., p. 113.

Chapter 2: Pomp and Circumstance

1 David Gilmour, *Curzon*, 1994, p. 234.

2 *Illustrated London News*, 9 January 1903.

3 Urdu was the lingua franca of northern India which, with some admixture of Hindi words, was used in the Indian army throughout the subcontinent.

4 E. W. C. Sandes, 'Kitchener – The Man', article in *Royal Engineers Journal*, December 1943, p. 233. Sandes, then a young officer, did not see K until the following year but his impression is typical.

5 See KRO, p. 82.

6 Maurice, op. cit., pp. 82–3.

7 Lady Winifred Renshaw to Sir Philip Magnus, 6 March 1961. CK. For the Renshaws, see KRO, p. 218.

8 Sir Bampfylde Fuller, *Some Personal Experiences*, 1933, p. 97.

9 Maurice, op. cit., p. 82.

10 Curzon to Hamilton, 13 January 1903. Curzon Papers, III 161.

11 Birdwood, *Khaki and Gown*, pp. 139–40.

12 Ibid., p. 140.

13 K to Lady Cranborne, 19 March 1903. Hatfield MSS.

14 Lady Lockhart to Marker, 6 August 1902. Marker Papers, NAM 6505.2.1.7 (3).

15 Smith-Dorrien, op. cit., pp. 318–19.

16 In a letter to Lady Cranborne, 16 July 1903. Hatfield MSS.

17 K to Lord Roberts, 12 March 1903. KP, 29.Q6. For an excellent account of K's reforms, see Birdwood, op. cit., pp. 142 ff.

Chapter 3: 'I Want Power to Do Good'

1 Sir Walter Lawrence, op. cit., pp. 247–8. For Elles, see *Royal Artillery Journal* 1934 and Roberts to K, 4 May 1901. KP, 20.O20.

2 K to Lady Cranborne (and for following conversation and comment), 25 January 1903. Punctuation supplied. Hatfield MSS.

3 Birdwood, op. cit., p. 146.

4 K to Lady Cranborne, 12 March 1903. Hatfield MSS.

5 Lord Ronaldshay, *The Life of Lord Curzon*, 1928, vol. 2, p. 251.

6 Curzon to Lord Cromer, 19 March 1903. David Dilks, *Curzon in India*, vol. 2, 1970, p. 22.

7 Curzon to Lord George Hamilton, 18 March 1903, Curzon Papers, 111.162.

8 Roberts to K, 19 March 1903. KP, 28 11 5.

9 Curzon to Lord George Hamilton, 25 March 1903. Curzon Papers, 111.162, p. 87.

10 K to General Sir A. Hunter, 3 April 1903. Duncan Doolittle, *A Soldier's Hero*, 1991, p. 250.

11 K to Roberts, 20 April 1903, KP, 29.Q7. For MacDonald, see KR, especially pp. 94 and 133–4; also Appendix 1.

12 Birdwood, op. cit., pp. 146–8.

Chapter 4: 'The Curzons Have Been Very Kind'

1 Maconchy's two-volume typescript Memoirs are in NAM (7908.62). These extracts are taken from a typescript compiled by his son and given to 3rd Lord Kitchener (checked against the original).

2 Ibid.

3 Curzon to Lord George Hamilton, 7 May 1903. Curzon Papers, 162.

4 Ibid., 4 June 1903. And see Ronaldshay, op. cit., p. 352. For K's very reasonable objections, see K to Lord Roberts, 6 May 1903. KP, 29.Q.9.

5 Ibid., 28 May 1903. Ronaldshay, op. cit., p. 354.

6 Ibid., 14 May 1903.

7 John Bradley, *Lady Curzon's India*, 1985, p. 92.

8 K to Lord Roberts, 13 May 1903. KP, 29.Q10.

9 K to Lady Cranborne, 13 May, 21 May 1903. Hatfield MSS.

10 Hubert Hamilton to Lady Cranborne, 9 August 1903. Hatfield MSS.

11 Maconchy typescript.

12 See KRO, p. 19.

13 Sir George Arthur, *Life of Lord Kitchener*, vol. 2, 1920, p. 131. See also E. F. Buck, *Simla Past and Present*, Bombay, 1925, p. 82.

14 See KRO, pp. 220–21.

15 Birdwood, op. cit., p. 149.

16 K to Renshaw, 16 July (1903). CK.

17 K to Renshaw, 13 May 1903. CK.

18 K to Lady Cranborne, 6 August 1903. Hatfield MSS.

19 Buck, op. cit., pp. 233–4.

20 K to Lady Cranborne, 16 July 1903. Hatfield MSS.

21 Curzon to Lord George Hamilton, 9 July 1903. Curzon Papers, 162.

22 K to Lady Cranborne, 23 July 1903. Hatfield MSS.

23 K to Lady Cranborne, 25 June 1903. Hatfield MSS.

24 The story is given, without source and with a different interpretation, in Philip Magnus, *Kitchener: Portrait of an Imperialist*, 1958, p. 205.

25 Sir Walter Lawrence, op. cit., p. 248.

26 K to Lady Cranborne, 26 July 1903. Hatfield MSS.

27 K to Balfour, 24 December 1903. Hatfield MSS. The volumes are referred to in a typescript note from Lady Salisbury (formerly Cranborne) to her son (later 5th Marquess) on 20 January 1928.

28 K to Lady Cranborne, 29 July 1903. Hatfield MSS.

29 Hubert Hamilton to Lady Cranborne, 9 August 1903. Hatfield MSS.

30 For Lady Cranborne, see KRO, p. 83.

Chapter 5: Exploring the Passes

1 Birdwood, op. cit., p. 152.

2 K to Lady Salisbury, 26 August 1903. Hatfield MSS.

3 Birdwood, op. cit., p. 154.

4 K to Lady Salisbury, 9 September 1903. Hatfield MSS.

5 Charlotte Maxwell, *Frank Maxwell*, 1921, p. 105; Birdwood, op. cit., pp. 154–5.

6 K to Renshaw, 6 October 1903. CK.

7 Maxwell Diary, 1 October 1903. In (Charlotte Maxwell) (ed.), *I am Ready*, 1955, p. 54.

8 Ibid.

9 K to Major-General Edmund Barrow, 6 October 1903. Barrow Papers, OIOL, E 420/18.

10 Raymond Marker to his sister, 6 October 1903. Marker Papers, NAM, 6803–4–5 f.b.

11 Hubert Hamilton to Raymond Marker, 16 June 1904. NAM, Marker Papers, letter 20.

12 Charlotte Maxwell, *Frank Maxwell*, p. 104.

13 K to Renshaw, 6 October (1903). CK.

14 Maconchy typescript, p. 3.

15 Birdwood, op. cit., p. 144.

16 K to Lady Salisbury, 11 November 1903. Hatfield MSS.

17 K to Brodrick, 4 November 1903. Midleton Papers, PRO, 67.10.18–19.

18 Ibid., 22 October 1903. MS cit. 20, 12–13 re Major Wilfred Malleson.

Chapter 6: Disaster in a Tunnel

1 H. Hamilton to Lord Roberts, 18 November 1903. KP, 29.Q 19–20. Also K to Roberts, 30 December 1903. KP, 29.Q.21. See also Edward Buck's

immediate account, quoted in Buck, op. cit., pp. 232–3.

2 K to Lady Salisbury, 26 November 1903. Hatfield MSS.

3 Ibid., 10 December 1903.

4 K to Renshaw (ND), CK; K to Lady Salisbury, 10, 17 December 1903. Hatfield MSS.

5 Frank Maxwell to his mother, 16 December 1903. Charlotte Maxwell, *Frank Maxwell*, pp. 107–8.

6 Maxwell Diary, 16 December 1903. In (Charlotte Maxwell) (ed.), *I am Ready*, p. 54.

7 Ibid., 5 January 1904, p. 55.

8 K to Edith Chevallier, 7 January 1904. CK. Information from John Monins's daughter, Bridget Toynbee.

9 K to Lady Salisbury, 30 December 1903. Hatfield MSS.

10 Balfour to Kitchener, 3 December 1903. Quoted in Dilks, op. cit., vol. 2, 1970.

11 Ibid., Curzon to Brodrick, 14 January 1904.

12 H. Hamilton to Lady Salisbury, 28 January 1904. Hatfield MSS.

13 K to Lady Curzon, 28 January 1904. Lady Curzon Papers, OIOL, 36B.f.

14 Records of the Coldstream Guards.

15 Birdwood to K (after Marker's death in action), 13 January 1915. KP, 61.WL1.

16 H. Hamilton to Lady Salisbury, 28 January 1904. Hatfield MSS.

17 Marker to his sister, 15 January 1903. Marker Papers, NAM, 5.f.4.

18 K to Lady Salisbury, 25 January 1904. Hatfield MSS.

19 E. W. G. Sandes, 'Kitchener – The Man', article in *Royal Engineers Journal*, December 1943, p. 233.

20 Frank Maxwell to Lady Salisbury, 9 March 1904. Hatfield MSS.

21 K to Lady Salisbury, 24 June 1904. Hatfield MSS.

Chapter 7: Assaulting Dual Control

1 Hubert Hamilton to Raymond Marker, 20 April 1904. Marker Papers, NAM (as are all Hamilton–Marker letters except otherwise stated), Letter 18.

2 Ibid.

3 Hamilton to Marker, 29 May 1904, Letter 19, and next quote.

4 K to Lady Salisbury, 23 June 1904. Hatfield MSS.

5 The best detailed political account of the Curzon–Kitchener controversy is in Dilks, *Curzon in India*, vol. 2, 1970, Chs. 1, 4, 7–9; also, more controversially, Gilmour, *Curzon*, 1994, Chs. 17–22. *The Fall of the Viceroy: How Kitchener Destroyed Curzon*, 1986, by Peter King, who had worked in radio and

television and edited two books of Curzon's writings, has factual errors, and the extensive quotations tend to be moulded rather in the manner of a television documentary to 'prove' a case against Kitchener.

6 Sir G. O'Moore Creagh, *Stray Recollections*, 1924, p. 256.

7 Valentine Chirol, *Fifty Years in a Changing World*, 1927, p. 228.

8 Lord Ampthill to Brodrick, 9 June 1904. Ampthill Papers, OIOL, 233/37.

9 Note by Lord Salisbury, ND, marked 'Very Private', forwarded to K by Lady Salisbury. Hatfield MSS.

10 Brodrick to K, 29 April 1904. KP, 22.Y166.

11 Largely printed in Arthur, *Life*, vol. 2, pp. 199–200. KP, 22.Y168.

12 K to Howard Vincent, 26 July 1904. Copy in Midleton Papers, PRO 67/21/1055. For Clarke and Curzon, family information.

13 K to Marker, 14 July 1904. Marker Papers, BL, 76A f.26.

14 O'Moore Creagh, op. cit., p. 257.

15 K to Lady Salisbury, 28 July 1904. Hatfield MSS.

16 See Dilks, op. cit., 21 September 1904.

17 As stated by Magnus, p. 214.

18 K to Lady Salisbury, 4 August, 14 September 1904. Hatfield MSS.

19 K to Marker, 15 September 1904. Marker Papers, BL, 76A ff. 28–30.

20 K to Lady Salisbury, 28 September 1904. Hatfield MSS.

21 Maxwell to her, same date. Hatfield MSS. (A rather illegible signature, but the writing is Maxwell's.)

22 Hamilton to Marker, 15 September 1904. NAM, Letter 22.

23 Frank Maxwell Diary, 12, 13 September 1904. *I am Ready*, p. 36.

24 Buck, op. cit., pp. 134–5. Unlike Curzon, Ampthill was a Freemason.

25 Maxwell Diary, 22 October 1904, *I am Ready*. This entry destroys King's assertion (p. 172) that Maxwell was sent home to intrigue against the Curzons.

26 For Repington see W. Michael Ryan, *Lieutenant-Colonel Charles à Court Repington. A Study of the Interaction of Personality, the Press and Power*, passim.

27 Ibid., p. 63.

28 Repington to Marker, 19 August, 10 October 1904. Marker Papers, BL, Add MSS 52277B, ff. 2, 10.

29 Hamilton to Marker, 22 September 1904. Marker Papers, NAM, Letter 24.

30 Chirol, op. cit., p. 228.

31 Hamilton to Marker, 20 October 1904. Marker Papers, NAM, Letters 26.

32 Ibid., ND (late October 1904), Letter 28.

33 Victor Brooke to Frank Maxwell, 29 October (1904). *I am Ready*, p. 58.

34 Hamilton to Frank Maxwell, 18 November 1904. Ibid., pp. 58–9.

35 Hamilton to Marker, 14 December 1904. NAM, Letter 29.

36 Hamilton to Maxwell, 18 November 1904. *I am Ready*, p. 59.

37 Sir George Arthur, *Not Worth Reading*, 1938, p. 187 (abbreviated henceforth to NWR).

38 K to Marker, 22 December 1904. Marker Papers, BL, 76A f. 34. Lieutenant G. G. E. Wylly, VC. He had won it on the North-West Frontier.

39 Hamilton to Marker, 14 December 1904, as above.

40 K to Renshaw, 14 December 1904. CK.

Chapter 8: 'Bitter and Unscrupulous Enemies'

1 K to Lady Salisbury, 22 December 1904. Hatfield MSS.

2 K to Lady Salisbury, 5 January 1905. Hatfield MSS.

3 Letters quoted in Nigel Nicolson, *Mary Curzon*, 1977, p. 199. See also K to Marker, 19 January 1905 (Marker Papers, BL, 79A f. 53), and Gilmour (op. cit., p. 307).

4 K to Birdwood, Calcutta, 3 March 1905 (misdated 3 May, when both were in Simla); next letter to Birdwood, 15 January 1905. Birdwood Papers, OIOL, 686/58.

5 K to Lady Salisbury, 19 January 1905. Hatfield MSS.

6 Earl of Midleton (formerly St John Brodrick), *Records and Reactions, 1859–1939*, 1939, p. 204; see also Hubert Hamilton to Marker, 27 October 1904 (Marker Papers, NAM, Letter 27): 'Curzon . . . finds the Mily Dept a most useful buffer against the possible eccentricities of Cs in C who are all assumed under existing system to be inefficient, and more particularly against the methods of an efficient C. in C. which on the grounds of expense alone are personally objectionable to him.' K's instructions re the memorandum are in K to Lady Salisbury, ND (context indicates January 1905). Hatfield MSS.

7 Hamilton to Marker, 12 January 1905. Marker Papers, NAM, Letter 30. Regimental records, Coldstream Guards, list Marker as Private Secretary, not assistant, i.e. *Military* Private Secretary, subordinate to the Principal Private Secretary, always a civil servant.

8 K to Birdwood, 10, 18 January 1905. OIOL, 686 58.

9 K to Lady Salisbury, 12 January 1905. Hatfield MSS.

10 K to H. A. Gwynne, 12 January 1905. H. A. Gwynne Papers, Part II, Imperial War Museum, enclosing a copy of the 'scurrilous reports' forwarded by Rawlinson.

11 Buck, op. cit., pp. 256–7. King's assertion (p. 156) that Buck was the channel for information to the press in England conflicts with Buck's own statement on his p. 234 and other evidence.

12 Maxwell Diary, 31 January 1905. *I am Ready*, p. 6.

13 Hamilton to Marker, 12 January 1905. NAM, Letter 30. See also Letter 31, 18 January.

14 Curzon to the King, 25 January 1905. RA VIC W3/21.

15 K to Maxwell, 23 December 1906. Maxwell Papers, NAM, 7807.25.37.

16 Nicolson, op. cit., p. 202.

17 Hamilton to Marker, 1 February 1905. NAM, Letter 32.

18 K to Lady Salisbury, 8, 16 February 1905. Hatfield MSS.

19 Hamilton to Marker, 9 February 1905. NAM, Letter 33.

20 K to Lady Salisbury, ND (February) 1905. Hatfield MSS.

21 Hamilton to Marker, 23 February 1905. NAM, Letter 35.

22 Nicolson, op. cit., p. 204.

23 Hamilton to Marker, 1 March 1905. NAM, Letter 37.

24 K to Lady Salisbury, 16 February 1905. Hatfield MSS.

25 Hamilton to Marker, 14 February 1905. NAM, Letter 34.

26 The replies are in KP, 32.CC3.

27 Hamilton to Marker, 1 March 1905. NAM, Letter 37. King's *Fall of the Viceroy* quotes very extensively from the Hamilton–Marker letters yet omits these paragraphs which compromise his contention that K manipulated the press to force Curzon's hand. On whether K should have written to the generals, see Gilmour, op. cit., p. 307. Re General Gaselee, mentioned two paragaphs later in this connection, see Repington to Marker, 2 January 1906. Marker Papers, BL, 77B f. 31.

28 Hamilton to Marker, 9 March 1905. NAM, Letter 38.

29 The only copy is in the Curzon Papers with C's later comments. See King, op. cit., pp. 152–3. Stedman's acknowledgement is KP, 33.AA 31.

30 K to Renshaw, 29 February 1905. CK.

31 K to Sir Reginald Wingate, 1 March 1905. Wingate Papers, Sudan Archive, University of Durham.

32 K to Birdwood, Sunday (postmark 12 March 1905). Birdwood Papers, OIOL, D686/58. For a more solemn account, see Ronaldshay, op. cit., p. 379.

33 Ibid., 24 March 1905.

34 Hamilton to Marker, 23 March 1905. NAM, Letter 40.

35 Ian Hamilton, *The Commander*, pp. 118–19. See also Margot Asquith, *More Memories*, 1933, pp. 177–8.

36 Frank Maxwell's Diary, 30, 31 March 1905. *I am Ready*, p. 62.

37 Frank Maxwell to his cousin Louisa Lockhart, 3 May 1905. *I am Ready*, pp. 63–4.

38 (Sir George Arthur), *Letters of a Man of No Importance*, 1928, pp. 187–8.

39 K to Birdwood, 21 April (1905). OIOL, D686/58.

40 Hamilton to Marker, 24 April 1905. NAM, Letter 11.

41 Hamilton to Marker, 3 May 1905. NAM, Letter 43.

42 Hamilton to Marker, 16 March 1905. NAM, Letter 39.

43 K to Lady Curzon, 'Thursday'. Lady Curzon Papers, OIOL, 368, f. 224; Hamilton to Marker, 3 May 1905. NAM, Letter 43.

44 K to Birdwood, Naini Tal, 21 April (1905). OIOL, 686/58.

45 Quoted in K to Marker, 24 April 1905. NAM, Letter 11.

46 Hamilton to Marker, 3 May 1905. NAM, Letter 43.

47 K to Marker, 11 May 1905. NAM, Letter 12.

48 The events of May 1905 in London are vividly described in King, op. cit., pp. 160–4, allowing for pro-Curzon bias: e.g. King says that Brodrick's claims in his memoirs that Curzon had influential people working for him at home 'are nonsense'. But Brodrick (Lord Midleton) was obviously referring to Roberts and Lansdowne.

Chapter 9: The Quarrel

1 Marker's wire quoted by Hamilton in Letter 46, 19 June 1905, and printed in King, op. cit., p. 164.

2 Hamilton to Marker, 1 June 1905. NAM, Letter 44.

3 Hamilton to Marker, 6 June 1905. NAM, Letter 45.

4 Brodrick to King Edward VII, 27 May 1905. Midleton Papers, PRO, 30.67.22.1145.

5 Brodrick to Lord Cromer, 8 June 1905, Cromer Papers, PRO FO 633/7, p. 289.

6 K to Marker, 22 June 1905. Marker Papers, BL, 76A f. 91.

7 K to Lady Salisbury, 29 June 1905. Hatfield MSS.

8 K to Lady Salisbury, 6 July 1905. Hatfield MSS. For the pistol, see Magnus, op. cit., pp. 219–20 (letter to Stedman).

9 K to Lady Salisbury, 10 August 1905. Hatfield MSS.

10 Sir Frederick Milner, letter in Morning Post, June 1916; Maurice, op. cit., p. 160.

11 Hamilton to Marker, 6 July 1905. NAM, Letter 48.

12 Ibid.

13 Lady Curzon to K, June 1905. KP, 33 AA 20.

14 Maxwell (Charlotte), I am Ready, pp. 65–7.

15 The telegram is printed in King, op. cit., pp. 177–8. King's account, however, is not reliable as he simply accepts Curzon's disputed version of the vital interview and writes off Kitchener's version as a pack of lies.

16 Curzon to King Edward VII, 6 July 1905, VICW 3/65.
17 Hamilton to Marker, 12 July 1905. NAM, Letter 49.
18 Hamilton to Marker, 29 July 1905. NAM, Letter 50.
19 Ibid.
20 K to Lady Salisbury, 16 July 1905. Hatfield MSS.
21 Brodrick to King Edward VII, 25 July 1905. RA VICR 26/55.
22 Ibid.
23 Balfour to King Edward VII, 25 July 1905. RA VICR 26/55.
24 Précis of Curzon to Barrow, 22 September 1903. Barrow Papers, OIOL, Eur. E 420/18.
25 K to Barrow, 6 October 1903. Barrow Papers. OIOL MSS Eur E420/19.
26 Hamilton to Marker, 12 July 1905 (misdated by King to 20 July). NAM, Letter 49.
27 K to Lady Salisbury, 16 June 1904. Hatfield MSS.
28 K to Marker, 3 August (1905). Marker Papers, BL, 76A f. 99/100.
29 Curzon to Clinton Dawkins, 3 August 1905 (MS missing; in print, misdated 1903, but context demands 1905). Curzon Papers, OIOL, F111/183.
30 Hamilton to Marker, 8 August 1905. NAM, Letter 51. For the Bishop, see K to Lady Salisbury, 10 August 1905. Hatfield MSS.
31 Curzon to Lord Ampthill, 12 August 1905. Curzon Papers, OIOL, 111/211. Curzon's account of the 'angry' interview of 5 August is in this letter.
32 Maconchy typescript Memoirs, vol. 2, p. 346. NAM.
33 See KRO, p. 161.
34 Hamilton to Marker, 8 August 1905. NAM, Letter 51.
35 K to Lady Salisbury, 10 August 1905. Hatfield MSS.
36 Brodrick to Lord Knollys, September 1905, copy in Midleton Papers, PRO, 30/67/1183—94.
37 Hamilton to Marker, 8 August 1905. NAM, Letter 51.
38 K to Lady Salisbury, 24 August 1905. Hatfield MSS.
39 K to Lady Salisbury, 3 August 1905. Hatfield MSS
40 K to Brodrick, 21 September 1905. Midleton Papers, PRO, 30/67/22.1195—1201.

Chapter 10: The Insult

1 K to General Scott, 26 August (1905), and to General Beauchamp Duff, 28 August. KP, 31. BB. 22—23.
2 Curzon to K, 28 August 1905. Indian Military Organization 1902—1905

(Private Correspondence). Privately printed, in Curzon Papers, OIOL 111/412, p. 122.

3 K to Marker, 30 August 1905. Marker Papers, BL, 76A f. 109–10.

4 K to Lady Salisbury, 30 August 1905. Hatfield MSS.

5 Curzon to Barrow, 30 August 1905. Barrow Papers, OIOL, E.420.19.

6 K to Brodrick, 21 September 1905. Midleton Papers, PRO, 30.67.22. 1195–1201.

7 Ibid.

8 Curzon to Valentine Chirol, 14 September 1905. Curzon Papers, OIOL, F.111.183.

9 Lady Curzon to Lieutenant-General Sir E. Barrow, 21 September 1905. Barrow Papers, OIOL, E.420.19.

10 Mary Curzon to Mrs Leiter, 2, 8 October 1905. Lady Curzon Papers, OIOL, 13A ff. 145, 151. She describes the farewell in her letter of 25 October, ff. 155–7. The letters are printed in Bradley, op. cit., pp. 164–6.

Chapter 11: India with Minto

1 K to Lady Salisbury, 27 September, 23 November 1905. Hatfield MSS.

2 Lord Minto to John Morley, 1 January 1906, quoted in Arthur, vol. 2, p. 244n., and January 1906, quoted ibid., p. 219n.

3 Raymond Marker to his sister Gertie, 4 January 1906. Marker Papers, NAM, 6803.4.5. f. 10.

4 K to Frank Maxwell, 2 April 1906. Maxwell Papers, NAM, 7807.25.39.

5 Unsigned pencilled note in the Midleton Papers, dated 26 October 1905. PRO, 30.67.22.1210.

6 K to Lady Salisbury, 24 May, 11 January 1906. Hatfield MSS.

7 K to Arthur Renshaw, 19 February 1906. CK.

8 Repington to Marker, 1 March 1906. Marker Papers, BL, Add MSS 52277 f. 41.

9 Repington to Marker, 18 May 1906. Marker Papers, BL, Add MSS 52277 f. 50.

10 K to Lady Salisbury, 24 May, 7 June 1906, 24 April 1907. Hatfield MSS.

11 K to Sir Arthur Bigge, 13 March 1906. RA GV A7A/5.

12 The Prince of Wales to K, 17 March 1906. RA GV, A visit to India, folder 1.

13 K to Lady Salisbury, 14 December 1905. Hatfield MSS.

14 RA QMD GV cc 68/21 p. 339.

15 Maconchy typescript Memoirs, pp. 8–9. Earl K.; Birdwood, op. cit., p. 165.

16 The Princess of Wales to Prince Alexander George ('Alge') of Teck, afterwards the Earl of Athlone, 8 January 1906. RA GV CC 53/369.

17 K to Birdwood, 20 February 1903. Birdwood Papers, OIOL, 58.

18 Several versions of this story exist. See Asquith, *More Memories*, p. 140; Frances Stevenson, *Lloyd George: A Diary*, 1971, p. 26.

19 See the catalogue of the twoday sale by the trustees of K's will at Sotheby, 16, 17 November 1938.

20 Birdwood, op. cit., p. 169.

21 Lady Wilson (A. C. MacLeod), *Letters from India*, Edinburgh, 1911, p. 323.

22 K to Lady Salisbury, 1 October 1908. Hatfield MSS.

23 Lawrence told this story to the Asquiths.

24 Lord Frederic Hamilton, *My Yesterdays*, 1926, pp. 39–40.

25 (Charlotte Maxwell) (ed.), *I am Ready*, 1955, pp. 71–9, 82, 91.

26 Birdwood to Clive Wigram, 12 June 1916. RA GV Q 2521/57.

27 *Emulation Ritual*, published by Lewis Masonic, 6th edn, pp. 67, 233.

28 Sir Henry McMahon, An Account of the Entry of HM Habibullah Khan Amir of Aghanistan into Freemasonry, typescript, January 1936; Birdwood, op. cit., pp. 176–7.

29 General Sir C. Monro to Lord Stamfordham, 28 December 1916. RA GV Q2521/174.

30 Minto to Bigge, 21 July 1909. RA GV A 12/2.

31 Birdwood to Lord Midleton, 26 August 1916. KP, 91 GA2.10.

32 K to Sir Reginald Wingate, 10 April (1908). Wingate Papers, 282/4/27.

33 K to Lord Roberts, 20 May 1909. KP, 29.Q46.

34 Arthur, *Life*, vol. 2, p. 275. The memoranda are printed in full, pp. 271–6.

35 Sven Hedin, *Grosse Männer denen Ich Begegnete*, 1952, p. 321; see other references on pp. 303–24, in Hedin's *TransHimalaya*, 1909, pp. 12, 15, 17, 18–19, 427–8, and *My Life as an Explorer*, 1925, pp. 336, 473–4.

36 K to Bigge, 25 February 1909. RA GV A 16A. King, op. cit., p. 241, is wrong in supposing that K chose Creagh.

37 K to Lady Salisbury, 6 April 1909. Hatfield MSS.

38 Minto to Bigge, 14 October 1909. RA GV A 6A/13.

Chapter 12: World Tour

1 The King's telegrams and K's replies, 25 July to 1 August 1909, are in RA VIC W 31. See also K to Lord Roberts, 5 August 1909, KP, 29 Q46; K to Wingate, 12 August 1909. Wingate Papers, 288/3/102.

2 Martin Gilbert, *Sir Horace Rumbold*, 1973, pp. 79–81.

3 KP, 74 WS 64.

4 Anonymous letter written on his death to Lord Derby 'as his greatest friend'. KP, 114.231.

5 See *The Australian Encyclopedia*, 1958, vol. 1, pp. 79–80, 'Military Defence' and related articles.

6 K to Lady Salisbury, 12 February 1910. Hatfield MSS.

7 The Parker interview was in the *Otago Daily Times*, Dunedin, 17 February 1910. For the 'fiasco', see ibid. and the Christchurch *Press*, 10 February 1910, in KP, 40. Also the *Otago Daily Times*, 12 February 1977, kindly sent by Millie Parker's granddaughter, the late Miss M. E. Cairns.

8 Birdwood, memo to Arthur, 25 August 1916. KP, 91 GA 2–10. See also K to General Sir Leslie Rundle (then Governor of Malta), 30 June (1910). Wingate Papers, 234/8/46.

9 Lord Roberts to K, 2 May 1910. KP, 28 11 49. D. Sommers, *Haldane of Cloan*, 1960, p. 230.

10 Viscount Morley, *Recollections*, 1917, vol. 2, pp. 330–31; Viscount Esher, *The Tragedy of Lord Kitchener*, 1921, p. 26.

11 Undated note by Lady Winifred Renshaw. CK.

12 Minto to Bigge, 15 June 1910. RA GV A6a/19.

13 Memorandum by Viscount Morley. RA GV N473/1.

14 K to Maxwell, 22 June 1920. NAM, 7807.25.44.

15 K to Prince Francis of Teck, 11 July 1910. RA GV CC 52.

16 See KRO, pp. 125–6, 135, 138, 150.

17 K to Raymond ('Conk') Marker, 30 October 1906. Marker Papers, BL, 76A f. 124.

18 Lord Desborough, *Kitchener as I Knew Him*. Address at the Canadian Hospital, Cliveden, memorial service, 11 June 1916. KP, 119.

19 Bridget *née* Monins (Mrs Philip Toynbee) to the author.

20 Birdwood Diary, 26 August 1910. NAM, 6707-19-23. Kitchener bought it for £1,400, not £14,000 as in Royale, *The Kitchener Enigma*, 1985, p. 234, which would have been an immense price in 1910.

21 K to Frank Maxwell, 17 September 1910. *I am Ready*, p. 90.

22 See KRO, pp. 135, 138.

23 K to Wingate, 7 December (1910). Wingate Papers, 298/3/53.

24 *Lantern Slides: The Diaries and Letters of Violet Bonham-Carter, 1904–1914*, ed. Mark Bonham-Carter and Mark Tottle, 1996. FR 245–6.

25 See KRO, p. 25.

26 For details of the East Africa property and negotiations, see Magnus, op. cit., pp. 255–7 (Songhor is misspelled). But K's great-nephew Charles, working in Kenya as a schoolmaster when he read Magnus, criticized him for implying that 'the intention was purely for personal financial gain and not for devel-

opment for its own sake, which I am sure was uppermost in K's mind'. Letter of Charles Kitchener to his mother, 1959.

27 KP, 100 PA 13/13.

28 K to Raymond Marker, 24 April (1911). Marker Papers, BL, 76B f. 93.

29 K to Arthur Renshaw, 13 April 1911. CK.

30 Birdwood, op. cit., p. 212.

Chapter 13: Portrait of a Pharaoh

1 Sir Edward Grey to K, 20 June 1911. KP, 36. JJ8.

2 Quoted in E. W. C. Sandes, The Royal Engineers in Egypt and the Sudan, 1937, p. 538.

3 Sir Ronald Storrs, Orientations, 1937, p. 122.

4 Lord Edward Cecil, The Leisure of an Egyptian Official, 1922, pp. 195–6.

5 As related to Lieutenant-General Sir Henry Meyrick Lawson, article on K in Lord Kitchener, The Nineteenth Century and After, 1921. Copy in KP, 94 GA 6; Cecil, op. cit., p. 194.

6 Storrs, op. cit., p. 131.

7 Ibid., p. 138; for the episode, see KRO, pp. 87–8.

8 Cecil, op. cit., p. 196.

9 Preserved in the Storrs Papers, Pembroke College, Cambridge.

10 'Lord Kitchener in Egypt', Part Two, dated Cairo, 10 January 1914 ('From A Correspondent').

11 Fitzgerald to Sir George Arthur, 4, 19 May 1912. KP, 42 KK14, 15.

12 Storrs, op. cit., p. 136.

13 Mrs Bonte Sheldon Elgood to Magnus, 1959. Copy in KP, 102 PA 2A; see KRO, pp. 62–3.

14 Letter from Hugo von Dumreicher, son of André and May von Dumreicher, to author, 12 April 1999.

15 Storrs, op. cit., pp. 129, 222; Clara Boyle, Boyle of Cairo, 1965; Kenneth Rose, The Later Cecils, 1975, p. 220.

16 Storrs to his mother, Mrs John Storrs, 27 October 1912. Storr's father was vicar of St Peter's Eaton Square and became Dean of Rochester in 1913. Storrs Papers.

17 Ibid., 30 November 1913. Storrs Papers.

18 See KRO pp. 43–4.

19 Storrs, op. cit., p. 125; Storrs to his mother , 4 November 1912. Storrs Papers.

20 Sybil (later Lady Sybil) Graham to Queen Mary, 4 December 1913, RA GV CC 47/34.

21 Sir Frederick Milner to Queen Mary, 15 February 1912. RA GV CC 47/296.

22 See K's letters to Wingate in the Wingate Papers.

23 K to Henry Kitchener (Hal) 6 August (1912) Hall Papers; Storrs to his mother, 10 February 1912, Storrs Papers; K to Bishop G. F. Blyth, Bishop of Jerusalem, 20 March 1912. Blyth Papers, Lambeth Palace MSS 2231.

24 Sir Frederick Milner, letter in *Morning Post*, June 1916, cutting in 3rd Earl Papers.

25 J. H. Molesworth, *Soldier of God*, 1916; H. C. Jackson, *Pastor on the Nile*, 1960, p. 144. When Molyneux retired, K ensured that he was presented to a good living (in the Diocese of Ely). I am grateful to Molyneaux's daughters, Mrs MacKinnon and Lady Mogg for information. A large portrait of K hung in the hall of the large rectory in the Fens.

26 Cecil to his wife, February 1912. Lord Edward Cecil Papers, Bodleian Library, No. 26. See Arthur, *Life*, vol. 3, p. 372.

27 Storrs to his mother, 31 March 1912. Storrs Papers.

28 K to Wingate, 19 August (1913). Wingate Papers, 187/2/212.

29 *Kentish Gazette*, 19 July 1913.

30 *Punch*, 12 November 1913.

31 FitzGerald to Arthur, 30 November (1913). KP, 44. MM 33.

32 Cecil to his wife, 6 May 1914. Lord Edward Cecil Papers, Bodleian Library (not numbered).

33 RA KGV Diary, 29 June 1914.

34 Fitzgerald to Arthur, 10 May 1914. KP, 45. 004.

Chapter 14: Into the Breach

1 K to Birdwood, 27 July (1914). OIOL, D686. 59.

2 K to Mrs Florence Marc, 27 July (1914). CK.

3 Winston S. Churchill, *The World Crisis* (1938 edn), vol. 1, p. 165.

4 K to Florence Marc, 31 July 1914. CK.

5 Storrs, op. cit., p. 146.

6 Asquith to K, 3 August 1914. KP, 76. WR.1.

7 F. S. Oliver, *Ordeal by Battle*, 1915, p. 254.

8 Quoted in George Cassar, *Kitchener: Architect of Victory*, 1977, p. 177. For further details of the political and newspaper background to K's appointment, see Cassar, pp. 174–86. His long magisterial book is essential reading for more extensive study of all aspects of K's wartime career.

9 Professor (ex-Major-General) K. Haushofer, *The Times*, 5 January 1937; Rt. Hon. Sir Guy Fleetwood-Wilson, *The Times*, 16 January 1937. In South

Africa K said 'muddlers', not 'statesmen'. Fleetwood Wilson was K's financial adviser, 1901.

10 Eric Field, *Advertising – The Forgotten Years*, 1959, pp. 28–9, 134, 135.

11 RA KGV Diary, 6 August 1914 and *passim*.

12 Viscount Long, *My Memories*, 1923, p. 216.

13 Ronald Storrs, op. cit., p. 147.

14 Viscount Long of Wraxell, *My Memories*, 1923, p. 162.

15 Lord Riddell, *The Riddell Diaries*, ed. J. McEwan, 1986, p. 88.

16 Denis Gwynn, *The Life of John Redmond*, 1932, p. 366.

17 Ian Colvin, *The Life of Lord Carson*, 1934, vol. 3, p. 27; Peter Simkins, *Kitchener's Army*, 1988, gives much detail about the raising of the New Armies.

18 KRO, p. 72.

19 Sir George Arthur, NWR, p. 191.

20 Ibid., p. 192.

Chapter 15: The Contemptibles

1 Information and viewing courtesy of the Lord Advocate's office, the then tenants; Lady Wantage to K, 12 August 1914. KP, 108. PA8.33; Arthur, NWR, gives many sidelights on life at 2 Carlton Gardens.

2 M. and E. Brock (eds), *H. H. Asquith: Letters to Venetia Stanley*, 1982, pp. 157, 158; see KRO, pp. 86–7.

3 See KRO, p. 19, for more detail.

4 From K's speech to Members of the House of Commons, 2 June 1916. Arthur, *Life*, vol. 3, p. 329. No record exists of his actual words to the Cabinet in August 1914.

5 Viscount Grey, *Twenty-Five Years*, 1925, II, p. 71.

6 Brock, op. cit., p. 160.

7 Quoted in Arthur, *Life*, vol. 3, pp. 25–6. Owing to the coincidence that the British C-in-C and the principal ally were both *French*, I tend to refer to the C-in-C as *Sir John*.

8 Arthur, NWR, p. 205.

9 Arthur, *Life*, vol. 3, p. 27.

10 Sir C. E. Callwell, *Field Marshal Sir Henry Wilson*, 1927, pp. 162–3.

11 Lady Salisbury to Lord Salisbury, 13 August 1914. Hatfield MSS.

12 The issues are well discussed in Cassar, *Kitchener*, pp. 195–201, and Simkins, op. cit., pp. 40–46.

13 Margot Asquith, *Autobiography*, 1922, p. 178.

14 King George V to the Duke of Connaught, 15 August 1914. RA VIC Add A15/6512.

15 Hunter to K, 9, 11, 21 August 1914. KP, 80. WV.7–8, 40.

16 Arthur, NWR, p. 216.

Chapter 16: Averting Defeat

1 Winston S. Churchill, op. cit., vol. I, p. 220.

2 Ibid. The telegram, French to K, 24 August 1914, is in KP, 49. WA 7 (pencil copy) and printed in Arthur, *Life*, vol. 3, pp. 35–6.

3 Margot Asquith, *Autobiography*, vol. 3, p. 205.

4 Ibid., pp. 205–7.

5 K to Lord Stamfordham, 25 August 1914. RA GV/Q 723A/5.

6 Lord Sandhurst, *From Day to Day*, 1928, p. 24.

7 French to K, August 1914. KP 49. W11.

8 Arthur, *Life*, vol. 3, p. 46.

9 Arthur, NWR, p. 217.

10 Arthur, *Life*, vol. 3, pp. 52–3.

11 Diary notes of Rt Hon. Jack Pease (later Lord Gainford). Gainford Papers, 40. f. 46. The two Cabinet Ministers were Pease (Board of Edcuation) and McKenna (Home Secretary).

12 Brock, op. cit., p. 213.

13 Arthur, NWR, p. 218.

14 Ibid., NWR, p. 219.

15 Written in 1928. Quoted in Cassar, *Kitchener*, p. 238.

16 Quoted in Martin Gilbert, *Winston S. Churchill*, 1971, vol. 3, p. 61.

17 Cassar, *Kitchener*, p. 241; Arthur, NWR, p. 220.

Chapter 17: 'An Enormous Asset'

1 Maurice Rickards, *Posters of the First World War*, 1968, pp. 10–12; Reginald Pound, *The Lost Generation*, 1968, p. 25.

2 Simkins, op. cit., pp. 74–5; Cassar, pp. 206–7.

3 O'Moore Creagh, VC, *Stray Recollections*, p. 275.

4 Lord Riddell, *War Diary 1914–18*, 1933, p. 48; (Sir George Arthur), *Letters of A Man of No Importance*, 1920, p. 42; Arthur, NWR.

5 Arthur, NWR, p. 210; Philip Ziegler, *King Edward VIII*, 1990, p. 51.

6 Princess Louise, Duchess of Fife, to K, 21 September (1914). KP, 104 PA 7.

7 Lord Stamfordham to K, 24 August 1914. RA GV Q 2554/2.

8 Arthur, NWR, p. 200.

9 John Vincent (ed.), *The Crawford Papers*, 1984, p. 343; Arthur, NWR, p. 201; Susan Mary Alsop, *Lady Sackville*, 1978, pp. 200–1.

10 Creedy Papers, PRO, 71.22.1.

11 Letter in *The Times* from Sir Harold Hartley dated 9 June 1934.

12 Information from Mr Hugo von Dumreicher.

13 Private information, but see Gordon Brook-Shepherd, *Between Two Flags*, 1972, chapter 14.

14 Brock, op. cit., pp. 260–1.

15 J. A. Spender, *Life, Journalism and Politics*, 1927, vol. 2, p. 48.

16 Viscount Halifax to K, 5 October 1914. KP, 73. WS7; E. L. Langston, *Bishop Taylor Smith*, 1938, pp. 127–30. For chaplains generally, see Sir John Smyth, VC, *In This Sign Conquer*, 1968.

17 For K's reaction in 1898, and how he put Gwynne to work among 'heathen' British troops, see KRO, pp. 163–4; Jackson, *Pastor on the Nile*, 1960, *passim*.

18 Bishop L. Gwynne to the Archbishop, 16 August 1914. Lambeth Palace Library, Davidson Papers, 343.20.

19 E. W. Swinton, *Eye-Witness*, 1932, pp. 39, 48–9.

20 Maurice, op. cit., p. 100.

21 Quoted in Winston S. Churchill, op. cit., vol. 1, pp. 305–6.

22 Arthur, NWR, p. 221.

Chapter 18: Nothing to Fight With

1 Sir Arthur Conan Doyle, *The British Campaign in France and Flanders, 1914–1916*, quoted in the Royal Surrey Regimental Association Newsletter, 5, 1989.

2 Edith, Lady Allendale, to K, 31 October 1914. KP, 108 PA 8.2. See KRO, p. 205.

3 Lord Birdwood, *Khaki and Gown*, 1941, pp. 144, 237.

4 F. Foch, *Memoirs*, tr. B. Mott, 1931, p. 162.

5 See Callwell, *Wilson*, pp. 186–7; Magnus, op. cit., pp. 304–5.

6 Tradition handed down in Barham, Kent.

7 Sir Walter Lawrence, op. cit., pp. 269–70.

8 Rudyard Kipling, *The Irish Guards in the Great War*, 1923, vol. 1, p. 51.

9 K to Lady Salisbury, 19 January 1905. Hatfield MSS.

10 Vincent (ed.), op. cit., p. 343 (27th Earl's Diary, 11 October 1914).

11 Arthur, NWR, p. 246. See the study, using this quote as a title, of the financial and industrial background to 1914 by John Hussey, *British Army Review*, No. 109, 1995.

12 Arthur, NWR, pp. 208–9; Winston S. Churchill, op. cit., p. 410.

13 The Marquis de Chasseloup Laubat in *The Lord Kitchener Memorial Book*, ed. Sir Hedley Le Bas, 1916.

14 Gainford MS 42, typescript Chapter IV, pp. 78–9; see KRO, p. 29.

15 Typescript memo on Lord Kitchener by Lord Beaverbrook. KP, 93, GA 3.24.

16 Arthur, NWR, p. 252.

17 Brock, op. cit., pp. 288–9, 291. See also Frances Stevenson, *Lloyd George: A Diary*, A. J. P. Taylor (ed.), 1971, p. 3.

18 Maurice, op. cit., p. 114.

19 Riddell, *The Riddell Diaries*, p. 94.

20 Lloyd George to K, 30 October 1914. KP, 80WV.14.

21 J. A. Spender, *Life, Journalism and Politics*, 1927, pp. 64–5.

22 Arthur, NWR, p. 199.

23 Hugh Sinclair, *Camp and Society*, extract quoted in letter to author from his granddaughter, Mrs Janet Winchester, 18 May 1998.

24 Letter of 2nd Lieutenant J. B. Nevitt, 25 January 1915. Imperial War Museum, 90.7.1.

25 Lieutenant-General Sir Henry Meyrick Lawson, *Lord Kitchener*, *The Nineteenth Century and After*, 1921, pp. 7–8.

26 Earl Haig in Arthur, *Life*, vol. 1, p. xvi; letter in the Museum of the Royal United Service Institution in 1936, quoted by the secretary, Captain E. Altham, RN, in *The Times*, 1936.

Chapter 19: Dardanelles Dilemma

1 Grey, op. cit., vol. 2, p. 72.

2 Violet Bonham-Carter, *Champion Redoubtable*, 1998, p. 17.

3 Milner, 8 December 1914, quoted in Cassar, *Kitchener*, p. 265.

4 See Cassar, *Kitchener*, pp. 261–3.

5 Sir Gerald Ellison, *The Perils of Amateur Strategy*, 1926, p. 27.

6 Lord Hankey, *The Supreme Command*, 1961, vol. 1, pp. 265–6; Brock, op. cit., pp. 372–7; see Robert Rhodes-James, *Gallipoli*, 1965, and Martin Gilbert, *Churchill*, 1971, vol. 3, and Cassar, op. cit., for detailed accounts of the 'drift to the Dardanelles'.

7 Sandhurst, Viscount, *From Day to Day, 1914–1915*, 1928, pp. 131, 136; David Gilmour, *Curzon*, 1944, p. 437.

8 Douglas Dawson to Lieutenant-Colonel Frederick Ponsonby (later 1st Lord Sysonby), 15 January 1915. RA PP GV 4/67/3.

9 Lord Stamfordham to Ponsonby, 16 January 1915. RA PP GV 4/67/3.

10 Arthur, NWR, p. 199.

11 See Gilbert, op. cit., p. 271, and Cassar, *Kitchener*, p. 280.

12 Maurice, op. cit., pp. 124–5.

13 Rhodes-James, op. cit., p. 41, and note.

14 Gilbert, op. cit., pp. 312–13.

15 Birdwood to K, 3 March 1915. KP, 61. WL 5.

16 Sir Ian Hamilton, *Gallipoli Diary*, vol. I, quoted in Rhodes-James, op. cit., p. 52.

17 Lord Fisher to K, 11 March 1915. KP, 80 WV 8.

18 Rhodes-James, op. cit., p. 65. Extracts from Dardanelles secret telegrams bound by Arthur are KP, 65.

Chapter 20: Conspiracy

1 Arthur, NWR, pp. 226–7, and *More Letters*, pp. 25–6.

2 Frances Stevenson, op. cit., p. 40.

3 Sir A. Hunter to K, 16 March 1915. KP, 73.WS 32.

4 Alan Clark (ed.), *A Good Innings: The Papers of Viscount Lee*, 1974, pp. 140–1.

5 Stevenson, op. cit., pp. 36–7.

6 Bonham-Carter, *Champion Redoubtable*, p. 36.

7 Brock, op. cit., p. 544.

8 Lord Crawford's diary, 15 February 1940. *The Crawford Papers*, (ed.) John Vincent.

9 Brock, op. cit., pp. 546, 550.

10 K to Asquith, 14 (April 1915). Asquith Papers, HHA/14/15. The note is reproduced facsimile in Margot Asquith's *Autobiography*.

11 E. M. House to President Wilson, 13 May 1915. Wilson Papers, vol. 33, p. 189.

12 C. E. Callwell, *Experiences of a Dug-Out 1914–1918*, 1920, p. 48.

13 Lord Esher to K, 19 May 1915. KP, 59.WI.39.

14 Lord Esher to FitzGerald, 24 May 1915. KP, 59.WI.48.

15 Lord Birkenhead, *Points of View*, 1922, vol. 2, p. 11.

16 Rawlinson to FitzGerald, 24 May 1915. KP, 51.WB.218.

17 Arthur, NWR, p. 253.

18 Asquith to K, 30 May 1915. 3rd Earl Papers.

19 (Arthur), *Some More Letters . . .*, p. 32.

Chapter 21: Two Triumphs

1 Churchill, *The World Crisis*, vol. 2, p. 807; Gilbert, *Churchill*, vol. 3, p. 469; information from Lady Soames.

2 Arthur, NWR, pp. 19–20.

3 Quoted in Lord Desborough's memorial address on Kitchener, 11 June 1916. KP, 119.

4 Margot Asquith, *Autobiography*, vol. 2, p. 228.

5 Ibid., *More Memories*, 1933, p. 157.

6 Interviews between the Archbishop and Curzon, 5 October, 18 November 1915. Davidson Papers, Lambeth Palace Library, Private Papers, vol. 13, pp. 35, 38.

7 Lord Birkenhead, op. cit., p. 30.

8 Lord Esher to Fitzgerald, 7 July 1915. KP, 59 W1 57–58.

9 Viscount Esher, *The Tragedy of Lord Kitchener*, 1921, pp. 140–41.

10 Haig to FitzGerald, 15 July 1915. KP, 53 WD4.

11 (Arthur), *More Letters . . .*, p. 31.

12 Esher to K, 11 July 1915. KP, 59 W1 59.

13 Mrs Asquith to K, 18 August 1915. KP, 106 PR9/5a.

14 Esher to FitzGerald, 2 November 1915 (referring to earlier events). KP, 59.WI.84.

15 The Marquis de Chasseloup Laubart in *The Lord Kitchener Memorial Book* (ed. Le Bas.), 1916.

16 Lord Derby in House of Lords, 15 June 1916.

17 Professor W. G. S. Adams, memo dated 6 November 1916. CK.

18 John Charteris, *At GHQ*, 1930, p. 105.

19 Jackson, *Pastor on the Nile*, pp. 150–1.

20 Charteris, op. cit., pp. 106–7.

Chapter 22: The End in Gallipoli

1 RA GVD 6 October 1915.

2 Arthur Henderson, 'Lord Kitchener and Labour', in *The Lord Kitchener Memorial Book* (ed. Le Bas.), 1916.

3 Asquith to K, 17 October 1915. KP, 76. WR 25.

4 From Lord Derby's tribute, read for him at the unveiling of the K memorial in Lakenheath church, Suffolk, 23 July 1917.

5 Hamilton to K, 27 June 1915. KP, 62 WL 62.

6 Brock, op. cit., p. 541.

7 (Arthur), *More Letters . . .*, p. 35; Viscount Esher, *The Tragedy of Lord Kitchener*, 1921, p. 173.

8 FitzGerald to Lady Salisbury, 9 November (1915). Hatfield MSS.

9 Captain C. E. W. Bean, *The Times*, 15 November 1915, quoted in Rye and Groser, *Kitchener in His Own Words*, p. 557.

10 Birdwood, op. cit., p. 280.

11 Sir Mark Sykes to Arthur, 16 September 1916. KP, 91 GA2 81.

12 Arthur, *Life*, vol. 3, pp. 210, 211. See also Duff Cooper, *Old Men Forget*, p. 56.

Chapter 23: Partnership for Victory

1 Sir William Robertson, *From Private to Field Marshal*, 1921, p. 237.

2 K to Robertson, 7 December 1915. Copy in KP, 55 WF4.

3 Robertson, op. cit., pp. 287–8.

4 Ibid., p. 243; for details, see Cassar, *Kitchener*, pp. 434–8.

5 Charteris, op. cit., p. 137.

6 Adolphus Duke of Teck to King George v, 19 February 1916. RA GV Q8 32/47.

7 Charteris, op. cit., p. 137.

8 Maurice, *Rawlinson*, op. cit., p. 153.

9 Cassar, op. cit., pp. 459–62. See J. F. C. Fuller, *Tanks in the Great War*, 1920; for air matters, see Cassar's summary and references, pp. 463–5.

10 Memorandum of Commander Viscount Broome to Sir George Arthur. KP, 93.8.

11 Duchess of Portland to K, Friday (28 April 1916). KP, 10.PA.26.

12 K to Asquith, 11 January 1916. Asquith Papers, Bodleian Library, HHA/16/14; copy in KP.

13 Typescript of eleven-page 'Interview with Lord Kitchener, London, 14 March 1916'. Report to President Wilson by Mr Strong of the Federal Reserve Bank, New York, and Mr Forbes, Receiver of the Brazil Railway Company. Woodrow Wilson Papers (National Archives, Washington), Series 2, Roll 78.

Chapter 24: Journey to Russia?

1 Stamfordham to K, 14 May 1916. RA GV Q 2554/31; K's reply same date, and the telegram (dated 13 May). RA GV Q 939/2,4.

2 Prince Felix Youssoupoff, *Lost Splendour* (original French edn 1952, English translation 1953), Folio Society edn 1996, pp. 155, 157. The Prince supposed the German spies had caused K's ship to be torpedoed but it hit a mine.

3 Hanbury-Williams to K from Petrograd, 12 May 1916. KP, 67 WN 57.

4 Note dated '1916' by Arthur Renshaw. CK. They lunched or dined together about once a fortnight.

5 Lady Scott's diary, quoted in Cassar, *Kitchener*, p. 474.

6 J. A. Pease, MS memo marked 'Very Private', 21 June 1916, recording Asquith's dinner conversation 20 June. Gainford Papers. See also Duff Cooper, *Old Men Forget*, p. 56, reporting a conversation wih Asquith on 16 July 1916. The debate is reported in Hansard, vol. LXXXII, pp. 2786 ff.

7 Undated, unaddressed note. KP, 85, WZ 10.

8 Randolph Churchill, *Lord Derby: King of Lancashire*, 1959, pp. 209–10; Arthur, NWR, p. 274.

9 Sir Mark Sykes to Sir George Arthur, 12 September 1916. KP, GA 91.81.

10 The statement is printed in full in Arthur, *Life*, vol. 3, pp. 326–42. Sir Arthur Markham's report to Lloyd George in Dublin, dictated that afternoon, shows several mishearings (dated 2 June 1916). Lloyd George Papers, House of Lords Record Office, D.20.2.99.

11 Sykes, MS cit.

12 Arthur, NWR, p. 264.

Chapter 25: 'A Splendid End'

1 Lord Stamfordham to Sir George Buchanan (Ambassador in Petrograd), 9 June 1916. RA GV/P 284A/22.

2 Margot Asquith, *More Memories*, 1933, pp. 140–1.

3 Ibid., p. 141, footnote. The Asquiths put the incident to the Sunday evening but it can only be the Friday.

4 Arthur, *Life*, vol. 3, pp. 350–5.

5 Information from Mrs Ralph Toynbee (*née* Bridget Monins), in 2000 the last survivor of those who had known K personally.

6 Baroness Bonnor of Main to Magnus, 12 August 1960. Magnus Papers. J. H. Bonnor went to Ottawa later in 1916 to carve decorations for the Parliament building but died of pneumonia. The plaster casts of the pairs of boys were shown at the Daily Mail Ideal Home Exhibition of 1920 but were never erected in bronze.

7 Arthur, NWR, p. 265 (and next quote).

8 Arthur, *Life*, vol. 3, p. 353.

9 Jellicoe Papers, p. 10 (statement of 23 July 1916); cutting of a letter from G. Hill, Dundee, in an unidentified newspaper (date probably *circa* 1965) among Lord Kitchener's personal papers.

10 Admiral Sir John Jellicoe's Report, 7 June 1916, copy in KP 85.WZ11. The Official Narrative, card 2710, 1926, is the principal source, together with the

German official history and a British Naval Staff Monograph (Historical) produced by the Naval Staff, Training and Staff Duties Division, October 1927: *Home Waters – Part VII. From June 1916 to November 1916*, Chapter 3. For a detailed modern study (but in error regarding U.75's movements), see Trevor Royle, *The Kitchener Enigma*, 1985, pp. 361–76.

11 See Cassar, *Kitchener*, p. 477.

12 Eyewitness account given to the late Mr Lindsay R. Phillips, Chairman of the Lord Kitchener National Memorial Fund, in 1981. Letter of L. R. Phillips to the 3rd Earl, December 1981. 3rd Earl Papers.

13 Memoranda and Minute Book of Petty Officer C. A. Kingswell, GPO telegraphist on HMS *Iron Duke*. Imperial War Museum. Kingswell's undated account, written probably some years later, conflicts somewhat in details with the official account, but the final incident would seem an authentic memory.

Epilogue

1 Ian Hamilton, *Listening to the Drums*, 1944, pp. 253–4.

2 Memo, 'Very Private', 21 June 1916. Gainford Papers.

3 Charteris, op. cit., p. 252.

4 Viscount Esher to Lord Stamfordham, 8 June 1916. RA GV Q 724/77.

5 King George V to the Duke of Connaught, 12 June 1916. RA VIC Add A15/6596; Connaught to the King, 8 June 1916. RA GV AA 42/41. In his reply to the King, Prince Arthur wrote that 'no one knows better than you how great his loss is to you, to the Army and to the Empire'. 16 June 1916. Ibid., 42.

6 Margot Asqith, *More Memories*, pp. 243–4; Colin Benbow, *Boer Prisoners of War in Bermuda*, Bermuda Historical Society, 1962, 3rd edn, 1994, quoting a book by the Revd. J. A. van Blerk; Lord Alfred Douglas went to prison for a criminal libel of Winston Churchill but this related to an alleged false communiqué about K's death.

7 Millie Parker to Mrs Hankey, 18 July 1916. Imperial War Museum, 89/1295.

8 Walter Page to President Wilson, 21 July 1916. Wilson Papers, vol. 37, p. 457.

9 Maurice, *Rawlinson*, pp. 159–60; Charteris, op. cit., p. 146.

10 RA GV Q 1591/5 p 1 (memo of 30 January 1920).

11 Sir Clive Wigram to Sir George Arthur, 7 March 1917. KP, 91. GA 2.87.

12 Rawlinson to Lord Stamfordham, 4 February 1918. RA GV Q 2522/2.

13 Haig in Arthur, *Life*, vol. I, p. xvi.

14 RA GVD, 13 June 1916.

15 Charlotte Knollys to Sir George Arthur, 12 June 1916. KP, 89 GA 1.13.

16 Lady Salisbury to Sir George Arthur, 7 June 1916. KP, 86 GA 1.22.

17 Order of service is in KP, 118; information was kindly supplied by Canon Michael Saward of St Paul's.

18 Charteris, op. cit., p. 147.

19 Sir Frederick Milner, *Morning Post* (letter), 19 June 1916.

SELECT BIBLIOGRAPHY
FOR VOLUME I

For the reader's convenience this list gives details of books cited in References and Notes. Many other biographies, memoires, journalists' accounts and historical works were consulted.

Place of publication London unless noted otherwise.

Arthur, Sir George, *Life of Lord Kitchener*, 3 vols, 1920
    A Septuagenarian's Scrapbook, 1933
    Not Worth Reading, 1938
    A Glance From His Letters, ed. Christopher Pemberton, privately printed, Birmingham, 1950
[Arthur, Sir George], *Some Letters of A Man of No Importance*, 1928
    More Letters . . ., 1930
Asquith, Margot, *More Memories*, 1933
Babikr Bedi, *Memoirs*, Vol. 2, translated by Ysuf Beolti and Peter Hogg, 1980
Bates, Darrell, *The Fashoda Incident 1898*, 1984
Beatty, B., *Kerry Memories*, Camborne, 1939
Benbow, Colin, *Boer P.O.W.'s in Bermuda*, Bermuda, 3rd edn, 1994
Besant, Sir Walter, *Twenty-One Years' Work in the Holy Land*, 1889
Birdwood, Lord, *Khaki and Gown*, 1942
Burleigh, Bennett, *Sirdar and Khalifa*, 1899
Caldwell, C. E., *Confessions of a Dug Out*, 1920
Cecil, Lord Edward, *Leisure of An Egyptian Official*, 1938
Charlton, C. E. C. G., *A Soldier's Story*. privately printed, 1963
Churchill, Winston S., *The River War*, 2 vols, 1899
Churchill, Randolph S., *Winston Spencer Churchill*, Vol. 1, *Youth*, 1966. Companion Volumes

Conder, C. R., *Tent Work in Palestine*, 2 vols, 1878

Daly, M. W., *Empire on the Nile*, Oxford, 1986

Daiches, Samuel, *Lord Kitchener and His Work in Palestine*, 1915

Doolittle, Duncan H., *A Soldier's Hero: The Life of General Sir Archibald Hunter*, Narragansett, Rhode Island 1991

Duncan, J. S. R., *The Sudan: A Record of Achievement*, 1932

Esher, Viscount, *The Tragedy of Lord Kitchener, Journals and Letters*, 4 vols, 1934–8

Fisher, John, *That Miss Hobhouse*, 1971

Frankland, Noble, *Witness of A Century: The Life and Times of Prince Arthur, Duke of Connaught 1850–1942*, 1993

Gaughan, J. Anthony, *The Knights of Glin*, Dublin, 1978 *Listowel and Its Vicinity*, Cork, 1973

Gilbert, Martin, *Sir Horace Rumbold*, 1973

Gordon, Charles, *The Journals of Major-General C. G. Gordon*, ed. E. Hake, 1885

Hamilton, Sir Ian, *The Commander*, ed. A. Farrar-Hockley, 1957

Hill, Richard, *A Biographical Dictionary of the Sudan*, 2nd edn, 1967

Hunter, Archie, *Kitchener's Sword-Arm: The Life and Campaign of Sir Archibald Hunter*, Staplehurst, 1996

Jackson, H. C., *Pastor on the Nile*, 1960

James, David, *Lord Roberts*, 1953

Keown-Boyd, Henry, *A Good Dusting: The Sudan Campaigns 1883–1899*, 1986 *Soldiers of the Nile: British Officers of the Egyptian Army 1882–1925*, Thornbury, 1996

Kruger, Rayne, *Good-bye Dolly Gray*, 1983 edn

Letters of Queen Victoria, Second Series, 3 vols; Third Series, 3 vols, ed. G. E. Buckle, 1928–32

Le May, G. H. L., *British Supremacy in South Africa, 1899–1907*, 1965

Liddell, A. G. C., *Notes From the Life of An Ordinary Mortal.*, 1911

Lyttleton, Sir Neville, *Eighty Years' Soldiering*, 1927

MacMichael, Sir Harold, *The Sudan*, 1955

Magnus, Philip, *Kitchener: Portrait of An Imperialist*, 1958

Mallet, Sir Victor, ed., *Life with Queen Victoria*, 1968

Marlowe, John, *Cromer in Egypt*, 1970

Maurice, Frederick, *The Life of General Lord Rawlinson*, 1928

Maxwell, Charlotte, *Frank Maxwell, V.C.*

Meintjès, Johannes, de la Rey, *Lion of the West*, Johannesburg 1966

Pakenham, Thomas, *The Boer War*, 1979
The Scramble for Africa, 1991

Pollock, John, *Gordon: The Man Behind the Legend*, 1993

Preston, Adrian, *In Relief of Gordon: Lord Wolseley's Campaign Journal*, 1967

[Pritchard H. L.], *The Sudan Campaign 1896–1899*, by 'An Officer', 1899

Repington, Charles à Court, *Vestigia*, 1919

Rose, Kenneth, *The Later Cecils*, 1975

Royale, Trevor, *Death before Dishonour: The True Story of Fighting Mac*, Edinburgh, 1982

    The Kitchener Enigma, 1985

Rye, J. B., and Groser, Horace G., *Kitchener in His Own Words*, 1917

Sandes, E. W. C., *The Royal Engineers in Egypt and the Sudan*, 1937

Scudamore, Frank, *A Sheaf of Memories*, 1925

Smith-Dorrien, Sir Horace, *Memories of Forty-Eight Years' Service*, 1925

Sommer, Dudley, *Haldane of Cloan*, 1960

Steevens, G. W., *With Kitchener to Khartoum*, 1898

Storrs, Sir Ronald, *Orientations*, 1937

Tulloch, Sir A. B., *Recollections of Forty Years' Service*, 1925

Warner, Philip, *Kitchener: The Man Behind The Legend*, 1985

Webster, William Bullock, *Ireland Considered for a Field of Investment or Residence*, Dublin, 1852

Wingate, Reginald, *Mahdism and the Egyptian Soudan*, 1896

Wingate, Sir Ronald, *Wingate of the Sudan*, 1955

Winstone, H. V. F., *The Diaries of Parker Pasha*, 1983

Wright, Patricia, *Fashoda*, 1972

Wood, Sir Evelyn, *From Midshipman to Field Marshal*, 2 vols, 1906

Ziegler, Philip, *Omdurman*, 1972

Zulfo, Ismat Hazan, *Karari*, translated by Peter Clark, 1980

Also *The Times*, *The Daily Telegraph*, *Morning Post*, *Daily News*, *Westminster Gazette*, *Army and Navy Gazette*, *Blackwood's Magazine*, *Contemporary Review*, *Cyprus Herald*, *The Nineteenth Century and After*.

SELECT BIBLIOGRAPHY
FOR VOLUME II

As in *Kitchener: The Road to Omdurman*, this list gives details of books cited in References and Notes. Many other biographies, memoirs and historical accounts and studies were consulted.

Place of publication London unless noted otherwise.

Alsop, Susan Mary, *Lady Sackville*, 1978
Arthur, Sir George, *Life of Lord Kitchener*, 3 vols, 1920
    A Septuagenarian's Scrapbook, 1933
    Not Worth Reading, 1938
    A Glance From His Letters, ed. Christopher Pemberton, privately printed, Birmingham, 1950
(Arthur, Sir George), *Some Letters of A Man of No Importance*, 1928
    More Letters . . ., 1930
Asquith, Margot, *Autobiography*, vol. 2, 1922
    More Memories, 1933
Australian Encyclopedia, vol. 1, 1958
Birdwood, Lord, *Khaki and Gown*, 1942
Birkenhead, Lord, *Points of View*, 1922
Bonham-Carter, Violet, *Diaries*, ed. Mark Bonham-Carter and Mark Tottle: *Lantern Slides*, 1996; *Champion Redoubtable*, 1998
Bradley, John, *Lady Curzon's India*, 1985
Brock, Michael and Eleanor, *H. H. Asquith: Letters to Venetia Stanley*, 1982
Brook-Shepperd, Gordon, *Between Two Flags*, 1972
Buck, E. F., *Simla Past and Present*, Bombay, 1925
Caldwell, Sir C. E., *Experiences of a Dug-Out 1914–1918*, 1920

Stray Recollections, 1923

Field Marshal Sir Henry Wilson, 1927

Cassar, George *Asquith as War Leader*, 1994

Kitchener: Architect of Victory, 1977

The Tragedy of Sir John French, 1985

Cecil, Lord Edward, *The Leisure of an Egyptian Official*, 1922

Charteris, John, *At GHQ*, 1930

Chirol, Valentine, *Fifty Years in a Changing World*, 1927

Churchill, Randolph S., *Lord Derby: King of Lancashire*, 1959

Churchill, Winston S., *The World Crisis*, 1938 edn

Clark, Alan (ed.), *A Good Innings: The Papers of Viscount Lee*, 1974

Colvin, Ian, *The Life of Lord Carson*, 1934

Conan Doyle, Sir Arthur, *The British Campaign in France and Flanders, 1914–1916*, vol. 1, 1916.

Cooper, Duff, *Old Men Forget*, 1953

Creagh, Sir G. O'M., *Stray Recollections*, 1924

Dilks, David, *Curzon in India*, 1970

Doolittle, Duncan, *A Soldier's Hero*, 1991

Ellison, Sir Gerald, *The Perils of Amateur Strategy*, 1926

Emulation Ritual (Lewis Masonic), 6th edn

Esher, Viscount, *The Tragedy of Lord Kitchener*, 1921

Field, Eric, *Advertising – The Forgotten Years*, 1959

Foch, Marechal F., *Memoirs*, tr. B. Mott, 1931

Fuller, Sir Bampfylde, *Some Personal Experiences*, 1933

Fuller, J. F. C., *Tanks in the Great War*, 1920

Gilbert, Martin, *Winston S. Churchill*, vol. 3, 1971

Sir Horace Rumbold, 1973

Gilmour, David, *Curzon*, 1994

Grey, Viscount, *Twenty-Five Years*, 1932

Gwynn, Denis, *The Life of John Redmond*, 1932

Hamilton, Lord Frederick, *My Yesterdays*, 1928

Hamilton, Sir Ian, *The Commander* (ed. Anthony Farrer-Hockley), 1957

Listening to the Drums, 1944

Hankey, Lord, *The Supreme Command*, vol. 1, 1961

Hedin, Sven, *Trans-Himalaya*, 1909

My Life as an Explorer, 1925

Grosse Männer denen Ich Begegnte, Wiesbaden, 1952

Hunter, Archie, *Kitchener's Sword-Arm*, Staplehurst, 1996

Jackson, H. C., *Pastor on the Nile*, 1960

Keown-Boyd, Henry, *Soldiers of the Nile*, 1996

King, Peter, *The Fall of the Viceroy*, 1985

Kipling, Rudyard, *The Irish Guards in the Great War*, 1923

Langston, E. L., *Bishop Taylor Smith*, 1938

Lawrence, Sir Walter, *The India We Served*, 1928

Le Bas, Sir Hedley, (ed.), *The Lord Kitchener Memorial Book*, 1916

Long, Viscount, *My Memories*, 1923

Magnus, Philip, *Kitchener: Portrait of an Imperialist*, 1958

Maurice, Sir Frederick, *The Life of Lord Rawlinson of Trent*, 1928

Maxwell, Charlotte, *Frank Maxwell*, 1921

(Maxwell, Charlotte), *I am Ready*, Aylesbury, 1955

Midleton, Earl of, *Records and Reactions, 1859–1939*, 1939

Molesworth, J. H., *Soldier of God*, 1917

Morley, Viscount, *Recollections*, vol. 2, 1917

Nicolson, Nigel, *Mary Curzon*, 1977

Oliver, F. S., *Ordeal by Battle*, 1915

Pound, Reginald, *The Lost Generation*, 1968

Rhodes-James, Robert, *Gallipoli*, 1965

Rickards, Maurice, *Posters of the First World War*, 1968

Riddell, Lord, *War Diary 1914–1918*, 1933

    The Riddell Diaries (ed. J. McEwan), 1986

Robertson, Sir William, *From Private to Field Marshal*, 1921

Ronaldshay, Lord, *The Life of Lord Curzon*, 1928

Rose, Kenneth, *The Later Cecils*, 1971

Royle, Trevor, *The Kitchener Enigma*, 1985

Ryan, W. Michael, *Lieutenant-Colonel Charles à Court Repington. A Study of the Interaction of Personality, the Press and Power*, New York, 1987

Rye, J. B. and Groser, H. G., *Kitchener in His Own Words*, 1917

Sandes, E. W. C., *The Royal Engineers in Egypt and the Sudan*, 1937

Sandhurst, Viscount, *From Day to Day*, 1928

Simpkins, Peter, *Kitchener's Army*, Manchester, 1988

Smith-Dorrien, Sir Horace, *Memories of Forty-Eight Years' Service*, 1925

Smyth, Sir John, *In This Sign Conquer*, 1968

Spender, J. A., *Life, Journalism and Politics*, 1927

Stevenson, Frances, *Lloyd George: A Diary*, ed. A. J. P. Taylor, 1971

Storrs, Sir Ronald, *Orientations*, 1937

Swinton, Sir Ernest, *Eye-Witness*, 1932

Vincent, John (ed.), *The Crawford Papers*, Manchester, 1984

Warner, Philip, *Kitchener: The Man Behind the Legend*, 1985

Wilson, Lady (A. C. MacLeod), *Letters from India*, Edinburgh, 1911

Youssoupoff, Prince Felix, *Lost Splendour*, 1953

Ziegler, Philip, *King Edward* VIII, 1990

Also *The Times, Morning Post, Times of India, Otago Daily Times, Contemporary Review, Fortnightly Review, The Nineteenth Century and After, Illustrated London News, Punch, Royal Artillery Journal, Royal Engineers Journal.*

INDEX
TO VOLUME I

Kitchener is referred to as 'K' throughout index

INDEX
TO VOLUME II

Kitchener is referred to as 'K' throughout the index